# CHALLENGING US HUMAN RIGHTS VIOLATIONS
## SINCE 9/11

"Ann Ginger has a clear sense of history, and her work has showed us how the struggle for justice must be waged today, while appreciating the insights and contributions of those who have struggled in the past. She also has a clear sense that the struggle for justice is a people's struggle that, while aided at crucial times by lawyers, is advanced only by an organized movement for change. This book is the most valuable possible contribution to the people's struggle for justice at the present historical moment, for it puts the struggle here and now into the context of a worldwide outcry for human rights."

Michael E. Tigar
Research Professor of Law, Washington College of Law;
human rights lawyer; author of *Fighting Injustice*

"We owe Ann Fagan Ginger a tremendous debt of gratitude for painstakingly compiling, in a single volume, a wealth of tools and resources for political activists. As the 'War on Terrorism' morphs into a war on civil liberties and human rights, Ann's call to action could not be more timely or more necessary."

Nancy Chang
Senior Litigation Attorney,
Center for Constitutional Rights

MEIKLEJOHN CIVIL LIBERTIES INSTITUTE

# CHALLENGING US HUMAN RIGHTS VIOLATIONS SINCE 9/11

EDITED BY **ANN FAGAN GINGER**

## Prometheus Books

59 John Glenn Drive
Amherst, New York 14228-2197

Published 2005 by Prometheus Books

*Challenging US Human Rights Violations Since 9/11.* Copyright © 2005 by Meiklejohn Civil Liberties Institute. Edited by Ann Fagan Ginger. All rights reserved. No part of this publication may be reproduced, stored in a retrieval system, or transmitted in any form or by any means, digital, electronic, mechanical, photocopying, recording, or otherwise, or conveyed via the Internet or a Web site without prior written permission of the publisher, except in the case of brief quotations embodied in critical articles and reviews.

Inquiries should be addressed to
Prometheus Books
59 John Glenn Drive
Amherst, New York 14228–2197
VOICE: 716–691–0133, ext. 207
FAX: 716–564–2711
WWW.PROMETHEUSBOOKS.COM

09 08 07 06 05    5 4 3 2 1

Library of Congress Cataloging-in-Publication Data

Challenging U.S. human rights violations since 9/11 / Meiklejohn Civil Liberties Institute; edited by Ann Fagan Ginger
    p. cm.
  ISBN 1–59102–279–7 (pbk.: alk. paper)
  1. Human rights—United States. 2. Victims of crimes—Legal status, laws, etc.
3. Crimes against humanity. 4. War on Terrorism, 2001–. I. Ginger, Ann Fagan.
II. Meiklejohn Civil Liberties Institute.
JC599.U36C37 2005
973.931—dc22

2004027189

Printed in the United States of America on acid-free paper

To all of the victims of human rights violations
since 9/11, and
to everyone who has been busy
exercising their human rights,
the men and women, young and old,
of all races, nations, languages, and religions,
the whistle-blowers, conscientious objectors,
peaceful pickets and demonstrators,
and
to the people in the government who did their job
of protecting human rights for all,
the Congress members and Judges and Inspector Generals
the Council members and Public Defenders,
and
to those who study their stories
and decide to work for human rights and peace law
in the future
this Report is dedicated.

# SHORT TABLE OF CONTENTS

# CHALLENGING US HUMAN RIGHTS VIOLATIONS SINCE 9/11

# ILLUSTRATIONS

# PREFACE

Every morning brings shocking news from Washington or Iraq, or somewhere else in the United States or the world. George Bush, Dick Cheney, or someone else in the Administration announces a new policy that sidesteps an act of Congress or a court decision—a new policy that often violates the oaths they took to "preserve, protect and defend the Constitution of the United States."

Now that George Bush and his colleagues are claiming a mandate to rule the United States until January 2008, all of us who know about the Administration's past human rights violations are asking: What new actions can we take to protect our freedom and our need for peace? *Challenging US Human Rights Violations Since 9/11* presents detailed evidence of violations that have occurred after 9/11 during the first Bush Administration and describes how activists have challenged them in order to maintain democracy in the United States based on the US Constitution.

This book opens with an account of the real score in the "war on terrorism" since 9/11. It is based on facts and statistics on how many "terrorists" have been arrested, tried, and convicted, and how many people have been killed or wounded in this "war." This discussion in Chapter 1 leads to a search for new strategies that citizens can use to continue the struggle for freedom here, for ending US wars abroad, and for bringing the troops home soon. This is a search for new paths for action that will be effective under these new conditions.

## NEW PATHS FOR ACTION

One new path described in Chapter 2 leads to the Office of Inspector General in all but one federal Government agency. Another is the traditional path of suing or defending in state or federal courts, using a new model brief for defending against a charge of terrorism that presents historical facts that can be widely used. Chapter 2 also presents several paths for action that have helped slow down some violations in the past. (Would that it could somehow combine the Crisis Papers, the Appeal to Reason, the Declaration of Independence, and the Gettysburg Address!)

The Bush Administration is required, under existing laws, to make a series of reports to international bodies on how well it is enforcing human rights in the cities, counties, and states of the United States, as well as at the federal and international levels. Chapter 3 describes how the mobilization of shame can lead to public dialogue about human rights violations and, then, to action. A recent resolution to the United Nations General Assembly on human rights violations in the United States is included. A letter issued by the Inter-American Human Rights Commission on US violations in Guantanamo and elsewhere is also included as a model for use on similar issues.

This Report tries to include every type of Government action from 9/11 through November 5, 2004, that violates the law. One-hundred-eighty reports in Chapter 4 give the names, dates, places, actions, and refusals to act of US Government officials. The reports describe what people are doing to challenge these violations of eleven basic rights of the people, starting with the "Right Not to Be Killed or Disappeared" summarized in Section1, followed by Reports 1.1–1.13. The reports then describe nineteen basic duties that the Government has violated since 9/11, starting with "The Government's Duty To Count the Votes Accurately and Report to the People Honestly" summarized in Section12, followed by Reports 12.1–12.9. The relevant laws pertaining to each of these rights and duties are listed at the end of each introductory section, 1 through 30, and Chapter 6 provides the basic text of the US Constitution, the UN Charter, and other ratified human rights and antinuclear weapons treaties. The specific statutes at issue, including the PATRIOT Act, are listed in each Report.

This Report can be a tool for people who rushed to the swing states to defeat the Bush agenda in 2004 and who want to figure out what to do next. It can be a tool for people who have been working against repression and war since the PATRIOT Act, since the First Gulf War, and since the Vietnam War. It can help people who worked for the Civil Rights Movement and against the McCarthy Cold War repression.

The Report is written for everyone who is working today for democracy and peace. It is written for activists, lawyers, the media, and legislators, for students, scholars, and educators; for civil servants, judges, and hearing officers. It is for people concerned about what is happening in this country, and the world, whether they are now active or not.

The Report is based on the right to plan and manage our communities as part of the global community. The text of city, county and state resolutions against the PATRIOT Act and the war in Iraq are set forth in Chapter 5 along with six resolutions that support new federal laws, from the Freedom To Read Act to An Inquiry on Impeachment.

# THIS IS THE FIRST TIME IN HISTORY

For the first time in the history of the world, one nation can destroy all life on this planet with its nuclear weapons or its ecological policies and practices. That nation is the United States. There is no countervailing national force of equal power. As a result of the November 2004 election, George Bush and Dick Cheney will serve as President and Vice President of this nation until January 2008.

Even before Bush felt he had a mandate to rule, after 9/11 the Bush Administration attacked the fundamental law in the US Constitution and Bill of Rights. And they attacked the commitments the United States made when it helped found the United Nations and when it ratified the UN Charter and other treaties.

How are they to be stopped—Bush, Cheney, Karl Rove, Condoleezza Rice, Alberto Gonzalez, and all the others? Each day they announce a new plan or policy that ignores certain fundamental laws, including the free press right to use the Internet, the basic right of every person under US jurisdiction to be represented by a lawyer, the right to habeas corpus, and the rights of combatants under international law. Daily, they attack some aspect of affirmative action for African Americans and Latinos or some effort to treat Islamic and Muslim Americans as equals.

Many people are asking: Where are the lunch counters we can sit down at to start a strong new movement against racism, sexism, and xenophobia? Where are the draft cards we need to collect and burn to stop the US war in Iraq (and plans for a US war anywhere else)? Where are the picket signs we can hold to support workers on strike? What rallies and sit-ins can we hold in Washington to convince Congress to save the New Deal legislation passed by men and women like them in the 1930s?

# NEW THOUGHTS, NEW BOOKS, NEW PATHS

This is a time for each of us to find our most basic beliefs, the principles by which we live. This is a time to recall the incidents that brought us into action. It is a time to contact the people we worked with on issues long ago, a time to read new books and delve into wise ones that we haven't read in years.

Can we think new thoughts that will help us find new ways of working with more people to stop Bush's White House? If we find strong new paths for action, we will encounter many people we never worked with before. We will meet some people who were part of the Establishment and then couldn't take it any more. We will meet people who are now writing books and making speeches about what they did, and what they learned, when they were part of The System —the Military Industrial Complex, the US Civil Service, the

Prison Industrial Complex, the Bechtel Corporation, FOX News, and their equivalents. Our paths for action must become more effective than the paths long traveled by these members of the Power Elite, the Globalists. While worrying about our student loans, mortgage payments, and doctors' appointments, can we use these revelations to make our actions more direct and meaningful?

This Report includes a series of revelations at this nodal moment by people who served the System for many years. Events have forced them to decide, one by one, that now is the time they must resign from the system, reveal the truth, and try to stop the juggernaut. John Perkins recently revealed the three steps to power he was taught to use for the US Government in other countries. First they use "Economic Hit Men" (EHM) to offer money, power, and sex to bribe progressive leaders of governments from Guatemala to Geneva (or New York). When that does not work, they call out the "Jackals." Soon some of the strongest leaders of the United Nations and individual countries die in accidents in airplanes and elsewhere. When that does not close down the forces for peace and democracy, these leaders start a War. In his "Confessions of an Economic Hit Man," Perkins lays out one situation after another in which he participated. The experiences of Joseph Wilson and Rep. Henry Waxman (D-CA) are described in Reports 12.2 and 12.6.

Knowing who is against democracy and peace helps. Knowing their action points helps. But many are now saying that we need to be sharper than they were in 2004. A whole generation of youth jumped quickly into the movement to stop Bush and the War. They tried new tactics that often worked to bring out new voters and help them stand in the cold, wet lines to vote. More people than ever worked with new strength to defeat Bush in November 2004 and failed. They failed to reach enough people in the "Red States" to vote against four more years of Bush/Cheney/Rove, of the PATRIOT Act, of Guantanamo, Abu Ghraib, and Fallujah, of secret memos approving the use of torture, of registration of immigrants, massive deportations, and more Bibles and less critical thinking in public schools. They failed to prevent voter fraud with no-paper-trail electronic voting.

## BUSH vs. THE CONSTITUTION

All this leads to the question before the house: How can everyone who knows what time of day it really is—or, more accurately, what time of night it is— find more effective ways of joining others to stop the war, repression, and rising unemployment? The Bush Administration openly took many steps after 9/11 to limit the powers of Congress and the courts as set forth in the US Constitution. They took many steps disguised as part of "the war on terrorism" against "enemy combatants." (See the defense brief on "terrorism" in US history by Professor Michael Tigar in *U.S. v. Lynne Stewart* in Chapter 2-B.) The Administration sent US troops to drop bombs and fight in the streets of Afghanistan (see Reports 13.1–13.2) and Iraq (see Reports 14.1–14.2), without getting Congress to exercise its constitutional power to decide whether or not to declare war and without getting UN Security Council or General Assembly support for the invasions under the UN Charter (see the text of the relevant laws in Chapter 6).

Just before the 2004 election, the Bush Administration announced that, under the Help America Vote Act, only the Attorney General could ask federal courts to enforce voting rights, not individuals or organizations. And the Internal Revenue Service began threatening to revoke the tax-exempt status of sixty organizations, including several Unitarian Universalist and other churches and the NAACP, a century-old nonprofit Nongovernmental Organization, for statements made in speeches and leaflets against actions of the Bush Administration, ignoring their criticisms of the Democratic Party for being spineless (*Washington Post*, Oct. 29, 2004, p. A-8). There have been no reports of churches or other NGOs being threatened by the IRS for preaching against John Kerry and supporting Bush.

## "THE WAR IN IRAQ IS ILLEGAL"

Many people in the United States and elsewhere in the world recognized the danger posed by these Bush Government actions before the 2004 election and said so. Finally, in mid-October 2004, UN Secretary-General Kofi Annan said, in London, that the US invasion of Iraq was "illegal" because the United States and its allies had not obtained Security Council backing before the invasion. (Associated Press interview, Oct. 17, 2004, International edition, CNN.com). Bush reacted immediately by "revealing" steps he said "the UN" did and did not take to prevent corruption in the Oil For Food program, steps taken, in fact, by the Security Council with US tacit or open approval.

After the 2004 election, every person in this country who believes in democracy and peace knows they have an unprecedented job to do. And it will not be easy. Facing Bush's second term, one is strongly tempted to write: "Now what we must do is . . ." and then spell out what activists have been saying for centuries. It is tempting to describe the massive rallies of the underpaid and the unemployed in Washington in the 1930s, moving Congress to establish the Social Security System, the National Labor Relations Board, unemployment compensation, equal pay for equal work, and beginning to end racial discrimination.

Instead, in the spirit of admitting that nobody knows today What Is To Be Done, Meiklejohn Institute is asking a series of questions.

Would this be a good time to reread the Constitution and the history of this country? And to read the UN Charter and other treaties the US Government has signed and sworn to uphold? (All in Chapter 6.)

Would this law give us the strength to think about how to rebuild the democratic process at the city, county, state, and national levels? Would it help us speak up at our work places? Would this history and law give us the energy to figure out how to end virtually unilateral control by the Bush Administration over the destruction and reconstruction of Afghanistan and Iraq? Could we then turn our attention to how to achieve cooperative control over global warming and destruction of the environment? (See Reports 27.1–27.9.)

Can we convince them to study Bush Administration statements until they are transformed, as Senator Barbara Boxer was, into conducting the most effective questioning she had ever done in the confirmation hearings on Condoleezza Rice for Secretary of State?

Can each of us find new ways to actually get to know our Congressional Representatives and Senators, to talk to them about the desperate situation we are in? Can we find ways to have a dialogue with them (and with their funders and trainers) about how to move forward in reconstructing democracy in the United States and building peace in the world?

On November 5, 2004, and again on November 8, 2004, six leading Members of the US House of Representatives acted on charges of election fraud brought by concerned citizens throughout the country. The Ranking Members of the Judiciary Committee and the Subcommittees on Crime, Terrorism, and Homeland Security, the Constitution, and on Commercial and Administrative Law wrote two "urgent" letters to the Comptroller General of the United States requesting that the Government Accountability Office "immediately undertake an investigation of the efficacy of voting machines and new technologies used in the 2004 election . . . and what we can do in the future to improve our election systems." Reps. John Conyers, Robert C. Scott, Jernold Nadler, Melvin Watt, Robert Wexler, and Rush Holt then requested that the GAO review and evaluate a sampling of more than thirty thousand voter complaints that are listed on http://voteprotect.org/index.php?display=EIRMap Nation and 265 specific complaints from Broward County, Florida; Cuyahoga and Warren Counties, Ohio; Sarper County, Nebraska; Guilford County, North Carolina; and others, that are reported at http://www.votersunite.org/electionproblems.asp?sort=date&selectstate=ALL&selectproblemtype=ALL.

These Representatives were soon joined by other Representatives, and the GAO announced it would make an investigation. NonGovernmental Organizations like the League of Women Voters can cite these Congressional letters to support their mission of nonpartisan political action, even when it requires reporting human rights violations by specific Government officials and political parties that may attack them (see Reports 12.1, 12.8).

The 9/11 family-member survivors have impeccable credentials to raise hard questions now and for many years to come. So do the workers injured at the World Trade Center. Many of them are following a well-known path for action by filing massive class action lawsuits against many corporate and Government leaders (see Reports 12.8 and 29.2). They are also taking the unprecedented step of filing a Complaint and Petition with the New York State Attorney General demanding that he open a criminal inquiry and/or grand jury investigation into the many still unsolved crimes of September 11, 2001, over which he has jurisdiction. And they took the twenty-first-century step of providing access to their complaint to everyone interested at http://www.justicefor911.org.

# 180 REPORTS OF HUMAN RIGHTS VIOLATIONS SINCE 9/11

Meiklejohn Institute's contribution to the process of countering the violations of human rights since 9/11 is this Report. Like many other affirmative actions since 9/11, it is based on the lively, hard work of interns working on the Internet, of traditional meeting-goers, and of activists in the Muslim, African American, Latino, and Native American communities.

This book is our effort to layout, in 180 reports, the problem we face in the United States today, in all its complex, contradictory aspects, and then to present many paths for action to consider, modify, refine, debate, and try out. This can help people act at their jobs and in the streets. It can help people meet their elected officials in government chambers in their cities, counties, states, and in Washington, DC. These Reports also suggest that we need to keep an eye on what the UN General Assembly is doing about the US Government under Bush, since clearly the whole world is watching what the people in the United States do now.

One little known example: On November 2, 2004, Belarus filed a draft resolution in the UN General Assembly on the Situation of Democracy and Human Rights in the United States of America. The resolution is based on critical reports by the US Commission on Civil Rights and other US Government bodies and NGOs. The complete document is presented in Chapter 3-A as a form that can be used on other issues. (And within a month, Bush called for two members of the Civil Rights Commission to be replaced.) A letter sent by the Inter-American Human Rights Commission to the President of the United States concerning treatment of detainees at Guantanamo Bay is presented in Chapter 3-D as another model for action.

All of the 180 Reports in Chapter 4 will be submitted by the Meiklejohn Institute to the US State Department for inclusion in their (past due) reports to the three UN human rights committees. And they will be submitted directly to the UN High Commissioner for Human Rights.

It is clear that it will not be enough if everyone works as hard as they ever have done—like they did during the Civil Rights Movement of the 1960s, the AntiWar Movement against the Vietnam War, and the First Gulf War. We must do more than we have ever done in the labor movement, the environmental movement, and the movement for the rights of veterans. We must do more than we have done for women's rights, gay rights, immigrant rights, disabled people's rights, prisoners' rights, the rights of youth and seniors, of journalists, librarians, and book readers, and indigenous peoples. Can we find new paths for action that we have never tried before to meet this challenge, what some are calling the political tsunami of 2005? Can everyone work together, all the organizations described in the Reports, and all the organizations that worked as hard whose reports did not make it into this compilation?

Can every one of the 1,200 organizations in Meiklejohn's 2003 *Human Rights Organizations and Periodicals Directory* work together now, in new ways? And can they work with the organizations that sprang up yesterday—to say nothing of the ones just forming in high schools and on the street? What new paths are being taken by older organizations like the American Association of University Women and the League of Women Voters, and what is the League of Young Voters doing, let alone Citizens' Alliance for Secure Elections and the League of Pissed Off Voters? What's new with the Sierra Club and Pacifica Network, with Earth First and Air America Radio and Peace Action and MoveOn.org, with Human Rights Watch, Amnesty International, Human Rights First, and the United Nations Association and World Federalists? What's the latest with the Women's International League for Peace and Freedom, the Gray Panthers, Veterans for Peace, and the Association of Community Organizations for Reform Now (ACORN) and the Applied Research Center? Are we hearing about new paths for action from the American Civil Liberties Union, National Lawyers Guild, National Conference of Black Lawyers, Center for Constitutional Rights, Association of Trial Lawyers of America, Lawyers Committee for Human Rights, NAACP Legal Defense, and the Mexican American Legal Defense Fund, National Asian Pacific American Legal Consortium, Lawyers Committee on Nuclear Policy, and Human Rights Watch? What about US Labor Against the War, the Coalition of Black Trade Unionists, the AFL-CIO, Food First, Food Not Bombs, Korean Immigrant Workers Advocates, Indian Law Resource Center, Women of Color Resource Center, American-Arab Anti-Discrimination Committee, National Immigration Law Center, Anti-Defamation League, Jewish Voice for Peace, National Gay/Lesbiana/Bisexual/Transgendered Labor Organization? What are we hearing from the Wellstone Action Network and Committee of Correspondence for Democracy and Socialism (CCDS) and Democratic Socialists of America (DSA)?

And what about the many faith-based organizations? What new steps will they suggest? And how will they all work together, and add to their numbers, the Quakers and the American Friends Service Committee, Mennonites and Brethren, to the Unitarian Universalist Service Committee, the Catholic Worker folks, the Episcopal Peace Fellowship, and the Union of Black Episcopalians, the Methodist Federation for Social Action, Interfaith Committee for Worker Justice, Ecumenical Peace Institute/Clergy and Laity Concerned, Catholic Charities, Pax Christi, Voices in the Wilderness, and the Buddhist Peace Fellowship?

And what about all of the university and college centers for human rights? And the local groups that have sprung up and are doing effective, and often innovative work in their communities without national affiliations?

The list of organizations in the United States that are in motion, and that are being moved into motion, is much longer than can be included here. Like everything in this massive report, many constructive organizations, significan events, and remarkable individuals could not be included for space reasons.

The goal of this book is to encourage so much action that these reports and ordinances and victories described here must be updated immediately.

# GLOSSARY

Working on the reports for this book led to the conclusion that there is a new form of governance in Washington since 9/11—not the three equally important branches of the federal system established in the US Constitution. George Bush, Dick Cheney, and other members of the executive branch have taken many steps to limit the power of the judiciary (e.g., as to detainees at Guantanamo) and the legislature (e.g., through interim appointments without Senate consent, and through statutes that "must be passed immediately without study and debate").

Many activists and scholars have described the Bush setup as a kingship. In this new era, it seems necessary to capitalize the word Government when referring to the US Government system under Bush's Administration, rather than the current rule of talking about the federal system or the government without capital letters set forth in the *Chicago Manual of Style* in a different era. For this reason, the words Administration, President, and Government are also capitalized, as well as the Secretary of Defense and others in Bush's Cabinet. (We also capitalize King of England, Church and State, Wal-Mart, and US Army.)

The New Deal created many administrative agencies, leading to the Administrative Procedure Act of 1946. This Act required many more hearings and decisions by administrators based on statutes and regulations. After

9/11, whole new departments were established that were to operate under "special procedures" formed in response to the "war on terrorism." Recently several federal agencies have changed the title of their Administrative Hearing Officers to Administrative Law Judges, or even Immigration Judges, even though they are not appointed as federal judges are appointed, and they do not preside over juries or enforce the Constitution and laws as federal judges are required to do. In this book we have retained the title "hearing officer," particularly for administrative decision makers in the new Bureau of Immigration and Customs Services, since the Immigration Service is an administrative agency, not a judicial body, and it is not even subject to the Administrative Procedure Act, which requires many due process protections in virtually every other administrative agency in the Government.

Because the Immigration and Naturalization Service was changed, after 9/11, and its functions were subdivided among other agencies, we have made many references to "Immigration officials" without stating where the action which began under the old INS is now being carried out, whether in the new Bureau of Immigration and Customs Enforcement (BICE) or the new US Citizenship and Immigration Services (USCIS).

The words "US citizen" and "US" are used in this book, rather than "American" and "America," to remind people in the United States that many "Americans" are living in Central America, South America, the Caribbean, and other countries in North America.

Technically, treaties are not ratified. This is just an abbreviation. In fact, the US Senate consents to their ratification by a two-thirds vote after they are signed by the President.

In order to avoid writing "he" or "his" when both men and women are included, we have used the plural "they," even when this is a little awkward. Few women really feel included, even now, when the male pronoun is used.


## THE INDICES

We have endeavored to include in the Indices the name of every person and place mentioned in the book, and all of the Government agencies and NGOs. We have not tried to include every reference to George Bush, "the President of the United States," "the US Government," or "the United Nations," because the index would then be endless. Hopefully the complete Table of Contents will lead readers to quickly find what they are looking for as to these people and institutions.

# APOLOGY

I want to apologize for leaving out some subjects and incidents that were really important, as well as for any commas or "www's" or other errors that crept in, despite all of our efforts at accuracy and completeness. Please let us know what should be corrected and included in the second edition!

# ACKNOWLEDGMENTS

As editor of this Report by the Meiklejohn Civil Liberties Institute, I want to thank all of the committed, remarkable people who helped find, research, write, check, and proofread the 180 Reports in Chapter 4.

The book would never have been finished, let alone corrected, without the dedicated work of MCLI office staff, Soula Culver and her sister, Sarah Kotzamani, who turned lengthy repetitive e-mails into readable reports, made corrections, updated material from Web pages, checked Web page citations, and prepared the two Indices and Table of Cases.

New lawyer Melody Saint-Saens really dug into checking the law and citations, updating case write-ups and doing last-minute editing in the summer and fall of 2004. Law students Rebecca Tennant, Kevin Cunningham, Jennifer Van Bergen, and Jenna Steele started the reports in summer 2003, with help from Rupneet Sidhu and Marc Petr. In summer 2004, the research continued with David Reed Saffold (Arthur Horowitz Meiklejohn Institute intern) and Joel Feinman (Haywood Burns National Lawyers Guild intern), working with Paul "Blaise" Bess, Cecelia Gutierrez, and Sally Sommer.

Richard Challacombe used his skillful eyes to find sharp images to illustrate the endless textual reports. Then he spent an incredible number of hours locating the photographers to get permissions and descriptions of the incidents. Jeffrey Melcher worked on raising awareness of the project and the funds to pay for it. Attorney Yolande Adelson and MCLI Board Members Jim Syfers and Zipporah Collins gave many helpful suggestions during the editing process, as did attorney Board Members Steven Birnbaum, Leslie Rose, and Colleen Rohan.

So many people answered e-mails and faxes and sent material from their Web pages, they cannot all be listed here. Many are in the Index.

Steven Mitchell and everyone at Prometheus Books has been indispensable in this enormous venture: Jeremy Sauer as Assistant Editor, Brian McMahon, Editorial Assistant, Christine Kramer, Production Manager, and the Production Department that had to make thousands of changes to the original manuscript.

# I
# THE MOBILIZATION OF SHAME

## A. AFTER SEPTEMBER 11

On September 11, 2001, hijackers killed themselves and 3,100 people by crashing airplanes into the World Trade Center, into the Pentagon, and en route to a Government building in Washington, D.C. Their actions forever destroyed the image of the United States as *the* untouchable world power.

The people of the United States were shocked, heartbroken, and frightened. They wanted their Government to find the attackers immediately. And they wanted their Government to take steps to assure their safety from future attacks. A few got angry and decided to take the law into their own hands.

This Report will try to do the impossible. It will try to describe what has really been happening since 9/11 in the United States and in Afghanistan, Iraq, and other parts of the world where the US Government and US corporations are active. To fulfill as much of this awesome task as possible, it will report what Government agencies or officials have admitted, or have been accused of, killing, torturing, arresting, or detaining a citizen or noncitizen in the United States, Afghanistan, Guantanamo, or Iraq. It will report significant budget cuts and regulations that are endangering the lives and cultures of whole communities.

Our Report will offer almost two hundred actions people have taken against these steps by the Government—demonstrations against the USA PATRIOT Act, against police arrests of demonstrators, and against the invasion of Iraq. We will report strong defenses of protesters, deportees, and affirmative lawsuits to stop violations. It will provide the text of proposed resolutions and statutes, and cite the failure of the major media to report many of these actions. It will describe the law that covers actions the Government can take, in the United States against citizens and noncitizens, and in Afghanistan, Iraq, and across the globe.

## 1. CONNECTING THE DOTS

As people began connecting the dots since 9/11, they began to see just how many dots there are—how many illegal arrests, detentions, and denials of visas; how many lies told on how many subjects; how many budgets shifted from human services to making "small" nuclear weapons; and how much Social Security reserve "loaned" to pay for the war in Iraq. The Chapters are divided into lettered Parts followed by numbered Sections, e.g., Chapter 1, Part A, Sec. 1. Chapter 4 is divided further into Reports, e.g., Chapter 4, Part A, Sec. 1, followed by Reports 1.1–1.13. The full citations to books, magazine and newspaper articles, radio programs, and Web pages are in the numbered End Notes after Chapter 6. Chapter 4 describes 180 dots, each a different event in which the Government apparently denied human rights since 9/11 either by its actions or by its failure to act.

The 180 Reports are presented in thirty sections to make it easier to see how one incident is connected to another and what laws govern each kind of violation. The dots are connected by the fact that all of these events happened since 9/11, and they are all governed by the same basic laws.

When people working to save the whales see how their work connects with people trying to save Native American land, those trying to stop the war in Iraq, and still others seeking to stop illegal detentions of immigrants and illegal shootings by the police, something wonderful happens. A Movement is born out of all the e-mails; Web pages; phone calls and letters to the editor; statements before boards of education, city councils, central labor councils, bar associations, interfaith councils, federal court judges, and Congressional Committees; and political party conventions. A Movement is born that the media cannot ignore.

## 2. SENDING A MESSAGE

People began wanting to send a message to the authorities to stop violating their rights. This book describes just how effective it can be to send such a message, especially since the US Government enacted a law after the Watergate scandal of the 1970s that *requires* every Government agency to investigate and reply to every complaint through the Office of Inspector General (see Chapters 2, 4.F-29, and 5.D-2).

Sending a message is a form of reporting on a violation of law to the Government agency or official allegedly responsible. This book describes new laws the US Congress adopted in the 1990s that require the federal Government to report its own violations of human rights as well as those committed by state governments. These new laws require officials from the Departments of State, Justice, Labor, Interior, and others to meet with international experts to determine how to stop, or at least limit, such violations in the near future. This book describes the treaties the United States ratified requiring these Reports to the UN Human Rights Committee, the UN Committee Against Torture, and the UN Committee on Elimination of Racial Discrimination. Chapter 6 includes the language of Article VI, Clause 2 of the US Constitution that makes these treaties part of the supreme law of the land. And it includes the language of each of these relevant treaties and laws.

## B. THE MOBILIZATION OF SHAME

People who join one small movement on one issue of human rights violations by their government soon find themselves marching with tens, then hundreds, then thousands, until a million people are marching together for their many issues. They have connected the dots. They are sending a message. They are making a Report. Although they may not have given it a name, they are engaged in the "mobilization of shame." This remarkable approach has caused ruthless dictators and their underlings to stop murdering, torturing, and detaining innocent people all over the world, from South Africa to East Timor in Indonesia.[1]

Before detailing how this new approach works, it is necessary to record the fact that the traditional system of hiring a lawyer and going to court to get justice on a human rights issue is not working effectively in the United States today.

## 1. WHY NOT JUST HIRE A LAWYER TO SUE?

Many people in the United States continue to think that the best way to enforce a human right is to "sue the bastards" and win before a judge and jury that will award damages. They remember the decisions of the US Supreme Court outlawing racial segregation in schools, upholding the rights of people who get arrested, the right to choose to have an abortion, and the right to damages for some personal injuries caused by corporate decisions to make less safe products.

It has been more than three decades since the end of the Warren Court Era when Chief Justice Earl Warren often helped the other eight Justices of the Court come to such affirmative decisions. For some time the Court has not handed down many broad decisions supporting human rights.

People who are defendants in criminal cases or who are sued in civil cases need to protect their rights before judges and juries. So do people who are arrested for deportation or brought before other administrative agencies where there are no judges or juries but only civil servants (now called Administrative Law Judges) who do not have to meet the strict standards of criminal law in their taking of testimony and making findings of facts.

For these reasons, since 9/11 a significant number of top-notch lawyers are spending their time seeking new ways to represent their clients who are being held by the Government or denied the right to vote. Sometimes they have been successful in slowing down deportations or limiting sentences. Sometimes they have won outright. They have been using every kind of law they can find: federal, state, and municipal law, as well as international and UN law. Several of their victories are recorded in Chapter 4. Some have already been reversed on appeal.

This situation has led many activists and lawyers to begin to use peace law to enforce human rights in the United States. Meiklejohn Institute uncovered this developing body of law as it worked with the UN Charter, the Nuremberg Principles, the antiweapons treaties, and World Court opinions during the 1980s to help the antiapartheid movement in South Africa and then to stop the Gulf War. (See Chapter 6 for relevant articles in these treaties.) Peace law can be used in courts and in nonlitigation efforts to stop violations of human rights, including the right to peace. The law of nations is older and also useful in domestic courts and struggles (and is more acceptable to some decision makers when given this name, rather than the traditional name of "international law").

There is a common misconception that there is no point in using international law or going to the United Nations because the UN can't enforce its decisions. The fact is that the Constitution does not give the Supreme Court the power to enforce its decisions. After the Court ruled that segregation is illegal in 1954 in *Brown v. Board of Education*, very little happened. Some obeyed the decision quickly, pushed by their communities, but it took decades before many local school districts obeyed the Court's ruling. Concerned parents had to get organized, hold meetings, run for the school board, and go back to the lower federal courts to seek injunctions against recalcitrant school boards. And then they had to go back again and again.

By now, activists, educators, and lawyers know that some of the media has not reported what they have been doing since 9/11. This leads some to believe that the media have not been accurately reporting what has been happening in other countries when the people insisted that their governments obey the UN treaties.

Miami, November 20, 2003: Riot police grab a protester off his bike after he expressed his views during a Free Trade protest. The Free Trade Area of the Americas talks were being held several blocks away. (AP Photo/David Adame)

## 2. A WORD OF CAUTION

No one is suggesting that connecting the dots, sending a message, and insisting on Government reports will quickly or automatically stop human rights violations by federal officials. For one thing, the Bush Administration did not make the reports the Government promised to make when it ratified the treaties (see Chapters 3 and 4.F-30). Furthermore, the UN Committees cannot try anyone for violating the laws, and the Bush Government has so far refused to join the new International Criminal Court where individuals can be tried for alleged abuses of internationally accepted human rights.

People in the United States know that slavery was not abolished quickly, nor was the twelve-hour day, the poll tax, or statutory racial segregation. We also know it took a long time to win voting rights for women, to tax the income of the rich, to end the Vietnam War, and to end the McCarthy "red scare" and rehabilitate its victims. But after the first victories, it takes constant vigilance to prevent a return to capital punishment; to prevent defunding of Social Security, medical care, and public education; or to the undermining of other human rights so hard won by the peoples of the United States over the decades and centuries.

In this book we describe many successful efforts to stop human rights violations by our own government through the mobilization of shame. In our current global economy, sending the message to the United Nations and the international media makes it more likely that the media in the United States will begin to report more of the facts.

## 3. A WORD OF HOPE

Some results of reporting on AIDS, Mad Cow disease, police misconduct, and habeas corpus include:

- When a few men became critically ill in San Francisco in the 1980s, and their doctors could not diagnose the cause, no one could help them, and they quietly died. When more and more men became similarly ill, some thoughtful people noticed that they seemed to come from one particular part of San Francisco, geographically and culturally. Keeping track of the patients led doctors very slowly to "discover" the AIDS virus. This led, more quickly, to raising funds for research and, in time, to laboratory work and putting together a series of drugs to alleviate pain and slow the effects of the disease. By this time, the media had learned to cover the story, first in the Bay Area, then in the gay community nationally, and, finally, in the general US population and in the world.
- Mad Cow disease struck the United States in the fall of 2003. While the media reported immediate actions across the country and the world to stem the spread of this fatal disease, experts began to say that the warning signals had been out for some time before anyone acted. But after a few weeks, this story no longer made page one, or even page twenty-one, in the general press.
- An African American man was killed while in the custody of the Cincinnati police department in the fall of 2003. This became news only when the Black community rallied and reported it to the media. They said that this was the eighteenth death of a Black man at the hands of Cincinnati police in recent years. The mayor and police chief at first defended the actions of the white police officers. But community demonstrations will lead to demands for further action against police misconduct (see Chapter 4.A-1.4).

There is no doubt that reporting a wrong can lead to action: first, action to do something for the people already wronged; and subsequently to find the cause of the problem and prevent its recurrence.

Some of the forces profiting from the system failures that led to the deaths from Mad Cow disease may not quickly submit to inspections or they may campaign vigorously against making the changes necessary to address the problem. This was true of the slow response of the pharmaceutical industry to the need to develop reasonably priced drugs to help improve the lives of those living with the AIDs infection. (There are many backdoor campaigns never reported to the public.) But widespread, prompt, and accurate reporting of a problem is a step toward meaningful affirmative action to resolve it.

The reporting tools used to begin to stop AIDS and Mad Cow disease are the same tools being tried by people horrified at police shootings, as well as those used to report government authorized detentions, deportations, instances of torture, and deaths, in addition to the lies about Weapons of Mass Destruction attributed to US Government actions since 9/11, and inefficiencies in acting on tips about terrorist attacks before 9/11.

Reporting is the very tool used by the UN Committees established to investigate and halt human rights violations. The Committees hold hearings and seek commitments by the Governments involved to take certain steps necessary to stop the violations. Then the Committees report to the world on these violations and the corresponding commitments so that the particular Governments will implement the agreed-upon actions.

Just as doctors and agriculture specialists must make a commitment to report contagious diseases to appropriate Government agencies and to the World Health Organization, so nations must make a similar commitment to report to the UN Committees charged with enforcing human rights treaties. The Committees then discuss with the nations' ambassadors what the obstacles are to enforcing human rights and ending abuses.

These reports should become as customary and commonplace as the reports by inspectors of beef shipments or by health departments on the cases of infectious diseases. They are spelled out in each of the international treaties and are to be made periodically.

The Bush Administration insists on constant reporting of the progress of each student in each grade of each public school in the United States, even though it does not continue funding many programs needed to improve public education. The Administration maintains that such reporting of test scores will lead to improvement by students and school administrations; and they will use the reports to deny federal funding to schools that do not show satisfactory results.

While there is great debate over the need for constant testing of students, the Bush Administration did not find the money or the determination to file *any* of the reports on human rights violations it owed to the three UN Human Rights Committees under the terms of three treaties ratified by the United States in the 1990s: the International Covenant on Civil and Political

Rights (ICCPR) (1992), the Convention Against Torture and other Cruel, Inhuman, or Degrading Treatment or Punishment (CAT) (1994), and the Convention on the Elimination of all forms of Racial Discrimination (CERD) (1994).

The US media largely ignores stories from the UN Committees when they report improvements in human rights in countries that result from their reporting to the UN Committees. In fact, the quiet, unobtrusive reporting system of the United Nations has changed many "customs" in many nations, including the treatment of women, children, indigenous people, and immigrants. (It is even causing people in the United States to use the plural "peoples" to describe the many different populations who reside in the United States today, as in most countries.)

## 4. WHAT COURT HAS THE POWER TO ENFORCE ITS DECISIONS?

The frequent comment that the UN lacks the power to enforce its decisions is based on insufficent information about how any governing body ultimately enforces its decisions. Concerned people take cases to court and testify in court; they publicize good decisions, demand that Government officials obey these decisions, and condemn bad decisions while they seek their reversal.

Activists can start reading the UN human rights reporting treaties, which are included in Chapter 6 of this book. They can collect material on human rights violations and do all they can to convince a local nongovernmental organization (NGO) to submit it to the US State Department. They can insist that State Department officials enforce the three reporting treaties by making the required reports and submitting them to the appropriate UN Committees. The Committees will consider these reports in public sessions that can receive broad media coverage. Activists can insist that Government officials take the final step in the reporting process and move to correct policies that violate human rights. This path will encourage whistle-blowing by conscientious people working in all levels of Government.

## C. GOALS OF THIS BOOK

- To spell out and publicize effective actions that individuals, groups, and their lawyers are now taking to redress human rights grievances.
- To present an accurate report of many violations of human rights by the US Government since 9/11 as well as examples of the Government's efforts to enforce these rights.

- To submit the Meiklejohn Institute Report in Chapter 4 to
    (1) the underutilized Office of Inspector General of the US Government agencies involved so that these offices can investigate the allegations and report to Congress. This could lead Congress to investigate and take action against confirmed wrongdoers, and, where necessary, change or strengthen the law.
    (2) the US Secretary of State to include in the reports the Secretary is required to make to the three UN Committees that administer the three ratified human rights treaties.
    (3) the UN High Commissioner for Human Rights and the three UN human rights committees that administer the three treaties.

## D. OUTLINE OF THIS BOOK

Chapter 2 will present the procedures that exist for beginning to deal with the violations of the fundamental rights of the people and the basic duties of the Government. It will describe two kinds of actions that individuals, organizations, and cities can take at the national and international levels. At the national level, readers can find the Web site of the appropriate Office of Inspector General (OIG), use the printed form (if available) to make a complaint, and see that the media gives wide coverage to the OIG procedure for dealing with complaints of misconduct.

The Chapter also describes litigation techniques lawyers can use to help defend people detained and arrested for deportation or demonstrations, and to file affirmative suits against the President, Attorney General, Immigration Service, FBI, and CIA, including a model brief on a charge of "terrorism."

Chapter 3 will describe how the UN Committees use the mobilization of shame to cause governments to improve their human rights records. It will then describe why making a report matters. It will spell out how the reporting process actually works:

(1) in the UN Human Rights Committee, which enforces the International Covenant on Civil and Political Rights (ICCPR) and
(2) in the Committee on Elimination of Racial Discrimination, which enforces the Convention on Elimination of Racial Discrimination (abbreviated as CERD), and
(3) in the Committee Against Torture, which enforces the Convention Against Torture (abbreviated as CAT).

Activists on local issues, and their lawyers, will find that the Second Reports of the Government under each of the three treaties must include state and local reports. People can visit city council members urging them to propose such municipal reporting. The budget costs of such reporting, raised by the Bush State Department, will be addressed in Chapter 3. A Sensible Federal Budget Resolution appears in Chapter 5.B-4.

Petitions on human rights violations in the United States can also be presented to the Organization of American States to the Inter-American Human Rights Commission (see the model letter on precautionary measures in Chapter 3.D).

Chapter 4 will present 180 reports on what actions people in the United States have taken since 9/11—people in the White House; the Pentagon; the Departments of Justice, State, and Labor; in the Congress; people in federal and state courts; in corporate America; in the media; and people in their communities, and in the streets, in libraries, schools, and city councils. This is the first effort to publish in one document summaries of the mass of information on alleged violations that fall into thirty categories. Each report includes the source(s) of the information and each Section lists the specific US and UN laws allegedly violated (or occasionally enforced).

The complete text of laws and resolutions passed by four states and more than 350 cities since 9/11 appears in Chapter 5. This includes resolutions against the USA PATRIOT Act, against the US War/Invasion in Iraq, against corporate personhood, and for worker rights in Iraq, for an Excess Profits/Windfall Revenue Tax on all war and reconstruction contracts, for freedom to read, and for Congressional hearings to investigate grounds for censure or impeachment of certain Government officials. Chapter 5 also presents resolutions encouraging local agencies to file complaints with the Office of Inspector General, to encourage local governments to make Reports to UN Committees, for the Precautionary Principles in making Government contracts, and for a broad city Human Rights Ordinances based on UN Charter Articles 55 and 56, like the Berkeley Ordinance in Chapter 5.C-1.

Chapter 6 will present the *text* of pertinent sections of major legal documents that have allegedly been repeatedly violated, including the US Constitution, the UN Charter, the Nuclear NonProliferation Treaty, and the three human rights treaties. Widespread knowledge of the commitments the United States has made in ratifying these treaties can encourage efforts to enforce their provisions, especially articles in recent treaties that elucidate and/or enumerate provisions in the Constitution, and older statutes and court opinions.

The Table of Cases lists lawsuits described in the entire book, with citations to pages.

The Index to Chapters 1, 2, 3, 5, and 6 includes page references to names, events, topics and laws.

The Index to Reports in Chapter 4 lists names, events, places, and laws described in the 180 Reports with references to the Reports in which the material is described (not to pages).

## E. THE ULTIMATE PURPOSE

The ultimate purpose of this book is to ensure that the facts about all US Government violations (actual and alleged) and the enforcement of human rights are made public. This information is critical for the media, educators, and all concerned people.

If the national path to human rights enforcement through the OIG is successfully followed, and if the international path through the UN Committees is also successfully followed, people will begin to find the strength to repeat the process periodically to the benefit of everyone.

## F. ACTIONS AFTER 9/11: A BRIEF, STARTLING SUMMARY

George W. Bush, as the Commander in Chief, told Congress on September 18, 2001, that he would attack Afghanistan and later Iraq. He did not make a clear statement of his criteria for ending the invasion and occupation. He did not seek a formal Congressional declaration of war against either country, but only the Authorization for Use of Military Force Joint Resolution (PL 107–40, 115 Stat. 224, Sept. 18, 2001). He ordered US troops to be sent to large areas where civilians lived and worked, and there they started dropping bombs.

The peace movement in the United States responded immediately with marches against war, which were joined by marchers in other countries around the world.

George W. Bush, as President, asked Congress to pass the USA PATRIOT Act (Uniting and Strengthening America by Providing Appropriate Tools Required to Intercept and Obstruct Terrorism) without time for study or debate, and Congress complied. Later the President asked Congress to pass the new Department of Homeland Security Act with limited discussion, and Congress complied. Not long thereafter, Congress was shut down for weeks due to the anthrax scare.

The President and Department heads issued a series of Executive Orders and Regulations on new forms of surveillance of residents of the United States, which administrative offices of the Government immediately began carrying out.

The President, as Commander in Chief of a country that had not formally voted to declare war on any country, ordered the arrest of hundreds of men in forty countries, and had them sent to a US base at Guantanamo Bay to be detained under harsh conditions leading to many suicide attempts.

The Environmental Protection Agency studies on Ground Zero after 9/11 were turned into press releases that did not tell the whole truth about the toxic dangers to clean-up workers there. They were "drafted or doctored by White House officials intent on reopening Wall Street," according to the EPA Office of Inspector General (see report 29.2).

The Department of Defense did not notify members of the military or veterans about the dangers of Gulf War Syndrome in 2002–2003, according to investigations by the Office of Inspector General and members of Congress.

George W. Bush, as President, invoked the Taft-Hartley Act for the first time in years to break the International Longshore and Warehouse Union that had been locked out by the Pacific Maritime Association. When union members and the community stood firmly behind the militant union, the Government's tactic failed (see report 23.1).

The then attorney general John Ashcroft issued a long series of Directives on Information Sharing after passage of the USA PATRIOT Act. Critics found few indications of respect for the right to privacy enshrined in the First and Ninth Amendments, and many indications of an effort by the head of one Department to take charge of many dispersed governmental units.

In late 2003, the new Department of Homeland Security issued new plans for surveillance of virtually everyone living in the United States. The plan called for the name, photograph, address, social security number, bank account, and other facts about each individual to become part of a database that can be called up by any Government official at any time for any, or no, reason under this plan (see Report 8.1).

Prior to the computer age, such universal surveillance was not possible even when earlier administrations acted autocratically. The reactions to this total destruction of the right to privacy were immediate. The American Civil Liberties Union, Human Rights Watch, the National Lawyers Guild, the Center for Constitutional Rights, Amnesty International, Human Rights First, and a great many other local, national, and international NGOs, as well as individuals protested loudly and often. They filed lawsuits and defended victims in courts and administrative hearings.

The FBI, the Attorney General, the CIA, Immigration officials, and state and local police arrested people based on their national origin, religion, race, or their association with such persons. These people were detained and many were subjected to torture or degrading treatment (see Chapter 4.A-2). Some people were killed; others committed suicide (see Chapter 4.A-1). Prison guards put many detainees in chains and deliberately served them food that violated the dietary restrictions of their religion. The Government required thousands born in specific designated countries to register with Immigration officials. The Immigration Service detained many and then deported thousands without hearings (see the reports in Chapter 4).

Citizens convinced four states and 350 cities to pass resolutions for repeal of the USA PATRIOT Act, condemning police misconduct toward peaceful protesters, and supporting the rights of their immigrant residents. Some members of Congress called for repeal of all or many sections of the Act, and sought to protect the right to privacy of library users. Representative Dennis Kucinich (D-OH) introduced an alternative act witch he dubbed The True Patriot Act.

In the face of citizen's anger at several actions of George W. Bush, on the recommendation of city staff, the City Council of Santa Cruz, California, took action. They wrote a letter to the House Judiciary Committee asking its members to determine whether President Bush had committed impeachable offenses in his actions in Iraq. Arcata, California, soon took similar action, as did the Conference of Delegates of California Bar Associations (see Chapter 5.B-6).

Immigration officials denied some admittedly valid petitions for political asylum until it was too late, sending some men to their deaths in the countries from which they had fled (see Report 1.1). Delays led to disruption of many families, widespread despair, and anger (see Chapter 4, Section20).

Immigration officials required the registration of all noncitizen males from a specified list of countries even though these individuals had lived in the United States for many years and a large number had US-citizen wives and children. Of the 83,000 who registered, Immigration brought deportation proceedings against 13,000. As a result, many thousands who wanted to stay in the United States followed the procedure called "voluntary departure" rather than face extended periods in confinement or trial on minor immigration law violations. A few were able to find counsel to defend them against deportation charges.

In the second required noncitizen registration which occurred in the fall 2003, registrants were also forced to give the names and addresses of family members and friends. In response to numerous complaints, Immigration officials announced that there would be no more such registrations; other means would be found to obtain necessary information on noncitizens (see Chapter 4, Section8).

The major media reported some of these events in full, others in part, and some not at all. Journalists did report the killing of men and women in the United States and abroad—killings by individuals and by groups, by prison guards, by FBI agents, and by US military personnel. Some of the killings were deliberate and planned and some were accidents, while others were part of US military attacks on soldiers of other countries and still others were suicides.

A few individuals and small hate groups felt justified in killing, detaining, and torturing people they decided were "terrorists" (see Chapter 4, Reports 1.5, 4.3, 6.3, 6.4). Some journalists were victims themselves as they worked on their stories (see Chapter 4, Report 7.5).

The Office of the Inspector General in some departments and agencies of the federal Government fulfilled their statutory duty to investigate and report on complaints of misconduct. But when the OIG of the Environmental Protection Agency made such a report to the House and Senate Judiciary Committee chairs and vice chairs, they did not succeed in their statutory duty to see that this report was widely publicized in the media (see Chapter 4, Report 29.2).

The Bush Administration convinced Congress to include in the Homeland Security Department Act permission for the Attorney General to decide by himself, without review, when complaints about the Department of Justice, customarily put in an Inspector General's report to Congress, shall not be reported.

The Secretary of State appointed by George W. Bush failed to file any periodic Second Reports on enforcement of human rights in the United States required under the three human rights treaties mentioned above. The Second Reports under the treaties which came due in 1997 and 1998 were not filed by the Bush Administration (see Report 30.1).

A few public radio and public TV programs began to air broad reports on some violations of rights and duties by some federal departments. On Oct. 5, 2004, the US Commission on Civil Rights issued its report, *Redefining Rights in America—The Civil Rights Record of the George W. Bush Administration, 2001–2004*. The 180-page report concluded that:

- The Bush Administration did not provide leadership to ensure the timely passage of the Help America Vote Act of 2002 or push for funding and swift enforcement before the 2004 election.
- The No Child Left Behind Act does not do enough to bridge the gap between white and minority children.
- The Administration did not push for affirmative action but "race neutral alternatives" that were not effective in maintaining diversity.
- The Administration did not take the initiative to stop environmental contamination of minority communities.
- The Administration instituted racial profiling of people from Arab and Middle Eastern countries, leading to increased scrutiny, interviews, registration, and removal.

(http://www.usccr.gov/pubs/bush/bush04.pdf.)

After the November 2004 election, President Bush announced that the terms of Commission Chair Mary Francis Berry and Commission member

Cruz Reynoso would end in December 2004. They said they understood that their terms ran into January 2005.

All of these events occurred against a backdrop of economic downturn, sometimes called "weak recovery." Between 2.3 and 3 million jobs in the United States were lost between the 2000 and 2004 elections. Many of the people who lost their jobs were men and women with secure positions in seemingly prosperous manufacturing corporations and in traditional Government agencies, libraries, and schools. Unexpected layoffs often lead to increasing rage within individuals and violence within families. At the same time, President Bush demanded massive cuts in income tax rates for the very wealthy. The Department of Justice AntiTrust and Criminal Divisions charged only a few corporate executives for their white-collar crimes, were slow to bring the cases to trial, and sought lower fines and sentences than their victims thought they deserved. These actions occurred within the United States and Guantanamo Bay while the US military was carrying out attacks on Afghanistan and Iraq without a formal declaration of war.

Some critics of the Bush Administration pointed out that President Franklin Roosevelt had asked Congress to declare war against Germany, Italy, and Japan after the attack on Pearl Harbor in 1941. And President Roosevelt helped to found (and later, turned to) the United Nations in 1945 near the end of that war in order to make future wars preventable by joint actions of concerned nations.

President Bush and his Cabinet members insisted that the reason the United States must go to war in Iraq was to stop Saddam Hussein from using, or continuing to build, Weapons of Mass Destruction. Almost from the moment he made this statement, UN observers and others challenged the assertion that Hussein had such weapons. In time, the challengers were vindicated.

President Bush did not follow the procedures the United States agreed to when it ratified the UN Charter in 1945 set forth in Chapter 6 on the Peaceful Settlement of Disputes, that required him to seek the assistance of the Security Council or the General Assembly, not simply to inform them of the actions he was about to take (see UN Charter Art. 33, 35, and 37, in Chapter 6.C). President Bush designated the military to carry out US policies in Iraq after he announced that "the war" was over. US military personnel, including many in the Army Reserves and National Guard, were killed by cluster bombs and attacks by angry Iraqis, whose relatives were also killed at the end of 2003 and in 2004 by cluster bombs, dirty water, and by the poverty accompanying 70 percent unemployment (see Report 23.4). By January 2004, twenty-four US service members in Iraq had committed suicide and thousands in Iraq and on rotation in the United States were suffering from post-traumatic stress syndrome.

On Veterans Day, November 11, 2003, members of Congress introduced a resolution urging President Bush to fire Secretary of Defense Donald Rumsfeld for misleading the people of the United States on assessments of progress in the war and the occupation, for sending forces to Iraq "without adequate planning and equipment," and for "demonstrated lack of sensitivity" in his statements about the war and about US casualties (Reuters, November 11, 2003). In 2003, the Departmen of Defense and the Joint Chiefs were in charge of 750 US military bases abroad.

Late in 2003, the US public began to hear about hundreds of men being held at Abu Ghraib in Iraq after US troops captured them somewhere in Iraq or in nearby countries. Then the media presented actual photographs of naked men being hit and humiliated in front of their US military guards. This led to an investigation by the DOD and Joint Chiefs, a series of reports, and arrests for possible court-martial of some of the troops in the photographs. These revelations also led many US NGOs to demand a full investigation (see Report 213).

Then the 9/11 Commission began to hold public hearings on March 31, 2003, that were broadcast live on some public radio stations. Many were not satisfied. They said the Commission's report raised many questions about what Presidents Clinton and Bush knew and when they knew about the threats of an attack on US cities before 9/11. Even more so, it led to many discussions about the failure of President Bush to act on information he and his staff had received from US intelligence sources (see reports 12.4 and 12.5).

In June 2004, the US Supreme Court ruled in *Rasul v. Bush* (124 S. Ct. 2686) that the US Constitution does apply to persons captured after 9/11 and taken to Guantanamo Bay, and designated as "enemy combatants." They are entitled to habeas corpus. The Court did not rule on a series of other issues (see Report 19.5).

In the summer of 2004, the Federal Communications Commission began to hold hearings around the country to listen to complaints by concerned TV viewers and radio listeners regarding the effects of recent media mergers permitted by the FCC. The outpouring of people wanting to make statements indicated to the FCC members present that there is, indeed, a serious problem, particularly in relation to news coverage. Also in the summer of 2004, millions of viewers went to the movies to see Michael Moore's *Fahrenheit 9/11*, Robert Greenwald's *Out FOXed*, and Jehane Noujaim's *Control Room*, depicting many current events as covered by the media.

The Democratic Party Convention in Boston in July and the Republican Party Convention in New York in August 2004 provided official forums for Government spokespersons, candidates, and some pundits to speak on prime-time TV. The Conventions stimulated many activists to speak, to ask questions, to demonstrate, and to hold public forums largely off camera.

The cordoning off of Free Speech Areas by local government officials far from the Party Conventions and surrounded by massive local and federal police drew widespread fury among concerned citizens. People began to say, "The Constitution doesn't limit where I can speak and demonstrate to a Free Speech Area far from the people I want to talk to!" Legal scholars began pointing out that the right "peaceably to assemble, and to petition the Government for a redress of grievances" is in addition to the right to freedom of speech. In order to petition the Government, a person has to be able to go where the Government is and petition—by means of speaking to the Government (that is, to a Government official), or by giving the official a petition in writing. The Conventions also led to criticism of some of the major media for having slanted the reporting of the Conventions, of the large gatherings outside the Convention areas, and of the massive arrests (see report 3.9).

Since 9/11, millions of individuals and hundreds of groups across the nation have been spending their time and energy—in some cases risking arrest, detention, and mistreatment—in order to defeat a mindset that they perceive condones killings; torture; scapegoating; racial profiling; and discrimination based on religion, color, national origin, immigration status, and gender.

Each month in 2004 seemed to bring to light some new Government report on some new problem or scandal. Many of the events mentioned above are described in detail in the 180 Reports in Chapter 4 and in the city council resolutions in Chapter 5. The relevant law is mentioned throughout Chapter 4 and is reprinted in Chapter 6.

## G. WHAT IS THE REAL SCORE IN THE "WAR ON TERRORISM"?

As a result of all of the actions by the US Government in the so-called war against terrorism, where are we at after more than three years?

In July 2004, then attorney general John Ashcroft issued his "Report from the Field: The USA PATRIOT Act at Work": "The information-sharing and coordination made possible by Section218 assisted the prosecution in San Diego of several persons involved in an al Qaeda drugs-for-weapons plot, which culminated in several guilty pleas. They admitted that they conspired to receive, as partial payment for heroin and hashish, four Stinger antiaircraft missiles that they then intended to sell to the Taliban, an organization they knew at the time to be affiliated with al Qaeda."[2] He did not mention that the conspiracy was actually with US undercover agents who offered them the weapons.

In October 2002, then Attorney General John Ashcroft called a national press conference to announce the arrest of four "radical Islamists" from Detroit, based on sketches and videotapes seized from them. He said they were conspiring to launch a holy war to drive US forces from the Arabian peninsula. A federal grand jury charged them with operating a "covert underground support unit for terrorist attacks within and outside the United States, as well as a sleeper operational combat cell." The grand jury also charged them with nonterrorist minor document fraud. After trial, the jury acquitted one defendant; found another guilty on one nonterrorist charge of document fraud, and found the other two guilty of both conspiracy and document fraud.

On December 12, 2003, the federal court judge admonished then attorney general Ashcroft for violating his gag order as defense counsel filed papers alleging systematic misconduct by the Assistant US Attorney. On August 24, 2004, the Department of Justice asked the judge to grant the defendants' motion to vacate the convictions, to drop all "terrorist" charges, and to conduct a new trial solely on minor "document fraud" charges.

On September 2, 2004, the judge threw out their convictions, which were the only convictions of "terrorists," out of more than 5,000 foreign nationals detained in "antiterrorism" sweeps since 9/11 (see Report 18.7).

After investigating numerous complaints, the American Civil Liberties Union and the New York Civil Liberties Union sued to enjoin Ashcroft and the Department of Justice from enforcing USA PATRIOT Act § 505 because it gave them unchecked authority to issue National Securtiy Letters to obtain sensitive customer records from Internet Service Providers and other businesses without judicial oversight. On September 29, 2004, Federal Judge Victor Marrero (SD-NY) granted their injunction (*Doe and ACLU v. Ashcroft*, et al., No. 04-CIV-2615).

The Humanitarian Law Project that provided aid to the Kurdish Workers Party in Turkey brought two suits challenging provisions of the Antiterrorism Act of 1996 and the PATRIOT Act that make it a crime to give "material support" to organizations without requiring proof of knowledge that the organizations were engaged in terorrism. The Ninth Circuit Court of Appeals held certain sections of the Antiterrorism Act unconstitutional on December 3, 2003. On March 17, 2004, the US District Court for the Central District of California enjoined Ashcroft and the DOJ from enforcing the USA PATRIOT Act §§ 8–5(a)(2)(B) against the plaintiffs for giving "expert advice or assistance" to the named Kurdish organizations (see report 18.6).[3]

On September 17, 2004, the *San Francisco Chronicle* (page 3) published a summary of the record in court of US charges brought against terrorist suspects by the US Department of Justice:

- Charges dropped against Army Capt. James Yee (see Chapter 4, Report 6.1), and Detroit "sleeper cell" defendants (see Koubriti, Chapter 4, Report 18.7).
- Idaho jury acquitted Student Sami Omar al-Hussayen on charges of

using his computer skills to foster terrorism, deadlocked on eight immigration charges. Al-Hussayen decided not to fight deportation so was not retried on those charges.

- The FBI apologized for mistakenly arresting Brandon Mayfield, a Portland, Oregon, lawyer and convert to Islam, based on fingerprints found near the scene of the Madrid train bombings March 11, 2004.
- No charges were filed against six hundred men being held at Guantanamo Bay, Cuba (see Chapter 4, Reports 19.1–3, 19.5–7). After US Supreme Court decisions in spring 2004, the Navy said it released one hundred fifty detainees and allowed them to return home. Navy Secretary Gordon England said more than two hundred cases are pending before a military tribunal.
- Jose Padilla (see Chapter 4, Report 18.1).
- Zacarias Moussaoui, the only US defendant charged with a role in the September 11 attacks (see Chapter 4, Report 18.5).
- Yaser Esam Hamdi (see Chapter 4, Report 19.2).
- Yasir Muhiddin Aref and Mohammad Mosharref Hossain—Albany, New York, mosque leaders—were released on bail in August 2004 when the federal judge concluded they were not as dangerous as the Government had claimed.
- John Walker Lindh pleaded guilty to aiding the Taliban and was sentenced to twenty years in prison.
- The Lackawanna Six pleaded guilty and were sentenced for up to ten years on charges of providing material support to al Qaeda in 2001.
- In 2002, the Portland Seven were indicted and later convicted for conspiring to wage war against the US by joining the Taliban after 9/11. They were sentenced to ten to eighteen years.
- In 2003, Richard Reid, the so-called shoe bomber, was sentenced to life in prison for trying to blow up a Paris-to-Miami flight with plastic explosives in his shoe.

These trials and court decisions raise a series of questions:

- How many of the alleged perpetrators of the acts of 9/11 have been charged and convicted of that crime?
- Have the reasons behind these terrorist actions been clearly spelled out?
- How many millions of people in the United States who are guilty of no crimes have been detained, lost their jobs, or have had their lives disrupted in the Government's "war on terrorism"?
- Did the loss of 180,000 union jobs through the Homeland Security Department Act actually "ensure airport security"? Was security heightened as a result of repeated efforts widely interpreted as

designed to break militant labor unions and destroy the right to organize? (see Report 23.1)

- Did millions of US workers feel more secure when they read what happened when some of their numbers went to Miami in November 2003 to demonstrate peacefully against the Free Trade Area of the Americas? The union members were building on the strong demonstrations in Seattle against the World Trade Organization in 1999. But here, the police attacked them using dangerous weapons in the most vicious police assault in recent times (see Report 3.6).
- When the Department of Defense demanded, and got, massive increases in the military budget, including funding for new types of nuclear weapons and other weapons of mass destruction, did this increase homeland security?
- Did it increase homeland security when, after joining the Service in order to get an education and "to be all you want to be," the DOD denied discharges to Service members who discovered they were conscientious objectors to war? (see Reports 16.1–16.3)
- Is the country more secure because the Government has made major cuts in the budget for education, health and human services, medical care, battered women's shelters, and for rehabilitation of parolees and first offenders, and has "borrowed" money from Social Security reserves? (see Chapter 4.E)
- Is the United States more secure because 83,000 people were required to register with the Immigration Service and 13,000 of these people were deported or currently face deportation? (see Reports 8.1–8.3)
- When thousands of foreign scholars and students had their academic work interrupted or ended as a result of denied visas or foreign work permits, even though they were not charged with any wrongdoing, did that help the war against terrorism? (see Chapter 4, Section10)
- Did it help that treaties were broken and the United States failed to honor its many commitments to other nations? (see Report 30.1 and Chapter 4.C)
- Did the people of the United States feel more secure when, in December 2003, the DOD announced that contracts for reconstructing Iraq after the massive damage by US and British bombing would be made only with corporations in nations that supported the United States war in Iraq? Did everyone agree to eliminate contracts to corporations in China, France, and Germany, among others, even if the costs involved were *much* less?
- Did people in the United States feel more secure when, just before the November 2004 election, the FBI began a criminal probe into how Halliburton got its war contracts?[4]

Some observers have noticed some interesting facts:

- No agency of the US Government has stated why it believes that its actions since 9/11 will reduce the number of people in the world who hate the United States, its institutions, and its people and might therefore commit terrorist attacks against us.
- No federal Government agency has made a point of working against terrorism with any of the UN bodies under the UN antiterrorism treaties that the US Government has ratified (see Chapter 4.15).
- Many US military officers, and Bush as Commander in Chief, have expressed concern that military staff may have taken, or may take, actions under the stress of battle (as in Kosovo, Afghanistan, or Iraq) that could lead to charges that they committed war crimes or crimes against peace or violated the Geneva Conventions. This fear caused Bush to announce US withdrawal from the new International Criminal Court, and to seek bilateral agreements with many nations that they would not seek to arrest or charge US Troops with violations of the law of nations.
- An unending war against terrorism has been declared, with daily reports of bombings and missiles, of deaths and destruction, and with rumors of new nations to be invaded by US troops.
- UN Secretary-General Kofi Annan said on October 17, 2004, "I cannot say the world is safer . . . when you look around you and see the terrorist attacks around the world and you see what is going on in Iraq. . . . We have a lot of work to do as an international community to try and make the world safer." He had earlier said the US-led war to topple Hussein was "illegal" because the US and its partners never got UN Security council backing for the invasion.[5]
- Just before the 2004 election, a scholarly study suggested the number of military and civilian deaths in Iraq was closer to 100,000 than to the 30,000 reported earlier.[6]

## H. WHAT HAS CLEARLY BEEN MISSING IN US GOVERNMENT ACTIONS SINCE 9/11

- Few Government officials have evidenced an understanding of the fundamental civil liberties spelled out in the First Amendment: that all of the people have a right to peaceably assemble to petition the Government for a redress of grievances; all people have a right to freedom of speech and of the press, this right is heightened in the exercise of academic freedom; all people have a right to free exercise of religion; and all people have a right to privacy.

- Few Government officials have evidenced an understanding of the fundamental and universal due process rights spelled out in the US Constitution in Article I, Section 9, and the Fourth, Fifth, Sixth, and Eighth Amendments: right to prompt notification of criminal charges immediately after arrest in the habeas corpus clause, no unreasonable searches or seizures, right to counsel, trial by impartial judge and jury of the community, no cruel and unusual punishment or unreasonable bail.
- Few Government officials have evidenced an understanding of some fundamental civil rights: no state or federal agencies shall "deny any person . . . the equal protection of the laws" regardless of race, color, national origin, religion, gender, or by judicial interpretation of statutes. (While this is explicitly stated in the Fourteenth Amendment to apply to the states, it has long been included in the Fifth Amendment due process clause by judicial interpretation, and all of the Civil Rights Acts are based on this concept.)
- Only a handful of federal officials have displayed awareness that the Government has ratified three treaties on human rights that include commitments to make periodic reports to three UN Committees and to dialogue with the Committee members on how to overcome obstacles to enforcing human rights in all territories under US jurisdiction.
- Only a handful of officials or members of the DOD or Joint Chiefs have indicated that they are aware that the federal Government helped to write and then ratified the UN Charter. They do not mention that Article 2.3 of that charter specifically provides that every member nation "shall settle their international disputes by peaceful means in such a manner that international peace, and justice, are not endangered." Nor do they mention that Article 2.4 provides that every member nation "shall refrain in their international relations from the threat or use of force against the territorial integrity or political independence of any state, or in any other manner inconsistent with the Purposes of the United Nations."
- To date no one from the DOD or the Joint Chiefs has prepared a report to the three UN Committees on the extent to which the United States has complied with its duty to protect life, and not to discriminate against people from certain countries or religious or national or racial groups, and not to use torture or other criminal or degrading treatment on anyone, as forbidden in the three treaties.
- To date no Government officials have reported on how the United States has or has not respected members of the military who have become conscientious objectors to war because they are no longer willing to kill or injure anyone labeled "the enemy" or to subject them to torture or to other cruel or degrading treatment.

- To date very few US Government officials have indicated that they are aware that the federal Government has a duty to its people and to the international community to live up to its commitments on human rights and peace to the same degree that they demand that other nations live up to commitments in North American Free Trade Agreement and FTAA Agreements to pay high-interest rates on loans and on other economic issues.

# I. MEIKLEJOHN INSTITUTE'S QUALIFICATIONS TO MAKE THIS REPORT

Meiklejohn Civil Liberties Institute (MCLI) is in a unique position to present this challenge to US human rights violations since September 11, 2001. The Institute was founded in 1965 to carry forward the heritage of Alexander Meiklejohn, the famous educator who worked within the traditional system for alternatives in the academic world as Dean at Brown University (1903–1911), president of Amherst (1912–1923), chair of the Experimental College at the University of Wisconsin (1927–1932), and founder of the San Francisco School of Social Studies (1932–1941), the adult evening school for workers. While serving on the ACLU national board (1927–1963), he developed a distinct, absolute interpretation of the First Amendment published in book form in *Free Speech and Its Relation to Government* (1948) that was respected, if not adopted, by several members of the US Supreme Court. (Cynthia Stokes Brown, "Alexander Meiklejohn: Teacher of Freedom"[MCLI 1981]).

In 1964 he gave permission to use his name in the new institute in Berkeley. In 1965 the Cold War/Truman/McCarthey period was claiming its last victims, the Civil Rights Movement was winning some important victories, and opposition to the war in Vietnam was just beginning.

The MCLI was founded as a center for human rights and peace law in order to document and help overcome violations of this basic law. The MCLI archival collections go back to the post–World War I raids of then Attorney General Mitchell Palmer when so-called radicals, workers, and immigrants were the targets of massive illegal arrests, detentions, and deportations.

From 1969 to 1995, law student interns at the Institute have helped prepare editions of the "Human Rights & Peace Law Docket," reporting the status of ten thousand cases alleging violations of civil liberties, due process, and civil rights, as well as economic, social, and cultural rights. These reports are now available on the Bancroft Library/University of California Web site at http://bancroft.berkeley.edu/collections/meiklejohn/project.html.

Washington, DC, October 23, 2004: Row upon row of more that 1,100 flag-draped symbolic coffins line the edges of the reflecting pool that stretches a third of a mile from the base of the Lincoln Memorial. The tribute was in honor of the US service men and women killed in Iraq up to that date. In the background is the Washington Monument. (AP Photo/Evan Vucci)

In 1994 the Meiklejohn Institute prepared and submitted its report on the status of human rights and weapons stockpiles in the United States to the US Department of State to include in the first US report to the UN Human Rights Committee enforcing the International Covenant on Civil and Political Rights in the United States. The MCLI report included descriptions of many human rights violations that the State Department did not include in the first US report under the Covenant. The MCLI also submitted its report directly to that UN Committee. The Institute then sent two representatives to attend the dialogue between the UN Committee and the US Government on this first US Report in New York in 1995. The Committee thanked MCLI for the material it provided.

Meiklejohn also presented testimony at Congressional hearings, State Bar Conferences, and at City Council meetings on human rights violations and enforcement in various jurisdictions.

In 1999 and 2000, the MCLI submitted shadow reports to the Department of State. to the UN Committee Against Torture and to the UN Committee on Elimination of Racial Discrimination. The Institute also made a statement to CERD at its meeting in Geneva just before the UN World Conference Against Racism in Durban, South Africa, at which the MCLI presented a workshop.

In 2003, the MCLI published "How To Use 'New' Civil Rights Laws after 9/11," describing sixty-nine US court decisions in favor of victims of human rights violations based on provisions of the UN Charter, the ratified UN treaties, and the US Constitution. These decisions had not been previously publicized.

On March 15, 2005, the Berkeley City Council voted unanimously to "submit . . . a copy of this Report to the U.S. State Department and to the UN High Commissioner for Human Rights and to the UN Human Rights Committee during its spring 2005 meeting in New York as one step in upholding the International Covenant on Civil and Political Rights, the Convention Against Torture, and the Convention on the Elimination of Racial Discrimination; and . . . to send a copy of this resolution to Governor Arnold Schwarzenegger, Senators Boxer and Feinstein, Representatives Lee and Pelosi, and be made available to interested media and NGOs."

The MCLI maintains a Web site at http://mcli.org.

# 2
# WHERE THE PEOPLE AND THEIR LAWYERS CAN GO TO REDRESS GRIEVANCES

Individuals whose human rights are violated by an agency of the US Government can pursue at least five paths in the United States to seek an end to the illegal practices and/or to seek damages for the loss of their rights. They can:

1. follow the procedures of the Office of Inspector General.
2. have their lawyers raise affirmative issues when they are defending them on criminal charges in federal and state court cases arising out of their campaigns to change Government actions.
3. ask their lawyers to file suit in federal court for these remedies.
4. ask their lawyers to file suit in state court for these remedies.
5. go to their legislative bodies and seek a change in laws, rules, or procedures.

Chapter 2 lays out paths 1 through 4. Chapter 5 includes successful legislative efforts.

## A. US OFFICE OF INSPECTOR GENERAL

Since 1978, virtually every US Government agency has had an Office of Inspector General (OIG) to receive and investigate complaints about misconduct by employees of the agency (including the new Department of Homeland Security) or by companies with government contracts. The USA PATRIOT Act acknowledges the requirements of OIG reports on complaints they receive. The OIG is required to file a report with the chair and vice-chair of the Senate and House Judiciary Committees every six months. The only exceptions are the Executive Office of the President, the CIA, the Government Accountability Office, and any entities of the judicial or legislative branches.

Organizations and individuals can use this procedure to get action on their complaints against many government agencies. This is particularly appropriate because the Office of Inspector General Act specifically requires each OIG to publicize its work so people will know how to file complaints. And it requires the OIGs to inform the media about their investigations and findings.

Representative John Conyers (D-MI) has been Vice-Chair of the House Judiciary Committee for several years, and he has made many reports to the House and the media based on the OIG reports he has received.

Each Office of Inspector General is required to be independent of all other parts of its Department. All OIGs are required to conduct independent investigations of all complaints. However, there were exceptions in the original Act as to the power of the Attorney General and DOD to limit OIG investigations of certain types. Under the statute, all OIGs are appointed by the President with the advice and consent of the Senate without regard to political affiliation, and no military officer can be an Inspector General.

## 1. SCANDALS LEAD TO INSPECTOR GENERALS

Until 9/11, the Office of Inspector General Act of 1978 (5 U.S.C. Appendix §§ 1–12) was only used by the handful of people who knew about it to complain about fraud by Government contractors and other misconduct by Government employees. The OIG procedure has yet to be used extensively by people who have a legitimate complaint about a human rights violation.

Many actions by Government agencies and individual officials after 9/11 have led to several significant, and shocking, reports by OIGs in the Immigration Service and the Environmental Protection Agency (see Chapter 4, Reports 29.1 and 29.2). Inspector General Glenn A. Fine of the (newly named) Bureau of Citizenship and Immigration Services (BCIS) of the new Bureau of Immigration and Customs Enforcement (formerly part of Immigration and Naturalization Service) filed *The September 11 Detainees: A Review of the Treatment of Aliens Held on Immigration Charges in Connection with the Investigation of the September 11 Terrorist Attack*. He filed his report in June 2003 describing systemic problems that arose during his investigation because the FBI detained people thought to have been involved in 9/11 on immigration law violations. He reported that 60.7 percent of the time detainees did not receive charging documents within the seventy-two hours required by law, and some did not receive the other documents concerning their status until a month after being detained. The BCIS detained people until the FBI had checked on them. This took an average of eighty days. The detainees were not released on bond and were confined under highly restrictive conditions, which included a detainee being escorted in handcuffs, leg irons, and heavy chains until released (See Chapter 4, Report 29.1). These conditions violate the basic rights of immigrants who are involved in civil, not criminal, cases and who violate administrative, not criminal, laws.

Inspector General Fine also reported the Government's restrictive policy on phone use, limiting detainees' conversations with their lawyers to one per week, even if this meant the detainee only left a message with the lawyer's office. Some guards limited such calls to three minutes. The report also documented allegations of physical assaults, bending of fingers, hitting heads against the wall, and putting detainees in a cell naked and without a blanket. His report did not indicate that the Bureau had changed any of these policies as a result of complaints or his report.

## 2. COMPLAINTS THAT CAN BE FILED WITH OIGs

*On Racial Discrimination and Hate Crimes*: Any time someone hears about an act of racial injustice by anyone in the US Government, he or she can send a complaint to the Office of Inspector General of the Civil Rights Division of the US Department of Justice, asking them to investigate the complaint and report their results to the Senate and House Judiciary Committees. The address of the OIG for each department is on the Web page of that department, or it can be obtained by a phone call to the Department. For example, the Web page of the Justice Department OIG is http://www.usdoj.gov/oig/. A complaint should be addressed to the Civil Rights Division. The postal address is US Department of Justice, Office of Inspector General, 950 Pennsylvania Avenue NW, Suite 4322, Washington, DC 20530–0001.

*On Misconduct by State and City Officials*: The Government funds a great many state, county, and city programs, so a discriminatory action by a state, county, or city employee can be the basis for a complaint to the federal agency funding the program. For example, complaints can be made to the US agency funding state prison guards asking for an investigation of cruel or inhuman treatment in a state prison. Complaints can be made to the federal agency funding state aid agencies if city or county personnel do not distribute federal aid fairly.

*On Corporate Misconduct*: Every complaint against a corporation that is subject to the Antitrust Acts of 1890 and 1914—that is, virtually every corporation—can lead to a complaint to the OIG of the Antitrust Division of the Department of Justice, which is required to investigate the complaint and make a report within six months to the Chair and Vice-Chair of the House and Senate Judiciary Committees (see Chapter 4.22).

*On Violations of Disarmament and Weapons Agreements*: It is possible for someone to file a complaint with the OIG of the Department of Defense asking for an investigation into whether the DOD is maintaining, upgrading, or repairing any weapons that are in violation of the 1996 World Court opinion that nuclear weapons are illegal. (*Legality of the Threat or Use of Nuclear Weapons*, Int'l. Ct. of Justice, July 8, 1996, General List No. 95.) (See Report 17.3.) An individual or organization can also file a complaint about the announcement that the DOD is planning to make "baby nukes," asking whether this would be illegal under that World Court opinion.

## A Note of Caution

Filing a complaint with the Office of Inspector General of each agency that is allegedly violating federal law does not mean that every OIG will investigate the complaint thoroughly and make a complete and accurate report to the Senate and House Judiciary Committees on April 30 or October 31, so that the reports can be released on July 1 and January 1. However, if individuals and organizations do *not* file such complaints, there is no chance of an honest OIG report. Many OIGs are determined to live up to their statutory responsibilities, as shown in the EPA OIG report below (and in Chapter 4, Reports 29.1 and 29.2).

## Steps To Take:

1. Determine the specific agency that allegedly committed an illegal act.
2. Access the Web page of the Office of Inspector General for that agency and read from the last report it made to Congress on the issue that concerns you.
3. Write a complaint including the date of the incident; the name(s) of the person(s) or company that violated your right; the person's title and the agency for which that person works; exactly what happened (who did what to whom); what right you feel was violated; what harm was done to you: physically, emotionally, financially; and the names of witnesses to the incident and how to contact them. Describe your attempts to solve the problem. Give the names of Government officials who failed or refused to discuss the problem in a constructive manner. Give your complete address, e-mail and postal, and your phone number and fax if you can take calls without undue stress (see Chapter 5.D-2).
4. If possible have the complaint cosigned by concerned organizations or individuals and send it to the OIG by snail mail with return receipt requested and by e-mail, keeping a copy with the date sent. At this point, or at any point, send a copy to the media.
5. If you are in a hurry because the misconduct is too brutal or immediate, let your Congress members know you have filed the com-

plaint. And if it won't cause further difficulty, let local Government officials know you have filed a complaint against them.

6. Expect some kind of contact from the OIG of the agency required to investigate your complaint.

7. When the Judiciary Committee issues its press release on the OIG complaints it has received over the past six months, check how your complaint was handled. (OIGs can lump complaints together or decide that some complaints are "frivolous" and don't require investigation.)

8. Send a copy of the complaint and the OIG action to the Secretary of State to include in the reports the secretary is required to make to the UN Committees (see Reports 29, 30 and Chapter 5.D-2).

9. Regardless of the action or inaction of the OIG and/or the Judiciary Committee chairs, send a copy of the complaint to the Meiklejohn Institute, Box 673, Berkeley, CA 94701–0673, or challenging @mcli.org. The MCLI will include the complaint in the report it makes on the enforcement of the three human rights reporting treaties.

10. Send a copy to the UN High Commissioner for Human Rights: Palais des Nations 8–14 avenue de la Paix CH–1211 Geneva 10, Switzerland.

11. Check the text of the three human rights treaties in Chapter 6. If it is appropriate, send a copy to the UN Human Rights Committee on any issue in the International Covenant on Civil and Political Rights. Send a copy to the UN Committee Against Torture, and/or the UN Committee on the Elimination of Racial Discrimination if the complaint is on an issue of concern to them.

## Bumps in the Road

Something happened to one critical report by the OIG of the Environmental Protection Agency after it was issued and given wide circulation. The OIG reported to the House and Senate Judiciary Committees that the EPA did not tell the truth when it said it was safe to work at Ground Zero immediately after 9/11 when they knew it was not safe (see Report 29.2). The Administration apparently caused the EPA to amend its original report. And the OIG issued its report to the media effectively. But, if you go to the OIG Web site for the EPA now, you will find that this report has been removed from distribution to the public. This is possible under a provision of the USA PATRIOT Act.

Many in the Office of Inspector General of many agencies continue to work hard at their jobs of investigating all complaints, however embarrassing to the agencies. We, as citizens, have a right and a duty to use this newly dis-covered old tool in our work on every issue on which the Government seems to be acting unfairly or illegally.

### Groups Can Act in Cities, Counties, States, and in Washington

There is widespread concern about how enforcement of the USA PATRIOT Act can destroy democracy in cities, counties, and states. This fear has led governing bodies of some cities, counties, and states to pass a series of resolutions calling for repeal of the USA PATRIOT Act, in whole or in part. In Minneapolis, Minnesota, this led to specific orders to local police officials not to cooperate with federal officials seeking to enforce certain provisions in the Act that are deemed unconstitutional (see Chapter 4, Section 6 introduction, and Chapter 5.A-1).

This concern can be the basis for NonGovernmental Organizations (NGOs) to propose that cities, counties, and states also pass resolutions calling on the Office of Inspector General to investigate complaints of misconduct by many federal agencies, including the Bureau of Customs and Border Protection (in the new Department of Homeland Security), the Department of Defense, the Department of Veterans Affairs, the Criminal Division of the Department of Justice, and other agencies (as described in many Reports in Chapter 4). If such resolutions are adopted, NGOs can quickly notify the media and urge coverage of these newsworthy events. They can see to it that the resolutions are actually sent to the OIGs, perhaps helping city officials find the addresses of the appropriate OIGs.

Some states have established OIGs in certain state agencies. California has separate OIGs to act on complaints concerning the California Department of Corrections, Board of Prisons, Youth Authority, Rehabilitation Center, Basic Correctional Officer Academy, Parole and Community Services Division of Department of Corrections, Optional Program, and Local Assistance Program (involving cities and counties). This kind of office could be encouraged in every state at every level of government. The cost of establishing such OIGs can be more than offset by the savings from costs now spent on paying damages or defending litigation against government officials.


## B. US FEDERAL COURTS

The third branch of government under the US Constitution is the judiciary. Most cases are filed in state courts under state law. Some are filed in federal courts under federal law; some challenge state laws; some also turn to international law.

### 1. DEFENDING DETAINEES, DEPORTEES, AND ARRESTEES

The US Government has been arresting tens of thousands of men and women since 9/11, and many youth. Many of the people arrested were charged with violations of immigration laws and came before administrative law judges. They did not get into federal courts until they had lost their cases in administrative hearings. Some of their cases are reported in Chapter 4.

Many people were detained by military personnel and taken to detention facilities that were not part of the US prison system and where they could not retain lawyers. When a few family members found out where their relatives were, they found lawyers to represent the detainees. Since these lawyers could not meet their clients they had to work very hard to get into a federal court to determine the charges. They also had to work hard to convince Government officials that customary US laws apply. Many of their cases are reported in Chapter 4.

Many US citizens of all ages were arrested on criminal charges as a result of participating in demonstrations against the war in Iraq, the FTAA, World Bank/International Monetary Fund, and against those arrests. While most of these cases were tried in state courts, some were tried in federal courts. Both kinds of cases are reported in Chapter 4.

In order to defend these cases successfully, lawyers and clients had to challenge Government practices, often proposing affirmative changes in procedures that otherwise would have been raised in civil suits by the plaintiffs bringing the cases. Some cases were won using UN Law (see Ginger, "How to Use 'New' Civil Rights Laws after 9/11," pp. 73, 79 [MCLI 2003]).

## 2. DEFENDING ATTORNEY LYNNE STEWART AFFIRMATIVELY

One of the most celebrated cases brought by the Government after 9/11 was the arrest of civil rights attorney Lynne Stewart at her home, taking files from her law office, and indicting her under the 1996 Antiterrorism Act. She was charged with misconduct in relation to her client, Sheik Omar Abdel Rahman, who was convicted of plotting terrorism in New York City in the early 1990s. Stewart and two legal assistants were charged with conspiracy to provide material support to a terrorist organization because Stewart allegedly passed information from her client that was received while she was visiting him in prison. The charges were based on prison officials wiretapping their conversations.

A brief history of the case is in Report 18.3. After reading briefs and hearing arguments, the federal trial court judge acquitted the defendant on felony counts under the Antiterrorism Act. The trial was postponed in January and began on May 19, 2004, on charges of lying to and defrauding the Government. The defense made its case in the fall of 2004.

The defendant's 171-page brief in support of the motion to dismiss filed in January 2003 was successful in getting the judge to dismiss several counts. The following excerpts suggest arguments to use in other post–9/11 cases.

New York, November 15, 2004: Lynne Stewart, lawyer, grandmother, public defender—shown here with her husband, Ralph Poynter—presented a strong defense to the US charge of providing support to terrorists, insisting on her rights and duties as a lawyer. (Photo coutresy of the Lynn Stewart Defense Committee)

## Model Defense Brief on Charge of "Terrorism"

UNITED STATES DISTRICT COURT
SOUTHERN DISTRICT OF NEW YORK
UNITED STATES OF AMERICA,
S1 02 CR 395 (JGK)

v.

AHMED ABDEL SATTAR, MOHAMMED YOUSRY
and LYNNE STEWART, Defendants.

MEMORANDUM OF LAW IN SUPPORT OF
LYNNE STEWART'S SECOND OMNIBUS
MOTION TO DISMISS THE INDICTMENT
AND FOR OTHER RELIEF

. . .

[Defendant seeks a motion]

4. Dismissing Count Four because it violated the *ex post facto*

clause of the Constitution, or, in the alternative, because it charges an offense that did not exist at the time of the alleged conduct;

5. Dismissing Count One because 18 U.S.C. sec. 371 fails to state an offense and is unconstitutionally vague as applied in this indictment;

8. Dismissing Counts Four, Five and Seven on the grounds that they are the result of the government's vindictive prosecution of Lynne Stewart or, in the alternative, granting Lynne Stewart's requests for discovery on the issue of vindictive prosecution or an evidentiary hearing on this issue;

9. In the alternative, as to any counts not dismissed, . . . striking all prejudicial, inflammatory, irrelevant, or vague wording in the indictment, including, but not limited to, references to "terror," "terrorize," "terrorism," "jihad," "fatal," and paragraphs . . . as prejudicial surplusage"; . . .

. . .

## C. *Terror, Terrorist, Terrorism*[114]

The original indictment used the word "terrorist" or "terrorists" 13 times and word "terror" three times, for a total of 16 references. In that indictment, the 18 U.S.C. § 2339B charge included an element referring to a terrorist organization. *Sattar*, 272 F. Supp. 2d at 352.

In the superseding indictment "terrorist" or "terrorists" appear 29 times, "terrorism" appears five times, "terrorize" appears twice, and "terror" appears once; a total of 37 references. Yet, none of the offenses charged contains an element that includes any of those words.[115]

None of the indictment's references is tied to a statutory definition,[116] or to the administrative definitions in the provisions at issue under the earlier indictment. The references are thus entirely gratuitous, inflammatory and irrelevant.

Moreover, the terms "terrorism" and "terrorist," divorced from any specific definition, are so vague as to invite speculation as to what

---

114. Our request to strike references to "terror" and "terrorism" is made with a reservation of rights. If there is a conviction in the case, we reserve the right to challenge the application, validity and procedural setting of any proposed reliance on "terrorism" as a sentencing enhancer, including without limitation arguments on separation of powers, vagueness and the right to jury trial as construed in *Apprendi v. New Jersey*, 530 U.S. 466 (2000), and its progeny.

115. The title of 18 U.S.C. 2339A does include the word "terrorists," but the term is not carried into the statute's text.

116. *See, e.g.*, 18 U.S.C. § 2331(1) and (5). Note that the definition of "domestic terrorism" was not added until the Patriot Act. *See generally* J. W. Whitehead and S. H. Aden, *Forfeiting "Enduring Freedom" for "Homeland Security": A Constitutional Analysis of the USA Patriot Act and the Justice Department's Anti-Terrorism Initiatives*, 51 AM. U.L. REV. 1081, 1092–1093 (2002) (*citing* USA Patriot Act, Pub. L. No. 107–56, 115 Stat. 272, 376 [2001]).

they mean. They are mere epithets. *See, e.g., Curtis Publ'g Co. v. Bird-song*, 360 F.2d 344, 348 (5th Cir. 1966) (the phrase "those bastards," when directed at members of the Mississippi Highway Patrol, were "mere epithets" and had "no real meaning"). *See also* BLACK'S LAW DICTIONARY 1484 (7th ed. 1999) (defining "terrorism" as: "The use or threat of violence to intimidate or cause panic, esp. as a means of affecting political conduct.") This adds nothing to any standard offense definition, nor to any offense here charged.

Of course, "terror" was an element of a common law crime that still survives in at least several American jurisdictions, but that offense has nothing to do with politics unless you are a member of the National Rifle Association. In its common law form, "terror" simply meant scaring people, and is a limit on the right to bear arms.[117]

---

117. The common law crime of affray (from the French word *"effrayer,"* meaning "to affright"-*See State v. Huntly*, 25 N.C. 418 [1843]) is defined as "the fighting of two or more persons in some public place, to the terror of his majesty's subjects." 4 W. Blackstone, COMMENTARIES 145 (1769) (cited in E. Dale, *A Different Sort of Justice: The Informal Courts of Public Opinion in Antebellum South Carolina*, 54 S.C. L. REV. 627, 628 n.2 [2003]).

Affray has also been defined as "a public offense to the terror of the people, and is an English word, and so called, because it affrighteth and maketh men affraid." Davies, *The Fictional Character of Law-and-Order Originalism: A Case Study of the Distortions and Evasions of Framing-Era Arrest Doctrine in* Atwater v. Lago Vista, 37 WAKE FOREST L. REV. 239, 284 n.132 (2002) (citing CONDUCTOR GENERALIS (J. Parker ed., printed by J. Patterson for R. Hodge in N.Y., 1788) (available in EARLY AMERICAN IMPRINTS, FIRST SERIES, no. 10935) (citing 2 Sir Edward Coke, INSTITUTES OF THE LAWS OF ENGLAND 158 [in four parts; originally published during the 1640s]).

The phrase "terror of the people" has also been used in legal parlance to identify traditional common law boundaries on the right to bear arms: "A Justice of the Peace may require surety from persons who "go about with unusual Weapons or Attendants, to the Terror of the People." D. B. Kopel, *The Supreme Court's Thirty-Five Other Gun Cases: What the Supreme Court has Said About the Second Amendment*, 18 ST. LOUIS U. PUB. L. REV. 99, 174 n.313 (1999) (citing W. Hawkins, A TREATISE OF THE PLEAS OF THE CROWN 126 (1716) (Garland Publ. 1978)). Some United States cases have used affray (or its criminal elements) to carve out an exception to the Second Amendment. *State v. Huntly*, 25 N.C. 418 (1843), recognized a crime that amounts to affray, quoting Blackstone: "the offence of riding or going armed with dangerous or unusual weapons is a crime against the public peace, by terrifying the good people of the land; and is *particularly* prohibited by the Statute of Northampton, 2 Edward 3d, Ch. 3d, upon pain of forfeiture of the arms, and imprisonment during the King's pleasure." *Huntly*, 25 N.C. at 420-421 (citing 4 W. Blackstone, COMMENTARIES 149 (1769) (emphasis in original)). In upholding Huntly's indictment, the North Carolina Supreme Court held: "It is the wicked purpose – and the mischievous result – which essentially constitute the crime. He shall not carry about this or any other weapon of death to terrify and alarm, and in such manner as naturally will terrify and alarm, a peaceful people." *Huntly*, 25 N.C. at 423.

Subsequent North Carolina Supreme Court decisions followed *Huntly*. State v. *Dawson* decided the issue of whether a citizen "has a right to bear arms to the terror of the people." 159 S.E.2d 1, 11 (N.C. 1968). In holding that he has no such right, the Court held that "[t]he right to keep and bear arms no more gives an individual the right to arm himself in order to prowl the highways or other public places to the terror of the people than the constitutional guaranty of free speech gives him the right to yell "fire" in a crowded theater." *Id.* at 11. . . .

Oxford University Professor Sir Adam Roberts notes that the word "terrorism" entered into European languages in the wake of the French Revolution in 1789, as the National Assembly sought to impose its views on the citizenry. This was what came to be called "The Reign of Terror." *See* A. Roberts, *The Changing Faces of Terrorism*, http://www.bbc.co.uk/history/war/sept_11/changing_faces_07.shtml.

Thus, the first meaning of the word "terrorism" was "system or rule of terror," as recorded by the Académie Française in 1798.[118]

In the nineteenth century, terrorism began to be associated with non-governmental persons or groups assassinating political leaders. *See id.* This association was symbolized by the assassination of Archduke Ferdinand by a Bosnian Serb student, and continued through the Second World War. *See id.*

Of the French "reign of terror," Mark Twain had a very different view than, say, Edmund Burke.[119]

Throughout American history, "terror" and "terrorist" have been chameleon words. From the earliest days of the American labor movement, they were epithets hurled at labor organizers and strikers. The historical parallel to this case is striking. Doubtless some labor leaders were involved in violent acts against property and people. *See, e.g.*, ATTORNEY FOR THE DAMNED (Weinberg ed. 1957) (containing many of Clarence Darrow's arguments in labor cases); M. Tigar, HAYMARKET: WHOSE NAME THE FEW STILL SAY WITH TEARS (1987). But judges, prosecutors and employers have used the terrorism epithet to brand all organized workers. *See, e.g.*, *United States v. Railway Employees' Dep't of American Federation of Labor*, 283 F. 79 (N.D. Ill. 1922) (a holding that required the Norris-LaGuardia Act to undo); *Lake Erie & Western Ry. v. Bailey*, 61 Fed 494, 495-97 (C.C.D. Ind. 1893) (a judicial harangue on whether labor unions should exist); *United States v.*

---

118. This terror was what is now known as state-sponsored terrorism, arbitrary governmental action such as practiced at least since 1981 by the government of Egypt.

119. Twain wrote:

There were two "Reigns of Terror," if we would but remember it and consider it; the one wrought murder in hot passion, the other in heartless cold blood; the one lasted mere months, the other had lasted a thousand years; the one inflicted death upon ten thousand persons, the other upon a hundred millions; but our shudders are all for the "horrors" of the minor Terror, the momentary Terror, so to speak; whereas, what is the horror of swift death by lightning compared with death by slow fire at the stake? A city cemetery could contain the coffins filled by that brief Terror which we have all been so diligently taught to shiver at and mourn over; but all France could hardly contain the coffins filled by that older and real Terror—that unspeakably bitter and awful Terror which none of us has been taught to see in its vastness or pity as it deserves.

M. Twain, A CONNECTICUT YANKEE IN KING ARTHUR'S COURT, ch. 13.

*Gregg*, 5 F. Supp. 848 (S.D. Tex. 1934) (unions as terrorists); *see also* the prosecutor's references to terrorism quoted in *Bridges v. California*, 314 U.S. 252, 275 n.19 (1941) ("union terrorism"). The criminal syndicalism statutes that were finally invalidated by *Brandenburg v. Ohio*, 395 U.S. 444 (1969), also contained references to terrorism.

Among other perpetrators of terror recognized in Supreme Court opinions are: monoplies and trusts, *United States v. South-Eastern Underwriters Ass'n*, 322 U.S. 533, 553 (1944); the Ku Klux Klan, *Virginia v. Black*, 535 U.S. 1094, 123 S. Ct. at 1544; federal tax collectors, *Warden v. Hayden*, 387 U.S. 294, 316 (1967); police who conduct unlawful searches, *Brinegar v. United States*, 338 U.S. 160, 180 (1949) (Jackson, J., dissenting); mob action to influence a jury, *Frank v. Mangum*, 237 U.S. 309, 347 (1915); courts of justice who should be a "terror to evil doers," *United States v. Castillero*, 67 U.S. 17 (1862); patent holders, *Hogg v. Emerson*, 47 U.S. 437, 473 (1848); and attacks by Native Americans, *Sim's Lessee v. Irvine*, 3 U.S. 425, 440 (1799).

In sum, these words have no generally accepted meaning. They are simply appeals to passion and prejudice. These words have no place in this indictment and all references to them should be stricken from Paragraphs 1, 4, 5, 6, 8, 11, 17, 20, 21, 22, 24, 25, 30(j), 30(p), 30(ee), 33(b), and 35.

## 3. FILING AFFIRMATIVE SUITS AGAINST BUSH, THE ATTORNEY GENERAL, THE IMMIGRATION SERVICE, THE FBI, AND THE CIA

Since 9/11, many aggrieved people have sought lawyers to file suits against US Government officials and agencies alleging major violations of their human rights. As with most such efforts by plaintiffs to win damages or injunctions against powerful defendants, few of these suits have gone to trial. A few have been won in trial court, and a handful have been won on appeal. Many of the cases reported in the media, by organizations, by email, and by aggrieved individuals are described in the Reports in Chapter 4. Concerned potential plaintiffs can watch for coverage in the media or on the Internet.

## C. STATE COURTS

### 1. DEMANDING JUSTICE BEFORE TRIAL

Many people who participated in large, successful demonstrations against the war in Iraq are good organizers. When federal, state, or local police made arrests during and after the demonstrations, some of these organizers were defendants.

They began to use their organizational skills to tell their neighbors and the media the facts about their arrests. And they began talking about the First Amendment and the right to petition the Government for a redress of grievances. As a result, many people signed petitions and attended city council meetings and picketed the office of the local district attorney—all demanding that the charges against peaceful demonstrators be dropped. Some unions, churches, and community organizations participated in these efforts.

Each effort had two aspects: Getting justice for the accused demonstrators and prompting further discussion of the underlying issue. As a result, some district attorneys dropped the charges before trial, some judges dismissed the charges before trial, and some juries acquitted after trial. Chapter 4 includes examples of all of these efforts.

### 2. USING THE UN CHARTER AND HUMAN RIGHTS TREATIES

Sometimes merely filing a well-drafted complaint against a city, county, or state official can shame the official or agency into changing a flawed administrative rule or practice.

Lawyers are using "new" laws that support their clients' claims, including, especially, the UN Charter human rights articles 55 and 56 and relevant articles in the three ratified human rights reporting treaties (all included in Chapter 6): the International Covenant on Civil and Political Rights, the Convention Against Torture, and the Convention on Elimination of Racial Discrimination.

There are some judges in state and county courts who have studied International Law and are prepared to use appropriate articles in these treaties, knowing they are part of the supreme law of the land that they are required to uphold under the US Constitution, Article VI, Clause 2. (Sixty-nine cases that were won in US courts based on the UN Charter or the human rights reporting treaties are described in Ginger, "How to Use 'New' Civil Rights Laws after 9/11" [MCLI 2003].)

# 3

# WHAT THE GOVERNMENT IS COMMITTED AND REQUIRED TO DO IN THE UN AND THE OAS

## A. THE MOBILIZATION OF SHAME, AGAIN

It is not difficult today for anyone to get on the Internet to find articles on the terrible violations of human rights going on in the United States today, including some of those described in the 180 reports in Chapter 4.

It is much more difficult to find on the computer or in the daily paper, or to hear on the radio or TV what is being done

- to investigate the facts in the articles,
- to stop these violations,
- to punish the violators, and
- to prevent future violations.

Every newspaper everyday describes all sorts of very serious problems. If a problem arises in an upscale area, concerned citizens get together to do something about it. They make campaign contributions to their City Council member, representative, Senator, or the President. So now they can make a phone call, and sometimes something is done immediately as Government officials are shamed into action. (A problem at the corner of Hollywood and Vine will be addressed shortly.)

Every religious body uses the mobilization of shame to raise money to give to the poor, and to fix the roof of the church, mosque, or temple. Franklin Roosevelt and Lou Gehrig mobilized healthy people to insist that money be spent on research *now* to cure or at least ameliorate the disastrous effects of polio and Lou Gehrig's disease. Prominent victims of AIDS and cancer have done the same.

It is not known to most people in the United States, but the UN uses the mobilization of shame to cause nations to stop violating the human rights of the people under their jurisdiction. When the African National Congress went to the UN in the early 1950s with a description of the horrors of the new apartheid regime in South Africa, the General Assembly passed a resolution condemning such actions. This led to other resolutions and, ultimately, to the declaration that apartheid is a crime against humanity. This caused many people to boycott South African goods and to stop visiting South Africa. These economic actions cut the income of everyone in that country. The heroic actions of the people of South Africa were the major force in bringing about the release of Nelson Mandela and the end of apartheid. But without constant pressure through the UN, apartheid would not have been ended by 1990.[1]

The experience in East Timor is quite different because East Timor is a much smaller country than South Africa and Indonesia is not ruled as South Africa was. However, the establishment of East Timor as a separate nation could not have happened without the strong and continuous concern expressed in the UN.

The mobilization of shame includes frequent public statements and small demonstrations organized by prominent people that lead to resolutions by small Government bodies, which in turn lead to more media coverage and massive demonstrations until, finally, the national Government and the highest court in the country are forced to act.

The first step is extensive, accurate reports on the wrongs being committed. Belarus, a small nation in Eastern Europe, made such a report to the UN in November 2004 about the human rights violations in a much larger nation, the United States. The Belarus resolution was apparently a first to target violations by the United States.

The Resolution was based on the European Parliament Resolution on Guantanamo (October 28, 2004); the Inter-American Commission on Human Rights of the Organization of American States declaration on no voting rights for residents of Washington, DC (December 23, 2003); and the needs assessment by the Organization of Security and Cooperation in Europe regarding US Presidential elections that was based in part on the Commission on Civil Rights report on the 2000 elections in Florida. The UN delegation from Belarus has received a copy of the research by the Economic Human Rights Project of Somerville, Massachusetts, which tried to get some part of the UN to help monitor the 2004 elections in the United States.

Belarus filed the resolution after the United States had introduced a resolution to the Third Committee attacking alleged electoral violations in the recent Belarus presidential election and the harassment of political opposition. The United S Ambassador to the UN did not explain why the United States filed this resolution regarding Belarus rather than filing resolutions as to several other nations facing allegations of similar recent electoral misconduct.

On November 11, 2004, Belarus withdrew the draft resolution so that "its friends and like-minded delegations" would not have to "face a tormenting choice in voting." On November 18, 2004, when the US resolution on Belarus came up in the General Assembly, Russia moved not to discuss it, supported by China and Malaysia. The vote on the Russian motion was: 75 for; 65 against; 28 abstained; killing the US resolution.[2] The text of the Belarus Resolution follows. (The coverage of the topics in the Resolution in reports in Chapter 4 is shown in references at the end of the document.)

UNITED NATIONS A/C.3/59/L.60
GENERAL ASSEMBLY
2 November 2004
Fifty-ninth session Third Committee Agenda item 105
Human rights questions: human rights situations and reports of special rapporteurs and representatives

## BELARUS: DRAFT RESOLUTION IN THE UN GENERAL ASSEMBLY ON THE SITUATION OF DEMOCRACY AND HUMAN RIGHTS IN THE UNITED STATES OF AMERICA

The General Assembly,

Guided by the purposes and principles of the Charter of the United Nations, the provisions of the Universal Declaration of Human Rights, the International Covenants on Human Rights and other applicable human rights instruments,

Reaffirming that all States have an obligation to promote and protect human rights and fundamental freedoms and to fulfill the international obligations they have freely undertaken,

Mindful that the United States of America is a party to the International Covenant on Civil and Political Rights, the Convention Against Torture and Other Cruel, Inhuman or Degrading Treatment or Punishment and the International Convention on the Elimination of All Forms of Racial Discrimination,

Recalling that each State party to the International Covenant on Civil and Political Rights undertakes to respect and ensure to all individuals within its territory and subject to its jurisdiction the rights recognized in the Covenant, without distinction of any kind, such as race, colour, sex, language, religion, political or other opinion, national or social origin, property, birth, or other status,

Reaffirming that improving security and the fight against terrorism should be conducted with full respect for human rights and democratic principles,

Bearing in mind the European Parliament resolution on Guantanamo of 28 October 2004,

Noting that the United States of America is a member of the Organization of American States and is obliged to observe the human rights standards under the Charter of that Organization, and aware that on 23 December 2003, the Inter-American Commission on Human Rights of the Organization of American States decided that the denial of equal participation by the residents of Washington, DC, in their own national legislature by duly elected representatives constituted violations of provisions of the American Declaration of the Rights and Duties of Man, adopted by the Organization of American States in 1948,

Taking note of the report of the needs assessment mission on the Presidential elections in the United States of America of the Organization on Security and Cooperation in Europe,

1. Expresses deep concern and dismay:

(a) At reports from credible sources on systematic violations of fundamental rights and freedoms in the United States, including alarming attacks on press freedom and tight control of news media; arbitrary, incommunicado and secret detentions and arrests; and continued and expanding intolerance, xenophobia and discrimination;

(b) That the electoral system in the United States does not comply with the obligations of the United States under the International Covenant on Civil and Political Rights to provide every citizen with the right and opportunity to vote and to be elected at genuine periodic elections which shall be by universal and equal suffrage and shall be held by secret ballot, guaranteeing the free expression of the will of the electors;

(c) That despite the report by the United States Commission on Civil Rights on the 2000 presidential election, which concluded that in Florida election policies and practices were in place that prevented some of Florida's residents, particularly African Americans, Spanish and Creole-speaking nationals with language assistance needs and persons with disabilities, from voting and from having their votes counted, such practices have continued during the current presidential election;

(d) That some election techniques, including verification requirements, disproportionately disenfranchise the poor, the elderly, minorities and immigrants;

(e) That despite promising to improve the electoral system after the 2000 presidential election, the United States has failed to reform the system, which remains fundamentally flawed and could disenfranchise some eligible voters and allow manipulation of the results of elections;

(f) That . . . it is not meeting its committment by prohibiting independent international and domestic observers of the Organization from monitoring the presidential election in 2004;

(g) That the United States continues to violate international standards in its use of the death penalty for people who were under 18 years of age at the time the crimes were committed and for the mentally ill;

(h) That the United States legislative measures to enhance security, including the adoption and implementation of the Patriot Act, have led to the limitation and abuse of vital civil rights and freedoms of nationals of the United States;

(i) About information on the deprivation of the rights of an undisclosed number of persons, including minors, detained as a result of military operations launched in Afghanistan and being held at present in detention camps located in the United States naval base in Guantanamo, as well as about the forced disappearances of some detainees;

(j) At the continued reports of ill-treatment, torture, death in custody and excessive use of force by police and prison officers, including the use of isolation, dogs, sensory and sleep deprivation, death threats and other forms of torture or cruel, inhuman or degrading treatment as interrogation techniques;

2. Urges the Government of the United States of America:

(a) To put an end to the violations of human rights mentioned above;

(b) To become a party to all core international human rights instruments, thus allowing the international community to monitor the situation of human rights in the United States in full;

(c) To fully cooperate with special procedures of the Commission on Human Rights to ensure that all necessary measures are taken to investigate fully and impartially all cases of arbitrary detention, forced disappearance, summary execution and torture and that perpetrators are brought to justice before an independent tribunal and, if found guilty, punished in a manner consistent with the international human rights obligations of the United States;

(d) To bring the electoral process and legislative framework into line with international standards;

(e) To take the necessary steps . . . to grant the residents of Washington, DC . . . the effective right to participate, directly or through freely chosen representatives and in general conditions of equality, in their national legislature;

(f) To abolish the death penalty for people who were under the age of 18 at the time the crimes were committed and for the mentally ill;

(g) To end immediately the practice of incommunicado and secret detentions and ensure that conditions of detention conform to international standards; . . .

(h) To implement a zero-tolerance policy on torture by investigating all allegations of torture and holding perpetrators of torture accountable so as to promote a culture in which torture is regarded as unacceptable, criminal behaviour;

(i) To invite all relevant human rights monitoring mechanisms, especially the Special Rapporteurs of the Commission on Human Rights on torture . . . extrajudicial, summary or arbitrary executions, and the Working Groups of the Commission on Enforced or Involuntary Disappearances and on Arbitrary Detention to visit all places of detention . . . ;

(j) To take urgent measures to bring legislation on national security into compliance with United States obligations under relevant international instruments;

(k) To bring the actions of its police and security forces into conformity with its obligations under the International Covenant on Civil and Political Rights as well as other relevant international standards;

3. Insists that the Government of the United States of America cooperate fully with and extend invitations to all the mechanisms of the Commission of Human Rights, including the Working Groups . . . ;

4. Decides to consider this question at its sixtieth session, under the same agenda item.


## REFERENCES

•Attacks on media members and freedom of the press, see Reports in Chapter 4, Section 7.

•Arrests leading to secret detentions in US detention centers, see Reports in Sections 2, 18, 19, 20, and 29.1.

•Discrimination, see Reports in Sections 4, 5, and 6.

•Charges of electoral fraud and discrimination against certain voters, see Reports 12.1 and 12.9.

•Deprivation of rights of people detained in Afghanistan and Guantanamo, see Reports in 2, 19, and 20.

•Excessive use of force by police in US jursdictions, see Reports in 1, 2.4, 2.15, 3, 18, and 19.

•Death penalty, see Report 24.2.


## B. PERIODIC REPORTING TO ENFORCE HUMAN RIGHTS

The method used by the UN to enforce human rights is periodic reporting. Each UN human rights treaty was drafted by a committee and adopted by the UN General Assembly. Each treaty provides that it will go into effect when a specific number of nations have ratified it. Each treaty requires each signatory nation to make periodic reports to a UN Committee on how it is fulfilling each duty and enforcing each right in the treaty.

Of the major UN treaties on human rights, the United States has signed six but has only completed ratification of three. The Human Rights Committee enforces the International Covenant on Civil and Political Rights (ICCPR). The Committee on Elimination of Racial Discrimination enforces the Convention on the Elimination of All Forms of Racial Discrimination (CERD), and the Committee Against Torture enforces the Convention Against Torture and other Cruel, Inhuman, or Degrading Treatment or Punishment (CAT). Since each Committee includes intelligent, often savvy representatives from varied nations, the reports will not stand scrutiny if they are clearly inaccurate whitewashes of Government misconduct.

This reporting requirement is not easy to carry out. It mandates that each national Government require each Government department to make a First Report on whether it is violating any of the rights in the treaty at the national level, and, if so, disclose the facts and statistics and state its procedures for stopping the violations. That is only the first step, and the United States took this step as to each of the three treaties in the Clinton and Bush Administrations.

For the Second Report, the national Government must require all local Governments to submit similar reports for each of their departments. In the United States, that means each of the fifty states and territories under US jurisdiction—from Puerto Rico to Guantanamo Bay to military bases in Colombia and the Philippines—and each of the cities and counties must submit a similar report to the states, which must submit a state report to the federal Government to include in its own Second Report to the UN Committees.

By 2004, the United Kingdom had submitted its initial national and four other reports, including local government reports; the Russian Federation also had submitted five reports at these levels. India had submitted its initial national, plus two other reports on its several large states.[3]

The need for statistics on the enforcement of existing laws (whether statutes or treaties) has gotten much coverage in the media as President Bush has insisted on the importance of testing each child in each public school each year to see whether the school is improving the scores under the No Child Left Behind Act (see reports 26.1–26.3). Many educators are insisting that these statistics are not helpful standing alone. It is necessary to know how many children are going to bed hungry or are homeless, which affects their test scores. They are saying that statistics are needed on the number of drivers stopped or arrested who are people of color compared with the number arrested or stopped who are white, and that such discrimination affects the children taking the achievement tests in ways that social scientists have spelled out in endless reports on racial discrimination in the United States.

And public health agencies in states with many antichoice voters are collecting statistics on the number of doctors in the state performing abortions and the number of abortions performed per year. They are carefully collecting statistics on the length of the pregnancies before the abortions were performed.

Civil rights advocates say they are insisting on the collection of facts and statistics on enforcement of human rights for inclusion in these US reports for the same reason managers of corporations insist on obtaining certain statistics. Without such facts, concerned citizens and legislators cannot know what changes to demand in the politics and practices of Government agencies at all levels. They say they are exactly the same as stockholders and bondholders who insist on knowing the value of their stocks and bonds, although no activists are demanding instantaneous numbers like those churned out on the Wall Street stock market and the Chicago Mercantile Exchange.

Reporting on torture at the Abu Ghraib prison facility in Iraq certainly made an immediate difference in mass media coverage of that scandal. And it made a difference in actions by US authorities at Abu Ghraib, including the removal of one US official heading the prison, arrests of some US military personnel, and so forth (see Reports 1.13, 2.12–2.15, 5.4, and 7.5). Reporting on human rights in that case had an immediate impact through the mobilization of shame.

Wal-Mart knows how many widgets were sold the previous day by its 1.3 million employees in each of its stores in nine countries. The pharmaceutical companies know, to the penny, the difference in the price of a drug produced by indigenous people in a country and the price they charge for producing it by mass production in the United States or in a third world country and they provide this information to their stockholders. The US Treasury knows how many bonds have been sold at what rates of interest and what is the US balance of payments per day, i.e., how many more dollars US residents spent on goods from every other country compared to how many other kinds of currencies were spent on US goods by consumers overseas. And they know how many corporations owe what amount of taxes, and how many are delinquent in paying. The US prison system knows how many occupants are in how many federal prisons, as each state knows how many prisoners are in their state prisons, guarded by what numbers of guards at what cost per prisoner.

Each city, county, and state can report to the US Government how many illegal arrests were made, how many people's votes were not properly counted, and how many hate crimes were committed by whom in the past year. Problems could arise when, for example, officials who hate African Americans decide to report every minor incident in which an African American allegedly commits a wrong against a European American but decide not to report incidents in which European Americans commit crimes against African Americans. This has happened in the last few years under the Hate Crimes Reporting Act (see, e.g., reports 4.2 and 4.4).

It is not only crimes that need to be reported. Every gated community that discriminates against people on the basis of their race, national origin, or religion, either overtly or covertly, needs to be reported. And the appropriate agency needs to report the steps they are taking to stop this discrimination. Why? So that the US Government can begin to live up to its constitutional responsibility to provide equal protection to every human being, without regard to race, color, or previous condition of servitude under the Fourteenth Amendment of 1868. And so that the Government can also live up to the commitment it made when it ratified the International Covenant on Civil and Political Rights to make no distinction based on race, color, sex, language, religion, political or other opinion, national or social origin, property ownership, birth, disability, or sexual preference. When President George H. W. Bush asked the Senate to ratify the ICCPR, he was saying that the United States should make a commitment to make periodic reports to the UN Human Rights Committee on the enforcement of the provisions in Article 2.1 (Text in Chapter 6).

Ratification made this treaty part of the "supreme law of the land" under the US Constitution, Article VI, Clause 2 (Text in Chapter 6). This means that the President, Congress, and the courts of the United States and of each state are required to enforce its terms even as they enforce the Constitution and federal statutes.

It certainly would have helped if the US media had given extensive coverage to the ratification of the International Covenant at the time. And it would have helped if the US media had sent journalists to cover the first dialogue on the first US Report between members of the UN Human Rights Committee and representatives of the Departments of State, Justice, Labor, Immigration, and others who attended the historic dialogue at UN headquarters in New York City in 1995. That did not happen. (The one US journalist present at the dialogue was from a Black Muslim newspaper.)

The same lack of reporting occurred when the Senate completed ratification of the Convention on the Elimination of All Forms of Racial Discrimination and the Convention Against Torture and other Cruel, Inhuman, or Degrading Treatment or Punishment in 1994.

Neither did the media report the dialogue that finally took place between the United States and the UN Committee Against Torture in 2000 and between the United States and the UN Committee on Elimination of Racial Discrimination in 2001. Each of these events only covered problems at the national level.

## C. REPORTING TO UN COMMITTEES

The United States Government made a solemn commitment to take certain steps when it ratified each of the three human rights treaties. One of those steps is to file periodic reports with the three UN human rights Committees administering the three treaties the United States has ratified. Colin Powell, the Secretary of State under President George W. Bush filed the last one of three First Reports required under the treaties. He did not file any of the three Second Reports that were due in 1997 and 1998. The Second Reports must include reports by each city and county in each state, and by each state and territory, on the successes and failures in enforcing the provisions of the three treaties.

The State Department says that its efforts to cause state and local governments to make their reports have been underfunded and unsuccessful.

## *1. WHY MAKING A REPORT MATTERS*

There are millions of good, conscientious people in the United States—private citizens and Government officials—who are busy and overworked, but concerned. When they know that the United States is violating a law, they want to do something about it. That is how studies of conditions in sweatshops employing immigrant women[4] led to crackdowns by health and labor departments.[5] That's how seemingly random, isolated incidents of pedophilia by a few men in religious garb came to be seen as a pervasive problem to be addressed by the whole religious community involved as well as by district attorneys. That's how AIDS stopped being "that dirty little disease that some of those, you know, uh, gay people give to each other" and became a health problem to be faced by society as a whole and by Government medical programs in particular. That is how the governments of South Africa and East Timor became free. And that is how Canada changed its policies and laws regarding Indian tribes. Inspired by the feedback from the UN Human Rights Committee on its reports submitted in accordance with the ICCPR, Canada changed its laws and practices to improve the lives of its indigenous peoples by establishing the Royal Commission on Aboriginal Peoples; creating a territory for the Nunavit in east Arctic; enabling aboriginal oversight of correctional services for aboriginal criminals; reaching land claim agreements and settlements; and forming aboriginal schools.[6]

Meiklejohn Institute has proposed that the number of people suffering housing discrimination should be a statistic in the daily paper right next to the number of home runs hit by the current Babe Ruth. The number of women who can't get glass ceiling jobs as partners in law firms, on corporate boards of directors, or as candidates for political office should be published next to the daily weather reports. The number of teenagers who cannot read the daily paper should be published next to the list of best-selling books.

Critics of this proposal said that most people who read the daily papers or listen to the news do not want to know these statistics, so there is no purpose in collecting and reporting them. They also said there is a good reason why the media report the value of each stock and the daily temperature in each region: some people invest in stocks and will act according to its daily value. And some people have work to do that will change if it is going to rain or if a hurricane is about to hit. But there is no similar number of people who want to know how many courts received petitions for habeas corpus from detainees at Guantanamo. There are not enough concerned readers who want to know how many complaints of police misconduct have been filed each day.

The Meiklejohn Institute could not come up with a method of gauging who was right in this argument, but each time the MCLI began to raise these issues, many people across the country responded affirmatively. A great many NGOs working on human rights had filed reports showing deep concern about their issues. These efforts were just beginning in the spring of 2001. The MCLI delegation to the World Conference Against Racism in Durban was enthused by its experiences there and returned home on September 10 prepared to push this project. Then came September 11.

Immediately afterward, the US Government took steps in the United States, in its territories, and around the world that the MCLI and thousands of other organizations felt they had to respond to immediately. No time was left to collect significant data on human rights violations and enforcement.

Concerned people were suddenly convinced they had to try to help friends who were being required to register, friends who went to the Immigration office and vanished. Concerned people felt that they had to try to slow down and stop US military actions in Afghanistan and Iraq. Concerned people felt they had to join picket lines at US ports to save the Longshore Union and other unions facing massive job loss through outsourcing or other corporate decisions. By summer 2004, concerned women's organizations were reporting on the decline in the standard of living of working mothers due to the slight increase in the cost of foods and the great increase in the cost of child care just when prekindergarten and after-school programs were being cut.

But the commitments the United States made to all of the other signatories to the three treaties we ratified did not end on 9/11. In fact, many people began to see that the violations of human rights in the United States—by corporations, by Government agencies and officials, and by individuals—could cause victims to become terrorists or to commit murder and suicide.

So the struggle against terrorism and the struggle for human rights reporting would seem to be inextricably connected. The demands that the Government obey the US Constitution and Amendments are beginning to include the demand that the Government live up to the commitments it made when it ratified the three human rights treaties.

These reports could be made much more easily and would be more accurate and complete if NGOs, Government agencies, and the media consciously accepted the challenge to collect and report data that belongs in the US Second Reports. As with reports of the Stock Market, the National League, Marriage Licenses, and Obituaries, concerned people would read them, and the rest of the public would know where to find them if they ever wanted to.

## 2. THE FIRST NATIONAL REPORT

Each nation when it ratifies a human rights treaty commits itself to make periodic reports to an appropriate UN Committee. The country report is submitted in one language of the six official languages of the UN: English, French, Chinese, Russian, Arabic, and Spanish. The UN is responsible for translating the report into the other five official languages and sending it to each member of the Committee.

Members come from every region of the world. They are men and women who take a certain number of days each season to go to New York or Geneva to hear a series of reports from various countries. Many are professors, retired judges, or local government officials. They must have a deep commitment to human rights to be able to listen to the horrific stories of racial discrimination, torture, and degrading treatment, and to participate in a meaningful dialogue with government representatives.

The method of work of the UN Committees has evolved over the years since the treaties were ratified by enough nations to bring them into force. In the Human Rights Committee, the procedure is for each country to present its report and hear the questions of Committee members on one day; the next day, country representatives prepare answers to these specific questions while the Committee spends that day with a second country; the third day, the first country's representatives answer the questions of the Committee members and listen to their concerns.

The goals are to state the actual facts on human rights enforcement and violations, to uncover the obstacles to enforcing the rights spelled out in the treaty, and to hear suggestions from the experienced Committee members on steps to be taken to quickly end the violations. But it goes much deeper than this. Anyone attending a meeting of any of the UN Committees is likely to gain some new insights into the universality of human rights violations and into specific steps that have repeatedly been successful in eliminating them. Certainly one's sense of US superiority is lost forever as one hears specific examples of widespread police misconduct before 9/11.

## 3. US GOVERNMENT RECORD ON REPORTING

Before 9/11, the United States had made three overdue reports under the three UN human rights treaties. The reports were very similar, mainly giving the history of human rights protections in the United States, the Constitution and laws, and some history of their enforcement. The three UN Committees made clear in their dialogues with the US delegation that the US Government had a lot of work to do in order to meet the standards it had committed to (see Reports in Section 30). After filing its First Report and participating in dialogue with the Human Rights Committee about it in 1995, the US Government was supposed to file its Second Report in 1998, five years after its First Report was due in 1993. The Government also made a commitment to file a Second Report on the enforcement and violations of the Convention on the Elimination of Racial Discrimination in 1997, two years after its First Report was due in 1995, and on the enforcement of the Convention Against Torture in 1998. The United States is listed as "very delinquent" in filing by each of the three UN committees to whom a US report is due.

When queried on this problem by the Meiklejohn Institute in June and October 2003, a representative of the State Department said that it would be too expensive to prepare the Second Reports due under the three treaties, and there was no budget for this purpose.

## 4. BUDGETING COSTS OF REPORTING

When Presidents George Bush and Bill Clinton asked the Senate to ratify the three human rights reporting treaties, they said there would be no budget costs. In fact, much of the information needed for the federal report is already collected by the agencies in order to make other reports required by other federal laws. The same is true at the state and local levels. Each administrative agency must make an annual report to the President so that he can use the material in his State of the Union speech. The actions of Government agencies on human rights issues requiring inclusion in the US report to the three UN Committees should all be included in the agencies' reports to the President. No new bureaucracy is needed to fulfill the treaty obligations. On the other hand, for each relevant federal agency and department to make a report every two or three or five years does take staff time and, therefore, does cost money. And for the federal Government to carry out its commitment to include reports from each of the fifty states, plus US territories, it must assign staff to convince each governor and head of a territory to make the required reports in a timely manner. State and local governments must pay someone to generate their reports as well.

However, it is also true that making such reports can save the Government money. Many people file lawsuits seeking damages from the Government for perceived violations of their rights. If accurate reports were compiled and published regularly, some such lawsuits would be averted because the complaints would be seen to be frivolous, or the fact of reporting would convince people that they could seek settlements of their grievances without litigation.

The bottom line is that Congress should know that reporting under any law, including human rights treaties, does cost some staff time and money, but that it is precautionary money that is better spent than it would be if it were spent on federal contracts for munitions and prisons.

Somehow the reporting problem was solved, often quickly and dramatically, when the Government was made to feel that a report must be made accurately and promptly, as with the reports on the economy for the Federal Reserve System.

And the US State Department spends the staff time to make a lengthy report to Congress each spring, "Country Reports on Human Rights Practices," in every nation in the world except the United States, as required under a Congressional act so that Congress will not fund any nation guilty of "a pattern of gross violations of internationally recognized human rights" (22 U.S.C. §2304 [a][2]) (see Report 15.1).

In the United States in the years following 9/11, many commentators noted a significant increase in discrimination against, and mistreatment of, people who are perceived to be "Muslims," "Black Muslims," "Islamic," "Arab," or who might be from the Middle East.[7] A report on this discrimination belongs in the reports due to the three UN Committees because such discrimination violates the US Constitution and Civil Rights Acts, the UN Charter, the UN Covenant on Civil and Political Rights, the UN Convention on the Elimination of Racial Discrimination, and the UN Convention Against Torture.

## *5. STATE DEPARTMENT STANCE ON REPORTING IN 2004*

On July 13, 2004, the MCLI called the State Department to ask when the United States will file the very tardy Second Reports due under the three treaties. Christopher N. Camponovo of the State Department Bureau of Democracy, Human Rights, and Labor, said, "There is no certain date as to when the reports will be filed." He couldn't say whether letters had been sent to states and cities seeking information for the reports. When the MCLI commented: "These reports are very late," Camponovo asked, "Your point?"

On July 27, 2004, the Human Rights Committee, which enforces the Covenant on Civil and Political Rights, addressed a letter to the United States requiring it to submit its overdue second and third periodic reports by December 31, 2004, and/or to submit specific information on the effects of measures taken to fight against terrorism after the events of 9/11, and notably the implications of the PATRIOT Act on nationals and nonnationals (ICCPR Articles 13, 17–19), and problems relating to the legal status and treatment of detainees in Afghanistan, Guantanamo Bay, Iraq, and other places of detention outside the United States (ICCPR Articles 7, 9, 10, and 14) (e-mail February 11, 2005, from Patrice Gillibert, Secretary of the Committee, to MCLI).

In November 2004, attorney Melody Saint-Saens tried to find out when the Government would be filing its reports. She looked up phone numbers on the Web pages of the White House and State Department. The State Department's Office of Human Rights, Democracy, and Labor at (202) 647–2126 transferred her to voice mail; they never called back. A call to the Special Assistant to the President for Multilateral and Humanitarian Affairs (part of the National Security Council), at (202) 456-9144 led her to Rosemary DiCarlo, Director of UN Affairs and International Operations, who did not return her call. Jean Garan, Director of Democratization and Human Rights referred her to Sandy Hutchison, Director of Contingency Planning and International Justice, who never responded to her e-mail. Another call to the DOS led her to the Office of Multilateral Affairs (202) 647-2264, where someone who called himself "Winston Man" said he did not know about the reporting requirement. He sent her to Linda Muncy, Human Rights Officer, who did not know about the three treaties or the reporting requirements (but did know the General Assembly Third Committee was meeting; see Belarus Draft Resolution in Chapter 30-A). She said she would ask around the office and call back; she did not.

## 6. THE SECOND NATIONAL REPORT MUST INCLUDE STATE REPORTS

One tactic that has proved very successful in at least one community is for the City Council to pass a resolution requesting city commissions to make reports on the enforcement and violations of applicable articles in a treaty. The Peace and Justice Commission of Berkeley, California, in 1994 convinced the Berkeley City Council to request that the Commissions on Labor, Women, Youth, and the Police Review Commission prepare written reports on the enforcement (and violations), of the rights in the International Covenant on Civil and Political Rights to be sent to the Department of State for inclusion in its First Report, and to send the reports directly to the UN

Human Rights Committee in the event the State Department did not include this information (see Chapter 5.C-2).

This small step by this one city *did* make a difference, as it turned out. Today every member of the City Council knows there is something called the United Nations Human Rights Committee and that there is a treaty connection between the City and this UN body. Frequently, now, in Berkeley, people who work for the city, who cover city news, who teach in the local schools and colleges, or work in the libraries all mention the UN as if it were a factor in city actions. No one any longer raises an eyebrow when copies of resolutions need to be sent to UN organs. UN Day in October is recognized as a meaningful anniversary of the founding of a body of international governance.

Since 9/11, whenever the US Government requires registration of foreign students and conducts surveillance of students from Middle Eastern countries—or allegedly from that region—human rights activists know to look in the UN Charter and UN treaties for support for their demands that these practices be stopped and that each person from every nation be treated with dignity.

If every city, county, and state police department made a report on every act in its jurisdiction violating the Fourth, Fifth, Sixth, or Eighth Amendments; the equal protection clause of the Fourteenth Amendment; the Convention Against Torture; the International Covenant on Civil and Political Rights; and the Convention on the Elimination of Racial Discrimination, a general awareness of the rights of each person and the duties of each police force and law enforcement official would emerge. The climate of fear and hatred that led to 9/11 can only be lifted by a climate of awareness of human rights and of Government commitments to enforce these rights for all.

## 7. NONGOVERNMENTAL ORGANIZATIONS CAN SUBMIT REPORTS

Nongovernmental Organizations that are concerned with human rights and that file complaints with OIGs can take the second step of writing to the Secretary of State to demand that the State Department immediately prepare the Second Reports of the United States for each of the three Committees and convince that the DOS to compel each state to collect information from cities, counties, and state officials so that state reports can be filed with the DOS for inclusion in the Second Reports.

If an NGO has sent any complaints to an OIG, they can send copies of these complaints with the action taken by the OIG to the Secretary of State to include in the required reports. NGOs can send a copy of the same OIG complaints and reports to the Office of the High Commissioner for Human

Rights in Geneva, Palais de Nations, 8–14 avenue de la Paix, CH–1211 Geneva 10, Switzerland. NGOs can also send a copy to the UN Human Rights Committee, the UN Committee Against Torture, and/or the UN Committee on the Elimination of Racial Discrimination. Finally NGOs can also send a copy of each complaint to the MCLI and describe what happened to the complaint. The MCLI will then include the complaint in the unofficial "shadow report" it sends to the State Department for inclusion in its official reports. The MCLI always also sends its shadow report directly to each of the UN Committees, since the State Department so far has not used this material.

Article 71 of the UN Charter specifically provides that the UN's Economic and Social Council "shall make suitable arrangements for consultation with nongovernmental organizations which are concerned with matters within its competence." (That is where the phrase NGO comes from.) This provision amplifies the relationship between a governing body and a NonGovernmental Organization set forth in the First Amendment to the US Constitution. The right to form an organization and to seek to affect Government policy is stated there in the double negative: "Congress shall make *no* law . . . *abridging* . . . the right of the people peaceably to assemble, and to petition the Government for a redress of grievances."

UN committee members are active in the civil societies from which they come. They have very small budgets and rely on material they receive in their official capacities with the Committees. When NGOs send delegates to attend the meetings in Geneva and New York between Committee members and US Government officials, the Committee members welcome their attendance and may meet informally with the NGOs. The Meiklejohn Institute sent a delegation to the UN Human Rights Committee when it was discussing the first State Department report and found that the Committee members were anxious to read the MCLI's written reports and to listen to the MCLI's oral comments between sessions. Other organizations have had similar experiences.

## D. REPORTING TO THE ORGANIZATION OF AMERICAN STATES: INTER-AMERICAN HUMAN RIGHTS COMMISSION

The United States is a member of the Organization of American States, which is a regional organization affiliated with the UN. The OAS has established the Inter-American Human Rights Commission to deal with alleged human rights violations by member nations parallel to the UN Human Rights Commission. These Commissions provide a venue for all involved parties to raise issues and present facts and then for the Commissions to reach a conclusion concerning human rights violations without violating the sovereignty of the nations in which the alleged violations occurred.

Since 9/11, many complaints have been made about US Government agencies mistreating citizens of other nations residing in the United States or in other countries in the OAS. One presentation to the Inter-American Human Rights Commission on the detainees in Guantanamo Bay was made by US attorneys representing the Center for Constitutional Rights, the Human Rights Clinic at Columbia Law School, and the Center for Justice and International Law, requesting that the Commission issue precautionary measures "to prevent irreparable harm to persons under the Commission's Rules of Procedure, Art. 25(1)."

The lawyers presented factual information to the Commission on the nature of the prisoners, the failure to charge them with any crimes, and the nature of their incarceration. They also briefed the specific violations of the law involved in the arrest and detention of detainees. As a result, the Commission sent a letter to President Bush on March 12, 2002, announcing its decision in this matter.

Guantanamo, 2002–2004: Afghani and Iraqi men taken as prisoners during the US invasions are given the specially invented label of "enemy combatants" and "softened" for interrogation by extreme sensory deprivation. They are shackled, blinded, deafened, and forced into uncomfortable positions for long periods of time, which it is presumed, will weaken their identity and purpose. (Photo: Shane T. McCoy/US Department of Defense)

## Model Letter on Precautionary Measures

The Inter-American Human Rights Commission letter to President Bush based on presentations to the NGOs can be used by lawyers and NGOs in lobbying Congress members to act on behalf of the Guantanamo detainees, and in press releases to the media. And it can be used in drafting complaints to the Commission on other cases of alleged violations by the United States in the Americas (see Report 19.1).

> Ref. Detainees in Guantanamo Bay, Cuba
> Request for Precautionary Measures

> After careful deliberation on this request, the Commission decided during its 114th regular period of sessions[1] to adopt precautionary measures, according to which we ask Your Excellency's government to take the urgent measures necessary to have the legal status of the detainees at Guantanamo Bay determined by a competent tribunal. Given the significance and implications of this request to and for the United States and the detainees concerned, the Commission wishes to articulate the basis upon which it reached this decision.

> The Commission notes preliminarily that its authority to receive and grant requests for precautionary measures under Article 25(1) of its Rules of Procedure[2] is, as with the practice of other international decisional bodies[3] a well-established and necessary

---

1. As this request was considered while the Commission was in session, these precautionary measures were approved by all eligible members of the Commission present, namely: Juan Méndez, President; Marta Altolaguirre, First Vice-President; José Zalaquett, Second Vice-President; Julio Prado Vallejo and Clare Kamau Roberts, Commissioners. Commissioner Robert K. Goldman did not take part in the discussion and voting on these precautionary measures, pursuant to Article 17(2) of the Commission's Rules of Procedure.

2. Article 25(1) of the Commission's Rules of Procedure provides: "In serious and urgent cases, and whenever necessary according to the information available, the Commission may, on its own initiative or at the request of a party, request that the State concerned adopt precautionary measures to prevent irreparable harm to persons."

3. See e.g. American Convention on Human Rights, Art. 63(2); Rules of Procedure of the Inter-American Court of Human Rights, Art. 25; Statute of the International Court of Justice, 59 Stat. 1055, Art. 41; Rules of Procedure of the United Nations Human Rights Committee, U.N. Doc. CCPR/C/3/Rev.6, Art. 86; Rules of Procedure of the European Commission of Human Rights, revised Rules updated to 7 May 1983, Art. 36; Rules of Procedure of the African Commission on Human and Peoples' Rights, adopted on 6 October 1995, Art. 111.

component of the Commission's processes.[4] Indeed, where such measures are considered essential to preserving the Commission's very mandate under the OAS Charter, the Commission has ruled that OAS member states are subject to an international legal obligation to comply with a request for such measures. [5]

The mandate given to the Commission by OAS member states, including the United States, under Article 106 of the Charter of the Organization of American States and Articles 18, 19 and 20 of the Commission's Statute is in turn central to the Commission's consideration of the matter presently before it. Through the foregoing provisions, OAS member states have charged the Commission with supervising member states' observance of human rights in the Hemisphere. These rights include those prescribed under the American Declaration of the Rights and Duties of Man, which constitutes a source of legal obligation for all OAS member states[6] in respect of persons subject to their authority and control.[7] The Commission has been directed to pay particular attention to the observance of Articles I (right to life), II (right to equality before law), III

---

4. See Regulations of the Inter-American Commission on Human Rights, approved by the Commission at its 660th Meeting, 49th session held on April 8, 1980, and modified at its 64th, 70th, 90th and 92nd sessions, Art. 29; Rules of Procedure of the Inter-American Commission on Human Rights, approved by the Commission at its 109th special session held from December 4 to 8, 2000, Art. 25; Annual Report of the IACHR 1996, Chapter II(4); Annual Report of the IACHR 1997, Chapter III(II)(A); Annual Report of the IACHR 1998, Chapter III(2)(A); Annual Report of the IACHR 1999, Chapter III(C)(1); Annual Report of the IACHR 2000, Chapter III(C)(1).

5. See IACHR, Fifth Report on the Situation of Human Rights in Guatemala, OEASer.L/V/II.111 doc. 21 rev. (6 April 2001), paras. 71-72; Juan Raul Garza v. United States, Case No. 12.243, Report No. 52/01, Annual Report of the IACHR 2000, para. 117.

6. See I/A Court H.R., Advisory Opinion OC-10/89, July 14, 1989, "Interpretation of the American Declaration of the Rights and Duties of Man within the Framework of Article 64 of the American Convention on Human Rights," Ser. A N° 10, paras. 43–46; James Terry Roach and Jay Pinkerton v. United States, Case 9647, Res. 3/87, 22 September 1987, Annual Report of the IACHR 1986-87, paras. 46-49; Michael Edwards et al. v. Bahamas, Case No 12.067, Report No. 48/01, Annual Report of the IACHR 2000.

7. The determination of a state's responsibility for violations of the international human rights of a particular individual turns not on that individual's nationality or presence within a particular geographic area, but rather on whether, under the specific circumstances, that person fell within the state's authority and control. See e.g. Saldaño v. Argentina, Report No. 38/99, Annual Report of the IACHR 1998, paras. 15-20; Coard et al. v. United States, Case No. 10.951, Report No. 109/99, Annual Report of the IACHR 1999, para. 37, citing, inter alia., IACHR, Report on the Situation of Human Rights in Chile, OEA/Ser.L/V/II.66, doc. 17, 1985, Second Report on the Situation of Human Rights in Suriname, OEA/Ser.L/V/II.66, doc. 21, rev. 1, 1985. See similarly Eur. Comm. H.R., Cyprus v. Turkey, 18 Y.B. Eur. Conv. Hum. Rgts. 83 (1975) at 118; Eur. Comm. H.R., Case of Loizidou v. Turkey, Preliminary Objections, Judgment of 23 March 1995, Series A No. 310, paras. 59-64.

(right to religious freedom and worship), IV (right to freedom of investigation, opinion, expression and dissemination), XVIII (right to a fair trial), XXV (right to protection from arbitrary arrest), and XXVI (right to due process of law) of the American Declaration.

In addition, while its specific mandate is to secure the observance of international human rights protections in the Hemisphere, this Commission has in the past looked to and applied definitional standards and relevant rules of international humanitarian law in interpreting the American Declaration and other Inter-American human rights instruments in situations of armed conflict.[8]

In taking this approach, the Commission has drawn upon certain basic principles that inform the interrelationship between international human rights and humanitarian law. It is well-recognized that international human rights law applies at all times, in peacetime and in situations of armed conflict.[9] In contrast, international humanitarian law generally does not apply in peacetime and its principal purpose is to place restraints on the conduct of warfare in order to limit or contain the damaging effects of hostilities and to protect the victims of armed conflict, including civilians and combatants who have laid down their arms or have been placed hors de combat.[10] Further, in situations of armed conflict, the protections under international human rights and humanitarian law may complement and reinforce one another, sharing as they do a common nucleus of nonderogable rights and a common purpose of promoting human life and dignity.[11] In certain circumstances, however, the test for evaluating the observance of a particular right, such as the right to liberty, in a situation of armed conflict may be distinct from that applicable in time of peace. In such situations, international law, including the jurisprudence of this Commission, dictates that it may be necessary to deduce the applicable standard by reference to international humanitarian law as the applicable lex specialis.[12]

Accordingly, where persons find themselves within the authority and control of a state and where a circumstance of armed conflict may be involved, their fundamental rights may be determined in part by reference to international humanitarian law as well

---

8. See generally Abella v. Argentina, Case No. 11.137, Report No. 5/97, Annual Report of the IACHR 1997; Coard et. al. v. United States, supra; IACHR, Third Report on the Situation of Human Rights in Colombia, OEA/Ser.L/V/II.102 doc. 9 rev. 1, 26 February 1999.

9. Abella Case, supra, para. 158.

10. Id., para. 159.

11. Id., para. 160-1

12. ICJ, Advisory Opinion on the Legality of the Threat or Use of Nuclear Weapons, ICJ Reports 1996, para. 25. See also Abella Case, supra, para. 161; Coard et al. Case, supra, para. 42.

as international human rights law. Where it may be considered that the protections of international humanitarian law do not apply, however, such persons remain the beneficiaries at least of the non-derogable protections under international human rights law. In short, no person under the authority and control of a state, regardless of his or her circumstances, is devoid of legal protection for his or her fundamental and non-derogable human rights.

This basic precept is reflected in the Martens clause common to numerous long-standing humanitarian law treaties, including the Hague Conventions of 1899 and 1907 respecting the laws and customs of war on land, according to which human persons who do not fall within the protection of those treaties or other international agreements remain under the protection of the principles of the law of nations, as they result from the usages established among civilized peoples, from the laws of humanity, and the dictates of the public conscience. And according to international norms applicable in peacetime and wartime, such as those reflected in Article 5 of the Third Geneva Convention and Article XVIII of the American Declaration of the Rights and Duties of Man, a competent court or tribunal, as opposed to a political authority, must be charged with ensuring respect for the legal status and rights of persons falling under the authority and control of a state.

Specifically with regard to the request for precautionary measures presently before it, the Commission observes that certain pertinent facts concerning the detainees at Guantanamo Bay are well-known and do not appear to be the subject of controversy. These include the fact that the government of the United States considers itself to be at war with an international network of terrorists,[13] that the United States undertook a military operation in Afghanistan beginning in October 2001 in defending this war,[14] and that most of the detainees in Guantanamo Bay were apprehended in connection with this military operation and remain wholly within the authority and control of the United States government.[15]

It is also well-known that doubts exist as to the legal status of the detainees. This includes the question of whether and to what

---

13. See e.g. Remarks by the President in Photo Opportunity with the National Security Team, Office of the Press Secretary, September 12, 2001, http://whitehouse.gov/news/releases/2001/09/20010912-4.html.

14. See e.g. Radio Address of the President to the Nation, Office of the Press Secretary, October 13, 2001, http://www.whitehouse.gov/news/releases/2001/10/20011013.html.

15. See e.g. Jim Garamone, 50 Detainees now at Gitmo; All Treated Humanely, American Forces Press Service, January 15, 2002, http://www.defenselink.mil/news/ Jan2002/n01152002_200201151.html.

extent the Third Geneva Convention and/or other provisions of international humanitarian law apply to some or all of the detainees and what implications this may have for their international human rights protections. According to official statements from the United States government, its Executive Branch has most recently declined to extend prisoner of war status under the Third Geneva Convention to the detainees, without submitting the issue for determination by a competent tribunal or otherwise ascertaining the rights and protections to which the detainees are entitled under US domestic or international law.[16] To the contrary, the information available suggests that the detainees remain entirely at the unfettered discretion of the United States government. Absent clarification of the legal status of the detainees, the Commission considers that the rights and protections to which they may be entitled under international or domestic law cannot be said to be the subject of effective legal protection by the State.

In light of the foregoing considerations, and without prejudging the possible application of international humanitarian law to the detainees at Guantanamo Bay, the Commission considers that precautionary measures are both appropriate and necessary in the present circumstances, in order to ensure that the legal status of each of the detainees is clarified and that they are afforded the legal protections commensurate with the status that they are found to possess, which may in no case fall below the minimum standards of non-derogable rights. On this basis, the Commission hereby requests that the United States take the urgent measures necessary to have the legal status of the detainees at Guantanamo Bay determined by a competent tribunal.

NOTE: In its letter to the NGOs who had sought this action, the Commission noted, "in accordance with Article 25(4) of the Commission's Rules of Procedure that the granting of these measures and their adoption by the State shall not constitute a prejudgment on the merits of a case."

---

16. See White House Fact Sheet, Status of Detainees at Guantanamo, Office of the Press Secretary, February 7, 2002, http://www.whitehouse.gov/news/releases/2002/02/20020207 13.html.

# 4
# REPORT ON HUMAN RIGHTS VIOLATIONS

## *DUTY TO MAKE THIS REPORT FOR USE IN OIG COMPLAINTS, LITIGATION, AND REPORTS TO UN COMMITTEES*

The Meiklejohn Institute is presenting this Report to the Inspector General of the United States, with copies, to the Judiciary Committees of the House and Senate in order to

- ensure that every complaint of a human rights violation by a US Government official (or someone acting for or under contract with the US Government) is investigated immediately and thoroughly, and that the Government takes steps to redress every proved grievance.
- help the media carry out its duty implicit in the First Amendment and UN Charter provisions; to accurately report events so that the people and the Government are kept informed.
- help libraries and educational institutions continue to carry out their primary functions of providing books and learning to all without distinctions, prejudices, or ideology-based surveillance.
- help the people of the United States, as individuals and groups, discover the full extent of the US violations of human rights since 9/11, and decide how to change US policies and practices immediately, before further damage is done.
- spur Congress to conduct investigations of human rights violations by federal, state, and local Government officials and by contractors using federal funds, leading to proposals for new legislation to ensure that violations do not continue and that violators are brought to justice.

We are presenting this Report to the UN human rights Committees to

- begin to meet the commitments the Government made when it ratified the three reporting treaties.
- help the UN Committees and the Inter-American Human Rights Commission conduct meaningful dialogues with Government officials about the reports, focusing, as the Committees do, on obstacles to correcting the abuses and how these obstacles can be overcome quickly.

## CATEGORIES OF RIGHTS AND DUTIES

Before presenting this lengthy Report, it may be helpful to look at the six large categories of rights and duties in the Table of Contents. The goal is to include every issue of concern to every individual victim and group affected by the actions or inactions of the US Government since 9/11—from Acts of racism, Attorney-client privilege violations, the Use of Uranium and Weapons of mass destruction; and violations perpetrated in Afghanistan, Guantanamo, the Philippines, and the Virgin Islands.

This is an almost impossible task and the Meiklejohn Institute did not undertake it lightly. But as the material was collected, it became obvious that a great many segments of American society have been attacked and affected by the post-9/11 actions by people with power. The goal is to present some examples of each type of violation, admitting that it is impossible at this time to include every one or to discover exactly how many people were victimized by each type.

To summarize the behavior of the Government, it has been following policies of guilt by association to build a climate of fear in and among political, racial, national, ethnic, and religious individuals and communities where the people have been denied their right to human dignity. The full text of the relevant laws is presented in Chapter 6.

## SOURCES FOR THIS REPORT

The facts in the following Report are from US Government reports, including Inspector General reports, from pleadings in cases and court opinions, from state statutes and city resolutions on the USA PATRIOT Act, from Nongovernmental Organization publications and special reports on aspects of the problems, from books; newspaper, magazine, and Web page articles; and from submissions by individuals.

The goal of this Report is to be inclusive of all issues, giving examples of individual victims and of individual perpetrators of the violations. Litigation handled by leading human rights organizations has been easier to collect and update than cases merely reported in the media, so the coverage is better for NGO cases. Community movements against violations are described throughout the reports. Fresno, California, was selected for more coverage as representative of communities across the country. It is a small agricultural community in Central California with an active group of organizations and publications working on many human rights violations.

The first draft of this Report was completed August 31, 2004. A great effort was made to update each report and to add the most important facts in new Reports through November 2004; this was not entirely successful. The Meiklejohn Institute will continue to collect information for future reports to the OIG and the three UN committees and summarize it on the MCLI Web site: http://www.mcli.org.

## FORMAT OF REPORT PAGES

Each report page begins with a description of the person whose rights have allegedly been violated, the name of the individual or Government agency that is allegedly guilty of the violation, and a description of the incident or practices. A list of the US and UN laws that govern the issues raised is presented in the introduction to Sections 1–30.

The goal is to answer this series of questions:

1. Which Government agency acted illegally or unwisely, or failed to react, to an illegal action by individuals or groups?
2. What supervisorial Government agency failed to investigate this illegal action and report it?
3. What agency that received a report of the misconduct either acted or failed to act?
4. Which agency failed to make a report to the highest US Government agency and/or to the appropriate UN Committee?
5. What is the present status of the complaint or problem?
6. What obstacles need to be overcome to prevent a recurrence of such incidents?

This information can lead to constructive work by the appropriate Office of Inspector General and to constructive dialogue between representatives of the US Government and the experts on the UN Committees. If additional questions are raised by a particular report, they will be listed at the end of the description of the incident.

## A. BASIC RIGHTS OF ALL PEOPLES UNDER US JURSIDICTION

Inspired by the Magna Carta of 1215 in England and the Petition of Right of the British Parliament in 1628, the people who fought against the King of England and his armies in order to establish the United States of America quickly declared, in writing, that they had rights that must be respected by their new government. The Bill of Rights begins with the First Amendment to the Constitution and proclaims the "right of the people peaceably to assemble, and to petition the Government for a redress of grievances." The First Amendment also proclaims freedom of religion, speech, and the press.

The people who fought against the Southern states in order to abolish slavery quickly voted, through their state legislatures, to adopt the Fourteenth Amendment, declaring the fundamental right to equal protection of the law to every person within the jurisdiction of the United States, regardless of race, color, or previous condition of servitude. This has come to include the right of women to equal protection.

The people who fought in World War II to defeat the fascist ideology and practices in Germany, Italy, and Japan quickly joined peoples from other nations in writing Articles 2.3 and 2.4 into the UN Charter, which committed the United States and all signatory nations to "refrain . . . from the threat or use of force" in the settlement of disputes. And they joined in writing Articles 55 and 56 into the Charter to commit the United States, and all other signatory nations, "to promote . . . universal respect for, and observance of, human rights and fundamental freedoms for all without distinction as to race, sex, language or religion." In 1945, the US Government helped write the Nuremberg Principles to define war crimes, crimes against peace, and crimes against humanity to limit all future legal actions of all nations.

By 1994, the US Government had joined most other nations in further defining these rights in the International Covenant on Civil and Political Rights, the Convention on the Elimination of all forms of Racial Discrimination, and the Convention Against Torture and other Cruel, Inhuman, or Degrading Treatment or Punishment. (The relevant text of all of these laws is in Chapter 6.)

After 9/11, people in the service of the US Government and under contract with the Government frequently took actions that US residents considered to be denials or abridgements of their basic rights, the rights of their neighbors, or people they learned of through the media. The violations and enforcement of these rights are described in this Part (A) in Sections 1–11 in eighty-six concise Reports. The Government must not only enforce basic human rights. It also has duties to the people under its jurisdiction and throughout the world. These duties are described in ninety-four Reports in Parts B–F in Sections 12–30.

The right not to be killed or disappeared is the most fundamental right of every human being. There are clear limits to killings even in wartime. Alleged violations of this right are spelled out in Reports 1.1–1.13 as they occurred from New York and Cincinnati to Afghanistan and Iraq. The right not to be tortured or subjected to cruel, inhuman, or degrading treatment or punishment is fundamental US and UN law. Alleged violations of this right are described in Reports 2.1–2.17. The Government officials who are alleged to have inflicted this treatment are members of the military, Immigration offices, the FBI, prison guards, and guards in Guantanamo and Iraq. The victims are people of many national origins residing on territory governed by the United States. One bright note: in October 2003, a federal jury awarded damages to the family of a victim of Pinochet's Chile in a suit under the Alien Tort Claims Act (Report 2.17).

Millions of people have been exercising their First Amendment rights to peaceable assembly and to petition the government since 9/11. Section 3 describes the Government-funded weapons, safety nets, and tactics used by the Secret Service, the FBI, and local police from Oakland to New York to "deal with" the people in Reports 3.1–3.7, 3.9. The US military allegedly punished one soldier for his wife's antiwar activities (Report 3.8). Peaceful protesters did defeat a "restitution" plan by weapons manufacturer Lockheed Martin (Report 3.4). More and more people began talking about the First Amendment and the illegality of "Free Speech Zones" after trying to raise their voices in many creative ways at the Democratic Party Convention in Boston and the Republican Party Convention in New York in summer 2004 (Report 3.9).

The basic right of every person under US jurisdiction to equal protection of the laws is one of the main issues since 9/11. Reports 4.1–4.11 enumerate the kinds of people allegedly being denied equal protection and the kinds of rights they allegedly are being denied. The victims range from a member of Congress (Report 4.1) to airport security personnel (Report 4.8). They are of every race and nationality, not just "Arabs," or "Iraqis," or "Muslims." In response, more people filed complaints with the Equal Employment Opportunity Commission than in several years (Report 4.9).

The right of women to equal protection of the laws was another victim of 9/11. On average women continue to earn only three-quarters of what men earn. Women in the US military allegedly suffer discrimination, and the military is charged with treating "enemy" women worse than it treats some enemy men. The Reports 5.1–5.4 detail these problems. The US media itself is also charged with sex discrimination (Report 5.2). In a step forward, female members of Congress demanded that the Senate Foreign Relations Committee vote to consent to US ratification of the Convention on the Elimination of Discrimination Against Women, and they won. However, their decision has yet to be sent to the whole Senate for a vote.

The right to freely exercise religion was an early victim of 9/11, and daily reports of the United States shelling of holy sites in Iraq caused people to wonder about the US Government's commitment to the First Amendment. Reports 6.2–6.4 detail actions of the FBI's arrests of US citizens who charged that those arrests were based on their religion, as well as attacks by city youth and ultra right-wingers on innocent people who turned out to not be Muslims. This is in addition to the Department of Justice's roundups of over one thousand people of Arab and Muslim backgrounds. One city responded strongly. The Minneapolis City Council passed a resolution requiring local law enforcement not to use city resources "to advance unconstitutional activities" (Section 6 Introduction).

The First Amendment covers not only the right of the people to read the news, but the right of the media to go where the news is being made to report it, and to have their reports published or aired. This necessarily includes the right not to be shot at by the military, and not to be so "embedded" as to be unwilling or prevented from finding all of the relevant facts in a story. All of these rights have been attacked since 9/11, from the killing of seven journalists in Iraq (Report 7.5) to the firing of many media staffers (Report 7.1). The United States censored and seized documents and detained journalists from many nations (Reports 7.2–7.7).

However the media made several unprecedented hits as well. Obtaining, and then publishing, in early 2004, the photographs of the treatment of prisoners at Abu Ghraib prison in Iraq led to major demands for an end to such practices, for an investigation of the accusations, and for trials of those in charge. In June 2004, *New York Times* columnist Paul Krugman put forth his opinion that John Ashcroft's misdeeds in office put him "head and shoulders below the rest" in comparison with all previous US attorney generals.[1]

US citizens and noncitizens at all levels of Government and income began to react to the passage of the USA PATRIOT Act the minute the first person was questioned or detained under its provisions. Reports 8.1–8.7 describe Government actions to obtain personal records, to require registration of aliens, and to infiltrate organizations like Peace Fresno. At least one city (Report 8.4) and one judge (Report 8.6) agreed to limit some intelligence gathering.

One of the noisiest groups to emerge after 9/11 was librarians (Reports 9.1–9.3). They told the press, the FBI, and the Department of Homeland Security what their lawyers told them about the right to privacy and the First Amendment. Then they told their patrons they would try to stop illegal actions. But the Republicans in Congress changed a rule to prevent the Democrats and certain other Republicans from stopping further oversight of libraries and their patrons (Report 9.3).

According to one estimate, since 9/11 six hundred thousand foreign students studying in the United States have been at risk of not being able to complete their college or graduate programs at US universities (Section 10,

Reports 10.2, 10.5). Many professors studying in the United States, and teaching at US universities, have faced arrest, detention, and deportation (Reports 10.3–10.4).

Citizens discovered that their Government kept two lists: one of countries and the other of scientific disciplines. Anyone from a listed country seeking to study a listed discipline faced heavy scrutiny and possible refusal of entry. All this was based on a new Student Exchange and Visitor Information System (Report 10.1). Some asked: where is our fabled academic freedom? Our right to education?

The right to travel is the basis for most of the current population of the United States. Many people have left other countries and immigrated to the United States. Some came with the proper papers. Some left their homelands in a hurry to avoid death or incarceration. From the earliest settlers to the immigrants who arrived yesterday, many have come without proper papers.

After 9/11, certain people heard their names called over the loud speakers at airports and found themselves in the custody of "security" officers who denied them entry into the United States and sent them back where they came from. Included among these people were a former member of Parliament (Bernadette Devlin), a Basque lawyer, a journalist (Report 11.4) and the fiancée of a US veteran (Report 11.6). Green, antiwar, and other activists were also prohibited from flying (Report ll.1). The Bush Administration took steps to stop visits by US citizens to Cuba while many members of Congress were seeking to lift the limitations on such travel (Report 11.5). The good news is that Congress rejected prescreening airline passengers when it adjourned in summer 2004.

It is impossible to add up the score of all alleged violations of the rights of people in the US since 9/11 described in the eighty-six Reports in Part A. It is even harder to count the number of times people challenged these alleged violations and either won a lawsuit, received damages, or saw a law or regulation changed. Certainly the firm decisions by a New York City Supreme Court judge ordering the immediate release of hundreds of protesters (and mere pedestrians) during the Republican National Convention in New York City in September 2004 (Report 3.9) will go down in history. Many of the rights described in Part A also involved failure of the Government to carry out its duties, described in Parts B through F.

## 1. RIGHT NOT TO BE KILLED OR DISAPPEARED

Every human being has a right not to be killed or disappeared by agents of the US or state governments, or by individuals. This right is clearly stated in the Fifth, Eighth, and Fourteenth Amendments to the Constitution; in the United Nations Charter, Article 55c; and in the three human rights treaties ratified by the United

States: the International Covenant on Civil and Political Rights, Article VI; the Convention Against Torture and other Cruel, Inhuman, or Degrading Treatment or Punishment, Article II; and the Convention on the Elimination of All Forms of Racial Discrimination, Article V. There are clear limits to killings even in wartime, defined in the Nuremberg Principles, the Geneva Conventions, and in the customary international humanitarian laws of war recently cited in the opinion of the International Court of Justice in the Nuclear Weapons Case (ICJ Advisory Opinion of 8 July, 1996, ¶ 105 F, D, 78, and see Report 17.3). Reports 1.1–1.13 briefly describe violations of this right since 9/11.

Every person in the jurisdiction of the United States has this right, regardless of the acts they have committed or with which they have been charged. This includes everyone in federal or state custody in the fifty states (Reports 1.1–1.6), the Virgin Islands (Report 1.7), or in any other property owned or controlled by the US Government located in another nation (Reports 1.8–1.13).

Since the fundamental law of the United States makes no distinctions as to who has this right, every person has this right, regardless of their status in the United States, whether citizen, permanent resident alien, foreign student, traveler, illegal immigrant, detainee, or enemy combatant. And the US Constitution, laws, and treaties do not permit killings or disappearances at times when the United States has not declared war against another country or when it has completed an "invasion." See reports on US actions in Afghanistan (Reports 1.8–1.11) in Iraq (Reports 1.12–1.13), and especially in Abu Ghraib prison (Report 1.13).

In September 2004, the US military brought murder charges, in three separate cases, against six US soldiers stationed in Iraq for murdering an Iraqi civilian, three Iraqis, and one US soldier. In early October 2004, the US military brought murder charges against four US soldiers for murdering an Iraqi general after torturing him in an interrogation. September was also the second deadliest month for US soldiers in Iraq, with eighty killed.[2]

**Relevant Law:**

U.S. Constitution: Art. I, §8, Cl. 11; Art. VI, Cl. 2; First, Fourth, Fifth, Sixth,
    Eighth, Fourteenth Amendments
UN Charter: Art. 2.3, 2.4, 55, 56
Nuremberg Principles
ICCPR: Art. 1, 2, 2.1, 3, 4, 6, 6.1, 7, 9, 10, 12-14, 20, 23, 26, 40
CERD: Art. 1, 2, 2.1, 4, 5, 5(b), 6, 7, 9
CAT: Art. 1, 2, 3, 4, 5, 7, 10, 16, 19
Third and Fourth Geneva Conventions
CRC: Art. 38, 39, 44

## Report 1.1: Asylum Applicant Deported, Then Killed

On January 25, 1991, Ahfaz Khan entered the United States in San Ysidro, California, from Pakistan. On August 11, 1993, he filed his application for political asylum with the Immigration and Naturalization Service (INS).

In his application, Khan reported that he "was harassed by Karachi police, who ransacked his house. 'If I were to return back to my country, I know I would continue to be persecuted, harassed, abused and even put in jail on fake charges. I would not be safe in the country. The police don't forget very soon when you report them to the authorities. They want to get even and they usually do'" (Louis Salmoe, "Deportation Becomes 'Death Sentence,'" *Palm Beach Post*, June 8, 2003, p. 1–A).

It was not until July 12, 1995, that an Immigration hearing officer in Los Angeles received Khan's application, and Khan's original asylum hearing was scheduled for July 7, 1995. Khan didn't know about the hearing because he had moved around and at that time was living in Boca Raton, Florida, so he was unable to attend. On the morning of February 8, 1996, an Immigration hearing officer ordered him deported in absentia.

On July 23, 1997, Khan's wife, a legal US resident, filed a petition to sponsor her husband for a residency visa. The Khans were scheduled to be called for an interview on Mrs. Khan's spousal visa petition on September 12, 2001. Then the September 11 attacks occurred.[3]

On January 8, 2002, officials arrested Ahfaz Khan in a post–September 11 Government sweep. On February 1, 2002, Khan was deported. His wife and two small children, US citizens, remained in the United States. On July 9, 2002, more than four months after he had been deported, his visa application was approved. Mrs. Khan was not interviewed until after her husband had been deported to Pakistan. The Immigration officials who interviewed her didn't even know that Khan had been deported.

In Khan's case, some Immigration officials knew that a visa was in the works for him, but nevertheless he was deported (Salmoe, "Deportation Becomes 'Death Sentence'").

A story dated September 12, 2002, stated that "the INS had deported over 750 people" with stories similar to Mr. Khan's. "These are people the government could not and did not charge with any terrorist related crimes."[4]

On March 26, 2003, Ahfaz Khan was murdered in the streets of his hometown in Pakistan, when he was close to receiving the documents necessary to return to the United States (Salmoe, "Deportation Becomes 'Death Sentence'").

## Report 1.2: NYC Police Kill Immigrant from Burkina Faso

On May 22, 2003, plainclothes New York police officer Brian Conroy was guarding counterfeit merchandise seized during a raid on a warehouse in Manhattan's Chelsea section. In the same warehouse, Ousmane Zongo, a recent immigrant from Burkina Faso, Africa, had been visiting a rental storage unit where he repaired African craftwork and drums. He was unarmed. Officer Conroy chased Zongo through the warehouse's hallways, then shot and killed him.[5]

Zongo suffered wounds to the abdomen, chest, and upper back and was grazed on the right arm. Officer Conroy stated that Zongo tried to take his gun. The *New York Times* reported that Zongo's friends and fellow vendors said it seemed impossible that he could have run afoul of the law. Kodjo Volta, a friend of Zongo's, said, "He wouldn't challenge anyone," and added that he did not even have the nerve to hound customers who owed him money.[6]

According to Zongo's roommate, Casmir Barry, the cops showed up at his apartment hours later "looking for evidence." "They searched everything; they threw everything on the floor," said Barry, who arrived at the apartment after police had searched the place. Civil rights lawyer Norman Seigel said, "They're looking to see if they could find something to discredit the guy—to make him look bad." New York Police Department (NYPD) spokesman Brian Burke said the cops went to Zongo's home to verify his identification and called the search normal police procedure. "It wasn't an attempt to gather any evidence," he said. But Barry said both of his roommates were taken to a police station where they were questioned for six hours (Douglas Montero and Heidi Singer, "Cop-Slay Victim's Pad Was Raided," *New York Post*, June 7, 2003, p. 11).

The media did not report any investigation of the killing by the Civil Rights Division of the Department of Justice or the US Civil Rights Commission. On June 9, 2004, a grand jury in Manhattan handed down charges of second-degree manslaughter against Officer Conroy. Reacting to the indictment, Patrick J. Lynch, president of the Patrolmen's Benevolent Association, defended Conroy. Lynch stated on behalf of the PBA, "We believe that the grand jury made a mistake indicting this police officer and are confident that he will be exonerated when all the facts are known." Sanford A. Rubenstein, a lawyer for Mr. Zongo's family, stated, "The charges, if true, [show that the] grand jury has done justice." According to the *New York Times*, no New York City police officer has ever been convicted of murder for actions in the line of duty (Sabrina Tavernise and William K. Rashbaum, "Grand Jury Said to Indict Officer in Fatal Shooting," *New York Times*, June 10, 2004, p. A27).

## Report 1.3: NYC Police Raid Kills Civil Servant

On May 20, 2003, New York City Police raided the apartment of Alberta Spruill, fifty-seven, an African American NYC civil servant. Using a "no knock" warrant, they entered using a flash grenade. As a result of the shock, Spruill had a heart attack and died.[7]

New York police told the media they believed, based on information from an informant, that Ms. Spruill's apartment had an arsenal of guns, drugs, and attack dogs and, as a result, used the Emergency Service Team to conduct the raid. It turned out the informant used by the police was unreliable and that he had misled police in the past.[8]

The public and the New York City Council asked for an investigation into this case by the Manhattan District Attorney, New York Attorney General, and the US Department of Justice. The City Council also looked into the use and legality of "no knock" search warrants, as well as stun grenades.[9] As of November 1, 2004, the media had not reported any investigation by the Civil Rights Division of the US Department of Justice or the US Civil Rights Commission of the killing.

## Report 1.4: Cincinnati Police Beat African American Man to Death

On November 30, 2003, Nathaniel Jones, a forty-one-year-old man, died in police custody in Cincinnati, Ohio. Jones was the eighteenth African American man to die in the custody of the Cincinnati police since 1995, compared to only one white man, in a city with only a 43 percent African American population.

Jones, a 350-pound man, was known as a gentle churchgoer and attentive to his teenage sons who lived in Cleveland. He had just returned from there early on a Sunday morning when he stopped at a White Castle restaurant to meet with two waitresses who were friends. Jones was not armed and not hostile. Due to the effects of drugs, fatigue, or illness, he started acting strange, dancing and jumping around. He went outside and passed out. The restaurant called for emergency medical assistance. When the paramedics arrived, Jones had revived, but they thought he was acting erratically; they called the police. When the police arrived, the paramedics left.

The police cruiser videotape shows Jones standing, looking away from the police. They asked Jones, "What is going on here?" Jones called the police officer a "nappy head redneck White boy." The officer sprayed mace on him, and Jones threw a punch at the officer. Two officers then tackled Jones to the ground. The videotape shows the officers hitting him repeatedly, more than forty times, with aluminum nightsticks. When four more officers arrived, they moved Jones so that his hands were behind his back, placed three sets of handcuffs on him, maced him, and left him lying on his face. Then the police videotape was turned off for one minute and thirty seconds.

When the videotape resumes, Jones can be heard whispering "Mama" three times and "Help." After a few minutes, the officers realized Jones was not breathing. They failed to begin CPR immediately. The police chief defended these actions, and the police union president said the police "exercised restraint."[10]

Jesse L. Jackson Sr., of Rainbow/Push Coalition, NAACP President Kweisi Mfume, National Urban League President Marc Morial, Cincinnati NAACP President Calvert Smith, and Rev. Fred Shuttlesworth called for an investigation and action by the US Justice Department, the Governor of Ohio, and the mayor and police chief of Cincinnati. Mfume said, "then attorney general John Ashcroft should direct the Justice Department to not only investigate the possible violation of civil rights laws, but to also consider whether federal funds should be cut off from the Cincinnati Police Department until the police are trained to handle this kind of situation without using excessive force." While the confrontation was airing on national TV, Jones's grandmother and aunt called for an investigation and justice, but also called on Cincinnatians to learn to live together, and called on the African American community to stay calm.

The Hamilton County Coroner's report stated that Jones's blood showed traces of cocaine and PCP, and that his heart was significantly enlarged. The report stated that the struggle with police was the primary cause of Jones's death because it affected his heart and escalated his condition; therefore, homicide was the official cause of death. A criminal investigation was launched into whether there had been criminal misconduct by the police officers involved.

On March 22, 2004, prosecutors closed the case. They said that Jones was the only one in the videotaped struggle who broke the law. Hamilton County Prosecutor Mike Allen said, "It's a tragedy that he's dead. . . . But he is the one who committed the crimes." Allen decided that the case was closed and would not be presented to a grand jury. He said that his conclusions were supported by the police investigation and an independent forensics expert who extensively reviewed the video.

Kenneth Lawson, the attorney representing Jones's family, said he was not surprised by the prosecutor's decision. "It was typical Mike Allen, demonizing another black male and making excuses for police misconduct."

There is also an internal police probe and another by a citizens' panel, and the Justice Department has said it was gathering information.[11] Lawson ordered an independent coroner's report.[12]

## Report 1.5: Gunmen Shot Sikh and Muslim Americans

The National Asian Pacific American Legal Consortium and its Affiliates, the Asian Pacific American Legal Center of Southern California, and the Asian Law Caucus in San Francisco, released their ninth annual *Audit of Violence Against Asian Pacific Americans: BACKLASH—Final Report on 2001*. It documents 507 hate crimes in 2001, a 23 percent increase over 2000, many occurring in schools and workplaces after 9/11.

The first incident occurred on September 15, 2001. A man shouting "I stand for America all the way!" shot and killed Balbir Singh Sodhi, a forty-nine-year-old Sikh American doing landscaping work outside his gas station in Mesa, Arizona.

"Sikh Americans, a religious group whose members are mostly of South Asian descent, were particularly targeted because many of their men wear turbans and long beards, similar to the publicly perceived image of Osama Bin Laden."[13]

The "ferocity and extent" of the backlash incidents are unparalleled, according to a report by the nongovernmental organization Human Rights Watch. The report recommended that law enforcement agencies need to "adopt pre-emptive policies, including building closer ties with local Muslim communities, to prevent violence against Muslim (or perceived to be Muslim) targets." The full extent of the backlash, otherwise, may remain unknown because of the "voluntary and incomplete nature of the various reporting systems [currently] used by police."

Public officials denounced the backlash incidents. At the same time, "mixed messages" were conveyed by actions such as federal authorities' detention of "some 1,200 people of almost exclusively Arab, Muslim, or South Asian heritage because of 'possible' links to terrorism" and FBI interrogations of 8,000 men of Arab and Muslim heritage in the first year after 9/11.[14]

## Report 1.6: County Sheriffs Investigate Deaths at Arizona Border

In July 2002, progressive attorneys and activists in Arizona decided to take a new path for action and started a group called The Samaritans to counteract the violence of "border militias" and to help migrants survive the dangerous journey through the desert. Rancher Glenn Spencer had formed the American Border Patrol in 2000 to "expose" a supposed Mexican conspiracy to reconquer the territory Mexico had lost in the aftermath of the Mexican-American War. From dawn to 10 AM and from 4 PM to sundown, three members of The Samaritans scour the desert in four-wheeled vehicles, ready to provide ailing migrants with emergency water, food, and medical assistance ("MCLI Helps Migrants to Arizona," *MCLI Newsletter*, Fall 2002, p. 4).

On October 24, 2003, the *Tombstone Tumbleweed* issued "a public call to arms" on its front page, demanding that citizens form a "Border Patrol Militia" to combat illegal immigration into Arizona, California, New Mexico, and Texas. On October 27, 2003, Glenn Spencer and two other ranchers, Roger and Don Barnett, allegedly used dogs to chase twenty-six illegal immigrants down a highway, pointed rifles and handguns at them, and forced them to march toward waiting border patrol agents. Also in October 2003, Gulf War veteran Jack Foote, in cooperation with various ex-military and law enforcement agents, created Ranch Rescue, a heavily armed paramilitary militia to conduct armed patrols along the border in search of what it labels "criminal trespassers and terrorists."[15]

In November 2003, the Arizona Pinal County sheriff's department and the Santa Cruz County sheriff investigated Ranch Rescue in connection with the murder of two migrants and the disappearance of nine migrants at a cattle pond near Red Rock, Arizona. Since 2003, both Ranch Rescue and the American Border Patrol have been accused of shooting holes in water tanks left in the middle of the desert by immigrant and border advocacy groups such as Humane Borders. The tanks are intended to help save the lives of hundreds of immigrants who die of thirst and exposure each year while attempting to make the overland border crossing between Mexico and the United States without legal papers.[16]

Other groups, with names like No More Deaths and Humane Borders, have formed in Arizona and other border states to put a stop to migrant deaths in the desert.[17]

In 2004, the nonprofit Border Action Network issued a report, *Justice on the Line*, chronicling a history of long-term, systematic racism and violence directed by the Bureau of US Citizenship and Immigration Services (formerly the INS) against legal and illegal Latino immigrants and US citizens.[18]

### Report 1.7: Police Murders in US Virgin Islands

On December 30, 2003, the *Virgin Islands Daily News* published a special report on the Virgin Islands police department's use of deadly force. Over the last twenty years it was found that police officers in the Islands, which are a territory of the United States, have used deadly force at a per capita rate far higher than the national average. Among other findings:

- Virgin Islands police officers used deadly force one hundred times, but were only prosecuted ten times. Only six prosecutions went to court, and only two cases resulted in jail time for the offending officers.
- Officers shot eighty-five people, killing twenty-eight.
- Of the one hundred victims of deadly force, thirty-five were armed and sixty-five were not.

- Of the seventy-two survivors, only seventeen were charged with a crime.
- Eighty-five of the shootings were criticized by experts as extrajudicial and illegal. Many of the shootings occurred while suspects were either running away from police or surrendering.

Mark Wallace, the Justice Department's law enforcement coordinator, studied the Virgin Islands police force and found that it lacks the most basic training in the proper use of deadly force. Local police union president Aaron King stated, "We need the basics." In addition to the police receiving poor training and the territory's refusal to prosecute officers, the Virgin Islands has no citizens review board to oversee complaints against police, nor does it have a grand jury system capable of investigating and charging individual officers. Attorney Generals for the islands have shown a historic reluctance to investigate police killings or file charges against members of the department (Lee Williams, "Deadly Force," *Virgin Islands Daily News*, December 30, 2003, p. 1).

## Report 1.8: Cluster Bombs Kill After Invasion of Afghanistan Ended

On October 10, 2001, the United States began dropping cluster bombs on "soft targets" (vehicles and people) in Afghanistan. "Eleven weeks later, US planes had dropped 1,210 cluster bombs, each containing 202 BLU-97 bomblets." In early 2002, Pierre Wettach of the International Committee of the Red Cross in Afghanistan said that unexploded weapons kill or wound more than one hundred Afghans a month. Seventy percent of the victims are civilians and more than 10 percent are children under age fourteen. The US Government defended its use of cluster bombs as an appropriate response to the killings at the World Trade Center, which it blamed on the al Qaeda network run by Islamic militant Osama bin Laden. The United States launched air strikes on Afghanistan to flush out bin Laden and punish his Taliban protectors. The British Halo Trust estimated that 20 percent of the bombs failed to explode. Accordingly, 48,884 yellow, soda-can-sized, deadly submunitions now litter the villages and fields of Afghanistan.

The cluster bomb is one of the cheapest air-delivered weapons available to the United States. Unlike most mines, cluster bomblets are not designed to break down over time, as this would raise their cost. "A single BLU-97 bomblet kills anyone within a 50-meter radius and severely injures a person within 100 meters."[19] The unexploded yellow bomblets look like toys and are very attractive to children. A significant number fail to explode when they reach the ground, but they can go off later at the slightest touch.[20] Concerned people are asking: how will the world ever know how many are ultimately killed by these cluster bombs?

## Report 1.9: Deadly US Attack on Afghan Wedding

On July 1, 2002, US helicopters, gunships, and jets fired on an Afghan wedding, killing or injuring at least 250 civilians. The attack occurred in the village of Kakarak in the Uruzgan province, where coalition troops were searching for remaining al Qaeda and Taliban fighters. The attack began shortly after midnight and continued for more than two hours until US Special Forces moved into the area. Most of the injured and dead were children and women.

According to a Pentagon spokesman, a "reconnaissance patrol that was flying over Uruzgan province reported coming under anti-aircraft artillery fire."[21]

Afghans claim that the wedding guests, who were celebrating, had been firing small caliber rifles into the air, as is the custom at Afghan weddings, when US armaments struck.

The US vehicles, including a B-52 bomber and an AC-130 helicopter gunship, dropped seven 2000-pound bombs.[22] A report from UN officials who visited the village on July 3–4 stated they found "no corroboration" for allegations by the Pentagon that its AC-130 had been fired upon first from the village. UN officials also found that coalition troops arrived on the scene very soon after the air strike and "cleaned the area," removing evidence of shrapnel, bullets, and traces of blood. They also reported that some of the women in the village had had their hands tied behind their backs.

The Pentagon claimed that removal of "blood samples, shell casings, and shrapnel" was part of an official investigation by US officials. The US investigative team, which arrived at the village on July 3, two days after the raid, immediately claimed that the physical evidence did not match the reported death toll. "There should be more blood. Where are the bodies?" they asked repeatedly. Villagers explained that Muslim custom requires that the dead be buried quickly. The lack of blood was allegedly due to the earlier US "cleansing" operation.

The Kakarak massacre is not an isolated incident. There is no official tally of civilian deaths caused by US bombing and other military operations. The Pentagon has refused to investigate most incidents or keep track of the number of people killed, maimed, or left homeless. Unofficial estimates based on careful analysis of media reports put the toll of civilian deaths in Afghanistan at over 3,000 by August 2002.[23] In fall 2004, some UN observers who tried to monitor the election process in Afghanistan were killed. This indicates that the number of civilian deaths in Afghanistan since 9/11 will never be known.[24] Human rights experts might comment that one of the tasks of military experts is to be sufficiently aware of the cultural patterns of people in a "hostile" country to avoid errors costly in human lives.

And see: Reports 2.9 and 2.10.

## Report 1.10: Afghan Prisoners Die After US Military Interrogation

In December 2002 at the US armed forces base in Bagram, north of Kabul, where the United States has held prisoners for questioning, two Afghan men died. One of the dead prisoners, known only as Dilawar, was a twenty-two-year-old farmer and part-time taxi driver. He was beaten and died "as a result of 'blunt force injuries to lower extremities complicating coronary artery disease.'" The autopsies "classified both deaths as homicides."

"Two former prisoners at the base, Abdul Jabar and Hakkim Shah, told the *New York Times* this week that they recalled seeing Dilawar at Bagram. They said that they had been kept naked, hooded and shackled and was deprived of sleep for days on end."

The death of Mullah Habibullah, the brother of a former Taliban commander, is also being investigated. "His death certificate indicates that he died of a pulmonary embolism, or a blood clot in the lung."

"In his State of the Union address in January 2003, President Bush announced that '3,000 suspected terrorists have been arrested in many countries.' He told Congress that many others "have met a different fate" and "are no longer a problem to the United States."[25]

## Report 1.11: US Troops Charged with Massacre of Afghan Prisoners

US soldiers and their allies, the Afghan Northern Alliance, had a role in "disappearing" around 3,000 men in northwest Afghanistan after the fall of the Taliban, according to witnesses.[26]

After intense fighting against the Taliban in Kunduz, Northern Alliance troops took control of the city and accepted the surrender of about 8,000 Taliban fighters that included al Qaeda, Chechens, Uzbeks, and Pakistanis. Almost 500 suspected al Qaeda members were taken to the Qalai Jangi prison while the remaining 7,500 were loaded in containers and transported to the Qala-I-Zeini fortress. Human rights advocates say that close to 5,000 of the original 8,000 are missing.[27] Two-hundred to three-hundred prisoners were forced into containers for a two-to-three day convoy. "The prisoners were crammed at gunpoint into large, oblong freight containers. When no more could be squeezed in, the metal doors were shut tight. Slowly they began to suffocate."[28]

"When the trucks arrived and soldiers opened the containers, most of the men inside were dead. Witnesses also said that US Special Forces directed that the containers carrying the living and dead be taken into the desert, and they stood by while the survivors were shot and buried."[29]

Jamie Doran, a veteran BBC filmmaker, included eyewitness accounts of this human rights disaster in his documentary film, *Afghan Massacre: The*

*Convoy of Death*: A local taxi driver said he smelled something awful when he stopped at a gas station. When he asked the petrol attendant where the smell was coming from, the attendant said "Look behind you." "There were trucks with containers fixed on them. . . . Blood was leaking from the containers." Two civilian drivers said they drove trucks carrying men to Dasht-e-Laile, near Shebargan, where the prisoners were shot. A driver told Doran that there were US soldiers present at Dasht-e-Laile. "How many Americans were with you?" Doran asked. The driver replied, "Thirty or forty."

An Afghan soldier claimed that he saw a US soldier break one prisoner's neck and pour acid on others. "The Americans did whatever they wanted. We had no power to stop them." At least two of the witnesses who appeared in *Afghan Massacre* were killed after the film's release.[30]

Physicians for Human Rights (PHR) personnel attached to the United Nations Assistance Mission for Afghanistan (UNAMA) investigated mass gravesites in Afghanistan. In May 2002, at the Dasht-e-Laile gravesite, PHR personnel dug a test trench that revealed the remains of fifteen people. Three bodies were exhumed and autopsied. The likely cause of death was determined to be suffocation.[31]

In March 2004, three British citizens who had been imprisoned for two years at Guantanamo Bay were released. One of the three, Asif Iqbal, had been one of the few survivors of the convoy of containers. He described the cramming of prisoners into containers by night, and said that spotlights were operated by American Special Forces.[32]

And see: Reports 1.9, 1.10, 2.9, 2.10.

## Report 1.12:
## After Iraq Invasion, US Soldiers Kill Unarmed Iraqi

On June 28, 2003, Mazen Nouradin, a thirty-two-year-old veterinarian with a private clinic, living in a suburb of Baghdad with his elderly parents, wife, and two daughters, was shot to death by US soldiers as he walked down the road from his house to hail a taxi to go to work. The soldiers fired eight bullets into Mazen's chest, legs, and arms.

The United States claimed that Mr. Nouradin "was holding a pistol." Mr. Nouradin's family claimed that he never owned a gun, and the "object he had in his hand was his daybook." When Mr. Nouradin's younger brother, Maher, came out of the house after hearing the shots, the US soldiers tied his arms behind his back. Mr. Nouradin's dead body was then taken to the Army hospital, and Mr. Nouradin's father, Antoine, was allegedly held for questioning when he went to claim the body. The United States offered no consistent explanation, nor issued an apology for Mr. Nouradin's death.

By contrast, when, on June 28, 2003, two US soldiers, Sergeant Philippe

Nine-year-old Ibtihal Jassem is rescued by her uncle, Jaber Jouda, in Basra, Iraq, in this photo dated Saturday, March 22, 2003, after the bombing of the Mshan neighborhood by coalition warplanes. Born deaf and mute, Jassem not only lost her right leg in the US bombing of Basra two days after the war in Iraq began, but also all seven members of her family. After she was rescued by Jaber Jouda, who found her with her right leg almost severed, Jassem has lived with her grandparents. (AP Photo/Nabil El Jourana)

Gladimir and Private Kevin Ott, were found dead outside of Baghdad, the United States conducted extensive raids and searches to find the killers, and four suspects were taken into custody.[33]

## Report 1.13:
## US Sergeant Reported Killing of Iraqi Prisoner at Abu Ghraib

In November 2003, Sgt. Ivan Frederick was responsible for the night shift at Abu Ghraib prison. He wrote to his family that around that time, the CIA and its paramilitaries interviewed an Iraqi prisoner. He stated, "They stressed him out so bad that the man passed away. They put his body in a body bag and packed him in ice for approximately twenty-four hours in the shower. . . . The next day the medics came and put his body on a stretcher, placed a fake IV in his arm and took him away." The prisoner was never given a number because he was never entered into the prison's inmate-control system.

Specialist Joseph Darby of the 372nd MP Company, 800th MP Brigade, got hold of a CD filled with photographs of naked Iraqi prisoners. On January 13, 2004, he reported incidents of torture and abuse to military investigators, including the Army's Criminal Investigation Division (CID). On January 14, 2004, the CID began an investigation by searching the room of Sgt. Frederick.

On March 3, 2004, US Maj. Gen. Antonio Taguba, who led an investigation on the conditions of Abu Ghraib, reported that some of the individuals in the 800th MP Brigade, the 372nd MP Company, and the US intelligence community used "sadistic, blatant and wanton criminal abuses" on some Iraqi prisoners, documented in graphic photographs.

On April 9, 2004, Sgt. Frederick was tried in an "Article 32 hearing" for his actions in the death of the unnamed Iraqi prisoner at Camp Victory near Baghdad. In October 2004, Frederick was sentenced to eight years in prison.[34]

On April 28, 2004, some of the photographs mentioned by Maj. Gen. Taguba appeared for the first time on CBS' *Sixty Minutes II*. Two of the photographs featured corpses. Others showed the bruised and bloody face of prisoner No. 153399, a room splattered with blood, and one focused on the body of the Iraqi man described in Sergeant Frederick's letter.[35]

## 2. RIGHT NOT TO BE TORTURED OR ORDERED TO TORTURE

Every human being has a right not to be tortured. The first US citizens insisted that this become the Eighth Amendment to their new Constitution: in the territories governed by the United States there shall be no "cruel and unusual punishments inflicted." The US citizens who helped write the United Nations Charter in 1945 included Articles 55c and 56: that each nation shall "promote . . . Universal respect for, and observance of, human rights and fundamental freedoms for all, without distinction as to race, sex, language or religion." In 1994, the US Senate consented to ratification of the Convention Against Torture and other Cruel, Inhuman, or Degrading Treatment or Punishment and then adopted the US regulation Implementing the Convention Against Torture, Article 3 (in 8 C.F.R. §208.18).

After 9/11, the US Administration took a number of steps in its announced "war against terrorism" that resulted in the torture or degrading treatment of many individuals and some groups. Legal immigrants to the United States from the Ivory Coast, Canada, Egypt, Saudi Arabia, and Palestine were tortured by guards in detention centers, by the FBI, and by Immigration agents (Reports 2.1–2.5). Finally, some deportees sued the Attorney General (Report 2.6).

Some US military personnel raped their fellow servicemen and -women at home and while deployed abroad (Report 2.7). Prisoners were tortured at Guantanamo Bay (Report 2.8). US troops "bagged prisoners" (Report 2.9), tortured Afghans and Iraqis (Reports 2.10, 2.12), used napalm on Iraqi civilians (Report 2.11), and tortured prisoners at Abu Ghraib Prison (Reports 2.13, 2.14). In June 2004, some of the tortured prisoners were able to sue Titan Corporation, CACI International, and some of their employees under the US Constitution, Third and Fourth Geneva Conventions, the Religious Land Use and Institutionalized Persons Act of 2000, the Racketeer Influenced and Corrupt Practices Act (RICO), and the Alien Tort Claims Act. In August 2004, the US Government awarded another contract to CACI to perform such services in Iraq prisons (Report 2.14). State prison guards tortured prisoners in US prisons without criticism by the Civil Rights Division of the US Department of Justice, then some of these guards were hired to run prisons in Iraq (Report 2.15). The US Government continues to refuse to close the School of the Americas, where it has trained hundreds of Central and South Americans on how to torture prisoners, renamed "Western Hemisphere Institute for Security Cooperation" (Report 2.16).

After 9/11, one powerful step was taken against torture when a federal jury in 2003 awarded damages to the family of a victim of Pinochet's Chilean dictatorship in 1973, in the first US case charging crimes against humanity forbidden by the Nuremberg Principles (Report 2.17).

**Relevant Law:**

U.S. Constitution: Art. I, §8, Cl. 11; Art. I, §9, Cl. 2; Art. II, §1, Cl. 8; Art. II §3; Art. VI, Cl. 2; First, Fourth, Sixth, Eighth, Fourteenth, Nineteenth Amendments

Alien Tort Claims Act, 28 U.S.C. §1350

Torture Victims Protection Act, 28 U.S.C. §1602

Religious Land Use and Institutionalized Persons Act of 2000, 42 U.S.C. 2000cc, et seq.

Racketeer Influenced and Corrupt Organizations Act (RICO), U.S.C. 1961, et seq.

UN Charter: Art 2.3, 2.4, 55, 55(c), 56

Nuremberg Principles

ICCPR: Art. 1-7, 9, 10, 14, 14.2, 16-21, 23, 24, 26, 27, 40

CERD: Art. 1, 1.1, 2, 5, 5(a), 5(b), 5(d)(i-iii), 7, 9

CAT: Preamble, Art. 1, 2, 4, 5, 5.2, 7, 10-16, 19

Third Geneva Convention (relative to the Treatment of Prisoners of War): Art. 13, 14, 17, 21, 25, 87, 103

Fourth Geneva Convention (relative to the Protection of Civilian Persons in Time of War): Art. 5, 27, 31-33, 37, 41, 42

CEDAW: Art. 3, 6, 18, 24

CRC: Art. 3, 6, 13-15, 37, 44

### Report 2.1: Detention Center Guards Beat Ivory Coast Pilot

On September 14, 2001, Tony Oulai went to the airport in Jacksonville, Florida, on his way home to Los Angeles. He was a thirty-four-year-old Roman Catholic pilot from the Ivory Coast. Airport screeners found in his luggage a stun gun, flight manuals, and commercially available CIA videos and newspapers annotated in a language the airline workers mistakenly took to be Arabic but was a native language. The FBI arrested him and charged him with overstaying his student visa, a minor immigration violation.

Authorities took Oulai to the Baker County, Florida, Detention Center and held him in isolation in an unlit cell that had a bed but no sheets or blankets. After midnight on September 17, 2001, two men wearing jeans and T-shirts, but carrying no identification or badges, came into his cell. They put handcuffs and shackles on him, and took him to another cell for interrogation. They asked him if he was a Muslim and if he was from an Islamic country. He replied "no" to both questions. One of the interrogators hit him from behind, after which Oulai fell on the floor and curled up to protect himself. One of the interrogators put his foot on Oulai's neck, while the other one repeatedly hit him on the back and in the face. Oulai said, "I was begging for my life." He estimated that the beating took less than an hour, and it left him bleeding from his nose, mouth, and ears.

The guards took Oulai to a cell where they were holding an Egyptian detainee. Oulai said he could not talk, and he fell asleep. In the morning he gave his sister's name to the Egyptian man and asked him to call her. He complained to the guards about his treatment, to which the guards responded, "They are going to take care of you where you're going." Oulai was then transferred to Bradenton Federal Detention Center in Manatee County and subsequently to three other East Coast prisons.[36]

On February 9, 2002, Human Rights Watch interviewed Oulai in the Alexandria, Virginia, City Jail. He told them that in November 2001, an Immigration hearing officer had ordered him deported. In December 2001, the Government held him as a material witness, but in January 2002, the deportation warrant was dismissed. The Government then charged Oulai with lying to federal agents the day of his arrest about whether he was living legally in the United States. After reporter Amy Goldstein reported these facts in the *Washington Post* based on an interview with Oulai at the Alexandria Detention Center, guards transferred him to solitary confinement.

In February 2002, Ivory Coast President Laurent Ghagbo was in Washington, DC where he repeatedly said his country would welcome Oulai back but would make him available to US authorities if they came up with any evidence against him.[37]

In March 2002, Oulai was returned to Jacksonville. His attorneys filed a motion to suppress the statements he made after his detention used to charge him with lying about his immigration status. US Magistrate Thomas Morris denied the motion "at a time of heightened securtiy interests in airports." Federal Judge Harvey Schlesinger denied a motion to free Oulai pending trial and set the trial date for August 14, 2002.[38]

On November 12, 2002, Oulai's brother-in-law, Mouhon Paul, announced that Oulai had been freed and had just arrived in Abidjan, Ivory Coast.[39]

## Report 2.2: INS Dentist Tortured Palestinian Canadian

Jaoudat Abouazza grew up in Palestine but became a Canadian citizen at age sixteen. He then moved to Boston, Massachusetts, where he joined a network of Palestinian solidarity activists. He became a highly visible leader in the movement, participating in weekly protest vigils in front of the Israeli Consulate, and in rallies against the Israeli occupation of Palestine.

After an April 6, 2001, demonstration of 2,500 people, Abouazza was shown on the front page of the *Boston Globe* as one of the leaders of the rally. At a subsequent rally on June 10, 2001, the police took close-cropped head shots of all the protesters and later shared this information with the FBI and the Israeli government. "Palestinian activists put special emphasis on this point in light of Israel's policy of assassinating its Palestinian opponents."

Late in the night on May 30, 2002, the city police approached Abouazza's car near Harvard Square in Cambridge, Massachusetts. Amer Jubran, a friend and fellow Palestinian, was present in the area and offered himself as a translator. The police refused him and called for backup, saying, "I think we've got something big." Abouazza was brought into custody and Jubran followed. As Jubran waited, he overheard police officers asking to see "the terrorist." At 3:00 AM Jubran was told that Abouazza was being held on "serious charges" and that his bail hearing would be set for 9:00 AM.

The hearing was delayed until 2:00 PM on Friday, May 31—too late for it to be appealed that day. At the hearing, Abouazza was charged with three traffic violations: driving without a license, driving a car without a registration, and driving with an illegal license plate. "These charges would usually warrant little or no bail," but the prosecution argued that the bail hearing should be continued until Monday on the ground that they found "suspicious papers" and "incendiary wiring" in the trunk of his car.

Over the weekend, Abouazza was held in jail. The FBI questioned him seven times. Some of the questions: "Are you suicidal?" "Do you know Osama bin Laden?" and "Are you planning any terrorist activities?" Also over the weekend the Immigration and Naturalization Service put a detainer on him so they could take him into custody as soon as he was released by the police.[40]

At the continuation of Abouazza's bail hearing, he was released into the custody of the INS. The INS took him to Bristol County Jail, "where he was greeted by a punch in the stomach by guards." The guards told other prisoners that he was a member of the Taliban, then they and other prisoners beat him repeatedly. Whenever he refused to talk, he was placed in solitary confinement.

On Sunday, June 16, 2002, Abouazza was awakened and brought to the prison dental facility. The dentist explained while examining Abouazza that he was going to remove several teeth, but Abouazza refused to let him. Guards wrestled Abouazza into the chair and placed metal retainers on his body. When he continued to resist, they forced open his mouth and gave him a tranquilizer. The dentist extracted four of his teeth, one only partially, leaving him bleeding and in tremendous pain. The guards supplied him with a few cotton swabs to stop the bleeding, and when those ran out, he used any kind of fabric he could find. Afterward he refused to sign a consent form for the procedure they had performed. So, the guards put him in the room they refer to as "the hole." Later prison officials said that only one of his teeth was removed, and they couldn't find the consent form.[41]

On June 20, 2002, Abouazza had his first INS hearing. Immigration hearing officer Leonard Shapiro ruled that there was no evidence that Abouazza was a security risk. Fearing an endless extension of INS mistreatment, Abouazza sought to leave the United States under so-called voluntary departure to Canada. The administrative judge granted this request and gave Abouazza until July 29 for the decision to be enforced or appealed. Guards removed Abouazza from Bristol County Jail to another jail and kept him incommunicado and in isolation in a bare cell without furniture or clothes for twenty-four hours, and then in lockdown for twenty-three hours a day until his departure. The INS refused to deliver him for his district court trial on the original vehicle violations warrant. The INS flew Abouazza to Canada on July 9, 2002. His outstanding warrant will prevent Abouazza from entering the United States in the future.[42]

## Report 2.3:
## INS and FBI Agents Tortured Legal Immigrant from Egypt

On September 12, 2001, the day after 9/11, Hady Hassan Omar heard a knock at his door in Fort Smith, Arkansas. Omar, an immigrant from Egypt, was married to a US citizen but did not yet have permanent resident status. He was scheduled to have an interview with the INS to get a green card on October 2, 2001. The men at the door were FBI agents who handcuffed Omar and took him away.

The FBI said it was investigating him because he had bought airline tickets for September 11 from the same computer terminal as one of the 9/11 hijackers. He was interviewed at a small FBI office in Fort Smith, where he was asked for the names and numbers of his friends and subjected to a lie detector test. After passing the polygraph, he was released.

The next day, Omar got another knock on his door. An INS agent served him with a notice to appear before the agency and took him in for mug shots and fingerprinting. The agent informed him that he had overstayed his tourist visa, even though he had a work permit and was in the country legally. Sometime after midnight, several INS agents placed Omar in leg irons and handcuffs, put him in a car, and drove him to an INS office in Oakdale, Louisiana.

At this point Omar had been in handcuffs for twelve hours and had not had any food for the same length of time. It is unknown whether he was given any water or not. Several hours later, they moved him again to the New Orleans Parish Prison. The guards strip-searched him, issued him a jump-suit, and allowed him to call his wife. The INS then moved him to the max-imum security penitentiary in Pollock, Louisiana. His family did not know he was there, and he was not permitted to make any calls.

In the penitentiary it is alleged that he was told to strip. A dozen officials, including two women, looked on. Someone produced a video camera as Omar undressed. He stood naked while his body cavities were searched for the third time in less than four days. As he stood wincing from the pain of the cavity search, he looked up at one of the female INS guards and saw that she was laughing.

Omar was then put in isolation in a cell ten feet by ten feet. It had a con-crete bunk at its center, a plastic chair, and a metal toilet. He asked if the guards could take his handcuffs off so he could use the bathroom; they said no. Two guards grabbed him and steered him to the bowl. Because he was handcuffed, he could not aim. The urine ran down his pant leg as the guards laughed.

The next morning the warden came to visit him and informed him that he was to be kept there until further notice. When Omar asked for an attorney, the warden denied the request, saying that there had been "special orders from DC." The warden then asked if he had any special dietary needs. Omar replied that he did not eat pork. Lunch was brought soon after—it consisted of bologna and ham. He decided to go on a hunger strike until he was allowed counsel. For the next ten days he was not allowed out of his cell.

Omar's wife retained an attorney to prepare for his immigration hearing. It took so long, however, for the attorney to locate him that there was no time to prepare and the hearing was rescheduled for two weeks later.

Omar used sleep to make the time pass. He did sit-ups and push-ups to keep fit, but his cell was so cold that he got chills whenever he broke into a sweat. Prison officials had turned off the hot water to his shower, so he stopped bathing. He was served pork at least twice a day. He formed a new-found desire to practice his religion and tried to guess the correct hours by following the changing of the guards, who would congregate outside his cell and make faces whenever he tried to pray.

On October 18, 2001, Omar had his immigration hearing. The INS hearing officer ordered him to be released on $5,000 bail. The next day he was informed that the INS prosecutor had appealed this bond decision and that under new antiterror measures, the Government could overturn hearing officers' decisions in "special interest cases." Weeks passed and Omar became depressed. He lost twenty pounds and hardly moved from his bunk. Omar decided to kill himself and made this intention known.

Suddenly everyone was concerned. The FBI decided that he was telling the truth and released him. Omar said he was convinced that during his seventy-three days of captivity they were trying to crush his spirit in order to be absolutely certain that he was telling the truth.[43]

## Report 2.4:
## US Guards Tortured Saudi Arabian Student in United States

On September 20, 2001, the FBI searched Yazeed al-Salmi's apartment. Three days later the FBI arrested him and his two roommates because of their alleged acquaintance with two 9/11 hijackers, and detained them as material witnesses. They took al-Salmi to the federal jail in San Diego, then to San Bernardino, California, then to Oklahoma, and finally to New York.

Al-Salmi, twenty-three, was a legal resident from Saudi Arabia enrolled at Grossmont Community College in El Cajon, California. He was in the United States legally on a two-year student visa that would expire in July 2002.

In jail, some of the guards beat him. They did not allow him to shower or brush his teeth for eight days. They held him in isolation without reading materials, television, or radio. Eventually they gave him the Koran he requested.[44]

Jail officials finally allowed al-Salmi's lawyer, Randall Hamud, to visit him. "I observed bruises on his upper body, arms, back of his neck, and welts on his wrists and ankles," Hamud said. "During the interview, I became very incensed about that because he informed me that the bruises were inflicted by the guards."[45]

On October 9, 2001, authorities released al-Salmi from prison. After seventeen days of detention, al-Salmi stated, "I knew I was innocent and they were wrong, so I have to be patient. They treated me as a terrorist. They stripped me and videotaped me. It was like a party for them with lots of jokes. It was humiliating. I was treated worse than an animal."[46]

### Report 2.5: Pakistani Immigrant Died in FBI Custody

After September 11, 2001, the FBI arrested Muhammed Rafiq Butt, a Pakistani immigrant in New York City. He was detained as a material witness but was not charged with a crime. The FBI sent him to the Hudson County Jail in New Jersey. On October 23, 2001, Butt died in captivity. The FBI stated that the cause of death was cardiac arrest. Butt's body was sent to Mayo Hospital, Lahore in Pakistan for an autopsy.[47]

Aziz Butt, a relative of Rafiq, claimed that the autopsy report from Lahore found multiple fractures in his cousin's legs and chest as well as deep bruises on the body. These marks on Muhammed's body suggested that he had been subjected to severe torture before his death.[48]

## Report 2.6: Deportees Sue Attorney General and FBI: *Turkmen, et al.*

After 9/11, the US Government detained many Muslims from Pakistan and Turkey, including:

- Ibrahim Turkmen, a native and citizen of Turkey;
- Asif-Ur-Rehman Saffi, a native of Pakistan and a citizen of France;
- Syed Amjad Ali Jaffri, a native of Pakistan who has immigrated to Canada.

Each of these men had overstayed his tourist visa and agreed to be deported.

The US Government continued to hold them far beyond the period necessary for their removal, never arresting or charging them with links to terrorist groups. They were held for six months in tiny, windowless cells; they said that guards beat and abused them solely because of their country of origin or their faith. The Government subjected them to degrading conditions, including strip searches and body cavity searches. They were manacled and shackled whenever they were taken from their cells. The Department of Justice, the FBI, and the INS said they could not say when they would clear the men for departure from the United States.

In 2002, the Center for Constitutional Rights (CCR) filed a class action lawsuit in US District Court in Brooklyn against then attorney general John Ashcroft and FBI director Robert Mueller. The suit alleged violations of the Constitution and international human rights and treaty law, including using ethnic and religious profiling in the roundup and detention of hundreds of people. The suit alleged that the Government made efforts to keep the plaintiffs from being able to practice their religion during their detention. These and hundreds of other post-9/11 detainees were presumed guilty of terrorism until some law enforcement authorities decided that they were innocent without a hearing or trial.

In mid-2002, the CCR amended the class action complaint to add more named victims. For example, Akil Sachveda, a native of India, was granted "landed immigrant status" in Canada in December 1998. While working as a travel agent in Canada, Mr. Sachveda married a US green-card holder who owned a gas station on Long Island, New York. For the next several years he lived with his wife and worked in the United States. In early 2001, Sachveda and his wife filed for divorce, and he returned to Canada. Sachveda reentered the United States in October 2001 to retrieve the last of his belongings and finalize his divorce.

In late November 2001, an FBI agent visited Sachveda's ex-wife's gas station looking for a Muslim employee. When the employee was not found, FBI agents asked Sachveda's former wife to contact them. She asked Sachveda to meet with FBI agents, and he was then questioned extensively about September 11 and his religious beliefs, without being advised about his right to counsel.

On December 20, Sachveda was arrested by INS agents and detained on charges of violating a voluntary departure order. On December 31, 2001, an Immigration hearing officer ordered Sachveda deported to Canada. Typically this would have resulted in his removal from the United States in a matter of days. Even though Sachveda was never charged with any offense or brought before a judge to determine whether he could be held, he was detained for another three and a half months. The CCR's suit was now on behalf of eight plaintiffs against Ashcroft; the heads of the FBI and INS; the Warden, Assistant Warden, Captain, nine Lieutenants, eleven Correctional Officers, and four Counselors at the Correctional Facility; John Does; and the federal Government. The Government moved to dismiss the CCR lawsuit, but the District Court did not grant the motion.

In June 2003, District Judge John Gleeson granted the CCR's motion to further amend its complaint to include disturbing information brought to light in a report issued on June 2, 2003, by the Office of the Inspector General (OIG) of the US Department of Justice. "The September 11 Detainees: A Review of the Treatment of Aliens Held on Immigration Charges in Connection with the Investigation of the September 11 Attacks" is described in Report 29.1.

"The Inspector General's report depicts a Department of Justice that turned its back on the Constitution by locking up hundreds of innocent men of the same ethnicity and religion as the September 11 suicide bombers for the weeks and months it took the FBI to clear them of terrorism," according to CCR Senior Staff Attorney Nancy Chang.[49] The Cato Institute and the Rutherford Institute filed amicus briefs supporting the plaintiffs' position.

On July 2, 2003, the defendants filed a motion to dismiss the claims in the second amended complaint, alleging, among other things, that the defendants were entitled to qualified immunity. While that motion was pending, the plaintiffs obtained leave from the Court to conduct limited discovery to ascertain the identities of all officers involved in the conduct alleged in order to name them as defendants. They also sought production of certain documents which the Government withheld on the basis of the deliberative process and law enforcement privileges.

On July 16, 2003, the CCR submitted a Supplemental Memorandum detailing how the new claims were properly brought before the Court since the Bush Administration violated the rights of those detained in the wake of September 11. On August 26, 2003, the Court ordered the Government to produce documents relating to interactions between officers and the named plaintiffs.

On July 29, 2004, Magistrate Cheryl Pollak found that information submitted on June 14, 2003, was not covered by any privileges and ordered the defendants to give all of the documents to the plaintiffs. The Court permitted the Government to redact the names of inmate witnesses other than the named plaintiffs, their disciplinary recommendations, and the social security numbers for either inmate witnesses or governmental employees. The Court noted that it appeared that the Government may have withheld certain documents that contained information relevant to the identification of officers involved in the alleged abuse of detainees. The Court ordered the defendants to give the plaintiffs any documents that identify any government employees potentially responsible for misconduct involving class members other than the named plaintiffs (*Turkmen, et al. v. Ashcroft, et al.* [2004 US Dist. LEXIS 14537]). The plaintiffs then added as defendants twenty-six more Metropolitan Detention Center (MDC) employees. The Government did satisfy this discovery order but plaintiffs' counsel was ordered not to discuss it with anyone. The defendants were required to submit their briefs on their motion to dismiss on January 25, 2005 (e-mail to MCLI November 8, 2004, from Nancy Chang of the Center for Constitutional Rights).

## Report 2.7:
## US Soldiers Rape US Servicewomen and Often Are Not Punished

Facing allegations that rape in the US military has become endemic in both combat and noncombat zones, and that even when reported the crime goes largely unpunished, in February 2004, Secretary of Defense Donald Rumsfeld created a task force to investigate. In late May 2004, the task force issued its report. "There is no uniformity in services for victims amongst the different branches of the Armed Forces, there are no victim advocates, and commanders regularly interfere in rape investigations, often tainting evidence and precluding a criminal investigation."[50]

In early July 2004, forty-eight members of Congress sent a letter to Secretary Rumsfeld demanding more answers than were provided in the DOD task force report. "Here's the situation: Our servicewomen in Iraq continue to make reports of sexual assaults, and DOD puts out a report that talks about convening summits and developing policies," Rep. Carolyn B. Maloney (D-NY) said.

As of July 2004, one hundred seventy-six US servicewomen who served in either Iraq or Afghanistan reported being sexually assaulted by fellow military

personnel. Many alleged that superior officers ignored their desire to prosecute fellow servicemembers, refused to post guards around bathrooms and
shower facilities where rape is most prevalent, and denied abortions in war
zones after they were sexually assaulted. US military policy allows for abortion
in the case of rape, but women must pay for the abortion themselves.[51]

As a result of the increasing number of men and women in the US military, the number of reported sex crimes has increased since September 11,
2001. US Air Force veteran Dorothy Mackey founded Survivors Take
Action Against Abuse By Military Personnel to help women and men in the
military cope with the physical, emotional, and psychological ramifications
of rape. Mackey herself was sexually assaulted by superior officers twice
during her nine-year career in the military. In her first year in the Armed
Forces, Mackey was raped three times, twice by military doctors. In a 2004
interview with Amy Goodman, Mackey stated, "The only way in which we
can truly see adequate changes given the decades of rapes is to have an outside investigative agency, independent of the Pentagon, able and willing to
prosecute generals and admirals, all the way down to those at the lowest
ranks."[52]

Civilians concerned about rape in the military may choose to take several paths for action. They may write letters to US advocacy groups such as
NOW, the League of Women Voters, and the American Academy of University Women asking them to write to the Civil Rights Division of the US
Department of Justice, the Women's Bureau in the Department of Labor,
and to Congressional representatives urging the creation of an independent
investigative agency to investigate sexual assault in the military. They can
also write letters to the UN Committee for the Elimination of All Forms of
Discrimination Against Women to ask the US Government to investigate
and report on sexual abuse in the military.

### Report 2.8: US Military Tortured Prisoners at Guantanamo: *Rasul, et al.*

In October 2003, Australian lawyer Richard Bourke charged that the US
military tortured some of his clients, who were being held without charge at
the US base at Guantanamo Bay, Cuba. Bourke said he began working soon
after 9/11 on behalf of dozens of the detainees at Guantanamo Bay. He
claimed that US military officials were using old-fashioned torture techniques to force confessions out of prisoners. Reports indicate that about 660
prisoners have been held without charges and without access to lawyers—
some since January 2002 (see Section 19 and Report 7.6).

Early in 2003, officials denied using torture and said detainees were
interrogated humanely, allowed to practice their religion, and given good
medical care. They continued to deny the families of the detainees access to

the prisoners, and heavily censored their mail. They gave advocacy groups and the media only limited and strictly controlled access to them.

Bourke told ABC radio that his claims were based on reports leaked by US military personnel and from descriptions by some detainees who had been released. "One of the detainees has described being taken out and tied to a post and having rubber bullets fired at them. They were being made to kneel cruciform in the sun until they collapsed," said Bourke.

He called on governments around the world to stand up to the US Government and demand that the United Nations investigate the reports of torture.[53]

In May 2004, two British citizens released from Guantanamo Bay said they were subjected to the same acts of torture at the hands of US troops that Iraqis suffered. Shafiq Rasul and Asif Iqbal wrote to President Bush to detail a string of abuses which, they claimed, were inflicted on them by US interrogators. Barbara Olshansky, the attorney representing Rasul and Iqbal, told BBC radio that "They were very clear that they were shackled for hours on end, and made to stand in stressed positions when being questioned by the military interrogators. . . . They were subjected to threatening dogs, freezing cold temperatures, being made to stand naked—the same type of humiliation and stress techniques that were used in Iraq."[54]

Rasul, Iqbal, and Ruhal Ahmed, another British former Guantanamo detainee, reported that they were beaten by US soldiers at Guantanamo and pressured into falsely confessing that they'd been associated with Osama bin Laden.[55] On August 4, 2004, the three men released a 115-page report detailing the abuses they had suffered.[56]

The next day the International Red Cross stated that the United States may have committed war crimes if the report is true, and that "Some of the abuses alleged by the detainees would indeed constitute inhuman treatment," which "constitutes a grave breach of the third Geneva Convention, and these are often also described as war crimes."[57]

## Report 2.9: US Troops "Bagged" Prisoners

After January 2002, US military personnel regularly subjected certain prisoners to the practice of hooding. In Shebarghan, Afghanistan, burlap bags were placed over the heads of suspected al Qaeda members and secured with metallic tape when they were on the way to interrogations by US authorities. On January 7, 2002, Amnesty International's Irene Khan sent a letter to Secretary of Defense Donald Rumsfeld protesting the practice of "hooding and blindfolding of suspects . . . as incompatible with the absolute prohibition of torture or other cruel, inhuman or degrading treatment contained under the UN Convention Against Torture. . . ."[58]

Mashahda, Iraq, July 13, 2003: US forces in Operation Ivy Serpent, an attempt to root out insurgents firing grenades on US convoys, lined hooded Iraqis up against a wall. They killed five Iraqis and detained more than eighty. (AP Photo/John Moore)

On January 24, 2002, US forces attacked the village of Uruzgan, Afghanistan, killing twenty-one people and taking another twenty-seven prisoner. "The US forces, who were wearing masks, tied the detainees' hands and feet, blindfolded them and slipped hoods over their heads, according to several of the prisoners." The hoods restricted breathing in the very hot desert climate. The captives were released two weeks later, as the villagers had been "misidentified . . . as al Qaeda and Taliban fighters."[59]

A December 26, 2002, front-page report in the *Washington Post* described the treatment of Afghan and Arab prisoners of war in the hands of the CIA: "Those who refuse to cooperate inside this secret CIA interrogation center are sometimes kept standing or kneeling for hours, in black hoods or spray-painted goggles, according to intelligence specialists familiar with CIA interrogation methods. At times they are held in awkward, painful positions or deprived of sleep with a twenty-four-hour bombardment of lights—subject to what are known as 'stress and duress' techniques."[60]

Khraisan al-Abally, an Iraqi businessman, said he was arrested and mistreated by US troops on April 30, 2003, because his family was mistakenly believed to know the whereabouts of a top official in the Saddam Hussein regime. US troops shot al-Abally's brother and arrested his eighty-year-old father. Al-Abally stated that "the US interrogators deprived him of sleep, forced him to kneel naked and kept him bound hand and foot with a bag over his head for eight days."[61]

On July 4, 2003, in Sulaymaniyah in northern Iraq, US troops from the 173rd Airborne Division, on an erroneous tip, raided a building housing the Turkish Special Forces (allies of the United States). Turkish "Captain Aydin" described how US troops forced him and his fellows to the ground, hand-cuffed and hooded them with plastic bags and herded them into trucks.[62] US troops put hoods on men captured in the Middle East and elsewhere, and sent them to Guantanamo Bay as "enemy combatants."[63]

One path for action is suggested by the experience of the United Kingdom. That government ordered its troops to put bags over the heads of Irish Republican Army (IRA) suspects in the early 1970s. In 1978, the European Court of Human Rights ruled that this "amounted to a practice of inhuman and degrading treatment" forbidden by the UN Convention Against Torture and other Cruel, Inhuman, or Degrading Treatment or Punishment (CAT), to which the UK was a signatory. The UK then stopped the practice.[64]

Concerned people in the United States are asking their Government to take the same step since it is also a signatory to the CAT, though not a member of the European Court of Human Rights.

## Report 2.10: US Troops Torture Then Kill Afghan Prisoners

In November 2001, Northern Alliance General Abdul Rashid Dostum accepted the surrender of 8,000 Taliban fighters while capturing the northern Afghan city of Mazar-i-Sharif with the aid of the US military. The prisoners were loaded into shipping containers for transport to Shebarghan Prison. Of the 8,000 who started the journey, only 3,015 arrived at Shebarghan alive (see Report 1.11, "US Troops Charged with Massacre of Afghan Prisoners").

At Shebarghan Prison, the Northern Alliance prisoner convoy was met by approximately 150 US soldiers and CIA officers, who ordered the Afghans to take the dead bodies outside of the city so they could not be filmed by satellite film teams. One Afghan soldier told Jaime Doran, a Scottish film-maker who was then working on a documentary about the alleged massacre, that "Everything (at Shebarghan) was under the control of the American commander."

One Afghan general told Doran that the Taliban members selected for interrogation by US personnel "were tortured and summarily executed in barbaric ways." He said, "They cut their legs; they cut their tongues; they cut their hair and cut their beards. They were Arab prisoners. Sometimes they did it for pleasure. They took the prisoners outside and beat them up and then returned them to the prison. But sometimes they were never returned and they disappeared, the prisoner disappeared. I was there."

Another Afghan soldier added that US soldiers "Broke their necks and cut their tongues. . . . The Americans had come to the prison to choose whoever they wanted to send to America. Then they came again after 10 or 15 days to choose some more to deliver to America. Many prisoners were killed. Some of them cried. No one listened to their cries. No one cared."[65]

In a separate incident in March 2003, US troops allegedly tortured eight Afghan soldiers, none of whom were linked to al Qaeda or the Taliban. US troops allegedly beat them, immersed them in water, gave them electrical shocks, hung them upside down, and tore off their toenails. One of them, eighteen-year-old Jamal Naseer, died. His body was described by a witness as "green and black" with bruises. After the *LA Times* and the Crimes of War Project questioned the Army about the incident, the Army opened an investigation.[66]

On March 20, 2004, US pathologists commissioned to investigate the massacre corroborated the claims by the UN that the US-backed Northern Alliance had tortured and killed Afghan prisoners. Forensic anthropologist William Haglund, who earlier led inquiries into mass graves in Bosnia, Rwanda, Sri Lanka, and Sierra Leone, told the *Observer* that he dug into desert soil outside the town of Shebargan and exhumed fifteen bodies—a tiny sample, he said, of what may be a very large total. Haglund visited the mass grave at Shebargan twice in 2002 in the wake of the Coalition's war against the Taliban. On the first occasion, he was part of a team from Physicians for Human Rights, which identified dozens of mass graves in northern Afghanistan, many containing the remains of prisoners killed by the proxy warlord forces that were backed by the United States. Haglund's conclusion "that they died from suffocation" corroborates the claim that many people died while being transported in suffocating containers.[67]

And see Reports in Sections 13 and 19.

### Report 2.11: US Troops Used Napalm in Iraq

Marine Corps fighter pilots and commanders who returned from the war zone in Iraq in 2003 confirmed that they dropped dozens of incendiary bombs (firebombs) near bridges over the Saddam Canal and the Tigris River. Col. James Alles, commander of Marine Air Group 11 based at Miramar Marine Corps Air Station, said, "We napalmed both those [bridge] approaches. Unfortunately, there were people there because you could see them in the [cockpit] video." This firebombing campaign "helped clear the path for the Marines' race to Baghdad" in March and April of 2003.[68]

Firebombs are similar to the controversial napalm used during the Vietnam War, and the explosions create massive fireballs. The Pentagon distinguished the Mark 77 firebombs that were dropped on Iraqi troops from napalm, stating that instead of using gasoline and benzene as fuel, the firebombs use kerosene-based jet fuel, which has a smaller concentration of benzene. John Pike, defense analyst with GlobalSecurity.org, stated, "You can call it something other than napalm, but it's napalm."

The Mark 77s are filled with a different mix of incendiary chemicals than napalm but have the same terrifying effect: a penetrating fire that seeps into dug-in infantry positions.[69]

## Report 2.12: US Troops Tortured Iraqis after Invasion

On April 29, 2003, US soldiers arrested As'ad, Ali, Uday, and Lu'ay Ibrahim Mahdi 'Abeidi (four brothers) in their house, after a shooting in Baghdad. The soldiers "hooded and tightly handcuffed" the brothers and made them spend their "first night in custody lying on the ground in a school" without access to a toilet, food, or water. At the time of arrest, a US second lieutenant took about $20,000 in savings and effects from the family's house.

On April 30, the brothers were taken to Camp Cropper Center at Baghdad International Airport, a US base, "where they were held in the open until tents were brought on the third day." On May 11, all four brothers were released, but their belongings and their savings were not returned to them.

On May 16, 2003, "US forces who were chasing looters" arrested Uday and Rafed 'Adel, thirty-one-year-old twin brothers. The two denied involvement with the looting, but the US forces handcuffed them tightly and took them to various transfer centers, and then to Camp Cropper. The brothers were not allowed to wash or have sufficient drinking water. They were not interrogated. After twenty days of detention, the brothers "were told that they would be released but instead were taken to Abu Ghraib prison."

On June 12, 2003, "all detainees demonstrated against their detention conditions." The "detainees arrested by US forces after the conflict have included both criminal and political suspects." Amnesty International delegates "saw numerous ex-detainees with wrists still scarred by the cuffs a month later." The Amnesty International delegation to Baghdad in June 2003 considered Paul Bremer, the head of the Office of the Coalition Provisional Authority and US Administrator in Iraq, responsible for "abuses" during arrests and detentions.

"US military lawyers who met Amnesty International delegates acknowledged that the failure to give information about the detainees' whereabouts was regrettable but claimed that it had been impossible until recently to set up logistics to do this." The lawyers asserted that "some detainees fall into the 'black hole' detention center at the airport . . . and they are only entitled to a review of their detention within three weeks by a US military lawyer." Others, however, arrested and "taken to Iraqi police stations" were entitled to "protection of the procedures in the 1971 Criminal Procedure Code: their files are brought before an Iraqi examining magistrate within 24 hours" and the arrestees are released "if there is insufficient evidence against them."[70]

## Report 2.13: US Guards at Abu Ghraib Tortured Prisoners

During Saddam Hussein's regime, Abu Ghraib, situated twenty miles away from Baghdad, served as a prison for up to 50,000 women and men simultaneously, who were subjected to daily tortures and executions.

On October 20, 2002, Suddam Hussein ordered the release of all prisoners, including those housed at Abu Ghraib, exept for those accused of spying for the United States or Israel. Abu Ghraib remained empty until the US military opened the prison's doors again in July 2003.[71] In April 2003, following the fall of Hussein, the US military took over Abu Ghraib, cleaned and repaired it, and converted it into a US military prison. The new prisoners were overwhelmingly civilians randomly gathered during military sweeps and checkpoints, including common criminals, individuals thought to have committed "crimes against the coalition," and suspected insurgents.

In June 2003, Brig. Gen. Janis Karpinski became commander of the 800th Military Police (MP) Brigade to head the military prisons in Iraq. She had no previous experience running a prison. On November 5, 2003, Provost Marshal Donald Ryder filed a report of his review of the prison system ordered by Lt. Gen. Ricardo Sanchez, senior US Commander in Iraq. His report highlighted the possible human rights issues and problems with training and manpower at Abu Ghraib arising from the tension between the assignments of the military police guarding the prisoners and the intelligence units in charge of interrogating them. However, Ryder added that the occurrences had not reached a crisis point.

In December 2003, the *St. Petersburg Times* interviewed Karpinski, who declared that "living conditions [at Abu Ghraib] now are better in prison than at home. At one point we were concerned that they wouldn't want to leave."

On January 13, 2004, Specialist Joseph Darby of the 372nd MP Company, 800th MP Brigade, reported incidents of torture and abuse to military investigators, including the Army's Criminal Investigation Division (CID), after obtaining a CD filled with photographs of naked Iraqi prisoners.[72]

On January 14, the CID began an investigation by searching the room of Ivan Frederick, the MP Sergeant responsible for the night shift at Abu Ghraib. On January 16, 2004, Defense Secretary Donald Rumsfeld learned about the probe but did not immediately notify President Bush. Two weeks later, in early February, Rumsfeld only told Bush that there is an "issue" concerning mistreatment of Iraqi prisoners.

On January 17, Sanchez admonished and suspended Karpinski, for "serious deficiencies in her brigade." On January 19, Sanchez launched another investigation to assess the "practices and procedures" of US soldiers at Abu Ghraib. On February 26, Pierre Gassman issued a report for the International Committee of the Red Cross warning that the treatment of the prisoners in Iraq is "tantamount to torture." The report was forwarded to Sanchez and L. Paul Bremer, head of the US Coalition Provisional Authority, and Gassman met with them.

On March 3, Maj. Gen. Antonio Taguba led an investigation on the conditions of Abu Ghraib and revealed in a Report that some of the individuals in the 800th MP Brigade, the 372nd MP Company, and members of the US intelligence community, including private contractors, effectuated "sadistic, blatant and wanton criminal abuses" on some Iraqi prisoners, documented in graphic photographs. He recommended firing two civilian contractors and reviewing the conditions at Abu Ghraib regarding the interrogation process.

On March 20, Brig. Gen. Mark Kimmit stated that six US military officers would be charged with conspiracy, dereliction of duty, cruelty, maltreatment, assault, and indecent acts. On April 6, Lt. Gen. David McKiernan issued his approval of Taguba's recommendations for giving letters of reprimand to six additional soldiers, two of whom were relieved of their duties.

On April 28, when Rumsfeld spoke with US Senators about the war in Iraq, he did not mention the photographs of abuse of Iraqi prisoners. Later that same day, CBS' *60 Minutes II* displayed the images. (This is reported to be the time when Bush first learned about these photographs.) These photos, and others released subsequently, show Iraqi prisoners sometimes hooded, forced into humiliating and sexual positions in the nude, and scared and bitten by attack dogs. Other photos show corpses, and a smiling US soldier looking at or pointing at the scene.

Shortly thereafter, Bush appeared on Arab Television and characterized the abuse of Iraqi prisoners as "abhorrent" behavior that "does not represent the America that I know." Upon hearing that the Muslim population was not pacified by his lack of apology, Bush went on the air again the next day to formally do so.

On May 1, the *New Yorker* revealed the existence of the Taguba Report, which was the first time the details were made public. On May 14, Rumsfeld testified before the Senate, indicating that more photographs and videos would appear. He added, "I failed to identify the catastrophic damage that the allegations of abuse could do to our operations in the theater, to the safety of our troops in the field, to the cause to which we are committed. . . . If I felt I could not be effective [as Defense Secretary], I'd resign in a minute."

US Rep. David Obey (D-WI), ranking Democrat on the House Appropriations Committee, formally asked President Bush to call for the resignations of Rumsfeld and Deputy Defense Secretary Paul Wolfowitz because of their mishandling of the war in Iraq. Bush said he would not ask him to resign, though his Administration reported that he had admonished Rumsfeld for not telling him about the photographs. The Administration has since taken the position that the abuse was the work of a few bad eggs on the night shift at Abu Ghraib.

In spring 2004, Maj. Gen. Geoffrey Miller, who had been in charge of the prisons at Guantanamo, was transferred to Baghdad and put in charge of the prisons there. "We have changed this—trust us," Miller told reporters in early May. "There were errors made. We have corrected those. We will make sure that they do not happen again."[73]

By the end of May, six soldiers of the 372nd MP were held in Iraq and charged with conspiracy, dereliction of duty, assault, maltreatment, and indecent acts. Another soldier was moved to Fort Bragg, North Carolina, where she was also charged with these offenses. Six other soldiers received reprimands that ended their military careers. Another soldier was reprimanded less severely. (Johanna McGeary, "The Scandal's Growing Stain," *Time*, May 17, 2004, p. 26.)

Two of the soldiers implicated in the prison abuse scandal were prison guards in the United States before going to Iraq. Lane McCotter, handpicked by John Ashcroft to direct the reopening of Abu Ghraib and the training of its guards, had previously resigned as head director of the Utah Department of Corrections when a schizophrenic inmate died after being shackled naked to a chair for sixteen hours. After his resignation, McCotter became a top executive for a private prison business, Management & Training Corporation, which the Justice Department criticized for maintaining unsafe conditions at its facilities. McCotter's comment about Abu Ghraib after the scandal broke was that the conditions there were similar to those in US prisons.[74]

Anthony Romero, Executive Director of the American Civil Liberties Union (ACLU), said, "The Bush administration's response to the daily shots of vicious inhumanity emerging from Abu Ghraib is to lambast them as an aberration." Gary Younge, in an editorial to the UK *Guardian*, said, "Americans are as disgusted by the evidence as everybody else. But they are pretty much alone in their shock that such things could happen under their flag. To the rest of the world, everything from detentions at Guantanamo Bay to the disregard for the UN points to a leadership at the White House which regards international law and human rights as at best an encumbrance and at worst an irrelevance."[75]

On June 4, 2004, UN Acting High Commissioner for Human Rights Bertrand Ramcharan said in his report to the Commission that "willful killing, torture or inhuman treatment" of detainees is a grave breach of international law.[76]

Reserve military police officer S.Sgt. Joseph Darby faced threats of attack when he returned home to Corriganville, Maryland, and testified in a hearing of one of the soldiers accused of abusing prisoners.[77]

On June 29, 2004, through the scope of his sniper rifle, Army National Guard S.Sgt. Kevin Maries saw an Iraqi guard hitting a blindfolded prisoner so hard "he made Babe Ruth look sick." He radioed Oregon Guard officers at nearby Patrol Base Volunteer. This triggered an investigation by Lt. Col. Dan Hendrickson, but the men were later ordered to return the prisoners to their captors and were ordered not to discuss the incident (Mike Francis, "Abuse by Iraqi 'Astonished' Guardsman," *Oregonian*, Oct. 9, 2004, front page).

On August 24, 2004, former Defense Secretary James Schlesinger released the "Final Report of the Independent Panel to Review DOD Detention Operations." The commission appointed by Rumsfeld to investigate the causes of detainee abuses and recommend policy changes confirms the facts and analysis by Seymour Hersh and the study by Asst. History Prof. Michael S. Bryant, University of Toledo, in "Atrocity by Frenzy or by Policy?" *National Lawyers Guild Practitioner* 61 (2004): 65–73.

University of Minnesota Professor Steven Miles reported in the *Lancet* medical journal that doctors or medics falsified death certificates to cover up homicides, hid evidence of beatings, and revived a prisoner so he could be further tortured (Emma Ross, Associated Press, *San Francisco Chronicle*, August 20, 2004, p. A8).

### Report 2.14: Abu Ghraib Prisoners Sued US Corporations for Torture, Alleging US Collaboration

In April 2004, US Army Maj. Gen. Antonio M. Taguba reported evidence of serious abuse of prisoners by US military personnel and private contractors at Abu Ghraib prison. Taguba found that a CACI International, Inc. employee, Steven A. Stefanowicz, "clearly knew his instructions equated to physical abuse" and recommended that he be fired for his actions. Stefanowicz denied any wrongdoing.[78]

Following Major General Taguba's report, approximately 1,050 persons were identified as actual or potential plaintiffs in a class action suit brought on behalf of Iraqi prisoners who allege torture at Abu Ghraib prison and elsewhere. The former and remaining Iraqi prisoners reported hoodings, beatings, sleep deprivation, electrocution, and sexual humiliation. They reported being urinated on, sodomized, raped, starved, exposed to extreme temperatures and weather conditions, and threatened with the death and murder of family members. They were denied medical treatment and prevented from abiding by religious practices. They said that some people were tortured to death.

On June 9, 2004, the Center for Constitutional Rights (CCR) and the law firm of Montgomery, McCracken, Walker, and Rhoads filed *Saleh v. Titan Corp.*, a class action suit (US Dist. Ct. for the S. Dist. of CA) alleging that two US corporations conspired with US Government officials to humiliate, abuse, and torture persons detained by US authorities in Iraq. The complaint alleged that, despite formal investigations and complaints by the International Committee of the Red Cross and the US Military Police, US Government officials allowed these activities to continue.

The suit named as defendants the Titan Corporation, CACI International, the two corporations' subsidiaries, and three individuals who work for the companies. The lawsuit charged the companies with violating the Racketeer Influenced and Corrupt Organizations Act (RICO), alleging that the companies engaged in horrible, illegal acts to demonstrate their ability to obtain large amounts of intelligence information from detainees captured by Northern Alliance Forces in Iraq in order to create a greater need for their services and thereby obtain more contracts from the US Government. CACI and Titan are publicly traded corporations that provide translation and interrogation services to the US Government as well as to state and local government agencies. The three individual defendants were charged with directing and participating in heinous, illegal conduct at Abu Ghraib and other US-controlled prisons and detention centers in Iraq, knowing that their actions were illegal and violated internationally recognized human rights law.

The suit also charged conspiracy to violate the Fourth, Fifth, Eighth, and Fourteenth Amendments of the US Constitution; violation of the Religious Land Use and Institutionalized Persons Act, 42 U.S.C. 2000 cc et seq.; RICO, 18 U.S.C. 1961 et. seq.; the Alien Tort Claims Act (ATCA) for summary execution; torture; cruel, inhuman, and degrading treatment; enforced disappearance; arbitrary detention; war crimes; crimes against humanity; numerous violations of the Third and Fourth Geneva Conventions; assault and battery; sexual assault and battery; wrongful death; false imprisonment; intentional infliction of emotional distress; negligent hiring and supervision; negligent infliction of emotional distress; conversion of contract payments to individual defendants; unjust enrichment (individuals receiving overpayment); and violations of laws governing contracting with the US Government.

The complaint sought compensatory and punitive damages including relinquishment of all profits the companies derived from these violations.

The complaint asked for an injunction against any continuing torture or abuse and an injunction against any future Government contract awards.

Susan Burke, the plaintiffs' attorney, stated, "It is patently clear that these corporations saw an opportunity to build their businesses by proving that they could extract information from detainees in Iraq, by any means necessary. In doing so they not only violated a raft of domestic and international statutes but diminished America's stature and reputation around the world."[79]

Baghdad, Iraq, 2003: Routinely terrorized by snarling attack dogs and humiliated by being stripped of clothes, Iraqi suspects were grilled by US personnel in Abu Ghraib and other prisons for knowledge of hidden weapons and of plans for resistance to the occupying powers. (New Yorker)

In July 2004, Phil Angelides, the Treasurer of California, recommended that the state pension fund divest itself from any CACI stock if the company remained in the interrogation business. On August 4, 2004, the Army awarded CACI another exclusive contract worth $23 million to continue providing private interrogators to gather intelligence in Iraq. The Army said that Coalition forces were "satisfied" with CACI's performance, and said that there had been no evidence to date that CACI itself was responsible for wrongdoing in connection with the scandal. CACI was awarded the contract without competitive bidding and the Army defended its use of privately hired interrogators, saying they are needed to relieve a huge backlog of work.

CACI repeatedly proclaimed its innocence. From April to August 2004, CACI's stock price dropped more than 10 percent. As of August 7, 2004, CACI had not terminated anyone in connection with the scandal.[80]

**Report 2.15: State Prison Guards in United States Tortured Prisoners, Then Were Sent to Iraq**

In recent years, both guards and other prisoners have tortured state prison inmates with greater frequency in the United States. In 2003, inmates sued Florida prison officials for allegedly spraying them with mace and pepper spray while they were locked in their cells. In Parchman prison in Mississippi, prison officials kept nearly one thousand inmates in insect-infested cells for twenty-three to twenty-four hours a day with insufficient water in the middle of the summer although many of them had severe mental illness. In New York state prisons, male guards allegedly sexually abused female prisoners (Amnesty International, *Amnesty International Report 2004*, [Oxford: Alden Press, 2004], p. 137).

It is well known among prison activists that racism is rampant in US prisons.

- One in eight (12.8%) black males aged 25–29 in the United States was in prison or jail at midyear 2002. One in 27 (3.7%) Hispanic males was also in prison or jail at the same time. This is in comparison to the 1 in 63 white males (1.6%) who was incarcerated at the same time.
- In 2002, 45% of prison inmates were black, and 18% were Hispanic.
- Black males have a 32% chance of serving time in prison at some point in their lives; Hispanic males have a 17% chance, and white males have a 6% chance.[81]

On February 1, 2004, sixty-year-old California state prison inmate Ronald Herrera pulled a dialysis shunt out of his arm. Nearby prison guards were busy watching the Super Bowl and ignored Herrera's cries for help. He bled to death in his cell. California state legislators subsequently held hearings on the nation's largest prison system that is, according to the *Contra Costa Times*, "plagued by out-of-control spending, inhumane disciplinary practices and outright brutality on the part of guards." In the fall of 2003, a 118-pound prison inmate at Corcoran, California, claimed he was repeatedly raped after guards purposely housed him with a 220-pound inmate. Both prisoners and parents have accused the California Youth Authority of overusing mace, drugs, physical restraints, and wire mesh cages while ignoring mental and physical health care.[82]

In July 2004, US District Judge Thelton Henderson for the Northern District of California wrote a letter to California Governor Arnold Schwarzenegger stating that he would consider placing the entire California Department of Corrections under federal judicial receivership if the state government does not take concrete, meaningful steps to correct the litany of human rights violations that plague the state's prisons.

The letter follows on Judge Henderson's findings in the 1994 case of *Madrid v. Woodford* (No. C90–3094–T.E.H.), a class action lawsuit that successfully exposed the torturous conditions of California's Pelican Bay supermax facility. After ruling in favor of the plaintiffs in 1994, Judge Henderson appointed a Special Master to reform Pelican Bay's Internal Affairs Division. According to Sara Norman, a staff attorney for the Prison Law Office in San Quentin, California, the corruption and abuse at Pelican Bay is indicative of far wider systemic problems that plague the California penal system as a whole. According to Norman, Judge Henderson wrote his letter to Schwarzenegger in recognition of this widespread crisis, amid mounting evidence that the state government has been either unwilling or unable to confront the issue of torture by prison guards in California prisons. (Sara Norman, in discussion with the editor of this book, Ann Fagan Ginger, July 26, 2004.)

In the spring of 2004, Equal Justice USA, a prisoners' advocacy group, reported that some of the US soldiers accused of torturing Iraqi prisoners at Abu Ghraib prison in Baghdad were former prison guards in the United States. A few examples: Specialist Charles Graner was a guard at Greene County State Correctional Institution in Pennsylvania, where former inmates accused him of physically assaulting them. Sgt. Ivan Frederick was a guard at Buckingham Correctional Center in Virginia for six years before going to Iraq.[83]

## Report 2.16: US Government Refuses to Close School that Teaches Torture

In 1997, Rep. Joseph P. Kennedy II (D-MA) led a bipartisan Congressional push to close the School of the Americas that was narrowly defeated. The Pentagon changed the name to the Western Hemisphere Institute for Security Cooperation (WHISC) in 2001.

In 1946, the United States opened the US Army Caribbean Training Center in Panama to help train and "professionalize" militaries across Latin America and the Caribbean. In 1963, the UACTC was renamed School of the Americas, (SOA), and it shifted to a cold war–driven focus on counterinsurgency. The SOA's 60,000 graduates include dictators and mass murderers Manuel Noriega and Omar Torrijos of Panama, Leopoldo Galtieri and Roberto Viola of Argentina, Juan Velasco Alvarado of Peru, Guillermo Rodriguez of Ecuador, and Hugo Banzer Suarez of Bolivia. Other graduates have been responsible for the assassination of Archbishop Oscar Romero and the El Mozote massacre in El Salvador, Contra massacres in Nicaragua, and the annihilation of entire indigenous villages in Guatemala and Peru during the 1970s and 1980s. In 1984, the SOA was moved from Panama to Fort Benning, Georgia.

Seven Spanish-language training manuals used at SOA up to 1991 taught military officers violent interrogation techniques, and ways to subvert union organization through the use of propaganda, blackmail, and methods of execution. According to the School of the Americas Watch, a pacifist organization that has sought the school's complete closure, the training reforms supposedly undertaken after 2001 have been "purely cosmetic." Former SOA human rights instructor Charles Call reported that human rights training is not taken seriously at the school, and it accounts for an insignificant amount of students' overall training."[84]

## Report 2.17:  Federal Jury Awards Damages for Murder in Chile

Armando Fernandez Larios was a member of the "Caravan of Death," a military squad acting under orders of Chilean dictator Augusto Pinochet. On October 17, 1973, Larios tortured and then murdered Chilean economist Winston Cabello in Copiapo, Chile.

In 1990, Pinochet was removed from power, but the Chilean amnesty law prevented Chile from prosecuting Larios in Chile. US criminal laws do not permit prosecution for summary killings committed outside the United States. However, there is another path for action in such situations. Two federal statutes, the Alien Tort Claims Act (ATCA), 28 U.S.C.A. §1350, and the Torture Victim Protection Act (TVPA), 28 U.S. Code §§102-256, permit human rights victims or surviving relatives to bring civil claims against perpetrators of torture in other countries if the torturers are later found in the United States. As a consequence, Cabello's family sued in US federal court in Miami under the ATCA.

On October 15, 2003, after hearing the evidence, the jury found Larios liable for all torts alleged: crimes against humanity, extrajudicial killing, torture, and cruel, inhuman, or degrading treatment or punishment. They awarded the family $4 million in compensatory and punitive damages. This is the first jury verdict in the United States holding a defendant liable for crimes against humanity under the Nuremberg Principles. It is also the first time that any Chilean has been held liable in the United States for crimes committed in Chile under Pinochet.

The verdict coincided with the fifth anniversary of the arrest of Augusto Pinochet in London on October 17, 1998, for having ordered the deaths that took place during the Caravan of Death. Pinochet was not brought to trial after he pleaded ill health.[85]

On May 28, 2004, the Santiago Court of Appeals ruled that Pinochet was not immune from suits stemming from the repression and murder he sanctioned as dictator of Chile in the 1970s and 1980s. Chile's Amnesty Law, passed while Pinochet was still in power, protected members of the Chilean military from prosecution for crimes committed during the first five years of the dictatorship. Although a loophole was found in the law whereby military officials could be prosecuted for "perpetual kidnappings" in cases where the bodies of those disappeared or murdered were never found, Pinochet himself had been judged by courts in Chile and England to retain immunity from prosecution based on his advanced age and ill health. According to prosecutors and victims who brought the 2004 suit, the court's decision to lift Pinochet's "ill health" immunity stemmed from an interview he gave in November 2003 to a Miami television station. In the interview Pinochet appeared lucid, belying his earlier claims of sickness. "Pinochet had been granting interviews, going to restaurants, going out shopping, and he continues to administer his assets," prosecution lawyer Hugo Gutierrez said. "He's not crazy or sick." Because of the appellate court's ruling, Chile's Supreme Court will have to revisit the issue of Pinochet's fitness for trial. [86]

*Note:* On June 29, 2004, in the case of *Sosa v. Alvarez-Machain*, the US Supreme Court affirmed the use of the Alien Tort Claims Act not only as a statute granting jurisdiction in federal court but also as a statute that provides a cause of action at common law. The vote was unanimous, with Justice Souter writing the Court's opinion in *Sosa v. Alvarez-Machain* (124 S.Ct. 2739 [2004]).

However, the Court rejected the claim of Sosa that his brief detention was sufficiently serious to entitle him to sue a non-US citizen for his actions in Mexico. The Court added dicta indicating that the plaintiff could not claim relief under the Universal Declaration of Human Rights because it is not a treaty, or under the International Covenant on Civil and Political Rights because it is a non-self-executing treaty.

## 3. RIGHT PEACEABLY TO ASSEMBLE AND PETITION THE GOVERNMENT

After 9/11, the President, Vice President, Attorney General, and the FBI and CIA Directors issued statements on the need to use the new PATRIOT Act to find and stop all "antigovernment" comments in every venue. Soon the President, Vice President, Secretaries of Defense and State, and other Government officials began to issue statements about the need to go to war, first in Afghanistan, and then in Iraq.

Many men and women of all generations disagreed. They followed a traditional path for action, from California (Report 3.1), to New York (Reports 3.2 and 3.9), and from South Carolina (Report 3.3), and Missouri (Report 3.3), to Pennsylvania (Report 3.3), from Lockheed Martin (Report 3.4), and Boston (Reports 3.5 and 3.9), to Miami (Report 3.6). Many protesters were US citizens; some were veterans of US military service; some were longtime resident aliens; many were students. One path of protest was massive peaceful demonstrations in major cities. Another was demonstrations at airports and along highways President Bush would traverse, often including the use of signs with slogans painted on them.

While the demonstrators were applying for the necessary city permits for their events, FBI, Secret Service, and Immigration agents were planning to stop the demonstrations. Some federal agencies met with local police to teach them "new" methods of "crowd control," including the use of new kinds of weapons against peaceful people without weapons, including wooden dowels and sting balls, which are rubber pellets to be shot at the ground in a cartridge or grenade, so that they explode out in a circle and must not be fired at close range or directly at people or they could cause death or serious injury.[87] They also used concussion grenades, tear gas, and other "less-lethal" weapons, including plastic nets to herd groups of protesters into tight areas for quick mass arrests.

Federal agents also encouraged establishment of "Free Speech Zones" where protesters would be hemmed in to protest a speaker who was blocks away, so that neither the speaker nor the protesters could see or hear each other. The Feds also encouraged, and sometimes financed, the building of barriers to prevent protesters from being seen anywhere near the President or other high Government officials. They detained and arrested some protesters directly while having local police disperse thousands and arrest hundreds of others.

In many instances, the people arrested could prove their actions were totally within their rights under the First Amendment: "peaceably to assemble, and to petition the Government for a redress of grievances."

On February 15, 2003, more than 100,000 people participated in a rally in New York City against President Bush's plan to invade Iraq. The city had denied them a permit at the last minute, and the police had erected barriers to make it impossible for many people to join the march. The mass of people walked peacefully, but police arrested between 350 and 400 people, charged most of them with disorderly conduct, and then released them.[88]

On March 20, 2003, ten thousand people in Chicago tried to march against the invasion of Iraq. The police herded, swept, and then penned in demonstrators and bystanders to prevent them from marching or leaving. They were held from four to thirty-six hours, and 800 people were injured. All charges were eventually dropped. The National Lawyers Guild filed suit for money damages and injunctive relief (*Keven Vodak, et al. v. City of Chicago*, Supt. Hillard, Cdr. Riley, Defendants Doe 1–400 [ND Ill], 03–C–2463). In June 2004, the city filed a counterclaim seeking costs and reimbursement.

Also on March 20, 2003, hundreds of seniors, students, parents, and children gathered in Albuquerque, New Mexico, to protest Bush's invasion of Iraq. The police used horses, struck people with batons, launched tear gas

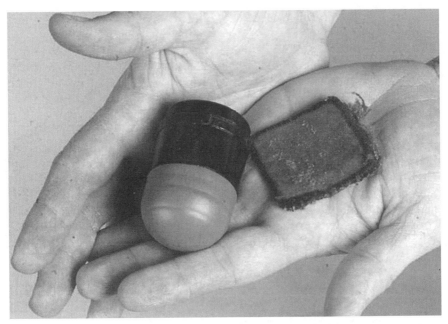

Today heavily militarized police go to demonstrations with large rubber-tipped bullets, cloth bags packed with metal pellets, wooden projectiles, tasers, pepper sprays, and other injury-inflicting devices to suppress citizen dissent. Called "less than lethal," they cause not only serious trama but have also killed. (Cincinnati Enquirer, Michael E. Keating photo)

Miami, November 22, 2003: As Nikki Hartman rose from her prayers at the FTAA protest and fled advancing police, she was hit repeatedly from the rear by their projectiles. Today she is actively researching the damage and deaths caused by these "less than lethal weapons." (Photo by Al Diaz/ Miami Herald)

canisters into the crowd, maced them, and hit them with bean bags and pepper rounds.

On November 20, 2003, Albuquerque's Independent Review Office issued its report that high-ranking police officers created a dangerous situation and failed to follow standard procedures. The National Lawyers Guild filed suit for declaratory and injunctive relief (*Lynn Buck, et al. v. City of Albuquerque; Mayor Martin Chavex, et al.*, CV 2004–01822).

The same thing happened in other cities across the country. In Washington, DC on April 12, 2003, hundreds of thousands demonstrated against the invasion of Iraq. Sean Taft-Morales was injured while marching on the permitted route when the police attacked him with their fists and clubs. The National Lawyers Guild and The Partnership for Civil Justice filed suit for damages and an injunction against using motorcycles and bicycles as weapons against demonstrators. (*Frucht et Morales v. District of Columbia* [U.S. District Ct. for DC], http://www.nlg.org/news/statements/pcj4132004 .http, August 2, 2004.)

Two years after 9/11, the ACLU and several other organizations filed a federal suit in Philadelphia seeking an injunction against the Secret Service for insisting on "Free Speech Zones," which, by definition, violate the basic commitments in the First Amendment[89] (Report 3.3).

On October 27, 2003, the US Secret Service filed a motion to dismiss, to which the plaintiffs answered on November 24, 2003. The Service replied on December 8, 2003. The case is pending.[90]

On May 25, 2004, FBI agents arrested seven domestic animal rights activists across the country for "conspiring" to shut down Huntington Life Sciences, a company that performs cosmetic testing on animals. The seven, charged with "interstate stalking" and with violating the federal Animal Enterprise Terrorism Act of 1992, face years of imprisonment and millions of dollars in fines if convicted on all counts. The Bush Administration hailed the arrests as a blow against terrorism.[91]

Three years after 9/11, before and during the Republican National Convention in Madison Square Garden, police from New York and elsewhere attacked scores of peaceful demonstrators, street theater participants, peaceful marches, and offices of legal defenders. They arrested 1,800 people in five days, took them to a pier with no bedding, water, clean floors, or telephones, where they were held one full day after a New York City judge ordered them released immediately (Report 3.9). On October 6, 2004, the District Attorney dropped all charges against 227 of the people arrested.[92] Subsequently, three lawsuits, including a class action, were filed by individuals arrested, the NYCLU, and other organizations, contesting the legality of the mass arrests and detentions and calling for a ban on such practices (Report 3.9).

**Relevant Law:**

US Constitution: Art. I, § 8, Cl. 11; Art. VI, Cl. 2
First, Fifth, Sixth, Seventh, Eighth, Fourteenth Amendments
UN Charter: Art. 2.3, 2.4, 55, 56
ICCPR: Art. 1, 1.1, 2–5, 7, 9, 10, 10.1, 12–14, 16–19, 21, 23, 26, 40
CAT: Art. 16, 19
Hague Conventions
Third and Fourth Geneva Conventions

## Report 3.1: Oakland Police Use "Less Lethal" Rubber Bullets, "Sting Balls"; DA Drops Charges

Antiwar protesters announced that a demonstration would take place on April 7, 2003, at the Port of Oakland, California. Days before the protest, the State of California's Antiterrorism Information Center (CATIC), which admits blurring the line between terrorism and political dissent, warned Oakland Police of violence at the Port of Oakland. Mike Van Winkle, spokesman for CATIC, said, "You can make an easy kind of link that if you have a group protesting a war where the cause that's being fought is international terrorism, you might have terrorism at that [protest]. You can almost argue that a protest against that is a terrorist act."[93]

On April 7, 2003, between 200 and 500 people held a peaceful demonstration against the Iraq war at the Port by the gates of two shipping lines. The Oakland police ordered them to disperse. When they refused, the police opened fire with wooden dowels, "sting balls," concussion grenades, tear gas, and other "less-lethal weapons."[94]

Scott Fleming, an Oakland attorney, was hit in the back and side. He showed reporters five purple, softball-sized welts. "As soon as I saw them raise their guns, I turned and ran. This guy kept shooting at my back. It obviously came from the same gun; it was rapid fire."[95]

At least a dozen demonstrators were injured; at least three were hit in the face, the others were hit in the back as they fled. The police also hit nine longshoremen waiting to go to work. They arrested twenty-five people on misdemeanor charges, including two legal observers who were taking pictures, and the International Longshore & Warehouse Union Local 10 business agent, who was pulled out of a car and arrested as he attempted to warn union workers that others had been shot.

Oakland Police Chief Richard Word accused protesters of throwing rocks, an allegation denied by eyewitnesses.[96]

Spectators and demonstrators say they never saw any "agitation" from the crowd and the only violence they saw was from the police.[97]

In May 2003, the twenty-five demonstrators appeared for arraignment, but no complaints had been filed against any of them. On June 24, 2003, the Oakland District Attorney filed misdemeanor charges against all of them.

On June 26, 2003, the National Lawyers Guild and the ACLU of Northern California filed a federal civil rights lawsuit [*International Longshore and Warehouse Union, et al. v. City of Oakland, et al.* (ND Cal, CO3–2962)] against Oakland on behalf of Local 10; the ILWU; the dockworkers' union; nine dockworkers who were shot while standing by awaiting a labor arbitrator's determination whether they should go to work; four Guild legal observers; three videographers; and thirty demonstrators, all of whom were shot and/or run over. The case is a class action seeking injunctive relief in the form of new police policies and training on crowd control and use of force, as well as damages for those individuals who were injured.[98]

"Local observers suggest that the Oakland Police Department's (OPD) disproportionate response may have been simultaneously: a local implementation of PATRIOT Act 'anti-terrorism' directives, an effort to 'send a message' to Oakland City Council critics of OPD, and part of a wider effort to contain anti-war dissent."[99]

On December 11, 2003, Oakland Police Chief Richard Word announced sweeping changes in how police will react to protestors in the future, stating that officers will no longer be allowed to fire wooden projectiles at protestors, or use motorcycles to break up crowds. In his public statement regarding these changes, Chief Word stated, "We have learned many lessons in light of the April 7 antiwar demonstration. . . . My goal is to see that something like April 7 never happens again in Oakland."[100]

On March 23, 2004, at UN Headquarters in Geneva, Switzerland, the Oakland arrests were included in the Report submitted by Hina Jilani, Special Representative of the UN Secretary-General Kofi Annan, to diplomats attending the UN Human Rights Commission sessions. The report was on the Situation of Human Rights Defenders: Addendum, Summary of Cases Transmitted to Government and Replies Received, in paragraph 476 of the three paragraphs on the United States (UNDoc E/CN.4/2004/94/Add.3).

On April 22, 2004, the Oakland District Attorney announced that he was dismissing all charges against those arrested at the protest in 2003.[101]

## Report 3.2: New York Police and the FBI Arrest Peaceful Protesters

On March 22, 2003, Liv Dillon and her husband attended a peace march in New York City. The organizers had obtained a permit for the march, despite dissent from the police. After the march itself ended in Washington Park, thousands of marchers stayed in the park.

Soon, there were lines of police on the street. To her right, Ms. Dillon saw a man talking with a friend suddenly get pulled from the sidewalk into the police line. "For no reason at all the cops grabbed the guy and put him in a paddy wagon. We saw this happen three more times. I was completely confused. It was random and pointless."

On April 7, 2003, Ms. Dillon attended another protest. A small, nonviolent civil disobedience was planned outside an office of the Carlyle Group, one of the world's most powerful military contractors. About two hundred people showed up. The folks planning on doing civil disobedience crossed the street and began a picket line. Another group, including Ms. Dillon and her husband, remained where they were as "supporters."

The police began to make arrests of the twenty or so people who were participating in the protest. "As the officers were finishing with arrests there, two lines of police suddenly came charging onto our side of the street." A young man was taking pictures of the supporters who were being penned in by the police. He was "thrown to the ground, smashed into the pavement by a dog pile of four officers, and then carted off to a paddy wagon. He had been doing nothing but taking pictures."

Ms. Dillon and her husband had been left outside the corral of supporters and observers. Officers ordered the two to disperse. Concerned for her fellow protesters, Ms. Dillon told the officer that he should let the penned-in people go; they had not been given an order to disperse, and he was in fact obstructing the sidewalk—she was not. The officer placed Ms. Dillon under arrest and when her husband said, "You can't arrest her; she hasn't done anything wrong," the officer arrested him, too, and put plastic cuffs on Ms. Dillon. When they were removed two hours later, they left lines and welts that stung for several days.

In the paddy wagon they saw the photographer who had originally been attacked. He had large clots of blood on his forehead and down his front. He was removed from the wagon a few minutes later to be taken to a hospital. Every person who had been on the sidewalk had been arrested. "When asked what we would be charged with, one cop replied with a grin, 'Oh, they'll make something up.'" Almost 140 people were arrested on April 7, 2003, although only twenty or so had had any intention of committing civil disobedience. Liv Dillon felt that the police were sending a message and it resonated clearly: "If you go to a protest, the police will try to arrest you. There is no safe space to express dissent."[102]

### Report 3.3: Secret Service Orders Arrests of Peaceful Protesters Against Bush

On October 24, 2002, Brett Bursey went to South Carolina Metropolitan Airport to protest President Bush's arrival. He carried a sign, "NO WAR FOR

OIL," and stood in an area designated for Bush supporters.[103] The federal agents singled him out and arrested him for trespassing. The local police later dropped the charges.[104]

However, the federal prosecutor pressed charges under a statute that allows the Secret Service to restrict access to areas while the President is traveling. Rep. Barney Frank (D-MA), along with eleven other members of Congress, sent a letter of protest asking then attorney general John Ashcroft to drop the charges against Bursey.[105]

On June 9, 2003, federal magistrate Bristow Marchant denied a jury trial for Bursey, because there is no jury trial for "petty offenses" such as the one Bursey was charged with.[106] On June 24, 2003, Bursey's trial was delayed for at least a month because of a technicality. Bursey's attorney, Bill Nettles, said, "it's extremely critical" that the technicality be cleared up before the trial.[107]

According to Wisconsin TV news, US Attorney John Barton had intended to use secret evidence against Bursey. In August 2003, Judge Marchant ordered Barton and the Secret Service to deliver all documents relating to Bush's visit so he could review them and determine if Bursey could use them in his defense. On September 18, Judge Marchant filed an order that gave the federal government five days to show a reason the documents detailing President Bush's arrival should not be disclosed.[108]

Bursey's trial ended on January 6, 2004, when he was found guilty of "willfully and knowingly remain[ing] in a restricted zone." Marchant said that, "In this age of suicide bombers, the establishment of a restricted area to protect the president was manifestly reasonable."

Marchant sentenced Bursey to only a $500 fine with no prison or probation, although the statute allows for up to $5,000 in fines, six months in prison, and five years' probation. He stated that he did not support the idea of a restricted area for demonstrators and told Bursey, "Your motives for being there that day played a large part in your sentence."[109]

On November 4, 2002, in St. Charles, Missouri, during a visit by President Bush at the local airport, Bill Ramsey of the Instead of War Coalition tried to show an antiwar banner and refused to go to the distant parking lot designated for protesters. The local police arrested him, saying "they'd been ordered [to] by the US Secret Service."

In January 2003, Andrew Wimmer displayed a sign "Instead of War, Invest in People" during a presidential visit to St. Louis. The police told him to move to a protest area two blocks away per the instructions from the Secret Service. When Wimmer refused, the police charged him with obstructing passage with his sign. The Secret Service claims that its policies and practices are "message-neutral," and that local police independently decide to remove protesters from the areas to be visited by Bush.

On Labor Day 2003, Bill Neel and his sister stood by the road that Bush was to pass through during his visit to Pittsburgh. When they displayed a handwritten sign stating, "THE BUSHES MUST LOVE THE POOR—THEY'VE MADE SO MANY OF US," Pittsburgh Detective John Ianachione, allegedly acting under the instructions of the Secret Service, informed them that they were to stand in the designated "free speech area," a baseball diamond far from the road and closed off by a chain-link fence. Because the field "looked more like a concentration camp than a free speech area," Neel told the detective, "I'm not going in there. I thought the whole country was a free speech area." The detective handcuffed and arrested him for disorderly conduct. When his sister protested, she was also handcuffed and arrested. Both were kept in a firehouse the local police and the Secret Service were using as headquarters for the occasion.

Pennsylvania District Judge Shirley Rowe Trkula later threw out the disorderly conduct charge against Neel, stating, "I believe this is America. Whatever happened to 'I don't agree with you, but I'll defend to the death your right to say it?'"[110]

On July 24, 2003, the Association of Community Organizations for Reform Now (ACORN) filed a verified complaint in the US District Court for the Eastern District of Pennsylvania in the pending case (C.A. No. 87–3975). ACORN asserted that the City of Philadelphia and its Police Department, in conjunction with the Secret Service, was violating an injunction from a 1988 case by preventing ACORN members from demonstrating near the scene of an appearance by President Bush and criticizing the Administration while permitting demonstrations supporting the current Administration. ACORN sought immediate judicial relief. Judge John P. Fullam entered an order allowing plaintiffs to demonstrate peacefully at a designated location no farther away from President Bush than other pro-Bush demonstrators.

On September 23, 2003, plaintiffs filed an amended complaint, adding USAction, United for Peace and Justice, and the National Organization for Women as plaintiffs. The plaintiffs sought: (1) a judgment that the Secret Service and police departments must provide equal treatment to demonstrators at public functions; (2) preliminary and permanent injunctive relief to the same effect; and (3) an order requiring all of the defendants to comply with the 1988 injunction. The amended complaint named the City of Philadelphia, the Philadelphia Police Department, and the US Secret Service of the Office of Homeland Security as defendants. The Judge found the Police Department to be a nonsueable entity and it was deleted as a defendant. The City of Philadelphia and the US Secret Service filed motions to dismiss the complaint for lack of subject matter jurisdiction, on the theory that the plaintiffs were not facing an imminent injury and therefore had no standing.

On May 6, 2004, Judge Fullam found that the "issue is whether the facts alleged by plaintiffs in their amended complaint suffice to permit this court to find that there is a clear likelihood that, at some identifiable future time and place, the defendants will violate plaintiffs constitutional rights if the requested injunction is denied."

Judge Fullam held that "plaintiffs' claims are too amorphous to be justiciable at this point in time. . . . The potential violations alleged by plaintiffs are simply not yet ripe. . . . I do not believe this court has subject matter jurisdiction. . . . I conclude that any injunctive relief which might be granted at this point would serve no useful purpose." He therefore dismissed the action. (*ACORN v. City of Philadelphia*, 2004 WL 1012693 [E.D.Pa.] May 6, 2004.) Plaintiffs decided not to appeal the decision (Sara Mullen, Director, Greater Philadelphia Chapter of the ACLU of Pennsylvania, e-mail message to the MCLI, August 9, 2004).

### Report 3.4: Peaceful Protesters Defeat Lockheed "Restitution" Plan

On April 22, 2003, demonstrators sat in the street in front of Lockheed Martin's Sunnyvale, California, facility to protest

- the company's production of illegal depleted uranium weapons and targeting mechanisms used in the US attack on Iraq,
- the company's central role in the international arms trade, and
- its repeated violations of the law, and corporate ethics.

The police arrested fifty-two protesters and charged them with disorderly conduct. Before trial, the Santa Clara County District Attorney agreed to Lockheed's demand that the defendants in the criminal case also be required to pay $41,000 to the company for costs it claimed it incurred in anticipation of the demonstration. There was no precedent for restitution in a case of this kind. Lockheed and the DA's office insisted this was "non-negotiable."

While most of the fifty-two defendants were willing to negotiate plea bargains on the criminal charges they faced, the group unanimously rejected several settlement offers that included restitution payments to Lockheed, the world's largest weapons manufacturer. The defendants, who were represented by volunteer lawyers from the National Lawyers Guild and court-appointed attorneys, prepared to go to trial on the criminal charges and, with support from the American Civil Liberties Union, to contest the application of restitution in the case.

"We engaged in civil disobedience to draw attention to Lockheed's crimes, and knew there would be legal consequences for that, but we weren't about to let the company succeed in setting a precedent that would chill everyone's right to dissent," said arrestee Jennifer Hansen, thirty-two, a nursing student from San Francisco.

In the face of the defendants' firm resistance and strong community sup-

Sunnyvale, CA, April 2, 2003: Early in the morning, antiwar protesters bind their arms together in "lock-down" pipes, forming a horizontal human chain to effectively block the entrance to US military contractor Lockheed Martin. Police keep watch in the background. (Photo, Eric Wagner)

port, Lockheed and the District Attorney finally agreed to drop the restitution claim. In response, most of the demonstrators agreed to plead "no contest" to disorderly conduct charges. On October 3, 2003, Judge Kenneth Barnum sentenced thirty-six of the defendants to a fine of $612.50 or equivalent amounts of public service or jail time, plus two years' court probation. Most of the defendants opted for public service; three chose to do jail time and one to pay the fine. "From the beginning, it has been our position that the restitution demand in these cases was unreasonable and without legal foundation," said Philip C. Andonian, attorney for the defense.

Defendant Larry Purcell, director of the Catholic Worker House in Redwood City, was among those who agreed to plead no contest, but when Judge Barnum asked if he accepted the settlement terms, which included "obey all laws" during the probation period, Purcell explained, "Your honor, you should know that I can't predict what the government is going to do in the next two years, so I can't promise not to engage in non-violent resistance again." Judge Barnum called Purcell "a hero" for his twenty-seven years' work on behalf of the hungry and the homeless, then proceeded to sentence him to forty-five days in jail.[111]

### Report 3.5: FBI Arrested Peaceful Palestinian Protester for Deportation

On November 2, 2002, Amer Jubran, a Palestinian legal resident of the United States for ten years, helped lead a peaceful march for Palestinian rights in Boston. Two days later, agents of the Immigration and Naturalization Service (INS) and the FBI arrested him. They threatened him with indefinite detention if he refused to waive his right to a lawyer, and he refused to talk about his political activity during an FBI interrogation. They released him after seventeen days.

The FBI visited Mr. Jubran's former wife and sister-in-law, claimed Jubran had links to illegal 9/11 activities, and tried to intimidate them into not testifying for Jubran in advance of the first round of his deportation hearing in administrative Immigration Court. In October 2003, after a year of repeatedly delaying the hearing, the Government released a fifty-two-page document detailing a secret FBI investigation into Jubran's political activities. On November 5, 2003, the Executive Committee of the San Francisco Labor Council demanded that the deportation proceedings against Amer Jubran be dropped immediately, and reaffirmed that the USA PATRIOT Act must be repealed.

On November 6, 2003, a broad coalition including Arab Americans, Jewish Americans, and human and labor rights activists held a rally and press conference in front of the Bureau of Immigration and Customs Enforcement (BICE or ICE, formerly INS) "to expose the illegal arrest and detention of Amer Jubran and other Arab human rights activists."[112]

On November 7, 2003, Jubran appeared before a federal judge in Boston. After the judge refused to grant a continuance in the case, Jubran asked that the court grant him "voluntary departure" from the United States before he was formally deported. In January 2004, Jubran left the country after living as a resident for more than ten years.[113]

### Report 3.6: Miami Police Used Federal Money Against Peaceful Union Demonstration

Before November 21, 2003, the United Steelworkers of America (AFL-CIO), the Citizens Trade Campaign, Public Citizen's Global Trade Watch, and United States Against Sweatshops secured permits for peaceful rallies and a parade in Miami, Florida, to protest the Free Trade Area of the Americas (FTAA) Ministerial.

On November 21, a manned armored personnel carrier sat within a few yards from the entrance to the venue. The Steelworkers told Congress members that, "It is doubly condemnable that $9 million of federal funds designated for the reconstruction of Iraq was used towards this despicable purpose."

The wife of a retired steelworker from Utah said the police slammed her to the ground facedown and aimed a gun point-blank at the back of her head. Other Steelworkers were returning to their hotel when they were directed by armed police to abandon the sidewalk and proceed down a set of trolley tracks. One was working as a parade marshal and was wearing a bright orange marshal's vest emblazoned with the words "AFL-CIO Peace Keeper." Once on the tracks, they were pounced on by armed riot police, handcuffed, and arrested. They were forced to remain in handcuffs for hours, even when visiting the washroom. While peacefully attempting to enter the AFL-CIO rally at the Bayfront Amphitheater, the codirector of the Citizens' Trade Campaign was forced to the ground and had a gun put to the back of her head.

Armed riot police surrounded the headquarters of the Citizens' Trade and Global Trade Watch and kept it under constant surveillance. Police shot other demonstrators with rubber bullets and sprayed them with tear gas. The International Executive Board of the Steelworkers Union chronicled such abuses in a letter sent to the Senate Republican Leader, the Democratic Leader, the Speaker of the House, and the House Democratic and Republican Leaders dated November 24, 2004.

During the trial of two protesters who were arrested, Judge Richard Margolius of Miami said he personally saw police officers commit at least twenty felonies during the demonstrations in Miami in November 2003. The judge asked how many police officers had been charged for their actions on the street.

The prosecutor answered, "None."

"That is a pretty sad commentary. . . . Pretty disgraceful what I saw with my own eyes. And I have always supported the police during my entire career. This was a real eye-opener. A disgrace for the community." He said he would have been arrested if a police officer had not recognized him as a judge.[114] Police Chief John Timoney subsequently began working for the city of Boston as a security consultant for the planning of the Democratic National Convention in July 2004.[115]

The Steelworkers Union Executive Board told Congress members that immediate action should be undertaken to punish the police; Chief Timoney should be fired, all charges against peaceful demonstrators should be dropped, and "Since federal funds helped finance the violation of our member's constitutional right of freedom of assembly, a Congressional investigation into the Miami Police Department's systematic repression should immediately be launched."[116] The AFL-CIO, the ACLU, and other organizations announced plans in November 2003 to file suits in December against the city and the police chief for their actions during the protests.

### Report 3.7: Police Pepper-Sprayed Baby at Antiwar Protest

On August 22, 2002, thousands of environmental and antiwar activists gathered in Portland, Oregon, to protest a fundraising visit by President Bush. The protestors staged a tree sit-in to voice their opposition to Bush's environmental policies, followed by a rally at the Portland waterfront organized by the Pacific Green Party. In the late afternoon, approximately five hundred protestors confronted Bush supporters attending a fund-raising event for US Senator Gordon Smith (R-OR) at a Hilton hotel. Police ordered the protestors to move away from the barricaded area in front of the hotel, then declared a "state of emergency" and began forcibly clearing out protestors with their batons. Police then fired pepper spray, tear gas, rubber bullets, and beanbag rounds into the crowd.[117]

Donald Joughin attended the protest with his wife and three small children. According to Joughin, "We brought our children to a peaceful protest; we stayed in the back and were walking on the sidewalk." As the family marched down the street, police moved up from behind the crowd, formed a barrier, and started pepper-spraying demonstrators. Joughin approached an officer and yelled to him to let his family through, at which point "[The Officer] looked at me, and drew out his can from his hip and sprayed directly at me. . . . The spray hit my right eye, and our three-year-old, who I was holding in my right arm. In this same motion he turned the can on my wife, who was holding our ten-month-old baby and doused both of their heads entirely from a distance of less than three feet."

Joughin then tried to pass through the police line in order to get medical treatment for his children, but was consistently refused permission even though officers could see his children, red-faced and screaming from their direct exposure to the pepper spray. When Joughin was finally allowed to pass through the police in order to call 911, he recalled that "the officers were laughing and said something to the effect of 'that's why you shouldn't bring kids to protests.' . . . On the way to the ER my three-year-old said that those guys back there were trying to get us and said we should call the police."[118]

Later in the day a local reporter asked Portland police spokesperson Henry Groepper about the children who were pepper-sprayed. Groepper told the reporter that "parents should not bring kids to a demonstration."[119] The National Lawyers Guild filed *Lloyd Marbet, et al. v. City of Portland, et al.* On September 8, 2003, the federal district court in Oregon ruled that pepper-spraying peaceful protesters violates the Fourth Amendment (CV-02-01448-MA).

## Report 3.8: Military Punished Soldier for Wife's Antiwar Protests

After the start of the war against Iraq in March 2003, Jari Sheese of Indianapolis became involved in antiwar protests. She participated in peaceful demonstrations and appeared on a television program in Paris, France. During this time, a general from the US military kept track of Sheese's antiwar activities.[120]

Sheese's husband, a US reservist, was deployed to Iraq to assist in setting up the Iraqi Media Network (which he characterized as broadcasting "mind control and propaganda"). According to Sheese, her husband had been "in and out of the military for 29 years and just wanted to get another year in as a reservist for his pension."[121]

After Jari Sheese began to organize against the war in Iraq, the military transferred her husband, with "only two hours' notice," to a different base with limited access to both the Internet and telephones.[122] Since her husband's transfer, Sheese has had difficulty communicating with him. Her husband thought his transfer was related to her speaking out, but he continued to support her opposition to the war in the hope that it would end the US occupation of Iraq.[123]

Interviews with the Families of Military and 9/11 Victims are available at the *Institute for Public Accuracy* at http://www.accuracy.org.

## Report 3.9: More Arrests at 2004 Republican National Convention than Ever Before

Months before the August 2004 Republican National Convention in Madison Square Garden, a very broad coalition of organizations sought a permit for a massive march through the streets of Manhattan leading to a rally in Central Park. City officials declined one proposal after another, finally forbidding any rally anywhere near the Convention but permitting a march on the Sunday before the Convention.

Hundreds of thousands of protesters marched in the largest political convention demonstration ever. Thousands took to the streets, staging hundreds of rallies, direct actions, and civil disobedience against the Bush Administration.[124]

The New York Police Department (NYPD), aided by federal agents, the FBI, and undercover operatives, arrested more than eighteen hundred people during the week, a record for a political convention (National Lawyers Guild, New York City Office). One of the protesters, Medea Benjamin of Code Pink for Peace, was arrested while unfurling a banner that said "Be Pro-Life: Stop the Killing in Iraq" inside the convention hall. She was removed and charged with assault (National Lawyers Guild, New York City

Office, in a conversation with the MCLI). On October 6, 2004, all charges were dropped by District Attorney Robert Morgenthau.[125]

The New York Civil Liberties Union (NYCLU) recorded several illegal actions by the NYPD:

- Preemptive arrests: Massive arrests followed on the heels of a negotiated agreement on the terms for a lawful march.
- Indiscriminate arrests: Members of the press, legal observers, medics, and even passersby found themselves caught in the orange mesh netting the police used to make mass arrests.
- Dangerous tactics: Police charged into protesters with metal barricades and drove scooters into the crowd. Both arrestees and bystanders reported being kicked, punched, or hit with batons by police. Some reported the incidents to local precincts and had their bruises photographed by police.
- Dangerous conditions at the Pier 57 detention facility: "Having announced for months that is was prepared to handle over 1,000 arrests a day during the RNC, the City chose to detain arrestees in this dank, filthy bus depot where people had to sit or lie on the floor covered with soot and quite possibly toxic automotive fluids. The conditions left many with rashes and respiratory problems during their detention stay and after they were released. The NYCLU is in the process of testing a sample gathered by a medic who was part of a sweeping arrest, although he was doing nothing more than monitoring a protest event."
- Excessive delays in processing arrestees: Hundreds whose arrests the police knew were unlawful were routinely held for thirty-six hours or more on minor offenses before receiving desk appearance tickets or being brought before a judge.
- Pervasive police surveillance: There were reports of pervasive videotaping and use of surveillance cameras to record lawful protest activity. A number of activists with a history of lawful protest activity also reported being followed by individuals who appeared to be Government agents. These practices appeared to be designed and had the effect of intimidating people from exercising their right to dissent.

The NYCLU filed suit just hours before President Bush was to speak at the RNC. State Supreme Court Judge John Cataldo ordered the immediate release of nearly five hundred protesters who had been held thirty-six to fifty-six hours. He then fined the city $1,000 for every protester held past a 5 PM deadline that he had set for their release. "These people have already been the victims of a process," Judge Cataldo told the district attorney. "I can no longer accept your statement that you are trying to comply" (Associated Press, "Judge Orders 470 GOP Protesters Released," September 2, 2004).

Immediately following the RNC, the NYCLU announced that it planned to:

- Continue to collect reports from individuals about police practices, including misconduct.
- Publish a report, based on these complaints and on the reports from the NYCLU's team of over 150 trained legal monitors, on what went wrong in the Government's response to protests at the RNC.
- Develop a campaign of reform, including litigation, legislative activity, and public education, to address the problems that arose during the RNC.
- Urge the City Council and state Attorney General to conduct a full investigation of police practices at the RNC.[126]

On October 7, 2004 the NYCLU and the Civil Rights Clinic of New York University's School of Law filed two lawsuits in the US District Court for the Southern District of New York against New York City officials for carrying out unconstitutional mass arrests during the Convention. *Schiller v. City of New York* challenged police tactics against antiwar protesters walking from the World Trade Center to Madison Square Garden. When the group marched along the sidewalk route previously approved by the police, officers arrested over two hundred people. *Dinler v. City of New York* challenged arrests at a demonstration in Union Square Park, when some protesters headed to East 16th Street. Police blocked off the street to arrest people confined in that space, including innocent bystanders. Many arrestees were not released until the court issued an order.

The NYCLU asked the court to declare these police practices illegal and to issue injunctions for the return of fingerprints and other records made during the arrests since, as NYCLU's Associate Director Christopher Dunn explains, "[t]he entry of fingerprints in government databases is a fundamental invasion of privacy that can have lifelong consequences and violates state law."[127]

On November 22, 2004, over twenty-three individuals, represented by the National Lawyers Guild, filed a class action suit in the US District Court for the Southern District of New York against the City of New York. *McNamara v. New York* alleges that city officials retaliated against protesters who expressed their political opinion by conducting mass arrests and detaining them for unreasonably long periods in overcrowded, dirty cells. The plaintiffs represented two thousand individuals arrested during the Republican National Convention.[128]

## 4. RIGHT TO EQUAL PROTECTION REGARDLESS OF RACE OR NATIONAL ORIGIN

After 9/11, discrimination on the basis of race and national origin increased markedly across the United States. The media focused largely on instances of hate crimes and police misconduct against men, and some women, based on their being, or suspected of being, "Muslim," "Arab," or "Middle Eastern." Attacks on African Americans did not make the news as often.

There were 751 active hate groups in the United States at the end of 2003, according to the Southern Poverty Law Center's Intelligence Project, up from 471 such groups in 1997.[129]

Many instances of discrimination were reported:

- A flight crew kept a US Congressman from boarding a plane (Report 4.1).
- Groups and individuals committed many more hate crimes against suspected "Muslims" and "Arabs" (Report 4.4).
- Police falsely arrested and accused Middle Eastern men (Report 4.6).
- The INS/ICE ousted a Lebanese-US citizen supervisor (Report 4.7).

The Government established US Operation Tarmac, a nationwide sweep of immigrant employees at tarmacs and other secure sensitive areas of airports, to prosecute those working illegally in the United States. This led to attacks after 9/11 on another large group of US citizens and resident aliens: Mexican and other Latin Americans. Tarmac caused the arrest of seven hundred Latinos, but no terrorists (Report 4.3), and similar incidents are reported (Reports 4.2, 4.10).

Discrimination on the job led to a record of almost 30,000 complaints being filed with the Equal Employment Opportunity Commission (Report 4.9). When the Transportation Security Agency established under the Aviation and Transportation Security Act of 2001, screened out noncitizens, 25,500 competent, trained people lost their jobs (Report 4.8). In the face of continuing massive unemployment in Mexico, thousands of Mexicans tried to enter the United States through desert areas. Racist practices by vigilantes and the US Border Patrol led to deaths (Report 1.6) and to widespread discrimination (Report 4.10).

More people in the United States committed hate crimes after 9/11 than before, based on skin color, race, national origin, or religion. Government agencies conducted investigations, made arrests, and blacklisted and isolated people based on their actual (or perceived) race or national origin. (Reports 4.3, 4.8). Neither the Civil Rights Division of the Department of Justice nor the US Civil Rights Commission took effective measures to stop these practices.

African Americans are better integrated into US life than Middle Easterners or Asian Americans because they were brought to this continent earlier than most other nonwhite racial groups. Violations of the human rights of African Americans are accordingly integrated into many of the thirty sections of this report, rather than all being described in Section 4. A summary of such incidents is in Report 4.11.

**Relevant Law:**

U.S. Constitution: Art VI, Cl. 2; First, Fourth, Fifth, Fourteenth Amendments
UN Charter: Art. 55(a), 55(c), 56
ICCPR: Art. 1, 1.1, 2, 2.1, 3, 5, 7, 9, 10, 12, 14-18, 18.1, 19, 20, 26, 27, 40
CERD: Art. 1, 2, 4(c), 5, 5(d)(i-iii), 5(d)(vii), 5(e)(i), 7, 9
CAT: Preamble, Art. 1, 2, 4-7, 10-14, 16, 19
ICESCR: Preamble, Art. 1, 2.2, 6, 16, 17

## Report 4.1: Racial Profiling of California Congressman and Others

Polls taken in December 2001 showed that 70 percent of people in the United States believed that some form of racial profiling was necessary and acceptable to ensure public safety. According to Michael Alexander of the American Civil Liberties Union of Northern California, prior to September 11, only 20 percent favored racial profiling.

For the new Department of Homeland Security and the airlines that engage in racial profiling, the profile of a terrorist apparently is "a man in his twenties or thirties who comes from Saudi Arabia, Egypt or Pakistan. He probably lives in one of six states—Texas, New Jersey, California, New York, Michigan, or Florida. And he is likely engaged in some sort of suspicious activity, such as taking flying lessons, traveling, or getting a driver's license."[130]

Darrell Issa fit the profile. Issa, an Arab American, was traveling to Saudi Arabia after September 11, 2001, when the crew of his flight refused to allow him to board the plane. When he proved he was an elected member of Congress from California, they let him board.

Since 9/11, airplane passengers who appear "Arab looking," including some who are South Asians and Latinos, have been asked to leave airplanes because both fellow passengers and crewmembers have refused to fly with them.[131]

Michel Shehadeh was profiled in December 2001 on his way to Washington, DC. He was pulled out of line at the Orange County, California, airport, questioned, and searched. "It was done in front of everyone's staring eyes. They made it a very humiliating experience. They want to give a message to non-Arab Americans, that they're doing something about 'it.' This has nothing to do with security," said Shehadeh.

Men belonging to the Sikh religion have been denied the right to board aircraft because they refuse to fly without their turbans. The Sikh Coalition documented 173 cases of racial profiling or incidents against Sikhs from September 2001 to December 2001.[132] Innumerable complaints have been made since that time.

In March and April 2003, the FBI questioned nearly 11,000 US residents of Iraqi origin as part of its "anti-terrorism campaign."[133] In 2004, the FBI interviewed more than 13,000 Muslims and Arabs in order to, they said, thwart terrorist attacks during the presidential elections.[134]

## Report 4.2: Hate Attack Against Mexican American Teacher

Robert Soza, thirty-one, is a Mexican American teaching assistant and PhD candidate in Ethnic Studies at the University of California, Berkeley. Soza is dark-skinned and had a full beard prior to September 11, 2001. As he drove to work on the morning of September 11, 2001, a blue pickup pulled over to let him pass. As Soza drove past the pickup, he made eye contact with the driver, a Caucasian man in his late thirties. The man in the pickup proceeded to follow Soza, who pulled into a parking place hoping the other driver would keep moving. Instead the driver slammed on his brakes, making it impossible for Soza to move his car. "The pickup driver runs around the car, reaches in and grabs me by the throat. He says, 'Do you know what's going on today?'" Soza said.

Soza finally got the man to back off, but he would not leave until Soza handed over the keys to his car, which the man then threw on the floor of Soza's car before he jumped back in his pickup and drove away.

The incident changed Soza in small but significant ways. He made "a conscious decision to 'look American,'" and shaved off his beard. He does not like to go out to eat alone and he says he's more aware of his surroundings. He has used the attack to educate his students and others. "I'm just asking people to think, 'Even I could become a victim,'" he says. The backlash continues to trouble him—particularly that "dissent is being so closely watched."[135]

## Report 4.3: Operation Tarmac Arrested 700 Latinos, No Terrorists

Shortly after September 11, the US Government arrested nearly seven hundred Latinos in a sweep titled Operation Tarmac. This was part of an antiterror campaign involving seven federal agencies. By March 2003, Tarmac had not turned up a single suspect linked to terrorism.[136]

In April 2002, then attorney general Ashcroft called the arrests "a wake up call for every airport in America. These individuals are charged with gaining access to secure areas of our airports by lying on security applications, using false or fictitious Social Security numbers or committing various immigration frauds."

Workers arrested in Operation Tarmac were charged with federal felonies, not violations of immigration law. In the Southern California sweep, about one hundred people were arrested, and eighty-five were hit with charges related to their work applications. The Government later reduced most of the charges to misdemeanors. Ashcroft said, "If convicted, many of the defendants face maximum penalties that range from two to ten years in prison, plus fines of as much as $250,000 and/or deportation."[137]

The INS arrested Juana Jimenez on August 22, 2002. She is a legal resident of the United States and had worked for twenty-one years at Los Angeles International Airport as a food service worker. The charges against her were dropped and she eventually got her job back.[138]

On September 9, 2002, authorities began arresting immigrants who used fraudulent Social Security numbers or made false statements to get jobs at George Bush Intercontinental Airport in Houston, Texas. Following an investigation of 23,000 Houston airport workers, the federal government indicted 143 former or current workers, most of them Mexican. By September 10, authorities had arrested sixty-four of those indicted. An additional forty-nine people were arrested on immigration violations.[139]

On January 7, 2004, the White House released a fact sheet outlining President Bush's Fair and Secure Immigration Reform proposal. The Administration boasted that "Operation Tarmac was launched to investigate businesses and workers in the secure areas of domestic airports and ensure immigration law compliance. Since 9/11, DHS has audited 3,640 businesses, examined 259,037 employee records, arrested 1,030 unauthorized workers, and participated in the criminal indictment of 774 individuals."[140] The Administration's discussion of Operation Tarmac did not mention any terror suspects being swept into the dragnet.

In August 2004, the Immigration and Customs Enforcement (ICE, formerly the Immigration and Naturalization Service) stated that since the inception of Operation Tarmac "ICE Special Agents have conducted investigations at 196 airports nationwide and audited more than 5,800 businesses as part of this operation. As a result, we've identified over 4,800 unauthorized airport workers, arrested 1,058 unauthorized alien workers, and obtained 775 criminal indictments."

Since September 11, 2001, the ICE has also initiated Operation Glow Worm. Glow Worm is a joint operation led by the ICE and the Department of Energy to screen the workforce at US nuclear power plants. Through Glow Worm, four unauthorized workers have been arrested out of the 64,835 that have been audited.

The ICE also conducts Operation Rollback, an ongoing investigation focused on violations at Wal-Mart retail stores targeting illegal aliens working for cleaning contractors employed at the stores. More than 245 undocumented alien workers have been arrested.[141]

### Report 4.4: Many More Hate Crimes Against "Arabs" and "Muslims"

In the three months following the 9/11 terrorist attacks, hate crimes against Middle Easterners and Muslims jumped from a total of fourteen in all of 2000 to 188 from 9/11 to December 11, 2001. People committed murders, batteries, arsons, and assaults with deadly weapons, although nearly two-thirds were acts of graffiti, vandalism, or criminal threats.[142]

Just ninety minutes after the attacks on 9/11, the principal of the Charlotte Islamic School in Charlotte, North Carolina, received a phone call. "We're going to get you," the anonymous caller said. The school closed for a week.[143] On September 12, 2001, unknown perpetrators firebombed a mosque in Denton, Texas.[144] On December 8, 2001, in Valencia, California, two men beat a Sikh owner of a convenience store while they asked him if he knew Osama bin Laden.[145]

"Initially after 9/11, Pres. Bush stood up and said we cannot tolerate hate crimes against anyone," said Will Harrell, a lawyer for the American Civil Liberties Union in Austin, Texas. "But the government teaches by example. When the government is discriminatory in applying laws, so are people in the way they go about their daily lives."[146]

According to Heidi Khaled, a journalist for the *Irvine Progressive*, many, if not most people in the United States still have the same feeling about Islam and Arabs that they did right after 9/11. Ethnocentrism has become widespread, especially stemming from conservative media, for whom "Muslim" has become synonymous with "terrorist."

Many people have been led to believe that Islam is the cause of terrorism. Others think that Islam in itself is an extremist religion and no one can be a moderate Muslim. In fact, Islam is the second-largest religion in the world, after Christianity. It has millions of followers worldwide. All Muslims do not agree with each other on every issue. The vast majority of Muslims are not extremists.[147]

### Report 4.5: Greek-born US Citizen Professor Investigated

Tony Koyzis is a Greek-Born, naturalized US citizen. He is an education professor at the University of Wisconsin–Oshkosh, who travels extensively to Cyprus to work with its Ministry of Education. In November 2002, the US Government sent a letter to Professor Koyzis informing him that he had been under investigation subsequent to USA PATRIOT Act (8 U.S.C.A. §1701) authority. The letter stated that he had been cleared of any suspicion of harboring, abetting, or being a terrorist.

"It apparently became a non-issue because I was cleared. But it bothered me because it happened without me knowing it," said Koyzis.

The USA PATRIOT Act gives a large number of Government agencies the authority to install wiretaps and to more easily access medical, financial, and library records, often without proof that any crime has been committed. Koyzis is still wondering which of the federal agencies investigated him and what they were looking for. He is one of a handful of US professors who know they have been investigated.

A special agent with the FBI said, "There may be situations when a person is never told that they've been investigated under the law even if they were found innocent."[148]

## Report 4.6: Police Falsely Accuse and Jail Middle Eastern Men

In January 2002, police in Evansville, Indiana, rounded up Tarek Albasti and eight other men, shackled them together, paraded them in front of a newspaper photographer, and jailed them for a week. A national crime registry listed four of them as having been accused of terrorism, although the Federal Bureau of Investigation (FBI) conceded that they were never charged with any crime. This stigmatization prevented the men from flying, renting apartments, and getting jobs.

In April 2003, Thomas Fuentes, Special Agent in Charge of the Indianapolis field office, went to an Evansville mosque to ask for cooperation in the fight against terrorism. Tarek Albasti's wife spoke up and described what had happened to her husband and the other men. As a result, Fuentes apologized and asked a federal judge to order the men's names erased from all federal crime records.

In December 2002, in Michigan, the police jailed Mohamed Alajji, a trucker born in Yemen, for seven days. Then agents interviewed his accuser, who turned out to be making false claims against him because of a family feud.

In Texas, the US Immigration and Naturalization Service (INS) detained Esshassah Fouad, a student from Morocco, after his former wife accused him of plotting to commit terrorist acts. The INS then brought immigration charges against Fouad for violating his student visa, despite his pleas that he had missed school because he was in jail. As a result, Fouad's immigration status was jeopardized.

In New York, the FBI jailed Abdullah Higazy after September 11, 2001, on suspicion that he had helped guide the hijackers into the twin towers. An informant, Mr. Ferry, told the FBI that he had found a ground-to-air radio in a hotel room occupied by Higazy. The FBI agent who took the tip failed to press Ferry for a sworn statement, to subject him to a lie detector test, or even to interview a second guard who helped search the room. Higazy was finally released after nearly a month in custody when the charges proved to be groundless.

In some cases, such as the one in Evansville, Indiana, the FBI realized that the people they arrested should not be held and their criminal records should be expunged. In most cases, however, the lives of those accused and detained are forever harmed by the detentions and accusations. Businesses are wrecked and reputations destroyed due to fraudulent tips acted on by the FBI.[149]

### Report 4.7: INS Ousts Lebanese-US Citizen Supervisor

On April 25, 2003, Simon Abi Nader sued then attorney general Ashcroft and others, alleging that he was ousted from his supervisory position at the US Immigration Service because he is of Middle Eastern descent.

Nader is a US citizen born in Lebanon, who had worked for the INS since 1980. From 1992 to 2002, Nader was the INS director for operations at Port Everglades, Florida. In 2002, the INS demoted him from port director to community relations officer. In his lawsuit, Nader alleged that he was the target of an internal smear campaign launched by ICE employees, including the then acting Florida district ICE director, depicting him as an "Arab terrorist." One of Nader's supervisors subjected him to constant offensive, insensitive, and discriminatory remarks and racial slurs. The lawsuit also alleged that Jack Garafano, then assistant INS district director for inspections, made comments about Nader's "camels" and his "tents in the desert." On one occasion, he allegedly said to Nader on the phone, "Simon Ali, are you kneeling on your prayer rug?"

Nader alleged that in 2002 he was accused of terrorist ties after he filed a discrimination complaint that led to the launching of an internal ICE probe. He also claimed that he was denied the "top secret" clearance needed for him to accept an ICE post in Athens, Greece; denied the opportunity to meet the agency's top official commissioner, James Ziglar; and refused permission to attend a conference on terrorism in Quantico, Virginia. Nader remained a federal employee while his suit was pending.[150] On July 30, 2004, Justice Donald Middlebrooks for the US District Court for the Southern District of Florida awarded Nader $305,000 as compensation for his claims. (*Simon Abi Nader v. United States Attorney General, et al.*, 03-CV-60781, [S.D. FL] July 30, 2004.)

### Report 4.8: Transportation Security Agency Screens Out 25,500 Noncitizens

At the end of 2002, after working fourteen years at the San Francisco International Airport, Erlinda Valencia, fifty-six, was fired from her job for not being a US citizen. The Aviation and Transportation Security Act of

November 2001 (49 U.S.C.A. §44901) made all airport screeners federal employees. By law, federal employees must be US citizens. This requirement cost thousands of immigrants like Erlinda Valencia their jobs.

Ms. Valencia arrived in the United States from the Philippines in 1988. She worked at the airport as a screener to support herself and her six children. She was promoted to supervisory positions, won numerous awards for her work, and became one of the top security personnel at the airport. Ms. Valencia was very proud of the job she held but worried about what may happen with so many new people being hired. "I've done this job for fourteen years, but they are going to hire people with no experience at all." She believes that "whether you are a citizen has nothing to do with the job, it is the skill and experience that count."[151]

Since the implementation of the Aviation and Transportation Security Act, the composition of new security screeners at US airports has changed dramatically. The Transportation Security Administration (TSA) reports that the new workforce is 61 percent white and only 31 percent of the new hires are women. According to the TSA, of the original 30,000 screeners working before the new law went into effect, only around 4,500 were rehired.[152]

### Report 4.9: Thousands of Workers File Discrimination Complaints with the EEOC

In November 2001, Damian Mandola, the co-owner of Pesce, an upscale seafood restaurant in Houston, Texas, fired Karim El-Raheb, the general manager. "Mandola fired El-Raheb after openly speculating that his Egyptian name and physical appearance were to blame for Pesce's decline in earnings in the months following the terrorist attacks," although El-Raheb has been a US citizen since 1986. On July 10, 2003, the Equal Employment Opportunity Commission (EEOC) announced it was filing a lawsuit against Pesce, Ltd. for firing El-Raheb because of his Egyptian ancestry.[153]

Between September 11, 2001, and September 10, 2002, the EEOC filed 654 Title VII charges against employers nationwide, alleging either discrimination in firing or on-the-job harassment. This backlash of post-9/11 discrimination has been aimed at individuals who are, or who are perceived to be, Muslim, Arab, Afghani, Middle Eastern, South Asian, or Sikh.[154]

The EEOC reports that in fiscal year 2001, it received 29,910 charges of race-based discrimination. It has resolved 33,199 race discrimination charges in FY 2002 and recovered $81.1 million in monetary benefits for aggrieved individuals, which did not include monetary benefits obtained through litigation.[155]

### Report 4.10: US Government Racism Plagues the Border

In October 2002, the US Border Patrol submitted plans to build one of the largest fences in the world on the US-Mexico border.[156] The proposed wall would be built by the United States on O'odham ancestral land. Tohono O'odham and Yaqui leaders told a UN representative that the wall would bring further misery to indigenous peoples already suffering from the militarization of the border. "They are planning to seal the border," said Tohono O'odham Ophelia Rivas, organizer of the O'odham Voice Against the Wall Project.

The proposed Fencing Project would stretch 330 miles across the entire Arizona-Mexico border. If completed, the wall would include seventy-four miles of O'odham lands. The first wall of railroad steel rails and steel sheets would have 400 high-security floodlights, lit twenty-four hours a day. A secondary wall would be of high-grade fencing material with razor-edged coils on top. In between the walls, the US military would build a paved road occupied by armed Homeland Security forces. The Border Patrol admitted that in Arizona, it will be bigger than the Berlin Wall.

O'odham members from Mexico, O'odham Lt. Gov. Jose Garcia, and Jose Matus, Yaqui ceremonial leader and director of the Indigenous Alliance Without Borders, said the USA PATRIOT Act and Homeland Security have increased the militarization of the border and made it more difficult for indigenous people to cross the border to conduct ceremonies or to visit family. The wall is an interference with the right of self-determination of indigenous people and preservation of traditional ways.

Matus said, "After 9/11, we had to deal with Homeland Security, the PATRIOT Act, the fight against terrorism and the fight against undocumented immigrants." The indigenous people who live along the US-Mexico border also face border-protecting vigilantes, death in the desert, and abuses by the Border Patrol. Matus also pointed out that the border separates Kumeyaay, Cocopah, Gila River O'otham, Yavapai-Apache, Tohono O'odham, Pascua Yaqui, and Kickapoo peoples in California, Arizona, New Mexico, and Texas from their relatives in Mexico.

Matus said when he attempted to bring ceremonial leaders from Rio Yaqui, Sonora, into Arizona, they were often halted because they lacked birth certificates and other documents for visas. When Matus attempted to cross the border at Juarez, Mexico, into El Paso, Texas, with a group of Raramuri (Tarahumara), they were halted by US immigration officials. "The interviewer made the people sing and dance. You talk about humiliating, you talk about a lack of respect for our indigenous people," Matus said.

In July 2004, Lieutenant Governor Garcia met with O'odham in four communities in Sonora, Mexico. "Their objection to the fence is it would cut off traditional routes. And they have not been consulted about building the fence."

Garcia said his people are losing their land because of encroachment by squatters, ranchers, mining companies, and cattle companies. He also says that the O'odham are people without a national identity. When the O'odham went to Mexico with their grievances, they were told to go to the Tohono O'odham Nation in Arizona. Then, when they took their grievances to Arizona and the US Government, they were told they were citizens of Mexico and to complain to the government of Mexico.

Rivas said O'odham have the inherent right to travel freely and safely through their traditional routes in O'odham territory. These rights are protected by the American Indian Religious Freedom Act (42 U.S.C. 1996) and recognized by the United Nations Universal Declaration of Human Rights and the Declaration of Human Rights for Indigenous Peoples.[157]

From the beginning of the consideration of the border-fencing project, environmental and human rights organizations also had serious objections to the proposal. Specifically, the construction of the fence would force migrants into perilous stretches of desert, significantly raise the number of deaths, disturb migratory patterns of endangered species, and destroy pristine animal habitats, in addition to bisecting the Tohono O'Odham nation.

Fencing projects carried out since the 1990s have not reduced the number of illegal immigrants to the United States, but simply redirected their travel routes to other border areas.[158]

On July 9, 2004, the UN International Court of Justice (ICJ) ruled 14–1 that the separation wall being built by Israel in the West Bank is in breach of international law, calling on Israel to tear it down and to compensate Palestinians harmed by its construction. The Court held that in building the fence, Israel violated international humanitarian law by infringing on Palestinians' freedom of movement. The ICJ said that the wall "cannot be justified by military exigencies or by the requirements of national security or public order."[159]

In its 2004 *Justice on the Line* report, the Border Action Network (BAN) evaluated the popular sentiment among residents of four Arizona border towns relating to immigration and human rights issues. The BAN found that 65 percent of those surveyed in Nogales, Arizona, think that the US Border Patrol treats white residents differently than nonwhite residents. One fifty-year-old Hispanic woman stated, "I have been stopped more than twenty times from the time I was thirteen years old up to today. I am a naturalized citizen and they constantly stop me in the city and on the road. They never give me a reason."

The vast majority of people questioned stated that racial profiling by US agents is a daily fact of life; 77 percent of Douglas, Arizona, residents and 70 percent of Nogales residents said they think the Border Patrol stops people because they have brown skin. Almost one-half of the respondents reported being stopped, questioned, or harassed by the Border Patrol, and nearly half of all respondents knew of incidents in which agents entered private property without permission. In addition, many border residents alleged that agents habitually engage in verbal and physical abuse while on patrol and that both individual agents and the Border Patrol as a whole are rarely held accountable for wrongful conduct. One Nogales woman, remarking on the overwhelming number of Caucasian agents in the Border Patrol's ranks, stated, "They're not from the community. They don't have any interest in what the community thinks." Another woman stated, "When the Border Patrol get people they treat them like criminals. Or even worse than criminals—even criminals have to be proven guilty. They grabbed my son—a citizen!—and beat him while I was watching."[160]

## Report 4.11: US Practices Deny Equal Protection to African Americans

The terrorist attacks on 9/11 not only killed and injured thousands of people in New York and Washington, DC at the sites attacked, they also permitted the continuation of policies causing racial disparity in the military, in zoning and environmental policy, and in higher education.

### Racial Disparity in the Military

In the months before the US invasion of Iraq, Rep. Charles Rangel (D–NY) introduced a bill calling for the reinstatement of the military draft. Rangel stated, "I truly believe that those who make the decision and those who support the United States going into war would feel more readily the pain that's involved, the sacrifice that's involved, if they thought that the fighting force would include the affluent and those who historically have avoided this great responsibility."

- Blacks make up 12 percent of the US population, but 20 percent of military enlistees.
- From the onset of the war on March 19, 2003, through February 26, 2004, seventy-nine black soldiers died in Iraq. This is 14.3 percent of the 549 combat deaths. This surpasses the percentage in two of the nation's bloodiest wars. In the Korean War, 3,075 of the dead (8.4 percent), were black. In the Vietnam Conflict, 7,241 of the dead (12.4 percent), were black.[161]

The people of the United States first became aware of these statistics on April 30, 2004, when the *ABC* news program *Nightline* showed photos of every member of the Army, Navy, Marines, and Air Force who had died in Iraq from the beginning of the invasion until the end of April 2004. This led to many talk-show discussions on recruiting practices of the military, targeting schools in African American, Latino, and poor white neighborhoods where many eighteen-year-olds see no future outside of the military.

### Racial Disparity in Zoning and Environmental Policy

Land-use and zoning policies are "a root enabling cause of disproportionate burdens [and] environmental injustice," according to a July 2003 report by the National Academy of Public Administration. These policies are often based on racial considerations. African Americans, other people of color, immigrant groups, the poor, and industries that are more likely to provide employment to minorities are often excluded from white and affluent communities.[162]

- In Ohio, the top four polluters in Cleveland are all located in or adjacent to minority communities.[163]
- In Chester, Pennsylvania, thirty-six thousand residents live near one of the largest collections of waste facilities in the United States. Seventy-five percent of Chester residents are African American, as are 95 percent of residents in neighborhoods closest to the facilities.[164]
- In Jefferson County, Texas, 240,000 people live in an area that ranks in the top 10 percent for the worst air quality in the country. They face a cancer risk more than one hundred times the goal set by the Clean Air Act (42 U.S.C. §7401). The two major cities in Jefferson County are Beaumont and Port Arthur. Beaumont, with a population of slightly more than 113,000, is 45.8 percent African American and 7.9 percent Hispanic, while Port Arthur, with 57,755 residents, is 43.7 percent African American and 17.5 percent Hispanic. Clark Refining and Marketing Inc. in Port Arthur and Mobile Oil Corporation in Beaumont each ranked in the worst 10 percent in the country for criteria air pollutant emissions in 1999.[165] (And see Section 27.)

### Racial Disparity in Higher Education

After 9/11 there were large drops in the percentage of African Americans entering leading state universities, due to the banning of race-sensitive university admissions policies in 2000. This was particularly true in states with large minority populations such as California, Georgia, Florida, and Texas. According to an article in the *Journal of Blacks in Higher Education*, "Bans on race-based affirmative action have done serious damage to black enrollments at the nation's flagship public universities."[166]

- In 2002, black enrollment at the University of Florida at Gainesville was 21 percent lower than it was in 2000.

- Black student enrollment fell by 40 percent at the University of Georgia after race-sensitive admissions policies were banned in 2001.
- At the University of California at Berkeley, 48.6 percent of African American applicants were admitted in 1997, the year the California ban went into effect. By 2002, only 21.2 percent of African American applicants gained admission.

Concerned activists called on the US Department of Education and the Civil Rights Commission to propose actions at the federal level to reverse these violations of the equal protection clause of the Fourteenth Amendment. (And see Section 26.)

## 5. RIGHT TO EQUAL PROTECTION FOR WOMEN

Since 9/11, women and girls living in the United States, or under US jurisdiction, have had a harder life. They continue to earn, on average, $760 whenever a man earns $1,000, and this gap increased after George Bush became President (Report 5.1). Every woman knows that she pays the same for food, rent, transportation, education, and medical care as a man pays. And every mother and grandmother knows she can't afford to pay another mother or grandmother to take care of her offspring the wages they would simply have to pay a plumber or locksmith to fix something in their apartment.

In July 2002, several of the sixteen women members of the House of Representatives marched to the Senate and joined several of the fourteen women Senators to insist that the Senate Foreign Relations Committee vote to ratify the Convention on the Elimination of Discrimination Against Women, which President Carter had signed in 1980. The Committee did so vote but the Senate did not on July 30, 2002, consider consenting to ratification. On January 7, 2003, the House passed a resolution (H.R. 21) suggesting that the Senate ratify the CEDAW. The State legislatures and forty-five city councils in twelve states have passed resolutions supporting ratification. As of November 1, 2004, 179 countries had ratified, most recently Micronesia and the United Arab Emirates.

The Bush Administration has appointed women who oppose ratification. Opponents of CEDAW list several problems that they say require the Senate not to ratify, answered by the Working Group on Ratification of the UN Convention on the Elimination of All Forms of Discrimination Against Women, a group of over 190 national nongovernmental organizations, which has studied the objections to CEDAW. Opponents say that CEDAW would violate US sovereignty, lead to frivolous lawsuits and unwise laws, require legalization of prostitution, and require "gender-neutral" textbooks. They say it would destroy traditional families, interfere in the proper role of parents in child-rearing, and could lead to the sanctioning of same-sex marriages.[167]

Stories like this are underreported by the US media, according to a recent study by the White House Project, perhaps partly because of the small number of women who host radio or TV shows, or are interviewed (Report 5.2). Even the remarkable Million Women's March on Washington on April 25, 2004, was only news for an instant and made no visible difference in general coverage of women's issues (Report 5.3).

Women are also subject to mistreatment when US forces act overseas. Reports from Iraq include unbelievable mistreatment of women detained by the US military at the Abu Ghraib prison. (Report 5.4). The Bush Administration has awarded a contract to train Iraqi women in political participation and democracy to the Independent Women's Forum, which explicitly opposes US ratification of CEDAW. It also opposes Government guarantees of maternity leave and child-care facilities.[168] There is no record of action by the Women's Bureau or the Civil Rights Division of the US Department of Justice on these issues since 9/11. Many other attacks on equal rights of women, and of girls, are reported in Reports 2.7, 5, 5.1–5.4, 8, 21, 21.5, 21.6, 22, 22.4, 24.1, 24.3, 25.1, 26.6, 27.1, and 30.3.

**Relevant Law:**

U.S. Constitution: Art. VI, Cl. 2; Fifth, Fourteenth, Nineteenth Amendments
UN Charter: Preamble, Art. 55, 56
ICCPR: Art. 1, 2, 2.1, 3- 5, 7, 9, 10, 16, 17, 19, 23, 24, 26, 40
CERD: Art. 1, 2, 4-7, 9, 13.1, 18
CEDAW
CRC: Preamble, 1-5, 29, 34, 35, 44

**Report 5.1: Women Earning 76.6 Percent of What Men Earn**

As reported by the US Census Bureau in 2002, on average, a woman performing the same work as a man who was paid $10 an hour was paid only $7.66 an hour. The wage gap between men's and women's earnings increased from 76.3 percent to 76.6 percent after George W. Bush came to office in 2001.[169]

There is no record of the Bush Administration's use of the Census Bureau figures to urge the Women's Bureau and the rest of the Labor Department and the Commerce Department to enforce equal pay laws more strictly. Title VII of the 1964 Civil Rights Act, 42 U.S.C. §2000, et seq., requires equal pay regardless of sex or race.

## Report 5.2: US Media Discriminating Against Women

On December 4, 2001, *NBC Nightly News* broadcast an interview with firefighter Lt. Brenda Bergman describing the events of September 11, 2001, when she raced into the flaming destruction that other people were fleeing, risking her life to save others. Her story was similar to hundreds of heartwrenching tales told by New York firefighters but also unfamiliar because the story was now being told by a woman. "The fact that the faces of women haven't been in the news or in the media is not reflective of reality," Bergman told NBC.

According to a study released in December 2001 by the White House Project, a nonpartisan women's leadership group, women were just 11 percent of guests and 7 percent of repeat interviewees on ABC, NBC, CBS, CNN, and FOX political debate shows between January 2000 and June 2001. In the six weeks after the 9/11 attacks, guest appearances by women plummeted 39 percent.

*FOX News Sunday* and ABC's *This Week* both interviewed just one female guest in the six-week period after September 11. The networks claimed this resulted from the fact that the supply of noteworthy political figures did not meet with the demands of diversity. "You tend to want to go to a committee chair or a leader of one of the parties, and right now they're mostly male," stated Marty Ryan, executive producer of *FOX News Sunday*. Nancy Nathan, executive producer of NBC's *Meet the Press*, told the *Washington Post* that its largely female audience would be "insulted" if the network "[tried] to manipulate the news to bring on women."

The White House Project study also found that female media guests were systemically underrepresented in every aspect of US civil society—from elected, government, and foreign officials, to media representatives and private professionals. For example, during the period covered by the study, Jerry Falwell appeared six times on network news programs. NAACP President Kweisi Mfume appeared five times, while Feminist Majority President Ellie Smeal and Human Rights Campaign President Elizabeth Birch appeared once each. According to journalist Jennifer L. Pozner, "Locking women out of these editorial forums gives us a skewed perception of America's political leanings. . . . Vigorous journalistic debate is intrinsic to a healthy democracy, but our media are neglecting the voices of half the population. The invisibility of women homogenizes public debate, distorts public opinion and fails not only women but America."[170]

The Federal Communications Commission under Chair Michael Powell has not taken any action to address this disparity after publication of the White House Project report. The Bush Administration has not supported the House call in 2003 that the Senate ratify the Convention on the Elimination of Discrimination Against Women, which the Senate subcommittee approved in 2003 after demands by Congresswomen.

## Report 5.3: One Million Women March for Women's Lives

On April 25, 2004, more than one million women marched through Washington, DC to protest the Bush Administration's threats to reproductive health services and the right to choose. In the largest rally for women's rights ever held in Washington, speakers criticized the Government's policies on abortion and condemned the disproportionate effect of cuts in reproductive health services for minority women.

Gloria Feldt, president of Planned Parenthood Federation of America, told the crowd, "My friends—make no mistake. There is a war on choice. We didn't start it, but we are going to win it . . . [The Administration's] not just after abortion rights. This is a full-throttle war on your very health—on your access to real sex education, birth control, medical privacy, and life-saving research."

"The reproductive health of Black women is in a state of crisis. Black women are suffering and dying too often, too soon and needlessly," said Dr. Lorraine Cole, president and CEO of the Black Women's Health Imperative. "When we leave here today, let's turn pain into promise, let's turn promise into partnership and let's turn partnership into power."[171]

Seven major organizing groups led the March, including the National Organization for Women, the Planned Parenthood Federation of America, the Feminist Majority, NARAL Pro-Choice America, and the National Latina Institute for Reproductive Health. The March was also cosponsored by an additional fourteen hundred organizations, including the NAACP and the National Association of Social Workers.[172]

## Report 5.4: US Troops Mistreating Women in Iraq

On October 29, 2003, Iraqi prisoner Saad Naif was released from US military detention at the Abu Ghraib prison outside Baghdad. Upon his release he told the Associated Press that "The worst thing [about the detention] was [the] treatment of the women." Naif reported that one detainee told him that when he shouted to his sister in a nearby women's tent, the guards punished the woman by putting her in "The Gardens"—a razor wire enclosure where prisoners were made to lie facedown on the burning sand for two or three hours with their hands bound. Seeing his sister lying bound in the sun, the brother started to cross through the razor wire ringing his tent, "and they shot him in the shoulder," Naif said. "Innocent women were kept for months in the same clothes." He remembered in particular an elderly woman "whose hands were tied up and she was lying in the dust."

Amnesty International said it has received credible reports of such incidents.[173] The Associated Press queried US military command in the United States about deaths in the camps in Iraq but got no response.[174] On May 7, 2004, the International Committee of the Red Cross/Red Crescent (ICRC) held a press conference about a confidential report concerning interviews with US detainees over the course of 2003, which had been leaked to the *Wall Street Journal*. The report indicated that the torture and "cruel, degrading, and inhumane treatment" of prisoners by US military intelligence officials were not isolated incidents but were instead systemic.[175]

## 6. RIGHT TO FREE EXERCISE OF RELIGION

One of the most basic rights in the US Constitution is the First Amendment protection of freedom of religion. The language is specific: "Congress shall make no law respecting an establishment of religion, or prohibiting the free exercise thereof." It is doubtful that any of the Founding Fathers envisioned a time two hundred years later when people from one region of the world would be targeted by US Government agencies in denial of their basic human rights.

After 9/11, President Bush began announcing that the attackers were from Saudi Arabia. People in the US know that every Italian is not a Roman Catholic, and the two categories are understood to be different: one is the Italian nationality of people born in Italy; the other is the religion of people whose church center is in Italy. But many people in the US do not know the difference between the words "Arab," "Muslim," "Moslem," and "Black Muslim," "Shiite Muslim," and "Sunni Muslim." Few people could list all of the countries in the Middle East or list the most common, or official, religion in each country. The Council on American Islamic Relations reported in October 2004 that a new study showed one in four people in the United States holds a negative stereotype of Muslims, and almost one-third responded with a negative image when they heard the world "Muslim." More than a quarter polled felt that Muslims value life less than other people and that Muslims teach their children to hate unbelievers. Harassment, violence, and discrimination against American Muslims had increased by 70 percent between 2002 and the summer of 2004.[176]

After 9/11, the ignorance of most people in the United States about Middle Eastern nations and religions led to many attacks on people in the United States presumed to be "the enemy," or "Muslims" or "Arabs," when in fact the people were actually citizens of the United States of various religions (Reports 6.3, 6.4).

In 2001, the Department of Justice (DOJ) rounded up and imprisoned over one thousand "individuals of Arab and Muslim backgrounds without providing official charges, giving them access to attorneys or even letting their families know of their whereabouts." These actions undercut the sense of security of the Arab, South Asian, Muslim, and Sikh communities, according to "Backlash: When America Turned On Its Own—A Preliminary Report to the 2001 Audit of Violence Against Asian Pacific Americans." The report was issued by the National Asian Pacific American Legal Consortium, the Asian Pacific American Legal Center of Southern California, the Asian American Legal Defense and Education Fund, and the Asian Law Caucus. Several of these arrests and detentions are described in Reports 6.1, 6.2, and 6.4.

In March 2003, the Attorney General authorized FBI agents and state and local law enforcement officers to make routine immigration arrests. "A secret memo reversed the policy" barring such actions. Until recently, only the Immigration and Naturalization Service was authorized to enforce immigration law "for two reasons. First, immigration law is complex and requires special training. And second, it interferes with criminal law enforcement. Foreign nationals with any immigration problems who are victims or witnesses to crimes simply will not come forward if it means they will face deportation."[177]

The strategy used by the Bush Administration was to lock up suspects for whom the Government lacked sufficient evidence to accuse of more serious crimes. The FBI affects arrests for minor immigration infractions such as failure to file a change of address within ten days of moving. These policies of then attorney general John Ashcroft led the Justice Department to transform immigration law into criminal law, in violation of the 1923 US Supreme Court decision that deportation is not punishment (*Bilokumsky v. Tod*, 263 U.S. 149 [1923]). This decision meant in effect that: (1) deportees do not have the same rights as criminal defendants to trial by judge and jury, using the standard of "guilt beyond a reasonable doubt," and, (2) they cannot be arrested by local or federal police or incarcerated in local or federal prisons.

The Justice Department also began entering immigration data into the National Criminal Information Center (NCIC) database, the system that state and local police check whenever they confront a person in traffic stops or other encounters. That database was supposed to be limited to criminal records. "Now the Justice Department is including civil immigration information from two programs selectively targeted at Arabs and Muslims."

In late March 2003, the Justice Department eliminated the government requirement to ensure that information in the NCIC database be accurate and current, saying the requirement was an impediment to investigations. This will result in state and local police arresting foreign nationals on immigration charges, without any training in the technicalities of immigration law, as well as Government reliance on information that may or may not be accurate.[178]

Florida revoked the driver's license of Sultana Freeman, a US-born Muslim woman, when she refused to remove her hijab (a traditional Islamic veil covering the face and/or head) for a photo for her license. She sued in state court and lost.[179]

In response to these actions and reactions, the Minneapolis City Council passed a resolution on April 4, 2003, titled "Defending the Bill of Rights" by an 11–2 vote, which contains a clause requiring local law enforcement agencies to "refrain from using city resources, including personnel and administrative or law enforcement funds, to advance such unconstitutional activities." The resolution requires police and city employees to report activities considered unconstitutional to the city council and the city's Human Rights Commission when legally possible. It also prohibits police from engaging in racial or political profiling and recommends city libraries post a notice to users that the USA PATRIOT Act allows the federal government to obtain their library records.[180]

During this period, there were also some attacks by Ultra-Right-Wingers on people of the Jewish faith in the United States.

And see: Chapter 5.

**Relevant Law:**

U.S. Constitution: Art. I, §9, Cl. 2; Art. VI, Cl. 2; First, Fourth, Fifth, Sixth, Seventh, Eighth, Fourteenth, Fifteenth Amendments
*Bilokunsky v. Tod*, 263 US 149 (1923)
UN Charter: Art. 55, 55(c), 56
ICCPR: Art. 1, 1.1, 1.2, 2.1, 3-5, 9, 10, 14, 14.2, 14.3, 16-20, 22, 26, 27, 40
CERD: Art. 1, 2, 4(c), 5, 5(a), 5(d)(vii), 6, 7, 9

**Report 6.1: DOD Detains US Army Muslim Chaplain**

In 2002, the US Armed Forces had ten thousand Muslim Americans in uniform, among them fifteen Muslim Chaplains, according to estimates by the American Muslim Armed Forces and Veterans Affairs Council. Until September 10, 2003, James Yee was one of these fifteen.

Yee, a Chinese American, was raised in New Jersey. He graduated from West Point in 1990 and served as an Air Defense military officer. He left the Army in the mid-1990s and moved to Syria, where he lived for four years. He returned to the United States and reenlisted in the Army as an Islamic chaplain. On October 25, 2002, Yee was quoted as saying: "An act of terrorism, the taking of innocent civilian lives is prohibited by Islam, and whoever has done this needs to be brought to justice whether he is Muslim or not."[181]

In November 2002, the Army assigned Yee to counsel terrorist suspects at Guantanamo Naval Base in Cuba.[182] On September 10, 2003, authorities took Yee into custody at Guantanamo Bay and told the media that Yee was in possession of documents that "a chaplain shouldn't have." Allegedly the documents included "diagrams of cells and the facilities at Guantanamo" and lists of detainees being held there, as well as lists of their interrogators. Yee "[is] believed to have ties to radical Muslims in the United States that are now under investigation." The military moved Yee to the Naval Consolidated Brig at Charleston, South Carolina, and held him without charges. The US military "[is] investigating whether Yee may have been involved in espionage or treason."[183]

The military held Yee for seventy-six days on suspicion of spying and aiding the enemy. In October 2003, charges were finally filed against Yee, accusing him of taking classified material to his home without proper security containers or covers. On December 9, 2003, the military admitted it did not know whether the material seized from Yee was classified. Then they charged Yee with committing adultery and having pornographic images on his computer.[184]

The Army announced that no one will be assigned to counsel the Muslim prisoners at Guantanamo who were formerly counseled by James Yee. The military made plans to bring a new Muslim chaplain to the base where it is holding some 660 accused terror suspects, but that chaplain will not be allowed to come into contact with the "enemy combatants" being detained there without trial.

A professional therapist with twenty years' experience who has known Yee personally for many years wrote that "I'm sure that the counseling regulations of the Federal Bureau of Prisons have not been applied to this government prison, which is in violation of the US Constitution and International Human Rights Laws" (anonymous letter to Marti Hiken of the National Lawyers Guild Military Law Task Force).

On November 6, 2003, Maj. Gen. Mitchell LeClaire, second in command of the interrogation operation, said that the military had arranged for a replacement chaplain to be sent to Guantanamo Bay by early December. However, while the new chaplain would continue Yee's role of advising command staff on Islamic practices, he would minister only to Muslim soldiers and not meet with detainees, as Yee did.[185]

On April 14, 2004, all charges against Yee were dropped, including the adultery and pornography charges. Two days later, the Army placed a gag order on Yee, preventing him from speaking publicly about the case.[186] On August 2, 2004, James Yee wrote a letter that his civilian attorneys released to the media. Yee wrote, "In 2003, I was unfairly accused of grave offenses under the Uniform Code of Military Justice and unjustifiably placed in solitary confinement for 76 days. . . . Those unfounded allegations—which were leaked to the media—irreparably injured my personal and professional reputation and destroyed my prospects for a career in the United States Army. . . . I have waited for months for an apology for the treatment to which I have been subjected, but none has been forthcoming. I have been unable even to obtain my personal effects from Guantanamo Bay, despite repeated requests. In the circumstances, I have no alternative but to tender my resignation."[187]

### Report 6.2:  FBI Arrests US Citizen, President of American Muslim Foundation

On September 28, 2003, at Dulles International Airport, the FBI arrested Abdurahman Alamoudi, a naturalized US citizen originally from Ethiopia. Alamoudi served as a goodwill ambassador to Muslim countries and as President of the American Muslim Foundation during Pres. Bill Clinton's administration. He is a founder of the American Muslim Council and cofounder of the American Muslim Armed Forces and Veterans Affairs Council, which helps the US military select Muslim chaplains for the armed forces.[188]

Alamoudi was arrested on charges that he made illegal trips to Libya and that in August 2003, he accepted $340,000 in cash from an agent of a Libyan front group.[189] Alamoudi was arrested without a warrant and held without bail. FBI Assistant Director Michael Mason said that Alamoudi's arrest was not related to alleged terror financing, but rather he was arrested on "probable cause."[190]

Justice Department prosecutors suggested that Alamoudi accepted cash from Libyan agents with the intention of flying to Syria and delivering it to the leaders of Palestinian terrorist groups. Prosecutors acknowledged they could not prove at this point Alamoudi's real intentions in taking the cash, but for their purposes it was irrelevant because Libya remains on the US sanctions list as a terrorist state.[191] Alamoudi contended that he was constantly looking for money for the Islamic advocacy group he heads and sought out Libya because it has renounced terrorism.[192]

Prominent legal activists fear that this is a case of selective prosecution driven by political motives. They are also concerned about legal maneuvers that may be used to misrepresent Alamoudi's character, omit his outstanding contributions to the Muslim community and to the United States, and deny his right to a presumption of innocence through the use of guilt by association.[193]

On June 14, 2004, in a memorandum order and opinion of the US District Court for the Southern District of New York in the case of *In re: Terrorist Attacks on September 11, 2001, Federal Insurance Co., et al., v. Al Qaida, et al.*, the court stated that the Government admitted that Abdurahman Alamoudi was still in US custody along with other Muslims named Ahmed Ressam, Enaam M. Arnaout, Mamdouh Mahmud Salim, Mohammed Ali Hasan al-Moayad,

Mohammed Sadeek Odeh, Wadih el-Hage, Wali Khan Amin Shah, Zacarias Moussaoui, and Mohammed Mohsen Yahya Zayed.[194]

### Report 6.3: US Citizens Perpetrate Hate Crimes Against Muslims

On February 22, 2003, a group of Orange County teens with bats and golf clubs attacked Rashid Alam, an eighteen-year-old Lebanese American. He suffered multiple head injuries, a broken jaw, and several stab wounds. Alam claims that his attackers shouted racial slurs. He filed a lawsuit against four named defendants and twenty-nine unnamed defendants and their parents. He said, "Just because I am Arabian or Muslim does not mean that I am bad or evil."

Laura Bosley, a spokesperson for the FBI, stated, "Nationwide, there have been more than 400 hate crimes directed against Muslim Americans since September 11, 2001."

Sabiha Khan, a spokeswoman for the Council on American-Islamic Relations, noted "a recent lull in attacks against Arab Americans, but that could change if Iraqi Americans start protesting over the presence of US troops in Iraq."[195]

On June 22, 2003, Saurabh Bhalerao, a twenty-four-year-old graduate student at the University of Massachusetts at Dartmouth, was making a pizza delivery when he was "kidnapped, beaten and stabbed, apparently because his attackers thought he was Muslim." Bhalerao, a Hindu from India, was tied up and gagged by four attackers who burned him with cigarettes before forcing him into the trunk of his car.

Later the police arrested two of Bhalerao's attackers, one of whom was a seventeen-year-old white male, Ryan Marsh. The two were "charged with crimes ranging from kidnapping and assault to intent to murder." A police official said that the attacks on Bhalerao were especially savage and brutal because of "their belief that [Bhalerao] was a Muslim." Marsh told the police that "one of the attackers told Bhalerao to 'go back to your own country.'" Bhalerao was in an intensive care unit at Rhode Island Hospital after the attack. "His face was swollen and stitched and he had difficulty moving."[196]

As of February 14, 2004, the Civil Rights Division (CRD) of the DOJ and US Attorneys offices had investigated 546 incidents since 9/11 involving violence, assaults with dangerous weapons, threats, vandalism, and arson and bombings against Arab Americans, Muslims, Sikhs, South Asian Americans, and other individuals perceived to be of Middle Eastern descent. The Government has brought federal charges in thirteen cases against eighteen defendants, with a 100 percent conviction rate. CRD attorneys have coordinated with state and local prosecutors in 121 nonfederal criminal prosecutions.

Some examples of Civil Rights Division cases include:

- On January 7, 2002, James Herrick pled guilty to pouring gasoline on the wall of a Pakistani American restaurant in Salt Lake City, Utah, and lighting it in an attempt to destroy the building. He was sentenced to fifty-one months.
- In February 2003, Charles Franklin was found guilty of a felony for intentionally damaging the Islamic Center Mosque in Tallahassee, Florida. Franklin crashed his truck into the mosque because he was angry with Arabs and Muslims. On May 19, 2003, he was sentenced to twenty-seven months and ordered to pay more than $60,000 in restitution.[197]
- Matthew John Burdick shot and wounded a Sikh postal carrier with a high-powered pellet rifle in Sacramento, California. Burdick pled guilty and was sentenced to seventy months in prison and ordered to pay $25,395 in restitution.
- On February 4, 2003, Earl Leslie Krugel of the Jewish Defense League (JDL) pled guilty to conspiring to manufacture and detonate bombs at a mosque in Culver City, California, and at the field office of Rep. Darrel Issa (R-CA). Using an informant within the JDL, the FBI monitored several discussions among Krugel and others in which they discussed destroying mosques and other Arab American institutions. Krugel faces a mandatory minimum of ten years on weapons-related charges.
- On April 3, 2003, four individuals who plotted to destroy the Islamic Education Center were sentenced in Florida. Dr. Robert Goldstein pled guilty to conspiracy to violate civil rights, attempted destruction of religious property, and firearms violations and was sentenced to 151 months in jail. Kristi Goldstein pled guilty to firearms violations and was sentenced to 37 months. Dr. Michael Hardee pled guilty to conspiracy to violate civil rights, conspiracy to detonate explosive devices, and firearms violations, and was sentenced to 41 months. Samuel Shannahan pled guilty to a firearms offense and was sentenced to 56 months.
- Patrick Cunningham pled guilty on May 9, 2002, for attempting to set fire to cars in the parking lot of the Islamic Idriss Mosque in Seattle, Washington. He then fired a gun at worshipers who exited the mosque before fleeing. Cunningham was sentenced to seventy-eight months.

## Report 6.4: US Muslims Feeling a "Chilling Effect"

In 2003, Muslim Americans felt "under siege," as "an unhealthy conservatism" arose. This marked a change from the 1990s, when Muslim Americans "led a tireless campaign to get mainstream Muslims portrayed in the media as just another group of patriotic Americans who go to work, raise their children, and believe in God."

According to Hamid Algar, a Muslim scholar at the University of California, Berkeley, after September 11, 2001, there was "a wave of self-promotion in the Muslim community," but it has since been chilled by the "deployment of more than 200,000 [US] troops to the Persian Gulf." The leaders of the Muslim American community replaced their "apocalyptic prediction" with "sudden patriotism" by shaving their beards and "[putting] on coats and ties." A few days before the United States invaded Iraq, US Muslims began "asking new questions about their role as the most studied and talked about religious minority in the United States." John Esposito, a professor at Georgetown University, feared that an invasion of a predominantly Muslim nation like Iraq might create more terrorism in the United States and around the world, and potentially "force the American Muslim community to pull back."[198]

In 2004, the Council on American-Islamic Relations (CAIR) reported that in 2003, the highest number of Muslim civil rights violations cases ever recorded by CAIR took place. Reports of harassment, violence, and discriminatory treatment increased nearly 70 percent over 2002 and represented a threefold increase since 2001. Incidents of hate crime alone more than doubled since 2001. Also, allegations of mistreatment by federal and local law enforcement personnel, including racial profiling and discriminatory application of the law, were the highest ever recorded in real and proportionate terms.

CAIR stated that four factors contributed to the sharp increase in reported incidents: "1) A lingering atmosphere of fear since the September 11 attacks; 2) The war in Iraq and the atmosphere created by the pro-war rhetoric; 3) The noticeable increase of anti-Muslim rhetoric, which often painted Muslims as followers of a false religion and as enemies of America; 4) The USA PATRIOT Act, the implementation of which has been associated with abuses."

CAIR recommended that a number of governmental actions be taken in order to stem the rise of anti-Muslim discrimination. These recommendations included a call for a public inquiry on post-9/11 policies impacting the Muslim community and a call for implementing reforms suggested by the Office of the Inspector General of the Department of Justice regarding post-9/11 investigations and detentions. CAIR also recommended a number of legislative actions to curb the use of profiling in law enforcement, strengthen hate crime prosecutions and end abuses associated with the USA PATRIOT Act.[199]

## 7. *RIGHT OF THE MEDIA TO REPORT FACTS AND NOT BE KILLED*

Freedom of the press is a basic right to be exercised by the media and by the people: the media to report, and the people to read, watch, and listen. It was enshrined in the First Amendment, as well as in the UN Charter and the International Covenant on Civil and Political Rights, because a free people must be able to hear many versions of "the truth" in order to decide whom to believe, and whom to vote for to run their government.

By September 15, 2001, a few reporters questioned what George Bush did immediately after September 11. The City Editor of the *Texas City Sun* and a prize-winning columnist for the *Daily Courier* of Grants Pass, Oregon were fired for their columns. In August 2002, a columnist for the *San Francisco Chronicle* was suspended for columns critical of Bush's foreign policy. And the *Chronicle* fired a technical reporter after his participation in the massive antiwar demonstration that led to his arrest. The publishers in each case denied that the reporters' writings were the reason for their being fired (Report 7.1).

The Government confiscated some sources of information being sent to journalists. An AP reporter in the Philippines tried to send an unclassified FBI document to a reporter in Washington, DC. Customs saw to it that the document was never delivered (Report 7.2). The Immigration Service detained another journalist on his return to the United States from assignments in Cuba and Mexico. It took six months of legal battles to regain permanent legal residence status (Report 7.3).

Journalists faced new threats after 9/11 when they tried to travel to wartorn areas to cover the US invasions of Afghanistan and Iraq and tried to report their conclusions about actions of Government officials. In March and April 2003, US forces killed several journalists from many nations as they traveled in Iraq to report their stories, and on April 8, 2003, the United States bombed the Al-Jazeera office on the bank of the Tigris River, and on the same day, a US tank fired on the Palestine Hotel in Baghdad, which was being used as a base by the foreign media (Report 7.5). Several journalists and cameramen were wounded while others died in these and similar attacks.

At the same time, for the first time the Pentagon arranged for journalists to be "embedded" with US troops in war zones. This permitted the media to see only what their "drivers" or "hosts" chose to let them see. And it made it impossible for the media to say, or write, what they thought for fear it would end their "embedded" status (Report 7.6).

In July 2003, a US military officer stopped documentary filmmakers for the Islamic Republic of Iran Broadcasting who were filming a US military base in Kut, southeast of Baghdad, in an area they had been told was "unrestricted." Authorities held them for 126 days. After endless questioning and mistreatment, they were released, thinner and exhausted (Report 7.7). When detainees at Guantanamo Camp Delta tried to talk to journalists from the BBC, guards seized their audio recordings and banned the BBC team from the rest of the tour (Report 7.4).

The Homeland Security Act of 2002 (6 U.S.C. § 101) calls for the development of "a comprehensive plan" for "securing . . . information technology," which independent media challenge as a clear violation of the First Amendment freedom of the press (Report 7.6).

In the face of widespread criticism of the Federal Communications Commission (FCC) and its then chair, Michael Powell, for encouraging monopoly media ownership, the US Court of Appeals for the DC Circuit, in *US Telecom Ass'n. v. FCC*, issued an order overturning new FCC rules.[200] The FCC held eight hearings across the United States to hear comments on media news coverage. Commissioner Michael Copps summed up the testimony of scores of witnesses in the Monterey hearing on July 21, 2004: media coverage of elections for local office and local propositions was miserable, amounting to either no coverage or coverage of less than ten seconds during the preelection stages, and coverage of what candidates in national elections actually said was sixty seconds per night on average, according to studies by the Stanford University Department of Communications "Grade the News" project and from Martin Kaplan of the University of Southern California funded by the Annenberg Foundation.

## Relevant Law:

U.S. Constitution: Art. VI, Cl. 2; First Fourth, Fifth, Sixth, Eighth, Four-
    teenth Amendments
UN Charter: Art. 55, 55(b), 56
CAT: Art. 1, 2, 4, 5, 10-13, 15, 16, 19
ICCPR: Art. 1, 6.1, 7, 9, 9.1, 10, 12.4, 14, 14.7, 16-20, 24, 26, 40
CERD: Art. 1, 2, 5, 5(a), 5(d)(viii), 6, 7, 9
CRC: Preamble, Art. 1-3, 5-10, 16, 18, 20, 22, 44

## Report 7.1: Media Fired Columnists for Criticizing Bush

On September 22, 2001, following President Bush's September 20 speech to Congress, the *Texas City Sun* ran a column by City Editor Tom Gutting that criticized Bush for not returning to Washington, DC after the September 11 attacks and for "flying around the country like a scared child seeking refuge in his mother's bed after having a nightmare." In the column Gutting also called Bush "a puppet."[201] The *Texas City Sun* publisher, Les Daughtry Jr., assured Gutting the day his piece ran that he would not be fired. There was a loud public outcry over the piece. The next day, Daughtry ran an apology on the front page and wrote an accompanying opinion piece: "Bush's Leadership Has Been Superb." Then Daughtry laid off Gutting "for administrative reasons."[202]

Dan Guthrie was a columnist and copy editor for the *Daily Courier* in Grant's Pass, Oregon. He won eleven awards for his column and a prize for best columnist in the state. In his September 15, 2001, column, he sharply criticized President Bush for flying around the country to secure locations following the 9/11 attacks. He wrote that the passengers of Flight 93, who presumably wrestled the terrorists on that plane off their target until the plane crashed into a Pennsylvania field, were the heroes. Guthrie wrote that Bush "skedaddled," that he was "hiding in a Nebraska hole" instead of returning to Washington, DC, and that he was "an embarrassment."[203] Readers of the *Daily Courier* complained. A few days later, the editor was pressured to apologize, and did so. The publisher fired Guthrie one week after his column appeared. He denied he fired Guthrie as a specific response to the article. Guthrie reportedly said, "I wish I had waited."[204]

Stephanie Salter, a *San Francisco Chronicle* columnist, wrote several pieces criticizing Bush and his post-9/11 foreign policy. On August 12, 2002, John Oppedahl, publisher of the *Chronicle*, suspended Salter. He claimed that her perspective did not "resonate," and that "people outside San Francisco are not interested" in the people and projects she was writing about.[205]

On March 20, 2003, Henry Norr, a technical reporter for the *San Francisco Chronicle*, participated in a massive demonstration against the war in Iraq and was arrested. The *Chronicle* suspended him for four weeks. On April 21, 2003, the *Chronicle* fired Norr for "falsifying his time card" by recording a sick day for the day he spent in jail. The *Chronicle*'s publishers sent an e-mail to all newspaper staff: all employees participating in war-related demonstrations must first obtain clearance from their supervisor.[206]

On July 29, 2004, Sarah Norr of *Beyond Chron* reported the purge of at least six staffers from the *San Francisco Chronicle* since 2002 because of suspected bias toward progressive causes. William Pates was replaced as the *Chronicle*'s Letters page editor (management labeled his $400 donation to the John Kerry campaign as an ethics violation).

Ted Glasser, director of Stanford's graduate journalism program, says that restricting workers' political rights is not a standard component of respectable journalism. Moreover, it is illegal. California State Labor C. Sections 1101 and 1102 bar employers from "forbidding or preventing employees from engaging or participating in politics."

Doug Cuthbertson, executive officer of the Northern California Media Workers Guild, which represents *Chronicle* staff, was unable to name any cases in which a staffer was transferred, suspended, or fired under suspicion of bias toward conservative causes.[207] Not one Government agency began investigating any of these alleged violations of the First Amendment.

## Report 7.2: FBI Seized FBI Document Sent to Journalist

An Associated Press (AP) reporter in the Philippines sent an unclassified FBI document to John Solomon, another AP reporter in Washington, in September 2002 as part of their research for an article they were writing, but the package never arrived. Federal Express originally said the parcel might have fallen off a delivery van. On April 3, 2003, the FBI acknowledged that its agents confiscated the package. The FBI did not offer any explanation for the seizure.

An inspector for US Customs in Indianapolis appears to have opened the Washington-bound package in a periodic routine inspection. Upon seeing that the package contained an FBI report related to terrorism in the Philippines, the inspector notified the FBI. The FBI seized the document without notifying FedEx or the AP.

This is the second time that the FBI has focused on John Solomon. In 2001, the Justice Department subpoenaed Solomon's home telephone records to try to determine the source of leaks he had used in writing about an investigation of Senator Robert Torricelli (D-NJ). Customs officials defended the actions of their employee by saying that the AP was not singled out and that "if I was an inspector and I opened something suspicious related to the FBI, I sure as heck would call somebody else in to look at it." The FBI also defended the actions of the FBI and its agents. They said that since it was an internal FBI document, it was not supposed to be released publicly.[208]

## Report 7.3: Immigration Service Detained Resident Journalist

On December 3, 2002, the US Immigration and Naturalization Service (INS) detained journalist Roger Calero for ten days after he returned to the United States through the George Bush Intercontinental Airport in Houston after completing assignments in Cuba and Guadalajara, Mexico. Calero has been a permanent resident of the United States since 1988.[209]

Calero's detention was based on a 1988 conviction for selling marijuana to an undercover police officer. The INS waived the conviction when Calero applied for and received permanent resident status in the United States. Because of the increased application of two 1996 Congressional acts that allow Immigration officials to retroactively use past convictions as grounds for deportation, Calero faced possible exclusion and deportation based on this previously overlooked charge.

"The effect of the Anti-terrorism and Illegal Immigration and Reform Act and immigration responsibility laws was to make most crimes the basis for deportation," according to Joe Vail, supervisor of the law department at the University of Houston. "The INS chose to take its interpretation a step further. The way the act was interpreted by the Immigration Service was that any crime at any time—even if it had been committed twenty to twenty-five years ago—could be resurrected to make a person deportable. Even if they had since obtained lawful residence status and if they lived a perfect life since that time, they could go back to any point in their life and pick up that crime and charge the person and possibly remove them."[210]

On May 1, 2003, the Department of Homeland Security moved to terminate the deportation case against Calero. Newark Immigration Judge William Strasser ordered the DHS to elaborate on its motion to terminate, which consisted of one sentence citing BICE rules and contained no other explanation. Twelve days later the DHS clarified the motion, saying the INS was correct in waiving the marijuana conviction, and had properly granted Calero permanent residency in 1988, invalidating the removal proceeding. On May 15, 2003, after a six-month legal battle, Calero received his permanent green card from the DHS.[211]

### Report 7.4: US Guards Threatened BBC Journalists on Guantanamo Tour

On June 22, 2003, a BBC Panorama team visited Camp Delta, a maximum security camp at Guantanamo Bay. As the journalists walked through the camp, four detainees shouted that they wanted to tell their stories. The soldiers that were present immediately halted the tour and ordered the press out. From behind a fence, one man with a Pakistani accent in his late twenties shouted out, "Are you journalists? Can we talk to you?" BBC reporter Vivienne White responded, "We're from BBC television; we are from BBC TV." Immediately US officials tried to hurry the reporters away. The detainee shouted, "We've been waiting to see you." A melee broke out as the reporters stood by only three meters away. One officer said, "Either you keep moving or the tour ends." One detainee said, "We've been here a long time . . . we will talk to you later."

US forces seized an audio recording made by the Panorama team and banished Vivienne White to a Sectionof the bay away from Camp Delta. Officials then forced some of the journalists onto a bus but allowed those reporters who were not with the BBC to continue the tour.[212]

### Report 7.5: US Fire in Iraq Killed Several Journalists

The US military has attacked many journalists reporting from Iraq since the invasion began. Aidan White, General Secretary of the International Federation of Journalists (IFJ), said that the killing and wounding of journalists is "evidence of what appears to be casual disregard of journalists' safety by military commanders. [When the journalists] identify themselves and seek permission from military units to do their work they are still being fired upon." Referring to the August 17, 2003, killing of journalist Mazen Dana, White said that it "was an avoidable tragedy" and "[t]here must be a full, independent and public inquiry. We need to know what went wrong and why. We cannot accept that this is brushed aside as just another regrettable incident in the chaos of war." Additionally, he questioned the safety of independent, as opposed to embedded, journalists working in Iraq.

The list of journalists killed and/or wounded by US forces in the Middle East is long, and it keeps growing.

- On March 22, 2003, Terry Lloyd, a news correspondent for ITN, was killed when his news team was fired upon by Coalition forces near Basra. Lloyd's cameraman, Fred Nerac, and translator, Hussein Osman, are still officially listed as missing.
- On April 6, 2003, Kamaran Abdurazaq Muhamed, a Kurdish translator working for the BBC in Northern Iraq, died after being seriously wounded, apparently by a US bomb.
- On April 8, 2003, Tareq Ayoub, an *Al-Jazeera* reporter, was seriously wounded, and later died, when *Al-Jazeera's* office near the Tigris River was hit by a US bomb.
- Also on April 8, 2003, Ukrainian cameraman Taras Protsyuk and Spanish cameraman José Couso were killed after the Palestine Hotel, a base for foreign media in Baghdad, was hit by a shell fired by a US tank.
- On August 17, 2003, Mazen Dana, a Palestinian cameraman working for Reuters, was shot dead by US troops near Abu Ghraib prison in broad daylight. The camera team had contacted soldiers in the vicinity and explained their mission to them, after which the soldiers had granted the crew permission to film the prison.[213]

On September 12, 2004, a US helicopter fired on a crowd in Baghdad to stop insurgents from attacking a military vehicle, killing a Palestinian TV journalist, Mazen al-Tomaizi. The IFJ General Secretary voiced support of the protests of Palestinian journalists and stated, "Once again a working journalist, carrying nothing more dangerous than a microphone is shot dead in the streets without any satisfactory explanation. This tragedy reinforces our demands for justice for journalists who have been killed in Iraq by so-called 'friendly fire.'" The IFJ called for "a detailed, independent inquiry."[214]

As of November 1, 2004, twenty-three journalists had died in Iraq in 2004 and thirteen had died in 2003. Nine deaths were directly linked to US fire. Five more deaths were caused by crossfire or other acts of war. Eighteen of the dead were Iraqi citizens.[215]

## Report 7.6: US Censored Embedded Journalists

During the invasion of Iraq, the Pentagon organized press pools in the Middle East and in Washington, DC that gave prescheduled reports on the war in Iraq to selected groups of journalists for distribution through their individual media organizations. For the first time in a war involving US troops, the Pentagon invited reporters to travel with coalition troops to observe and report on the war efforts. These "embedded reporters," working directly with military units in the field, had to maintain cooperative working relationships with unit commanders as they fed breaking news back to the US public. "Cooperative reporting is vital to continued access to government news sources. Therefore, rows of news story reviewers back at the corporate media headquarters rewrite, soften, or spike news stories from the field that threaten the symbiotics of global news management."

Government publication specialists and media experts from private commercial interests provide ongoing news feeds to the national media distribution systems. Journalists who fail to recognize their role as cooperative news collectors may be disciplined in the field or barred from reporting. Journalists working outside of this mass media system may face ever-increasing dangers from "accidents" of war and the corporate media may dismiss such independent reports.

Massive civilian casualties caused by US troops, extensive damage to private homes and businesses, and reports that contradicted the official public relations line have been downplayed, deleted, or ignored by the corporate media, which uses retired generals and other approved "insiders" to comment on and filter the news for the general public.

The Homeland Security Act (6 U.S.C.A §111) empowers the "directorate" to "develop a comprehensive plan for securing the key resources and critical infrastructure of the US including . . . information technology and telecommunications systems . . . and emergency preparedness communications."

The director of Project Censored at Sonoma State University states that "Symbiotic global news distribution is a conscious and deliberate attempt by the powerful to control news and information in society. The government's goal is total information control and the continuing consolidation of media."[216]

Consolidation of media outlets has led to more and more US citizens getting their news from a smaller and smaller handful of corporations. Media companies have an ever-increasing dependence on prearranged content, and many, such as MSNBC, FOX and CNN, are closely interconnected with various governmental and private industry sources of news.

In July 2004, MoveOn.org helped publicize a two-hour documentary on one of the biggest US media conglomerates, titled *OutFoxed: Rupert Murdoch's War on Journalism*, describing in hundreds of short film clips the degree of control over the men and women hired to "present" the news on FOX stations. The documentary reproduces a score of the daily memos prepared by FOX management telling newscasters and commentators which stories to emphasize or skip, and what spin to give these stories. The film includes lengthy commentaries by a number of former FOX employees describing their frustrations, and ultimate defeats, in seeking to fulfill their roles as "journalists" rather than "propagandists."

### Report 7.7: US Detains Iranian Journalists 126 Days

On July 1, 2003, journalists Saeed Abu Taleb and Sohail Karimi were working as documentary filmmakers for the Islamic Republic of Iran Broadcasting (IRIB) in the town of Kut, southeast of Baghdad, filming a US base in what the military said was an unrestricted area. A US military officer spotted them, arrested them, and took them to the town of Diwaniyah, and then to Baghdad, before handing them over, some four months later, to British troops in Um Qasr prison in southern Iraq to be released.

"After 48 hours of detention and after they were sure we were documentary filmmakers and they had looked at our films, the torture and the harassment began," Abu Taleb told Iranian state television as he and his freed colleague Sohail Karimi crossed back into Iran. "The detention was unimaginable. The first ten days were like a nightmare. We were subjected to severe torture. The other four months were terrifying. I would rather not remember it. It was very bad, very bad," he said as the pair were greeted at the southern Iranian border post of Shalamcheh, near the Iraqi city of Basra.

Both journalists were visibly thinner and exhausted by their 126 days in detention. Abu Taleb said that a US officer had apologized to them before they were released and admitted their arrest had been a mistake. "In our last interrogation, which happened a week or ten days ago, they themselves said it was a mistake by the soldier or officer who arrested us. And I told them that this mistake could have been solved after three days, not four months," Abu Taleb said.[217]

## 8. RIGHT TO PRIVACY VS. SURVEILLANCE AND REGISTRATION

Immediately after September 11, President Bush called on Congress to swiftly pass the USA PATRIOT Act ("Uniting and Strengthening America by Providing Appropriate Tools Required to Intercept and Obstruct Terrorism"), a 131-page bill that became Public Law 107–56. The PATRIOT Act amends many sections of many statutes and changes the powers of many federal agencies in many Departments.

It includes expansion of the powers of the Foreign Intelligence Surveillance Act (FISA) of 1978 (50 U.S.C. §1801), which created a court to oversee FBI surveillance in foreign intelligence investigations. Only Government staff may appear before the FISA court, which meets in secret. In addition, the Government established a new technology called MATRIX (the Multistate Anti-Terrorism Information Exchange System) to make it easier for local, state, and federal law enforcement agencies to exchange information they consider related to terrorism and other criminal activity, again without an avenue for public review.

The convergence of these Governmental powers led many people to become concerned about violations of the right to privacy of everyone living in the United States. The Supreme Court accepted the formulation by Justice William O. Douglas that the right to privacy is the penumbra of the First and Ninth Amendments. That is, it is a fundamental human right. The Constitution and Bill of Rights do not specifically state that women shall be treated equally with men and that children shall have due process rights. But every lawyer, judge, and legislator knows that unequal treatment of women and denial of due process to children will lead to litigation. In the same way, the fact that the right to privacy was not spelled out by the framers of the Constitution does not lessen its standing as a basic human right.

One of the sharp examples of the operation of the USA PATRIOT Act began in October 2003, when Prof. Sally Frank of Drake University Law School in Des Moines, Iowa, discovered that her e-mail was being monitored. As adviser to the school's chapter of the National Lawyers Guild, Frank notified the national Guild office of the surveillance. On February 3, 2004, federal authorities issued subpoenas to four antiwar protesters in Des Moines, Iowa, to appear before federal grand juries.

The US Attorney also subpoenaed records from the University concerning the Guild chapter, the names of its officers, information concerning its November 2003 antiwar conference, and other activities spanning the years 2000 to 2003. The US Attorney also obtained a gag order on Drake University employees. The Guild quickly filed a motion to quash the subpoena, and the Society of American Law Teachers (SALT), the National Conference of Black Lawyers (NCBL), the Bill of Rights Defense Committee, and United for Peace and Justice publicly denounced the Government's actions. The US Attorney first made a statement confirming the existence of a criminal investigation, then withdrew the subpoenas.[218]

After the Attorney General began to implement a new registration system for noncitizens (Report 8.1), the Immigration Service failed to notify so many noncitizens of the second registration date that the system had to be changed (Report 8.3). The new Bureau of Immigration and Customs Enforcement threatened to deport a Pakistani teenager (Report 8.2), which led to so many complaints that the City of Denver agreed to limit intelligence gathering (Report 8.4).

Similar complaints arose when Peace Fresno discovered its organization had been infiltrated (Report 8.5) and many organizations are complaining that the privacy of medical records is now being jeopardized (Report 8.7).

A District Judge in the Central District of California first ruled that some language in the USA PATRIOT Act was unconstitutional under the First and Fifth Amendments, then amended her opinion to say that the issue would have to be dealt with on a case-by-case basis (Report 8.6).

## Relevant Law:

U.S. Constitution: Art. VI, Cl. 2; First, Fourth, Fifth, Ninth, Fourteenth
    Amendments
UN Charter: Art. 55, 55(c), 56
ICCPR: Art. 1.1, 1.3, 2, 2.1, 4, 5, 9.1, 9.2, 10.2, 13, 16-21, 22.2, 23.1, 25-27,
    40
CERD: Art. 1, 2.1(a), 2.2, 4, 5(d)(iii), 7, 9

## Report 8.1: Attorney General Implements His Registration System

On June 6, 2002, then attorney general John Ashcroft announced the implementation of the National Security Entry-Exit Registration System (NSEERS) without consulting Congress. NSEERS is intended to increase the Justice Department's ability to track and monitor the movement of foreign nationals currently residing in the United States. NSEERS requires certain foreign residents to "call in" to the INS when required, then appear and register in person at a nearby INS office.

Registration for those foreign nationals "called in" consists of them being photographed, fingerprinted, and questioned under oath before an Immigration officer, as well as requiring them to present any government-issued identification documents such as a passport and an I-94 card. The called-in foreign nationals are also expected to bring proof of employment, school matriculation, and proof of residence from both the United States and abroad.

On November 6, 2002, Ashcroft announced the first group of people expected to call in to the INS and register. This group consisted of males born before November 15, 1986, who are citizens of Iran, Iraq, Libya, Sudan, and Syria, who entered the US on or before September 10, 2002, and with plans to remain until at least December 16, 2002. On November 22, 2002, Ashcroft expanded the list to include citizens of Afghanistan, Algeria, Bahrain, Eritrea, Lebanon, Morocco, North Korea, Oman, Qatar, Somalia, Tunisia, United Arab Emirates, and Yemen. On December 16, 2002, Ashcroft added Saudi Arabia and Pakistan to the list. On January 16, 2003, Ashcroft further expanded the list to include Bangladesh, Egypt, Indonesia, Jordan, and Kuwait. By the fall of 2003, the media reported eighty-three thousand non-citizens had registered for the first time (late 2002–early 2003). As a result, thirteen thousand were deported.[219]

### Report 8.2:  ICE Threatened to Deport Pakistani Teenagers after "Registration"

On February 10, 2003, two teenage Pakistani brothers, nineteen-year-old Hassan Amin and seventeen-year-old Ahmad Amin, went to the San Jose Immigration and Customs Enforcement (ICE; formerly the INS) office for "special registration," where Hassan was promptly arrested and Ahmad was accused of a minor visa violation. Their attorney had told the family that the brothers were here legally because their petitions for green cards were pending with the Immigration authorities.[220] The Amin brothers had applied for green cards four years earlier, but in 2003 they were declared "out of status" and faced deportation. Hassan was taken to the Yuba City jail where he was "kept in a cell with criminals."[221] He was released the next day after his older brother posted a $4,000 bond to bail him out.[222]

The brothers must now undergo deportation proceedings. The Amin brothers say they feel more American than Pakistani and worry they have no future in the country of their birth. "With the deportation process, my family will be separated again," said Hassan. Ahmad said that he has to skip school once every three weeks to sign a form at the Immigration office declaring that he remains in the country.[223]

"This program has created a culture of anxiety, humiliation, and despair in communities throughout this country," said Samina Faheem, Executive Director of the American Muslim Voice and Pakistani Alliance. "It has made people feel like common criminals, to register and re-register every time they leave the country. We are wasting precious resources on this program."[224]

Since December 2002, an estimated thirteen thousand Muslim boys and men have been deported from the United States as a result of "Special Registration."[225]

And see: Chapter 4.A, Sections 9 and 11.

## Report 8.3: Immigration Failed To Notify Noncitizens of Second Registration

In 2002, the Bush Administration initiated the National Entry-Exit Registration System (NSEERS) Special Registration program. Immigrants who voluntarily registered in 2002 under the program were mandated to reregister within ten days of the anniversary of their individual original registration date. The anniversary of some 2002 registrations—which were carried out in four phases—was November 15, 2003. The members of that first group included men and boys age sixteen and older from Iran, Iraq, Libya, Sudan, and Syria. In 2002, "the initial registration deadlines resulted in mass confusion, detentions, and ultimately, the initiation of deportation proceedings against more than 13,000 men from predominantly Islamic nations," according to Dalia Hashad, the American Civil Liberties Union's Arab, Muslim, and South Asian Advocate. "In most cases, it was apparent that the Immigration Service had arrested men who were simply waiting for approval of their green card applications, or those with minor visa problems caused by incompetence in the agency itself, which has been plagued by an inept bureaucracy for years."

"NSEERS is a poorly implemented plan that has failed to advance our national security or improve efficiency within our immigration system," Hashad said. "The failure to publicize the new deadlines appears to be a continuation of the pattern of selectively arresting, detaining, and deporting Middle Eastern and Muslim men in the United States." Earlier in 2003, the ACLU and a coalition of advocacy groups sent a letter to Immigration and Homeland Security officials detailing a host of other problems with the NSEERS program and requesting a meeting to discuss them.[226]

In December 2003, the ICE and the Department of Homeland Security announced they were ending the NSEERS program, which would be replaced by the US Visitor and Immigration Status Indication Technology (US-VISIT) system, a "check-in/check-out" mechanism that, when fully implemented, could record the entry and exit of all foreign visitors to the United States, scan each visitor's fingerprints and photographs against national security and law enforcement databases, and maintain each visitor's travel history.

The system will involve information sharing among Immigration and Customs Enforcement, Customs and Border Protection, Citizenship and Immigration Services, the Transportation Security Administration, the General Services Administration, and the Departments of State and Transportation.[227]

And see: Chapter 4.A, Sections 9, 11, and 12.

### Report 8.4: City Agreed to Limit Intelligence Gathering

In April 2003, the City of Denver, Colorado, agreed to settle a lawsuit filed by the American Civil Liberties Union of Denver, which alleged that the Police kept illegal intelligence files on the general public, including law-abiding protesters, pro-gun activists, people who might be affiliated with militia groups; a person possibly involved in an illegal motorcycle gang; and a file on a person in the Russian mafia. The department also kept files on people who support Columbus Day and those who would rather do without this holiday out of respect for Native Americans. The files date back to the 1950s.

The City of Denver agreed in the settlement to ensure that its police officers and personnel would be supervised when entering data into a file or sharing information from that file with other law enforcement agencies. In addition, if the file is inactive for five years, it must be purged. Files stored on computers would be purged after the people documented in the files had the opportunity to view them. As part of the settlement, the Denver Police agreed not to keep files on lawful protesters and demonstrators, while continuing to keep files on people "reasonably suspected" of committing crimes. The settlement also confirmed that the Denver Police cannot gather intelligence on people solely based on their support of unpopular causes, or because of their gender, race, age, ethnicity, religion, or political beliefs. Under the new policy, files kept by the police are subject to audit by an independent agency.[228]

And see: Section 3.

### Report 8.5: Police Infiltrated Peace Fresno

On February 20, 2003, community leaders from Fresno, California, and Mark Schlosberg from the ACLU of Northern California wrote to Fresno Police Chief Jerry Dyer expressing concern about the possibility of the Fresno Police Department (FPD) joining the Joint Terrorism Task Force (JTTF). The community leaders requested that the FPD not join the JTTF, and if it did, the FPD should take steps to ensure that the privacy rights of Fresno residents were protected and that FPD officers would not violate the California Constitution, which provides that law enforcement does not have the right to investigate and infiltrate groups unless they have a reasonable suspicion of criminal activity.

The police chief replied in a letter stating that the FPD had not joined the JTTF at that point but told them that the participation of the FPD in the JTTF was vital to the safety of the citizens of Fresno. He also assured them that "it is the duty and goal of the FPD to safeguard the constitutional rights of all the people they come in contact with while attempting to guard the physical well-being of all the citizens of the City of Fresno."[229]

In August 2003, the peace activist group Peace Fresno discovered that they had been infiltrated by an agent who worked for the JTTF of the Fresno Sheriff's Department. The FPD told community members that Fresno is a hotbed of terrorist activity with possible "sleeper cells," and that was why the JTTF had been established in the area. They were also concerned about the alleged connection between the "sleeper cells" and illegal methamphetamine production to fund terrorist activities.

Peace Fresno leaders said they were concerned that an undercover officer was attending their meetings in violation of their personal liberties and civil rights. "The revelation that the Sheriff's department placed an agent in Peace Fresno begs the question of what other groups are being investigated, what has happened to our civil liberties? . . . A united community defending their Constitutional Rights to civil liberties will be the best defense against future attacks. The goal is not only to stop these current intrusions against peaceful and nonviolent groups engaged in civil participation but return the rights that were taken away with the passage of the PATRIOT Act."[230]

## Report 8.6: Judge Limited PATRIOT Act Application, Then Amended Opinion

In 2002 and 2003, five organizations and two US citizens advised groups involved in the Kurds' movement for self-determination in Turkey on how to use peaceful means. The US Government informed them that, under the USA PATRIOT Act, they risked fifteen years in prison for assisting Kurdish refugees in Turkey, who were designated members of a "foreign terrorist organization," even if engaged only in lawful and peaceful activities.

On August 27, 2003, the Humanitarian Law Project brought a lawsuit against John Ashcroft, the Department of Justice, Colin Powell, and the Department of State, on behalf of these organizations and citizens. In their suit, the plaintiffs sought to enjoin the defendants from enforcing the PATRIOT Act to prevent them from assisting the Kurdish refugees.

On January 24, 2004, the District Judge for the Central District of California, Audrey Collins, held that the language of §805(a)(2)(B) of the PATRIOT Act that forbids the provision of "expert advice or assistance" to groups labeled as "foreign terrorist organizations" is unconstitutionally vague and violates First and Fifth Amendment rights. Specifically, "[T]he USA PATRIOT Act places no limitation on the type of expert advice and assistance which is prohibited and instead bans the provision of all expert advice and assistance regardless of its nature." She indicated that the flaw in the PATRIOT Act is its failure to delineate permissible forms of expert advice and assistance. This was the first ruling to hold part of the Act unconstitutional. The Justice Department immediately appealed the ruling.[231]

On March 17, 2004, the judge amended her decision (*Humanitarian Law Project v. Ashcroft*, 309 F.Supp.2d 1185). The amended decision held that the PATRIOT Act's prohibition of "expert advice or assistance" to foreign terrorist organizations was not overbroad, in violation of the First Amendment. Judge Collins ruled that, although some protected speech may have been prohibited, the Act's prohibition was aimed at furthering legitimate state interest, and litigation on a case-by-case basis would provide sufficient safeguards from First Amendment violations. On December 14, 2004, the Ninth Circuit Court of Appeals heard arguments *en banc* (with all judges sitting) (9th Cir. Docket nos. 02–55082 and 55083).

And see Report 18.6.

### Report 8.7: Federal Legislation Threatens Right to Privacy of Medical Records

Many people might not care if their broken leg is public knowledge, but when it comes to mental health treatment, it's another matter. As a result, a number of mental health organizations began expressing concerns after 9/11, exploring legal options and/or taking action regarding the erosion of citizen rights to privacy over their medical and other health care records. Lack of medical privacy became the norm with the passage of the Health Insurance Portability & Accountability Act (HIPAA) in 1996. Medical record privacy further deteriorated with the passage of the USA PATRIOT Act (PL 107–56).

In 2004, seventeen organizations and individuals representing nearly 750,000 citizens and practitioners filed a civil suit against Secretary of Health and Human Services, Tommy Thompson, to challenge HIPAA. Plaintiffs alleged that, while HIPAA ostensibly guarantees patient confidentiality, it actually opens the door for violations of privacy by making it easier for federal officials to access health information without the consent of the patient. The American Civil Liberties Union said that under this act, "law enforcement is entitled to your records simply by asserting that you are a suspect or the victim of a crime." Two other sections of HIPAA also allow for the release of medical records for "national security and intelligence activities."

On April 2, 2004, the District Court for the Eastern District of Pennsylvania decided against the plaintiffs. The judge ruled that HIPAA does not violate the plaintiffs' constitutional rights because HIPAA does not actually compel anyone to use or disclose the plaintiffs' health information for routine purposes without the plaintiffs' consent. Therefore, the court found that HIPAA was not per se violative of constitutional rights (*Citizens for Health, et al. v. Tommy Thompson, Secretary of Health and Human Services*, No. 03–2267, April 2, 2004).

Practitioners have the option of circumventing HIPAA and instead maintain their patients' privacy by not transmitting any patient information electronically. Practically speaking, this means receiving full payment from patients out-of-pocket and/or corresponding with insurance companies by mail instead of online or by fax. For many health professionals and their patients, this choice is not a realistic economic or logistical option. The focus for most professionals, therefore, has been on "how" to comply with HIPAA, rather than a more fundamental civil liberties question of "whether" to participate at all.

HIPAA does require standard written consent by patients to allow sharing actual session content (as opposed to other parts of a patient's record where there is no such consent requirement). No such protections exist under Section 215 of the USA PATRIOT Act, which covers libraries and their patrons, as well as medical records that could include psychotherapy, hypnotherapy, massage therapy, and any other facet of health care, whether the practitioner is licensed or not.

A spokesperson for the American Mental Health Alliance, a plaintiff in the lawsuit challenging HIPAA, characterized the PATRIOT Act "as essentially exploiting vulnerabilities exposed by" the earlier law. For instance, while HIPAA allows practitioners to decide whether or not to notify patients if their records have been obtained by the Government, the PATRIOT Act makes it illegal for the practitioner to tell anyone, including the patient. Plaintiffs claimed this places mental health practitioners in particular in an unethical position, for the extension of government secrecy into the therapeutic relationship negates one essential purpose of psychotherapy itself: the discussion of anything that might impact the client's well-being. The legal counsel of the California Association of Marriage and Family Therapists wrote, "Therapists have unique relationships with their patients, which may be permanently damaged by gag provisions of the Act."

Despite this secrecy requirement, the American Psychological Association (APA) encourages its members "to contact us if you become aware of any practitioner whose records are seized as a result of this Act." The only way for mental health professionals to fulfill the APA request is by breaking the law.[232]

## 9. RIGHT OF LIBRARIES NOT TO REPORT ON READERS

The USA PATRIOT Act (PL 107–56) expanded the FBI's authority to obtain people's records. Section 215 of the Act gives the FBI the authority to seize any record of any entity, including libraries and bookstores. It also removed the requirement that the FBI must have some evidence that the person whose records were being sought was a member of a terrorist group or otherwise involved in terrorism. Section 215 of the PATRIOT Act allows the FBI to obtain whole databases, including records of citizens not suspected of any wrongdoing. In addition, Section215 has a built-in gag order; those who are asked to turn over records are not allowed to say that the search has occurred or that records were given to the Government.

By October 2002, the FBI had visited 178 libraries to ask for their records. Some librarians in New Jersey and Ohio questioned such actions and won some victories (Report 9.1). And many library boards, as well as city councils, passed resolutions opposing provisions of the PATRIOT Act. Santa Cruz librarians began shredding the library's Internet-use log, and many libraries are posting signs that the FBI can get a court order to access records (Report 9.2). When the Democrats had enough votes to amend this PATRIOT Act provision, the Republicans held up the roll call till they could stop it (Report 9.3).

See Chapter 5.4-1.

**Relevant Law:**
US Constitution: Art. VI, Cl. 2; First, Fourth, Ninth Amendments
UN Charter: Art. 55, 56
ICCPR: Art. 1, 17, 18, 19

### Report 9.1: FBI and Department of Homeland Security Checking Out Library Patrons

A survey conducted by the University of Illinois in October 2002 was sent to 1,505 directors of 5,094 US public libraries. It showed that the FBI was busy making visits. "In the year after the World Trade Center and Pentagon attacks," the survey said, "federal and local law enforcement officials visited at least 545 libraries to ask for these records. Of these, 178 libraries received visits from the FBI itself."

At the height of the anthrax scare, two FBI agents visited Temple University's computer center and ordered two student staff members to copy the hard drive of a library employee and give it to them. If anyone asked what they were doing, the FBI agents said, the students were to say they were ridding the computer of a virus. The plan collapsed when the students found that the employee's office door was locked. When the University's chief librarian heard what was going on, she went to the University's lawyers, one of whom asked the FBI about it. The agents said they needed the info because the library employee had received an e-mail mentioning the word "anthrax." After the call from the University's lawyer, the agents left and did not return.

A librarian in Bluffton, Ohio, reported that an unidentified woman recently entered the city public library and asked for the local hazardous materials plan. The librarian got out the folder and handed it to the woman, as she would to any library patron. "When I gave her the binder," the librarian wrote, "she took out the contents and handed me a letter stating the document would no longer be available at public libraries because it contained 'highly critical' information and would be available 'at a controlled location where proper ID of the user can be readily obtained.'" The letter was signed by the director of the local office of the Department of Homeland Security and Emergency Management. Soon thereafter, a woman from the local Homeland Security office removed the same file from the Lima, Ohio, public library.[233]

## Report 9.2: Libraries Shredding Against PATRIOT Act

In February 2003, the library board and the City Council of Santa Monica, California, passed resolutions opposing provisions of the USA PATRIOT Act that require monitoring what patrons read and buy. Monterey Park's Bruggemeyer Memorial Library's board of trustees also formally opposed the legislation on June 17, 2003.

In Santa Cruz, California, the librarians began shredding the library's Internet-use log and information requests to minimize the amount of historical data kept about their patrons. They also started distributing a handout that outlines objections to the enhanced FBI powers and explains that the libraries are reviewing all records to "make sure that we really need every piece of data" about borrowers and Internet users. The move is part of a campaign by the Santa Cruz libraries to demonstrate their opposition to the PATRIOT Act, especially Section 215.[234] Libraries throughout Southern California are fighting against the federal law that makes it easier for authorities to find out what patrons are reading. Librarians have posted warning signs to readers that state: "The FBI has the right to obtain a court order to access any records we have of the library's transactions."[235]

After public pressure from Congress, the American Civil Liberties Union, and the American Library Association (ALA), the Justice Department disclosed the libraries that it had investigated. The ALA and legislators also asked the FBI, pursuant to the Freedom of Information Act (FOIA), to disclose the individual case information that the FBI had gathered.

## Report 9.3: Republicans Change Rules To Keep Library Oversight

On July 8, 2004, Republican leadership of the House of Representatives blocked a proposed Democratic Party amendment to the PATRIOT Act that, if passed, would no longer have allowed US officials to get special court orders requiring book stores and libraries to disclose records of customer reading habits and book purchases. When the amendment appeared to be succeeding within the House roll call's normal fifteen-minute time limit, GOP leaders quickly altered procedural rules to allow the vote to remain open for an additional twenty-three minutes while they persuaded ten Republican members to switch sides and recast their votes against the amendment. Lawmakers switching their votes from 'yes' to 'no' included GOP Reps. Michael Bilirakis of Florida, Rob Bishop of Utah, Tom Davis of Virginia, Jack Kingston of Georgia, Marilyn Musgrave of Colorado, Nick Smith of Michigan, and Thomas Tancredo of Colorado.

Democratic members shouted, "Shame, shame, shame," as the votes were switched. The vote, which required a House majority to pass, failed with a vote of 210–210. "You win some, and some get stolen," Rep. C. L. Butch Otter (R-ID), a sponsor of the defeated provision and one of Congress's more conservative members, told a reporter.[236]

## 10. RIGHT OF UNIVERSITIES TO ACCEPT FOREIGN SCHOLARS AND STUDENTS

Since 9/11, when foreign students have been accepted to do graduate work in US universities, they must go to the US Consul in their country to apply for student visas. US Consular officers have been given the Government Technology Alert List and the List of State Sponsors of Terrorism. If a student is from one of the countries on the second list, and is interested in studying one of the "sensitive" subjects on the first list, the Consular officials must send the application to Washington, DC, for review. This process can take six months or more.

The Government revised its Technology Alert List after 9/11, adding many "sensitive" academic subjects. As of August 2002, the List included: global positioning systems, genetic engineering, biochemistry, microbiology, pathology, flight training, neurology, and urban planning. The Department of State also issued a List of State Sponsors of Terrorism: Cuba, Iran, Iraq, Libya, North Korea, Sudan, and Syria. And it listed five "non-proliferation export control countries": China, India, Israel, Pakistan, and Russia.[237] The Immigration Service also created the Student and Exchange Visitor Information System (SEVIS) to store computerized records on students (Report 10.1).

According to the magazine *Physics Today*, these lists and procedures in the visa process may place nearly six hundred thousand international students studying at colleges and universities in the United States "at risk of not being able to return to their schools if they leave the country."[238]

In 2002–2003, foreign students from countries in the Middle East, Pakistan, Malaysia, and Indonesia had their visa applications delayed for months or denied because of security checks (see Report 10.2). These delays can prevent foreigners from attending or teaching classes in the United States (see Report 10.2).

The Association of American Universities and the Association of International Educators revealed in a survey that in the 2002–2003 school year, hundreds of students and scholars, mostly from China, India, or countries with large Muslim or Arab populations, were unable to attend their universities in the United States despite the timely filing of their visa applications (see Report 10.2).

The Immigration Service instituted the Student and Exchange Visitor Information System in 2002 to track foreign students by means of an electronic monitoring system from the time they apply for a visa (Report 10.1).

A student who left Kuwait after participating in prodemocracy actions there went on to get a Master's degree in mathematics and a teaching job in California. After 9/11, he was arrested, questioned, jailed, beaten, knocked unconscious, and called a terrorist by other prisoners. The judge dismissed all charges at the preliminary hearing for lack of evidence, and the professor filed suit for damages (Report 10.3). After Bill O'Reilly put Prof. Sami Al-Arian on his show, the computer science professor at the University of Southern Florida (USF) was first put on leave, then fired. In 2003, the Department of Justice indicted him and seven other Muslim men for alleged connections with Islamic Jihad (Report 10.4). The US Department of Education did not issue a report on the actual impact these events had on defeating terrorism, the advancement of science and technology, or on the academic freedom enshrined in the First Amendment.

**Relevant Law:**

U.S. Constitution: Art. VI, Cl. 2; First, Ninth, Fourteenth Amendments
UN Charter: Art. 55(b)-(c), 56
ICCPR: Art. 1, 2, 2.1, 3-5, 9, 10, 10.1, 12-14, 16-19, 26, 40
CERD: Art. 1, 2, 2.1(a), (e), 2.2, 5, 5(d)(iii), 5(e)(v), 9

### Report 10.1: New Student Exchange and Visitor Information System Targets International Students

Late in 2002, the Immigration Service created a new system to store computerized records of international students. The Student and Exchange Visitor Information System (SEVIS) shares the records of international students with the Immigration Service.[239] Institutions wishing to enroll foreign students had to be approved for SEVIS by January 30, 2003.

An electronic system for monitoring international students was originally mandated by the Illegal Immigration Reform and Immigrant Responsibility Act of 1996. It was amended by the USA PATRIOT Act and the Enhanced Border Security and Visa Entry Reform Act. According to the

Association of International Educators (NAFSA), SEVIS is the most cumbersome of the new regulations. SEVIS tracks international students and exchange visitors from the time they apply for a visa in their own country, throughout their stay in the United States, to their return home.

"SEVIS poses the greatest threat to institutions enrolling large numbers of international students, which have had to develop or purchase software enabling them to upload to SEVIS the required data for many students at one time. The University of Buffalo (UB), which has more than thirty-two hundred international students, had to purchase commercial software at great expense to meet SEVIS requirements for 'batch processing.' As of early March 2003, the system is still being tested, and until it is ready, the UB must submit data for each student individually."[240]

Section 1761 of the Enhanced Border Security and Visa Entry Reform Act requires collection of data that includes the student's date of entry, port of entry, date of school enrollment, date of departure from school, and the degree program or field of study. Student visa applicants must also provide additional information including their addresses, the names and addresses of relatives, the names of contacts in their country of residence who can verify information about the student visa applicant, and previous work history, if any, including the names and addresses of employers (8 U.S.C. §1701 [2002]).

Section 1761 also establishes an interim system under which the State Department is prohibited from issuing student visas unless the agency has received electronic evidence of acceptance documentation from an approved academic or other institution and the department officer has adequately reviewed the applicant's visa record. Once the visa is issued, the Secretary of State must transmit to Immigration notice that the visa has been issued; Immigration must notify the academic institution that the alien has been admitted to the United States, and the institution must notify Immigration not later than thirty days after the class registration deadline if the alien fails to enroll.

Under the interim system, several students in Colorado were jailed in December 2002 for enrolling in fewer than the required twelve credit hours. In Florida, a student was jailed for reporting to the Bureau of Immigration and Customs Enforcement (ICE; formerly the INS) a day late, which was the result of the student's having to complete a class project on which his grade and continued visa eligibility depended.[241]

Section 1762 of the Enhanced Border Security Act requires the ICE to conduct reviews of educational institutions certified to receive nonimmigrants to determine their compliance with reporting requirements. The Secretary of State is required to conduct similar reviews of entities designated as sponsors of visitor exchange programs. If an institution or program fails to comply materially with the reporting requirements, its authorization to accept foreign students will either be suspended for one year or revoked in its entirety.

## Report 10.2: Mandatory Security Checks Hit Certain Foreign Students: 600,000 May Be Affected

According to the magazine *Physics Today*, "The security clampdown on the US visa system in the wake of the September 11 terrorist attacks has created problems throughout the scientific and higher-education communities that are so numerous and complex that a comprehensive solution may be years away."

Visiting scientists, even those with well-documented records of working in the United States, are finding it increasingly difficult to return if they leave. Those who do leave, even briefly, must go through the entire visa process again on their return to the United States, as if they were applying for the first time. That process often takes eight or nine months, especially for researchers and advanced science students whose work is related to one of the many categories on the special technology alert list.

At the University of Connecticut, nine students from Beijing who had been accepted into the University's graduate research program in physics for the 2002/2003 school year were denied visas.[242] A Chinese student, who went back to China when his parents were killed in an accident, couldn't obtain a visa to return to school. A Russian woman, who had worked as an associate scientist at the US Department of Energy's Ames Laboratory in Iowa for eleven years went to Germany and wasn't allowed to return. There were seventy-eight such cases of denied or delayed visas reported to the American Physics Society between August 2002 and February 2003.[243] Also according to *Physics Today*, new visa and security laws and stricter regulations and enforcement throughout the visa process may place nearly six hundred thousand international students studying at colleges and universities in the United States "at risk of not being able to return to their schools if they leave the country."[244]

It has been estimated that security checks over the past year led to "Severe delays in the issuance of visas to students from countries on the Department of State's 'watch list.'" Many students from countries in the Middle East, as well as Pakistan, Malaysia, and Indonesia, faced delays of three to six months or outright denials of their visa applications."[245] The State Department has said applicants can expect delays of six to eight weeks as a result of the tougher rules. "Such delays can cause international students and teachers to be unable to attend or teach class in the United States."[246]

More than a dozen foreign students entering Harvard for the 2002/2003 school year experienced significant delays in getting their visas; some students weren't able to attend school because of these delays. Adrian Ow Yung Hwei, a student from Malaysia slated to enter Harvard in the fall of 2002, expected to receive his visa within a matter of weeks. Instead he had to wait three and a half months. The Malaysian government, which is funding his education, considered sending him to Australia or New Zealand. When his US student visa finally arrived, the Malaysian government decided to let Hwei enter Harvard after all, this time in fall of 2003.[247]

According to a survey released by the Association of American Universities and the Association of International Educators, hundreds of students and scholars missed their program start dates because of delays in visa issuance even though more than half indicated they applied more than six weeks in advance of their start dates, and more than a third said they applied more than eight weeks before their programs were scheduled to begin. Nearly 80 percent of the delayed students for fall 2002 at the responding institutions were from China, India, or a Muslim or Arab country.[248]

And see: Report 10.4.

## Report 10.3:
## The INS Detained Kuwaiti Immigrant Mathematics Professor

In December 2001, Hasan Hasan received a Master's degree in mathematics at the California State University at Long Beach. He had emigrated from Kuwait in August 1996 to learn English and to escape the climate of fear that had resulted from his being jailed on several occasions for his vocal stance in favor of democracy in Kuwait. Shortly after arriving in the United States, federal agents detained him for questioning concerning his political activities in Kuwait.

According to a story by Ben Ehrenreich in the *Orange County Weekly*, Hasan went to Cal State soon after he was permitted entry into the United States. He was arrested in March 2001 for allegedly making threatening phone calls to Dr. Arthur Wayman, the chairman of the Mathematics department. Dr. Wayman soon dropped all charges.

After graduation, Hasan got a job at Cerritos College. In January 2002, local police picked him up for questioning relating to accusations of stalking and sending a sexually explicit e-mail to another professor. When the police radioed in to check for warrants, they found that the "INS want[ed] to talk to him."

The INS, local police, and the FBI spent the next seven hours interviewing Hasan, then released him. He had no further problems until April 2002, near the end of the semester at Cerritos. Dean Norman Fujimoto called Hasan to his office to tell him that he was fired effective immediately and gave no reason for the dismissal. While leaving the dean's office, Hasan was arrested by the INS for being in the United States illegally, even though he had a work visa valid through December 2002. According to Hasan, when he told the arresting INS officer this the officer responded, "You are not working now." Upon his arrest he was told that the college needed his grades for the students in his class. The INS officers took him to his house and they searched it for the grades for "over two hours," even though he had offered to find the grades himself. While searching they found a propane tank and a receipt from the Jewish Community Center and questioned him about the two items. They took Hasan to jail. Bail was set at $5,000 and Hasan spent the next two and a half weeks behind bars until his bail was lowered and he was released.

After his release, Hasan attended a mathematics conference in Miami, Florida. Upon his return, Hasan was informed by his roommate, Edgar Lanchippa, that while he had been gone, the FBI had come by asking questions and had searched the apartment. Shortly thereafter, Hasan and Lanchippa got into a disagreement, and Hasan asked his roommate to move out. Lanchippa called the police and told them that Hasan had threatened to "disappear" him and that Hasan was "involved in terrorist activities." Hasan was arrested and charged with "criminal threats," a felony.

Hasan spent the next three months in jail. On one occasion he was beaten, knocked unconscious, and called a terrorist by other prisoners. At his preliminary hearing on August 30, 2002, the judge dismissed the case for lack of evidence. Hasan sued the college and all agencies involved for conspiracy to violate his civil rights. The case is pending.[249]

## Report 10.4: Palestinian Professor on TV; Put on Leave; Indicted

On September 26, 2001, Bill O'Reilly invited Prof. Sami Al-Arian to appear on his FOX News Channel show *The O'Reilly Factor*. Al-Arian had been in the United States since 1975. He was a computer science professor at the University of South Florida (USF). O'Reilly asked him about an Islamic think tank he founded and ran in conjunction with USF, which O'Reilly said was a haven for radical Palestinians and anti-Israeli terrorists. These were old allegations that USF and an Immigration Service hearing officer had investigated and rejected in 2000, which Al-Arian tried to say on the air. O'Reilly concluded by saying that if he were with the CIA, "I'd follow you wherever you went."

The interview was widely reported by NBC, FOX News, and Clear Channel Communications. USF received a torrent of angry calls after the show, including death threats against Al-Arian. USF first put him on paid leave and later fired him. The basis for his dismissal was that he had not stated that his views did not necessarily reflect those of USF.

On February 20, 2003, the Department of Justice arrested Al-Arian and three other Muslim men in a predawn raid. They were indicted for alleged connections to the Palestinian group Islamic Jihad. Al-Arian was charged with providing material support to the group and being a chief financier. Palestinian Islamic Jihad was designated by the State Department as an international terrorist organization previous to Al-Arian's arrest, but he had been cleared of connections to that organization in October 2000 by federal Judge R. Kevin McHugh.

One of Al-Arian's attorneys, Nicholas Matassini, said Al-Arian was a political prisoner. If convicted, Al-Arian could face a sentence of life in prison.[250]

In July 2004, Linda Moreno, another attorney, said that Al-Arian had been held since March 2003 in an eight-by-twelve-foot cell in a maximum security federal penitentiary in Coleman, Florida. Amnesty International protested the conditions of his imprisonment. Al-Arian was kept under twenty-three-hour lockdown. He was also subjected to strip searches, chains and shackles, severely limited recreation, lack of access to any religious service, and denial of a watch or clock in a windowless cell where the artificial light was never turned off. When he had to be let out to meet with his attorney, his hands were manacled behind his back. Guards would not help him carry any needed papers or articles; he was made to bend over and carry the items on his back. His trial was set for January 2005.[251]

And see Chapter 4.A, Section 2, and 4.B, Section 18.

## Report 10.5: ICE Detained and Degraded Student Registrant

In February 2003, Chicago-area resident and Pakistani citizen Asim Salam went to register with US Immigration and Customs Enforcement (ICE; formerly the INS) as part of the Department of Homeland Security's Special Registration Program. Salam felt comfortable with the procedure since he was in the United States on a student visa. After completing his master's degree program at the University of Southern California, Los Angeles (USC), he had applied for a one-year extension to allow him to work in his field of study. He had also spoken with immigration lawyers at USC to make sure his papers were in order. The School had given him a letter of good standing.

The ICE agent who reviewed Salam's case said she did not understand the type of visa Salam had. The ICE subsequently detained him and sent him to prison. According to Salam, the prison guards gave him a prison uniform, handcuffed him, and insulted him. Salam's family was required to post a $7,500 bond to affect his release from custody.[252]

On December 30, 2003, the Immigration Judge (hearing officer) for Salam's case ruled that immigration officials should adjust his status to permanent resident since Salam is married to a US citizen. As of September 2004, US Citizenship and Immigration Services (USCIS) had not completed processing Salam's case, so he was not allowed to travel outside the US (e-mail correspondence with MCLI from Asim Salam, September 7, 2004).

## 11. RIGHT TO TRAVEL

Before 9/11, it was fun to go on a trip by plane. Rushing to the airport just before takeoff, people quickly found their gate, showed their ticket to the agent, and boarded with all sorts of packages. There weren't many clerks or airport personnel around, but the majority of those who were on duty were friendly. After the Government instituted "antiterrorism" rules that caused layoffs of more than twenty-five thousand noncitizen airport personnel (Report 4.8) and required everyone to come to the airport two hours early to go through a "routine" check, it stopped being fun. Some people, but not all, had to sit down and take off their shoes, even those with leg and back problems which made it difficult for them. Some people, but not all, were pulled out of line and made to undergo a further individual search by an austere airport guard.

In November 2001, officials barred several people from getting on their flights, including a Green Party official and two women founders of the newspaper *War Times*, who faced police and a long wait because their names were on a "master list" (Report 11.1). US Immigration officials stopped, then deported a Syrian Canadian citizen to a Syrian jail (Report 11.3). They stopped a former member of the British Parliament and a renowned Basque lawyer from entering the United States, immediately putting them on return flights to Ireland and Spain respectively. They held a British journalist in the airport for hours, then returned her to England (Report 11.4).

When security at the Atlanta airport stopped the Pakistani German fiancée of Trevor Hughes, a US Navy veteran, from entering, he said he would fight back (Report 11.6).

By 2004, first-class airline passengers were insisting on some way to avoid these demeaning, unpleasant, and time-consuming searches. Many other people just gave up on the idea of traveling by air for fun. And airlines increasingly filed for bankruptcy.

After both the Senate and the House voted to lift the ban on travel to Cuba, Bush stopped their action by threatening a veto (Report 11.5).

Congress rejected the Computer Assisted Passenger Prescreening System II (CAPPS II), but the Department of Homeland Security and the Transportation Security Administration continued working on it (Report 11.2).

On January 3, 2004, the Department of Homeland Security unveiled its new US-VISIT program at fourteen seaports and 115 airports around the country. Under the VISIT program, travelers to the United States from all but twenty-eight (mostly European) countries will be subjected to more stringent background and ID checks, including fingerprinting, each time they attempt to enter the United States.

Some organizations, including the National Council of Pakistani Americans, welcomed the program as less discriminatory than past US polices that specifically targeted men from predominantly Muslim nations. Some countries reacted with sharp criticism. A week before US-VISIT was implemented, a federal judge in Brazil ruled that his country would begin fingerprinting and photographing US visitors to counter US "xenophobic" actions.[253]

On September 21, 2004, pop singer Cat Stevens, fifty-seven, boarded a flight in London headed for Washington, DC. He was listed as Yusef Islam, the name he adopted when he converted to Islam in the late 1970s. En route, the plane was diverted to Bangor, Maine, where he was detained on "national security grounds." He was ordered off the plane. "I was simply told that the order came from on high," he said. He was deported back to London because his name was on a "no-fly" list.

It turned out that the name on the list was not his but Youssouf Islam. He initiated a legal process challenging his treatment.[254]

### Relevant Law

US Constitution: Art. VI, Cl. 2; First, Fourth, Fourteenth Amendments
War Crimes Act of 1986, 18 U.S.C. §2441 as amended by War Crimes Act
of 1997
UN Charter: Art. 55, 56
ICCPR: Art. 1-3, 9, 12-14, 17, 26, 40

### Report 11.1: Activists Kept Off Airplanes

In November 2001, Nancy Oden, a Green Party official, was barred from flying from Maine to Chicago on the grounds of national security.[255] In April 2002, Alia Kate, sixteen, a high school student in Milwaukee, wanted to go to Washington, DC, for protests on the twentieth. She checked in for her flight, then was pulled aside and questioned by a sheriff's deputy. Kate never made it onto her flight, and neither did most of the thirty-seven other activists with her, including a seventy-four-year-old Catholic nun.[256]

Shortly after 9/11, Jan Adams, fifty-five, and Rebecca Gordon, fifty, joined with other activists to found the *War Times*. "We've spent most of our lives working against unjust violence. We couldn't be more opposed to terrorism," Jan Adams said. As they checked in for a flight in August 2002, an airline employee said that both their names had shown up on an "FBI no-fly" list and asked if there was any reason that their names could be on that list. "Right away I thought *War Times* is bothering the government." The newspaper has criticized the Government's war in Afghanistan, the erosion of civil liberties in the United States, and the invasion of Iraq. Agents alerted the police and told the women that if their names appeared on the "master list," they would be held for the FBI. "Here we were, two middle-aged women, detained by three police officers in the middle of the airport, when what we were held for was the most normal, most American thing in the world." The police permitted the women to fly, but marked their boarding passes with a big red "S," singling them out for special searches at every stop. On the return flight, an airline employee trailed them to the gate.[257]

## Report 11.2: Congress Rejects Prescreening Airline Passengers

On June 17, 2003, the House Appropriations Committee voted to withhold 2004 fiscal funding for the Computer Assisted Passenger Prescreening System II (CAPPS II), pending review by the Government Accountability Office (GAO), formerly the General Accounting Office.[258]

CAPPS II would be the largest domestic surveillance system ever deployed in the United States. Under CAPPS II, which is currently being tested by Delta Airlines, passengers would be required to provide their full name, address, telephone number, and date of birth before boarding an airplane. The airline's computer system would then link to the Transportation Security Administration (TSA) for a computer background check. The TSA would then assign a red, yellow, or green score to the passenger, based on the agency's risk assessment of that traveler. Green would allow the passenger to proceed; yellow would allow the passenger to proceed but with extra security checks; and a red score would ground the passenger. In July 2003, the Senate Appropriations Committee also denied any funding for CAPPS II until the GAO produced a study on the privacy impact of the program.[259]

An amendment to the legislation, spearheaded by Rep. Martin Olav Sabo (D-MN), directed the National Academy of Sciences to study the program's effects on passengers' privacy and civil liberties. Sabo expressed concern that CAPPS II databases will not be well protected from hackers and that law-abiding citizens who are mistakenly flagged by the system will have no adequate means to correct erroneous records.[260] On August 25, 2003, the US Department of Homeland Security (DHS) and the TSA said that, despite the lack of funding, they will continue to "refine and improve plans" for CAPPS II.[261]

In January 2004, the General Accountability Office reported that the TSA failed to meet seven out of eight Congressional requirements for CAPPS II. Specifically, TSA failed to:

- adequately assess the accuracy of information in the databases that will be used for CAPPS II;
- stress test the CAPPS II system and demonstrate its efficacy and accuracy;
- install safeguards to protect CAPPS II from abuse;
- install security measures to protect unauthorized access to travelers' personal data;
- establish effective oversight of the system's use and operation;
- address privacy concerns regarding CAPPS II; and
- create redress procedures for passengers to correct erroneous information.

Congress then stated that it did not intend to release funds for CAPPS II until the TSA satisfied these criteria. Bush made it clear that he believed these requirements to be merely advisory and would not serve to prevent CAPPS II from being implemented as scheduled.[262]

On July 14, 2004, Homeland Security Secretary Tom Ridge told a reporter that CAPPS II was effectively "dead." Homeland Security spokeswoman Suzanne Luber, however, said, "The name CAPPS II may be dead, but the process of creating an automated passenger prescreening system to replace the current CAPPS will continue."[263]

## Report 11.3: INS Stopped, Deported Syrian Canadian Man to Syrian Jail

On September 26, 2002, Maher Arar, a Canadian citizen born in Syria, departed from Tunisia, where he was vacationing with his family, to return to Montreal. During a stopover in New York, Mr. Arar was detained by the INS.[264] While in detention Arar was denied access to counsel by the INS, and was refused legal representation at his deportation hearing. The Hearing Officer ordered Arar deported to his country of birth, not to the country where he is a citizen, despite the fact that he was traveling with a Canadian passport.

US officials acknowledged that they never charged Arar under any US law and that they had no authority to charge Arar under Canadian antiterrorism laws.[265] On October 7 or 8, 2002, the INS deported him to Syria.[266] The Syrian government held Arar for 365 days in a three-by-six-foot cell and made him sign documents and confessions that he was not allowed to read. "I was ready to confess to anything if it would stop the [daily] torture."[267]

Attorney Michael Ratner of the Center for Constitutional Rights (CCR) maintained that in its action toward Arar, the US Government violated the War Crimes Act of 1996, 18 U.S.C. Section 2441, as amended by the expanded War Crimes Act of 1997; the Canadian Crimes Against Humanity and War Crimes

Act of 2000, c. 24; the Canadian Geneva Conventions Act, R.S. 1985, c. G-3; and the Canadian Prisoner-of-War Status Determination Regulations, SOR/91–134.

On October 6, 2003, the Syrian government allowed Arar to return to Montreal, one year after the United States had deported him.[268] On November 25, 2003, Arar filed suit against the Syrian Arab Republic and the Hashemite Kingdom of Jordan, officially seeking $6 million in damages and $25 million in punitive damages as a result of the injuries he suffered while being detained in the Middle East and unofficially seeking media coverage of the issue.[269] On January 23, 2004, Arar filed suit against then attorney general John Ashcroft for injury stemming from his allegedly unlawful deportation, seeking financial compensation and an admission of wrongdoing. The lawsuit, filed by the CCR, alleged that US officials deported Arar knowing that Syria practices torture.[270]

On January 28, 2004, the Canadian government began an investigation into the Arar case as to whether the information gathered and shared with the United States was done legally. On July 5, the Syrian government stated that it would not cooperate with the inquiry, saying there is no treaty on legal cooperation between Canada and Syria. On July 6, the Canadian government found that it was in contact with the US authorities from Arar's arrest in New York to his deportation to Syria. It found that none of the communications were improper or inaccurate, but some may not have been authorized by law. Arar's lawyer said that the documents show there were multiple exchanges between Canadian and US authorities.[271]

Then attorney general John Ashcroft did not file an answer promptly. The CCR expects the Government and individual defendants to file motions to dismiss.[272]

### Report 11.4:  US Denied Entry to Ex-UK Official, Spanish Lawyer, British Journalist

On February 21, 2003, Bernadette Devlin McAliskey, a former member of the British Parliament, arrived at the O'Hare Airport with her daughter to attend a christening. Her name was called over the loudspeaker, and when she responded she was immediately stopped by two INS agents who threatened to arrest and jail her if she insisted on entering the United States. They then photographed and fingerprinted her and told her that she must return to Ireland against her will on the ground that the State Department had declared that she "poses a serious threat to the security of the United States." McAliskey told INS agents that she had cleared US Immigration in Ireland prior to boarding and had received routine permission to travel. She was told that the order to ban her came from US officials in Dublin.

One INS officer said, "If you interrupt me one more time I'm going to slam the cuffs on you and haul your ass to jail," according to Deirdre McAliskey, her daughter. Another officer said, "Don't make my boss angry. I saw him fire a shot at a guy last week and he has the authority to shoot."

McAliskey was denied access to a lawyer and was put on a plane back to Ireland. "She's not in the best of health and the thirteen hours of travel put her at further risk," said to her daughter. Bernadette McAliskey announced plans to file a formal complaint with the US Consul in Dublin.[273]

In October 2003, Urko Aiartza Azurtza, a Spanish human rights attorney from the Basque region of Spain, got off a plane in Chicago on his way to speak at the national convention of the National Lawyers Guild in Minneapolis. Azurtza's name was called over the loudspeaker at the airport. Immigration officials stopped and interrogated him for two hours. Immigration and Customs Enforcement (ICE; formerly the INS) confiscated all of his belongings, including the files of legal cases on which he had been working on the plane. They denied him access to counsel and put him back on the plane to return to Spain.[274]

Azurtza has never been charged with committing crime, and he was never disciplined by the Spanish bar for misconduct. The ICE questioned him at length about his activities, including whether he had been involved in events in Colombia, which he said he had not. He had represented many defendants in criminal cases in Spain, including members of the left-wing faction of the Basque separatist movement, and others who sought independence legally. He had been elected to sit in the regional government. The National Lawyers Guild convention adopted a resolution condemning this action of the Bush Administration and sent copies to the US State Department.[275]

On May 3, 2004, Elena Lappin, a credentialed British journalist, was detained at Los Angeles International Airport for twenty-six hours after she landed on assignment, then sent back to England for not having the proper visa. She was traveling on a British passport without a press visa, a requirement for foreign journalists entering the United States which had been law for years but rarely enforced as to journalists from Western Europe and other "friendly" nations before 9/11.

Although she would have been allowed entry as a tourist had she declared herself as such, after she declared that she was a member of the press but that she had no press visa, airport security personnel detained, groped, searched, fingerprinted, and handcuffed her, and took a mug shot. Then they publicly paraded her through the airport. They released her the next morning after a twenty-six-hour detention. She said later, "As a detainee, [I saw] a glimpse of a country hiding its deep sense of insecurity behind an abusive façade, and an arbitrary (though not unintentional) disrespect for civil liberties."[276]

### Report 11.5: Bush Preventing US Citizens from Traveling to Cuba

In late 2003, the Office of Foreign Assets Control (OFAC) in the US Department of the Treasury referred fifty cases of US citizens traveling to Cuba to administrative law judges. These referrals could result in the enforcement of civil penalty fines as high as $6,500 and possible jail sentences, according to Cindy Domingo of the Women's International League for Peace and Freedom (WILPF).[277]

The Government threatened two African American members of Milwaukee's Central United Methodist Church with fines for their 1999 trip to participate in the one hundredth anniversary of their sister church in Cuba. After a public campaign by church members that asked why only the two African Americans in the six-person delegation were threatened with fines, the Government also threatened the four white members with fines in September 2003.

The OFAC has asked the US-Cuba Labor Exchange for information on each person who has traveled to Cuba with the Exchange and threatened the officers of the organization with ten years in prison and fines up to $55,000 per violation. The Government took this action after the Senate voted 59–36 on October 23, 2003, to join a majority in the House of Representatives in adopting language that would effectively end the travel ban on visiting Cuba that was first enacted in 1960. This vote was followed in November by a 13–5 vote by the Senate Foreign Relations Committee calling for a separate bill that would explicitly overturn the travel ban altogether.

"Bush also ordered the Department of Homeland Security to increase inspection of travelers to Cuba. US charter companies report that agents of US Customs and Border Patrols and the Treasury Department are now questioning passengers about their licenses before allowing them to board flights to Cuba," according to Cindy Domingo.[278]

Domingo also reported that the WILPF's license to travel to Cuba after April 2003 was not renewed by January 2004. The Office of Foreign Assets Control began an inquiry of the WILPF's past licensing, and took similar action as to other organizations that had been previously licensed. Facing a Presidential veto, the Senate and House Conference Committee agreed not to oppose eliminating the Cuba travel ban from the Treasury and Transportation appropriation bill, despite the majorities in both Houses who favored the elimination.[279]

### Report 11.6: US Veteran Protests When Pakistani German Fiancée Denied Entry

In October 2003, Trevor Hughes, who had served in the Navy and diplomatic corps, awaited a visit from his fiancée, Beate Killguss, a Pakistani who was adopted at birth by German missionaries. Beate, a German citizen, tried to visit Hughes in Colorado Springs, Colorado, on a six-month tourist visa, her third trip to the United States.

As Beate was leaving Stuttgart, a German customs officer warned Beate that in recent months many Germans attempting to visit the US were turned back at the Atlanta airport, including the wife of a US soldier and a German musician who was invited to perform with several US orchestras. She disregarded the officer's warning and flew to Hartsfield International Airport in Atlanta to catch her connecting flight to Colorado. In Atlanta, Beate was ordered into an "Immigration Second" area. Border Agent Barry Carter interrogated her, inspected her belongings, and made copies of all of her personal papers, including a journal. He questioned her about her birthplace.

Although her visa had been approved by the US Consul in Frankfurt, Carter kept insisting that she hadn't proved that she was a permanent German resident, even though she owned an apartment near Stuttgart, where her family lived. Carter went through her address book and telephoned Hughes and Hughes's mother; both vouched for Beate.

Hughes wondered whether Carter made judgments based on Beate's ethnicity and if there was a bias against Germans because their country did not join the United States in the war against Iraq.

Agent Carter told Beate, "I looked you up on Amazon.com and you like books about second languages." Her field of study is languages. The INS held her for six hours, then told her she would be sent home. Then Border Officials took all her belongings, including her diamond engagement ring, photographed her, and transported her in handcuffs, along with other accused people, to and from a jail, treating her "like cattle." Twenty hours after landing in Atlanta, she had eaten nothing and had to bang on the locked door to beg for some food. A border agent brought her a pancake. Hours later she was escorted onto a nonstop flight back to Stuttgart. Her visa had a case number written on it and was marked "cancelled."

Hughes began to seek redress against US officials for this mistreatment of his fiancée. Hughes had attended college in New Zealand and Dallas, Texas, and worked for humanitarian causes in Afghani and Pakistani refugee camps before enlisting in the Navy. In October 2001, he had been recalled to duty and was assigned to Central Command as an intelligence analyst and then to the defense attaché's office in the US Embassy in Pakistan, where he worked on air space issues for US flights into Afghanistan. All these prior experiences and contacts helped Hughes to investigate the matter:

- The German Consulate in Atlanta told Hughes he'd heard of no such case and that it was odd Beate was not allowed to seek help.
- Agent Carter did not return Hughes's telephone call seeking a comment.

- The Atlanta Border Patrol said it would look into the matter.
- The Immigration and Customs Enforcement Agency (ICE) did not return any of his phone calls.
- The Department of Homeland Security (DHS) would not discuss the case.
- The DHS Office of Inspector General said that "no comment" could be made on policies that guide border agents' treatment of detainees or how Deportation decisions are made.
- Officials with Sen. Wayne Allard (R-CO) and Rep. Joel Hefley (R-CO) offered to look into the case if Hughes filed a complaint with them but were not willing to get into the issue of Immigration officials' discretionary powers.
- A spokesperson for Sen. Ben Nighthorse Campbell (R-CO) said she looked into the matter and had suggested several steps Hughes could take.

Hughes said, "When the superpower of the world, the country that lauds freedom and democracy, is the one that's causing this injustice to a person who has gone through the system perfectly legally and has done nothing wrong and yet their response is the exact same as to a felon, obviously we're distraught. . . . I'm for homeland defense. My whole life is in service to this nation. But there's a vast difference between someone who has not broken the law and a felon."[280]

In December 2003, Trevor Hughes received a letter from Senator Ben Nighthorse Campbell (R-CO) who forwarded the response he received from US Customs and Border Protection. Hughes was not satisfied with the response, saying, "Why did it take so long to get a wrong answer based on inaccurate information to a potentially very easy investigation? This is just ridiculous." Hughes quit his job with Homeland Defense and moved to Germany to begin studies in international relations. He and Beate Killguss planned to marry in June 2004.[281]

## B. THE GOVERNMENT'S DUTY TO COUNT THE VOTES ACCURATELY AND REPORT TO THE PEOPLE HONESTLY

The Bush Administration is not only required to protect the rights of the people in the United States and under its jursdiction, as described in Sections 1–11. Every branch of the US Government also has duties spelled out in the Constitution, in statutes, in the UN Charter, and in treaties ratified by the United States as described in Sections 12–30.

After 9/11, George Bush and other leaders in his Administration made statements on three critical issues to Congress, the media, the people of the United States, and to other nations:

- the need to go to war against Iraq because it possessed Weapons of Mass Destruction (see Reports 12.2 and 12.6);
- the validity of the presidential elections of 2000 and 2004 (see Reports 12.1 and 12.9); and
- the safety of working at Ground Zero and other facts about the 9/11 disaster (see Reports 12.4–12.5, and 12.8).

Other violations of the Government's duty to report to the people truthfully are described in many reports in chapter 4, sections A–F.

## 12. CONGRESS AND THE PEOPLE CHALLENGE ADMINISTRATION WORDS AND ACTIONS

On January 6, 2001, a special joint session of Congress met to formally count the electoral vote and declare George W. Bush the forty-third president of the United States. During the count, Democratic Representatives, most of them members of the Congressional Black Caucus, rose and formally objected to the awarding of Florida's twenty-five electoral votes to Bush. Although twenty Representatives stood to declare their formal opposition, 3 U.S.C. Section 15 (on Counting Electoral Votes in Congress) requires at least one Senator to cosign a Representative's written objection to a Presidential election. None of the one hundred Senators present, half of whom were Democrats and none of whom were African American, agreed to support the House members' objections. After walking out of the joint session before Bush was declared President, Rep. Corrine Brown of Florida stated, "We keep hearing 'get over this.' We will never get over this. The Supreme Court selected George Bush as President. He was not elected." Speaking at a news conference later, Rep. Eddie Johnson (D-TX), Vice Chair of the Black Caucus, asked, "How long will we suffer injustice in America? How long will we have to fight to perfect the Fifteenth Amendment? How long will we have to struggle for something that should be every American's birthright?"[282]

After 9/11, voters also mistrusted the results of the 2002 election in several districts where the polls and the counts differed significantly (Report 12.1). As the 2004 election approached, the state of Florida did announce it was putting ex-felons back on the voting rolls. Then, just before November 2004, members of the Congressional Black Caucus took the unprecedented step of asking the UN to monitor the 2004 presidential election.

And on November 5, 2004, Congressman John Conyers (D-MI) and other members of Congress wrote to the Comptroller General asking that the Government Accountability Office investigate the efficacy of using voting machines, and to evaluate complaints about the treatment of voters and counting of ballots in the 2004 presidential election. Then Conyers chaired a Forum on December 8, 2004, in the Rayburn Building, on Preserving Democracy: What Went Wrong in Ohio? (see Report 12.9).

Meanwhile, former US Ambassador Joseph Wilson proved that the Administration used evidence on Iraq's possession of Weapons of Mass Destruction known to be false in promoting the US invasion of Iraq (Report 12.2). In response, someone in or near the Administration committed the crime of revealing the identity of Wilson's wife, a CIA agent (Report 12.3), leading to another investigation.

On November 3, 2002, the government of Iraq delivered its official 11,800-page report to the UN on the status of its nuclear, chemical, and biological weapons programs. One of the Bush Administration's main justifications for the subsequent invasion of Iraq was the alleged inaccuracy and untruthfulness of this report, and the Hussein regime's failure to abide by UN resolutions. According to a December 19, 2002, story published in the German newspaper *Die Tageszeitung*, the US Government itself removed 8,000 pages of the original official report before it was accepted by the UN Security Council. US reporter Michael Niman claimed that "The missing pages implicated twenty-four US corporations and the successive Ronald Reagan and George Bush Sr. Administrations in connection with the illegal supplying of Saddam Hussein's government with myriad weapons of mass destruction and the training to use them."[283]

Congress member Henry Waxman (D-CA) publicized a report chronicling 237 misleading statements by the Bush Administration leading up to the US invasion of Iraq (Report 12.6).

One 9/11 widow filed suit against Bush and other Cabinet members for not heeding warnings of 9/11 (Report 12.4). Many 9/11 victims' families demanded that an independent commission study all aspects of the 9/11 attacks, without prejudice or protection of Government officials. The 9/11 Kean Commission held extensive hearings, collected a huge number of documents, and finally issued its massive report in July 2004. Its findings are summarized in Report 12.5. The Commission's proposal for a new US Office of Strategic Influence is reported in 12.7.

Thousands of people worked on the clean up of Ground Zero at the World Trade Center, and thousands more continued to work in that vicinity at their various occupations. Report 12.8 sets forth the types of hazards people encountered and the inaccurate information they were given by officials at various levels of Government concerning the safety of continuing to work. For an insightful summary, see David Corn, *The Lies of George W. Bush: Mastering the Politics of Deception* (New York: Crown, 2003).

**Relevant Law:**

U.S. Constitution: Preamble, Art. I, §4; Art. I, §5, Cl. 1; Art. I, §8, Cl. 11; Art. II, §1, Cl. 2-4, Cl. 8; Art. II, §2, Cl. 1, Cl. 3; Art. II, §3; Art. IV, §4; Art. VI, Cl. 2; First, Fourth, Fifth, Sixth, Eighth, Ninth, Twelfth, Fifteenth, Nineteenth Amendments
UN Charter: Preamble, Art. 1.3, 2.2, 2.3, 2.4, 2.7, 25, 55, 55(c), 56
ICCPR: Preamble, Art. 1, 2, 2.1, 3-6.1, 7, 16-20.1, 21, 23, 25, 25(b), 26, 40, 41.1, 44, 46, 47
CERD: Art. 1.1, 2.1(a)-(c), 5(c), 5(d)(iii), 5(d)(ix), 6, 9
CAT: Preamble, Art. 1, 2, 4, 5, 15, 19
CEDAW: Preamble, Art. 1, 2(d), 2(e), 7(a), 7(b); 8; 18, 24; 28
ICESCR: Preamble, Art. 1.1, 2.2, 3. 16, 17
CRC: Preamble, Art. 1-3, 5-10, 16, 18, 20, 22, 44

### Report 12.1: Voters Mistrust 2002 Election Results

The disputed election results in Florida in the presidential election of 2000 ended in a 5–4 vote by the US Supreme Court upholding the election of George W. Bush based on the official Florida results (Bush v. Gore, 531 U.S. 98 [2000]).

The November 2002 elections for state and Congressional seats led to renewed concerns about the fairness and accuracy of election procedures in Colorado, Florida, Georgia, Minnesota, and New Hampshire. In each state, the Republican candidates were behind in the polls the day before the election, then proceeded to win their elections by 3 to 5 percent, according to election officials. Consequently, control of the Senate passed to the Republicans, giving them control of Congress, since they already had a majority in the House.

Three major grounds of electoral concern included: (1) not every qualified person who had registered to vote was permitted to vote (people of color were especially likely to be disenfranchised); (2) some qualified voters who went to vote did not have their votes counted at all, or they were counted inaccurately; and (3) voting machines used to count the ballots were not reliable and miscounted some ballots.

Some of the specific charges of irregularities grew out of the following election results:

- For Colorado Senate:
  November 3 poll by MSNBC/Zogby—
    Tom Strickland (D) 53%; Wayne Allard (R) 44%
  November 5 Diebold Electronic Voting Machines results—
    Tom Strickland (D) 46%; Wayne Allard (R) 51%
- For Minnesota Senate:
  November 3 poll by *Minneapolis Star-Tribune*—
    Walter Mondale (D) 46%; Norm Coleman (R) 41%
  November 5 Diebold Electronic Voting Machines results—
    Walter Mondale (D) 47%; Norm Coleman (R) 50%
- For Georgia Senate:
  November 1 poll by *Atlanta Journal-Constitution*—
    Max Cleland (D) 49%; Saxby Chambliss (R) 44%
  November 5 Diebold Electronic Voting Machines results—
    Max Cleland (D) 46%; Saxby Chambliss (R) 53%
- For Georgia Governor:
  November 1 poll by *Atlanta Journal-Constitution*/WSB-TV of eight
  hundred likely voters—
    Roy Barnes (D) 51%; Sonny Perdue (R) 40%
  November 5 Diebold Electronic Voting Machines results—
    Roy Barnes (D) 46%; Sonny Perdue (R) 51%[284]

In jurisdictions using electronic voting machines, concern was sharpened by the fact that the machines did not produce paper receipts that could be used to check the machines' results. Additional concern arose because election officials stopped taking exit polls, and local media exit polls did not produce the same results as the voting officials announced. These concerns were heightened by the fact that the owners of the companies that manufacture voting machines were described as "well-known Right-wing Republicans."[285]

## Report 12.2:  Wilson Stated Administration Used Information Known To Be False

In July 2003, Joseph C. Wilson, who helped direct African policy for the National Security Council (under President Bill Clinton), said, "Some of the intelligence related to Iraq's nuclear weapons program was twisted to exaggerate the Iraqi threat." He said that it was his experience in Africa that led him to play a small role in the effort to verify information about Africa's suspected link to Iraq's nonconventional weapons programs.

In February 2002, officials at the Central Intelligence Agency (CIA) had informed Wilson that Vice President Dick Cheney's office had questions about a particular intelligence report. "While I never saw the report, I was told that it referred to a memorandum of agreement that documented the sale of uranium yellowcake—a form of lightly processed ore—by Niger to Iraq in the late 1990's. The agency officials asked if I would travel to Niger to check the story so they could provide a response to the vice president's office."

While in Africa, Wilson met with Ambassador Barbro Owens-Kirkpatrick at the embassy. The ambassador told Wilson that the embassy staff always kept a close eye on Niger's uranium business, that she already knew about the allegations of uranium sales to Iraq, and that she felt she had already debunked the allegations in her reports to Washington.

Wilson spent the next eight days in meetings with people associated with Niger's uranium business. "It did not take long to conclude that it was highly doubtful that any such transaction had ever taken place." The night before Wilson left Niger, he briefed the ambassador on his findings, which were consistent with her own. He also shared his conclusions with members of her staff. "In early March 2002 I arrived in Washington and promptly provided a detailed briefing to the CIA. I later shared my conclusions with the State Department African Affairs Bureau," Wilson stated.

In September 2002, the British Government published a "white paper" asserting that Saddam Hussein and his unconventional arms posed an immediate danger. As evidence, the report cited Iraq's attempts to purchase uranium from an African country. In January 2003, President Bush, citing the British dossier, repeated the charges about Iraqi efforts to buy uranium from Africa. One of the pieces of evidence used to support this assertion was documents, allegedly printed on a Nigerian-Government letterhead, detailing Iraqi attempts to purchase the uranium.

*New Yorker* journalist Seymour Hersh reported that when the International Atomic Energy Agency inspected these documents, it took them "only a few hours" to determine that they were forgeries. Hersh further wrote that "Forged documents and false accusations have been an element in US and British policy toward Iraq at least since the fall of 1997, after an impasse over U.N. inspections."[286]

Commenting on the Bush Administration's assertions that Iraq possessed WMD, Joseph Wilson wrote, "[Bush's] conclusion was not borne out by the facts as I understood them. The vice president's office asked a serious question. I was asked to help formulate the answer. I did so, and I have every confidence that the answer I provided was circulated to the appropriate officials within our government.

"The question now is how that answer was or was not used by our political leadership. If my information was deemed inaccurate, I understand. If, however, the information was ignored because it did not fit certain preconceptions about Iraq, then a legitimate argument can be made that we went to war under false pretenses."[287]

On July 8, 2003, the White House formally admitted that President Bush overstated Saddam Hussein's alleged efforts to obtain uranium for nuclear arms. Specifically at issue was a line in Bush's State of the Union speech in January 2003, when he alleged: "The British government has learned that Saddam Hussein recently sought significant quantities of uranium from Africa."[288]

On July 9, 2003, former Ambassador Wilson said, "This is not some minor dispute over a footnote to history, but rather raises the possibility of one of the most egregious misrepresentations by a US Administration. What could be more cynical and impeachable than fabricating a threat of rogue nations or terrorists acquiring nuclear weapons and using that to sell a war?"[289]

Also see the next report.

### Report 12.3: Investigation of Administration Leak of CIA Agent's Identity

On July 14, 2003, two senior Bush Administration officials told conservative columnist Robert Novak that Wilson's wife, Valerie Plame, was an undercover CIA operative. Such public revelations of an intelligence agent's identity are illegal under the Intelligence Identities Protection Act of 1982 because they threaten the security of the agent.[290] Wilson charged that the exposure of his wife's position was an act of vengeance by the Bush Administration against him because of his op-ed piece in the *New York Times* on July 6, 2003, alleging that the Bush Administration used information known to be false regarding Iraq's possession of Weapons of Mass Destruction (Report 12.2). [291]

On October 1, 2003, the White House announced that its staff had begun to go through records and telephone logs in search of any information relevant to the investigation by the Justice Department and the FBI into the disclosure of Plame's identity. No facts or names were released during the first six months of the investigation.[292]

On January 2, 2004, then attorney general John Ashcroft recused himself from participation in the Department of Justice probe and appointed US Attorney Patrick J. Fitzgerald as special prosecutor for the case. On March 6, a federal grand jury impaneled to investigate the revelation of Plame's CIA identity and to bring charges against those found culpable began to subpoena records of July 2003 contacts between the White House and over two dozen journalists and news media outlets. The grand jury also issued a subpoena for Air Force One telephone call logs, in an effort to determine who may have been responsible for leaking Plame's CIA identity to the press.[293] On June 3, President Bush consulted a lawyer about representing him were he to be called before the grand jury.[294]

## Report 12.4: 9/11 Widow Files RICO Lawsuit Against Bush

Ellen Mariani is the widow of Louis Neil Mariani, who died in the airplane that struck the South Tower of the World Trade Center on 9/11. On November 26, 2003, she and her lawyer, Philip J. Berg, filed an amended complaint in the US District Court for the Eastern District of Pennsylvania (*Mariani v. Bush*, Case No. 03–5273). The complaint alleged that President Bush, Vice President Cheney, then attorney general Ashcroft, and Secretary of Defense Rumsfeld had knowledge/warnings of 9/11; failed to warn or take steps to prevent the attacks; and were covering up the truth of 9/11 and, therefore, violated the laws of the United States. The suit was filed under the Racketeer Influenced and Corrupt Organizations Act (RICO–18 U.S.C. § 1961).

Attorney Berg issued a press release stating, "Mrs. Mariani was the first victim's family member to bring civil action regarding the events of 9/11 against United Airlines. Since then the truth of 9/11 has not been forthcoming and Mrs. Mariani, for the good of her country, now seeks the truth via this courageous action under the RICO Act."

The sixty-two-page complaint also alleged that the defendants were liable to answer for failing to act to prevent the murder of Mrs. Mariani's husband and for obstructing justice in the aftermath of these criminal acts and omissions.[295]

Among questions that Mrs. Mariani wanted answered were:

- "Why did your brother Jeb [the Governor of Florida] go to the offices of the Hoffman Aviation School and order that flight records and files be removed? These files were then put on a C130 government cargo plane and flown out of the country. Where were they taken and who ordered it done?"
- "Why were 29 pages of the 9/11 committee [Joint Congressional Intelligence Committee Inquiry] report personally censored at your request?"[296]

Mrs. Mariani said that President Bush used a long-standard operating procedure of invoking national security and executive privilege claims to suppress the lawsuit. She also said that she would present compelling evidence that will prove that Bush failed to act to prevent 9/11, knowing the attacks would lead the United States to an "International War on Terror" and would benefit the defendants both financially and politically.

Mrs. Mariani announced plans to call as witnesses former federal employees with firsthand knowledge of and expertise on military intelligence and other matters. This would support the underlying RICO Act foundational basis to prove that the defendants engaged in a "pattern of criminal activity and obstruction of justice" in violation of the public trust and laws of the United States for personal and financial gains.[297]

## Report 12.5: National Commission Issued Report on 9/11

1. In late 2001, Congress members proposed authorizing a committee to investigate the September 11, 2001, attacks. The Bush Administration argued against it. In January 2002, both President Bush and Vice President Cheney personally asked Senate majority leader Tom Daschle to limit Congressional investigation into the events of September 11, saying that "a wide-reaching inquiry could distract from the government's war on terrorism."[298]

In mid-February 2002, the two houses of Congress, controlled by different parties, responded by setting up the Joint Congressional Intelligence Committee Inquiry to be chaired by Florida Democrat Bob Graham, with Florida Republican Porter Goss to serve as vice chair.

The Joint Committee petitioned the Bush Administration for access to National Security Council documents. The Administration denied the request, stating that the information was outside the scope of the investigation. In July 2003, the Joint Congressional Committee issued its report. The investigation had been limited to intelligence failures. The Report put most of the blame on the intelligence agencies and very little on the Bush Administration. As a consequence, some argued that the Committee's final report "represented the results of engineering by the Bush administration to produce a report that minimized political damage."[299]

2. In May 2002, the families of some of those killed in the 9/11 attacks began to push for an Independent Commission with a much wider scope than the Joint Committee inquiry. Kristen Breitweiser, one of the New Jersey widows who banded together to lobby for a new commission, said, "If my husband had been killed in a car accident there would have been an investigation immediately. This was 3,000 people. We just assumed it would happen."

The Administration continued to argue against an Independent Commission. On May 19, 2002, Cheney told FOX News, "I think it's the wrong way to go." He claimed that national security concerns trumped the families' appeals. Many lawmakers from both parties made statements indicating their outrage at the Administration's position and said the benefits of a wide-ranging investigation would detail the intelligence failures that permitted the attacks. It was reported that many people believed that the real motivation behind the White House position was its desire to avoid embarrassing revelations about what it knew and failed to do to prevent the tragedy on 9/11.

On November 14, 2002, the Administration finally agreed to a compromise satisfying White House specifications: the President would appoint the chair of the Commission, and six out of ten members of the Commission would be needed to issue a subpoena. Supporters of a new investigation got some concessions: the Commission would have eighteen months to complete the probe; six months longer than the Administration wanted but less than the two years asked for by the families.[300]

This independent "National Commission on Terrorist Attacks Upon the United States" was tasked to include an inquiry into the causes of the attacks on 9/11, the US response to terrorism, and (more generally) diplomacy, immigration, commercial aviation, and the flow of assets to terrorist organizations.[301]

Bush selected Henry Kissinger to chair the Independent National Commission. This immediately led to a flurry of negative reactions. Kissinger resigned after less than three weeks on the job. The White House then selected Thomas Kean, former Governor of New Jersey.[302] The 9/11 Commission requested documents from the White House, the CIA, the Department of Defense, and the FBI. These bodies were slow to respond.

On October 27, 2003, Senator Joseph Lieberman (D-CT), coauthor of the legislation that created the Commission, said he would urge the 9/11 Commission to take the Administration to court if it continued to refuse to turn over the documents.[303]

In November 2003, 9/11 Commissioner Max Cleland, former US Senator, stated, "As each day goes by, we [on the 9/11 Commission] learn that this government knew a whole lot more about these terrorists before September 11 than it has ever admitted." He also stated that the Commission's investigation had been deliberately compromised. Cleland left the Kean Commission shortly thereafter.[304]

3. On June 16, 2004, the Commission issued a preliminary report based on research and interviews by its staff. This report found:

- "No credible evidence" of a link between Iraq and al Qaeda in regards to the 9/11 attacks.
- Although Osama Bin Laden requested arms and support from Iraqi intelligence agents in 1994, there was no evidence that the government of Iraq gave such aid.[305]

On June 17, 2004, the *New York Times* stated in an editorial that "it's hard to imagine how the commission investigating the 2001 terrorist attacks could have put it more clearly yesterday: there was never any evidence of a link between Iraq and Al Qaeda, between Saddam Hussein and Sept. 11. Now President Bush should apologize to the American people, who were led to believe something different. . . . There are two unpleasant alternatives: either

Mr. Bush knew he was not telling the truth, or he has a capacity for politically motivated self-deception that is terrifying in the post-9/11 world."[306]

4. On July 22, 2004, the 9/11 Kean Commission issued its final unanimous report on 9/11. The Commission:

- faulted both the Clinton and Bush Administrations for "[failing] to grasp the gravity of the threat from Al Qaeda before the September 11, 2001, attacks and [leaving] counterterrorism efforts to a disparate collection of uncoordinated, underfinanced and dysfunctional government agencies";[307]
- called on the Government to institute reforms of its foreign and domestic intelligence operations.
- recommended creating a Cabinet-level office of "National Intelligence Director," who would control the budgets of all fifteen federal agencies and oversee the efforts of both the CIA and the FBI; and
- proposed that Congress create a joint House-Senate Committee on Intelligence, which would have budget authority over all US intelligence agencies.[308]

5. On July 23, 2004, a group called "9/11 Citizens Watch" released a sixty-four page critique of the Kean Commission and its investigatory process, criticizing the failure of the Commission:

- to release the full, unredacted transcripts of various interviewees, including Dick Cheney and George W. Bush;
- to obtain sworn public testimony from Bush or Cheney, who would only agree to testify one time, together and in private, and not under oath;
- to address differences in the chronology of the events of 9/11 (the "timeline") initially issued by NORAD (North American Aerospace Defense Command) and other sources right after 9/11 from the chronology that NORAD gave the Commission; and
- to address the loss of forensic evidence after 9/11, including the destruction of audio recordings and surveillance-camera footage.

The group also criticized the refusal of the Commission:

- to insist on recordings or transcripts of the private interview sessions it held, as well as the White House censoring of notes taken during these sessions before the notes were released to the public;
- to use its subpoena power to obtain testimony;
- to include any of the family members of 9/11 victims on their panel as

well as its refusal to address almost all of the questions family members had posed to it; and

- to admit facts such as that several of the named suspects were using the IDs and photos of people still living, as noted by the BBC and other mainstream media.

Additionally, the group criticized the commission about:

- the cancellation of certain important public hearings;
- its acceptance of a deal with the White House which radically limited its access to White House documents that it had requested;
- the appointment to the Commission of people with personal and family connections to the airline and oil industries; and
- the appointment of Philip Zelikow as Executive Director of the Commission because of his ongoing deep-seated ties to the Bush Administration. (He had also coauthored a book with Condoleezza Rice.)[309]

On July 30, 2004, Senator Mark Dayton (D-MN), during a Senate Governmental Affairs Committee hearing, charged that the timeline presented by NORAD and the FAA in the Commission report was not the same as that made public soon after the 9/11 attacks.[310]

On August 1, whistle-blower Sibel Edmonds, a former FBI translator who was hired shortly after 9/11 to translate intelligence gathered over the previous year related to the 9/11 attacks, objected to the report in an open letter to the Commission. Edmonds had testified before the Commission, but she could find no trace of her testimony in the Report. She pinpointed grave problems with the FBI's mishandling of 9/11-related information and said, "I find your report seriously flawed in its failure to address serious intelligence issues that I am aware of, which have been confirmed, and which as a witness to the commission, I made you aware of. Thus, I must assume that other serious issues that I am not aware of were in the same manner omitted from your report. These omissions cast doubt on the validity of your report and therefore on its conclusions and recommendations."[311]

The Kean 9/11 Commission paid PR agency Edelman Public Relations Worldwide $194,000 to promote its report. Commissioners went on the road across the country to publicize it. It quickly became a nationwide best-seller. Buyers were quoted as saying, "It's probably the most important document that will come out in my lifetime."[312] One week after the report was issued, on August 2, 2004, President Bush charged Congress with creating the proposed position of National Intelligence Director and a "Center For Counterterrorism." Bush urged that the position be appointed by, and report directly to, the President, and suggested Rep. Porter Goss (R-FL) for the position.

Some commentators saw the move to integrate foreign and domestic spying as a threat to civil liberties in the United States, particularly having the CIA participating in domestic intelligence. Ray McGovern, a twenty-seven-year career analyst with the CIA and cofounder of Veteran Intelligence Professionals for Sanity, said that the FBI was designed to work under the rule of law of the United States, while the CIA was not, and that the position of National Intelligence Director would have more power than J. Edgar Hoover had, "and that's pretty scary." Many in Washington criticized Porter Goss's nomination; McGovern labeled Goss "a shill for the Bush Administration."[313]

## Report 12.6: Waxman Report Exposes Administration's Misleading Statements

On March 16, 2004, the minority staff of the Committee on Government Reform of the US House of Representatives prepared a report for Rep. Henry A. Waxman (D-CA) chronicling 237 misleading statements made by senior members of the Bush Administration relating to the US invasion and occupation of Iraq.

Congressman Waxman requested the report after the United States failed to discover weapons of mass destruction that the administration repeatedly cited as proof of the imminent, deadly threat the Hussein regime presented to US citizens and interests at home and abroad. Among the most misleading statements cited are the following:

- On October 2, 2002, President Bush stated in a speech, "On its present course, the Iraqi regime is a threat of unique urgency . . . it has developed weapons of mass death." According to the Waxman report, "This statement was misleading because it suggested that Iraq posed an urgent threat despite the fact that the US intelligence community had deep divisions and divergent points of view regarding Iraq's weapons of mass destruction." As Director of Central Intelligence George Tenet noted in February 2004, "Let me be clear: analysts differed on several important aspects of these programs and those debates were spelled out in the Estimate. They never said there was an 'imminent' threat."
- On November 14, 2002, Secretary of Defense Donald Rumsfeld stated in an interview with Infinity CBS Radio, "Now, transport yourself forward a year, two years, or a week, or a month, and if Saddam Hussein were to take his weapons of mass destruction and transfer them, either use them himself, or transfer them to the al Qaeda, and somehow the al Qaeda were to engage in an attack on the United States, or an attack on US forces overseas, with a weapon of mass

destruction you're not talking about 300, or 3,000 people potentially being killed, but 30,000, or 100,000 . . . human beings."

The Committee on Government Reform staff wrote that this statement was misleading: "by evoking the specter of thousands of deaths in a time frame as short as a week, or a month, it suggested that Iraq posed an urgent threat."

- On March 16, 2003, Vice President Dick Cheney said on the television program *Meet the Press*, "He's had years to get good at it and we know he has been absolutely devoted to trying to acquire nuclear weapons. And we believe he has, in fact, reconstituted nuclear weapons."

The Waxman report claims that this statement was misleading, "because it failed to acknowledge the intelligence community's deep division on the issue of whether Iraq was actively pursuing its nuclear program."[314]

## Report 12.7: US Office of Strategic Influence Proposed to Issue Lies

On February 20, 2002, the BBC reported that the Pentagon set up a new office called the Office of Strategic Influence (OSI), the admitted aim of which is to influence public opinion abroad.[315] In February 2002, the *New York Times* reported that the Pentagon was "developing plans to provide news items, possibly even false ones, to foreign media organizations."[316] This news was met with outrage. Within a week the Pentagon closed down the OSI.[317]

According to Fairness and Accuracy in Reporting (FAIR): "The plan was troubling for many reasons: it was profoundly undemocratic; it would have put journalists' lives at risk by involving them in Pentagon disinformation, and it is almost certain that any large-scale disinformation campaign directed at the foreign press would have led, sooner or later, to a falsified story being picked up by the US media."

In a media briefing on November 18, 2002, Defense Secretary Donald Rumsfeld told reporters, "And then there's the Office of Strategic Influence. You may recall that . . . I went down the next day and said, 'Fine, if you want to savage this thing, fine; I'll give you the corpse. There's the name. You can have the name, but I'm going to keep doing every single thing that needs to be done and I have."[318]

## Report 12.8:  Bush Administration Agencies Lied About Ground Zero Dangers

"Many hundreds of people in New York City are sick today because of exposure to the pollution from the September 11, 2001 attack on the World Trade Center." These are the opening words in the dramatic, carefully researched 184-page report, "Pollution and Deception at Ground Zero," by Suzanne Mattei for the Sierra Club, issued in Fall 2004. It is based on hundreds of interviews with firefighters, rescue/recovery workers, service restoration workers, privately hired dust cleanup workers, nearby residents, employees of small businesses, students at neighborhood schools and colleges, and parents and doctors of newborn babies.

The Report describes the problems of the men and women who worked in the cleanup or policing of the area as well as the problems of nearby residents. It presents the facts and research of scores of top-notch researchers, conclusions as to what the US agencies did not do that they should have done for the people working at and near Ground Zero after 9/11, and recommendations for actions that must be taken now to prevent a similar tragedy in the future.

The Report describes the types of hazards, both well known and little known but knowable. Then it continues:

> The Bush Administration failed to obtain and provide health risk information to limit the harm from the toxic aftermath of the attack.
>
> - This Pollution Was Not Completely 'New'—Federal Agencies Already Had an Extensive Expert Knowledge Base
> - EPA Misrepresented the Meaning of Asbestos Test Results by Knowingly Mischaracterizing Its Own Technical Detection Limits as Health Standards
> - The White House Council on Environmental Quality Provided Misleading Data to US Senators While Implying that Most Lower Manhattan Homes Were Not Asbestos-contaminated
> - EPA Did Not Find Health Hazards Because It Did Not Look for Them—PAHs, Asbestos, Ultra-fine Particles, Indoor Contamination
> - The Federal Administration Failed at Least a Dozen Times to Correct Its Improper Assurances of Safety Even After More Data on Health Risks Became Known
> - Both the Federal Emergency Management Agency (FEMA) and the EPA Assured Residents that They Could Just Clean Up the Contaminated WTC Dust Themselves—Instead of Warning Them Against It. The Federal Administration Failed to Give Special Warnings for Children and People with Certain Diseases—Who Are More Vulnerable to the Effects of Pollution.

The Report maintains that the failure of the federal government to warn the public against the pollution cannot be justified, claiming that the Bush

Administration seemed to place reopening Wall Street above public safety. The Administration has continued to refuse to disclose who engineered the cover-up of the dangers. The Government chose not to enforce its occupational safety and health standards at Ground Zero and failed to respond properly to the toxic release as a terrorist attack. One of the most important sections of the Report warns that the Bush Administration plans to implement its mistakes at Ground Zero into national policy by eliminating OSHA's enforcement role in future terrorist attacks and weakening cleanup standards.

The Report describes very specific problems faced by rescue and recovery workers, including the inadequate safety gear of low-income, privately hired dust and debris cleanup workers. Some were even denied permission to protect themselves. Some owners of small businesses had trouble convincing their insurers of their need for coverage to pay for cleanup. New exposure to indoor WTC dust may still occur and be particularly dangerous to children.

The Report states that many hundreds of people are suffering adverse health effects from exposure, and warns that victims will continue to need help after the WTC Medical Monitoring Program stops being funded after five years. This is particularly serious because many area employees are uninsured.

On June 3, 2004, Det. John R. Walcott, of the narcotics division of the NYPD, who has terminal cancer, filed a personal injury lawsuit with his wife for damages caused by his work at Ground Zero. The defendants are the City of New York, Silverstein and Trade Center Properties, Bovis (and other) Lend Lease companies, Turner (and other) Construction companies, and Consolidated Edison companies—forty-one in all. Richard J. Volpe, thirty-six, along with his partner who has kidney disease, filed a similar suit (Paul J. Napoli, Esq., e-mail to the MCLI, Sept. 24, 2004.)

On September 10, 2004, eight hundred people, including many members of police unions, who had worked at the WTC, filed a similar class action suit against similar defendants. Plaintiffs were represented by Worby, Croner, and Edelman as well as Napoli Bern. Many suits were brought because of diseases. The defendants include airport security companies, the Port Authority of New York and New Jersey, and the Environmental Protection Agency (EPA).[319] The suits will be in the pretrial phase for many months or, perhaps, years.

The Report concludes with a series of Recommendations:

THE BUSH ADMINISTRATION MUST RESTORE TRUST IN ITS AGENCIES CHARGED WITH PROTECTING HEALTH AND SAFETY
   I. The Federal Government must Act Now to Prevent More Harm from Its Failure to Ensure Proper Clean-up of the WTC Contamination.

    II. The Federal Government Must Provide Medical Monitoring and Treatment as Needed for Those Who Suffer Health Effects or Are at Risk From Exposure to WTC Pollution—Especially Given Its Own Failure to Warn About the Hazards.

    III. The Bush Administration Must Issue a Retraction of Its Safety Assurances, Disclose Who Suppressed the 9/11 Health Warnings and Take Strong Measures to Ensure that This Does Not Occur in Any Future National Emergency.

    A. The Bush Administration Must Reveal the Top Official Involved in Altering the EPA Statements—and that Official Should Be Censured to Send a Clear Message that Failing to Warn the Public Truthfully About Health Hazards Is Unacceptable.

    B. The Administration Must Work with Ground Zero-affected Communities, Labor Unions and Environmental Health Groups to Develop Effective National Policies and Practices that Promote Truthfulness in Communication of Health Hazards from National Emergencies and Proper Response Actions

    IV. The Bush Administration Must Abandon Plans to Eliminate Health and Safety Enforcement Protection for Those Who Respond to Terrorist Attacks and Other National Emergencies.

And see Report 29.2.

## Report 12.9: US Lawmakers Turn to the UN and the Government Accountability Office on 2004 Election

In June 2004, Florida Circuit Judge Nikki Clark ruled in favor of *CNN* and other media organizations after they sued in the attempt to see copies of the list that was intended to keep more than 47,000 "suspected felons" from voting in the 2004 elections. The list included the names of 28,025 registered Democrats; 9,521 registered Republicans; 24,197 Whites; 22,084 Blacks; and 61 Hispanics. Historically, Florida's large Cuban population tends to vote Republican. On July 12, 2004, Florida Secretary of State Hood announced that Florida was going to scrap the list.[320]

Without a statewide list of suspected ex-felons, all of Florida's forty-seven county supervisors were left to come up with their own lists of former felons in their counties who should not be allowed to vote.[321]

On July 1, 2004, Rep. Barbara Lee (D-CA), a member of the Congres-

sional Black Caucus, and twelve other members of the US House of Representatives asked UN Secretary-General Kofi Annan to monitor the 2004 US
presidential election. Their main concern: Experts have concluded that over
half of the votes that went uncounted nationwide during the last election
were cast by 'nonwhite voters.'"

The letter to the Secretary-General stated:

> Given the deeply troubling events of the 2000 election and the growing con-
> cerns about the lack of necessary reforms and potential for abuse in the 2004
> election, we believe that the engagement of international election monitors
> has the potential to expedite the necessary reform as well as reduce the likeli-
> hood of questionable practices and voter disenfranchisement on Election
> Day. . . . In addition, we believe that international oversight is critical in this
> election not only because of the role the US has in the world, but also because
> the issues related to the methodology of elections inside the United States,
> such as the use of electronic and paperless voting technology, are likely to
> have international impact. The danger that these methodologies could
> become a standard to be exported and emulated involves broader issues of
> democracy that should be of concern to the United Nations and the interna-
> tional community as a whole. (Letter from Rep. Barbara Lee to the Honor-
> able Kofi Annan, Secretary-General of the United Nations, July 1, 2004)

UN policy prohibits the body from observing a nation's election unless
asked by the country's government, "not just a few elected officials," UN
spokeswoman Marie Okabe said. The General Assembly would have to
approve the monitoring.[322]

On July 8, 2004, Rep. Bernice Johnson (D-TX) and other Congressional
colleagues wrote a letter to Secretary of State Colin Powell asking him to
formally request that the UN monitor the election. The letter stated:

> Unofficially, reports indicate that the UN has denied our request because it
> was not submitted by the 'national government.' Therefore, in the interest
> of ensuring democracy and transparency in our electoral process, we are
> asking that you officially make the request to the UN for election observers.
> The UN did not question the merits of our request or imply that it is not
> needed. Reports indicate that the denial is based on procedural grounds
> only. . . . As you are aware, Ambassador Stephan M. Minikes, Chief of Mis-
> sion, US Delegation to the Organization for Security and Cooperation in
> Europe [OSCE] in Vienna invited the OSCE Office for Democratic Insti-
> tutions and Human Rights [ODIHR] to observe the November 5, 2002
> general elections. At the request of the Department of State, the ODIHR
> deployed an Election Assessment Mission to the US from October 30 to
> November 7, 2002. That mission submitted a report dated November 5,
> 2002 on the shortcomings of the 2000 election, remedial measures adopted
> for the 2002 election, and recommendations for improvement for 2004

elections. (Letter from Rep. Bernice Johnson to the Honorable Colin Powell, US Secretary of State, July 8, 2004)

The other Congressional signers of the original UN letters included Democrats Julia Carson (IN), Jerrold Nadler (NY), Edolphus Towns (NY), Joseph Crowley (NY), Carolyn B. Maloney (NY), Raul Grijalva (AZ), Corrine Brown (FL), Elijah E. Cummings (MD), Danny K. Davis (IL), Michael M. Honda (CA), and Barbara Lee (CA). On July 15, 2004, the US House of Representatives approved Rep. Steve Buyer's (R-IN) amendment to the 2005 foreign aid bill, blocking UN involvement in US elections by barring any US funds being used by the UN to monitor US elections. The vote was 243–161 with 33 Democrats joining 210 Republicans.[323]

During the following week, Corrine Brown (D-FL) announced that the Democratic Institutions and Human Rights Office of the Organization for Security and Cooperation in Europe [OSCE] confirmed that it would be present in the United States, specifically in Florida, on Election Day 2004. State election authorities in Florida announced that such observers would not be allowed access to the voting process and would have to remain at a distance of more than fifty feet from the polls.[324] Then Secretary of State Powell did not answer the Representatives' letter.

Starting on November 5, 2004, six leading members of the US House of Representatives acted on charges of election fraud brought by concerned citizens throughout the country. The Ranking Members of the Judiciary Committee and the Subcommittees on Crime, Terrorism, and Homeland Security; on the Constitution; and on Commercial and Administrative Law wrote two "urgent" letters requesting that the Government Accountability Office "immediately undertake an investigation of the efficacy of voting machines and new technologies used in the 2004 election . . . and what we can do in the future to improve our election systems." Representatives John Conyers, Robert C. Scott, Jerrold Nadler, Melvin Watt, Robert Wexler, and Rush Holt then requested that the Comptroller General of the US review and evaluate a sampling of more than 30,000 complaints listed on https://voteprotect.org/index.php?display =EIRMapNation&tab=ALL (accessed December 13, 2004) and 265 specific complaints from Broward County, FL; Cuyahoga and Warren Counties, OH; Sarper County, NE; Guilford County, NC; and others, reported on at http://www.votersunite .org/electionproblems.asp ?sort=date&selectstate=ALL &selectproblemtype=ALL (accessed December 13, 2004). These Representatives were soon joined by other Representatives and the GAO announced it would make an investigation.

Nongovernmental Organizations can cite these Congressional letters to support their mission of nonpartisan political action, even when it requires reporting human rights violations by specific Government officials and political parties that may attack them.

On December 8, 2004, Conyers chaired a Judiciary Democratic Forum on Preserving Democracy, "What Went Wrong in Ohio?," with several Congress members spelling out violations of the voting rights of African American and low income citizens. People active in organizations that worked frantically in the election described specific people and groups whose voting rights they had seen being violated. Several participants insisted that the issue would not be over until Congress met in January 2005 to vote to accept the ballots of the Electoral College. For a list of participants and statements made, see http://www.house.gov/judiciary_democrats/voteforum .html (accessed December 13, 2004).

On December 14, 2004, the Berkeley City Council adopted Resolution 62, 762–N.S. Supporting the Request that the Government Accountability Office Immediately Undertake an Investigation of Voting Irregularities in the 2004 Elections. After seven "Whereas" clauses describing the problems, the Resolution supports the work of Representative Conyers and expresses Berkeley's endorsement of seventeen "measures to improve access to and fairness of elections" covering all known serious proposals for election reform:

1. Democracy Day, a holiday for voting, or moving elections to weekends.
2. Early voting in all jurisdictions throughout the United States.
3. A voter-verifiable paper record of every vote cast.
4. Consistent national standards for security, including physical and electronic security, of election systems, including tallying systems.
5. Mandatory, automatic recounts of a statistically significant percentage of votes cast.
6. Public access to computer coding that operates election systems so that such software may be widely reviewed by independent analysts.
7. Consistent national standards for the number of voting machines and poll workers per 100 voters in each precinct to ensure reasonable and uniform waiting times for all voters.
8. A requirement that the top elected official responsible for overseeing elections in each jurisdiction be elected in a nonpartisan race, and may not serve in any capacity in any political campaign other than her or his own.
9. Uniform and inclusive voter registration standards.
10. Accurate and transparent voting roll purges, based on fair and consistent national standards.

11. Uniform, reliable, and voter-friendly standards for development, distribution, collection, and counting of provisional ballots.
12. National standards for ballots that are consistently clear and minimize the likelihood of voter error.
13. Fair and uniform rules about requiring voters to produce identification to register to vote.
14. Protections to prevent minority vote suppression such as Election Day challengers turning away qualified voters or causing needless slowing of voting in minority precincts.
15. In all jurisdictions, rescinding laws that disproportionately disenfranchise minorities, such as prohibitions on allowing former felons to vote once they have completed their sentences.
16. Consistent, national standards for the distribution and return of absentee ballots to ensure timely receipt of ballots by the voters, timely return of voted ballots to election officials, and voter privacy.
17. Requiring that sample ballots be provided to all registered voters in every election.

Copies of the Resolution were sent to the County Registrar of Voters, the Secretary of State, the State Senate Majority Leader, the Berkeley Assembly member, US Representatives John Conyers and Barbara Lee, US Senators Barbara Boxer and Dianne Feinstein, and the UN High Commissioner for Human Rights.

## C. THE GOVERNMENT'S DUTY TO OBEY THE CONSTITUTION, THE LAW OF NATIONS, AND THE LAWS OF WAR

When the person elected President of the United States takes the oath of office, that person must swear or affirm "I will . . . to the best of my ability, preserve, protect and defend the Constitution of the United States." Article VI, Clause 2 of the Constitution pronounces that "all treaties . . . which shall be made, under the authority of the United States shall be the supreme law of the land." And Article I, Sec. 8, Cl. 10 specifically recognizes that the United States is bound by international law that is "the law of nations," and gives Congress, not the President, "the Power to define and punish . . . Offences against the Law of Nations."

On June 16, 2004, Phyllis Oakley, former Assistant Secretary of State for Intelligence and Research, presented a statement at the National Press Club that President Bush should not be reelected because his tenure in office was such a "complete and terrible disaster." Twenty-two former Ambassadors, two retired Generals, and two retired Admirals joined in the statement.[1]

The statement of the Diplomats and Military Commanders for Change (DMCC) summarized the record of the Bush Administration on peace and human rights issues:

> From the outset, President George W. Bush adopted an overbearing approach to America's role in the world, relying upon military might and righteousness, insensitive to the concerns of traditional friends and allies, and disdainful of the United Nations.[2]
>
> Instead of building upon America's great economic and moral strength to lead other nations in a coordinated campaign to address the causes of terrorism and to stifle its resources, the Administration, motivated more by ideology than by reasoned analysis, struck out on its own. It led the United States into an ill-planned and costly war from which exit is uncertain. It justified the invasion of Iraq by manipulation of uncertain intelligence about weapons of mass destruction, and by a cynical campaign to persuade the public that Saddam Hussein was linked to Al Qaeda and the attacks of September 11. The evidence did not support this argument.
>
> Our security has been weakened. While American airmen and women, marines, soldiers and sailors have performed gallantly, our armed forces were not prepared for military occupation and nation building. Public opinion polls throughout the world report hostility toward us. Muslim youth are turning to anti-American terrorism.
>
> Never in the two and a quarter centuries of our history has the United States been so isolated among the nations, so broadly feared and distrusted. No loyal American would question our ultimate right to act alone in our national interest; but responsible leadership would not turn to unilateral military action before diplomacy had been thoroughly explored. . . .
>
> We face profound challenges in the 21st Century: proliferation of weapons of mass destruction, unequal distribution of wealth and the fruits of globalization, terrorism, environmental degradation, population growth in the developing world, HIV/AIDS, ethnic and religious confrontations. Such problems can not be resolved by military force, nor by the sole remaining superpower alone; they demand patient, coordinated global effort under the leadership of the United States. . . .
>
> The United States suffers from close identification with autocratic regimes in the Muslim world, and from the perception of unquestioning support for the policies and actions of the present Israeli Government. To enhance credibility with Islamic peoples we must pursue courageous, energetic and balanced efforts to establish peace between Israelis and Palestinians, and policies that encourage responsible democratic reforms.
>
> The Bush Administration has shown that it does not grasp these circumstances of the new era, and is not able to rise to the responsibilities of world leadership in either style or substance. It is time for a change.[3]

Diplomats and military leaders who served under Republican and Democratic presidents signed the DMCC's Official Statement: Avis Bohlen, Assistant Secretary of State for Arms Control in 1999 and Ambassador to Bulgaria in 1996; Adm. William Crowe, Chairman of the President's Foreign Intelligence Advisory Committee in 1993 and Chairman of the Joint Chiefs of Staff in 1985; Charles Freeman, Assistant Secretary of Defense for International Security Affairs in 1993 and Ambassador to Saudi Arabia in 1989; William Harrop, Ambassador to Israel in 1991 and Ambassador to Zaire in 1987; Gen. Joseph Hoar, Commander-in-Chief of the US Central Command in 1991 and Deputy Chief of Staff of the Marine Corps in 1990; Princeton Lyman, Assistant Secretary of State for International Organization Affairs in 1997 and Ambassador to South Africa in 1992; Gen. Merrill McPeak, Chief of Staff of the Air Force in 1990 and Commander-in-Chief of the Pacific Air Forces in 1988; and twenty other former Ambassadors, Assistant Secretaries of State, Assistant Secretaries of Defense, and Air Force, Marine, and Navy Chiefs-of-Staff.[4]

The specific types of alleged violations of US domestic and international law include the duty not to send US military to bring about regime change in Afghanistan over a period of years (Reports 13.1–13.2) or in Haiti in one dramatic incident followed by denials and confusion (Report 13.3), not to send troops for invasion of Iraq (Reports 14.1–14.4), and not to support abusive regimes in Egypt, Israel, and Colombia (Reports 15.1, 15.3) or violations of World Court opinions (Reports 15.2, 17.3).

The laws related to these issues include the Human Rights and Securities Assistance Act of 1974, the Hague Conventions, the Geneva Conventions, and the opinions of the International Court of Justice (World Court).

The US military also has a set of duties to its own troops. Since 9/11, the military has been challenged to deal fairly with people who, in every era, join the military and then become conscientious objectors to participation in war (Reports 16.1–16.3).

The Bush Administration has withdrawn the United States from several treaties banning various types of weapons (Report 17.1). The Department of Defense is trying to change US nuclear weapons policies, and so is the Congress but in a different way (Report 17.2). Neither the DOD nor Congress acknowledged the unanimous opinion of the World Court that there is a duty to complete nuclear disarmament (Report 17.3). US forces used depleted uranium in Iraq (Report 17.4) and the United States is charged with contaminating Afghanistan with uranium (Report 17.5).

## 13. *NOT TO SEND MILITARY FOR REGIME CHANGE IN AFGHANISTAN OR HAITI*

Numerous legal, economic, social, cultural, and moral problems were created when the US sent military forces into Afghanistan (Reports 13.1–13.2) and Iraq. President Bush did not seek a declaration of war from Congress against a particular nation in order to achieve certain clearly stated goals when he invaded Afghanistan and Iraq. Additionally, the US Government made an ongoing commitment not to go to war with any nation or against any people when it ratified the UN Charter. Finally, a military attack on a particular national group within a sovereign state is legally governed by the laws of war even if the conflict is not technically referred to as a "war" (see Report 13.3).

Beyond the issue of the illegality of Bush's actions, the sending of soldiers to invade another nation requires an enormous amount of supplies of weapons and troops. The rate of profit on selling such weapons and supplying such soldiers can be much higher than the customary rate of profit on civilian products and supplying civilian employees. As a consequence, military action provides US corporations with opportunities for war profiteering in violation of domestic law.

Members of the Bush Administration have themselves admitted the illegality of the invasion of Iraq. Richard Perle, an influential member of the Defense Planning Board and an ardent proponent of the invasion, has since stated that, "International law . . . would have required us to leave Saddam Hussein alone," but that this would have been morally unacceptable.[5]

### Relevant Law:

U.S. Constitution: Art. I, §8, Cl. 11; Art. II, §1, Cl. 8; Art. VI, Cl. 2; First, Thirteenth, Fourteenth, Fifteenth Amendments
Human Rights and Securities Assistance, 22 U.S.C. §2034
War Crimes Act of 1986, 18 U.S.C §2441 OLD amended by War Crimes Act of 1997
UN Charter: Art. 2.3, 2.4, 55, 56
*Legal Consequences of the Construction of a Wall in the Occupied Palestinian Territories*, International Court of Justice Advisory Opinion of July 9, 2004
*Legality of the Threat or Use of Nuclear Weapons*, International Court of Justice Advisory Opinion of July 8, 1996, ¶¶105 (F) and (O).
Hague Conventions
Third and Fourth Geneva Conventions
ICCPR: Preamble, Art. 1, 2, 2.1, 3, 4, 4.2, 5-7, 18, 20, 26, 40
CERD: Art. 1, 5, 9

CAT: Art. 1, 2, 5, 19
CRC

## Report 13.1: US May Have Directly Killed 3,400 Afghans, Indirectly Killed 20,000

On Sunday, October 21, 2002, the United States began bombing Afghanistan. On that day, a thirty-eight-year-old Afghan named Maroof stated that he saw a massive fireball rising from the ground outside his Torai village. He realized that "bombs had fallen over the little cluster of houses a mile away," where his sister and other relatives lived. Once the fireball cleared away, the dead included his mother-in-law, two sisters-in-law, three brothers-in-law, and four of his sister's five young children, all under the age of eight."[6]

As of February 2004, Prof. Marc Herold of the University of New Hampshire, who has studied Afghan casualty rates extensively, estimated that the number of Afghans killed as a result of American bombings had reached 3,421. This number is in addition to the 6,158 Afghans wounded by aerial bombing in the same time period and does not include deaths due to uranium poisoning that allegedly resulted from US use of depleted uranium munitions.[7]

It has been supremely difficult for investigators to accurately estimate the number of "noncombat" deaths, due in part to the Muslim practice of burying the dead within twenty-four hours and the lack of time and opportunity needed to adequately interview survivors and check their stories. However, it has been estimated by various NGOs that as many as twenty thousand additional Afghans may have been killed as an indirect consequence of the US military intervention.

According to the British *Guardian*, US intervention effected the humanitarian situation in Afghanistan in three main ways: (1) it caused massive internal dislocation, (2) it disrupted aid supplies to Afghans who were depending on emergency food and water relief, and (3) it provoked renewed fighting between the Taliban and the Northern Alliance. As a consequence, from mid-September to mid-December 2001, there occurred huge, unrecorded population movements of internally displaced people (IDPs). Of the two hundred thousand Afghan IDPs who found their way to refugee camps, it has been estimated by NGOs such as the Massachusetts-based Commonwealth Institute that as many as sixteen hundred died from malnutrition or exposure from September to the end of December.

If the approximately one million IDPs outside the camps who were not provided with even minimal international aid suffered comparable death rates, another eight thousand Afghans may have died preventable deaths in the same time period. Such statistics do not reflect the effect the US offensive had on the five million Afghans who remained at home during the war. These people may have suffered as many as ten thousand deaths as a consequence of the disruption of relief aid and the escalation of intra-Afghan fighting.[8]

## Report 13.2: US Bombing Killed Children in Afghanistan

On June 29, 2002, the International Committee of the Red Cross (ICRC) issued a warning to children in Afghanistan not to play with or around the yellow unexploded cluster bombs that litter the countryside. "The size and color of the bomblets are unfortunately very attractive, especially to children," read an ICRC newsletter. "Do not touch or play with them. As they are unstable, do not go near or throw anything at them." It is estimated that millions of unexploded munitions are scattered around the country, a remnant of twenty-three years of almost nonstop warfare that has recently culminated in large-scale US air strikes against suspected Taliban and al Qaeda positions. Approximately one hundred Afghans are killed each month by such weapons. It is estimated that of those killed, 70 percent are civilians, and 10 percent are children under fourteen.[9]

In early July 2002, the US Air Force bombed a wedding party in the Uruzgan province of Afghanistan, killing between 30 and 140 civilians, most of whom were women and children. In responding to the incident, the Pentagon stated that an AC-130 gunship and a B-52 bomber were on an air reconnaissance patrol when they reportedly came under antiaircraft fire and responded by dropping their bomb loads. A military spokesman stated later that "At least one bomb was errant. We don't know where it fell." As Afghans traditionally fire guns into the air during weddings, some reports suggested that this gunfire was mistaken by the US planes as hostile and was what led to the bombing.[10]

On December 5, 2003, bombing and secondary explosions collapsed a wall during an assault by US forces in the Paktia province in eastern Afghanistan, killing two adults and six children. US military spokesman Lt. Col. Bryan Hilferty stated afterward that "If noncombatants surround themselves with thousands of weapons and hundreds of rounds of ammunition . . . in a compound known to be used by a terrorist, we are not completely responsible for the consequences. . . . I can't guarantee that we will not injure more civilians. I wish I could."[11]

On December 6, 2003, US bombing near the city of Ghazni in southern Afghanistan killed nine children. According to military spokesman Maj. Christopher West, US forces were acting on information that a suspected terrorist, believed to be behind the murders of two foreign contractors, was hiding in the house that was bombed. Major West stated that "The coalition forces regret the loss of any innocent life."[12]

On January 28, 2004, a US air raid in the Uruzgan province, Afghanistan, killed eleven Afghan villagers, including four children. Abdul Rahman, a district chief in Uruzgan told the Associated Press that a US warplane dropped a bomb on a house in the village of Saghatho in southern Afghanistan. The eleven who were killed "were simple villagers, they were not Taliban," said Rahman. "I don't know why the US bombed this home." The provincial governor later confirmed the deaths of seven adults and four children in the attack.[13]

## Report 13.3: Bush Charged with Orchestrating Removal of President Aristide in Haiti

On September 26, 2003, Jean-Bertrand Aristide, the democratically elected president of Haiti, told the UN General Assembly that the government of France had a duty to repay Haiti $21.7 billion in reparations for three hundred years of genocide and slavery. This figure was presented by Aristide as restitution for the ninety million gold francs Haiti paid France during the nineteenth century as "compensation" for the Haitian appropriation of French plantations after the victorious Haitian revolution of 1804. Stating that French colonialism used African slaves to extract billions of dollars in material wealth from Haiti until its independence, Aristide called on the UN to assist his country in development and stabilization: "Haiti is the mother of liberty, and its sons and daughters are the product of that liberty."[14]

On January 1, 2004, Haiti celebrated its bicentennial Independence Day. Progressive organizations in the United States and around the world hailed the day as a benchmark in the progress of human liberty. In December 2003, the San Francisco Labor Council had passed a resolution honoring the Haitian bicentennial. Recognizing Haiti as the first free republic in the Americas, the Council called the abolition of slavery and the end of colonial rule "an earth-shattering development in the struggle for the emancipation of labor all over the world."[15]

In January and February 2004, a well-financed armed opposition movement demanded Aristide step down as President. The Bush Administration had announced it supported the replacement of Aristide. On March 4, 2004, US Marines landed in Haiti, and US troops led Aristide to a plane that flew him to exile in the Central African Republic. Aristide immediately claimed that the coup that drove him from Haiti was manufactured by the United States, and that he departed at the behest of the US ambassador and armed US military personnel. Aristide also claimed that any legal documents he signed relinquishing legal power as the President of Haiti were done at the demand of "US agents."[16]

On March 9, 2004, Rep. Barbara Lee (D-CA) introduced House Resolution 3919 in the House of Representatives. The bill, cosponsored by forty-nine other members as of June 14, 2004, called for the establishment of an independent commission to "examine and evaluate the role of the United States Government in the February 2004 coup d'etat in the Republic of Haiti." According to Representative Lee, "The Bush Administration's efforts in the overthrow of a democratically-elected government must be investigated. All of the evidence brought forward thus far suggests that the Administration has, in essence, carried out a form of regime change."[17]

On July 20, 2004, investigative reporter Max Blumenthal told *Democracy Now's* Amy Goodman that he believes the International Republican Institute (IRI), a federally funded nonprofit group backed by the Bush Administration, may have helped to overthrow President Aristide. The IRI is active in over fifty countries and, according to Blumenthal, "Has a penchant for backing opponents to regimes hostile to the US, specifically conservative interests." Over the past six years, the IRI has funneled $3 million into Haiti, allegedly to help destabilize the government and bring about the destruction of the Aristide regime. Stanley Lucas, the IRI's program officer for Haiti, used a $2 million grant from the US Agency for International Development to host Aristide opponents in political training sessions, then helped merge Haiti's disparate opposition groups into one big party called the Democratic Convergence (DC). US Ambassador to Haiti Brian Dean Kern found evidence that Lucas encouraged the DC to reject internationally approved power-sharing agreements with the Aristide government. Max Blumenthal alleges that Lucas had been seen with opposition leader Guy Phillipe in Ecuador in the 1990s while Phillipe, a former Haitian police chief, was being trained by US Special Forces.[18]

## 14. NOT TO SEND TROOPS FOR INVASION OF IRAQ

The US Constitution contains a clause giving Congress the power to declare war against another country. It does not mention going to war against poverty, drugs, or terrorism. After the disastrous and costly US undeclared war against Vietnam, the Congress passed the War Powers Act to provide some Congressional oversight on military actions by the President and the DOD taken without a declaration of war (50 U.S.C. §§1541–1548).

Immediately after 9/11, President Bush and other members of the Cabinet began discussing starting a war against Saddam Hussein and his regime in Iraq. On September 20, 2002, Bush asked Congress to support a possible US-led military attack on Iraq in order to topple the regime of Hussein because he was manufacturing or stockpiling weapons of mass destruction.[19]

On October 16, 2002, Congress complied with the President's request, voting 77–23 in the Senate and 296–133 in the House to authorize a unilateral US attack against Saddam Hussein's regime if other approaches failed to force Iraq to disarm.[20]

The United States did not seek (nor did it receive) approval by the UN General Assembly or the Security Council for its military actions in Iraq. During the one-month official war in Iraq in March 2003, many Iraqi civilians were killed, as well as many Iraqis carrying weapons. Many Iraqis demonstrated against US policies after the United States announced that the "war" was over. Some Iraqis threw stones; the US forces fired shots. The media reported demonstrators saying "Saddam Hussein is better than the Americans," and "Americans offer no jobs, or democracy, or security." The US military particularly targeted civilians protesting against US actions (Report 14.1).

In July 2003, while searching for Hussein's two sons, US soldiers shot at a car carrying the El Birhana family, killing everyone inside (Report 14.2).

By September 2004, more than one thousand US troops had died in Iraq as a result of the invasion that had starting in March 2003. Over twelve thousand US troops were injured so badly they had to be evacuated. These figures do not include troops suffering from Post-Traumatic Stress Syndrome, whose illnesses will only become evident in succeeding months and years (Report 14.3).

In its role as head of non-Iraq forces in Iraq, the United States participated in the selection of Iyad Allawi as interim Prime Minister. In June 2004, an Australian reporter interviewed two witnesses to Allawi personally shooting to death six men suspected of involvement in attacks against the United States and Iraqi police forces (Report 14.4).

Human Rights Watch and other US-based NGOs continue to ask the DOD and Congressional committees to investigate these and hundreds of other charges of killings and misconduct by forces under US supervision. Many also urge appeals to the UN High Commissioner for Human Rights and/or other appropriate UN bodies to investigate and report illegal actions by the United States and other forces in Iraq in order to strengthen the ability of the new Iraq governing bodies to achieve actual sovereignty. In September 2004, UN Secretary General Kofi Annan repeatedly stated that the US war in Iraq was illegal under the UN Charter.[21]

The Web site *Iraq Body Count* tracks the deaths of Iraqi civilians as reported by official agencies and the media. As of December 3, 2004, they reported that a minimum of 14,591 and a maximum of 16,771 Iraqi civilians have died. (Iraq Body Count, http://www.iraqbodycount.net accessed December 3, 2004.) The medical journal *Lancet* projected that "the death toll associated with the invasion and occupation of Iraq is probably about one hundred thousand people, and may be much higher."[22]

## Relevant Law:

U.S. Constitution: Art. I, §8, Cl. 11; Art. VI, Cl.2, First, Fifth Amendments
War Powers Act, 50 U.S.C. §§1541-1548

War Crimes Act of 1986, 18 U.S.C. §2441 as amended by War Crimes Act
  of 1987
UN Charter: Art. 2.3, 2.4, 55, 56
Hague Conventions
Third and Fourth Geneva Conventions
Nuremberg Principles
ICCPR: Art. 1, 2.1, 3, 4.2, 5, 6, 7, 9, 10, 14, 18, 26, 40
CAT: Preamble, Art. 1, 2, 4, 5, 5.2, 7, 10-16, 19
CERD
CEDAW
CRC

## Report 14.1: US Troops Open Fire, Kill Iraqi Protesters

According to news reports, on April 28, 2003, "US troops shot dead seventeen and injured seventy in Fallujah without provocation. No evidence has
emerged that Iraqis shot at the US soldiers first." Witnesses to this incident
claimed that troops from the Eighty-second Airborne Division fired without
provocation on an unarmed crowd of protesters outside a local school. In
response, the Pentagon stated that its soldiers were fired on by gunmen
among the demonstrators.

The NonGovernmental Organization Human Rights Watch raised
questions as to what actually happened, with one spokesman stating,
"Human Rights Watch believes that the information provided by US officers
in al-Fallujah regarding the scope and focus of the Commander's Inquiry, as
well as the April 29, 2003, statement by US Central Command headquarters
asserting that US troops had been fired on by twenty-five armed individuals
amid the demonstrators and on rooftops, underscores the need for a thorough, independent, and impartial investigation into these incidents. If the
required investigation is carried out by US military authorities, it should be
by a body that is fully independent and has no links to those units implicated
in the incidents or previous investigation, including the 82nd Airborne Division and the Central Command."[23]

On October 1, 2003, six months after the US Government announced
the end of the "hostilities" in Iraq and in the midst of massive unemployment, Iraqi protestors stormed a police station in Baghdad to demand jobs
with the police force. Many had paid bribes to get their names onto a
recruiting list but had not been hired. The police told the protestors that
they had no business being there and then opened fire into the crowd.

On the same day, the followers of a Shiite Muslim cleric in Baghdad
gathered outside their mosque where US forces were detaining and questioning him about allegedly inflammatory sermons. They threw stones at US

soldiers in protest. The soldiers fired warning shots over the heads of the crowd. Afterward, several Shiites warned that if they did not receive a written apology from the soldiers and Iraqi police within three days, they would turn against the US occupation.[24]

On June 18, 2003, US troops opened fire on Iraqi demonstrators during a protest outside the main gate of the presidential compound in Baghdad; Iraqi protesters later said that two demonstrators were killed. The US military claimed that a soldier opened fire after the demonstrators started throwing stones at a military convoy. Demonstrations outside the Republican Palace had been frequent since coalition forces captured the Iraqi capital in April, with protests often sparked over unpaid wages to civil servants and the army.[25]

## Report 14.2: After Iraq Invasion, US Troops Killed Thousands of Civilians

Around 6 PM on July 27, 2003, the el-Birhana family was driving toward their mosque in Baghdad. While approaching the end of an alley, the family came upon a unit of US soldiers in the process of searching for Saddam Hussein's two sons. The soldiers sprayed the car with gunfire. The entire el-Birhana family was killed instantly, along with two passengers in a car right behind theirs.

US soldiers did not allow any journalists to remain at the scene or report about the incident. Afterward several soldiers grabbed an Al-Jazeera Network journalist and took him away, then closed off the sector.[26]

In December 2003, the US occupation authority brought pressure to bear on Iraq's Health Ministry officials to halt a count of civilians killed and injured since the US-led invasion. The head of the Ministry's Statistics Department, Dr. Nagham Mohsen, said she had been summoned by the Director of Planning, Dr. Nazar Shabandar, and told to stop a survey of hospitals aimed at tallying civilian casualties. He also ordered her not to release any of the partial information that had been collected to date. Mohsen said Shabandar had been acting on behalf of Health Minister Dr. Khodeir Abbas—a member of the US-imposed Iraqi Governing Council. Moshen said that the US-led Coalition Provisional Authority (CPA) influenced this decision.

Abbas issued a statement denying that either he or the US occupation authorities had anything to do with the order. "I have no knowledge of a civilian war casualty survey even being started by the Ministry of Health, much less stopping it," he stated, adding, "The CPA did not direct me to stop any such survey."

Mohsen claims that the ministry began its survey in July 2003 by sending letters to all hospitals and clinics in Iraq, asking them to send details of civilians killed or wounded in the war. The study was reported in the media as early as August 2003 and a preliminary figure of 1,764 deaths was made public. The Pentagon has not kept (or released) a tally of Iraqi casualties. A comprehensive tally by the Associated Press based on information from about half of Iraq's hospitals put the civilian death toll at 3,240 for the month following March 20, 2003.

In October 2003, the Project on Defense Alternatives published a report based on hospital records, official US military statistics, and news reports. It estimated that between March 20 and May 1, 2003, when Bush declared the end of major combat operations, between thirty-two hundred and forty-three hundred noncombatant civilians were killed in the fighting.[27]

In December 2003, Human Rights Watch (HRW) released a report pointing out that even hospital figures would not tell the full story. "Though hospitals have records of some of the deaths in the war, a certain percentage of casualties, due to religious practices, were not taken to hospitals, not even to obtain death certificates. Finally, as in any war, in some instances, there were few if any remains by which to identify the dead."

The HRW report found that the methods of the US military and its allies had directly contributed to the high death toll. "The widespread use of cluster munitions, especially by US and UK ground forces caused at least hundreds of civilian casualties. . . . Although cluster munition strikes are particularly dangerous in populated areas, US and UK ground forces repeatedly used these weapons in attacks on Iraqi positions in residential neighborhoods."

The HRW report also criticized the United States for the indiscriminate use of air strikes. "Many of the civilian casualties from the air war occurred during US attacks targeting senior Iraqi leaders. The United States used unsound targeting methodology that relied on intercepts of satellite phones and inadequate corroborating intelligence." Satellite phone signals can provide bombing coordinates only to an accuracy of 100 meters. Based on such inaccurate information, an air strike in a built-up urban environment would put hundreds, if not thousands, of innocent people at risk.

As the HRW report noted, the Geneva Conventions not only bar direct attacks on civilians but also prohibit indiscriminate attacks. These include strikes against "military objectives and civilians or civilian objects without distinction" and those that are expected to cause civilian casualties "which would be excessive in relation to the concrete and direct military advantage anticipated."[28] On July 19, 2004, US air forces fired two missiles into a residential area of the Iraqi city of Fallujah, killing twenty-two people.[29]

### Report 14.3: Over Twelve Thousand US Casualties from Iraq Invasion

On November 14, 2003, Mark Benjamin of United Press International concluded that the total US casualties in Iraq at that time exceeded 9,200, a figure representing an increase of 3,000 noncombat medical evacuations since the first week of October 2003. The new total of 6,861 reported non-combat evacuations marked a rise of 57 percent. The Army offered no immediate explanation for the increase.

Steve Robinson, executive director of the National Gulf War Resource Center, said, "We are shocked at the dramatic increase in casualties. . . . We are especially concerned about the psychological and neurological evacuations from this war. We request a clarification of the types of illnesses people are suffering from so we do not have a repeat of the first Gulf War. We need to understand the nature and types of illnesses so scientists can determine if significant trends are occurring."[30]

As of early October 2003, the Army Surgeon General's office said that 3,915 soldiers had been evacuated from Operation Iraqi Freedom for non-combat injuries and illnesses, including 478 with psychological problems and 387 for neurological reasons. The data on noncombat evacuations included 1,628 orthopedic (bone) injuries, 831 surgeries for injuries, 289 cardiology cases, 249 gastrointestinal cases, 242 pulmonary (lung) cases, 634 evacuations for general surgery, 319 gynecological cases, and 290 urological cases. The many pulmonary evacuations included soldiers who suffered from pneumonia as part of a cluster that was investigated by the Army in August 2003, according to Army Surgeon General's Office spokeswoman Virginia Stephanakis.

The numbers do not include service members treated "in theater" or those whose illnesses—such as Post-Traumatic Stress Disorder—were not apparent until after they returned to the United States. [31] On August 8, 2004, *ABC News* reported that the Landstuhl Medical Center in Germany had already treated over twelve thousand battlefield casualties from Iraq.[32]

In late March 2004, the Pentagon issued a survey revealing that twenty-four US soldiers had committed suicide in Iraq. The survey did not take into account the additional seven suicides of US soldiers who had returned from Iraq.[33]

As of December 3, 2004, there have been 1,262 US deaths in Iraq, of which 992 were in combat, since the beginning of the invasion of Iraq on March 19, 2003. Within that same period, 9,326 US troops were wounded according to the official numbers although it is estimated that the actual number is between 15,000 and 20,000.[34]

### Report 14.4: US Appointed Ex-CIA Operative Head of Iraq After He Allegedly Murdered Six

On May 28, 2004, Iraq's US-appointed Governing Council chose Iyad Allawi to serve as the country's interim Prime Minister. On June 28, 2004, the United States "transferred sovereignty" over to the Allawi government.[35]

In the 1970s, Iyad Allawi, an Iraqi citizen trained as a neurologist and a member of Saddam Hussein's Baath Party, went to London to work as a covert agent for Iraqi intelligence. According to former CIA officer Vincent Cannisatraro, "If you're asking me if Allawi has blood on his hands from his days in London, the answer is yes, he does. He was a paid Mukhabarat [intelligence] agent for the Iraqis, and he was involved in dirty stuff."[36]

In the mid-1970s, Allawi broke from Hussein and founded the Iraqi National Accord (INA) to undermine Saddam's regime. In 1992, Allawi began to receive support and funding from the CIA, which assisted Allawi's INA in an organized bombing campaign in Baghdad in the 1990s aimed at toppling the Hussein regime. (There are conflicting reports as to whether this campaign led to any casualties.)[37]

In July of 2004, Paul McGeough, an investigative reporter for the *Sidney Morning Herald*, interviewed two Iraqi men who reported to him that in June 2004 they witnessed Iyad Allawi personally execute six men suspected of involvement in attacks against US occupation and Iraqi police forces. They said the six were handcuffed and blindfolded, then lined up in a courtyard of Baghdad's Al-Amariyah. "The prisoners were against the wall and we were standing in the courtyard when the Interior Minister [Falah al-Naqib] said that he would like to kill them all on the spot. Allawi said that they deserved worse than death—but then he pulled the pistol from his belt and started shooting them. . . . He was very close. Each was shot in the head." One eyewitness further told reporters, "Allawi wanted to send a message to his policemen and soldiers not to be scared if they kill anyone—especially, they are not to worry about tribal revenge. He said there would be an order from him and the Interior Ministry that all would be fully protected. . . . He told them: 'We must destroy anyone who wants to destroy Iraq and kill our people.'"

Five or six US citizens, members of the security team that acts as bodyguards to Allawi, were supposedly present and also witnessed the killings. While the identities of the men are unknown, it is understood that such positions are usually filled by members of the US Special Forces.[38] On July 19, 2004, Bakhtiar Amin, Iraq's Human Rights Minister, stated he would investigate the claims made in the *Herald* against Allawi. Amin stated, "I will check this and I will talk to the Prime Minister as well."[39]

## 15. NOT TO SUPPORT ABUSIVE REGIMES OR VIOLATIONS OF WORLD COURT OPINIONS

The attacks on 9/11 violated many treaties and principles of international law. The attacks did not change national or international law, or permit the US to ignore this law or to ignore treaty law. In fact, the attacks on US business and government buildings led to calls for more enforcement of national and international laws in order to avoid recurrences of 9/11.

When the United States joined the UN in 1945, it made a commitment to not support abusive regimes anywhere in the world. That is, the United States would not support any nation that behaved as Germany, Italy, and Japan had behaved under Hitler, Mussolini, and Tojo. To carry out this policy, in 1974 Congress passed the Human Rights and Security Assistance Act, requiring the State Department to make a report each year on the human rights record in each nation so that no US funds would be awarded to the government of any nation that violated human rights. However, the Act does not revoke US Government aid to human-rights-violator nations that are already receiving aid (22 U.S.C. §§ 2303 [a] [2–3]).

For example, the reports on human rights abuses in Egypt and Israel for 2003 must be compared with the budget items to fund those countries in 2003 and thereafter (Report 15.1). One of the six organs of the UN is the International Court of Justice, also known as the World Court. On July 9, 2004, the World Court issued its answer to the question asked by the General Assembly as to whether the separation wall being built by Israel in the West Bank is legal or illegal. The Court ruled (14–1) that the wall is illegal (Report 15.2).

The United States admittedly had between two hundred and three hundred troops in Colombia in 2004 in an undeclared war against two groups of Colombians known as the People's Army and the National Liberation Army. Many US citizens knowledgeable about the ongoing struggles in Colombia consider the use of US troops totally outside legal US policy (Report 15.3).

Political scientists and activists are concerned about the threat of US militarism spreading even further throughout the world. They are calling on people in the United States to question all candidates for public office on how they will uphold the rule of law. They are insisting that US delegates to UN bodies must answer the hard questions about what the US military is actually doing in so many countries. And they are insisting that no nation should receive funding in the US budget if it is guilty of gross violations of human rights against any people in its own territory or in territories it controls.

## Relevant Law:

U.S. Constitution: Art. II, §3; Art. VI, Cl. 2
Human Rights and Securities Assistance, 22 U.S.C. §2034
UN Charter: Art. 1, 12.1, 14, 23.1, 24.1, 24.2, 27.1, 32, 33, 36.3, 37.1, 37.2, 39, 41, 42, 48.1, 51, 52.3, 55, 56, 62.1, 62.2, 68, 69, 92, 93.1, 94.2, 96.1, 103
Fourth Geneva Convention of 1949
Additional Protocol I to the Geneva Conventions
Hague Convention Respecting the Laws & Customs of War on Land of 1907

Regulations annexed to the Fourth Hague Convention of 1907
ICCPR: Preamble, Art. 1-5, 6.1, 7, 9, 10, 12-14, 16-21, 26, 27, 40, 41.1, 44, 46, 47
CERD: Art. 1, 2, 3, 5, 9
CAT: Art. 1, 2, 16, 19
International Convention on the Suppression of the Financing of Terrorism, ratified by the US on June 26, 2002
International Convention for the Suppression of Terrorist Bombings, ratified by the US on June 26, 2002
ICESCR: Preamble, Art. 1, 2, 6, 11, 12, 15-17, 25
Resolutions of the Tenth Emergency Special Session of the General Assembly, May 2002, on Illegal Israeli Actions in East Jerusalem and Palestine Territory, and Not to Threaten or Deport Yasser Arafat

### Report 15.1:  US Provides Aid to Abusive Regimes in Violation of Federal Law

On February 25, 2004, the State Department's Bureau of Democracy, Human Rights, and Labor issued its annual country reports on human rights practices for 2003, as required by The Human Rights and Security Assistance Act (22 U.S.C.A. § 2304). Passed by Congress in 1974, the Act requires the federal government to abide by international law and consider human rights standards when providing military assistance for foreign governments. Section (a)(2) states that "No security assistance may be provided to any country the government of which engages in a consistent pattern of gross violations of internationally recognized human rights."

In its report on Egypt, the Bureau wrote that:

* Egypt's human rights record remained poor;
* the security forces and local police mistreated, tortured, and killed prisoners;
* freedoms of press, assembly, and association were significantly restricted;
* tradition and law discriminated against women and non-Muslims; and
* workers' rights were limited, and child labor was widespread.

In 2003 the United States sent Egypt $1.2 billion in military and $911 million in civilian foreign assistance funds, for a total of $2.111 billion, the third-highest total dollar amount of all recipients of US aid.[40]

In its statement on Israeli actions in the occupied territories of the West Bank and Gaza Strip, the Bureau reported that:

- Israel's overall human rights record in the occupied territories remained poor and worsened in the treatment of foreign human rights activists as it continued to commit numerous serious human rights abuses;
- Israeli forces undertook targeted killings of suspected terrorists in areas where civilian casualties were likely, killing forty-seven bystanders, including children;
- Israeli forces often used excessive force in confronting Palestinian demonstrators;
- Israeli forces sometimes arbitrarily destroyed Palestinian property;
- Israel conducted mass arbitrary arrests;
- prison conditions for Palestinian detainees were poor, with detainees often subjected to beatings and torture by Israeli police; and
- Israel strictly limited Palestinians' freedom of assembly and movement.

In 2003, the Bush Administration requested more than $2.1 billion in military aid, $600 million in economic assistance, and $60 million in migration resettlement assistance funds for Israel, second only to Iraq in the total dollar amount of all recipients of US aid.[41]

## Report 15.2:  US Supported Israel's Rejection of World Court Opinion

On July 9, 2004, the UN International Court of Justice (ICJ) ruled 14–1 that the separation wall being built by Israel in the West Bank is in breach of international law, called on Israel to tear it down, and to compensate Palestinians harmed by its construction. The sole dissent was by US judge Thomas Buerghenthal. The ICJ issued the advisory opinion in answer to the question posed by the General Assembly on the legality of the wall. The ICJ opinion called on the UN Security Council and General Assembly to consider further action to end the illegal situation and to stop the construction of the barrier. ICJ president Judge Shi Jiuyong of China read the opinion.

The Court held that in building the fence, Israel violated international humanitarian law by infringing on Palestinians' freedom of movement and freedom to seek employment, education, and healthcare. "Israel is under an obligation to terminate its breaches of international law; it is under an obligation to cease forthwith the works of construction of the wall being built in the Occupied Palestinian Territory, including in and around East Jerusalem, to dismantle forthwith the structure therein situated," the Court ruled.

The ICJ also urged the UN to "redouble its efforts" to end the conflict between Israelis and Palestinians, which it said posed a threat to international peace, saying that the wall "cannot be justified by military exigencies or by the requirements of national security or public order."

The barrier could become tantamount to annexation of Palestinian land if it is completed and it "thus severely impeded the exercise by the Palestinian people of its right to self-determination. . . . The Court considers that the construction of the wall and its associate regime creates a 'fait accompli' on the ground that could well become permanent, in which case, and notwithstanding the formal characterization by Israel, it would be tantamount to de facto annexation." The Court questioned the route of the fence, saying that it would encompass 80 percent of the settlers in the West Bank, while cutting off more than 230,000 Palestinians from their surrounding areas.

"The Court cannot accept the view . . . that it has no jurisdiction because of the 'political' character of the question posed," Judge Shi Jiuyong said. All countries "are under an obligation not to recognize the illegal situation resulting from the construction of the wall and not to render aid or assistance in maintaining the situation created by such construction."

The Court also stated that Israel violated many treaties and international laws, including the UN Charter; the Regulations annexed to the Fourth Hague Convention of 1907; the Fourth Geneva Convention of 1949; the Applicability of the Fourth Geneva Convention in the Occupied Palestinian Territory; the International Covenant on Civil and Political Rights; the International Covenant on Economic, Social, and Cultural Rights; and the Convention on the Rights of the Child. The court acknowledged Israel's right to build such a barrier within its own territory. The court did not include in its decision the parts of the fence constructed within the Green Line. (The Green Line is the 1949 armistice line established between Israel and Lebanon, Syria, Jordan, and Egypt [the Arab nations] after the 1948 War of Independence for Israel.) Israel, with the assistance of the United States, immediately sought to block the issue from reaching the Security Council.[42]

### Report 15.3:  US Plan Colombia Led to Poisoning People and the Environment

In 2004, the United States admitted it had between two hundred and three hundred combat troops in Colombia at any one time as part of Plan Colombia that began in December 1998. At that time, the US Government began its massive military aid program to assist the Colombian government in two struggles: the first against The Revolutionary Armed Forces of Colombia-People's Army (FARC-EP) and the National Liberation Army (ELN), and the fight against the country's burgeoning involvement in cocaine production and smuggling. Plan Colombia allocated $1.3 billion and as many as five hundred military personnel and three hundred civilian personnel to the intervention program. The United States began to build a joint

US-Colombia military base in Colombia and also sent Green Berets to train a Colombian Army counterinsurgency battalion.[43]

One main aspect of Plan Colombia involves the aerial spraying of herbicide on tens of thousands of acres of Colombian farmland in order to eradicate cultivation of the coca plant. The chief herbicide is Glyphosate, a chemical manufactured by the Monsanto Corporation (often marketed as "Roundup"). It is sprayed by US planes owned and operated by the US company DynCorp. Following a 1996 lawsuit, Monsanto was forced to label every can of Glyphosate with a label warning users to "avoid direct application to any body of water. . . . Do not apply this product in a way that will contact workers or other persons, either directly or through drift," and "only protected handlers may be in area during application." Monsanto no longer claims that Glyphosate is free of risk and has made public the dangers involved in using it.

Environmental researchers have found Glyphosate to be toxic to most plants and many species of animals and to have a toxic effect on soil, rivers, and oceans. David Olson, Director of Conservation Science at the World Wildlife Fund, "likens actions being taken by the US to the spraying campaign of Agent Orange in the Vietnam War that disturbed wildlife and natural ecosystems to such a large extent that they have never recovered. The spraying campaign in Colombia will, and already is, having devastating environmental effects." Colombian farmers in the spraying zones, and South Americans thousands of miles beyond the borders of Colombia, have seen the contamination and destruction of their food and water supplies as a result of the US-sponsored Glyphosate spraying. It has been claimed that Glyphosate also causes damage to humans at the genetic level, and may lead to sickness and birth defects in unborn children.[44]

On November 2, 2000, Aldo Lale-Demoz, a senior official with the United Nations Drug Control Program (UNDCP) sent a letter to NGOs on behalf of UNDCP Director Pino Arlacchi stating that "UNDCP is not in the game of developing and promoting biological weapons for use in eradicating coca in Colombia or anywhere else in South America." The letter was sent to the Sunshine Project in response to the Project's inquiry about the UNDCP's stance on US-sponsored herbicide spraying in Colombia.[45]

In February 2001, the European Parliament voted to voice its opposition to the US Plan Colombia. The next month, President Bush increased US funds for Plan Colombia by $500 million. Called the Andean Initiative, Bush's action continues the Clinton Administration's crop-spraying program and provides even more arms and counterinsurgency training for the Colombian armed forces.[46]

After 9/11 the Bush Administration continued to push for increased US financial and military aid to Colombia. In January 2002, Bush asked Congress to authorize a further $98 million in aid to train and equip Colombian troops to guard an Occidental Petroleum pipeline in Colombia. Since September 11, the war on terrorism has been repeatedly used to justify the continuation of Plan Colombia and the Andean Initiative.[47] In 2003, Colombia received $605 million in military aid from the US Government, which is more than any other nation except Israel and Egypt.[48]

## 16. TO DEAL FAIRLY WITH CONSCIENTIOUS OBJECTOR CLAIMS AND STOP-LOSS ORDERS

Every male in the United States is requested to register with the Selective Service System when he turns eighteen, including legal and illegal aliens unless they have visitor, student, or diplomatic visas. The No Child Left Behind Act of 2001 (PL 107–110) includes a clause that permits school districts to automatically turn over the names, addresses, and telephone numbers of every high school student in the district to the US military unless the parents of a student request otherwise. The information is used to solicit recruits among students as they register for the draft. The Peace Fresno Foundation Committee responded to this problem on December 3, 2003, when Vincent J. Lavery, chair of the Peace Fresno Education Committee, presented to the Superintendent of the Fresno Unified School District a request that teachers from each high school grade read a statement to their students regarding parent/student approval to have their directory information released to military recruiters, and instructions on how to notify the School District if they did not want this information released. In its presentation, the Committee also pointed out that the District failed to notify all parents that they could opt out of the system before the date on which opting out ended.[49]

Since January 2004, at least several hundred US soldiers have applied for Conscientious Objector (CO) status, although relatively few of them have gone public. Only a small number of people who apply for CO status receive a discharge. Military statistics relating to such cases lag about one year behind their actual occurrence. Decisions on CO applications take an average of six months to one year and sometimes as long as two years. As a consequence, the exact number of COs in the present war in Iraq will not be known for some time. The military also does not count CO applications from servicemembers absent without leave (AWOL).

Some veterans' organizations are alleging that the DOD consistently denies applications for conscientious objector status, regardless of their merits, including the case of Gabriel Johnson, who was sent to the war zone (Report 16.1) and Stephen Frank, who was sentenced to six months for unauthorized leave after he became a CO (Report 16.2).

The military not only denies many CO claims of service members; it seeks to keep them in the service through stop-loss policy. In November

2002, the Army's Reserve Component Unit Stop-Loss policy took effect, barring soldiers in the Reserve and National Guard deployed in the Bush Administration's war on terror from leaving their units from the moment their units were notified of the policy until ninety days following their return to their home stations.[50]

On November 13, 2003, the Acting Secretary of the Army, Les Brownlee, approved a new Active Army Unit Stop-Loss Program to enable the Army to continue the "Global War on Terrorism" and to ensure that "unit formations are ready, cohesive and at their best to effect forthcoming rotational Plans." This program covered soldiers selected for rotations of Operation Enduring Freedom in Afghanistan and of Operation Iraqi Freedom.

On June 1, 2004, the US Army's Assistant Secretary for Manpower and Reserve Affairs signed an order expanding the stop-loss program. It forces soldiers whose units are scheduled to deploy in the Middle East or Central Asia to remain with their units until ninety days after their tour of duty ends.[51]

Both Democratic Senator John Kerry and Republican Senator John McCain criticized these programs as an attempt by the Bush Administration to create a "backdoor draft." Retired military officers also worry that stop-loss orders will discourage current service members and new enlistees at a time when the troops are already stretched thin by the occupation of Iraq and Afghanistan and the reduction of the Army's troops following the end of the Cold War in 1989.[52]

On June 2, 2004, reporter Martha Raddatz revealed on *ABCNEWS.com* that the Pentagon faces a decline in recruitment, which translates into less manpower, especially in the Air National Guard. Gen. Peter Pace, vice chair of the Joint Chiefs of Staff, informed a Senate panel that recruitment decreased by 23 percent.[53] The Army last used stop-loss during Operation Shield/Desert Storm in 1990.[54] The Army also issued stop-movement policies to prevent "the normal rotation of soldiers into and out of affected units" and soldiers from transferring out of their units.[55]

*USA Today* reported in September 2004 that more than six hundred former soldiers did not show up when they were called as part of the Army Individual Ready Reserve. They were more than one-third of the sixteen hundred retired soldiers being reactivated for duty in Iraq. Many requested exemptions for health and personal reasons. Fourteen were immediately declared to be AWOL (Report 16.3).

**Relevant Law:**

U.S. Constitution: Art. I., §8, Cl. 11; Art. VI, Cl. 2; First, Fifth, Eighth, Fourteenth Amendments

War Powers Act, 50 U.S.C. §§1541-1548

Selective Services Act of 1948, 50 U.S.C. App. §454(d)(1)-(2)

Uniform Military Training and Services Act Amendments of 1951, 50 U.S.C. App. §454(c)(1)

Armed Services Act of 1968, 10 U.S.C. §506

UN Charter: Art. 2.3, 2.4, 55, 56

ICCPR: Preamble, Art. 1, 4, 5, 8.3(c)(ii), (iii), 9, 9.3, 10, 11, 14, 16, 18, 19, 26, 40

CAT: Preamble, Art. 2, 4, 6, 13, 14, 16, 19

## Report 16.1: The DOD Consistently Denies Conscientious Objector Status

There were an estimated 200,000 Conscientious Objectors in the Vietnam War, forty-three hundred in the Korean War, and thirty-seven thousand in World War II. In World War I, CO status was not officially recognized, but thirty-five hundred men claimed conscientious objector status. Many were subsequently convicted of refusing to be drafted and were sentenced to prison.

In the Gulf War, the military granted only 111 CO discharges and thereafter denied all CO applications. During the Gulf War, COs being held at Camp LeJeune in North Carolina alleged that they were beaten and harassed. In some cases, COs were put on planes to Kuwait and told that they could not apply for CO status, or they could apply only after going to war.[56]

Father Michael Baxter, a former counselor of the Central Committee for Conscientious Objectors (CCCO), said that during the Gulf War, COs were forcibly deployed to the Middle East, some in handcuffs and leg irons. Many COs were arrested and held without even the right to receive letters from their families. Reports after the Gulf War showed that of the twenty-five hundred CO applications submitted, almost none of them were processed correctly. Many COs were prosecuted and brought to trial for unauthorized absence and desertion.[57]

Military statistics do not include the cases of US Army Pvt. Wilfredo Torres, or Army National Guard S.Sgt. Camilo Mejia. Torres was AWOL for nearly a year before surrendering to US military police on Veterans Day 2002. Torres claimed CO status after coming out of hiding, stating, "I have decided that it would be wrong for our country to attack Iraq on its own, without working as part of the U.N. . . . . I'm no expert, but I think that such an attack will undermine the U.N. and affect America's standing in this world. . . . If we do [attack], I won't be going with them." The Army detained Torres at Fort Knox, Kansas, then gave him an "other than honorable" discharge.[58]

In October 2003, S.Sgt. Camilo Mejia returned from service in Iraq on a two-week furlough. He failed to report back to his unit. When he surrendered at Fort Stewart on March 16, 2004, he submitted the first application for discharge as a conscientious objector in the Iraqi war. In his application, he provided details of the torture and abuse of detainees by US troops he witnessed at a detention center at al Assad airbase. Mejia stated, "I think this war is particularly immoral." His unit was reprimanded by a commander for celebrating their escape from an ambush when "their job was to kill the enemy, not run away."[59] On May 21, 2004, a military court-martial found Mejia guilty of desertion and sentenced him to one year in prison for refusing to return to Iraq.[60]

And see Report 16.3.

### Report 16.2:  Marine Corps Sentences Conscientious Objector Applicant

On February 9, 2003, twenty-year-old Stephen Funk, a Filipino Marine Corps reservist, did not join his unit when it was deployed for active duty in Iraq. Funk claimed Conscientious Objector status. "There are so many evil things about war," said Funk. "There is no way to justify war because you're paying with human lives." On April 1, Funk showed up at the gates of his San Jose military base with conscientious objector papers in hand, ready to be punished for not joining his unit when it was deployed. At the base, Capt. Patrick O'Rourke, USMC, said that Funk must report for duty at 7:30 each morning while his application was being reviewed. Funk said his moral quandary began at boot camp, where he was trained to shout, "Kill! Kill!" as he slashed with his weapon. He shared his problem with military chaplains.[61]

On April 22, 2003, the Marine Corps sent Funk to the Fourth Force Service Support Base in New Orleans, Louisiana, away from his family, friends, legal team, and supporters. He was placed in a unit of nearly twenty Marine Corps Conscientious Objectors who were all waiting for discharge hearings or court martial proceedings.

On May 2, 2003, the Marine Corps filed Desertion charges against Funk, claiming that he "shirked important duty." On May 13, the Corps initiated investigative hearings to determine the validity of his Conscientious Objector beliefs. On September 6, 2003, a military jury acquitted Funk of desertion but found him guilty of Unauthorized Absence during the Iraq War. On September 10, the Marine Corps flew Funk to its base at Camp Lejeune, North Carolina. (E-mail titled, "Stephen Funk Transferred to Camp Lejeune, NC," *NLG Military Law Task Force*, sent to the MCLI and others, Sep. 12, 2003.)

On November 15, 2003, the organization Refusing to Kill stated, "On October 5th, the *New York Post* reported there are at least 50 more

San Jose, CA, April 1, 2003: Marine Corps reservist Stephen Funk, center, reads a statement before turning himself in at his reserve unit. The twenty-year-old Marine reservist, called to active duty, refuses to serve in the Iraqi conflict, claiming conscientous objector status. Behind Funk is his sister, Caitlin Funk, left, and his mother, Gloria Pacis, right. (AP Photo/Eric Risberg)

reservists facing charges for refusing to report to duty. Stephen is a political prisoner. The US government jailed Stephen to make him an example to the potentially thousands of soldiers who want to resist this war."[62] On March 14, 2004, Funk was released. Despite numerous requests for clemency, Funk served a six-month sentence in military prison for unauthorized absence.[63]

The US military acknowledged that recruits may change their views during training, and allows service members an exit if they prove a religious, ethical, or moral objection to war. However, the consequences of claiming CO status can range from a noncombat job to court martial and possible prison term.[64]

## Report 16.3: Military Uses Stop-Loss Program Unfairly

On August 16, 2004, attorneys Michael S. Sorgen and Joshua Sondheimer, assisted by the Military Law Task Force of the National Lawyers Guild in San Francisco, filed the first lawsuit, *Doe v. Ashcroft*, challenging the issuance of stop-loss orders, in the North District of California.

The petitioner, a married man with two young daughters, served during the invasion of Iraq and had nine years of active military service. A reservist in the California Army National Guard under a one-year enlistment, he received a stop-loss order on July 6, 2004, impeding him from leaving the

Guard after finishing his one-year enlistment on December 21, 2004. The order declared that his unit would spend six months in Fort Bliss, Texas, for training and then would be deployed to Iraq for two or more years of military service. Although John Doe was allegedly excused from being deployed to Fort Bliss, the stop-loss order prevented him from exiting the military upon the end of his enlistment.

He filed for writs of habeas corpus and mandamus and/or declaratory relief alleging violations of his due process rights and of the terms of his enlistment agreement, which specifically forbade the extension of his enlistment without his consent. He also alleged that the order violated the Selective Service Act of 1948, 50 U.S.C. App. §§ 454(d) (1)–(2), the Uniform Military Training and Services Act Amendments of 1951, 50 U.S.C. App. § 454 (c) (1), and the Armed Services Act of 1968, 10 U.S.C. §506, which codify that a soldier's enlistment may be extended only during a period of war or a national emergency. The National Lawyers Guild said it acted to prevent the Army from creating "a new category of indentured servitude."[65]

The Army settled the suit by issuing John Doe a notification that he was no longer under a stop-loss order and would not be deployed to Iraq. Attorneys Sorgen and Sondheimer have filed a similar suit in Central California. The total number of such lawsuits is unknown and the Army has not revealed how many complaints it has received from soldiers affected by the stop-loss programs.

## 17. *NOT TO MAINTAIN WEAPONS OF MASS DESTRUCTION OR DESIGN NEW NUKES*

Since 9/11, the concerned public has read, and talked, a great deal about the wars in Afghanistan and Iraq and about some of the weapons used there. At the same time, the Lawyers Committee on Nuclear Policy issued a list of the treaties the Bush Administration said would no longer apply to the United States (Report 17.1).

While some argue that the invention, maintenance, and upgrading of nuclear weapons are not human rights issues, others quote the World Court opinion that nuclear weapons are illegal, based on the humanitarian laws of war (Report 17.3). More lives and cultures are at stake from one nuclear blast than from hundreds of violations of human rights, they say, and they urge everyone to visit Nagasaki and Hiroshima and to read the opinion of the World Court (International Court of Justice [ICJ]) (Report 17.3). In fact, while twelve nations have nuclear weapons programs, all but 2 percent of the nuclear warheads in the world have been built by the United States and Russia. And the US Trident submarine fleet alone still carries over three thousand nuclear warheads one of which could destroy a city with one million people.[66]

After September 11, the Department of Defense began proposing changes in nuclear weapons policies. Members of both Houses of Congress also sought changes but not the same ones (R 17.2). In 2003, US Forces used depleted uranium in Iraq (Report 17.4), which sharpened the debate. And then reports were made that US Forces were contaminating Afghanistan with Uranium (Report 17.5).

## Relevant Law:

U.S. Constitution: Preamble, General Welfare Clause; Art. I, §8, Cl. 11; Art. II, §3; Art. VI, §2; Fifth, Eighth, Fourteenth Amendments
Genocide Convention Implementation Act, 18 U.S.C. §1091
UN Charter: Preamble, Art. 1, 2.3, 2.4, 2.6, 24.2, 33, 55, 56, 93, 103
ICCPR: Preamble, Art. 1, 2, 4-6, 6.1, 7, 17, 23.1, 26, 40.1, 47
CAT: Preamble, Art. 1, 2, 4, 10, 14, 19
Nuremberg Principles
Hague Convention Respecting the Laws and Customs of War on Land of 1907: Art. 22, 23, 26
Third and Fourth Geneva Conventions
Additional Protocol I of the Geneva Convention Art. 35, 36, 48, 49, 51, 52, 54, 55, 57, 58
Convention on the Prevention and Punishment of Crime of Genocide of 1951
Nuclear Non-Proliferation Treaty
ICESCR: Preamble, Art. 1, 2, 11, 12, 16, 25
CRC: Preamble, Art. 2, 6, 16, 24, 27.1, 37.1(a), 38.1, 38.4, 44
Comprehensive [Nuclear] Test Ban Treaty of 1996
Antiballistic Missile Treaty of 1972
Biological and Toxin Weapons Convention of 1972
UN Agreement to Curb the International Flow of Illicit Small Arms of 2001
The International Criminal Court Treaty of 1998
Land Mine Treaty of 1997
*Legality of the Threat or Use of Nuclear Weapons*, International Court of Justice Advisory Opinion of 8 July, 1996, ¶¶ 74-87, 31, and 105(F). Also see, *Nuclear Weapons Are Illegal: the Historic Opinion of the World Court and How It Will Be Enforced*, ed. Ann Fagan Ginger (New York: Apex Press 1998).

## Report 17.1: Administration Acts Against Treaty Commitments to Limit Arms

The Bush Administration withdrew the United States from several anti-weapons treaties:

- Comprehensive [Nuclear] Test Ban Treaty, 1996. In November 2001, the United States forced a vote in the UN Committee on Disarmament and Security apparently to demonstrate US opposition to the Treaty and announced its intention to enhance US readiness to resume testing of new short-range tactical nuclear weapons.
- Antiballistic Missile Treaty, 1972. In December 2001, the United States officially gave notice of its withdrawal to take effect in June 2002—the first time in the nuclear era that the United States renounced a major arms control accord.
- Biological and Toxin Weapons Convention, 1972, ratified by 144 nations including the United States. In July 2001, the United States walked out of a London conference to discuss negotiations of a protocol proposed in 1994 to strengthen the Convention by providing for on-site inspections. At Geneva in November 2001, Undersecretary of State for Arms Control John Bolton stated, "The protocol is dead," while at the same time accusing Iraq, Iran, North Korea, Libya, Sudan, and Syria of violating the Convention, offering no specific allegations or supporting evidence.
- UN Agreement to Curb the International Flow of Illicit Small Arms, 2001. The United States was the only nation in opposition to this proposed action plan.
- The International Criminal Court (ICC) Treaty, 1998. In December 2000, President Clinton signed. In May 2002, Bush announced he was "unsigning" the ICC Treaty—a move that the United States had never done before. By mid-2003, the United States had signed thirty-seven mutual immunity pacts, mostly with poor, small countries in Africa, Asia, Central America, and Eastern Europe that pledged to give US citizens immunity from charges before the new ICC. In July 2003, the Bush Administration suspended all military assistance to thirty-seven countries that refused to sign such pacts.
- Land Mine Treaty, 1997. Banning the use, production, and shipment of antipersonnel bombs and mines, the treaty has been ratified by 142 countries, not including the United States. President Clinton committed the United States to cease using mines and to join the treaty by 2006 if alternatives were identified. In February 2004, the Bush Administration reversed this policy, announcing that the United States will not join the treaty and that US use of mines is permissible without restriction.[67]
- UN Resolution calling for the prevention of an arms race in outer space. This resolution was overwhelmingly adopted 174–0. Four countries abstained: the United States, Israel, Micronesia, and the Marshall Islands.[68]

Also in 2004, the US voted against two antinuclear resolutions:

- an omnibus resolution in the UN General Assembly, "Towards a Nuclear-Free World: A New Agenda," approved by 133 nations. The United States was one of only six countries to vote against it, and
- a resolution, "A Path to the Total Elimination of Nuclear Weapons." One hundred sixty-four countries voted for it; only two nations, India and the United States, voted against it. The US representative at the General Assembly said that the resolution stressed the importance of member states ratifying the Comprehensive Nuclear-Test-Ban Treaty, which the United States does not support.[69]

## Report 17.2: The DOD and Congress Trying to Change Nuclear Weapons Policies

Shortly after September 11, 2001, Congress instructed the Department of Defense (DOD) to plan and report on the direction for US nuclear forces over the next decade. On December 31, 2001, Secretary of Defense Rumsfeld submitted the Nuclear Posture Review to Congress, made public on January 8, 2002. The Review announced the formation of a "New Triad," consisting of:

- new nuclear and nonnuclear offensive strike systems;
- new active and passive defenses; and
- a new "defense infrastructure that will provide new capabilities in a timely fashion to meet emerging threats."[70]

The report did not mention the unanimous holding in the International Court of Justice decision in 1996 that "There exists an obligation to pursue in good faith and bring to a conclusion negotiations leading to nuclear disarmament in all its aspects under strict and effective international control" (¶ 105F). The ICJ judge from the United States joined in this holding.[71]

On June 3, 2004, the Bush Administration announced the submission to Congress of a classified plan for the future size of the US nuclear arsenal which states that in 2012, the United States will have more than six thousand warheads. Critics noted that in 2004, the total world count of in tact nuclear warheads was about thirty thousand (including more than 10,455 in the US arsenal along with the stockpiles of Russia, China, France, Britain, Israel, India, and Pakistan).[72] There are approximately four thousand US and Russian nuclear bombs on continued hair-trigger alert, according to the Council for a Livable World.

Every nation signing the Nuclear Nonproliferation Treaty (NPT) made a commitment to verify its warhead withdrawals and dismantling, including the United States. The Bush administration resisted requests to discuss the matter seriously. The Administration gave the impression that it saw the planned reductions more as a matter of reorganization and efficiency than as compliance with international disarmament obligations. Lengthy private negotiations by the five permanent nuclear powers in the Security Council (the United States, the United Kingdom, Russia, France, and China) led to Resolution 1540 on nonstate actors and terrorists.

On April 28, 2004, the Council passed the Resolution unanimously. It requires all states:

- to criminalize terrorist and other nonstate actor acquisitions of nuclear, biological, and chemical (NBC) weapons and their delivery systems; and
- to establish export controls, methods of accounting, physical protection, border controls, and law enforcement efforts to prevent nonstate actor trafficking in nuclear, chemical, and biological weapons, as well as related materials.

Critics pointed out that nothing in the UN Charter confers the authority on the Security Council to adopt global legislation. The Charter authorizes multilateral agreements to be entered into by states as the mode of global lawmaking.

Attorney John Burroughs of the Lawyers Committee on Nuclear Policy told the Barcelona Forum that "A concern about the resolution is that it will reinforce the current emphasis on the imperative of preventing the spread of NBC weapons to the virtual exclusion of the . . . obligation under the Nuclear Nonproliferation Treaty (NPT), to reduce and eliminate existing arsenals of nuclear weapons held by the world's most powerful states." Furthermore, "the resolution comes in the context of a US refusal to meet NPT commitments to ratify the Comprehensive Test Ban Treaty, to reduce nuclear arms in a verifiable, transparent, and irreversible manner, and to negotiate a treaty banning production of fissile materials for nuclear weapons."[73] Worldwide military spending rose by 11 percent in 2003, according to the Stockholm International Peace Research Institute on June 9, 2004. That is over $30,000 every second of the year, amounting to one trillion dollars per year. The increase can be attributed to the US invasion of Iraq, according to the Institute and other observers.

On June 15, 2004, the Senate voted 55–42 to preserve $36.6 million of the latest Pentagon spending measure that had been earmarked for the research and development of new nuclear weapons. According to the *New York Times*, Senate Democrats who voted against the funding claimed that renewed nuclear weapons development would "spur other nations to turn to such weapons and that even bombs exploding underground would pose risks of fallout far beyond their targets."[74] Each year the United States spends $27 billion to prepare to fight a nuclear war, according to the Center for Defense Information (http://www.cdi.org).

On June 25, 2004, by a vote of 370–16, the House of Representatives approved an Energy Department spending bill that pointedly omitted funding for new nuclear weapons. The House vote cut $27.5 million the Administration wanted for a nuclear bunker buster; $9 million for low-yield weapons, or mini nukes; and $30 million to begin building a new factory to make the pits that are the heart of nuclear weapons. Rep. David Hobson (R-OH) led the opposition to the nuclear initiatives because

- the US already has a stockpile of more than ten thousand, and
- "building new nuclear weapons would be inconsistent with US efforts to stop other countries from arming themselves with nuclear weapons."[75]

### Report 17.3: Bush Ignores World Court Opinion that Nuclear Weapons Are Illegal

The Bush Administration ignored the opinion of the International Court of Justice (ICJ), also known as the World Court. In March 2002, Walter C. Uhler, a weapons acquisition executive for the Defense Department, wrote "America's undue fascination with dropping the bomb on somebody became further unhinged in the wake of Sept. 11."

In 1996, in response to a General Assembly vote asking for an advisory opinion, the ICJ issued its opinion in the "Legality of the Threat or Use of Nuclear Weapons" (July 8, 1996, General List No. 95), holding unanimously that:

- "There is in neither customary nor conventional international law any specific authorization of the threat or use of nuclear weapons" (¶105[2]A);
- "A threat or use of force by means of nuclear weapons that is contrary to Article 2, paragraph 4, of the UN Charter and that fails to meet all the requirements of Article 51, is unlawful" (¶105[2]C);
- "A threat or use of nuclear weapons should also be compatible with the requirements of the international law applicable in armed conflict, particularly those of the principles and rules of international humanitarian law, as well as with specific obligations under treaties and other undertakings which expressly deal with nuclear weapons" (¶105[2]D); and

- "There exists an obligation to pursue in good faith and bring to a conclusion negotiations leading to nuclear disarmament in all its aspects under strict and effective international control" (¶105[2]F).[76]

As Joseph Gerson, Director of the American Friends Service Committee's Peace and Economic Security Program, wrote before September 11, "on more than 20 occasions since the atomic bombing of Nagasaki, and at least 5 times since the end of the Cold War, US presidents have prepared and threatened to initiate nuclear war during international crises and wars."

According to Walter C. Uhler of the *Philadelphia Enquirer*, both the *Los Angeles Times* and *New York Times* revealed the contents of the Bush Administration's secret "Nuclear Posture Review." They reported that the Administration's Review showed that "the President and the Pentagon are taking numerous steps to be able to explode nuclear weapons: (1) against targets impervious to conventional weapons, (2) in retaliation for an attack using nuclear, biological, or chemical weapons and (3) "in the event of surprising military developments."

"Seven countries—China, Russia, Iraq, North Korea, Iran, Libya, and Syria—have been listed as potential recipients of such explosions."[77]

### Report 17.4: US Forces Use Depleted Uranium in Iraq; Many Affected

On May 15, 2003, Scott Peterson, a staff writer for the *Christian Science Monitor*, reported that in downtown Baghdad, where children play on burnt-out Iraqi tanks, and spent shell casings litter the ground, his Geiger counter readings measured radiation levels one thousand to nineteen hundred times higher than "normal" background radiation levels.[78] On August 4, 2003, the *Seattle Post Intelligencer* reported that "The Pentagon and the United Nations estimate that the US and Britain used 1,100 to 2,200 tons of armor-piercing shells made of depleted uranium during attacks on Iraq in March and April, 2003."[79]

Depleted uranium (DU) is a waste byproduct generated when uranium is enriched for use in atomic weapons and nuclear power plants. It is both toxic and radioactive, like natural uranium. The Army Environmental Policy Institute warns that the radiation and heavy metal of DU weapons makes food and water unsafe for consumption and can cause kidney, lung, and liver damage, and increased rates of cancer among those exposed to such munitions. Army training manuals require anyone who comes within seventy-five feet of any DU-contaminated equipment or terrain to wear respiratory and skin protection.

The Bush Administration publicly denies that DU weapons can cause sickness and refuses to let a team from the United Nations Environmental Program

(UNEP) study the environmental impact of DU contamination in Iraq. The Government says it has no plans to remove the debris left over from DU weapons. It has stated that "No cleanup is needed, because research shows DU has no long term effects."

Dr. Asaf Durakovic of the Uranium Medical Research Center disagrees. He explains that the initial effects of toxic and radiological uranium contamination are neurological, showing up as headaches, weakness, dizziness, and muscle fatigue. Long-term effects include cancers and radiation-related illnesses, such as chronic fatigue syndrome, joint and muscle pain, rashes, neurological and nerve damage, lung and kidney damage, vision problems, autoimmune deficiencies, miscarriages, maternal mortality, and genetic birth defects.

Sara Flounders, a contributing author of *Metal of Dishonor: How Depleted Uranium Penetrates Steel, Radiates People and Contaminates the Environment* (ed. Helen Caldicott, et al. [New York: International Action Center, 2005]) alleges that hundreds of thousands of Iraqi and US soldiers will suffer the ill effects of DU, as will the British, Polish, Japanese, and Dutch soldiers sent to join the occupation. The real extent of the injuries they will endure, including chronic illnesses, long-term disabilities, and genetic birth defects, won't become apparent for five to ten years.[80]

The humanitarian laws of war forbid weapons that (1) cannot distinguish between civilians and military personnel; (2) cause unnecessary suffering; and (3) have long-term effects on human beings and on the environment.[81]

On April 3, 2004, the *New York Daily News* released a special investigation report that it had commissioned called "Poisoned?" The report stated that four soldiers from a New York Army National Guard company—Sgt. Hector Vega, Sgt. Ray Ramos, Sgt. Agustin Matos, and Cpl. Anthony Yonnone—are the first confirmed cases of inhaled depleted uranium exposure from the current Iraq conflict. Dispatched to Iraq in April 2004, the company's members have been providing guard duty for convoys, running jails, and training Iraqi police and have not been involved in active combat. The soldiers said that they have been battling persistent physical ailments that began in the summer of 2003 in the Iraqi town of Samawah. "I got sick instantly in June," said S.Sgt. Ray Ramos, a Brooklyn housing policeman. "My health kept going downhill with daily headaches, constant numbness in my hands and rashes on my stomach."

As part of the investigation, Dr. Asaf Durakovic, a nuclear medicine expert who has conducted extensive research on depleted uranium, examined the nine soldiers from the 442nd Military Police in late December 2003, and collected urine specimens from each. Several of the men also had minute traces of another uranium isotope, U-236, that is produced only in a nuclear reaction process. "These men were almost certainly exposed to radioactive weapons on the battlefield," Dr. Durakovic said.

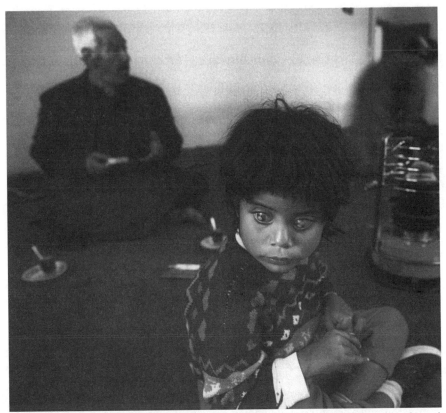

The village of al-Abarra, north of Baghdad, 2004: Alarming numbers of Iraqi children, such as Zara, are now born blind from cataracts and eye deformations. Their fathers were heavily exposed to DU during the Gulf War—the depleted uranium ammunition now commonly used by the United States. (Photo/J. B. Russell, photojournalist)

Dr. Durakovic was a colonel in the Army Reserves who served in the 1991 Persian Gulf War. While working at a military hospital in Delaware, he was one of the first doctors to discover unusual radiation levels in Gulf War veterans. He has since become a leading critic of the use of DU in warfare: "These are amazing results, especially since these soldiers were military police not exposed to the heat of battle. . . . Other American soldiers who were in combat must have more depleted uranium exposure."

"A large number of American soldiers [in Iraq] may have had significant exposure to uranium oxide dust," said Dr. Thomas Fasey, a pathologist at Mount Sinai Medical Center and an expert on DU. "And the health impact is worrisome for the future." The test results for the New York guardsmen—

four of nine positives for DU—suggest the potential for more extensive radiation exposure among coalition troops and Iraqi civilians.[82]

### Report 17.5:  US Forces Contaminating Afghanistan with Uranium

In 2002 and 2003, the Uranium Medical Research Centre (UMRC) of Canada tested soil and urine samples obtained in areas of Afghanistan that had been bombarded with US weapons. The UMRC found the levels of uranium contamination to be much higher than what would be expected because of contamination from so-called depleted uranium (DU) weapons. "The results were astounding: the donors presented concentrations of toxic and radioactive uranium isotopes between 100 and 400 times greater than in Gulf veterans" that the UMRC had tested in 1999. Dr. Asaf Durakovic, Director of UMRC, was "stunned" by the results.[83]

In 2003, Chicago-based Afghan researcher Dr. Daud Miraki sent out an Afghan survey team to talk to people in some of the areas that had been most heavily bombarded. People told the team that severe and unusual health problems began just weeks after the bombings, often far away from actual battlegrounds.

US uranium weapons cause a pyrophoric explosion, creating a fine, highly poisonous dust that travels with the wind. As a consequence, many Taliban soldiers and civilians died from "internal bleeding and other bizarre symptoms including uncontrolled vomiting, diarrhea, and blood loss in urine and stool" whether they had been wounded or not. Many people began to experience kidney disease/failure, and other problems such as skin lesions, confusion, auto immune deficiencies, and joint pain. Pregnant women miscarried or bore babies with deformities. It was estimated that 25 percent of children born in Afghanistan since November 2001 have been affected by uranium poisoning. As the half-life of uranium is 4.5 billion years, it is probable that this percentage will rise over time.

According to Dr. Miraki, "Subsequent to the contamination, newborn children have physical deformities and those that do not have physical deformity are suffering from mental retardation. . . . many children are born with no limbs, no eyes, or tumors protruding out from their mouths and their eyes." A father in the Paktia province testified, "When I saw my little boy with those monstrous red tumors, I thought to myself, 'Why is it difficult for Americans to understand that they are hated in our country?' If I do this to the child of an American family, that family has the right to pull my eyes out of my eye sockets. I would like to tell the Americans that they love to live their lives of luxury at the expense of our extermination."

Dr. Miraki wrote, "The father of one of the victims from Kundoz whose wife had given birth to a deformed child that hardly resembled an infant said this to our survey team in Kabul: 'My wife was pregnant and we were happily waiting for the moment to see our second child. On the day of the delivery, my wife felt weird, saying that she did not feel good and had pain in her abdomen. When the baby was born, it was hardly a human. It looked as if some one had beaten a baby and then covered its body with flour. My poor child looked like someone had rolled it in a basket of flour. When my wife saw the baby, she went into shock and died after 5 hours.'"[84]

Near Rish-Khor military base in Kabul, multiple witnesses reported seeing dead birds on tree branches with blood coming out of their mouths. A witness stated, "We were amazed to see all these birds sitting quietly on [tree] branches; but when we shook the tree the birds fell down and we saw blood coming out of their mouths. Then we climbed the trees to see those that were still stuck on the tree branches, all of them had bled from their mouths. Two of the birds appeared to be partly melted into the tree's branches."[85]

There has been DU contamination of the land and of the groundwater. Eyewitnesses reported in Kabul "waterspouts rising from bomb craters immediately following impact. These points of impact are . . . reported to be natural springs and underground watercourses. . . ."[86]

The testimony collected by Dr. Miraki's teams corroborated earlier findings of the UMRC: "The UMRC field team was shocked by the breadth of public health impacts coinciding with the bombing. Without exception, at every bombsite investigated, people are ill. A significant portion of the civilian population presents symptoms consistent with internal contamination by Uranium."[87]

An Afghan grandfather told the research team, "After the Americans destroyed our village and killed many of us, we also lost our houses and have nothing to eat. However, we would have endured these miseries and even accepted them, if the Americans had not sentenced us all to death. When I saw my deformed grandson, I realized that my hopes of the future have vanished for good, different from the hopelessness of the Russian barbarism, even though at that time I lost my older son Shafiqullah. This time, however, I know we are part of the invisible genocide brought on us by America, a silent death from which I know we will not escape."[88]

## D. THE GOVERNMENT'S DUTY TO PROTECT PEOPLE'S RIGHTS

Traditional US studies of human rights violations might begin with the first cases in Section D: to guarantee due process of law, right to counsel, and habeas corpus (Reports 18.1–18.8). Before 9/11, human rights focused to some extent on the need to release famous political prisoners like Leonard Peltier (Report 24.1) and Mumia Abu-Jamal (Report 24.2) among a list of almost one hundred others (Report 24.3). After 9/11, human rights activists had to learn the new language of the Government ("detention" of "enemy combatants" at "Guantanamo Bay" and elsewhere), and had to figure out how to cause Government officials to learn or relearn basic due process standards and admit that they apply to every person under US jurisdiction (Reports 19.1–19.7).

In view of Government efforts to enforce many provisions of the USA PATRIOT Act and other regulations of immigrants and resident aliens, concerned people began to demand that the officials deal promptly and fairly with political asylum petitions (Reports 20.1–20.4).

In the face of many statements by President Bush and his Administration about leaving no child behind, shocking reports of US mistreatment of unaccompanied minors entering the United States were released (Report 21.1) while the Administration cut housing vouchers for poor families (Report 21.2) and limited sex education funding to abstinence only (Report 21.5). Youthful students got in serious trouble when one permitted an acquaintance to put something on his Web site (Report 21.3) and a teacher called in the Secret Service when students made comments in class (Report 21.4). One affirmative step: Hawaii passed a law to end sex tourism (Report 21.6).

The duty of the US Government to enforce Antitrust laws and Anticorruption laws (Reports 22.1–22.5) was ignored as often as the duty to protect the rights of workers and their unions from California to Iraq (Reports 23.1–23.5). While corporate employees were carrying weapons in Iraq (Report 22.5), whistle-blowers were winning their suit against DynCorp (Report 22.4). The campaign to abolish capital punishment (Report 24.4) was almost lost until the Governor of Illinois removed everyone from death row in his state as he left office.

## 18. TO GUARANTEE DUE PROCESS OF LAW, RIGHT TO COUNSEL, AND HABEAS CORPUS

The Founding Fathers had two basic concerns about the rights and liberties of themselves and their fellow residents of the new United States: fairness and freedom. They spelled out freedom of religion, speech, press, assembly, and petition in the First Amendment. They spelled out fairness in the habeas corpus provision in Article I and in the Fourth, Fifth, Sixth, Seventh and Eighth Amendments, often summed up as "due process of law."

It is instructive to note that the people who had just defeated the King of England in battle immediately put into their written Constitution in Article I, Section 9, Clause 2: "The Privilege of the Writ of Habeas Corpus shall not be suspended, unless when in Cases of Rebellion or Invasion the public Safety may require it." Everyone arrested or detained or incarcerated for any reason has a right to immediately file a petition for the writ to find out why they are being held. A hearing on a habeas corpus petition is the moment when the jailer must tell the judge, in the presence of the detainee, on what charge the detainee is being held. At the habeas hearing, the detainee, often for the first time since being jailed, gets to see his lawyer and a judge who is supposed to listen impartially to the charges set forth by the US Attorney or attorney for the head of the jail or prison where the detainee is being held.

Even as the Civil War was beginning in the United States in the 1860s, President Lincoln was criticized for lifting the habeas corpus rights of men who were quite openly advocating overthrowing the US Government and its control over the Southern (slave) states.

The revolutionary citizens of 1787 were willing to wait to spell out further rights in civil and criminal cases in the Bill of Rights, adopted in 1791. The Seventh Amendment protects the right to a jury trial in civil cases and forbids appellate courts to reexamine facts decided by the jury. The Fifth Amendment "right to due process of law" covers both civil and criminal cases.

The Fourth Amendment prohibits the Government from conducting unreasonable searches and seizures of the person and the property of a person suspected of a crime. The Sixth Amendment guarantees the right to counsel in all criminal prosecutions, and a speedy and public trial by an impartial jury. The defendant has a right to know the charges against him and to "be confronted with the witnesses against him." He can have "compulsory process" to bring people to court to testify for him, and he has the right to have a lawyer assist in his defense. The Eighth Amendment spells out the right to be freed on bail that is not "excessive" and "no cruel and unusual punishments" shall be "inflicted."

The Fifth Amendment "right to due process of law" in criminal cases includes: (1) the right not to be held for a serious crime ("capital or otherwise infamous") unless a grand jury has heard the prosecution's case and voted to send the case to trial "except in cases arising in the land or naval forces, or in the Militia, when in Actual service in time of War"; (2) the right not to be forced to be a witness against one's self; and (3) the right not to be tried twice for the same crime.

The eight reports in Section 18 detail repeated denials of habeas corpus petitions and violations of each of the due process rights. Perhaps the most pervasive attack on due process rights started before 9/11 but was exaggerated by the budget crisis caused by the expenses of the military actions in Afghanistan, Iraq, and elsewhere. The President sought, and the Congress agreed to, budgets that did not adequately address the need of poor and homeless people for legal advice and counsel in civil and criminal cases. That is mentioned first here because it receives the least coverage in the media and is pervasive rather than being raised sharply in a particular case (Report 28.1).

The case of a US citizen, Jose Padilla, detained by the US Government as an "enemy combatant" (Report 18.1), received considerable media attention until the Supreme Court rejected his plea on the technical ground that his lawyers had sued in the wrong court. The defeat for Padilla on this ground does not bode well for other detainees getting a "speedy trial."

President Bush demanded immediate passage of the USA PATRIOT Act after 9/11. The Act labels many ordinary crimes as "terrorism," permitting much higher penalties (Report 18.2). In this climate, the FBI arrested Lynne Stewart, a well-known civil rights lawyer on her way to court and charged her with four counts of assisting terrorism based on secretly taped conversations with her client, an Egyptian sheik (Report 18.3). Immigration officials detained Rabih Haddad, an executive of the Global Relief Foundation, denied him asylum, and then deported him (Report 18.4). The Eleventh Circuit Court of Appeals upheld a District Court informal ruling keeping secret a habeas hearing of a detained Algerian (Report 18.5).

The Ninth Circuit Court of Appeals struck down sections of the 1996 Antiterrorism Act (Report 18.6). A Detroit jury, after hearing the evidence, acquitted one Middle Eastern defendant on charges of terrorism and the trial judge reversed the convictions of two others based on misconduct by the Assistant US Attorneys (Report 18.7).

On April 17, 2003, House Judiciary Committee Chair Jim Sensenbrenner (R-WI) said that a proposal to eliminate the USA PATRIOT Act's sunset provision early would only pass "over his dead body." The PATRIOT Act includes a sunset clause requiring that certain sections not be enforceable after a certain date.

On June 5, 2003, then attorney general Ashcroft stated that the PATRIOT Act "has several weaknesses which terrorists could exploit, undermining our defenses," and endorsed three provisions of the PATRIOT Act II, which had been rejected as too extreme. On September 10, 2003, President Bush announced in a speech at FBI headquarters that the PATRIOT Act contained "loopholes" that erected "unreasonable obstacles" to law enforcement. Bush urged Congress to "untie the hands of our law enforcement officials" and pass three provisions of PATRIOT Act II, each of which was introduced as a separate bill at that time:

1. H.R. 3037, "The Antiterrorism Tools Enhancement Act of 2003" would allow the Government to seize records and compel testimony in terrorism cases without prior review by a court or grand jury.
2. H.R. 3040 and S. 1606, "The Pretrial Detention and Lifetime Super-

vision of Terrorists Act of 2003" would allow Government to deny bail without proving danger or flight risk for a laundry list of federal crimes said to be terrorism-related. (Under current law, pretrial detention is available for all federal crimes, but a presumption of detention only applies to terrorism crimes if they are "acts of terrorism transcending national boundaries.")

3. H.R. 2934 and S. 1604, the "Terrorist Penalties Enhancement Act of 2003," would create a new death penalty for "domestic terrorism" as defined by the PATRIOT Act—a definition that applies not only to specific crimes of terrorism but also to any violation of federal or state law if it involves a dangerous act and is intended to influence Government policy. This broad definition could cover some acts of civil disobedience by protest groups.

Section 501 of the PATRIOT Act II was not immediately incorporated into any proposed bill. Under that proposed section, any US citizen could be stripped of citizenship for providing "material support . . . to a terrorist organization." This could be extended to include the forcible expatriation of citizens who financially support only the legal activities of any organization the US Government deems a terrorist organization.[89]

**Relevant Law:**

U.S. Constitution: Preamble, General Welfare Clause, Art. I, §8, Cl. 3, Cl. 18; Art. I, §9, Cl. 2; Art. II, §1, Cl. 8; Art. II, §3; Art. III, §2, Cl. 1; Art. VI, Cl. 2, Cl. 3; First, Fourth, Sixth, Eighth, Tenth, Fourteenth, Fifteenth Amendments
Treaty with the Western Shoshone, 1863. (18 Statutes at Large 689)
*Harris v. Nelson*, 394 U.S. 286 (1969)
*Hensley v. Municipal Court*, 411 U.S. 345 (1973)
UN Charter: Preamble, Art. 55, 55(c), 56, 93
ICCPR: Preamble, Art. 1, 2, 2.1, 3-7, 9, 10, 12-19, 22, 23.1, 26, 27, 40.1, 47
CERD: Preamble, Art. 1, 2, 3, 5(a), 5(b), 5(e)(iii), 7, 9
CAT: Preamble, Art. 1, 2, 11, 16, 19
ICESCR: Preamble, Art. 1, 2, 3, 11, 12, 16.1, 17, 25

**Report 18.1:  US Detains Citizen Padilla as "Enemy Combatant"; Habeas Denied on Technicalities**

On May 8, 2002, US citizen José Padilla flew from Pakistan to Chicago's O'Hare International Airport. As he stepped off the plane, Padilla was apprehended by federal agents executing a material witness warrant issued by the

US District Court for the Southern District of New York in connection with its grand jury investigation into the September 11 terrorist attacks. The Government then transported Padilla to New York, where he was held in federal criminal custody.

On May 22, 2002, acting through appointed counsel, Padilla moved to vacate the material witness warrant. On June 9, while Padilla's motion was pending, President Bush issued an order to Secretary of Defense Rumsfeld designating Padilla an "enemy combatant" and directing the Secretary to detain him in military custody, using his authority as Commander in Chief and the Authorization for Use of Military Force Joint Resolution PL 107–40, §§ 1–2, 115 Stat. 224 (AUMF), enacted September 18, 2001. That same day, the Department of Defense took Padilla into custody and transported him to the Consolidated Naval Brig in Charleston, South Carolina, without charging him.

On June 11, Padilla filed a habeas corpus petition in the Southern District of New York. In December 2002, the District Court (233 F.Supp.2d 564) ruled that the President has authority to detain as enemy combatants US citizens captured on US soil during a time of war. On July 3, 2003, a bipartisan group of prominent New York lawyers, former federal judges, and former government officials filed an amicus brief on behalf of Padilla. The brief charged that the detention of Padilla was unconstitutional.

In December 2003, the Court of Appeals for the Second Circuit (352 F.3d 695) reversed, granted the writ of habeas corpus, and directed the Secretary to release Padilla from military custody within thirty days. The Government did not release Padilla and appealed. The US Supreme Court granted certiorari, agreeing to hear the case.

On June 1, 2004, the Justice Department held a press conference in which they restated the allegation that Padilla sought to explode "uranium wrapped with explosives" in the hope of spreading deadly radioactivity. On June 9, 2004, the Associated Press reported that such a bomb would most likely have been a dud. Peter D. Zimmerman, a nuclear physicist at Kings College in London, and expert in the analysis of "dirty bombs" for the US National Defense University, said that the Justice Department's announcement was "extremely disturbing because, even if exploded, such a bomb presented 'no significant radiation hazard.'" Ivan Oelrich, a physicist with the Federation of American Scientists, came to the same conclusion.[90]

On June 28, 2004, the Supreme Court reversed the judgment of the Court of Appeals and remanded the case for dismissal without prejudice (*Rumsfeld v. Padilla*, 124 S.Ct. 2711 [2004]). The Court did not reach the question whether the President has authority to detain Padilla militarily (p. 2714). The 5–4 decision, written by Chief Justice Rehnquist, held that:

• The Southern District lacks jurisdiction over Padilla's habeas petition,

which ought to have been filed in the District Court of South Carolina (p. 2723).
- Cdr. M. A. Marr of the Consolidated Naval Brig is the only proper respondent to Padilla's petition because she, not Secretary Rumsfeld, is Padilla's custodian under federal habeas statute (p. 2722).

The Court rejected the dissent arguments that exceptions exist to the "immediate custodian" and "district of confinement" rules whenever exceptional, special, or unusual cases arise. Justice Kennedy filed a concurring opinion, in which Justice O'Connor joined.

Justice Stevens wrote the dissenting opinion, joined by Justices Souter, Ginsberg, and Breyer.

The dissent argued:

- The order vacating the material witness warrant that the District Court entered in the ex parte proceeding on June 9, 2002, terminated the Government's lawful custody of Padilla. His custody between May 8 and June 9 was pursuant to a judicially authorized seizure; he has been held for two years pursuant to a warrantless arrest (FN 2).
- "It is not apparent why the District of South Carolina, rather than the Southern District of New York, should be regarded as the proper forum . . ." (p. 2730). The dissent quoted *Harris v. Nelson*, 394 US 286 (1969): "The very nature of the writ demands that it be administered with the initiative and flexibility essential to insure that miscarriages of justice within its reach are surfaced and corrected" (p. 2732).
- The dissent also quoted *Hensley v. Municipal Court, San Jose—Milpitas Judicial Dist., Santa Clara Cty.*, 411 US 345 (1973): "[W]e have consistently rejected interpretations of the habeas corpus statute that would suffocate the writ in stifling formalisms or hobble its effectiveness with the manacles of arcane and scholastic procedural requirements" (p. 2733).
- The writ of habeas corpus reaches the Secretary as the relevant custodian in this case (20).
- "Executive detention of subversive citizens, like detention of enemy soldiers to keep them off the battlefield, may sometimes be justified to prevent persons from launching or becoming missiles of destruction. It may not, however, be justified by the naked interest in using unlawful procedures to extract information. Incommunicado detention for months on end is such a procedure." (p. 2725).
- "For if this Nation is to remain true to the ideals symbolized by its flag, it must not wield the tools of tyrants even to resist an assault by the forces of tyranny" (p. 2735), (*Rumsfeld v. Padilla*, 124 S.Ct. 2711 [2004]).

On February 28, 2005, Judge Henry Floyd (D.C. S.C.) held the President had no authority to hold Padilla and must act to charge or release him within forty-five days. The Government filed an appeal.

Paul Krugman of the *New York Times* compared the case of Padilla, who did not have any bomb-making materials "or even a plausible way to acquire such material," with the case of white supremacist Texan William Krar. Krar possessed a cache of weapons including remote-controlled explosive devices disguised as briefcases, sixty pipe bombs, automatic machine guns, and a cyanide bomb capable of killing thousands. Krar was discovered in April 2003 only because of a misdelivered package. Then attorney general Ashcroft put Padilla on front pages around the world. He said nothing about Krar. Krugman asked "Is Mr. Ashcroft neglecting real threats to the public because of his ideological biases?"[91]

### Report 18.2: PATRIOT Act Labels Ordinary Crimes "Terrorism," Increases Penalties

Since the passage of the USA PATRIOT Act (PL 107–56) on October 25, 2001, federal prosecutors have brought more than 250 criminal charges under the law, resulting in more than 130 guilty pleas or convictions.

Dan Dodson, a spokesman for the National Association of Criminal Defense Attorneys, says that "Within six months of passing the PATRIOT Act, the Justice Department was conducting seminars on how to stretch the new wiretapping provisions to extend them beyond terror cases." In early November 2003, then attorney general John Ashcroft completed a sixteen-city tour defending the PATRIOT Act as key to preventing a second catastrophic terrorist attack. The Act lifted many of the restrictions that barred the Government from spying on its residents, granting federal agents new powers to use wiretaps, to conduct electronic and computer eavesdropping, and to access private financial data.

In June 2003, federal prosecutors used the Act to file a charge of "terrorism using a weapon of mass destruction" against a California man after a pipe bomb exploded in his lap, wounding him as he sat in his car. In addition, local law enforcement agencies have begun increasing charges and possible sentences based on definitions in the PATRIOT Act that were added to state laws. In North Carolina, Martin Dwayne Miller was arrested under a new state law barring the manufacture of chemical weapons, for operating a methamphetamine lab. This new law increased the maximum possible sentence for the crime to life imprisonment, up from the previous maximum of six-to-twelve years. Prosecutor Jerry Wilson said he was not abusing the PATRIOT Act, which defines chemical weapons of mass destruction as "any substance that is designed or has the capability to cause death or serious injury" and contains toxic chemicals. The US Justice Department said it has used authority given to it by the PATRIOT Act to crack down on currency smugglers, and to seize money hidden overseas by alleged bookmakers, con artists, and drug dealers.[92]

The San Francisco Labor Council (SFLC) pointed out that "[USA] Patriot [Act] I created the new category of 'domestic terrorism'. . . . [I]t's important to note that the legal definition of domestic terrorism is now so broad that it encompasses traditional forms of job actions and concerted activities by unions, such as non-violent picket lines, civil disobedience or strikes. Resistance to corporate and government domination becomes 'terrorism.'"

The SFLC also pointed out, "The Patriot Act at 18 U.S.C. § 2331 (5) defines domestic terrorism as including acts that 'appear' to be intended to influence the policy of a government 'by intimidation or coercion.' This language is dangerously vague and can be used to apply to labor union actions such as strikes, slowdowns, boycotts, informational picketing, organizing, or even engaging in aggressive collective bargaining." During the International Longshore and Warehouse Union (ILWU) collective bargaining negotiations of 2002 in Oakland, "Secretary of Defense Rumsfeld all but made this very accusation of 'terrorism' by stating that an ILWU strike would not be in the interest of 'national security.'"

Denis Mosgofian of the SFLC stated that the April 7, 2003, "anti-war demonstrations at the Port of Oakland were met with excessive force by the police. Protestors and ILWU Local 10 members standing nearby were shot in the face, neck and body with wooden dowel bullets and concussion grenades. If someone had died in this melee, the anti-war organizations could have been labeled as 'terrorist' for causing the death. If law enforcement agencies suspected that the union cooperated or was involved in any capacity with these organizations, they too could be labeled 'terrorist,' subjecting the leadership and members to surveillance, arrest, and seizure of union assets."[93]

On December 13, 2003, while pictures of a captured, deloused Saddam Hussein were flashed around the world, President Bush quietly signed into law the Intelligence Authorization Act of Fiscal Year 2004. An expansion of federal surveillance powers originally intended to be part of PATRIOT Act II, the IAI redefines "financial institutions" to include "stockbrockers, car dealerships, casinos, credit card companies, insurance agencies, jewelers, airlines, the US Post Office, and any other business whose case transactions have a high degree of usefulness in criminal, tax, or regulatory matters." The records of such institutions are thereby open to examination by the FBI if they are requested in a "National Security Letter," even without a showing of probable cause.[94]

### Report 18.3: Attorney General Arrested Well-Known Defense Lawyer for Egyptian Sheik

On April 9, 2002, the FBI arrested Lynne Stewart, a sixty-three-year-old civil liberties attorney practicing in New York City, in front of her home as she was on her way to court. Stewart has a long career as a criminal defense attorney who represents high-profile clients. Her arrest was based on her relationship with her client Sheik Omar Abdel Rahman, convicted in 1995 of plotting terrorism against the United States, including planning to bomb public buildings in New York. Stewart was his court-appointed attorney.

On April 9, the FBI handcuffed Stewart and took her to FBI headquarters in Manhattan, while FBI agents searched her empty office all day. They removed computer hard-drives, address books, appointment books, and Rolodex files of Stewart's clients. After three hours at FBI headquarters, she was locked up.

Stewart was indicted under the 1996 Antiterrorism Act and charged with four criminal counts: providing material support to a terrorist organization, conspiracy to provide material support to a terrorist organization, defrauding the US Government, and lying to the US Government. The first two charges are felonies carrying a maximum sentence of fifteen years in prison. The latter two carry maximum sentences of five years each.

The indictment indicated that Stewart's communications with her client Abdel Rahman had been the subject of government wiretaps for more than two years. Stewart assumed the FBI got Foreign Intelligence Surveillance Act warrants that do not require probable cause, but only a suspicion that one is engaging in terrorist activities.

The indictment alleged that Stewart passed information from her client, Rahman, incarcerated at Federal Medical Center in Rochester, New York, to the media. It also alleged that she allowed a letter to be read to Rahman that was in violation of a Special Administrative Order (SAM) she signed with the Department of Justice in order to see her client.

Civil libertarians and lawyers protested the use by the Government of Stewart and Rahman's attorney-client conversations in building a case against Stewart because of the privileged nature of such conversations. Nevertheless, she was held until outraged colleagues posted her $500,000 bail.[95]

On the evening of Lynne Stewart's arrest, then attorney general John Ashcroft announced the criminal indictment of four defendants, including Stewart. Later that evening, Ashcroft appeared on the TV program *Late Night With David Letterman* and announced Stewart's arrest as a significant development in the fight against terror.

Stewart retained Michael Tigar, a prominent professor of constitutional law at American University, to represent her. Dozens of defense attorneys attended her arraignment in a showing of support. Because of the charges against her, all of Stewart's clients who were charged with federal crimes were questioned by judges, who asked them whether they wanted to continue to be represented by Stewart or not.

On June 13, 2003, in the US District Court for the Southern District of New York, presiding Judge John G. Koeltl questioned government prosecutor Christopher J. Morvillo on the distinction between political activities protected by the US Constitution and criminal conduct in terrorism cases. The prosecutor replied, "You know it when you see it, your Honor" (see Chapter 2.B-2, "Model Defense Brief on Charge of Terrorism").

On July 22, 2003, Judge Koeltl issued his seventy-seven-page opinion granting the defendant's motion to dismiss the felony counts of providing material support to terrorists because the Government applied the 1996 AntiTerrorism Act in a way that was unconstitutionally vague. The judge ruled that the defendants were correct to argue against a prosecution that was based on the mere use of telephones and other means of communication.

Four months later, Ashcroft and NY Southern District US Attorney James B. Comey brought a superseding indictment, although there were no new facts in the case, charging Stewart and her codefendants Ahmed Abdel Sattar (a postal worker who worked as a paralegal for the Sheik), and translator Mohammed Yousry with providing support for terrorists.[96] Judge Koeltl did not dismiss these charges.

Trial began on May 20, 2004, and lasted nine months. The Government sought to subpoena reporters from the *New York Times*, Reuters and *Newsday*, all of whom challenged the subpoenas.[97]

On February 10, 2005, after a seven month trial, the jury returned a verdict of guilty on all counts against each of the three defendants. They remained free on bail pending sentencing on July 15, 2005. Stewart's license to practice law was immediately suspended. Attorney Michael Tigar announced that he and the other defense lawyers would file a strong appeal.[98]

### Report 18.4: Immigration Officials Detained Global Relief Foundation Executive, Then Deported Him

In December 2001, the US Government froze the assets and raided and closed the Chicago offices of the Global Relief Foundation (GRF). On December 14, 2001, three Immigration and Naturalization Service officers arrested Rabih Haddad, who had legally entered the United States from Lebanon in 1988, for overstaying his visa.

Haddad cofounded the humanitarian-focused GRF in 1992 and served as chairman of its board and as its CEO between 1992 and 1996. Recently he served as GRF's public relations director, and raised funds extensively for GRF projects. Haddad is married and has four children.

Haddad's visa had expired, but he was in the process of applying for permanent resident status. In accordance with a visa amnesty law passed under the Clinton administration, Haddad's immigration status did not require him to leave the country. Nevertheless, the INS refused Haddad bond on the basis that he might be a flight risk and might pose a danger to the community. After his arrest, the Government transferred Haddad to the Metropolitan Correctional Center in Chicago, where he was held in solitary confinement. Haddad's 2002 INS hearings were closed to the public. The Government said Mr. Haddad and GRF were suspected of links to al Qaeda.[99]

In the case of *Haddad v. Ashcroft*, 303 F.3d 681 (6th Cir. 2002), the ACLU and the *Detroit Free Press* sued the federal Government for having illegally closed Mr. Haddad's INS hearings. *Detroit Free Press v. Ashcroft* was heard by Judge Nancy G. Edmund on April 3, 2002. Her decision denied the Justice Department's claim that secrecy was more necessary than individual rights.[100] The Sixth Circuit Court affirmed August 26, 2002. In June 2002, the Government transferred Haddad to Monroe County Jail in Michigan to await an INS hearing.

On July 15, 2003, US Immigration and Customs Enforcement (ICE; previously the INS) denied Haddad asylum and deported him to Lebanon after holding him in jail for nineteen months. Haddad was never charged by the US Government with any crime.[101] On July 28, 2003, the United States deported Rabih Haddad's wife, Salma Al-Rushaid, and her four children, aged five to thirteen. They were flown to Kuwait.[102]

### Report 18.5: US District Court Kept Secret the Habeas Corpus Case of Detained Algerian

In 2001, the INS detained Mohamed Kamel Bellahouel, an Algerian waiter in south Florida, and the FBI questioned him. They held Bellahouel for five months in federal prison in Miami, and took him to testify before the federal grand jury in Alexandria, Virginia, that indicted the so-called twentieth hijacker, Zacarias Moussaoui. They questioned Bellahouel because he had allegedly served meals to two 9/11 hijackers in the weeks before the attack and had watched a movie with one of them.

Because he was not charged with a crime, Bellahouel filed a petition for writ of habeas corpus to challenge his detention. He posted a $10,000 immigration bond on the charge that he had overstayed his student visa, issued in 1992, and was released in March 2002. Bellahouel continues to challenge his detention and the secret handling of his case. His petition for certiorari is publicly listed only as *M.K.B. v. Warden, et al.*, 03–6747.[103]

In 2002, US District Court Judge Paul C. Huck sealed the records of this Habeas Corpus suit and ordered the case kept off the public docket. He did not issue a formal order to keep the case secret, which is the standard practice. The Eleventh US Circuit Court of Appeals upheld Huck's actions, also without ordering that the case be kept secret. Miami public defender Paul Rashkind filed an appeal for Bellahouel "to preserve and protect the public's common-law and First Amendment rights to know, but also to reinforce those rights in a time of increased national suspicion about the free flow of information and debate."

The Administration told the Supreme Court that it did not plan to file a response to the appeal. On November 4, 2003, the Court agreed to hear a petition for certiorari, but case files and records remained sealed. In a brief notice released November 4, the Court said it told the Administration to present its side, with no specific deadline.

"It's the case that doesn't exist. Even though two different federal courts have conducted hearings and issued rulings, there has been no public record of any action. No documents are available. No files. No lawyer is allowed to speak about it. Period." The case has come to light only because a brief docketing error identified MKB by name.[104]

The Reporters Committee for Freedom of the Press filed a friend of the court brief on November 3, 2003, accusing the Eleventh Circuit of approving the "drastic departure" from judicial norms by Judge Huck. The brief argued that "The district court's failure to issue a sealing order, make findings, explore less restrictive alternatives, or give the public an opportunity to be heard constitutes an egregious violation of well-settled law."

Bellahouel's appeal includes blank page after blank page, where the ruling would have been. The nine justices will be able to see all the information that is withheld from the public. "The fact that someone can be held like this, and there be no trail of the existence of the case is mind-boggling," said Michael Greenberger, a counterterrorism expert and former senior official in the US Justice Department during the Clinton administration.[105]

"When the government classifies things like that, they're usually trying to cover up their own mistakes," said Abner J. Mikva, who served as a Democratic Congressman, chief judge of the US Court of Appeals for the DC Circuit, and a top aide to the Clinton Administration.[106]

In February 2004, the Supreme Court refused to take up Bellahouel's appeal. According to legal scholars Floyd Abrams and Neal Sonnett, by refusing to review the Bellahouel case "the Supreme Court set 'precedent' that implicitly gave federal judges and prosecutors room to keep cases completely secret."[107]

### Report 18.6: Courts Reject Sections of Antiterrorism Act and USA PATRIOT Act

After passage of the USA PATRIOT Act, the Humanitarian Law Project of Los Angeles amended the complaint they had filed in 1998 challenging sections of the 1996 Antiterrorism and Effective Death Penalty Act (18 U.S.C. § 2339 [B]) to include sections of the PATRIOT Act.

For years the Humanitarian Law Project provided humanitarian aid to the Kurdish Workers Party (PKK) in Turkey. In Northern California, Sri Lankan Tamils sent money to members of their group abroad. The HLP and others who supported legal humanitarian activities had filed the suit, prepared by the Center for Constitutional Rights (CCR), challenging the constitutionality of sections of the AntiTerrorism Act, and its enforcement by the US Department of Justice. The amended complaint in *Humanitarian Law Project v. Ashcroft* alleged that enforcing the PATRIOT Act has a "chilling effect" on people making badly needed donations to medical clinics, schools, churches, mosques, grassroots organizations, and other humanitarian causes in countries the US Government has designated as places where "terrorist groups" are active.

On December 3, 2003, the US Court of Appeals for the Ninth Circuit in San Francisco declared significant sections of the Antiterrorism Act unconstitutionally "void for vagueness under the First and Fifth Amendments because they bring within their ambit constitutionally protected speech and advocacy." The Court ruled that the Government must prove beyond a reasonable doubt that the donor knew the organization was designated or was aware of the unlawful activities that led to the designation. "[A]ccording to the government's interpretation of 2339B, a woman who buys cookies from a bake sale outside of her grocery store to support displaced Kurdish refugees to find new homes could be held liable so long as the bake sale had a sign that said that the sale was sponsored by the PKK, without regard to her knowledge of the PKK's designation or other activities" (*Humanitarian Law Project v. Ashcroft*, 353 F.3d 382, 9th Cir., 2003).

Prof. David Cole, who argued the case, said the statute imposes guilt by association. The opinion calls into question the legality of several convictions, including those of the Lackawanna Six who pleaded guilty to violating the law by attending an al Qaeda training camp. Nancy Chang of the CCR, says the opinion is particularly important because "the PATRIOT Act was amended to increase the penalty for the provision of material support from ten years to 15 years and possibly a sentence of life."[108]

And see Report 8.6.

## Report 18.7: Jury Acquits One; DOJ Agrees To Drop "Terrorism" Charges Against Two After Conviction

In October 2001, then attorney general John Ashcroft called a national press conference to announce the arrest of four young men from Detroit, Michigan, as terrorists. On August 29, 2002, they were indicted for being "radical Islamists" conspiring to launch an international holy war to "drive American military forces from the Arabian peninsula, end American support of Israel, and undermine American support to moderate regimes throughout the Middle East that they viewed as insufficiently Islamic." (*United States v. Iarim Koubriti, et al.*, ED MI S. Div., #01–80778.)

The defendants were granted a jury trial on one or more of four counts: providing material support or resources to terrorists; conspiracy to engage in fraud and misuse of visas, permits, and other documents; fraud and misuse of visas, and the like; and fraud and related activity in connection with identification documents and information (under 18 U.S.C. §§ 2339(A) 371, 1546(a), and 1028(a)(6) and 2).

In June 2003, the jury acquitted Farouk Ali-Haimoud of all charges, found Ahmed Hannan guilty of fraud and misuse of his visa, and convicted Karim Koubriti and Abdel-llah Elmardoudi of conspiracy to support some unspecified terrorist acts at some unspecified place in the unspecified future (District Attorney Richard Helfrick in a conversation with the MCLI, July 26, 2004).

The case marked the only conviction of "terrorists" from the DOJ detention of more than five thousand foreign nationals arrested in antiterrorism sweeps between 9/11 and January 2005.

On December 12, 2003, Federal District Court Judge Gerald F. Rosen held a hearing to determine whether to vacate the convictions on the ground that federal prosecutors had failed to disclose evidence that the principal Government witness had lied on the stand. On December 16, 2003, Judge Rosen admonished then attorney general Ashcroft for interfering with the trial by violating a gag order and officially praising the Government's principal witness while the jury was deliberating.[109]

On June 11, 2004, the Justice Department delivered to defense attorneys thirty to forty relevant documents that had not been disclosed to the defense before trial. In addition, theDOJ's Public Integrity Section announced it had launched a criminal investigation of Assistant US Attorney Richard Convertino, the lead prosecutor in the case who was responsible for the decision not to grant the defense full disclosure.[110]

On August 24, 2004, the DOJ submitted a sixty-page memo to the trial judge that harshly criticized its Assistant US Attorney, and stated that it would no longer pursue terrorist charges against any of these defendants. The memo also supported their request for a new trial solely on charges of document fraud.

On September 2, 2004, the District Court judge threw out the convictions. The three defendants remained in custody after three years, awaiting trial on the minor nonterrorist charge (*US v. Koubriti*, 307 F.Supp.2d 891 [E.D. MI, 2004]).

## Report 18.8: US Takes Native Land for Nuclear Waste Repository and Resource Extraction Despite 1863 Treaty

The 2003 Western Shoshone Distribution Act (H.R. 884) is one in a long series of actions by the US Government to take land and resources from Native American tribes. The Act authorized compensation by the United States of approximately fifteen cents an acre for tens of millions of acres of disputed Shoshone lands in Nevada, Idaho, Utah, and California. The authority cited by Congress for this action was an Indian Claims Commission (ICC) decision, docket # 326–K, which allegedly determined that the Western Shoshone's aboriginal title to the land had been extinguished. The Government signed the Treaty with the Western Shoshoni (the Treaty of Ruby Valley) in 1863.

The Treaty provided that "the boundaries of the country claimed and occupied by said bands are defined and described by them as follows: On the north by Wong-goga-da Mountains and Shoshonee River Valley; on the west by Su-non-to-yah Mountains or Smith Creek Mountains; on the south by Wi-co-bah and the Colorado Desert; on the east by Po-ho-no-be Valley or Steptoe Valley and Great Salt Lake Valley [Article 5]." The Treaty also put many restrictions on the Shoshones' use of the land and provided for many actions of settlers, miners, and the US Government that the Shoshone would have to tolerate. Article 6 stated that the tribes "agree that whenever the President of the United States shall deem it expedient for them to abandon the roaming life, which, they now lead, and become herdsmen or agriculturalists, he is hereby authorized to make such reservations for their use as he may deem necessary within the country above described." Finally, Article 7 stated that the United States, "being aware of the inconvenience resulting to the Indians in consequence of the driving away and destruction of game along the routes travelled by white men, and by the formation of agricultural and mining settlements, are willing to fairly compensate them for the same. . . . And the said bands hereby acknowledge the reception of the said stipulated annuities as a full compensation and equivalent for the loss of game and the rights and privileges hereby conceded."[111]

Article 6 §2 of the US Constitution provides that treaties are the supreme law of the land. Historians agree that the Government has seldom lived up to its treaties with many Native American tribes. The land base at issue is the third-largest gold-producing area in the world and is considered an excellent investment opportunity for extraction companies. It has been the home of numerous tribes for centuries. It is also the site where the Yucca Mountain nuclear waste repository would be located, and home to the Nevada Test Site and Federal Counterterrorism Facility, where the Bush Administration advocated resuming nuclear testing.

The majority of tribal councils representing approximately 80 percent of the population of the affected area, the Western Shoshone National Council, and most of the traditional people of the area strongly opposed the bill that became law in 2004. The National Congress of American Indians and Amnesty International supported them. The Bush Administration ignored this formidable opposition and used an undocumented, unverified straw poll to justify the legislation.

In the opinion of many of the elders of the community, the Act does not change the fact that the Western Shoshone still hold title to the land. Their assertion stems from three facts. First, some Shoshone claim that the Indian Claims Commission process was illegitimate because it was co-opted by a relative minority of Shoshone who claimed to have authority to adjudicate the claims of all Shoshone. Hugh Stevens, Chairman of the Te-Moak Tribe of the Western Shoshone Nation, described the ICC as "the self-described, private group who pushed for this money," and said that they "are not members of any federally-recognized council and have no authority to speak on behalf of our Tribe or the Western Shoshone Nation. The Nevada legislators and the Bush Administration have been well-advised of this fact. The way this legislation was handled makes an absolute sham of the stated government-to-government relationship and responsibility of the US government."[112]

Second, even if the ICC were a legitimate process, Section 21 of the Indian Claims Commission Act (ICCA) required the ICC to promptly file a report with Congress when it completed a given case. The Commission never carried out this requirement in this instance. Western Shoshone docket 326–K is listed in the ICC's "Final Report" as one of the dockets "not reported to Congress" because the case was still on appeals (by both the US Government and the traditional Western Shoshone) before the Court of Claims when the ICC went out of existence. Although the ICC issued a Final Award judgment in the case, the ICC had a clear and explicit statutory obligation to file a final report with Congress on the case. Because the Commission failed to do so, finality was never achieved. The report of the Commission's judgment to Congress was an essential prerequisite for the United States to compensate the Western Shoshones for the unsettled land that the United States claimed the Western Shoshone were dispossessed of within the boundaries described in the 1863 Treaty of Ruby Valley.

Finally, the Western Shoshone assert that the Ninth Circuit Court of

Appeals was correct when it ruled in 1978 that "the title issue in this case was neither actually litigated nor actually decided in the proceedings before the ICC" (*United States v. Dann*, 572 F. 2d 222, 226). Thus, the question of title to land held by Shoshone families, such as the Danns and others with land similarly held, is necessary for determination of compensation.[113]

On July 7, 2004, President Bush signed the Western Shoshone Distribution Bill into law. Carrie Dann then called on the United States to prove how it received title to the land. She alleged that the sole legal theory stated by the ICC was that the Western Shoshone land title was extinguished through "gradual encroachment" by nonindigenous miners and settlers. Dann claims that such legal theory cannot be found in US law prior to its use in this case.

Raymond Yowell of the Western Shoshone National Council stated, "I am utterly disappointed. It's unbelievable that the US body that makes the laws has acted in this manner. The fight is not over. A fraud is a fraud—Individuals cannot sell out a nation. . . . [T]he bill, although a threat politically, does nothing to change our inherent rights or our Treaty rights. Congress and the President were informed of all the facts that touch upon this issue. We will use the Treaty of Ruby Valley to stop Yucca Mountain and to protect our lands. Our title is still intact."[114]

## 19. NOT TO "DETAIN" "ENEMY COMBATANTS" AT GUANTANAMO OR ANYWHERE ELSE

The most pervasive human rights violations since 9/11 occurred during the detentions of people on various grounds. Every person in US custody has a series of clear rights:

- not to be tortured or subjected to cruel and unusual punishment,
- to be notified of the charges on which they are being held or to go before a judge in a habeas corpus proceeding and be told the charges, and
- to be tried within a reasonable time on these charges.

The Bush Administration uniformly denied all of these due process rights to detainees in violation of federal and international law.

- Most of the people who were killed or disappeared by the US Government were first detained (Section 1).
- Most of the people who were subjected to torture by the US Government ment were first detained (Section 2).
- Most of the people who were arrested by the US Government while

exercising their right to assemble were detained before being released or tried (Section 3).

- Many people who went to register at the request of the US Government were immediately detained by Immigration authorities (Section 8).
- Many of the people were detained while they were trying to exercise their right to travel (Section 11).
- People seeking political asylum were often detained while awaiting decisions on their applications (Section 20).
- Some US Armed Forces personnel who applied for conscientious objector status were kept in detention while the military decided what to do with them (Section 16).
- Political prisoners continued to be detained (Section 24).

The largest single category of detainees, and those held the longest without any due process or procedure for determining why they should be detained, were the men arrested all over the world and held by US military forces at Guantanamo Bay, Cuba.

On January 20, 2002, a group of journalists, lawyers, professors, and members of the clergy filed a petition for habeas relief before the US District Court for the Central District of California on behalf of the class of unidentified individuals detained at Guantanamo Bay. The petition named President Bush, Secretary Rumsfeld, and a number of military personnel as respondents (*Coalition of Clergy v. Bush*, 189 F. Supp. 2d 1036 [C.D. Cal., 2002]). The Court dismissed the petition for lack of "next-friend" standing, or, in the alternative, for lack of jurisdiction.

The mistreatment of prisoners at Guantanamo Bay quickly became known internationally. In early 2002, the UN High Commissioner for Human Rights and later the Inter-American Commission on Human Rights of the Organization of American States requested the US Government to ensure a "competent tribunal" to determine the legal status of the Guantanamo detainees (Report 19.1 and Chapter 3.D).

In May 2004, Spc. Sean Baker, a former soldier, accused the military of causing him brain damage during a training exercise at Guantanamo Bay with the 303rd Military Police Company. In January 2003, Baker's superior told him to pose as a prisoner, which involved wearing an orange jumpsuit, so that four MPs could practice the techniques used by the Emergency Response Force (ERF) at Camp Delta, Guantanamo Bay. The MPs were not told that Baker was a military official and not an inmate, as had been done previously. During the exercise, the MPs entered the cell in riot gear and grabbed Baker, twisting his legs and hitting and choking him. The MPs exerted pressure on his head and slammed it several times against the steel floor.

Baker kept saying, "I'm a US soldier."

The MPs did not stop until they ripped the orange jumpsuit and saw Baker's military uniform underneath.

Baker was sent to the infirmary and declared fit for duty after being given a brainscan. Several months later, he went to Walter Reed Medical Center for treatment. Subsequently, he was hospitalized for two months for seizures. In April 2004, the military gave him a medical discharge, leaving him unemployed, disabled with seizures, and still experiencing flashbacks of the assault.

The Pentagon claims there was no connection between his condition and the Guantanamo assault. The Southern Command declared that Baker's injuries were a "foreseeable consequence" of the training exercise. The military physical evaluation board reported that Baker's mood and seizure disorders were caused by a traumatic brain injury sustained while "playing [the] role of detainee who [was] non-cooperative and was being extracted from [a] detention cell in Guantanamo Bay, Cuba. Soldier is mentally competent."[115]

In June 2004, the Supreme Court granted the habeas corpus petition of Yaser Hamdi, a US citizen arrested in Afghanistan, sent to the US detention camp at Guantanamo Bay, and then transferred to a prison in Virginia. The Court clearly held (8–1) that he is entitled to a hearing before a neutral decision maker (Report 19.2). Before, and after, that decision, the military announced it would try fifteen detainees held at Guantanamo Bay, amid numerous charges by reporters that prisoners are subjected to systematic torture and cruel treatment there, with no notice of the charges against them or an opportunity for contact with any living being other than the guards (Report 19.3).

The US Navy arrested a Syrian-US citizen interpreter at Guantanamo, charged him with thirty-two counts of aiding the enemy, and conducted an illegal search of his legal papers (Report 19.4). The United States sent to Guantanamo men from the Middle East (Report 19.3), Syria (Report 19.4), Australia (Report 19.5), and the United Kingdom (Report 19.7). All attempted to charge that they were detained illegally. Several alleged that they were tortured (Report 19.3). The Department of Defense (DOD) denied an Australian the right to a habeas corpus hearing (Report 19.5). After the Supreme Court agreed to hear other detainee cases, the military released several British detainees from Guantanamo Bay who went home and talked about the cruel treatment they suffered there (Report 19.7).

On June 28, 2004, the Supreme Court ruled that US courts have jurisdiction to consider charges of illegality of detention of foreign nationals at Guantanamo Bay (Report 19.5), which sent the cases of other detainees back to US District Courts for hearings on the merits of their habeas petitions (Report 19.6).

In mid-October 2004, several employees at Guantanamo Bay, under anonymity, revealed to the *New York Times* that detainees had been subjected to "harsh and coercive treatment" regularly, contrary to Pentagon military officials' claims that allegations of torture were exceptional and rare. These employees, including military guards and intelligence agents, spoke of stripping uncooperative inmates to their underwear and forcing them to sit in a chair with their hands and feet shackled to a bolt on the ground. The guards would then turn on strobe lights, loud rock and rap music, and the air conditioner to the maximum, knowing most inmates were used to high temperatures in their birth countries. At the end of the procedure, the inmates were completely confused. Guards also followed Operation Sandman, in which guards wakened an inmate out of deep sleep, interrogated him, and put him in a different cell. When he had fallen back to sleep, they wakened him and started all over again, repeating the procedure five or six times during the night.

David Sheffer, a former Department of State human rights official, now a professor at George Washington University, said, "I don't think there's any question that treatment of that character satisfies the severe pain and suffering requirement, be it physical or mental, that is provided for in the [Geneva] Convention Against Torture."

The Defense Department, through Lt. Cdr. Alvin Plexico, issued a statement that the military is providing a "safe, humane and professional detention operation at Guantanamo Bay that is providing valuable information in the war on terrorism."[116]

People concerned about the condition of prisoners at Guantanamo Bay are closely following the slow path of these cases challenging the detentions. And they are telling their Congress members to vote against any budget items to expand detention facilities at Guantanamo and to vote for the funding of public defenders to represent the detainees when hearings are ultimately held. Lawyers and activists maintain that the proper treatment of detainees is essential to stop the spread of terrorism in each country from which detainees come. (See *Guantanamo: What the World Should Know*, by Michal Ratner and Ellen Ray [White River Junction, VT: Chelsea Green, 2004]).

## Relevant Law:

U.S. Constitution: Preamble, Art. I, §8, Cl. 11; Art. I, §9, Cl. 2; Art. II, §1, Cl. 8; Art. II, §2, Cl. 1; Art. II, §3; Art. VI, Cl. 2; First, Fourth, Fifth, Sixth, Eighth, Fourteenth Amendments
*Hamdi v. Rumsfeld*, 124 S.Ct. 2633 (2004)
*Rasul v. Bush*, 124 S.Ct. 2686 (2004)
UN Charter: Preamble, Art. 1.3, 2.2, 55, 56, 73 (a)-(d), 74

Nuremberg Principles
Hague Conventions
Third and Fourth Geneva Conventions
OAS Charter: Art. 106
ICCPR: Preamble, Art. 1-7, 9, 9.4, 10, 10.1, 10.2(a), 12.3, 12.4, 14, 16-19, 20.2, 23.1, 26, 27, 40.1
CERD: Art. 1, 2, 5, 6, 9
CAT: Preamble, Art. 1, 2, 2.2, 2.3, 3-5, 7, 10.1, 10.2, 11-14, 14.1, 15, 16, 16.1, 19.1, 21.1(c)
ICESCR: Preamble, Art. 1.1, 1.2, 2-4, 12, 15, 16, 25
Inter American Commission on Human Rights (IACHR) Statute: Art. 17-20
American Convention on Human Rights

## Report 19.1: The UN and the OAS Concerned about Competent Tribunal for Guantanamo Detainees

President Bush declared a "war on terror" on September 20, 2001. In October 2001, the US military launched air and ground strikes against Taliban forces and members of al Qaeda in Afghanistan. On November 13, 2001, Bush issued a Military Order permitting the Secretary of Defense to detain individuals whom the president had determined were members of al Qaeda, or who had participated in some manner in international terrorist acts "or acts in preparation therefore, that have caused, threaten to cause, or have as their aim to cause, injury to or adverse effects on the United States, its citizens, national security, foreign policy, or economy," or who "knowingly harbored any such person."

This Military Order did not obligate the US Government to bring each detainee to trial. However, all such trials of any detainee must occur before military commissions, which may wield the power to impose death sentences without a unanimous verdict. The Military Order also stated that such detainees could not, individually or through a third party, "Seek any remedy or maintain any proceeding" in any state or federal court in the United States, or convened by or in a foreign nation or international tribunal.

In early January 2002, the US military started transporting prisoners from the armed conflict in Afghanistan to its naval station at Guantanamo Bay, Cuba, stating that these prisoners were to be tried, if at all, according to the terms of the Military Order.

On January 16, 2002, the UN High Commissioner for Human Rights released a statement:

- reminding the US Government that the Guantanamo detainees were "entitled to the protection of international human rights law and

humanitarian law," including "the International Covenant on Civil and Political Rights (ICCPR) and the Geneva Conventions of 1949";
- indicating that a competent tribunal should determine their "legal status" as detainees, and determine if they qualify for "prisoner-of-war" (POW) status under article 5 of the Third Geneva Convention; and
- requiring that all trials should follow basic principles of fairness, "including the presumption of innocence," as found in the ICCPR and the Third Geneva Convention.[117]

On February 7, 2002, the Office of the US Press Secretary responded by releasing a fact sheet stating that the United States was treating the Guantanamo detainees "humanely." It specified that the al Qaeda detainees did not qualify for POW status because al Qaeda, as "a foreign terrorist group," was "not a state party to the Geneva Convention." The US Government announced that the Taliban detainees did not qualify as POWs under the terms of the Geneva Convention despite recognizing that Afghanistan was a party.[118]

On February 25, 2002, the Center for Constitutional Rights (CCR), the Human Rights Clinic at Columbia Law School, and the Center for Justice and International Law presented a request to the Inter-American Commission on Human Rights (IACHR) of the Organization of American States (OAS). They urged that "precautionary measures" be taken so that the approximately three hundred detainees at Guantanamo Bay would be treated as POWs, and their human rights would be protected from unlawful detentions, interrogations, and military trials where they could face the death sentence.[119]

On March 12, 2002, the IACHR sent a letter to President Bush asking the US Government to "take the urgent measures necessary to have the legal status of the detainees at Guantanamo Bay be determined by a competent tribunal," and that the United States respond within thirty days of receiving its letter regarding its compliance with these measures and provide periodic updates. In a separate letter of the same date, the IACHR notified the CCR and the other US NGOs of its decision (see the text of the letters in Chapter 3.D).

On April 15, 2002, the IACHR informed the CCR of the US Government's rejection of its decision regarding the adoption of precautionary measures, arguing that the IACHR lacked jurisdiction to apply precautionary measures and the right to interpret the Geneva Convention. In October 2002, the IACHR held a hearing to evaluate the US Government's position. On June 28, 2004, the CCR requested that the IACHR expand the "Precautionary Measures" previously adopted in relation to detainees in Guantanamo, based on new evidence regarding the conditions and treatment of persons detained by the United States.

On July 29, 2004, the IACHR sent a letter to President Bush that:

- suggested that the United States had contradicted its previous statements that all measures would be taken to prevent the torture or other cruel, inhuman, or degrading treatment of detainees at Guantanamo;
- chastised the Bush Administration for lapses in information: "This information appears to contradict previous assurances provided to the Commission by your Excellency's government that it is the United State's policy to treat all detainees and conduct all interrogations, wherever they may occur, in a manner consistent with the commitment to prevent torture and other cruel, inhuman or degrading treatment or punishment";
- expressed concern over the legal status of the detainees and doubts over the legitimacy of the planned military tribunals; and
- held that the United States is not effectively protecting the fundamental rights to which the detainees may be entitled.[120]

## Report 19.2: US Sends US Citizen Hamdi to Guantanamo; Supreme Court Exercises Jurisdiction

In November 2001, during the US invasion of Afghanistan, the Northern Alliance captured Yaser Hamdi, a US citizen, and handed him over to the US military who took him to Camp X-Ray in Guantanamo Bay, Cuba, and labeled him an "enemy combatant." When they discovered he was a US citizen, they transferred him to a military brig in Norfolk, Virginia, where he was denied counsel, detained without charges, and held in solitary confinement.

In June 2002, Hamdi's father filed a petition for writ of habeas corpus. The petition stated that, although Hamdi was in a zone of active combat when captured, he is a US citizen and is, therefore, entitled to the full protection of the Constitution. In January 2003, the Fourth Circuit Court of Appeals dismissed Hamdi's petition because he had been labeled an "enemy combatant" (*Hamdi v. Rumsfeld*, 316 F.3d 450).

The Supreme Court granted certiorari and on June 28, 2004, rendered its decision. In an opinion by Justice O'Connor, the Court ruled (8–1) that even though Congress authorized the detention of combatants in the narrow circumstances alleged by the Government, due process requires that a US citizen being held as an enemy combatant be given meaningful opportunity to contest the factual basis for his detention before a neutral decision maker. And the Court ruled unanimously that, "It does not infringe on the core role of the military for the courts to exercise their own time-honored and constitutionally mandated role of reviewing and resolving claims like those presented here." (*Hamdi v. Rumsfeld*, 124 S.Ct. 2633 [2004]).

The Court also held:

- Habeas corpus remains available to every individual detained within the United States unless suspended (p. 2633) (8–1);
- Separation of powers principles do not mandate a heavily circumscribed role for the Court in such circumstances (p. 2650) (8–1);
- "Any process in which the Executive's factual assertions go wholly unchallenged or are simply presumed correct without any opportunity for the alleged combatant to demonstrate otherwise falls constitutionally short" (p. 2651) (8–1); and
- "Hamdi has received no process. An interrogation by one's captor, however effective an intelligence-gathering tool, hardly constitutes a constitutionally adequate fact finding before a neutral decision maker" (p. 2651) (8–1).

Justice Souter, along with Justice Ginsburg, wrote a concurring opinion; Justice Scalia, along with Justice Stevens, wrote a dissenting opinion; Justice Thomas also wrote a dissenting opinion.

Justices Souter and Ginsberg maintained that: "The threshold issue is how broadly or narrowly to read the Non-Detention Act, the tone of which is severe: 'No citizen shall be imprisoned or otherwise detained by the United States except pursuant to an Act of Congress.' Should the severity of the Act be relieved when the Government's stated factual justification for incommunicado detention is a war on terrorism, so that the Government may be said to act 'pursuant' to congressional terms that fall short of explicit authority to imprison individuals? With one possible though important qualification, the answer has to be no" (p. 2653).

They also insisted that the focus of the Authorization for Use of Military Force (AUMF; PL 107–40), passed by Congress and signed by President Bush on September 18, 2001, "never so much as uses the word detention, and there is no reason to think Congress might have perceived any need to augment Executive power to deal with dangerous citizens within the United States, given the well-stocked statutory arsenal of defined criminal offenses covering the gamut of actions that a citizen sympathetic to terrorists might commit" (p. 2656). "The Government has not made out its claim that in detaining Hamdi in the manner described, it is acting in accord with the laws of war authorized to be applied against citizens by the Force Resolution" (p. 2658).

The O'Connor Four and Justice Thomas clarified their position: "Enemy combatant proceedings may be tailored to alleviate their uncommon potential to burden the Executive at a time of ongoing military conflict. Hearsay, for example, may need to be accepted as the most reliable available evidence from the Government in such a proceeding. Likewise, the Constitution would not be offended by a presumption in favor of the Government's evidence, so long as that presumption remained a rebuttable one and fair opportunity for rebuttal were provided" (p. 2649). They also held:

- There is no bar to the United States holding one of its own citizens as an enemy combatant (p. 2640);
- Congress has clearly and unmistakably authorized detention in the narrow circumstances considered in this case (p. 2641) (5–4);
- The Executive has the authority to detain citizens who qualify as "enemy combatants" pursuant to Congressional Authorization for the Use of Military Force (AUMF) (5–4); and
- Indefinite detention of citizen enemy combatants for the duration of active hostilities is legal under the laws of war. Since US forces are still actively combating Taliban fighters in Afghanistan, Hamdi's detention is justified (p. 2641) (5–4).

Justice Scalia and Justice Stevens stated in their dissent:

- "The very core of liberty secured by our Anglo-Saxon system of separated powers has been freedom from indefinite imprisonment at the will of the Executive. Blackstone stated this principle clearly: 'Of great importance to the public is the preservation of this personal liberty: for if once it were left in the power of any, the highest, magistrate to imprison arbitrarily whomever he or his officers thought proper... there would soon be an end of all other rights and immunities'" (p. 2660);
- "Where the Executive has not pursued the usual course of charge, committal, and conviction, it has historically secured the Legislature's explicit approval of a suspension" (p. 2664);
- "In *Ex parte Milligan*, the Court issued the writ to an American citizen who had been tried by military commission for offenses that included conspiring to overthrow the Government, seize munitions, and liberate prisoners of war. The Court rejected in no uncertain terms the Government's assertion that military jurisdiction was proper under the 'laws and usages of war'" (p. 2667); and
- "The proposition that the Executive lacks indefinite wartime detention authority over citizens is consistent with the Founders' general mistrust of military power permanently at the Executive's disposal" (p. 2667) (*Hamdi v. Rumsfeld*, 124 S.Ct. 2633 [2004]).

After the Supreme Court's decision in *Hamdi*, it emerged that the US Government has threatened to indefinitely detain other US citizens at Guantanamo as "enemy combatants." On June 11, 2003, Ahmed Abu Ali, a US citizen, was jailed without charges in Saudi Arabia at the US Government's request on suspicion that he was a member of al Qaeda. In September 2003, he was visited in his jail cell by a US consulate, who reportedly "threatened him with being declared an enemy combatant and [sending him] to Guantanamo."[121]

On July 28, 2004, the parents of Abu Ali filed suit against the US Government, claiming that their son's detention was a deliberate attempt to keep him out of the United States and in the hands of jailers who could abuse or torture him for information. The family's lawyer cited the *Hamdi* case in support.[122]

On September 22, 2004, the Director of Public Affairs for the DOJ, Mark Corallo, announced that Hamdi and his attorney had negotiated and signed an agreement with the United States for his release. The conditions of the release include Hamdi's renunciation of his US citizenship, his relocation to Saudi Arabia where he is also a citizen, and restrictions on his traveling. Corallo added, "[T]he United States has no interest in detaining enemy combatants beyond the point that they be permitted to consult an attorney."[123]

On September 24, 2004, the United States filed the agreement (in the Eastern District of Virginia District Court) providing: Hamdi cannot leave Saudi Arabia for five years; then for ten years he must first notify the US Embassy before doing so; he cannot go to Afghanistan, Iraq, Israel, Pakistan, or Syria, and he is prohibited travel to the United States for ten years; thereafter he must request permission from the Secretaries of Defense and Homeland Security. He cannot sue the United States for wrongful imprisonment; he must report any details of terrorist activity that he knows about; and he cannot participate in terrorist activity or be involved with the violent jihad.[124]

On October 10, 2004, the United States finally flew Hamdi to Saudi Arabia after three years of detention as an "enemy combatant." Deborah Pearlstein, Director of the US Law and Security Program at Human Rights First declared, "The release calls into question the government's vigorous insistence that Mr. Hamdi ever posed a significant threat. Most important, it's another lesson in why the United States has always relied on courts to test the truth of its accusations."[125]

## Report 19.3: Middle Eastern Men Detained at Guantanamo, Tortured, Denied Rights

After September 11, 2001, the US Government captured more than 650 alleged members of the Taliban and al Qaeda in Afghanistan and Iraq, and, beginning in January 2002, sent them to Guantanamo Bay, a military base in Cuba leased by the United States. As of May 2003, the detainees were from forty-two countries: most were from Saudi Arabia, Yemen, and Pakistan; others were from Canada, Sweden, Australia, Britain, France, and Kuwait. Three detainees were juveniles between the ages of thirteen and fifteen. No US Government agent informed any of the detainees what crimes they were being held for. They were also denied access to lawyers.

US treatment of the detainees became the subject of immediate, vocal, international protest, with many critics alleging torture and systemic violations of basic human rights. After their arrival in January 2002, the detainees were photographed kneeling on the ground in orange jumpsuits with blacked-out goggles blocking their vision, their mouths and eyes covered, and their hands shackled together and covered in heavy mittens.[126]

In June 2003, investigative journalist Ted Conover went to Guantanamo and reported that each prisoner lives in a separate cell six feet eight inches by eight feet. Each prisoner is allowed out of the cell only three times a week, for twenty minutes of solitary exercise in a large concrete-floored cage, followed by a five-minute shower. Before coming out of the cell, prisoners must submit to leg shackles connected to handcuffs. Guards escort them on either side.[127]

Since 2002, there have been reports of thirty-four suicide attempts by twenty-one individual detainees. One lapsed into a persistent vegetative state and must be fed through a medical device in his stomach. Almost one hundred detainees are under mental health supervision, with about half receiving psychiatric drugs regularly[128]

On July 4, 2003, senior Bush Administration officials announced that Bush had officially ruled that six of the detainees in Guantanamo were eligible for trial before military tribunals as alleged members of al Qaeda on charges ranging from terrorism to war crimes.[129]

As of August 2003, the United States had released approximately seventy detainees, and one hundred twenty prisoners had been moved to a medium security wing where they could get more exercise, and read books and exercize other liberties, reportedly for cooperating in interrogations or because they "provided good intelligence." Two of the sixteen Afghan prisoners released on July 21, 2003, said that they were beaten and kept or restrained in cold, overcrowded rooms.

On August 26, 2003, the Government announced that it was building a fifth camp to hold more detainees and expand interrogation facilities. The Camp V could house one hundred more detainees, increasing the capacity at the naval base to 1,100.[130]

On March 15, 2004, the US military announced the release of twenty-three Afghan and three Pakistani citizens from the US Navy prison in Guantanamo. The released prisoners were flown back to their native countries. The US military did not state the reasons for their release although it did admit that 610 more detainees remained at Guantanamo.[131]

On July 7, 2004, after the Supreme Court decisions in *Hamdi v. Rumsfeld* and *Rasul v. Bush*, the Pentagon announced its intention to try nine more detainees currently being held at Guantanamo Bay as "enemy combatants." They would be tried in a military court along with the six others already approved by President Bush. According to a DOD spokesperson, "The President determined that there is reason to believe that each of these enemy combatants was a member of al Qaeda or was otherwise involved with terrorism directed against the United States."[132]

Both military and civilian defense lawyers have criticized the military commission that is scheduled to try the detainees as "An inherently unfair process that does not allow for review outside the military."[133]

This is based on the tribunal's announced rules of rights and procedure:

- The tribunal is to consist of five US military Colonels, and no impartial civilian judges or jurors;
- The detainees are to be provided with military counsel at no charge, but if they choose to hire a civilian lawyer, they must do so at their own expense; and
- The accused will be considered innocent until proved guilty; a death sentence will require a unanimous vote, and guilt must be established beyond a reasonable doubt. However, unlike the unanimous vote required for a guilty verdict in civilian criminal courts, only a two-thirds vote of the tribunal will be required to hand down a conviction.

The Pentagon has yet to release the names or nationalities of those to be tried, or to list the formal charges being made against them.

### Report 19.4:  US Navy Arrested US-Syrian Airman al-Halabi; Seized His Defense Papers; Released Him

Senior US Airman Ahmad al-Halabi served as an interpreter for the Navy at Guantanamo Bay, Cuba, for nine months. On July 23, 2003, the Navy arrested him (also referred to as "Halabi"), a native of Syria, at the US Naval Air Station in Jacksonville, Florida. The Navy flew him to Travis Air Force Base in California, then jailed him at Vandenberg Air Force Base. The military did not disclose his arrest until two months after his initial detention. The military charged him with thirty-two counts, including espionage, aiding the enemy, making false official statements, and disobeying orders.[134]

Al-Halabi allegedly e-mailed information about the US base in Cuba and its prisoners to someone he knew was "the enemy." Air Force officials did not identify that "enemy" to Halabi's defense lawyers or to the public. Halabi was also accused of having improper contacts with the Syrian government, and planning to send classified information to Syria. Syria has denied any connection to him.

The military also charged Halabi with giving prisoners unauthorized treats such as baklava pastries. Military officials said this special treatment could have undermined interrogations of the prisoners. They also accused him of making "anti-American" statements. Al-Halabi denied all charges and retained both military defense counsel and a private lawyer, Donald G. Rehkopf Jr.[135]

On December 9, 2003, while transporting al-Halabi from Vandenberg AFB to Travis AFB for his arraignment, Government agents took all of his trial preparation files "for safe keeping." These files were clearly marked "privileged." The agents also took a laptop computer which had been approved and given to al-Halabi for use in preparing his defense, and to allow him to work on the voluminous paperwork associated with his case. The computer itself was clearly marked as containing "Privileged" material. It was only after al-Halabi's attorney complained to authorities that they returned the files and computer, without informing his counsel who had been given access to the material.

On December 10, 2003, armed Air Force Security Forces personnel invaded the defense counsel's office at Travis AFB, without a search warrant, while al-Halabi was working with his military attorneys and defense paralegals. Travis AFB officials then issued an order prohibiting the accused from using "any computer connected to the Internet," even when working with and in the presence of his military defense attorneys, which included a threat of punitive action against anyone who violated the order.

On December 11, 2003, federal agents conducted an official, warranted search of the Area Defense Counsel's office at Vandenberg AFB while defense counsel were preparing for a preliminary hearing. During the course of this search, a computer in that office was seized for unknown reasons.

Counsel for the defense vigorously protested that these were unwarranted invasions into the attorney-client relationship and requested that the military judge both abate the court-martial proceedings and grant a stay of any and all matters that affect their client.

On May 12, 2004, a military judge decided Halabi no longer represented a risk of fleeing from prosecution, and he was released from jail. According to the Reuters News Service, "Judge Col. Barbara Brand said she made her decision based on new evidence in the case after Halabi's lawyer charged that prosecutors had tampered with evidence and obstructed justice." Although now free, Halabi is still facing trial on charges of espionage and misusing classified information, with a possible maximum life sentence.[136]

### Report 19.5: US Supreme Court Grants Guantanamo Detainees Rasul and al Odah Habeas Review

After 9/11, Congress adopted a joint resolution, Authorization for the Use of Military Force, "as necessary and appropriate against nations, organizations, or persons that planned, authorized, committed, or aided in terrorist attacks" (Authorization for Use of Military Force, September 18, 2001, PL 107–40, §§ 1–2, 115 Stat. 224). Congress did not declare war on any country.

On October 7, 2001, President Bush sent US Armed Forces into Afghanistan to wage a military campaign against al Qaeda and the Taliban regime that had allegedly supported it. The United States captured over 640 non-US citizens suspected of associations with and giving aid to the terrorists and transported them to the Naval Base at Guantanamo Bay, where they were simply labeled "enemy combatants" and detained in military custody "indefinitely."

On February 19 and May 1, 2002, relatives of alien detainees at Guantanamo filed *Rasul v. Bush* and *al Odah v. United States.* The petitioners were two Australians, twelve Kuwaitis and two British citizens captured abroad during the hostilities. Their suits challenged the legality of their detention, alleging that they had never been combatants against the United States or engaged in terrorist acts, and that they had never been charged with wrongdoing. They alleged that they were never permitted to consult counsel and never provided access to courts or other tribunals.

The US District Court for the District of Columbia combined the suits and construed them as habeas corpus petitions and dismissed them for want of jurisdiction (215 F.Supp.2d 55). The Court of Appeals for the DC Circuit affirmed (321 F.3d 1134). After the Supreme Court granted certiorari, the United States released the two British detainees and they returned to the UK.

On June 28, 2004, the Supreme Court, in a 6–3 decision in *Rasul* and *Al Odah*, 124 S. Ct. 2686, written by Justice Stevens, held:

- US courts have jurisdiction to consider challenges to the legality of the detention of foreign nationals captured abroad in connection with hostilities and incarcerated at Guantanamo (p. 2696);
- The writ of habeas corpus is available in "all cases where any person may be restrained of his or her liberty in violation of the constitution, or of any treaty or law of the United States" (p. 2692);
- The allegations of the detainees that, although they were not terrorists or combatants, they have been held in Executive detention for more than two years in territory subject to the long-term, exclusive jurisdiction and control of the United States, without access to counsel or being charged with any wrongdoing, unquestionably

describe "custody in violation of the Constitution or laws or treaties of the United States" (FN 15);

- Nothing categorically excludes aliens detained in military custody outside the United States from the privilege of litigation in US courts, which have traditionally been open to nonresident aliens (p. 2698); and
- The federal courts have jurisdiction to determine the legality of the Executive's potentially indefinite detention of individuals who claim to be wholly innocent of wrongdoing (p. 2699).

Justice Kennedy filed a concurring opinion. Justice Scalia filed a dissenting opinion in which Chief Justice Rehnquist and Justice Thomas joined.

The Supreme Court ruling in *Rasul v. Bush* specifically held that the finding of jurisdiction in that case overturned denial of jurisdiction in Habib's case (*Rasul v. Bush*, 124 S. Ct. 2686 [2004]), and the ruling applied to *Gherebi v. Bush* and other cases.

## Report 19.6: US Supreme Court Vacated Judgment for Detainee Gherebi, Remanded

The US military arrested Falen Gherebi of Libya after the US invasion of Afghanistan and detained him at Guantanamo Bay. In February 2002, his brother, Belaid Gherebi, filed an amended next-friend habeas petition in the Ninth Circuit Court of Appeals on behalf of his brother. He alleged violations of the US Constitution and the Third Geneva Convention arising from his brother's involuntary detention at Guantanamo, "a naval base 'under the exclusive and complete jurisdiction of the respondents,'" and further claimed that Bush, et al., have characterized his brother as an 'unlawful combatant,' denied him status as a prisoner of war, denied him rights under the US Constitution and access to US Courts, and have denied him access to legal counsel." The Government did not respond to this petition.

On December 18, 2003, Judge Stephen Reinhardt issued the opinion of the Ninth Circuit that:

- Habeas jurisdiction existed over the petition filed on behalf of "enemy combatants" detained at the naval base in Cuba but is under territorial jurisdiction of the United States pursuant to the lease granting the United States complete jurisdiction and control over the property;
- Where the United States exercises "exclusive jurisdiction" over a territory, territorial jurisdiction lies;
- For habeas purposes, the naval base in Cuba was a part of the sovereign territory of the United States, which was granted complete juris-

diction and control over the property pursuant to lease that provided for the continuance of Cuba's ultimate sovereignty;

- For habeas purposes, the United States exercised sovereignty over the naval base in Cuba by virtue of its insistence on its right to use the territory for any and all purposes desired, and its refusal to limit its dominion and control to the use permitted by the lease and continuing treaty;
- A court has personal jurisdiction in a habeas case so long as the custodian can be reached by service of process. Habeas jurisdiction is proper even though the custodian is not physically present in the relevant district, as long as the custodian is within reach of the court's process (28 U.S.C.A. § 2241);
- Although not physically present in the district, the District Court for the Central District of California had personal jurisdiction over the Secretary of Defense in habeas proceedings brought on behalf of "enemy combatants" detained at the naval base in Cuba; activities of the Secretary and Defense Department were substantial, continuous, and systematic throughout the state of California, which had the largest number of military facilities in the nation, and therefore the Secretary had the requisite "minimum contacts" to satisfy California's long-arm statute (US Constitution Fifth Amendment; California C.C.P. § 410.10); and
- Transfer should not be granted if the effect is simply to shift the inconvenience to the party resisting the transfer (28 U.S.C.A. § 1404[a]).

On June 28, 2004, the Supreme Court, in *Bush v. Gherebi*, 124 S.Ct. 2932 (2004), vacated the Court of Appeals opinion and remanded to the Ninth Circuit for further consideration in light of *Rumsfeld v. Padilla* (124 S.Ct. 2711, [2004]), see Report 18.1.

Mamdouh Habib is an Australian citizen captured and detained in Camp Delta in Guantanamo Bay, Cuba, where he has been held virtually incommunicado, and has not been informed of any of his rights. Habib filed a petition for habeas corpus, represented by the Center for Constitutional Rights (CCR), which charged the US Government with violating Article 14 of the International Covenant on Civil and Political Rights.

On July 31, 2002, the US District Court for the District of Columbia dismissed Habib's petition. The CCR appealed, arguing that it is a violation of the law for the executive officers of the US Government to imprison persons for prolonged, indefinite periods, acting on secret information, with no judicial review whatsoever. The DC Circuit Court of Appeals rejected the CCR appeal, which combined *Rasul v. Bush*, *Habib v. Bush*, and *al Odah v. U.S.*, declaring that courts in the United States lack jurisdiction to provide habeas relief to these detainees (*al Odah v. U.S.*, 321 F.3rd 1134, 1141, [DC 2003]).

On April 20, 2004, these cases were heard together by the Supreme Court. On June 28, 2004, the Supreme Court held 6–3 that the detainees at Guantanamo have the right to challenge their detention in US courts (*Rasul v. Bush*, 124 S.Ct. 2686, 159 L.Ed.2d 548 [2004]).

Habib's case will, however, be considered after June 28, 2004, in light of the Supreme Court opinion in *Padilla* (Report 18.1).

## Report 19.7: Released British Detainees Allege Abuse at Guantanamo

After the US invasion of Afghanistan, US and Northern Alliance forces captured nine British citizens and sent them to Guantanamo Bay for interrogation. On November 26, 2003, Lord John Steyn, one of Britain's most senior judges, labeled conditions at Guantanamo Bay detention center Camp Delta as "utter lawlessness." In a speech broadcast on British television, Steyn stated that "As a lawyer brought up to admire the ideals of American democracy and justice I would have to say that I regard this as a monstrous failure of justice," and that the detainees in US prisons in Cuba were being held "beyond the rule of law, beyond the protection of any courts and at the mercy of the victors."[137]

On March 9, 2004, the US military released five of the nine British detainees from custody and returned them to the UK. In an interview with the British *Observer*, three of the released men claimed to have been tortured while being interrogated by US officials. The "Tipton Three," as they are known in the British media, claimed that within the confines of the larger detention facilities at Guantanamo Bay, there exists a supermaximum security facility, Camp Echo, "Where prisoners are held in tiny cells in solitary confinement twenty-four-hours a day, with a military police officer permanently stationed outside each cell door."

The three stated that they were subjected to an interrogation process so relentless that conditions eventually forced them to falsely confess to charges that they were members of al Qaeda. While being interrogated by the US military when they were still being held in Afghanistan, the Three told the *Observer* that "Guns were held to [their] heads during [their] questioning . . . and physical abuse and beatings were rife." They also claimed that few, if any, terrorists were being held at Guantanamo, and that as far as they could tell the worst "terrorists" were "a few mullahs who had been loyal to the Taliban."[138]

On June 25, 2004, British Attorney General Lord Peter Goldsmith reported that the British Government is unable to accept the Bush Administration's proposals for military tribunals at Guantanamo Bay. In a speech before an international lawyers' conference in London, Goldsmith stated, "We in the U.K. have been unable to accept that the US military tribunals proposed for those detained at Guantanamo Bay offer sufficient guarantees of a fair trial in accordance with international standards. . . . Any restriction on fundamental rights must be imposed in accordance with the rule of law." In commenting on the four British citizens who remained in US custody in Cuba, the Attorney General, along with British foreign secretary Jack Straw, repeatedly insisted that the United States should either try the accused according to the principles of international law, or release them to British custody.[139]

Moazzem Begg, a British citizen, was held at Guantanamo Bay for two years without charge or trial. He wrote a letter on July 12, 2004, stating that he had been subjected to "vindictive torture" and death threats by US soldiers who forced him to make a false confession. And he wrote that he had witnessed the murder of two men in Afghanistan by US troops. Apparently, the Pentagon accidentally released the letter to Begg's US lawyers in September 2004. On October 2, 2004, the British media published the letter.[140]

## 20. TO DEAL PROMPTLY AND FAIRLY WITH POLITICAL ASYLUM PETITIONS

Throughout history, people from many nations and cultures have sought asylum in the United States of America from persecution in their native lands because of their political actions and beliefs. Some refugees were called refugees from starvation, like the Irish farmers starved off their land by British policies in the droughts of the nineteenth century. Some were called refugees from fascism, like the Jews and communists fleeing Hitler in the twentieth century. The problem is worldwide. UN treaties and programs directly address the need for political asylum from repressive regimes.

In the face of these problems, in 2003, the new Department of Homeland Security initiated Operation Liberty Shield to detect, and discriminate against, asylum seekers from certain Arab and Muslim countries (Report 20.1). Azmy Elghazaly, a 1990 Palestinian Muslim immigrant to the United States, was denied political asylum in 1998, detained for ten months after 9/11, and continues to seek asylum (Report 20.2). The nine members of the Palestinian Kesbeh family sought political asylum from Jordan. After 9/11, the INS arrested the father and one brother, detained them for six months, then denied their political asylum petitions and deported them to Jordan (Report 20.3).

While Muslims and Arabs from Middle Eastern countries were the targets of many arrests, detentions, and denials of political asylum, they were not the only ones targeted in the aftermath of 9/11. After spending seven years in a prison in Northern Ireland, Ciaran Ferry and his family came to the United States where, in 2003, the Immigration Service arrested him for investigation for ties to the Irish Republican Army (IRA), and detained him. The Board of Immigration Appeals denied his appeal from the charge he had overstayed his visa (Report 20.4).

Organizations of US citizens from many nations and regions, especially members of the Islamic/Muslim/Middle Eastern communities, are seeking out and taking up the cases of community members arrested and detained while awaiting action on their applications for political asylum. They find that it is difficult to "win" a "case" because the administrative hearings and procedures of the Immigration Service are not as open as are the public trials in civil and criminal cases, and "administrative" law does not provide many of the protections in civil and criminal law, i.e., proof beyond a reasonable doubt of a person presumed to be innocent. It is much easier for the Government to get an administrative law judge to order a person deported to a country where he fears incarceration, persecution, or death than it is for a prosecutor to get a federal judge or jury to convict someone charged with the rape or murder of another human being.

In several communities, Middle Eastern organizations are beginning to meet with Irish organizations and with Haitian and Colombian groups to make common cause to protect the rights of everyone seeking political asylum in the United States from repressive regimes throughout the world. As NGOs concerned about their fellows around the world are beginning to come together to face the common problem of political asylum denials, they are making a troubling discovery. FBI agents, Immigration officials, and other Government agents in the case of a Palestinian from Syria, for example, are often the same agents involved in a case from Northern Ireland. And the lack of constitutional protections and respect for dissidents and "their side" is much more cohesive and organized than for "our side." Their network of agents is much better organized and has much more federal funding than the networks beginning to be built among communities with common refugee problems.

Actions of Government agents in dealing with applicants for political asylum belong in the required reports by the US Government to the three UN human rights committees administering the International Covenant on Civil and Political Rights (ICCPR), the Convention Against Torture (CAT), and the Convention on Elimination of Racial Discrimination (CERD). Complaints about the behavior of Immigration and Customs agents and others in the system can be made to the Office of Inspector General in the appropriate agency. Changes in political asylum law can be proposed to members of Congress.

And concerned people can constantly remind the media, and other Government officials, that this is, very largely, a nation of immigrants who came to these shores to seek asylum from political persecution and its attendant economic consequences.

**Relevant Law:**

U.S. Constitution: Art. I, §8, Cl. 4; Art. VI, Cl. 2; Fourth, Fifth, Fourteenth
    Amendments
UN Charter: Preamble, Art. 55, 55(c), 56
ICCPR: Art. 1-5, 7, 9, 10, 12-14, 23, 26, 27, 40
CERD: Art. 1.1, 1.4, 2, 5, 7, 9, 13.1
CAT: Preamble, Art. 1-5, 7, 10-14, 19

### Report 20.1: "Operation Liberty Shield" Detains Asylum Seekers

On March 18, 2003, the new Department of Homeland Security (DHS) initiated Operation Liberty Shield to detain asylum seekers who seek refuge from certain countries.[141] "The plan specifically targets individuals who come from a country 'where al Qaeda sympathizers and other terrorist groups are known to have operated.' While that description includes many nations in the world, there is a clear possibility that asylum seekers from Arab and Muslim countries will be disproportionately targeted. According to the DHS, the asylum seekers will be detained for the 'duration of their processing period,' which may mean years of incarceration for people whose only crime is that they sought refuge from repressive regimes."

According to the Center for Constitutional Rights (CCR), "This program involves racial and ethnic profiling, thereby violating the equal protection clause of the Constitution and the right of all persons within the US to be free from seizure on less than probable cause."[142]

### Report 20.2: INS Detained Palestinian Muslim After He Filed an Asylum Petition

In 1990, Azmy Elghazaly, a Palestinian Muslim, entered the United States on a tourist visa. During his stay in the United States, Elghazaly twice applied for political asylum. After both attempts were denied in 1999, he actively evaded deportation hearings for two years. He was issued a work visa during the time his asylum case was pending.

On October 12, 2001, police arrested Elghazaly based on a tip they had received from someone who knew him. Upon his arrest, it was discovered that he had a gun that had been obtained legally, but that his possession of it was illegal due to his immigration status.

In November 2001, Elghazaly was found to be on the Attorney General's list of suspected terrorists. As a consequence, Elghazaly ended up in a maximum security prison for his "own protection."[143] On August 21, 2002, the Government finally released him after ten months of incarceration and after he posted a $25,000 bond. Bruce Burns, Elghazaly's lawyer, asked that his asylum hearing be reopened.[144]

### Report 20.3: US Denied Asylum to a Palestinian Family, Deported Them to Jordan

After September 11, 2001, the INS arrested Sharif Kesbeh and his oldest son, detained them for six months, and scheduled them for deportation.

The Kesbehs, a Palestinian family of nine, had been in the United States for eleven years. They came to the United States from Jordan on tourist visas in 1991 and applied for political asylum. They were rejected and, in 1998, the INS ordered them deported. "If we go back to Jordan we go to jail," said Noor Kesbeh.

The deportation order was put on hold for six months after Rep. Sheila Jackson Lee (D-TX) introduced a bill that would have offered the Kesbehs permanent residency. In March 2003, the deportation order was reactivated, and the Immigration Service deported the Kesbeh family to Jordan.[145] "The deportation of the Kesbehs is a bitter pill. It leaves them in a precarious situation in Jordan, a country in the middle of a war zone with a well-documented history of human rights abuses against Palestinians and others. They are being forced to live in a refugee camp, and have no means of support. They are under the threat of arrest or worse."[146]

### Report 20.4: United States Detains Irish Immigrant Seeking Asylum

In late January 2003, Ciaran Ferry walked into the office of the Immigration and Naturalization Service (INS) in Denver, Colorado, for what he thought would be a routine interview. In 1993, he had been a member of the Irish Republican Army, and was arrested in Northern Ireland and convicted on charges of possession of weapons and conspiracy to murder persons unknown, and sentenced to twenty years in prison. In July 2000, Ferry had been released as a result of the Good Friday Peace Accord. In order to gain his release under the Accord, he had had to prove that he no longer had ties to the IRA and that the offense he had committed was only a "scheduled [political] offense."

After being informed by the Royal Ulster Constabulary (RUC) that he was on a pro-British death list, Ferry and his wife immigrated to the United States with the hope of gaining asylum status.[147] At his Immigration interview in January 2003, the INS arrested Ferry on charges of overstaying his visa. Immigration and Customs Enforcement (ICE, a bureau under the Department of Homeland Security since March 2003—formerly INS) kept him in solitary confinement for nine months in Denver County Jail and, in September 2003, moved him into the convicted criminal population at Jefferson County Jail, despite having no criminal charges pressed or pending against him.[148]

After his arrest, two FBI agents allegedly visited Ferry in jail and asked him to assist them in investigating a dissident Irish group on the East Coast, in exchange for his freedom. He refused and alleges that, as a result of this refusal, his case is being given "extreme treatment" in retaliation.[149] As of March 2004, Ferry's habeas corpus petition was still pending with the US District Court in Colorado. On May 12, 2004, the Board of Immigration Appeals denied Ferry's appeal challenging the administrative decision that he had overstayed his visa.[150]

## 21. TO PROTECT THE FAMILY, ESPECIALLY CHILDREN

In 1787, the founders of the United States proclaimed in the preamble to their Constitution that they were establishing the United States to "secure the Blessings of Liberty to ourselves and our Posterity." That is the only mention of children in this basic document; "family" and "women" are not mentioned. The preamble does say that the United States was being established to "insure domestic Tranquility" and to "promote the general Welfare." These phrases have been read as proclaiming that the US Government has a duty to protect the family, especially children.

After 9/11, the Bush Administration frequently talked about the family and the need to help children, promoting a program known as "Leave No Child Behind" (PL 107–110). The actions of Bush Administration officials at all levels challenge this stated goal in four ways: (1) the failure to properly fund many city, county, state, and federal agencies providing services to children and families, described in E, Sections 25 and 26; (2) the promotion of policies that endanger the environment that will, in the future, impact the children of today, described in Section 27; (3) decisions that hurt the development of individual youth, especially youth of color and immigrant youth in the United States; and (4) military actions in Afghanistan and Iraq that hit children especially hard as their fathers are detained or killed, their whole family life is disrupted, and they often must move from their homes.

In his 2004 State of the Union address, President Bush announced his support of an amendment to the US Constitution that would define marriage as between a man and woman building on the federal Defense of Marriage Act of 1996 defining marriage as between a man and a woman.[151] In response, the mayor of San Francisco, two small-town mayors in New York, and commissioners in Oregon, issued marriage licenses to thousands of gay couples. In March 2004, the California Supreme Court banned the issuance of marriage licenses to same-sex couples and invalidated those already issued.[152] As of November 2004, Massachusetts is the only state that issues marriage licenses to same-sex couples. Connecticut, New Jersey, New Mexico, New York, Rhode Island, and the District of Columbia do not expressly forbid same-sex marriages as many other states do.[153] Human rights activists increasingly faced rigid religious and political preachers and organizations seeking to forbid same-sex marriages everywhere.

The Bush Administration did not push the Senate to consent to ratification of the UN Convention on the Rights of the Child, which spells out many specific protections needed for children to survive and prosper in the twenty-first century. All nations in the world except the United States and Somalia have ratified this treaty. The United States and Iran are the only UN members that continue to execute juvenile offenders. In 2004, the United States was the only country to vote against a UN General Assembly Resolution on the Rights of the Child, calling on all nations to implement measures to stop child labor, sexual exploitation, and abuse of children, among other steps (*UN Chronicle*, no. 1, 2004, p. 24).

One of the most dramatic examples of US Government failure to protect children and their families is the actions of officials in rounding up unaccompanied minors, detaining them in prisons, and failing to tell them about their right to a lawyer, as Amnesty International discovered in a survey in 2003 (Report 21.1). Many minors from poor families who have lived all their lives in the United States were subjected to the loss of their Section 8 housing due to a Bush Administration policy of cutting the amount of money available to poor families through federal vouchers (Report 21.2).

The FBI and Secret Service arrested an African American youth after he returned from protesting the 2002 World Economic Forum in New York City. He was arrested for material he had permitted on his Web site written by an affluent Euro youth about bombmaking. The Euro youth was not arrested; the African American youth was tried and sentenced to one year in prison and three years in very restrictive supervised conduct (Report 21.3). A teacher in Oakland, California, called the Secret Service to deal with two fifteen-year-old Asian American students who, in a class discussion on the US war in Iraq, casually made provocative comments about George Bush (Report 21.4).

The issues of sex education and sex exploitation continued to be raised after 9/11. A Louisiana federal court ruled that sex education in the public schools based on abstinence-only material would violate the First Amendment separation of church and state (Report 21.5). The government of Hawaii took an affirmative step and urged the federal Government and other states to follow them in making sex tourism a crime with serious penalties for travel agencies and others engaged in sex tourism (Report 21.6).

Concerned parents, teachers, government officials, and activists see many paths to action to protect the family, especially children, after 9/11. All of these paths call on busy, effective people to join their parent/teacher associations (of whatever name); to attend meetings of the local school board to express opinions on school policies; to tell members of state legislatures, Congress members, and candidates for President and Vice President that a commitment to children, and families, means funding programs that uphold the First Amendment and promote the general welfare for all residents of the United States. All this, and ending US military actions abroad, would bring enormous changes in the lives of hundreds of millions of children.

**Relevant Law:**

U.S. Constitution: Preamble, General Welfare Clause; Art. I, §8, Cl. 3, Cl. 18; Art. II, §1, Cl. 8; Art. II, §3; Art. VI, Cl. 2; Fourth, Fifth, Sixth, Eighth, Ninth, Tenth, Thirteenth, Fourteenth, Nineteenth Amendments
Section 8, Home Ownership Program, 42 U.S.C. §1437 et seq., 24 CFR §982.625, et seq.
UN Charter: Art. 1, 23, 24, 24.2, 55, 56, 103
ICCPR: Preamble, Art. 1-7, 12.1, 17-19, 19.2, 23, 23.1, 24, 26, 27, 40, 41.1, 44, 46, 47
CERD: Preamble, Art. 1, 1.1, 2, 4 ,5, 5(b), 5(e)(iv), (v), 6, 7, 9
CAT: Art. 1, 2, 3, 4, 16, 19
CRC: Preamble, Art. 1-4, 6, 9.1, 11.1, 16, 18.2, 19, 24, 27, 34-36, 44
CEDAW: Preamble, Art. 1, 2.1(a)-(b), 2.1(e)-(f), 3, 5.1(a), 6, 15.1, 11.1, 11.2, 11.3, 18, 24, 28.2
ICESCR: Art. 2-4, 6, 7, 9, 10.3, 11, 12, 16, 17

## Report 21.1: US Mistreating Unaccompanied Minors Entering United States

R.D., age twelve, fled India to escape religious persecution. On arrival in the United States, he applied for asylum. He had an uncle, a US citizen, willing to sponsor him, pending determination of his immigration status. Immigration officials placed R.D. in detention and held him for over fifteen months. When Amnesty International (AI) met with him, he said the staff in the facility were very strict. If children forgot to wear their name tags, the authorities would make them stand facing the wall. He said when children failed to obey instructions they did not understand because they did not understand English, they would get into trouble. R.D. told AI: "It's been a long time. . . . I just want to get out of here."

Near An Najaf, Iraq, March 31, 2003: An Iraqi man comforts his four-year-old son at a regroupment center for POWs of the 101st Airborne Division. The man was seized in An Najaf with his son, and the US military did not want to separate them. (AP Photo/Jean-Marc Bouju)

In 2002, five thousand minors under the age of eighteen entered the United States by themselves. When a city, state, or federal authority found and identified them, the agency turned them over to a federal agency that sent them to one of the 115 facilities in the United States for detention, pending rulings on the legality of their staying in the country.

Amnesty International distributed a questionnaire that was answered by thirty-three facilities in 2003. Almost half said they put these minors, charged with no crime, into cells with juvenile offenders who had been convicted of crimes. Eighty-three percent routinely restrained children when taking them outside the facility, or to the dentist, for example. More than half the facilities said they used solitary confinement as punishment. Sixty-five percent did not explain to the children why they were detained in jail nor that they had a right to have a judge review their detention. Federal law requires that each minor receive weekly psychological counseling. Only 13 percent of the facilities surveyed provided the children with this basic necessity.

Under the new Homeland Security Act, the Department of Homeland Security is responsible for "apprehending" unaccompanied minors and turning them over to the new Office of Refugee Resettlement (ORR) in the Health and Human Services Department. Responsibility for detaining unaccompanied immigrant children was shifted from the INS to the ORR without sufficient increased funding. Amnesty International found that this shift in federal departments' responsibility did not improve the treatment of the children, most of whom were kept in the same penal facilities as before.

Congress did not debate a bill proposed by Senators Dianne Feinstein (D-CA) and Sam Brownback (R-KS) in 2003 that would have required immigration officials to return children without asylum claims to their homes more quickly, establish minimum standards for their custody, expand foster care programs to supply more appropriate living conditions, and provide guardians and facilitate pro bono legal advice.[154]

## Report 21.2: Bush Cuts Housing Vouchers

In January 2004, the Bush Administration proposed that 250,000 rental vouchers currently in use by families across the United States be eliminated. A rental voucher is a full or partial payment from the US Government to be used by low-income tenants to pay their rent. Bush later signed the 2004 budget.

In April 2004, the Government informed public housing agencies across the country that reimbursements from the Department of Housing and Urban Development (HUD) for fiscal year 2004 would not be based on current renters' voucher costs. They would be based on the much lower cost of vouchers in August 2003, adjusted only minimally for inflation.

Many US public housing agencies already had to terminate low income rental vouchers previously given to some tenants. Welfare activists across the United States believe that HUD incorrectly interpreted the will of Congress since Congress had already funded the existing stock of housing vouchers for fiscal year 2004.

The crisis is nationwide: New York City could not fully fund 118,000 housing vouchers already distributed for the fiscal year 2004. Warrenton, Oregon, had to cut off funding for 110 families in May 2004 and another 50 families on June 1, 2004. Alameda, California had to send letters to 1,659 families on May 15, 2004, in order to inform them that the city would not be able to pay any part of their rent for June 2004. Fargo, North Dakota, had to terminate vouchers for 46 out of 1,100 families.

Massachusetts housing officials announced that they would send termination notices to 650 families unless the state can come up with a solution immediately. Minnesota took 2,000 families off their voucher list in June 2004. California faced the loss of 294,708 fully funded vouchers that are already in use and a stop on future vouchers for the state's scores of homeless.

Rep. Barney Frank (D-MA) introduced H.R. 4263 to resolve the problem. The bill would amend the FY04 VA-HUD Appropriations Act to fully fund Section 8 vouchers based on the agency's per-unit cost, as originally intended by Congress. He quickly got 85 co-sponsors to support the bill. According to House Minority Leader Nancy Pelosi, "The Bush Administration is breaking a 30-year promise to help low-income families, the elderly and the disabled to afford decent, safe housing."[155]

### Report 21.3:  US Judge Sentenced African American Teenager for Web Site

On January 24, 2002, twenty-five armed FBI and Secret Service agents surrounded the home of eighteen-year-old African American Sherman Austin in Los Angeles. For six hours the agents proceeded to seize computer equipment, protest signs, and other items under a warrant that contained two allegations: (1) "distribution of explosives information with the intent that the information be used for or in furtherance of an activity that constitutes a federal crime of violence," and (2) "alleged illegal computer activity." Three agents questioned Austin at length (with no attorney present), then left the premises.[156]

According to the FBI, Austin and www.raisethefist.com, the "anarchist" Web site he ran from his home, had been under surveillance by the Government because of the Web site's provocative language and links to other sites that provided bombmaking instructions.[157] One item was the "Reclaim Guide," a Web site authored by another teenager that existed in a subsectionof Austin's site known as a "free hosting area" where people could post, remove, and alter Web pages they created. Austin could have hosted Web sites there without knowing their content.[158]

The Web site containing the explosives information was uploaded and authored by an affluent, Euro American teenager from Orange County, California. FBI Agents interviewed him, and the agents' reports show that the teen admitted to authoring the Reclaim Guide. Agents did not arrest the Euro American teenager, nor charge him with any crime.

On February 2, 2002, the NYPD arrested Austin and twenty-five others for protesting against the World Economic Forum. After their release, the FBI arrested Austin and questioned him for eleven hours without an attorney present. Authorities held him for eleven days in two New York facilities, where he was called "terror boy" by the guards. The authorities then transferred him to a Bureau of Prisons facility in Oklahoma, where authorities held him for two days, then released him.

In August 2002, federal prosecutors offered Austin a plea agreement: plead guilty to "distribution of information with intent," get one month in prison, three months in a community correctional facility, and three years of supervised release. Austin decided to accept the plea after learning that not doing so might result in a twenty-year sentence.

On September 30, 2002, federal Judge Stephen V. Wilson rejected the plea as too light. During Austin's trial, the FBI and the prosecutor told the court that Austin had authored the Reclaim Guide. Austin's Public Defender did not challenge this until the last court hearing. At Austin's sentencing hearing on June 30, 2003, the prosecutor recommended four months in prison. Again Judge Wilson said that the sentence was too lenient.

On August 4, 2003, Judge Wilson sentenced Austin to one year in federal prison and three years of very restrictive supervised release, plus a $2,000 fine.

When Austin turned himself in on September 3, 2003, he was immediately transferred to San Bernardino Detention Center where he received death threats from the Aryan Brotherhood, saying that there was a price on his head. Sherman was thereafter moved into a segregated prison block.[159] On July 12, 2004, he was released from prison in Arizona, and left for Los Angeles to serve the remainder of his sentence in a halfway house. Sherman will be under federal probation for the next three years. The terms of his probation bar him from having any contact with "anarchist groups," and dictate that he not use a cell phone, computer, or "digital device" unless approved by the Government.[160]

### Report 21.4: Teacher Called Secret Service to Interrogate Students

On April 23, 2003, John and Billy, two sixteen-year-old Asian American high school students in Oakland, California, participated in an in-class discussion on the war in Iraq. One of the boys said, "We need a sniper to take care of Bush." The other student responded, "Yeah, I'd do it."

The teacher, Sandy Whitney, soon called the Secret Service to ask what her responsibilities were when one of her students made a threat. As a result of this call, two Secret Service Agents came to the school, and the two students were pulled out of class and questioned about their comments in the presence of the principal.[161] According to Larry Felson, a teacher at the school who spoke to the boys after the incident, when one of the students asked to speak to a lawyer, he was told by the Secret Service agents, "You do not have any rights; we own you."

The parents of the children were never notified about the questioning (California law allows law enforcement to question students on school grounds without notifying their parents). Several members of the community who recalled some of their teenage indiscretions, including School Board President Greg Hodge, expressed outrage over the incident. The School Board held weekly meetings with students, parents, and faculty to prevent similar incidents in the future. The California State Assembly began looking into a law requiring principals of state high schools to notify students that they can request to have a legal guardian present if and when they are questioned by law enforcement.[162]

### Report 21.5: United States Limited Sex Education Funding to Abstinence-Only

In 2002, the American Civil Liberties Union (ACLU) of Louisiana filed a lawsuit in federal court, *ACLU of Louisiana v. Foster*, to protest abstinence-only programs in public schools funded by state and federal grants. In their suit the ACLU alleged a violation of the separation between Church and State, based on the fact that some abstinence-only programs "present theater skits with Jesus as a character, feature a chastity curriculum entitled 'God's Gift of Life,' and minister to teens about the 'scriptural, spiritual, and practical foundation for combating the issues of premarital sex.'"

In 1996, Republican members of the House of Representatives convinced Congress to fund abstinence-only sex education as part of the Welfare Reform Act. Districts that encouraged abstinence from sex until marriage could receive direct grants and matching grants, roughly $4 in federal funds for every $3 in local tax funds. Since then, such programs have received more than half a billion dollars in federal funds.

As part of his 2000 platform, George Bush promised that he would augment federal funding to a minimum of $135 million per year to equalize the funding provided to traditional "comprehensive" sex education programs, which present abstinence as "the only sure way to prevent pregnancy and disease" but include information on birth control and "safer sex." Abstinence-only sex education mentions contraception solely in terms of "failure rates." Sex education teachers participating in abstinence-only programs "agree not to tell youngsters how to reduce risk of disease and pregnancy if they are sexually active" on the theory that such discussion will encourage adolescents to engage in sex.

The US birth rate among fifteen- to nineteen-year-old women decreased by 26 percent in the 1990s. Some experts say there is no evidence that abstinence-only sex education generated this drop. They maintain that concern about AIDS and improved use of contraception are likelier causes of the decline. After Bush became President in 2001, funding for traditional "comprehensive" sex education programs remained stagnant while abstinence-only programs received increasing amounts of federal money.[163]

On July 25, 2002, the US District Court ruled for the ACLU in its suit and mandated that the Louisiana Governor's Program on Abstinence (GPA), which was receiving federal funds, "Cease and desist from disbursing GPA funds to organizations or individuals that convey religious messages or otherwise advance religions in any way . . . using GPA funds."[164] On November

13, 2002, the GPA and the ACLU reached a settlement under which programs that receive GPA funds are to report monthly and submit their curricula to the GPA while demonstrating that the program did not use any of the funds for religious purposes. If found in violation of this settlement, such programs have a designated period of time to correct themselves. Those that persist in engaging in religious activities will not receive any more GPA funds. This decision marked the first time a program funded with federal abstinence-only funds under the 1996 federal welfare reform legislation was challenged.[165] In 2003, Congress renewed funding for abstinence-only sex education programs.[166]

In March 2004, the Food and Drug Administration (FDA) announced they had "developed a regulatory plan to provide condom users with a consistent labeling message and the protection they should expect from condom use." The plan came in response to recent studies indicating that condoms do not provide users protection against HPV, or human papillomavirus, a sexually transmitted disease that can cause genital warts or cervical cancer if left untreated.

Some federal lawmakers, including Rep. Henry Waxman (D-CA) fear that such new warnings could cause people to stop using condoms. Representative Waxman asked, "Are condoms perfect? Of course not. But reality requires us not to make a public health strategy against protection, but rather to ask a key question: compared to what? . . . The evidence . . . indicates that abstinence-only education works rarely, if at all."[167]

### Report 21.6:  Hawaii Passed Law To End Sex Tourism

In 2004, the legislators in Hawaii described the dangerous increase in sex tourism: "The sex industry has rapidly expanded over the past several decades. It involves sexual exploitation of persons, predominantly women and girls, including activities related to prostitution, pornography, sex tourism, and other commercial sexual services. The low status of women in many parts of the world has led to a burgeoning of the trafficking industry. Discouraging sex tourism, which is an estimated $1,000,000,000-per-year business worldwide, is key to reducing the demand for sex trafficking." Yet the President and Congress have taken no action on the issue.

On May 19, 2004, the Lieutenant Governor of Hawaii signed into law Act 82, that makes it a criminal offense to sell, or offer to sell, travel services for the purpose of engaging in prostitution, with a sentence of up to five years in prison and suspension or revocation of a travel agency's registration. Hawaii is the first state to specifically criminalize the activities of sex tour operators, not simply to criminalize prostitution.

Act 82 states, "Prostitution and related activities, which are inherently harmful and dehumanizing, contribute to the trafficking in persons, as does sex tourism. . . . The Purpose of this Act is to promote and protect the human rights for women and girls exploited by sex tourists. . . . In so doing, the legislature forcefully declares Hawaii's unequivocal opposition to any form of sex tourism, whether it is child sex tourism or sex tourism involving adults."

The Act makes clear to law enforcement authorities in Hawaii that they can prosecute for promoting sex tourism, even if the act of prostitution does not take place in the state of Hawaii. The Hawaiian legislators indicated their hope that the passage of Act 82 would inspire Congress and state legislatures to explicitly mandate prosecution and criminal penalties for sex tour operators.[168]

## 22. TO ENFORCE ANTITRUST AND ANTICORRUPTION LAWS

Mass movements of citizens throughout the United States demanded that corporations be curbed in the 1890s. Railroad workers and steelworkers could see that a few large corporations were making deals among themselves to speed up production by workers even if it meant cutting safety standards and the quality of products. The new trusts cut competition between corporations so that a small number of corporate leaders could make huge profits. In 1890, Congress passed, and the President signed, the Sherman Antitrust Act (15 U.S.C. §1). Corporations quickly hired lawyers to fight the new Act, but the Supreme Court upheld its constitutionality in *Standard Oil v. US*, 221 US 1(1911). Then corporations hired lawyers to find ways to get around the law.

By 1914, the labor unions demanded, and Pres. Woodrow Wilson supported, a second antitrust act called the Clayton Act (15 U.S.C. §12). The Antitrust Division of the Department of Justice was established to enforce the letter and the spirit of these laws, that is, to prevent a few huge corporations from forcing smaller companies to close or be bought out by price-cutting and other unfair practices. The Act was intended to prevent a few large corporations from stopping innovations by small companies and forcing their own quality standards on all consumers.

During the Great Depression, after the stock market crash, thousands of people knew that the big corporations had lied to them about the value of stocks. As a result, Congress established the Securities and Exchange Commission to oversee actions by corporations chartered by the various states to protect the interests of investors (15 U.S.C. §77a).

After 9/11, more and more pundits began to comment on the total inactivity of the Antitrust Division in the face of mergers by many huge corporations in many industries, from computers to grocery outlets to TV and radio stations. In July 2004, hundreds of concerned citizens began attending hearings of the Federal Communications Commission (FCC) to express their rejection of proposed rules that would permit even more mergers of huge TV and radio networks because they would provide even less uncensored news than the inadequate coverage since 9/11.

The Department of Defense (DOD) awarded Iraq reconstruction contracts to a handful of corporations without competitive bidding (Report 22.1). By June 2003, US Labor Against the War issued a report detailing the percentage of US Government contracts in Iraq awarded to antilabor monopolies (Report 22.2). By September 2003, Congress members were complaining to the Bush Administration about massive overcharging on gasoline by a few corporations (Report 22.3). It took two years, but at least two whistle-blowers on DynCorp Corruption proved they were telling the truth when they alleged that some DynCorp employees were "buying" foreign women and underage girls from the Serbian Mafia in Bosnia (Report 22.4). By April 2004, the traditional media was reporting that corporate armies were waging the war in Iraq and Afghanistan (Report 22.5). Labor unions, activists, and good government NGOs were on the path of action to enforce basic US laws against corporate misconduct.

**Relevant Law:**

U.S. Constitution: Preamble, General Welfare Clause; Art. I, §8, Cl. 11; Art.
    II, §1, Cl. 8; Art. II, §3; Art. VI, Cl. 2
Sherman Anti-Trust Act, 15 U.S.C. §1 (1890)
Clayton Act, 15 U.S.C. §12 (1914)
Securities Act of 1933, 15 U.S.C. §77a (1933)
*Standard Oil v. U.S.*, 221 U.S. 1 (1911)
UN Charter: Art. 2.3, 2.4, 2.5, 2.6, 55, 55(a), 56
ICCPR: Art. 1.1, 1.2, 2, 2.1, 4, 5, 16, 22.1, 26, 40
CERD: Art. 1, 5, 6, 7
ICESCR: Preamble, Art. 1-2, 6-8, 16, 17

### Report 22.1:  DOD Awarded Iraq Reconstruction Contracts without Competitive Bidding

In July 2003, the United States Agency for International Development (USAID) and the Army Corps of Engineers invited only twenty-one firms to bid on eight Government contracts relating to the rebuilding of Iraq for $1.7 billion. USAID is in charge of advancing "America's foreign policy interests in expanding democracy and free markets while improving the lives of the citizens of the developing world." Most of the details of the contracts were hidden from US taxpayers and the Iraqis. Many of the firms that received a contract have had previous contracts with USAID, such as ABT Associates Inc., Creative Associates International Inc., Research Triangle Institute, and Bechtel.[169]

By October 2003, of "the $4 billion being spent monthly in Iraq, as much as a third is going to the private US contractors who have flooded into the country," said Deborah D. Avant, a political scientist at George Washington University.[170] On October 30, 2003, the Center for Public Integrity revealed that major contracts for rebuilding Iraq and Afghanistan were awarded either without competitive bids, or by closed-bidding only. The nonpartisan study disclosed that the companies that were awarded contracts to rebuild in Iraq were major campaign donors to President Bush and that their executives had important political and military connections. The seventy US companies and individual contractors surveyed had donated more than $500,000 to the Bush 2000 campaign, more than they gave collectively to any other politician over the past twelve years.

Kellogg, Brown & Root, a subsidiary of the Halliburton Corporation, has received more contract money in the aggregate than any other US company: over $4 billion for work in both Afghanistan and Iraq, including task orders on oil contracts and large-scale construction contracts.[171] Vice President Dick Cheney was the former head of Halliburton before he resigned to join the Bush 2000 campaign. Since his departure, Halliburton has continued to pay Cheney between $100,000 and $1,000,000 per year in deferred compensation.[172] Bechtel received the second-biggest contract: $1 billion for capital construction involving Iraq's utilities, telecommunications, railroads, ports, schools, healthcare facilities, bridges, roads, and airports. The company's chairman and chief executive officer, Riley Bechtel, was appointed to the President's Export Council in 2003 to advise Bush on programs to improve US trade. The Center for Public Integrity's study concluded that most of the ten largest Iraq contracts went to companies that employed former high-ranking Government officials, or executives with close ties to members of Congress and agencies in charge of awarding the contracts. [173]

## Report 22.2: Contracts in Iraq Awarded to Antilabor Monopolies

In June 2003, US Labor Against the War issued a lengthy report detailing US Government contracts to rebuild Iraq that were awarded, without competitive bidding, to monopoly corporations with strong antilabor records. Such corporations include: Halliburton; Kellogg, Brown & Root; Bechtel Group Inc.; MCI WorldCom; Stevedoring Services of America; DynCorp/Computer Sciences Corporation; and Fluor Corporation.

"The record recounted in the pages of this report is marked by cost overruns, accounting irregularities, financial dereliction, fraud, bankruptcy, overcharging, price-gouging, profiteering, wage-cheating, deception, corruption, health and safety violations, worker and community exploitation, human and labor rights abuses (including use of forced labor), union-busting, strike-breaking, environmental contamination, ecological irresponsibility, malpractice, criminal prosecutions, civil law suits, privatization of public resources, collusion with dictators, trading with regimes in violation of international sanctions, drug-running, prostitution, excessive executive compensation, and breach of fiduciary duty to shareholders and the public."[174]

## Report 22.3: Congress Members Complain about US Awarding Contracts to Political Contributors

US Congressional Representatives Henry Waxman (D-CA) and John D. Dingell (D-MI) complained to the Bush Administration on September 30, 2003, that Halliburton's subsidiary, Kellogg, Brown & Root, was billing the US Army in the Middle East between $1.62 and $1.70 per gallon of gas, while the average price for gasoline in the Middle East was $0.71. They also complained that Iraqis were being charged between $0.04 and $0.15 per gallon at the pump for the imported gasoline. Waxman and Dingell accused Halliburton of gouging US taxpayers while importing gasoline into Iraq. "Although Iraq has the second-largest oil reserves in the world, the US taxpayer is, in effect, subsidizing over ninety percent of the cost of gasoline sold in Iraq."[175]

On September 30, 2003, Representative Waxman wrote to the Office of Management and Budget (OMB) that much of the rebuilding in Iraq could be done at one-tenth the cost if Iraqi contractors and companies were employed rather than US corporations. He cited the fact that the United States spent $25 million refurbishing twenty police stations when local firms could have done the work for $5 million. In one instance, he reported that the United States spent $80,000 to restart production at a cement factory using local contractors, even though the US Army Corps of Engineers wanted to spend $15 million to repair the plant.

Waxman also stated, "Sometimes, the reconstruction process is structured so that low-cost Iraqi contractors are excluded from even bidding on the projects." He said that a journalist from the *Santa Monica (CA) Daily Press* told his staff that she attended a meeting in Baghdad where a Bechtel executive interviewed Iraqi contractors seeking jobs rebuilding the Iraq airport. The Bechtel executive informed the Iraqis that they could not participate in rebuilding their country's airport unless they got three different types of insurance. When one Iraqi contractor asked how to obtain such insurance, which Iraqis never had to obtain before and which is not available in Iraq, he was told, "Don't worry, there will be American insurance companies coming to sell you insurance."

Waxman contended that "when inordinately expensive reconstruction projects are awarded to high-cost federal contractors with close political ties to the White House, the Administration can create a lose-lose situation: not only do US taxpayers vastly overpay for reconstruction services, but Iraqis are denied urgently needed employment opportunities."[176] On October 16, 2003, while addressing the US Senate, Senator Edward Kennedy (D-MA) asked, "Why not scale back the lavish resources being provided to US contractors and consultants and provide larger sums directly to the Iraqi people?"[177]

### Report 22.4:  Whistle-blowers on DynCorp Corruption Win in Two Courts

In August 2002, DynCorp agreed to the settlement of a lawsuit brought by Ben Johnston, an employee hired in 1998 to maintain helicopters and airports for the Army at Comanche Base Camp in Bosnia. The DynCorp Corporation has its main office in Fort Worth, Texas, and has many contracts with the US Government in former Yugoslavia and in Iraq. In March 2000, Johnston had reported to his supervisor that DynCorp employees were "buying" foreign women and underage girls from the Serbian Mafia to exploit them sexually and then sell them to each other. They were also buying and selling weapons in the same way. Johnston's supervisor warned him "to mind his own business." Johnston then informed the US Army Criminal Investigation Command (CID), after which the CID placed Johnston and his wife in protective custody to safeguard them from retaliation.

On June 2, 2000, the Forty-eighth Military Police Detachment, as part of CID's investigation, set up a sting at DynCorp's Comanche Base Camp in Bosnia. The CID's raid revealed such evidence as a videotape of DynCorp's site manager having sex with two prostitutes he had "bought," a machine gun a DynCorp employee had obtained from the Serbian mafia, and evidence that other DynCorp employees had "bought" women.

At the end of June 2000, the CID turned over its case to the Bosnian authorities, who did not take action allegedly because they thought DynCorp employees had immunity from Bosnian laws under the Dayton Peace Accords. On June 9, 2000, Johnston received a letter of discharge signed by his supervisor at DynCorp stating that he was fired for bringing "discredit to the company and the US army," without stating any rationale.

In August 2000, Johnston filed suit against DynCorp in the Seventeenth District Court of Fort Worth, Texas, accusing them of racketeering in violation of the Racketeer Influenced and Corrupt Organizations Act (RICO) and of wrongful termination after he had refused to commit an illegal act. Dyn-Corp argued that Johnston had been fired for cause. In February 2001, one DynCorp employee testified that Johnston's "unverifiable statements" to CID was the reason for his termination.[178] In August 2002, *Johnston v. Dyn-Corp* ended in a settlement, the exact amount of which was kept confidential. Johnston's attorney, Kevin Glasheen stated, "This settlement would not have happened if DynCorp hadn't, at least internally, accepted some responsibility for what happened in the Balkans."

Also in 2000, Kathryn Bolkovac, a US citizen, who worked as a UN police officer in Bosnia as part of the international police force that the US State Department recruited through DynCorp, uncovered similar evidence of racketeering. She authored e-mails to her supervisors alleging that some UN police officers went to brothels and participated in the sex trade in Bosnia. DynCorp thereafter fired Bolkovac, and she subsequently sued Dyn-Corp Aerospace Operations Ltd., Dyncorp's British subsidiary, under Britain's 1998 Public Interest Disclosure Act, for unfair dismissal. DynCorp argued that she had been fired for falsifying time sheets. In August 2002, the Southampton Employment Tribunal found no evidence of her doing so.[179] In November 2002, a hearing was held to set the amount of damages. The employment tribunal ordered DynCorp to pay Bolkovac £10,117 in lost wages, £81,254 in lost future earnings, and £15,000 for injury to feelings.[180]

## Report 22.5: Corporate Armies Wage War in Afghanistan and Iraq

By April 2004, approximately fifteen thousand military contractors were working for the US Government in Iraq and Afghanistan, with more contractors expected after the transfer of sovereignty from the Coalition Provisional Authority to the Provisional Iraqi Government. In the past, the US military employed civilian contractors as noncombat logistical support staff, hiring them to serve food, do the laundry, and drive trucks. Due to a dearth of specially trained troops in Iraq and the dismantling of the Iraqi military and police force in the weeks following the US invasion, the US Army turned over more and more "mission-critical" functions to private contractors as well, such as interrogating prisoners, providing security for coalition personnel, and combating Iraqi insurgents alongside US soldiers.

After the death of four private contractors in street fights in Fallujah on March 31, 2004, heightened press scrutiny revealed an alarming lack of corporate accountability and government control over some of the largest private firms with a presence in Iraq, such as Blackwater Security Consulting, DynCorp, and Combat Support Associates. According to one US Government official, "Each private firm amounts to an individual battalion. . . .

Now they are coming together to build the largest security organization in the world."[181]

On April 23, 2004, Common Dreams News Center reported that "The contractors are simultaneously creating opportunities for the government to evade public accountability, and, in Iraq at least, are on the verge of evolving into an independent force at least somewhat beyond the control of the US military. And, as the contractors grow in numbers and political influence, their power to entrench themselves and block reform is growing. . . . They do not fall under international law on mercenaries, nor does the national law of the United States clearly apply to the contractors in Iraq—especially because many of the contractors are not Americans."[182]

Individual contractors come from the United States, South Africa, Great Britain, India, Chile, and many other countries. They are paid very well, often in excess of $100,000 a year, but many allegedly lack the proper background and training necessary for providing security in a combat zone such as Iraq. One private contractor, interviewed by *Common Sense* under the pseudonym "Jerry," stated that many of the other contractors he encountered in Iraq were unfamiliar with basic military terminology and tactics, and lacked experience. "Navy SEALs and former Marines, a bunch of hot rodders, wild cowboys, all they want to do is kill people. They had their machine-gun mentality. A little too young, a little too green. Not enough combat experience in my opinion. They had launched bullets, but never had bullets coming back at them."[183]

On June 18, 2004, David Passaro, a civilian contractor working for the CIA in Afghanistan, was charged with four counts of assault after being accused of beating an Afghan detainee, Abdul Wali, in a prison in northern Afghanistan. The day after the alleged beating, Mr. Wali died of a heart attack, according to US officials. Mr. Passaro, a former Special Forces soldier, joined the Army after being fired from the Hanford, Connecticut, police force; months after he graduated from the police academy, Passaro was arrested on felony charges for beating a man in a parking lot. After leaving the Army, Passaro was given a contract by the CIA in December 2002, and traveled to Afghanistan in June and July of 2003, assisting in paramilitary operations there. If convicted of assaulting Mr. Wali, Passaro could face up to forty years in prison.[184] Photographs of tortured detainees which came to the world's attention in the summer of 2004 made clear the case of Mr. Passaro is not an isolated incident.

## 23. TO PROTECT THE RIGHTS OF WORKERS AND UNIONS

Members of labor unions across the United States participated in strong demonstrations against the Fair Trade Agreement for the Americas in Miami in November 2003. They were building on the successful Seattle demonstrations against the World Trade Organization in November and December 1999, which led to the decision not to hold further such gatherings in the United States. The Miami demonstrators were met by the most dangerous police actions against demonstrators in recent times (Report 3.6).

One of the victories won by workers in 1978 was the passage of the Humphrey-Hawkins Full Employment and Balanced Growth Act. It requires the President to report to Congress during preparation of the annual budget on what the unemployment rate is and to propose a plan to bring it down to 3 percent for adults and 4 percent for workers under twenty. The report filed by President Bush in 2004 was totally inadequate in light of massive plant closures and job outsourcing (Report 23.3).

The International Longshore and Warehouse Union (ILWU AFL-CIO) is often called one of the most militant unions in the United States, with strong ties to longshore unions around the globe. In the face of more and more mechanization in this trade, as in so many others, the ILWU members rejected employer contract changes until President Bush after 9/11, for the first time in several presidencies, got a Taft-Hartley injunction against the union. As it turned out, even that did not stop the ILWU (Report 23.1). Its leaders went on to participate in a delegation to Iraq after the war was declared over, to meet with Iraqi union leaders and workers to report back to their members and the US labor movement on the effects of US invasion policies on enforcement of basic labor rights (Report 23.4).

Also see union resolutions on the war and Iraqi workers' rights in 5.D-1.

Union workers in Oklahoma locked out by their employer, located in Taiwan, after years of no action on their demands, went to Taiwan and conducted a hunger strike (Report 23.5). The Immigration Service conducted raids in Wal-Mart stores across the country seeking illegal immigrants on the janitorial staffs for deportation (Report 23.2). Organized labor, led by the International Longshore and Warehouse Union Local 10, called for a massive march of workers on Washington, DC, on October 17, 2004. The demands of the march included: universal healthcare, a national living wage, guaranteed pensions, and the repeal of the USA PATRIOT Act.[185]

According to organizers, "This mobilization is being proposed in response to the attacks upon working families in America and the millions of jobs lost during the Bush administration and with the complicity of Congress. The working class has not suffered such hardships since the Great Depression. . . . Now is the time for organized/unorganized labor, the interfaith and community organizations to show solidarity and demand that all elected officials address the needs of working people."[186]

**Relevant Law:**

U.S. Constitution: Preamble, General Welfare Clause; Art. II, §1, Cl. 8; Art.
    II, §3; Art. VI, Cl. 2; First, Fourth, Fifth Amendments
Humphrey-Hawkins Full Employment and Balanced Growth Act, 15 U.S.C.
    §§1021, 3101, et seq. (1978)
UN Charter: Preamble, Art. 2.3, 2.4, 55, 56
ICCPR: Art. 1-3, 5, 9, 13, 14, 22, 26, 40
CERD: Art. 5(b), 5(d)(ix), 5(e)(i)-(iv), 6, 9
ILO Convention of 1948
ICESCR: Preamble, Art. 1, 6-8, 16, 17

## Report 23.1: Bush Uses Taft-Hartley Act Against Militant Union

On September 29, 2002, the Pacific Maritime Association (PMA) shut US
West Coast ports and locked out members of the International Longshore
and Warehouse Union, accusing them of engaging in a slowdown. The
major issue in the dispute was the management's proposal to introduce new
technologies to speed cargo handling and its refusal to honor previous agreements stipulating that when union jobs were lost due to the introduction of
new technology, alternative jobs would be offered to union members. The
militant, interracial union's 10,500 members were also fighting to defend
healthcare and pensions.[187]

The PMA refused to negotiate with the ILWU and had the backing of
forty-five multinational corporations, including Wal-Mart and the Gap.
With 7 percent of the US Gross Domestic Product flowing through West
Coast ports, the PMA pressured the Bush Administration to act to prevent a
longshore strike or slowdown. Bush threatened to replace the ILWU on the
West Coast with federal troops if they did go on strike. There was also talk
of using the new USA PATRIOT Act and the Office of Homeland Security
to investigate the background of all workers on the waterfront.

ILWU spokesman Steve Stallone explained the central issue: "What
power does a union have other than withdrawing its labor? These have
been recognized as legitimate worker rights since 1934 and are still the law
of the land."[188]

On October 8, 2002, Bush successfully obtained a court order to stop
the employers' lockout of the longshoremen for eighty days. Bush became
the first president to invoke the Taft-Hartley Act since 1971. Passed in
1947, the Act allows presidents to seek injunctions against strikes and lockouts that "imperil the national health or safety."

Bush said he was worried about the movement of military supplies. The
Pentagon often uses commercial shipping lines to send supplies and equipment

overseas. West Coast lines have been used when fighting has erupted in Iraq or elsewhere in the Middle East, as the route avoids the Panama Canal. In a statement, Bush said, "The crisis in our Western ports is hurting the economy. It is hurting the security of our country, and the federal government must act. Americans are working hard every day to bring our economy back from recession. This nation simply cannot afford to have hundreds of billions of dollars a year in potential manufacturing and agricultural trade sitting idle."[189]

The AFL-CIO denounced the President's decision. "We're absolutely furious," said Rich Trumka, secretary treasurer of the AFL-CIO. "The PMA locked the workers out, contrived a phony crisis and then gets rescued by the administration. They're getting their way and have the weight of the government behind them."[190] Before the eighty days were up, the ILWU won its demand for continued collective bargaining with the PMA. The two sides signed a contract protecting job security for thousands more ILWU members than in the original PMA proposal, although the PMA did successfully eliminate many jobs.

### Report 23.2: Immigration Service Raids Wal-Mart Janitorial Staff

On October 23, 2003, federal agents raided sixty Wal-Mart stores in twenty-one states across the United States and arrested 250 janitors employed by Wal-Mart contractors for alleged violations of immigration law. Government officials and Wal-Mart executives declined to state why these unprecedented raids were made on employees of one company at this time, or name the cleaning contractors whose employees were arrested.

In fact, Immigration Enforcement conducted the raids as unions were conducting organizing drives on large supermarkets nationwide and as unionized supermarkets were seeking pay cuts after 9/11. Victor Zavala Jr. said the cleaning contractor for whom he worked paid him $400 for working fifty-six hours per week and paid his wife the same. That would come to $6.25 an hour if it included time and a half for all hours worked in excess of forty. "We don't know nothing about days off," said Mr. Zavala, whose hometown is Mexico City. "We don't know nothing about nights off. We don't know health insurance, we don't know life insurance, and we don't know anything about 401(k) plans."

Misha Firer, an illegal immigrant from Russia, said he worked for three months in 2002 as a cleaner at Wal-Marts in Ephrata, Pennsylvania, and Glens Falls, New York, working ninety consecutive days without having a day off. Firer said that he earned $6 an hour, working the midnight-to-8 AM shift, washing, waxing, and buffing floors. He said the chemicals were so strong that some workers had nosebleeds, sore eyes, and skin irritations.[191] The Immigration and Customs Enforcement Service (formerly INS, now part of the

Department of Homeland Security) spent a large budget on simultaneously arresting employees in different states as they were leaving work.[192]

## Report 23.3: Bush Filed Inadequate Report Under Humphrey-Hawkins Act

The Humphrey-Hawkins Full Employment and Balanced Growth Act of 1978, 15 U.S.C. § 1022a(b)(1), requires the President, within ten days of submitting the budget, to truthfully report the nation's unemployment rate to Congress. The law also requires the President to propose steps to bring unemployment down to 3 percent for adults and 4 percent for workers under twenty years of age. If indications are clear that the private sector cannot provide this many new jobs in a year, the President shall propose creating jobs by means of WPA New Deal–type government jobs, as President Roosevelt did in the New Deal period, or as President Johnson did in the 1960s with the war on poverty and the Office of Economic Opportunity.

In February 2004, President Bush made the required annual Economic Report to Congress. In it, Bush stated that the "unemployment rate has fallen from its peak of 6.4 percent last June [2003] to 5.7 percent in December, and employment is beginning to rise as new jobs are created, in small business." He added, "I will not be satisfied until every American who wants a job can find one. I have outlined a six-point plan to promote job creation and strong economic growth."[193] He did not deal with his duty to present a plan to Congress to bring unemployment down to 3 percent for adults despite the daily reports of the closing of large manufacturing, mining, transportation, and state and local government jobs across the United States. He did not state the widely known truth that millions of workers are not listed in the unemployment statistics because they are "discouraged workers" who are no longer receiving unemployment compensation and are not officially looking for work. Nor did he make any proposal to stem the outsourcing of jobs from the United States to developing countries where workers can be paid a fraction of what they receive in the United States in wages, medical coverage, and pensions.

The absolute urgency of reducing unemployment was spelled out to Congress in a statistical study in 1984 by Prof. M. Harvey Brenner PhD, of Johns Hopkins University, for the Subcommittee on Economic Goals and Intergovernmental Policy of the Joint Economic Committee of Congress. The study found that, as national economic conditions deteriorated, within less than two years, the rates of the following illnesses all increased:

- suicide;
- cirrhosis mortality;

- homicide;
- motor vehicle accident mortality;
- infant, fetal, and maternal mortality;
- mental hospitalization; and
- indicators of alcohol abuse.

Statistics show increases in cardiovascular-renal diseases within two to nine years. "For individuals of comparatively low socioeconomic status, including a significant proportion of the nonwhite population, the consequences may be particularly severe. . . . Studies since the 1960s have found strong relationships between crime indices and lack of employment . . . [property crimes, admissions to state and federal prisons]."[194] In March 2004, the MCLI brought this study to the attention of the Firemen's Union in Richmond, California, which faced major cuts in jobs and services. Some members of a union coalition opposing budget cuts proposed that an additional category be added to each proposed budget beyond the short-term savings in dollars achieved by cutting education, libraries, fire and police protection, and health and human services. Since society will pay for every additional inmate in a prison and for every additional patient in a mental health ward that results from budget cuts, these figures should be included in every projected budget as additional costs.

The coalition members said that there are also economic costs resulting from unemployed people who are more likely to fall into patterns of domestic violence and child abuse that must be paid by every person still employed.

### Report 23.4:  US Government Not Protecting Union Rights of Workers in "New" Iraq

In the United States, the Wagner Labor Relations Act of 1935 guarantees the rights of workers to organize labor unions. Among signatory nations, the United States included, the International Covenant on Civil and Political Rights (ICCPR, Art. 22.1) binds member governments to uphold the same rights.

Prior to Saddam Hussein's regime, Iraq had a history of strong labor unions. Under Hussein, unions had survived in the large public/private sector of government-owned enterprises. Starting in March 2003, US and UK military forces destroyed Iraq's infrastructure and then made contracts for its reconstruction.

In May 2003, the International Confederation of Free Trade Unions (ICFTU) issued a statement concerning actions needed to be undertaken in Iraq, "Ensuring respect for workers' rights including freedom of association must be central to building a democratic Iraq and ensuring sustainable economic and social development. Democracy ... requires ... mass based, democratic trade unions that help secure it and protect it as well as being schools of democracy. Free trade unions, an irreplaceable pillar of civil society, also bring together people of different backgrounds to promote and defend their interests at work. . . . The UN's International Labour Organization (ILO) must play a central role in supporting economic reconstruction, in generating decent employment and in supporting the development of tripartite processes and social dialogue."

In July 2003, US Labor Against the War (USLAW) reported that the United States and the UK gave the large, highly profitable reconstruction contracts to eighteen corporations, including Halliburton; Kellogg, Brown & Root; Bechtel; MCI WorldCom; Stevedoring Services of America; Dyn-Corp; and Fluor. These companies have long expressed interest in the exploitation of Iraqi oil resources, but they had never expressed a commitment to respect the rights of Iraqi workers. A survey of these eighteen corporations revealed that, "Half or more are privately owned and therefore not required to account to public shareholders, nor to file even the minimal financial reports required of publicly traded corporations."

Several of these firms have often engaged in "wage-cheating, . . . health and safety violations, worker and community exploitation, human and labor rights abuses (including use of forced labor), union-busting, strike-breaking" and many violations of laws governing corporations and protecting the environment.[195]

In June 2003, Paul Bremer, President Bush's special envoy to Iraq, issued a regulation prohibiting the encouragement of anyone to organize any kind of strike or disruption in a factory or any kind of economically important enterprise. It was also decreed that the Occupation Authority could arrest anyone found in violation of this edict, and treat them as a prisoner of war.

In July 2003, Bremer promised a 30 percent wage increase of an additional $18 a month, plus the granting of additional loans and land.

In October 2003, the International Occupation Watch Center (IOWC) in Baghdad, which toured Iraq with a delegation from USLAW, reported that the promised increase in wages had not been fulfilled, and employed Iraqis at the time of the report still earned an average of $60 a month, the "emergency" pay decreed by the US Coalition Provisional Authority (CPA), and the same wage paid by the Hussein regime. However, since food and housing subsidies were no longer provided under US rule, the actual income of Iraqi workers fell sharply in comparison to preinvasion levels. In addition, the CPA legalized 100 percent foreign ownership of Iraqi enterprises, and set the corporate tax rate at 15 percent. Other countries have a corporate income tax rate much higher than the one the United States proposed for Iraq—e.g., in 2000, at least ten countries had corporate income tax rates above 30 percent, including the

United States, Australia, Germany, the Netherlands, Italy, Greece, Turkey, and Mexico. The low rate proposed for Iraq will attract foreign investors and make it harder for Iraqi-owned companies to compete in the market.[196]

Also in October 2003, three-fourths of the work force at a brick factory in a major industrial complex thirty miles east of Baghdad decided to react to terrible working conditions and a wage of 3,000 dinars a day ($1.50) for a fourteen-hour shift. They walked off the job and marched to the management's office to demand a wage increase, a formal contract, on-site medical facilities, and retirement payments. The owner of the factory threatened to dismiss them and hire replacements. The workers went home, retrieved their guns, and returned as an armed picket line to guard the factory and defend their strike from scab labor. Overpowered, the owner granted them a raise of 500 dinars (25 cents), and agreed to negotiate on social and health benefits.[197]

On the return to the United States of the USLAW two-person delegation (a labor leader and a labor media expert) in October 2003, USLAW issued a resolution based on their findings:

- seventy percent unemployment in Iraq after Bush declared an end to the war in April, 2003;
- widespread hunger and dislocation;
- drop in income of Iraqi workers as a result of the US freeze on Iraqi wages at $60 per month;
- elimination of bonuses, profit sharing, and food and housing subsidies; and
- discovery that, of the $87 billion Congress appropriated for reconstruction in Iraq, none had been used to raise Iraqi wages or provide unemployment benefits.

The delegation found that these conditions led to rekindling of the Iraqi trade union movement after April 2003, though it was undermined by the lack of resources and US withholding of union assets and funds.

The United States preserved the 1987 law issued under Hussein barring unions and collective bargaining in the public sector and in state enterprises (which employ most Iraqi workers), including the oil industry. The United States announced it would sell off state enterprises, even those belonging to the Iraqi people. Issuance of Public Order 39 by the US permitted 100 percent foreign ownership of Iraqi businesses and the repatriation of profits to the country of ownership, rendering illegal any resistance by Iraqi unions. USLAW feared this privatization would result in massive layoffs of Iraqis.[198]

On December 6, 2003, without reason or explanation, US occupation forces in ten armored cars attacked the Iraqi Federation of Workers' Trade Unions (IFWTU) at its temporary headquarters in Baghdad. They arrested eight Union leaders, handcuffed them, and took them away to an unknown location. They also destroyed IFWTU possessions, tore down banners and posters condemning acts of terror, defaced the name of IFWTU and the General Union of Transport Workers on the building's main front with black paint, and smashed windows.

The Executive Bureau of the IFWTU immediately issued a statement condemning "this unjustified terrorizing act by the occupation forces which targeted trade unionist cadres and leaders who are well-known for their struggle against the hated dictatorship." The Union leadership demanded the release of their captured colleagues and the complete cessation of any further arrests of trade union leaders. They asked the Iraqis, the Arab community, and the international trade union organizations to protest the US action, call for the release of the detained leaders, and mandate "compensation for the damages" caused by the attack. On December 7, 2003, the US forces released the eight union leaders unharmed.[199]

And see Resolution in Chapter 5.D-1.

## Report 23.5: Oklahoma Workers Hunger Strike in Taiwan

In Ponca City, Oklahoma, on May 8, 2001, eighty-six union workers were locked out of their jobs at the Continental Carbon Company plant. Unyielding in its resolve to make annual wage and benefits cuts of $15,000 to $20,000 per employee, the company proceeded with the lockout in spite of numerous concessions from the union.[200] Continental Carbon had been bought out in 1995 by the Koos Group, controlled by the billionaire Koo family of Taiwan.[201] After the lockout, workers made several trips to Taiwan to protest at the corporate headquarters, and received support from local unions and other groups. On June 26, 2002, representatives from the PACE Union joined Taiwanese and international labor and environmental organizations in confronting board members and stockholders of Koos Group's China Synthetic Rubber Company at the company's annual meeting in Taipei, Taiwan.[202]

Carbon black, the main product of Continental Carbon Company, is a reinforcing material used in the manufacture of tires. Substandard carbon black can cause tire defects including tread separation. In September 2002, Goodyear Tire Company stopped the receipt of shipments from Continental Carbon. Goodyear Tire discovered defective carbon black produced in the Ponca City plant. On May 8, 2003, Goodyear sued Continental Carbon, stating it had been forced to shut down tire production for more than two days.[203]

In Oklahoma on August 25, 2003, members of the Ponca Tribe and their attorneys announced a pending lawsuit against the Continental Carbon Company for personal injuries and property damage resulting from increased pollution from the plant since the lockout. They linked the increase to the Company's replacement of experienced union employees with fewer and less experienced temporary workers.[204]

By 2003, five people had been killed in accidents linked to Firestone Steeltex tires, and attorney Joseph L. Lisoni brought a national class action suit against Bridgestone/Firestone Inc. for alleged defects in its Steeltex tires. In February 2004, Firestone recalled 490,000 Steeltex tires. On March 26, 2004, Lisoni called on the tire manufacturer to stop using carbon black produced by Continental Carbon Corporation (CCC) at its Ponca City plant because it could lead to large-scale tire tread separations.[205]

The CCC lockout is the longest lockout by a foreign corporation in US history. United Steelworkers of America (USWA), which represents workers at most of CCC's customer companies, stated that they were fully committed to assist PACE in bringing the lockout to an end. The USWA and PACE established a new strategic alliance to coordinate activities.[206]

In June 2004, after three years of not getting the desired results, five US members of PACE went to Taiwan to protest the lockout. They held a hunger strike in front of the offices of Koos Group's Taiwan Cement Corporation, where a shareholders meeting was taking place. Leslie Koo, one of the heads of the Koos Group, asked police to use any means necessary to stop the protest, including arrest and deportation.[207]

One path for action to prevent such situations from recurring: the US Department of Labor could write a letter to the Corporation saying that such lockouts do not conform to either the 1935 Wagner Labor Relations Act or the UN Charter, and any corporation operating in the United States should follow US labor laws. Another path would be for the Department of State to notify the Corporation that the fundamental human rights provisions of the UN Charter, Articles 55 and 56, and Article 22 of the International Covenant on Civil and Political Rights prohibit such actions. The State Department should include this violation in the second, long overdue US periodic report to the UN Human Rights Committee.

## 24. TO RELEASE POLITICAL PRISONERS; TO STOP CAPITAL PUNISHMENT

The deaths of innocent civilians on September 11 set in motion greater concern for the deaths of innocent defendants on Death Rows across the United States.

Throughout US history, some prosecutors have asked grand juries to indict activist men (and a few women) for committing crimes the defendants said they had not committed. Often the defendants could not pay top-notch lawyers to defend them in cases that raised sharp political issues and had received extensive media coverage. Often the trials were conducted in the same jurisdiction where the incidents had occurred, so it was very difficult, often impossible, to find jurors who had not heard of the cases. Often the trials were conducted before judges who were part of the political party or structure the activist defendant had opposed before the incident or the trial. The media often covered the original event in a way that assumed the guilt of the person ultimately put on trial. When the same reporter covered the trial, it was unlikely that the defendant's counterview would be given coverage equal to that given the prosecution's case. The struggles to free political prisoners often finally bring more support than the issue the prisoner espoused that put him in the spotlight in the first place.

One of the most successful efforts to free political prisoners and to avenge their wrongful incarceration grew around the detention of Japanese Americans after Japan attacked the United States at Pearl Harbor in 1941. US citizens of Japanese descent had to leave their homes and businesses on very short notice to go to distant camps where they were forced to live in cramped quarters with inadequate education for their children and inadequate care for their elders. They were kept in the camps until World War II was over, even as many of their sons and grandsons were fighting in the US military, many receiving medals for their bravery. In 1988, after years of effort by second and third generation Japanese Americans, Congress agreed to compensate the surviving detainees (Civil Liberties Act of 1988, 50 App. U.S.C. § 1989). By February 5, 1999, 82,219 people had received $20,000 each. Many families received nothing because the grandparents and parents who were detained had died, although their descendants continued to suffer the loss of the property and businesses their parents had been forced to give up in 1942.[208]

There have been many efforts to investigate the violations of the rights of Native Americans from different tribes, and the financial losses they suffered due to US seizures of their lands and destruction of their cultures. Young Native American scholars have found support for their efforts among some white scholars and activists. Some tribes have received some compensation for some specific illegal acts. But the issue of reparations for Native peoples has not yet begun to be addressed. The events since 9/11 seem to have pushed this issue to the background for many people, while it remains in the foreground for many tribal members. And retrial for Native American activist Leonard Peltier remains a goal (Report 24.1).

The issue of reparations for African Americans for their torture, deaths, and mistreatment as slaves in much of the United States remains unresolved. One of the strongest and most effective proponents of reparations, Mumia-Abu Jamal, remains imprisoned for a crime he says he did not commit (Report 24.2).

All around the globe, these cases and causes are receiving more attention than they are in the United States. And the global campaigns to end capital punishment and to achieve full rights for indigenous peoples are growing, especially in countries considered Third World or "underdeveloped" (Report 24.3).

One path for action for concerned men and women, and especially youth, in the US after 9/11 is to study the provision in the International Covenant on Civil and Political Rights that all of the nations signing the treaty adhered to. Article 10, Section 3 clearly sets forth the basic purpose of punishment: "The penitentiary system shall comprise treatment of prisoners the essential aim of which shall be their reformation and social rehabilitation. Juvenile offenders shall be segregated from adults and be accorded treatment appropriate to their age and legal status."

A second useful subject for study is the current policies followed in prisons in Finland. With a high crime rate thirty years ago there scholars proposed changing the whole atmosphere in prisons, and the government agreed. Prison guards stopped wearing uniforms and stopped requiring prisoners to wear them. Walls and fences were removed, replaced by unobtrusive camera surveillance.

It turned out the scholars were right! The number of prisoners decreased, partly because the recidivism rate decreased. Today the percentage of Finnish people in prison is 0.052 percent, which is comparable to Denmark (0.062) and Sweden (0.064). The rate in the United States is 0.702 percent and 0.664 in Russia.[209]

## Relevant Law:

U.S. Constitution: Art. VI, Cl. 2; First, Fourth, Fifth, Sixth, Eighth, Ninth,
   Fourteenth, Fifteenth Amendments
Civil Liberties Act of 1988, 50 App. U.S.C. §1989
UN Charter: Preamble, Art. 55, 56
ICCPR: Art. 1. 1.1, 2, 2.1, 4, 5, 5.1, 6, 7, 9, 10, 14, 16-19, 21, 26, 27, 40
CERD: Art. 1, 2, 5, 6, 9
CAT: Preamble, Art. 1-3, 10-14, 16, 19
CRC: Preamble, Art. 1, 37, 44

## Report 24.1: Leonard Peltier, Native American Political Prisoner

Leonard Peltier, an American Indian and citizen of the Anishinabe and Lakota Nations, is currently serving two consecutive life sentences in the federal penitentiary in Leavenworth, Kansas. Amnesty International considers Peltier a "political prisoner" who should be "immediately and unconditionally released."[210]

On June 26, 1975, two FBI agents allegedly searching for a young Indian man spotted several men in a red pickup truck in Pine Ridge, South Dakota. The occupants of the truck pulled into the Jumping Bull ranch south of Oglala and shots were fired; no one knows who fired first. Soon the situation exploded into a firefight involving approximately thirty Native American men, women, and children, and over 150 law enforcement agents, including FBI and US Marshals. Before it was over, two FBI agents and a young Native American activist had been killed.

The American Indian Cultural Support organization has published extensive material on the case. "Peltier had been identified as a member of the American Indian Movement by the FBI and targeted by COINTELPRO, a program which 'neutralized' people by slander, attack, and arrest." Fearing no possibility of a fair trial and at the request of his elders, Peltier fled to Canada. He was later arrested and extradited on the basis of affidavits that the US Government now concedes were "false" and "fabricated."

Four men were initially accused of murder in the deaths of the FBI agents. One was the young man the FBI had come to the camp to arrest. All charges against him were dropped. Two of the men were acquitted before a jury, found not guilty by reason of self-defense. The jury had concluded that the men had no way of knowing that the two agents, in plainclothes and unmarked cars, were federal agents. Peltier was in the camp that day, and fired in the direction of the two vehicles, but "had no more idea of what was going on than the two men acquitted."

Because Peltier had fled to Canada, he did not stand trial with the two men who were acquitted. The FBI "decided to concentrate their 'full prosecutorial weight against Leonard Peltier.'" They had Peltier tried before a judge in North Dakota who had a reputation for being hard on Indians. The judge refused to allow Peltier to present any evidence of self-defense. He also ruled that the jury could not be told that his codefendants had been acquitted.

"Manufactured evidence was presented by the FBI in the form of false ballistics tests, and illegally withheld evidence in the form of ballistics tests that proved that the evidence was false." The prosecution never proved that Peltier owned the gun that they said fired the fatal shots that killed the FBI agents. In 1977, Peltier was convicted and sentenced to two consecutive life terms.

The Government has since changed its theory on the Pine Ridge killings, and now admits they have no idea who killed the federal officials.

According to a decision of the US Eighth Circuit Court of Appeals, Peltier's trial and previous appeals were riddled with FBI misconduct and judicial impropriety, including coercion of witnesses, perjury, fabrication of evidence, and the suppression of exculpatory evidence that could have proved his innocence. The court called the FBI's misconduct "a clear abuse of investigative process." Yet they ruled against a new trial for Peltier because they were "reluctant to impute further improprieties to them" (*US v. Peltier*, 585 F2d 314 [8th Cir. 1978]).[211]

During a parole hearing in December 1995, US prosecutor Lynn Crooks admitted again that no evidence exists against Peltier. He further stated that the Government never really accused him of murder and that if Peltier were retried, the Government could not reconvict.[212] In January 2001, President Clinton received a petition for executive clemency for Peltier but decided against it after FBI director Louis Freeh argued that canceling Peltier's life sentence would "signal disrespect" for law enforcers and the public.[213] In December 2002, a federal appeals court rejected Peltier's request for reduction of his two consecutive life sentences, saying the appeal came far too late. Peltier is still incarcerated in Leavenworth, Kansas. His next full parole hearing will be in 2008. He will be sixty-three. He has been incarcerated since he was thirty-two.[214] In August 2004, the California Peace and Freedom Party nominated Leonard Peltier as its presidential candidate.[215]

### Report 24.2: Mumia Abu-Jamal, African American Political Prisoner on Death Row

Mumia Abu-Jamal was an award-winning African American journalist who exposed police violence against Philadelphia's minority communities. He was known as the "Voice of the Voiceless," and at one time was a member of the Black Panther Party.[216]

On December 9, 1981, Mumia Abu-Jamal was driving a taxi in Philadelphia, Pennsylvania, when he saw that the police had stopped his brother. He got out of the car to make sure police were not violating his brother's civil rights. In the altercation that followed, Philadelphia Police Officer Daniel Faulkner was shot and killed; Abu-Jamal was shot and lived. Witnesses saw a man flee the scene who did not look like Abu-Jamal. When police arrived, they arrested him.

Judge Albert Sabo presided over Abu-Jamal's trial in 1982, and his 1995 Post Conviction Relief Act hearing. A member of the Fraternal Order of Police, Sabo had been openly hostile to the defense. During the initial trial, he prevented Abu-Jamal's court-appointed attorney from getting the money necessary to investigate and prepare an adequate defense and allowed the prosecution to use what were later ruled illegal means to keep African Americans off the jury. Sabo also refused to let Abu-Jamal represent himself, even though he was defended by a "reluctant incompetent" attorney who was later disbarred and who still later filed an affidavit in Abu-Jamal's support, detailing his delinquencies.

Officer Daniel Faulkner was shot with a .44 caliber weapon. Ballistics reports prove that the gun found on Abu-Jamal on December 9, 1981, a .38 caliber weapon, was not the gun that killed Faulkner. Police did not test Abu-Jamal's weapon to see whether or not it had been fired. Eyewitnesses who were not called to testify in the 1982 trial came forward later claiming, "Abu-Jamal was not the shooter." Eyewitness Veronica Jones said the police threatened to jail her if she testified. Other witnesses who testified against Abu-Jamal in the original trial later changed their stories, claiming police threatened and intimidated them in order to elicit their original testimony. Some eyewitnesses who saw a man flee the scene of the crime on December 9 claimed that the man they saw did not look like Abu-Jamal.[217]

On October 30, 1998, the Pennsylvania Supreme Court reviewed the evidence in the Abu-Jamal case but refused to grant a new trial. In 1999, Arnold Beverly, who admitted to being a mob hit man, confessed on videotape to having killed Faulkner. In November 2001, Judge Pamela Dembe ruled that the court could no longer hear new defense witnesses who had not been present at the 1995 hearing. In December 2001, Federal District Judge William Yohn overturned the death sentence, but upheld Abu-Jamal's conviction. Pennsylvania continued to hold him on death row. On October 8, 2003, the Pennsylvania Supreme Court dismissed an appeal by Abu-Jamal and upheld Judge Dembe's decision, saying that the petition to present new witnesses was "untimely." The Court also dismissed Abu-Jamal's petition stating that the original trial had been tainted by the racism of the trial court judge. Judge Sabo had made a racist remark against Abu-Jamal in a conversation overheard by white court stenographer Terri Maurer-Carter. Sabo had been heard to say: "Yeah I'm gonna help 'em fry the nigger."[218]

After many years of monitoring Mumia Abu-Jamal's case, Amnesty International concluded that "The proceedings used to convict and sentence Abu-Jamal to death row were in violation of minimum international standards that govern fair trial procedures." Amnesty believes that "the interests of justice would best be served by granting a new trial to Mumia Abu-Jamal."[219]

On June 29, 2004, the US Court of Appeals for the Third Circuit lifted a stay that had been placed on the case. According to attorney Robert Bryan, the case "is now moving forward on the fast track. . . . Pennsylvania state authorities want to silence his voice and pen and are pressing hard once again for the death penalty. . . . In over three decades of litigating death penalty cases, I have never seen one in which the government has so badly wanted to kill a client."[220]

On July 16, 2004, the National Association for the Advancement of Colored People (NAACP) passed an "emergency resolution" on the last day of its national convention calling for a new trial for Abu-Jamal. This is the first time the organization has gone on record in support of a new trial in the case.

The resolution received overwhelming support from convention delegates and passed with only one dissenting vote. Abu-Jamal stated through his attorney, "I am humbled by and very grateful for the NAACP's support. The NAACP has taken stands through the years on behalf of so many people who have been victimized in society because of their race. I hope this resolution will help many others in situations similar to mine."[221] Late in the 2004 election campaign, the IRS began questioning the tax-exempt status of the NAACP (see the preface).

### Report 24.3: Almost One Hundred Political Prisoners on US List

In April 2004, the Prison Activist Resource Center compiled a list of ninety men and women serving time in federal and state prisons whom they considered political prisoners. In addition to well-known prisoners like Leonard Peltier and Mumia Abu-Jamal (see Reports 24.1 and 24.2), the Center list includes men and women in twenty-five states as well as Puerto Rico. Of this number, almost one-fourth had names that suggest that they are Muslim or Arab, or are from the Middle East.

Since 1986, six political prisoners have died in US prisons. In 2002, twenty-three political prisoners were released.[222] All of the people arrested in peaceful demonstrations against the war and on other issues who were taken to a jail were political prisoners. They are not included in the statistics above, which cover people tried and convicted and serving sentences (see Section 3). And all of the noncitizens arrested and detained without charges in the United States can be considered political prisoners, since they were arrested not for their actions but because of a political fact: they were from a country that the US Government was either invading or seeking to neutralize (see Sections 18 and 20). The detainees at Guantanamo Bay (and elsewhere in the world) who are never brought up on criminal charges must also be considered political prisoners—men held because of their actual or alleged political beliefs, associations, and commitments, not for criminal acts (see Sections 2 and 19).

### Report 24.4: Failure to Abolish Capital Punishment

After 9/11, the campaign to end capital punishment was met by the campaign to punish wrongdoers even more harshly because some of them might be "terrorists." The opponents of capital punishment quoted the decision by the Republican Governor of Illinois, George Ryan, in January 2000, to declare a moratorium on all executions in his state because thirteen men had been found to have been wrongfully executed. Then he called for the creation of a special commission to review the administration of the death penalty in the state and make recommendations to him before the moratorium was lifted.

He said, "I cannot support a system, which, in its administration, has proven to be so fraught with error and has come so close to the ultimate nightmare, the state's taking of innocent life. . . . Until I can be sure that everyone sentenced to death in Illinois is truly guilty, until I can be sure with moral certainty that no innocent man or woman is facing a lethal injection, no one will meet that fate. . . . I am a strong proponent of tough criminal penalties, of supporting laws and programs to help police and prosecutors keep dangerous criminals off the streets. We must ensure the public safety of our citizens but, in doing so, we must ensure that the ends of justice are served."[223]

In 1976, the international community tried to end capital punishment by including such a provision in the International Covenant on Civil and Political Rights. Facing opposition from the United States and other countries, the Covenant includes two provisions on the subject: (1) Art. 6, Sec. 2: in countries that have not abolished the death penalty, it may be imposed only "for the most serious crimes," and (2) Art. 6, Sec. 6: "Nothing in this article shall be invoked to delay or to prevent the abolition of capital punishment by any State Party to the present Covenant."

The US Government ratified the Covenant in 1992, including the comment that capital punishment continues to be legal both at the federal level and in several states. Since 1976, the US Government has executed three men, including one in 2003. In several states, 188 prisoners have been legally executed between September 11, 2001, and August 5, 2004.[224] The FBI Uniform Crime Report for 2002 shows that the murder rate in the Southern states is higher than in the rest of the country although they execute over 80 percent of all those executed in the United States. The Northeast, which carries out less than 1 percent of all executions in the country, has the lowest murder rate.

Opponents of the death penalty say that the strongest argument against executions is that they do not cut the murder rate.

- Of death row inmates 46% are White, 42% are Black, and 10% are Hispanic. (2003 Census Bureau figures show that the US population is 80.5% White, 12.9% Black, and 13.7% "Hispanic or Latino.")
- Of the 921 prisoners executed since 1976, 58% were White, 34% were Black, and 6% were Hispanic.
- Over 80% of completed capital punishment cases involve White victims, even though nationally only 50% of murder victims are White. The odds of receiving a death sentence rise 3.5 times among defendants whose victims were White.
- Of the chief district attorneys in death penalty states, 98% are White; 1% are Black.
- Twenty-one people have been exonerated and freed from death row since 2001, after proof of their innocence surfaced.

- As of June 30, 2004, there were seventy-two juveniles (under eighteen at the time of the crime) on death row across the United States.
- Since 1976, twenty-two defendants have been executed for crimes committed while they were juveniles.
- Florida, Georgia, New Hampshire, North Carolina, and Texas place the minimum death penalty age at seventeen.
- Of criminologists surveyed, 82% rejected the notion that the death penalty acts as a deterrent to murder.

On March 1, 2005, the US Supreme Court (5–4) abolished the death penalty for juveniles (under eighteen) in *Roper v. Simmons*. The opinion covers all those on death row who committed their crimes before they were eighteen, based on the Eighth Amendment and Convention on the Rights of the Child.[225]

## E. THE GOVERNMENT'S DUTY TO PROPERLY FUND THE GENERAL WELFARE

In Spring 2004, the San Francisco Bay Area Progressive Challenge prepared the "Sensible Federal Budget Resolution" for adoption by the California state assembly, a copy of which was to be sent to both houses of Congress, the President and Vice President, and the media. The Resolution calls on Congress and the President "to enact a budget that redirects sufficient amounts of money from the military budget to the states," to allow for increased funding of social programs that provide "a decent level of health-care and safety for all our citizens." Many organizations have prepared similar resolutions in cities and states all across the country (the full text of the Bay Area Sensible Federal Budget Resolution is in Chapter 5.B-4).

President Bush's budget proposal for 2005 provided $401.7 billion for the Department of Defense's base budget, an annual increase of 7 percent, for a total increase in defense spending of 35 percent since 2001.

**The 2005 Discretionary Budget Authority Sought by Bush:**

| | |
|---|---|
| 1. Dept. of Defense | $401.7 billion |
| 2. Dept. of Health and Human Services | $ 66.8 billion |
| 3. Dept. of Transportation | $ 57.4 billion |
| 4. Dept. of Education | $ 57.3 billion |
| 5. Dept. of Homeland Security | $ 33.8 billion |
| 6. Dept. of Housing and Urban Development | $ 31.3 billion |
| 7. Dept. of Veterans Affairs | $ 29.7 billion |
| 8. Dept. of Energy | $ 24.3 billion |
| 9. Dept. of Agriculture | $ 19.1 billion |
| 10. Dept. of Justice | $ 18.7 billion |
| 11. National Aeronautic and Space Administration | $ 16.2 billion |
| 12. Dept. of Labor | $ 11.9 billion |
| 13. Dept. of the Interior | $ 10.8 billion |
| 14. Dept. of State and International Econ. Assistance | $ 10.3 billion |
| 15. Social Security Administration | $  9.1 billion |
| 16. Environmental Protection Agency | $  7.8 billion |
| 17. National Science Foundation | $  5.7 billion[1] |

The President's Department of Defense budget proposal for fiscal year 2005 is $25.3 billion more than all of the other sixteen departments of the Government (above) combined. After 9/11, the Bush Administration limited the funding for health and human services (see Section 25), education for all (see Section 26), environmental protection (see Section 27), and the judicial system (see Section 28).

## 25. HEALTH AND HUMAN SERVICES

In November 2001, the World Trade Organization (WTO) ministerial conference in Doha, Qatar, concluded an agreement among all 144 member states of the WTO, except the United States, to help poor nations buy medicines to fight AIDS, tuberculosis, malaria, and other diseases, by relaxing patent laws that kept prices of drugs beyond their reach. In December 2002, the US Government single-handedly destroyed the agreement by insisting that strong international patent protection be left in place. Sources at the WTO in Geneva said that this decision to scuttle the agreement came directly from the White House, following intense lobbying from US pharmaceutical companies.[2]

In July 2002, the US Government cut off its $34 million annual contribution to the UN family-planning program and in November 2002, it withdrew its support of the Cairo Action Plan of 1994. The Plan promotes "reproductive health services and health care" as a means of curbing population growth in developing countries. The State Department's population office stated that the Plan implied a right to abortion and undermined the US international campaign for sexual abstinence as the only method to avoid pregnancy.

In August 2003, the Congressional Budget Office (CBO) reported that the US Government would experience eight more years of budget deficits, including a record $480 billion shortfall in 2004. The CBO also warned that these numbers would get worse if Congress failed to rein in spending and the additional tax cuts that the White House advocated (which were passed).

Rep. John Spratt (D-SC) said the Administration was draining the Government's ability to pay for Social Security and Medicare at a time when seventy-seven million baby boomers are approaching retirement, and it is saddling future generations with repayment of a national debt that could rise to $7 trillion by 2013 (Report 25.6). Senator Kent Conrad (D-ND) said a deficit "of this magnitude coming at this time fundamentally threatens the long-term economic security of this country."

The CBO also stated that the budget outlook has worsened substantially since its review in March 2003. "Much of that is the result of subsequent acts of Congress to cut taxes and increase spending for security, defense, and the war in Iraq."[3]

At the same time, Bush Administration budget cuts sent more single mothers into poverty (Report 25.1), created a crisis for many cities like Richmond, California (Report 25.5), and threatened to make cancer care (Report 25.2) and mental health care (Report 25.7) out of reach of ordinary people, at the same time cutting Social Security payments (Report 25.6). Critics found a certain irony in the Bush Administration seeking more funding for the invasions of Afghanistan and Iraq (Report 25.4) while proposing cuts in veterans' benefits (Report 25.3).

## Relevant Law:

U.S. Constitution: Preamble, General Welfare Clause; Art. I, §8, Cl. 1, Cl. 2, Cl. 11; Art. VI, Cl. 2; Fourteenth, Nineteenth Amendments
UN Charter: Preamble, Art. 2.3, 2.4, 55, 55 (a)-(b), 56
ICCPR: Preamble, Art. 1, 2, 2.1, 3-5, 16, 20, 23-26, 40
CERD: Art. 1-5, 9
ICESCR: Preamble, Art. 1.1, 9, 11-13, 16, 17
CEDAW: Art. 1-3, 5, 10-14, 16, 18
CRC: Preamble, Art. 1-3, 6.2, 23, 24, 26, 27.3, 44

## Report 25.1: Administration Budget Cuts Sent More Single Mothers into Poverty

In 2002, the number of people living in poverty in the United States increased for the second year in a row, according to the US Census Bureau. As of 2002, 1.7 million more people were classified as living below the poverty line than during 2001, for a total of 34.6 million people, including 12.1 million children. There were 3 million more poor people in 2002 than in 2000.[4] In August 2004, statistics concerning poverty in the United States were not available for 2003 and 2004 from the Census Bureau.

In 2003, 50 percent of all families living in poverty were headed by single mothers although only 20 percent of all US families were headed by single mothers. The poverty rate for female-headed households was three times that of other households.

"The Bush administration excuses the increase in poverty rates over the past two years as a side effect of a nation emerging from a recession," said the president of the National Organization for Women, Kim Gandy, "but we know that the increase is due to a deliberate government policy to encourage and reward states who kick poor women off welfare regardless of whether they have stable employment, safe and decent childcare and living conditions or are paid enough to support their families."[5]

Presidents of the United States have signed the Convention on Elimination of Discrimination Against Women (CEDAW)—Carter in 1980—the Convention on the Rights of the Child (CRC)—Clinton in 1985—and the International Covenant on Economic, Social, and Cultural Rights (ICESCR)—Carter in 1977. By their signatures, the Presidents made commitments to seek ratification by two-thirds of the Senate and to not violate the treaties. For example, President Carter carefully did not violate the Strategic Arms Limitations Talks (SALT II), a treaty between the United States and the then Union of Soviet Socialist Republics (USSR) that imposed limits on each country's strategic offensive arms, which was signed in 1976 but never ratified. All three treaties contain the commitment of signatory nations to take steps to abolish child poverty (CEDAW Preamble, Art. 1.8.3, 11(1)(a), (e), 12(2), 14(2)(h), 14; CRC Art. 6, 24, 26, 27; ICESCR Art. 9, 11, 12). CEDAW requires the commitment of signatory nations to protect the rights and lives of all women, including single mothers (Art. 11(2)(d), 12(2), 13(a), 16).

The Humphrey-Hawkins Full Employment and Balanced Growth Act of 1978 requires the President to present a plan to Congress each February to bring unemployment down to 3 percent for adults and 4 percent for youths under twenty. In 2004, President Bush made an inadequate report (Report 23.3).

One path for action in 2004 was the Sensible Federal Budget Resolution, authored by the San Francisco Bay Area Progressive Challenge, that would reverse the Bush Administration cuts to health and human services, education, and environmental protection (see Chapter 5.B-4).

## Report 25.2: Administration Urged Budget Cuts for Cancer Care

The overwhelming majority of adults in the United States surveyed from September 5 to 9, 2003, stated that they were unaware that the Medicare prescription drug benefit bills before Congress contained multibillion-dollar cuts for cancer treatment. Nearly eight out of ten said that Congress should remove the cancer care cut provision before the legislation was finalized. Three out of five said they would prefer that Congress pass no drug benefit bill at all rather than pass one containing the cancer treatment cuts. The proposal called for reductions of up to $16 billion in Medicare reimbursements for chemotherapy and other cancer treatments. Patients, physicians, and nurses who had experienced cancer firsthand were convinced the cuts would lead to a massive disruption in access to treatment, including the closing of community cancer treatment centers in every part of the country.[6]

On September 25, 2003, President Bush urged Congress to work quickly to pass the bill. "I think it's the right thing to do," Bush said at a Cabinet Room meeting.[7] In November 2003, Congress complied with the President's wishes, voting to approve the Medicare Prescription Drug Improvement and Modernization Act of 2003, with the Senate voting 54–44 and the House voting 220–215. On December 8, President Bush signed the bill into law.

## Report 25.3: Administration Proposed Shrinking Veterans' Benefits

In January 2004, the Bush Administration considered a proposal that would cut the number of military personnel who qualify for disability benefits. The proposal, if retroactive, could disqualify 1.5 million veterans, about two-thirds of those now in the Veterans Affairs (VA) disability program. The Administration also considered dramatic increases in the fees veterans must pay for prescription drugs. These new fees would generate more than $728 million income for drug companies by 2005 and nearly $4.2 billion by the end of 2009.[8]

As the law stood, disabled veterans eligible for military retirement pay had their retirement reduced by the amount they received in disability payments. Veterans' groups argue that civilian federal employees on disability receive full retirement benefits and these rights should be extended to veterans.

Giving veterans both retirement and disability benefits would cost $58 billion over ten years. The White House and House Republican leaders proposed a less costly compromise that would phase in retirement benefit increases over the next four or five years and narrow the service-connected benefits. The proposal would define qualified disabilities as those injuries and illnesses "directly resulting from the performance of official military duties." The Veterans Committee Republicans estimated that 50 to 90 percent of veterans would not qualify if these standards were applied to current disability claims. They added that future payments to widows could also be jeopardized.[9] On June 1, 2004, the Associated Press reported that if President Bush were elected in 2004 his 2006 budget would have a provision in it to cut funds for Veterans Affairs by 3.4 percent or, roughly, $1 billion. In June 2004, the United States was spending $1 billion dollars a day on the war in Iraq.[10]

### Report 25.4: Administration Budgeted for Expanding War Powers, Not US Needs

On September 17, 2003, the White House formally requested $87 billion from Congress to fund operations in Iraq and Afghanistan. Rep. David Obey (D-WI) criticized the "huge disparity between what this administration is willing to spend on Iraq and what it is willing to spend here" on "homeland security," education, and infrastructure.

Obey and other Democrats and some Republicans called for more funding of homeland security, veterans benefits, and infrastructure spending inside the United States. Obey said that, while he supported balancing the federal budget, "we not only need a balanced budget but we need a balance in the budget between what we do abroad and what we do at home."

In February 2004, the Bush Administration requested $420.7 billion for the military for the 2005 fiscal year, including $401.7 billion for the Defense Department and $19 billion for the nuclear weapons program of the Department of Energy.[11]

On July 30, 2004, the Bush Administration released its Mid-Session Review of the budget for the 2005 fiscal year, estimating the largest deficit in history at $455 billion.[12] The Bush Administration renewed its request for $402 billion for the Department of Defense. The Administration also requested $25 billion for a "contingency reserve for continuing operations in Iraq and Afghanistan," although it admitted that the "full cost of these operations in 2005 is uncertain, but they are expected to require additional funding beyond this request." The Mid-Session Review did not mention nuclear weapons programs.[13]

### Report 25.5: National Budget Crisis Cuts City Services

In a sequence of events mirrored across the US, especially in low-income neighborhoods and communities of color, the city of Richmond, California, went from having a large budget surplus before 9/11 to an enormous deficit by the year 2004, as the energy crisis of 2000–2001, the war economy, and layoffs hit home.

To deal with the deficit, the Richmond City Council did not seek federal funding but cut city staff and public services. By April 2004, Richmond's once-excellent public library was in danger of closing because of the layoffs of most of its employees. The Council shut some fire stations and cut police and fire staff as well as three hundred other unionized city infrastructure jobs (street, equipment, and park maintenance workers and community center staff). The Council also closed half of the city's recreational centers.[14]

In response to the budget crisis, the Richmond school district laid off hundreds of teachers and other staff. School libraries were closed, and high school sports, art, and music programs were curtailed. Residents of Richmond feared the effects these cuts would have on young people. Deborah Doctor, a twelve-year resident of Richmond, said, "One of the real tragedies here is that services for children are being cut out from several angles. The idea of cutting back on library time for kids in Richmond is just inconceivable."[15]

Chevron Corporation operates a large, very profitable refinery in Richmond. Richmond residents repeatedly called for Chevron to pay more to help out the city in this financial crisis. They suggested that the City Council stop giving Chevron tax breaks amounting to millions of dollars per year and suggested imposing a "clean air tax" on Chevron and other polluting industries, as well as fining industries that release toxins into the air without first setting off warning sirens. Concerned Richmond citizens, some with sons and daughters in the military service, also proposed that the City Council and the Board of Education seek federal funding to make up for the municipality's deficit. The City Council and the School Board ignored these and many other creative suggestions from town residents.[16]

After a closed-session vote by the City Council to lay off nearly 40 percent of Richmond's workforce, attorneys for the Service Employees International Union (SEIU) Local No. 790 filed a legal challenge against the city based on the Brown Act, California's open-meetings law. "We are filing a lawsuit," said Millie Cleveland, SEIU field representative. "The vote was illegal."[17] Another path for action calls for a federal investigation of the profits made from the "2000–2001 energy crisis," leading to fines that could fund grants to cities and counties suffering from the "crisis." Some critics believe that there was no real energy crisis; others disagree. Certainly it was a crisis for consumers, but some corporations made huge profits off of this "crisis."

### Report 25.6: Bush Plan Endangers Social Security

On January 15, 2003, the comptroller of the nonpartisan General Accounting Office testified before Congress that the Bush Administration's plan to partially privatize Social Security would have a negative impact on benefit recipients. Testifying before the Senate's special committee on aging, GAO comptroller John Walker stated that the privatization plan allowing for Social Security benefits to be invested in the stock market would "require tax increases, raising the retirement age and benefit cuts."[18]

In June 2002, economists Peter Diamond, with the Massachusetts Institute of Technology, and Peter Orszag, with the Brookings Institute, had released a report concluding that under two of the Administration's three Social Security reform proposals, for those who retire in 2075, "Total benefits would be ten percent below current-law benefits for low-income people, twenty-one percent below current-law benefits for middle-income people and twenty-five percent below current-law benefits for upper-income people." These projected reductions would be even larger if they were adjusted to reflect the risk of investing in the stock market.[19] On October 27, 2004, just before the election, the *Iconoclast* in Crawford, Texas, "the President's hometown newspaper," which had supported George Bush's candidacy in 2004, issued its endorsement of his opponent because of Bush's policies on Social Security and six other issues.

> The Social Security Trust Fund actually lends money to the rest of the government in exchange for government bonds, which is how the system must work by law, but how do you later repay Social Security while you are running a huge deficit? It's impossible, without raising taxes sometime in the future or becoming fiscally responsible now. Social Security money is being used to escalate our deficit and, at the same time, mask a much larger government deficit, instead of paying down the national debt, which would be a proper use, to guaranteee a future gain.
>
> Privatization is problematic in that it would subject Social Security to the ups, downs, and outright crashes of the Stock Market. It would take millions in brokerage fees and commissions out of the system, and, unless we have assurance that the Ivan Boeskys and Ken Lays of the world will be caught and punished as a deterrent, subject both the Market and the Social Security Fund to fraud and market manipulation, not to mention devastate and ruin multitudes of American families that would find their lives lost to starvation, shame, and isolation.

## Report 25.7: Administration Failed to Face Rising Mental Health Problems

According to the National Mental Health Association (NMHA), federal and local governments have addressed the nation's physical security and health since 9/11 but have neglected to fund and care for the mental health of US residents. According to Michael Faenza, president and CEO of the NMHA, "Since the 9-11 attacks, the need for mental health services has risen dramatically, with increased anxiety, Post Traumatic Stress Disorder (PTSD) and other mental health problems. But our nation still has not prioritized mental health. In fact, many actions—such as state budget slashing—further ignore the mental health needs of Americans." In analyzing the parity between different countries' physical and mental health care insurance coverage, the NMHA gave the United States a D+.[20]

In April 2002, President Bush announced his support for mental health parity legislation that would require private health insurance benefits "to cover treatment for all mental disorders, including substance abuse, at the same level as other medical illnesses."[21] This legislation, the Senator Paul Wellstone Mental Health Equitable Treatment Bill (S. 486/H.R. 953), has sixty-nine cosponsors in the Senate and 245 in the House of Representatives, and has received wide support from the US medical community. None of the responsible Congressional committees has taken action or scheduled a hearing on the bill.[22]

Many vulnerable groups are particularly susceptible to mental health problems and as a consequence are disproportionately forced to suffer when the President and Congress fail to act. Among them are:

- *US Iraqi war veterans*: A US Army study of soldiers returning from Iraq in 2003 reported that up to 17 percent suffered from post-traumatic stress disorder (PTSD), major depression, or other serious mental afflictions within months of ending their deployment—but less than half of them sought treatment. The prevalence of PTSD among Vietnam veterans was 15 percent in studies conducted years after the end of service. Studies of first Gulf War veterans show rates from 2 to 10 percent, versus 3 to 4 percent among the general public.[23]
- *POWs and other detainees*: The International Committee of the Red Cross, in February 2004, in a rare public rebuke, identified humiliation and "psychological coercion" as unacceptable treatments of captives being held by the United States and its allies. Psychological symptoms resulting from interrogation methods and duration included "concentration difficulties, memory problems, verbal expression difficulties, incoherent speech, acute anxiety reactions, abnormal behaviour and suicidal tendencies."[24]

- *US Prisoners*: In September 2003, Human Rights Watch (HRW) reported that a high proportion of people with mental illnesses are incarcerated. A two-year HRW study found that one in six US prisoners is mentally ill and suffering "from serious illnesses such as schizophrenia, bipolar disorder, and major depression." Some seventy thousand are psychotic. The rate of mental illness in US prisons is three times higher than found in the general population.[25] The statistics are mind-boggling. Many critics are convinced that the presence of mentally ill individuals in US prisons is tied directly to the cutting of services and the disappearance of mental health institutions and programs. Prison conditions in the United States have themselves created or exacerbated mental illness in the prisoners.

The American Psychiatric Association praises a Bush Administration plan to integrate the mentally ill into their communities, but a whistle-blower says the initiative serves the pharmaceutical industry's interests by focusing on medication as treatment. The plan includes recommendations to screen for mental illness fifty-two million students, including preschool students, and six million adults who work in schools.[26]

Since 9/11, several organizations have expressed growing concerns about the predisposition of Government, private industry, and health care professionals to limit treatment options to the medical model, which favors pharmaceutical and electroshock treatments and institutionalization. The Law Project for Psychiatric Rights files lawsuits challenging "unwarranted court orders requiring people diagnosed with mental illness to submit or be forcibly subjected to brain damaging treatments, primarily psychiatric medications."[27] MindFreedom Support Coalition International united one hundred grassroots groups and thousands of members to win campaigns for human rights of people diagnosed with psychiatric disabilities.[28]

## 26. EDUCATION FOR ALL

One purpose of the US Constitution, found in the Preamble, is to "promote the general Welfare." In 1979, Congress echoed these words in its passage of the United States Department of Education Organization Act, to establish a Department of Education so as to "promote the general welfare of the United States, [to] help ensure that education issues receive proper treatment at the Federal level, and [to] enable the Federal Government to coordinate its education activities more effectively." The right to education includes the right to attend high-quality public schools (K–12), even in low-income neighborhoods, community colleges, efficient facilities for training and rehabilitation of first offenders and parolees, and workable schools for disabled students.

Since 9/11, the US budget for military missions has led to budget cuts for education. After-school programs were cut while more and more children had no parent at home to return to after school (Report 26.1). Federal funds that used to help cities and counties pay for schools in low-income areas were cut (Report 26.2), along with funds for training and rehabilitation of people in prison and getting out of prison (Report 26.3). At the same time, the Bush Administration promoted religious education and school vouchers for private schools (Report 26.5), continued federal administration of the schools in the District of Columbia (Report 26.4) against strong community opposition, and cut funding for athletics programs for girls (Report 26.6).

## Relevant Law:

U.S. Constitution: Preamble, General Welfare Clause; Art. I, §8, Art. VI, Cl. 2; First, Fifth, Thirteenth, Fourteenth, Fifteenth, Nineteenth Amendments

*Brown v. Board of Education*, 347 U.S. 483 (1954)

UN Charter: Preamble, Art. 55, 56

ICCPR: Preamble, Art. 1, 2.1, 5, 16, 20, 24-26, 40

CERD: Art. 1, 2, 4(c), 5, 7, 9

ICESCR: Preamble, Art. 1-3, 13, 14, 16, 17

CRC: Preamble, Art. 1-3, 6.2, 23, 28, 44

CEDAW: Preamble, Art. 1-3, 10, 15.1, 18

## Report 26.1: Budget Cut 475,000 Kids out of After-School Programs

Four hundred thousand children in the United States fell into poverty during 2002. In 2004, 58 percent of Black children were living in low-income families, as were 62 percent of Latino children and 25 percent of Caucasian children. These percentages are highly disproportionate to the population and show that Black and Latino children have a much higher chance of living in poverty than do White children.[29]

The Bush budget cut 475,000 kids out of after-school programs. It cut $8 billion from the promised funding of Bush's own No Child Left Behind Act, almost all of it from schools serving the poorest children in the country. Bush cut all funding to help build new schools, even though the schools in the United States are flooded by the largest wave of children since the baby boom.

There is no money in the 2004 budget for an enlarged teachers corps, even though the United States faces the largest wave of teacher retirements ever. Bush's budget does not fully fund Head Start, the one program all agree can help children get ready to learn.

Bush says that the commitment he made in Iraq will cost $87 billion in 2004. About $67 billion will pay for US troops. The other $20 billion will go to rebuild life in Iraq destroyed by US bombing: constructing schools, improving roads and infrastructure, building public housing, and putting people to work. Eighty-seven billion dollars is more than twice what the federal government will spend on schools in 2004. It is eighty-seven times the cost of after-school programs.[30]

In addition, President Bush signed a $368 billion defense budget for 2004. The bill includes an average military pay raise of 4.1 percent, funding for twenty-two F-22 stealth fighters, $9 billion in missile defense programs, and $11.5 billion for shipbuilding.[31]

## Report 26.2: Funding Cut for Ghetto Schools, Community Colleges

On February 3, 2003, President Bush released his proposed education budget for 2004. The budget had increased by an average of 13 percent a year over the past seven years. Bush proposed a 5.6 percent increase. His budget included cuts to numerous programs, cuts that would have a dispro-portionate effect on low-income students attending inner-city schools and community colleges, the majority of whom are people of color. Federal funds for health, education, and nutrition provided under the Head Start program were frozen, and the power of disbursement of federal funds was transferred to state governments in the form of block grants.

Funding for the Title I programs that teach mathematics and reading to disadvantaged children was one-third less than the total that Bush and Congress had agreed to provide under the No Child Left Behind Act. As a consequence, 2.2 million disadvantaged children would have no "critical education programs."[32] The Government completely eliminated funding for "Close Up Fellowships," which helped fund educational visits to Washington, DC, by low-income students and their teachers. The budget also abolished $32.5 million in funding for "Community Technology Centers," which pro-vided economically disadvantaged neighborhoods with access to computers and high-technology training, and $23.5 million in funding for dropout-prevention programs.[33]

The Fiscal Year 2004 budget also froze federal funding for Perkins Loans, which assisted students from low-income communities in paying for college. The Thurgood Marshall Legal Educational Opportunity Program, which helped pay law school tuition for minority and disadvantaged students, has added scores of committed public interest lawyers to the bar. It was elimi-nated. Five million dollars in funding for the "Tech-Prep Demonstration Pro-gram," which established secondary technical education programs on the campuses of community colleges, was eliminated. Bush and Congress also terminated $1 million in funding for "Loan Forgiveness for Child Care Providers," which partially forgave the college loans of child care providers who worked in low-income communities after they graduated.[34] The Administration's FY 2004 budget did provide for the extensive funding of "choice programs," including $300 million in private school vouchers.[35]

In 2004, in Richmond, California, the federal budget cuts led to the state budget crisis that led to announced layoffs of many teachers and counselors, the closing of all school libraries, and the ending of all school athletic, music, and drama programs in West Contra Costa Unified School District (WCCUSD), a district where 29 percent of K–12 schoolchildren are African American, 36 percent are Hispanic, 11 percent are Asian, and 15 percent are White.[36]

To highlight the dire situation, students, teachers, parents, and activists in the School District came together and organized a seventy-mile march to Sacramento. When Gov. Arnold Schwarzenegger refused to meet with the marchers, some of them began a hunger strike, which lasted for twenty-six days. Dolores Huerta, of the United Farm Workers of America, joined the effort. On the final day of the strike, state legislators granted the school district a reduction in the interest rate on the large "bailout loan" it had been paying interest on to the State since its near-bankruptcy in 1991.[37]

### Report 26.3: Funding Cut for Training, Rehabilitation, and Special Education

The theory behind free public education from kindergarten to high school is that every young person is entitled to an "education," including philosophy, critical thinking, history, political science, the natural sciences, and the arts. To limit a child's education to "training," without a broad education, is discriminatory. But, when a child only has access to training programs, cutting them means eliminating that child's opportunity to have any education.

On February 3, 2003, President Bush issued his 2004 education budget, ending many vocational training, rehabilitation, and special education programs. Bush indicated that other programs could fulfill the cut programs' objectives, that state and local governments were better funding sources, or that the cut programs had "only indirect or limited effect on improving student outcomes."

Terminated vocational training programs included the $9.5 million Occupational and Employment Information grants for state academic counseling programs; the $67.5 million Regional Educational Laboratories, which produced research and development products and provided training and technical assistance; the $5 million Tech-Prep Education State Grants, which integrated academic and vocational education in secondary and post-secondary institutions; and the $12 million Vocational Education National Programs, which gave "assessment, evaluation, dissemination, and technical assistance."

Bush also ended many other programs: the $9.5 million Adult Education National Leadership Activities, which provided technical assistance for rehabilitation; the $5 million Literacy Programs for Prisoners which funded state and local correctional agencies to teach life skills to decrease recidivism; the $17 million State Grants for Incarcerated Youth Offenders, which enabled state correctional agencies to help incarcerated youth become literate and gain job and life skills; and the $50 million State Grants for Community Service for Expelled or Suspended Students.

Bush also stopped federal funding of special education programs: the $7 million Demonstration Projects to Ensure Quality Higher Education for Students with Disabilities, which created "professional development activities" for higher education faculty and administrators of disabled students programs; the $22.1 million Projects with Industry, which employed disabled individuals; the $2.6 million Recreational Programs that assisted disabled students "in their employment, mobility, independence, socialization, and community integration"; the $38.2 million Supported Employment State Grants for "collaborative programs" with "nonprofit organizations to provide supported employment services" for disabled students; and the $2.4 million Migrant and Seasonal Farmworkers program for rehabilitation services to disabled farmworkers.[38]

Simultaneously, US corporations transferred many manufacturing jobs to foreign countries, cutting US labor costs and raising profits. Dean Baker, the codirector of the Center for Economic and Policy Research, pointed out that "[t]he federal government had the chance to create good jobs by investing in the states, which desperately need the work on run-down infrastructure such as schools and bridges—but it blew that on money [for] millionaire tax cuts."[39]

### Report 26.4: DC Schools Run by the Federal Government

On September 15, 2003, despite opposition from the National Education Association (NEA), the House of Representatives passed the DC Parental Choice Incentive Act of 2003, (H.R. 2556) by one vote. The Act would create vouchers for private and religious school students in the District of Columbia. On November 18, 2003, the Senate struck a proposed DC school voucher program from legislation. Yet, in December 2003 and January 2004, the House and Senate passed the DC Parental Choice Incentive voucher program as part of an omnibus spending bill, thereby approving the DC school voucher program.[40]

In February 2004, DC Mayor Anthony Williams and US Secretary of Education Rod Paige signed a Memorandum Of Understanding (MOU). The MOU detailed how, within the US Department of Education, the Office of Innovation and Improvement will be responsible for establishing the voucher program and the Institute of Education Sciences will evaluate the program. On February 4, 2004, Paige announced, in a *Federal Register* notice, the beginning of the competition to select a group that will manage the $14 million DC School Choice initiative to start in Fall 2004. The five-year federally funded program will provide vouchers of up to $7,500 to about two thousand low-income DC children to study at parochial or private schools. Paige proclaimed, "A good, wise, just and compassionate country makes certain that educational opportunities are available for all of its citizens regardless of economic circumstances, race or zip code. No child can be left behind."[41]

Opponents do not believe that the DC School Choice Initiative will turn Paige's vision into reality. People For the American Way (PFAW) indicated that this voucher program offers very little "choice" because "at best 2% of DC students [will get] fully funded vouchers in FY 2004, while diverting resources that could be used in the public schools that educate over 90% of DC's students" for safety and maintenance. This voucher program affects "the local control of DC residents," since School Superintendent Paul Vance, US Representative Eleanor Holmes Norton, and 76 percent of DC voters opposed "taxpayer-funded vouchers if they mean less money for public school students." Only 17% of DC voters favored such vouchers.

This voucher program also suffers from a lack of accountability for failing "to require participating schools to adopt any of the standards under the No Child Left Behind Act of 2001," and allowing them "to exclude students based on gender, limited English proficiency and disability." Because such schools tend to "expel students easily," many admitted students will be "turned away" the following year. Finally, no study of school voucher programs has shown any "findings to suggest that a larger voucher program would produce significant gains for students."[42]

### Report 26.5: Bush Administration Promotes Religious Education and School Vouchers

On January 8, 2002, President George W. Bush signed the No Child Left Behind Act of 2001 (NCLB). He announced, "We affirm the right of parents to have better information about the schools, and to make crucial decisions about their children's future."[43] The NCLB rested on the ideal to provide "more choices for parents."[44]

In June 2002, the Ohio Supreme Court ruled on the Ohio Pilot Scholarships Program, providing vouchers to low-income and minority parents who desire to take their children out of their current public schools to send them to better public or private schools. The Court held that this did not violate the separation between Church and State delineated in the Establishment Clause of the First Amendment. Applicable to states through the Fourteenth Amendment, the Establishment Clause impedes states from passing laws whose purpose or effect advances or inhibits religion. In his majority opinion, Chief Justice Rehnquist distinguished between unconstitutional school voucher programs, "government programs" that give "direct aid to religious schools," and constitutional "neutral programs," "programs of true private choice, in which government aid reaches religious schools only as a result of the genuine and independent choices of private individuals." (*Zelman v. Simmons-Harris*, 122 S. Ct. 2460 [2002]).

On February 3, 2003, Bush unveiled his 2004 education budget with $756 million for choice programs. To address capacity problems, Bush allocated $75 million to the new Choice Incentive Fund for "competitive awards to states, school districts and community-based nonprofit organizations" to enable low-income parents to transfer "their children to high-performing public, private or charter schools." A portion of these funds were set aside for school-choice programs in DC. He also earmarked $25 million for the Voluntary Public School Choice grants to states and school districts "to increase the capacity of schools to accept students exercising a choice option." To fund partial tax credits for parents transferring their child from an underperforming public school, as defined by the NCLB, to another public or private school, the Government disbursed $226 million. They can obtain a credit of 50 percent of the first $5,000 they pay for "tuition, fees, and transportation." Because the NCLB lists "public charter schools as an option when districts are required to permit students to transfer from a school identified for improvement to a better public school," Bush provided $220 million for grants to help about eighteen hundred charter schools obtain facilities, including "a new per-pupil facilities aid program," which gives "funds to states to assist charter schools." Also, the Credit Enhancement for Charter School Facilities program received $100 million to award "competitive grants to public and nonprofit organizations" helping "charter schools finance their facilities" by "providing loan guarantees, insuring debt," and other methods for "private lending."

The Magnet Schools Assistance Program got $110 million to disburse grants "to eligible local education agencies" to create and maintain magnet schools operating "under a court-ordered or federally approved voluntary desegregation plan."[45] For these programs, which include a total of $300 million for private school vouchers and tax credits, Bush decreased funding for after-school programs by $400 million and for vocational education by $300 million. He did not increase funding for Pell Grants, a higher education program for low-income college students, or for Head Start, which gives "health, education, and nutrition services to disadvantaged children."[46] Consequently, on February 3, 2003, Rep. George Miller (D-CA) of the House Education and the Workforce Committee, criticized the Bush Administration, "Our nation's public schools do not deserve to be cut at the expense of private school vouchers. Our public school children do not deserve to suffer because of a demand by the Republicans to defund public education."[47]

### Report 26.6: Bush Jeopardizes Programs Against Gender Discrimination in Schools

In January 2003, President Bush's Title IX Commission issued a report with recommendations to change the thirty-one-year-old law that mandates public educational institutions to provide equal access to sports teams for men and women. Key recommendations from that report were adopted by the Department of Education at a meeting on January 29–30, 2003, in Washington, DC.

One of the reforms mandates that schools conduct "interest surveys" to assess in advance girls' demands for sports. Another reform permits schools to weigh "ghost slots" on women's teams, that is, positions that are not filled by women on the teams. Simultaneously, schools can overlook male "walk-ons" (ones that have not been recruited). According to the National Organization for Women (NOW), such reforms would deter first-time girl participants from joining or creating a sports team at their schools and would lead to the misrepresentation of the quantities of boys and girls on sports teams, thereby affecting the amount of funds received by teams made up mostly of girls.

Several legislators responded to the attacks of the Bush Administration on Title IX. Sen. Joseph Biden (D-DE) introduced a resolution (S. Res. 40) that "reaffirms Congressional Commitment to Title IX . . . and its critical role in guaranteeing equal educational opportunities for women and girls, particularly with respect to school athletes" (Title IX of the Educational Amendments of 1972, 20 U.S.C. §§ 1681–88).

Simultaneously, Senators Ted Kennedy (D-MA) and Tom Daschle (D-SD) circulated a letter to senators for their signatures to be sent to Education Secretary Rod Paige criticizing the recommendations of Bush's Title IX Commission, also known as the Opportunity in Athletics Commission, and expressing support for Title IX.[48]

Pro-Bush women's advocacy groups such as the Independent Women's Forum have denied that Bush is antiwomen. Margaret Carroll, press coordinator for the Independent Women's Forum stated, "[Bush] acknowledges the successes of women in society, culturally and in the workforce." She added that Title IX in its current status harmed men by cutting some of their teams in the name of proportionality and women by creating sports teams they had no interest in. White House spokeswoman Claire Buchan pointed to Bush's proposal to relieve some of the taxes imposed on single mothers, and his plans to increase opportunities for small businesses, many of which are owned by women.[49]

On February 3, 2003, the US Department of Education issued the 2004 Education Budget. One of the programs slated for termination was the Women's Education Equity, which ensured that women and girls have opportunities in education. The Bush Administration reasoned that "activities promoting educational equity for girls and women may be supported through larger, more flexible programs like ESEA Title V-A State Grants for Innovative Programs."[50]

## 27. ENVIRONMENTAL PROTECTION

September 11, 2001, in one morning created an environmental disaster for many years to come and human disasters without end. That day changed many Government policies, but it did not change the policies of the Bush Administration concerning environmental protection. Before 9/11, President Bush had withdrawn the United States from the Kyoto Protocol on climate change (Report 27.4). After 9/11, the Bush Administration took many steps based on the assumption that climate change is not as serious a problem as scientists predict (Reports 27.1, 27.4, 27.5) and that there is less urgency about working for clean air (Report 27.3), saving wildlife habitat (Report 27.7), or enacting strict standards for nuclear waste management (Report 27.2).

At the same time, the US Military decided to ignore the outcry from the peoples of Hawaii not to build more military bases there (Report 27.6) as they sought to ignore testimony by the Inuits of Alaska that their whole culture will be destroyed if global warming is not stopped (Report 27.5).

The Administration moved forward to continue subsidies to large corporate farms and to continue collecting import duties on agricultural goods from underdeveloped countries, ignoring the cries of the international community that this dooms millions of people to poverty and early death (Report 28.8). At the same time, the Administration did nothing to stop factory farming that destroys the water supply and the concept that an animal to be slaughtered can be treated no different than an inanimate piece of machinery (Report 27.9).

In February 2004, twenty Nobel laureates, nineteen recipients of the National Medal of Science, and twenty other prominent scientists issued a statement accusing the Bush Administration of "deliberately and systematically" distorting scientific facts and misleading the public in order to further its own political objectives. The eminent scientists, including Republican Russell Train, who served as EPA Administrator under Presidents Nixon and Ford, detailed examples of the Administration's relentless abuse of science: censoring Government studies, gagging agency scientists, refusing to confer with or ignoring independent experts, misinterpreting information to fit its predetermined policy objectives, appointing unqualified and industry-connected individuals to federal advisory committees, and disbanding those government panels for offering unwanted information. According to these experts, the Administration's unprecedented tactics put at risk the US environment, health, security, and prosperity.[51]

Their statement describes years of frustration with actions, and inaction, of the Environmental Protection Agency, the Food and Drug Administration, the Departments of Health and Human Services, Agriculture, the Interior, and Defense since Congress and the Presidents began dealing with environmental issues.

In 1969, Congress passed the National Environmental Policy Act (42 U.S.C. §4321). In 1970, Congress passed the Clean Air Act which requires power plants and large factories to minimize their emissions of harmful pollutants. It also established national air-quality standards to be met by 1975 (42 U.S.C. §7401). Congress acknowledged that forcing polluters to retrofit every plant immediately would be prohibitively costly. In the face of strong industry opposition, Congress agreed to apply the tough standards only to newly built facilities. In response, many companies simply patched and upgraded their old, dirty plants. In 1977, Congress updated the Act and introduced New Source Review (NSR) requiring companies to install the best available pollution-control technology on all new plants.

In 1990, the EPA mounted a major investigation into the energy industry. It found that the biggest energy companies in the United States had updated their plants without installing any new pollution controls and were illegally releasing millions of tons of harmful pollutants. At the same time, a growing body of medical research indicated that industrial air pollution was making a lot of people sick. According to the EPA, long-term exposure to fine particulates (the tiny particles of air pollution spewed out of smokestacks that become lodged deeply in the lungs) caused asthma attacks, raised the risk of chronic bronchitis, and shortened the lives of more than thirty thousand US residents every year.

The EPA found that pollution-controlling technology cut emissions up to 95 percent. In 1997, the EPA started collecting data and threatened subpoenas if companies did not comply. By 1999, the EPA had collected overwhelming evidence of wrongdoing by the coal-burning power industry. The EPA filed complaints against the polluting corporations, sought compliance rather than fines, and won court verdicts against them. The industry refused to address EPA complaints. In November 1999, the EPA asked the Justice Department to file suits against seven electric utility companies, charging that their power plants had illegally released enormous amounts of pollutants: more than two million tons of sulfur dioxide every year and 660,000 tons of nitrogen oxides, in some cases for twenty years or more. Then attorney general Janet Reno announced the suits herself, saying, "When children can't breathe because of pollution from a utility plant hundreds of miles away, something must be done."

Potential penalties ran to $27,500 per plant for each day it had been in violation. Fines could reach tens of millions of dollars. The cost of fitting plants with new scrubbers and reconfiguring plants to run on cleaner-burning natural gas were estimated at hundreds of millions of dollars. At the same time, in 1999, the Southern Company reported profits of $1.3 billion. In early 2000, Tampa Electric agreed to spend more than $1 billion on new pollution controls and to pay a $3.5 million civil penalty. The agreement took 123,000 annual tons of pollution out of the sky, and the penalty amounted to less than 2 percent of the company's profits in 1999. Officials at some other companies followed a similar path.[52]

This was the situation in the EPA/power plant controversy when the Bush Administration took office in January 2001. Parallel histories of confrontation, regulations, lawsuits, settlements, and violations can be found for struggles for clean air (Report 27.3) and saving sequoia and redwood trees and other endangered species of plants and animals (Report 27.7).

In the face of all of these challenges, some people have taken to the trees. Julia Butterfly Hill helped save one redwood tree by living in it for years to prevent a lumber company from cutting it down. Other concerned environmentalists are increasingly joining forces with concerned immigrants' rights advocates to preserve natural resources, including human beings.

The paths for action are numerous. All require a little training in how to be an effective lobbyist for preservation of all natural resources and how to help the media give coverage of events as they are happening, so that catastrophes can be averted.

### Relevant Law:

U.S. Constitution: Preamble; Art. I, §8, Cl. 3, Cl. 10, Cl. 18; Art. II, §2, Cl. 2; Art. II, §3; Art. IV, §2, Cl. 1; Art. IV, §4; Art. VI, Cl. 2; Fifth, Ninth, Tenth Amendments
Treaty with the Western Shoshone, 1863 (18 Stats. At Large 689)
Endangered Species Act, 7 U.S.C. §136; 16 U.S.C. §460 et seq. (1973)
Clean Water Act, 33 U.S.C.A. §1251
Clean Air Act, 42 U.S.C.A. §7401

National Environmental Policy Act, 42 U.S.C.A. §4321-4347
Nuclear Waste Policy Act, 42 U.S.C.A. §10101
UN Charter: Preamble, Art. 1, 11.1, 11.3, 13.1, 23, 24.2, 55, 56, 57, 93, 103
ICCPR: Preamble, Art. 1, 2, 4, 5, 6.1, 7, 23.1, 24.1, 26, 40.1, 41.1, 44, 46, 47
UN Framework Convention on Climate Change of 1992 (UNFCCC)
Kyoto Protocol of 1997
ICESCR: Preamble, Art. 1, 2, 4-7b, 11, 12, 15.1-2, 16.1, 17, 25
CRC: Preamble, Art. 3.1, 6, 24.1, 24.2(a)-(c), 27.1, 30-31, 32.1, 44.1

## Report 27.1: Bush Charged with Replacing Government Science with Corporate Science

In October 2001, Secretary of the Interior Gale Norton responded to a Senate committee inquiry on the effects of oil drilling on caribou in the Arctic National Wildlife Refuge. She claimed that the caribou would not be affected because they calve outside the area targeted for drilling. Later Norton explained that she had somehow substituted "outside" for "inside." She also substituted findings from a study financed by the oil industry for one that the Fish and Wildlife Service had prepared for her.

In 2002, Environmental Protection Agency (EPA) scientists studying a process used in extracting oil and gas known as hydraulic fracturing found that it contaminated groundwater supplies in excess of federal drinking water standards. Halliburton, Vice President Cheney's former company, was the leading practitioner of this process. One week after reporting its findings to Congressional staff members, the EPA revised the data to indicate that contamination levels would not exceed Government standards. In a letter to Rep. Henry Waxman (D-CA), EPA officials said the change was made based on "industry feedback."

In June 2002, the EPA also held back a report exposing the impact of mercury on children's health, "as a favor to utility and coal industries, America's largest mercury dischargers." The report, released in February 2003 after being held up for nine months, found that the bloodstream of one in twelve women in the United States "is saturated with enough mercury to cause neurological damage, permanent IQ loss and a grim inventory of other diseases in their unborn children." In April 2003, the EPA disbanded an advisory panel that had spent almost two years developing stringent rules for reducing industrial emissions of mercury.

In July 2003, the EPA's Everglades regional office accepted a report which stated that wetlands discharge more pollutants than they absorb. The study was accepted without public comment or peer review and was used by the EPA to justify giving credit to developers for "improving water quality" by developing in wetland areas. The study contradicted a determination by more than twenty-five scientists at the Tampa Bay Estuary Program that wetlands do not generate nitrogen pollution.[53] Robert F. Kennedy Jr., attorney for Riverkeepers and the Natural Resources Defense Council, asserted that the primary force behind this study was Rick Barber, a consultant for a proposed golf course that had been denied a permit by the EPA. After the study was accepted, EPA water quality specialist Bruce Boler resigned in protest. "It was like the politics trumped the science," he said.

In November 2003, the Administration took the studies away from EPA scientists and made an agreement giving control over the federal research to Syngenta, the manufacturer of Atrazine, which is the most heavily utilized weedkiller in the United States. Scientists recently identified it as a potential carcinogen associated with a high incidence of prostate cancer among workers at manufacturing facilities. The European Union immediately banned this dangerous chemical. Sherry Ford, a spokesperson for Syngenta, praised the advantages of having the company monitor its own product. "This is one way we can ensure it's not presenting any risk to the environment."

Mr. Kennedy stated, "The Bush Administration has so violated and corrupted the institutional culture of government agencies charged with scientific research that it could take a generation for them to recover their integrity even if Bush is defeated." Michael Oppenheimer, a Princeton University scientist, stated, "If you believe in a rational universe, in enlightenment, in knowledge and in a search for the truth, this White House is an absolute disaster."[54]

### Report 27.2: US Department of Energy Weakens Standards for Nuclear Waste Storage

In December 2001, the General Accounting Office (now the Government Accountability Office [GAO]) reported that the Department of Energy's (DOE) 2000 assessment of the proposed permanent nuclear waste storage site at Yucca Mountain was "fatally flawed" in that the DOE environmental assessment did not meet DOE regulations. The GAO is the nonpartisan, independent investigative arm of Congress, which studies how the federal government spends taxpayer dollars and advises Congress and the heads of executive agencies about ways to make the government more effective and responsive. Its report urged the Bush Administration to postpone indefinitely a decision on whether to move forward with plans to license the Yucca Mountain site in the Nevada desert as the sole repository for a substantial part of the nation's high-level radioactive waste until other sites could be considered.

Energy Secretary Spencer Abraham then changed the regulations. The DOE decided that the Government no longer must prove that Yucca Mountain's underground rock formations would prevent radioactive contamination of the environment. Instead, the DOE plan would rely on "engineered waste packages" that it asserted would adequately contain the highly radioactive waste. The Natural Resources Defense Council (NRDC) asserted that the DOE is required by the Nuclear Waste Policy Act (42 U.S.C.A. §10101) to bury all of its high-level radioactive waste deep underground in a sound geologic repository. The NRDC maintained that leaving the waste in tanks and covering it in concrete would ensure it would eventually leach into groundwater and rivers.

On December 17, 2001, the State of Nevada filed suit against the DOE for its new "Yucca Mountain rule." Geoffrey H. Fettus, NRDC's nuclear program attorney, stated, "We share Nevada's and GAO's concerns about uncertainties over the planning, design, cost estimates and ultimate potential for success of the Yucca Mountain project. We think it unfortunate the Energy Department continues to plow forward without a solid foundation in science or law. . . . When our society considers dumping several thousand tons of dangerous waste that will be highly radioactive for literally thousands of years, the last thing the Bush administration should do is force the decision to meet artificial or political timelines."[55]

In the first quarter of 2002, another GAO report stated that the DOE considered relaxing requirements on transporting nuclear waste in order to speed cleanup at old nuclear weapons sites and to do so inexpensively. The GAO report also revealed that the DOE had given itself the authority to "illegally" reclassify one hundred million gallons of high-level nuclear waste as low-level or "incidental" waste. Much of the waste that was reclassified was in storage tanks that were damaged and leaking. By reclassifying the materials, the DOE asserted that it did not have to handle or store the material as carefully or with as much concern for human health.

Fettus stated, "It's stunning that the Energy Department is trying to cut corners when dealing with a substance as dangerous as high-level nuclear waste . . . by stashing thousands of tons of the nation's most radioactive waste under a concrete cap in leaky tanks and hoping no one notices."[56]

On July 9, 2004, the US District Court of Appeals for the District of Columbia decided the case of *Nuclear Energy Institute, Inc. v. Environmental Protection Agency* (373 F. 3d 1251[2004]), including the state of Nevada's challenge to the EPA's and the DOE's Yucca Mountain rule. The court issued a per curiam decision (with no judge listed as the author) holding that

- the EPA violated the Energy Policy Act (EnPA) by choosing a ten thousand-year compliance period for its radiation exposure standards because the compliance period is not "based upon and consistent with" the recommendations of the National Academy of Sciences;
- the Nuclear Regulatory Commission of the Department of Energy

(NRC) did not have to require that the repository rely primarily on its geologic setting to isolate waste from human environment;

- the NRC did not have to specify minimum performance standards for each of the "multiple barriers" required by the Nuclear Waste Policy Act (NWPA);
- the NRC acted reasonably by evaluating the proposed repository based on overall system performance, rather than barrier-by-barrier performance evaluation;
- the "Property" clause of the US Constitution gave Congress authority to designate a particular site as a repository; and
- designation of site was otherwise constitutional.

The court decided that the remaining challenges to the EPA rule are without merit and thus denied Nevada's petition for review challenging the NRC rule. The court also decided that the DOE's and the President's actions leading to passage of the Yucca Mountain rule are unreviewable (*Nuclear Energy Institute, Inc. v. Environmental Protection Agency*, 373 F. 3d 1251[2004]).

## Report 27.3: Bush Administration Cut Clean Air Act Protections; EPA Leader Resigned

In 2002 and 2003, the Bush Administration made a series of rule changes that effectively eliminated "new source review" regulations. In 1970, Congress passed the Clean Air Act. In 1977, Congress updated the Act and introduced the New Source Review (NSR) regulations that required companies to install the best available pollution control technology on all new plants. The changes to the NSR were portrayed by the President and his advisers as a compromise. "Now we've issued new rules that will allow utility companies . . . to make routine repairs and upgrades without enormous costs and endless disputes," the President said.

In the last months of the 1990s, many of the nation's biggest power companies were facing expensive court-imposed fines or expensive out-of-court settlements with the United States. The Environmental Protection Agency (EPA) investigators had caught them breaking the law. FirstEnergy's president, Reliant Resources's CEO, and Reliant's chairman raised at least $100,000 for the 2000 George W. Bush election campaign. Southern Company's executive vice president raised more than $200,000. Each of their companies was either in litigation or expected soon to be under investigation for NSR violations. Six other lawyers or lobbyists for companies charged with NSR violations raised at least $100,000 for Bush.

After Bush took office, the electric utilities sought relief from the EPA and its NSR program. Bush asked Congress to pass major environment-related legislation like the so-called Clear Skies Initiative and a sweeping energy bill, which he knew would face considerable opposition. The Bush political appointees at the Department of the Interior, the EPA, the Department of Agriculture, and the Office of Management and Budget began to carry out policies in closed-door legal settlements and obscure rule changes. These appointed officials came directly from industry into low-visibility positions within Bush's Administration. They knew exactly which rules and regulations to change because they had been trying to change them in their previous positions.

On March 18, 2001, Joseph Kelliher, a top assistant to Energy Secretary Spencer Abraham, e-mailed the American Petroleum Institute, an energy-industry lobbyist: "If you were King, or Il Duce, what would you include in a national energy policy?" In May 2001, President Bush issued Executive Order 13211, which is nearly identical in structure and impact to the document that the American Petroleum Institute had suggested.

On May 16, 2001, President Bush's final National Energy Policy (NEP) was published. The policy's defining notion: environmental regulations have constrained US domestic energy supply. The Administration directed the Justice Department to review its cases against the Southern Company, American Electric, and others to see if any of the suits might be dropped outright.

Also in 2001, the US General Accounting Office (GAO) called on the EPA to improve its oversight of emissions reporting. The GAO study found that only 4 percent of all emissions determinations were made using direct monitoring or testing and 96 percent were made based on estimates using "emissions factors." The EPA acknowledged that emission factors were not accurate.[57]

Bush appointees at the EPA and the Energy Department continued to undo the long-standing NSR rules even though the EPA's own documents showed that from 1997 to 1999, the NSR program reduced emissions nationwide by a total of more than four million tons. In January 2002, the Justice Department (DOJ) delivered its report on the legality of the EPA's lawsuit against the large power companies for NSR violations. The Department found all of the lawsuits were legal and warranted. In fact, DOJ lawyers said they intended to prosecute the cases "vigorously."

On February 14, 2002, Bush unveiled his "Clear Skies Initiative." He declared that his proposed legislation "sets tough new standards to dramatically reduce the three most significant forms of pollution from power plants—sulfur dioxide, nitrogen oxides and mercury." Clear Skies allowed 50 percent more sulfur dioxide, nearly 40 percent more nitrogen oxides, and three times as much mercury as the Clean Air Act.

On November 22, 2002, the EPA revealed its overhaul of the NSR. The new rules gave utility companies much more maneuverability under the NSR. The American Lung Association, in a report issued with a coalition of environmental groups, called the rule changes "the most harmful and unlawful air-pollution initiative ever undertaken by the federal government." The report estimated that, compared with enforcement of the old NSR rules, the new rules would result in emissions increases of 7 million tons of sulfur dioxide and 2.4 million tons of nitrogen oxides per year by 2020. Investigations into seventy companies suspected of violations of the Clean Air Act were abandoned.[58]

Eric Schaeffer, who had directed the EPA's Office of Regulatory Enforcement from 1997 to 2002 and had worked on the NSR lawsuits since their inception, denounced the proposal two weeks after it was introduced. In 2002, Schaeffer resigned because he was tired of "fighting a White House that seems determined to weaken the rules we are trying to enforce" and founded the Environmental Integrity Project (EIP).[59]

On December 24, 2003, the US Court of Appeals for the District of Columbia Circuit granted a motion to stay implementation of Bush's proposed changes to the NSR program (*State of New York, et al., v. United States Environmental Protection Agency* [No. 02–1387 and consolidated cases]). New York Attorney General Eliot Spitzer initiated the lawsuit against the EPA. Other plaintiffs in the case included fourteen states, several environmental groups and a number of cities including New York, San Francisco, Washington, DC, and several municipalities in Connecticut. The court declared that the plaintiffs "demonstrated the irreparable harm and likelihood of success," therefore meeting the legal threshold required to prevent a regulation from taking effect. The court will not lift the stay unless it ultimately decides the Administration's rule change is legal.

On August 9, 2004, the EPA and the DOJ filed the Government's brief in the lawsuits. On its Web site, the EPA stated that the 2002 rule "which grew out of more than 20 years of experience with the NSR program and over a decade of working with states, industry, and environmental groups on NSR reforms—provides greater regulatory certainty, increases flexibility and promotes administrative efficiency, while ensuring the current (or a greater) level of environmental protection."[60]

On June 22, 2004, Schaeffer's EIP and the Galveston-Houston Association for Smog Prevention (GHASP) released a new study concluding that the EPA and state governments were still underreporting refinery and chemical plant toxic air emissions, including the known carcinogens benzene and butadiene, on the magnitude of at least 330 million pounds per year. The EIP-GHASP analysis found that the presence of the carcinogens in the air in the United States may be four to five times higher than the level the EPA reports to the public, based on findings by the Texas Commission on Environmental Quality (TCEQ). A copy of the full report is available at http://www.environmentalintegrity.org.[61]

## Report 27.4: Bush Administration Ignored Global Warming and the Kyoto Protocol

In May 2002, the Environmental Protection Agency (EPA) released the Climate Action Report 2002. The Bush Administration report admitted that global warming is a real problem that could have drastic and costly effects on the environment, the economy, and the health of the America. The report also acknowledged that emissions from human activities are to blame for climate changes. The Administration's solution to reducing greenhouse gas emissions was to replace legally binding pollution cuts with a voluntary plan. Under the plan, corporations are encouraged, but not obligated, to voluntarily reduce their emissions. Under this plan, emissions levels are permitted to rise at exactly the same rate as they have been.

This was the first act of the Bush Administration on climate change after March 2001, when Bush announced that he was informally withdrawing from the Kyoto Protocol.[62] The United States signed the Kyoto Protocol on November 12, 1998. The Protocol of 1997 is the document conceived and adopted in 1992 at the third session of the Conference of the Parties to the United Nations Framework Convention on Climate Change (UNFCCC). The United States ratified the UNFCCC on October 15, 1992, and the UNFCCC subsequently entered into force on March 21, 1994, when the required number of nations ratified it. Under the UNFCCC, the United States as a signatory had the obligation to reduce emissions of certain greenhouse gases, to negotiate further reductions of other greenhouse gases in the future, and to act in accordance with the spirit and letter of the treaty.[63]

In 2002, Bush also opposed various plans to reduce carbon dioxide emissions from power plants and vehicles. His Administration drafted an energy plan that the Natural Resources Defense Council (NRDC) said was guided by fossil fuel lobbyists. It will inevitably lead to increased emissions and provide minimal support for cleaner energy alternatives, according to Dan Lashof, science director of the NRDC Climate Center. "[R]ather than recommending reductions in greenhouse gases to control global warming, the EPA report suggests adapting to the inevitable, including heat waves, the disruption of snow-fed water supplies, and the permanent loss of Rocky Mountain meadows and some coastal marshes."[64] In September 2002, the EPA, with White House approval, deleted the chapter on global warming from its annual report on air pollution: "Latest Findings on National Air Quality: 2001 Status and Trends." The report noted significant reductions in most emissions.[65] In December 2002, the Bush Administration called for at least five more years of study before taking any substantial action to stem the problem of global warming.

Investors around the world continue to invest in and build expensive new energy plants that use highly polluting, outdated technologies, even though cleaner technologies exist. The International Energy Agency forecast that $4.2 trillion will be spent on electricity-generating plants by 2030, at an average investment of $140 billion a year.[66]

In June 2003, the EPA deleted a sentence from its Report on the Environment that read, "Climate change has global consequences for human health and the environment," along with other information on the potential harm to humans and wildlife from pesticides and industrial chemicals. The final report included only a few inconclusive paragraphs on global warming, leading to controversy over the findings in the report that the nation's air is cleaner and better protected than it was thirty years ago, according to environmentalists. They said that even if the findings were accurate, none of the improvements cited in the EPA's report reflect actions taken by the Bush Administration. In response to this report, David Hawkins, director of the NRDC Climate Center, said, "The Bush administration is hiding the facts on the most serious environmental challenge that we face."[67]

In September 2003, the *Observer* released the results of an independent investigation of internal documents and e-mails of the Bush Administration. One e-mail dated June 3, 2002, to a top official at the White House Council on Environmental Quality, came from the head of the Competitive Enterprise Institute (CEI), the think tank that filed the lawsuit against the Administration for access to documents on climate change. The e-mail reveals that Bush officials wanted the CEI to publicly discredit the EPA's Climate Action Report 2002 containing evidence of global warming, and it admits that industrial activities contribute to the problem.

Other documents, such as a confidential memo from the EPA, detail the Bush Administration's efforts to suppress research to the point that EPA staff warned that the Section "no longer accurately represents scientific consensus on climate change." White House and industry officials denied any collusion.[68]

After the 2004 report of sixty scientists,energy supplies that could cause riots around the globe and culminate in nuclear warfare.[69]

## Report 27.5:  US Inaction on Global Warming Threatens Inuit Cultural Extinction

In 2003, the Inuit people of Canada and Alaska accused the Bush Administration of pushing their culture closer to extinction through policies and actions on global warming. Inuit means "the people" and is the name that the indigenous people of the Arctic gave to themselves. Inuit populations include Canadian Inuit, Alaska's Inupiat and Yupik people, and the Russian Yupik. The Inuit are descendants of the Thule people who arrived in Alaska about 500 CE and reached Canada in 1000 CE. Alaskan Inuit now live mainly in the North Slope boroughs and the Bering Strait region and rely heavily on subsistence fishing and hunting whales, walruses, and seals for their survival.

The Inuit claim that the US Government is violating their human rights by repudiating the Kyoto Protocol and refusing to cut US carbon dioxide emissions, which make up 25 percent of the world's total. Sheila Watt-Cloutier, chairwoman of the Inuit Circumpolar Conference, represented all 155,000 of her people inside the Arctic Circle in international relations concerning global warming. Watt-Cloutier said, "We are already bearing the brunt of climate change—without our snow and ice our way of life goes. We have lived in harmony with our surroundings for millennia, but that is being taken away from us." At the end of 2003, the Inuit announced their human rights abuse claim against the Bush Administration at the talks concerning the UN Framework Convention on Climate Change in Milan, Italy (UNFCCC COP 9).[70]

When governments adopted the Framework Convention on Climate Change of 1992 (UNFCCC), they knew that its textual commitments would not be sufficient to achieve its ultimate objective. The governments therefore included a series of review mechanisms in the Convention to ensure that its commitments could be tightened in the future. The first review mechanism kicked in at the first session of the Conference of the Parties (COP 1), held in Berlin in March/April 1995, where, in a decision known as the Berlin Mandate, Parties agreed that the specific commitments in the Convention for Annex I Parties were not adequate. The governments therefore launched a new round of talks to decide on stronger and more detailed commitments for these countries.

After two and a half years of intense negotiations, the Kyoto Protocol was adopted at COP 3 in Kyoto on December 11, 1997, that actually provided concrete commitments to reduce greenhouse gases. The countries that ratified the Kyoto Protocol continue to negotiate further formal and informal amendments to the Kyoto Protocol, which in turn are amendments to the UNFCCC.[71] Under the terms of the Protocol, it will not go into effect unless either the United States or Russia ratifies it. The Bush Administration withdrew from it. The Inuit stated their claim in reaction to the US attempt to persuade Russia not to ratify it either so that it would not enter into force.

Watt-Cloutier comes from Pangirtung, north of Iqaluit, in Canada. In December 2003, she stated, "We now have weeks of uncertainty about when the ice will come. In the spring the ice melts not at the end of June but weeks earlier. Sometimes the ice is so thin hunters fall through. The ocean is too warm. Our elders, who instruct the young on the ways of the winter and what to expect, are at a loss. Last Christmas after the ice had formed the temperature rose to 4C [39F] and it rained. We'd never known it before."

Among the problems the Inuit face is permafrost melting, which has destroyed the foundations of houses, eroded the seashore, and forced people to move inland. The infrastructure of the area, including airport runways, roads, and harbors, is also collapsing.[72]

### Report 27.6: US Military Ignores Environmental/Cultural Standards in Hawaii

On July 7, 2004, the US Army announced the approval of a $1.5 billion brigade of 291 eight-wheeled armored Stryker vehicles to be built, tested, and used in various training exercises in Hawaii. The armored vehicles are to be brought to Hawaii as part of a new "fast-strike" operation. In order to provide infrastructure for the activities of the vehicles, the Army had to acquire 1,400 acres of the island of Oahu, and an additional 23,000 acres to expand the 109,000-acre Pohakuloa Training Area on Hawaii proper. In addition, hundreds of millions of dollars of construction projects and networks of private trails for the twenty-ton vehicles are planned.

The National Environmental Policy Act (42 U.S.C.A. §4321 et seq.) (NEPA) requires all federal agencies to examine the environmental consequences of federal projects like the Stryker plan that are likely to have significant environmental impacts and to prepare environmental impact statements (EISs) on each project. The three thousand-page EIS for the Stryker plan stated that 1,736 tons of dust would be generated annually from increased vehicle traffic because of the nearly five hundred soldiers and four hundred vehicles that would be added to the islands' environments.[73]

According to the Malu 'Aina Center for Non-Violent Education and Action, the Pohakuloa Training Area has more endangered species than any US Army installation in the world. The Army admitted that many "significant unavoidable adverse impacts" will occur in the area where these species are located. These significant impacts include:

- soil loss from training activities;
- biological impacts from fire on sensitive species and habitats;
- biological impacts from off-road training on sensitive species and habitats;
- cultural resource impacts to historic buildings in the Ke'amuku Village;
- cultural resource impacts to archaeological resources from range and facility construction and from training activities;
- cumulative impacts to biological and cultural resources;
- cumulative impacts to human health and safety hazards; and
- environmental justice impacts to areas of traditional importance.[74]

The DMZ Hawaii Aloha Aina organization issued an Impact Statement that precious water will be contaminated in the demilitarized zone unexploded ordnance will be left on the ground, toxic/mutagenic chemicals and other health hazards will threaten the health of native Hawaiian people, and almost nothing will be done by the Department of Defense to mitigate these harms.

The DMZ stated, "In assembling this Community Impact Statement, we are building on the testimony of the people, who called for a broader and more profound analysis and response on how the Stryker Brigade will affect us and our families, both alone and also in conjunction with the century-long amassing of American military forces in Hawaii, with the cumulative impact of all of the toxins, carcinogens, and mutagens we have been exposed to; the social and economic effects of so much of our land being consumed by militarism, as well as the increase in violence that occurs when families are saturated in the carnal violence of war making."[75]

Jim Albertini, of the Malu 'Aina Center for Non-Violent Education and Action, stated, "The EIS was a legal requirement but the process was a complete fraud. Hawaii's senior senator, Daniel Inouye, said on June 18, 2003, months before the EIS public hearings and comment period even began, that he was assured 'Hawaii will get its Stryker Brigade.'" In addition, the Army made its announcement about commencement of the project the day after the community comment required by NEPA ended, thus appearing not to have even considered the community's concerns.[76]

### Report 27.7: US Further Endangers Endangered Species

On August 18, 2003, the US Fish and Wildlife Service (FWS) published a draft policy on enhancement-of-survival permits. On September 10, 2003, the FWS proposed a rule revising the permit regulations under the Endangered Species Act (ESA). On March 4, 2004, 359 professional scientists wrote to the FWS to express their concern over the proposals by the FWS that would allow the importation into the United States of endangered and threatened species killed or collected in the wild for conservation purposes. The scientists urged the FWS to withdraw these proposals and to reiterate its commitment to strictly control international trade in globally endangered species.

As set forth in the draft policy and the proposed rule, the FWS proposed to alter its long-standing interpretation of the ESA to expand the circumstances under which the importation of endangered species might be allowed. Specifically, the FWS proposed to authorize imports of foreign endangered species for virtually any purpose including sport-hunted trophies, skins and hides for commercial sale, and live specimens for the pet and entertainment industries if the Secretary of the Interior decides the import is "reasonably likely" to have a net conservation benefit for the species. This rule would apply, without limitation, to any of the more than 550 foreign species currently protected by the ESA.

The 359 scientists were concerned that neither the draft policy nor the proposed rule reflected a critical inquiry. The scientists asserted that the FWS proposed to allow imports of endangered species killed or collected from the wild in the name of conservation without defining any standards by which proposed conservation programs will be evaluated. The FWS did not identify the mechanisms through which it would monitor the implementation or outcomes of the conservation programs. Jane Goodall et al. stated: "It is our shared view that opening the door to commercial imports of endangered species without fully defining these parameters will put the hundreds of species potentially affected by this rule at serious risk. We do not believe such risks are acceptable for species already on the brink of extinction."

The scientists went on: "As currently crafted, the proposal poses a significant threat to the very species it is designed to benefit. For too many of these species, this new threat could mean the difference between survival and extinction. Accordingly, we respectfully urge the FWS to immediately withdraw its draft policy on enhancement-of-survival permits and remove any reference to 'in-situ conservation' of foreign listed species from the proposed rule of September 10th."[77]

*Bush Green Watch* reported that FWS biologists estimated that about two hundred species currently listed as endangered are on the verge of extinction primarily because of a lack of funding. President Bush's FY 2005 budget cut ESA recovery by $9.8 million, or 14.4 percent below FY 2004 levels. The 2005 budget for ESA implementation was cut by $7.5 million, or 5.5 percent below 2004 levels. Instead of reductions, experts cited by *Bush Green Watch* said an increase of at least $50 million for recovery programs is needed.

The Bush budget did include a $5 million increase for programs that list new species as endangered, but it was offset by the cuts to the other endangered species accounts. The current listing backlog is $153 million, which includes more than 250 candidate species in need of protection that have been awaiting listing for years.

Mary Beth Beetham, director of legislative affairs at Defenders of Wildlife, said, "The Bush Administration cries poverty when it comes to implementation of the Endangered Species Act, claiming the 'ESA is broken.' . . . Yet it is trying to transform this statement into a self-fulfilling prophecy by refusing to request the funds needed to carry out its responsibilities under the law to protect imperiled wildlife."[78]

## Report 27.8: US Farm Subsidies Are Starving the World

The events of 9/11 did not change the trends in US agriculture. Statistics indicate that it is increasingly an industry run by large corporations. Any tourist crossing the farm belt in the United States sees the death of family farming with diverse crops and natural irrigation. Agriculture is a very big business run by big corporations that have lobbied Congress to continue the subsidies to "farmers" started in hard times to help small farmers keep their farms. These subsidies are now an issue around the globe.

Agriculture is the driving force in almost all economies of developing countries. World Trade Organization (WTO) statistics show that agriculture accounts for over one-half of export earnings for almost forty developing countries. About a dozen more developing countries depend on the agricultural sector for over one-third of export earnings.[79] Nations in Africa depend on agriculture for about one-quarter of their total economic output. A healthy agricultural sector is essential to achieving the 3.5 percent annual growth needed for African nations to meet developmental needs: eliminating poverty, expanding education, combating HIV/AIDS, and increasing potable water supplies.[80]

In September 2003, talks by the 146 members of the WTO collapsed over trade-liberalization disputes between "developed" and "developing" countries. The most contentious issue was the extent to which the governments of the United States, Europe, and Japan were willing to slash their huge subsidies to their farmers. More than twenty developing countries banded together to fight these nations' agricultural subsidies. The Bush Administration provided US exporters guarantees against default on loans used to purchase US agricultural commodities, reimbursed trade groups and private companies for promotional activities overseas, and subsidized exports of dairy products and other farm commodities.[81]

The UN Food and Agriculture Organization (FAO) Web site states, "Subsidies to farmers in the developed world have negative ramifications for agriculture in the developing world in a number of ways. By enabling farmers and agro-companies to sell on the international market at prices far below production value, they leave growers in the developing world unable to compete. They also encourage excess supply, which further lowers world agricultural prices—reducing the money that poor farmers make, or pushing them out of the business entirely."

Alexander Sarris, Director of FAO's Commodities and Trade Division, added that the increased profile of cheap food imports can also be a disincentive to investment in domestic agriculture in importing countries, leading governments to neglect the sector. "High import growth can undermine otherwise viable domestic production with few opportunities for alternative uses of productive resources," Sarris said.[82]

The director of the FAO, Jacques Diouf, traveled to Washington after the WTO meeting in Cancún to voice the concerns of thousands of farmers in dozens of developing countries. Diouf estimated that the billions of dollars that the United States spent yearly on subsidies is destroying the livelihood of millions of farmers in developing countries. A World Bank study estimated that reducing agricultural subsidies in the developed countries and ending tariffs on imports from developing countries could pull 144 million people out of poverty.[83]

World Bank President James Wolfensohn warned that efforts by institutions such as the World Bank to tackle poverty are irrelevant unless wealthy countries cut farm subsidies. Wolfensohn pointed out that the $50 billion spent by developed countries like the United States in development assistance annually worldwide is dwarfed by the $350 billion ploughed into agricultural subsidies to farm owners in the United States and other developed countries every year.[84] On July 16, 2004, the WTO proposed that its 147 member countries eliminate agricultural subsidies in a new attempt to broker a compromise in deadlocked global trade talks.[85]

### Report 27.9: Bush Administration Allows Concentrated Animal-Feeding Operations Unabated

On December 15, 2002, the Environmental Protection Agency (EPA) announced a new rule on controlling concentrated animal feeding operations (CAFO) as required by a 1992 judicial consent decree between the Natural Resources Defense Council (NRDC) and the EPA.

In 1972, Congress identified agricultural feedlot operations (CAFOs) as point sources of water pollution to be regulated under the Clean Water Act (CWA) and created regulations to control the discharge. Since then the amount and size of CAFOs has changed drastically. The EPA found that the earlier regulations had become inadequate.[86]

The NRDC reported that thousands of domesticated animals "produced" for human consumption are crowded into small areas on CAFOs. The animals' physical and mental health conditions are poor; their manure and urine are funneled into massive waste lagoons. These lagoons often leak, overflow, or break, sending dangerous microbes, bacteria, and heavy metals into water supplies. CAFO lagoons also emit toxic gases such as ammonia, hydrogen sulfide, and methane. When CAFOs sell manure from these lagoons to neighboring farmers as fertilizer, these harmful substances are emitted into the air and water.[87]

The EPA proposed initiatives that would have protected the environment. Agribusinesses complained about the economic costs. The Bush Administration removed them. The new rule allows agribusinesses to continue to apply liquid waste on land and foul the nation's waterways to such an extent that the NRDC says it is killing fish, spreading disease, and contaminating drinking water supplies. The new rule also legalized the discharge of contaminated runoff into rivers and streams, failed to update technology standards to tighten controls on water pollution, allowed factory farms to write their own permit conditions, shielded factory farms from liability for animal wastes running off the land into waterways, and shielded corporations that own the livestock from liability for the environmental damage they cause.[88]

In May 2003, the NRDC announced that behind closed doors the EPA discussed giving CAFOs amnesty from federal air quality and toxic waste cleanup laws. The EPA and industry representatives confirmed the private negotiations. Allegedly under the tentative plan, the EPA monitors pollution levels at thirty or more CAFOs through a planned $11 million research program. The negotiations were unnecessary because the EPA already had the authority to order the CAFOs to adhere to the Clean Air Act and Superfund laws regardless of the industries' input or approval. Environmental groups said this unprecedented scheme would let polluters off the hook by offering factory farms safe harbor from environmental law and give amnesty for any past violations. John Walke, director of the NRDC's Clean Air Program, said that these negotiations are "yet another example of the Bush administration trying to dismantle our bedrock environmental laws at the expense of public health."[89]

## 28. THE US JUDICIAL SYSTEM

The Government of the United States consists of three branches: legislative, executive, and judicial. The legislative branch writes the laws, the executive administers them, and the judiciary decides whether the laws are constitutional and whether they are being properly enforced at both the federal and the state levels.

Because of the struggles of poor and working people since the 1930s, Presidents and members of Congress have had to grant some services to people in trouble with the law. During the war on poverty under Pres. Lyndon Johnson, the third branch was granted funding to establish a national system of lawyers to provide legal services to people without money to pay fees in suits against landlords and other civil suits against corporations, government agencies, and other groups. These legal-service lawyers joined the public defenders who provide counsel to defendants in federal criminal cases who cannot pay for their own lawyers. Today the judicial branch also provides drug testing of criminal defendants and rehabilitation services by probation officers.

All of these services cost money. But, several also save money, as when a person who has served time in prison (paid for by taxpayers) is released and rehabilitated, which means he has become a law-abiding person who pays taxes. It strengthens the democratic spirit when innocent people without funds can prove that they are innocent. It also saves money when innocent defendants are not sent to prison for long, expensive terms.

And the federal legal service program to provide lawyers to poor people in civil cases also helps ensure justice by funding some attorneys in suits against gouging landlords and unscrupulous employers and merchants. Many of these facts about the judicial branch are seldom mentioned in the media. Few actions by judges in civil suits by poor people receive the coverage that is typically given to actions of the President or Congress.

Yet actions by each branch affect the operation of the other two. And the personnel selected for each branch affect the selections for the other two. While the people vote for the President and Vice President in the executive branch, the President selects the people to act as judges in the judicial branch, with the advice and consent of the legislative branch (Congress). The legislative and executive branches decide on the budget for all three branches; the judicial branch has no representative in the decision making on the budget for courts.

The judicial branch has the power to order members of the executive branch to stop taking certain actions that it rules are unconstitutional or violate statutes. And judges at various levels try cases involving alleged violations of the criminal law by members of Congress when they are not engaged in Congressional activities. Judges also try some civil cases brought by or against members of Congress.

As a result of these relationships, when the federal budget must be cut, it is much easier to convince Congress members to cut the budget for the judicial branch than to cut the budget for the executive branch. Members of the President's cabinet and staff can attend all of the meetings to discuss the budget. And they can subtly, or openly, remind Congress that no budget they pass will go into effect unless the President signs it, or they pass it over his veto by a two-thirds vote.

After 9/11, all of these relationships began to be challenged. As cases were filed challenging sections of the USA PATRIOT Act and the deportations and detentions of "enemy combatants," the money being spent by the Department of Defense (DOD) on the invasions of Afghanistan and Iraq cut an enormous hole in the federal budget.

In drafting the budget for all federal Government spending in 2005, the President told Congress that the budget for the DOD must go up to meet the costs of the invasion and continued occupation of Afghanistan and Iraq and for the production and construction of new types of weapons (see Section 17). After submitting the budget, President Bush asked for "emergency" funds to deal with the situation in Iraq. The President also made clear that he opposed any increase in income taxes to meet the additional costs.

One problem with seeking a budget for the judiciary is that the judges are not in charge of how many cases are filed in the federal courts. That is determined by how many federal crimes are committed and how many defendants federal attorneys decide to try criminally. It is also determined by how many lawsuits corporations and human beings decide to file civilly. Budgets for the judiciary also depend on how many criminal defendants and civil parties decide they want trials by jury because each juror is paid out of the federal judicial budget. In 2004, Congress addressed the needs it knew about from each department, with particular concern paid to the DOD. Congress agreed with the President to cut all nondefense discretionary-budgetary spending by 1 percent. This created a crisis in the court system.

**Relevant Law:**

U.S. Constitution: Preamble, General Welfare Clause; Art. I, §8, Cl. 1; Art. III; First, Fourth, Fifth, Sixth, Eighth, Fourteenth, Nineteenth Amendments
UN Charter: Art. 55, 56
ICCPR: Art. 2, 14, 40

**Report 28.1: Federal Budget Creates Crisis in the Judiciary**

For Fiscal Year 2005, Congress and the Bush Administration agreed to cut all nondefense spending. In the federal courts, the 1 percent cut in discretionary-budgetary spending translated into a cut of 32 percent. The reason for this is that only 60 percent of the federal judiciary's budget is fixed, while the remaining 40 percent is discretionary, that is, in a sense, up to the agency.

In addition to the cuts in discretionary spending of the courts, in 2004, Congress and the Bush Administration considered keeping the 2005 budgetary allowances for fixed costs of the federal judiciary at the same rate as in 2004. Since the "fixed" costs such as rent and security go up each year, not increasing "fixed cost" budgetary needs means that the federal judiciary will not be able to cover all of its costs and thus not be able to properly function. Just to stay even, Chief Judge Carol King of the Fifth Circuit Court of Appeals says, the federal judiciary needs a 6 percent increase in funding each year. Since 2002, the federal judiciary's budget has been cut despite ever-increasing caseloads. The judiciary's portion of the national budget is just two-tenths of one percent (0.2%). The judiciary has enormous responsibility as one of the three branches of the US government, established to ensure that the other two branches obey the law. The judiciary depends on the legislative process since it is the legislature that controls the budget and the judiciary has no lobbyist working in Congress.

If the federal judiciary does not get the funding that it needs in 2005, the result will be "draconian."

- The money to pay attorneys representing indigent defendants will run out by summer 2005;
- there will be no trials of indigent defendants, since a trial cannot take place without attorneys;
- many criminals will be freed since federal statutes require defendants to be released if they are not tried within seventy days of their arrest, and the courts will be so backed up that they will not be able to process defendants quickly enough;
- in many jurisdictions the systems will run out of money to pay jurors in civil cases;
- up to five thousand of the federal judiciary system's twenty-one thousand employees could be laid off;
- the technological systems that courts rely on in order to operate efficiently will fall into disrepair;
- probation and parole officers will not be able to process parolees as quickly, which will mean that more money will have to be spent to keep these people in jail or prison until they are processed;
- probation officers as well as essential programs—drug testing and rehabilitation services—which probation officers oversee, may have to be cut; and
- personnel cuts mean that investigations and various other services will not be done as well.

In summer 2004, the federal judiciary asked Congress to exempt it from any across-the-board budgetary freezes or cuts.[90]

## F. THE GOVERNMENT'S DUTY TO REPORT VIOLATIONS TO CONGRESS AND THE UN

The duty of the Government to file reports did not begin with 9/11. It certainly did not end with 9/11, as new and old issues required actions by the Government. Three types of actions by the Bush Administration in its war on terrorism led to reports by the Office of Inspector General (OIG) which discovered the mistreatment of many detainees by Immigration authorities (Report 29.1), the suppression of an EPA report on the dangers of working at Ground Zero (Report 29.2), and the failure to conduct an investigation of those responsible for suspending the report. These reports led concerned people to file additional complaints with the OIG on many issues (see the text of an NGO's complaint to the OIG in Chapter 5.D-2).

The US Government continued a policy after 9/11 of not filing the reports that are required under treaties ratified by the United States even as the Government was demanding that other governments file the required reports under the Free Trade Area of the Americas (FTAA) Agreement. The reports that are not prepared and filed by the State Department are required by the three human rights treaties ratified by the United States: the International Covenant on Civil and Political Rights, the Convention Against Torture, and the Convention on Elimination of Racial Discrimination (Report 30.1). This failure meant that the Second Report due under each treaty was not filed, and city, county, and state reports required under those treaties were never sought by the US Government. This continued the situation in which most government officials at all levels remain ignorant of the content of these human rights treaties and the procedures used in UN committees for enforcing the treaties (Report 30.2). One city, Berkeley, California, did make reports under the first UN ratified treaty, with affirmative results (Report 30.3).

## 29. TO REPORT THROUGH THE OFFICE OF INSPECTOR GENERAL

In 1978, Congress passed the Office of Inspector General Act, which requires the Office of the Inspector General (OIG) in each agency of the US Government to investigate every complaint received at that agency and to submit a report describing each complaint and the results of the investigation to the chairs and vice chairs of the House and Senate Judiciary Committees every six months (PL 95–452).

The OIG procedure was little known to the US public and media from 1978 until after 9/11, when two reports by OIGs hit front pages across the country. One was the report of the OIG finding physical assaults and other violations of the rights of people detained by the FBI and the Immigration officials (Report 29.1).

A few months later, almost two years after 9/11, the OIG issued a report on the Government's suppression of a study on the dangers of working at Ground Zero prepared by the EPA (Report 29.2). This study documented Administration officials making changes in the scientific findings of a federal agency in order to calm the public, which led to massive medical problems for workers and residents of the area (Report 12.8).

These two seminal reports led many people throughout the United States to decide to use the procedure of filing complaints with the OIG in working in their communities on their major complaints against Govern-

Downtown Miami, November 20, 2003: With an estimated budget of $16.5 million, more than forty US police agencies elaborately weaponized their troops with armor and guns to disperse and crush the surge of protesters expected at the Free Trade Area of the Americas conference. (AP Photo/J. Pat Carter)

ment action or inaction. While there can be no guarantee that this action will be successful whenever the complaints are valid, it certainly opened up a new path that concerned residents can follow whenever they find a link to a federal agency or to federal funding of a program of a city, county, state, NGO, or contractor.

## Relevant Law:

U.S. Constitution: Art. I, §9, Cl. 2; Art. II, §1, Cl. 8; Art. VI, Cl. 2; Fourth, Fifth, Sixth, Eighth, Fourteenth Amendments

Office of the Inspector General Act of 1978, 5 U.S.C.A. Appx §1 (2001)

UN Charter: Art. 55, 56

ICCPR: Preamble, Art. 1, 2, 4, 5, 6.1, 9.2, 9.3, 9.4, 10.1, 14.1, 14.3(a), 14.3(b), 40, 47

CERD: Art. 1, 2.1(a), 9

CAT: Preamble, Art. 1, 2, 4-7, 13, 14, 16, 19

## Report 29.1: Inspector General Finds that Detained Aliens Were Physically Assaulted

After the attacks on September 11, 2001, the FBI frequently used alleged violations of immigration laws as the basis for detaining suspects. Its use of these laws led to the filing of numerous complaints with the Office of Inspector General (OIG), alleging misconduct and discrimination based on national origin, religion, or race.

On June 4, 2003, Department of Justice Inspector General Glenn A. Fine released a report titled "A Review of the Treatment of Aliens Held on Immigration Charges in Connection with the Investigation of the September 11 Terrorist Attacks." In the report, Fine presented the results of his investigation into the detention and legal processing of alleged illegal immigrants connected in any way to 9/11. He encountered systemic problems during his investigation.

- Before 9/11, the Immigration and Naturalization Service (INS) had a policy of serving immigrants with notice of charges within forty-eight hours of detention. After 9/11, the INS extended this to seventy-two hours. The OIG report found that 60.7 percent of the time detainees did not receive the charging documents within the seventy-two hours and, in some cases, did not receive the documents until up to a month after being initially detained.
- In order for the FBI to check whether the person detained was involved in September 11 or was a known terrorist, it used immigration laws to detain people until they were investigated. This process took an average of eighty days. As a result of not knowing whether the detainee was a terrorist or part of a terrorist group, the detainees were not released on bond and were confined under highly restrictive conditions. Guards forced handcuffs and leg irons onto detainees and moved them with heavy chains until they were cleared by the FBI.
- The Government had a restrictive policy on phone use, which limited detainees' conversations with their lawyers to one call per week. If a message machine answered the detainee's call, this often counted as their weekly call. One guard asked the detainees if they wanted legal counsel in a confusing way: "Is everything all right?" If the detainee answered yes, the guard decided that he did not need to make a call to his lawyer. Some detainees alleged that Government employees limited the amount of time they could talk to their lawyer to only three minutes. There were also examples of detainees not getting lists of lawyers who would provide free counsel, or getting lists that included bad phone numbers and lawyers who did not take their type of case.

- Prison guards engaged in bending the fingers of detainees, hitting their heads against the wall, and putting them naked in a cell without a blanket. The allegations of verbal abuse included calling people "Bin Laden Junior," or guards telling detainees, "You are going to die here," or, "You will never leave here."
- In one detention center, guards left the lights on twenty-four hours a day for several months. As a result, some detainees complained of lack of sleep, exhaustion, depression, stress, acute weight loss, fevers, panic attacks, rapid heart beat, and reduced eyesight.[91]

After media coverage of this report, the Government announced it was investigating further the complaints of verbal and physical abuse.

### Report 29.2: Administration Suppresses EPA Reports on Ground Zero Dangers

On August 21, 2003, the Environmental Protection Agency (EPA) Office of Inspector General (OIG) published a report stating that the White House Council on Environmental Quality (CEQ) and the National Security Council suppressed EPA warnings about potentially dangerous environmental contamination and ordered the EPA to replace warnings with misleading statements that there was no cause for concern. The OIG report presented detailed comparisons between press releases drafted by the EPA staff and the final text that was released at the end of 2002 after discussions between EPA and CEQ officials. "The CEQ official's suggested changes added reassuring statements and deleted cautionary statements," the report says. "Every change that was 'suggested' by the CEQ contact was made." According to the EPA chief of staff, "Final approval came from the White House." According to the OIG, the chief of staff "told us that other considerations, such as the desire to reopen Wall Street and national security concerns, were considered when preparing the EPA's early press releases."

The changes resulted in the EPA publishing information that was the reverse of what was in the draft. For example, an asbestos level that was originally described as "hazardous in this situation" was changed to "no significant levels of asbestos." One EPA draft said that "buildings contaminated by the collapse should be cleaned by professionals." The advice in the published version was to follow the instructions of New York City officials, who said that the cleanup could be performed with mops and wet rags. The OIG called on the EPA to begin a new cleanup designed to remedy the flaws identified in the first attempted cleanup. Acting EPA Administrator Marianne Horikno rejected most of the OIG report's conclusions, saying, "Under unbelievably trying conditions, EPA did the best that it could."

Senator Hillary Clinton (D-NY) said the report was evidence of the "highest breach of faith" by the EPA and the White House, adding, "They knew and they didn't tell us the truth." Senators Clinton and Joseph Lieberman (D-CT) wrote to President Bush that the OIG's allegations were "galling and beyond comprehension" and requested that Bush identify who on the White House staff was responsible for changing the EPA press releases.

Public health experts also expressed concern after reading the OIG report. Steven Levin, codirector of the Mount Sinai–Irving J. Selikoff Center for Occupational and Environmental Medicine, said that workers and residents were harmed by the EPA's misleading statements. "There are people who would have worn respiratory protection on that pile, but had been told, everything is okay. There were office workers who were required to come back down to this area by their employers, who said, 'The EPA has told us it's safe; you can come back.'"[92]

On September 10, 2003, Detection and Evaluation of Long Range Transport of Aerosols (DELTA) released a study about the air quality around the World Trade Center. The study, headed by Thomas Cahill, Professor of physics and engineering at the University of California at Davis, found that the gases of toxic metals, acids, and organics were capable of penetrating deeply into the lungs of the workers at Ground Zero.

According to the study, "tons of concrete, glass, furniture, carpets, insulation, computers, and papers burned until December 19, 2001." The study said samples from Ground Zero found four types of particles listed by the EPA as likely to harm human health: fine metals that can damage lungs, sulfuric acid that attacks lung cells, fine insoluble particles of glass that can travel through the lungs to the blood stream and heart, and high-temperature carcinogenic organic matter.[93]

"The debris pile acted like a chemical factory," said Cahill. "It cooked together the components and the buildings and their contents . . . and gave off gasses of toxic metals, acids, and organics for at least six weeks."[94] "For each of the four classes of pollutant, we recorded the highest levels we have ever seen in over 7,000 measurements we have made of very fine [*sic*] air pollution throughout the world, including Kuwait and China," Cahill said.[95]

## 30. TO MAKE PERIODIC REPORTS UNDER UN TREATIES

The US Government took on the duty to make periodic reports on the enforcement of human rights under each UN human rights treaty it ratified. Reporting and dialogue are the basic methods of enforcement used in the UN. The result can be summarized very briefly:

- the Government filed its first report to each of the three UN Committees late;

- after meeting with the UN Committees, the Government did not announce any steps it would take to carry out the recommendations made by the UN Committees to US Government representatives (Report 30.1);
- the Government reorganized the agency connected to the White House responsible for making the reports;
- the Bush Administration has not filed any of the Second Reports required under each of the three treaties;
- between August 2004 and November 2004, State Department staff members contacted about when the reports would be made became less knowledgeable. Before the 2004 election, someone knew about the reports but thought their filing was not important—after the election, no one knew that reports were required (see description in Chapter 3.C-5); and
- the Bush Administration has done nothing publicly to cause states, counties, and cities to prepare material required for the Second Reports (Report 30.2).

**Relevant Law:**

U.S. Constitution: Art. VI, Cl. 2; First, Fourth, Fifth, Thirteenth, Fourteenth, Fifteenth, Nineteenth, Twenty-fourth Amendments
UN Charter: Art. 55, 56
ICCPR: Preamble, Art. 7, 10.1, 10.2(a), 12.1, 13, 17.1, 17.2, 18, 19, 22, 23, 40
CERD: Art. 1, 2.1, 5, 6, 7, 9
CAT: Art. 1.1, 6, 13, 14, 16, 19

**Report 30.1: US Delinquent in Filing Three Required Reports to UN Committees**

Before 9/11, President Bush renamed and reorganized the agency that President Clinton had established in the White House to enforce the three UN treaties, putting Elliot Abrams in charge of the Policy Coordination Committee on Democracy, Human Rights, and International Operations. In August 2001, in compliance with the International Convention on the Elimination of all forms of Racial Discrimination, this Administration Committee presented the US report to the UN Committee on the Elimination of Racial Discrimination (CERD), far past the due date and just before the UN World Conference Against Racism (WCAR) in Durban, South Africa, which began on August 31, 2001. The UN Conference used the words "race," "color," "national or social origin," "language," and "birth" to try to include everyone who is subjected to racist discrimination.

Anthropologists at the Conference recognized that the word "race" is not a scientific word, that in fact there are no valid categories of "races"—no "black," "yellow," "brown," "white," or "red" races. The word continues to be used in treaties and laws worldwide to describe people who seem to have certain features in common—skin, hair, or eye color.

The World Conference against Racism brought together people from many countries whose ancestors had been taken from Africa to become slaves of white masters. There were poignant meetings between black and white activists from the United States, the United Kingdom, France, Belgium, Holland, Spain, Portugal, and people from Africa whose ancestors had been sold as slaves to work in the southern colonies of the United States, and in the Caribbean, Brazil, and Central and South America. In this setting, the NGO Conference held before the UN Conference addressed the issue of reparations. There was a strong consensus in the NGO Conference that the descendants of slaves should be compensated for the value of the services their ancestors had performed for hundreds of years in many countries. This issue was then raised at the governmental Conference.[96] After much debate over the issue and the proper language to use, all of the nations except the United States and Israel agreed to a declaration on the right to reparations and the desirability of finding a path to determining the amount of reparations that should be paid as well as to whom they should be paid. The United States and Israel walked out of the Conference on September 5.

The US State Department said the conference had erred by "suggesting that Israel practices apartheid." But many delegates felt that the prime motive for the US walkout was to avoid facing the issue of reparations for slavery and colonialism in the United States. The State Department made it clear before the conference that if the transatlantic slave trade were labeled a "crime against humanity," it would most likely refuse to participate in the conference further.[97] Since that time, the State Department has not filed any of the reports required under the three ratified human rights treaties.

## Report 30.2: United States Failing to Collect and Report at State and Local Levels

Since 9/11, the US Government, through the Secretary of State, has not confirmed that it sent letters to the Governor and Attorney General of each state asking them to prepare a report on the status of their enforcement of the UN Convention on the Elimination of Racial Discrimination, the UN Convention Against Torture, or the International Covenant on Civil and Political Rights.

Before 9/11, the State Department under President Clinton sent one letter to each state Attorney General and Governor seeking a report under one or two of these treaties. None of the states filed reports and none relayed the letters to city mayors or chairs of the county governing bodies asking them to make such reports. Nor have letters gone to each Native American tribe, who are part of the Indigenous Peoples included in the treaties. Nor have letters gone to officials in Puerto Rico, the Virgin Islands, or other territories under US jurisdiction. In fact, very few officials at the city, county, or state level have ever heard of any of the three treaties or know that reports are required at this time.

In the one city that has prepared such a report, Berkeley, California, members of the City Council and city commissions, and the media, all know about the three treaties because they have become part of the known law that governs the city (Report 30.3). The experiences in the city of Miami, Florida, make clear why such reporting on human rights violations is essential to the protection of those rights. In late November 2003, the Miami Police Department received $8 million from the US budget to quell demonstrators expected at rallies against the Free Trade Area of the Americas (FTAA) meetings in Miami. Miami city officials requested the money in advance, which came from the federal appropriation for the invasion of Iraq. Afterward, city officials reported to federal officials on how the money was spent—riot gear, pepper spray, rubber bullets, extra police forces, and other crowd-control apparatus.[98]

Every city, county, and state agency that receives federal funding must file a report on how the money was spent. This includes virtually every local agency dealing with expenditures for highways, education, hospitals and health care, parks and recreation, and state and local police. In addition to these fiscal reports, agencies must file reports that cover allegations of violations and enforcement of laws against discrimination on the basis of race, color, sex, language, religion, national or social origin, political or other opinion, disability, sexual orientation, or property (ICCPR: Art. 2.1, and CERD: all articles). The reports should also include steps taken to ensure the protection of the right to life against nuclear dangers under Article 6 of the ICCPR, as interpreted by the UN Human Rights Committee (see Reports in Section 17).

In telephone conversations with the official in charge of the reporting process in the Department of State in mid-November 2003, the MCLI was told that very few local governments had made the reports after the first request and that there was no budget for enforcing the production of them. When asked how other government agencies obtain reports from local governments under other laws, the State Department official said she did not know. The State Department had not even prepared or submitted the Second Reports of the United States at the *federal* level by Fall 2004.

In view of the fact that a great many of the violations of human rights alleged in the media and by many NGOs in the United States since 9/11 occurred at the local or regional level, it is clear that no US report can be complete or accurate unless it includes coverage of local events. Federal funding of various local government departments requires local reports to be submitted to federal funding agencies. These local reports could then be used in the reports to the DOS to fulfill treaty obligations. Where necessary, the rules for state and local expenditure of federal money could be amended to include requirements to make the mandatory reports.

### Report 30.3: One City Made Required Reports to Department of State, Others Did Not

After 9/11, the Berkeley (California) City Commission on Peace and Justice held public forums and meetings to discuss several resolutions it was proposing for adoption by the Berkeley City Council. As a result, the Council adopted a resolution against the USA PATRIOT Act (Chapter 5.A-1), for the precautionary principle (Chapter 5.B-3), for an excess profits tax on contracts during US wars (Chapter 5.B-2), and against corporate personhood (Chapter 5.B-5).

Each of these resolutions included a Whereas clause indicating that this action was based, in part, on the Human Rights Ordinance adopted by the City Council in 1990 (Ord. No. 5985 NS). This Ordinance (Chapter 5.C-1) is a restatement of the human rights articles of the UN Charter (55 and 56), committing the City "to promote higher standards of living; full employment; . . . solutions of local economic, social, health and related problems; and regional, cultural and educational cooperation; and universal respect for and observance of human rights and fundamental freedoms for all without distinction as to race, sex, language or religion."

In a pioneering move, at its April 20, 1993, meeting, the Berkeley City Council adopted Resolution 56,919 NS, supporting the ratification of the International Covenant on Civil and Political Rights (ICCPR) and widespread publication of it. The Council then encouraged all concerned City Commissions to establish Task Forces to work with NGOs to prepare reports for inclusion in the US Report.

On September 27, 1993, the Peace and Justice Commission voted to recommend to the City Council that the reports from the Commission on the Status of Women and the Berkeley Labor Commission be forwarded to the State Department for inclusion in its first report to the UN Human Rights Committee, to President Clinton, and to Hillary Rodham Clinton as the Head of the Capital Task Force on Health Care Reform (Chapter 5.C-2). As a result of these actions by city commissions and the City Council, Council members, activists, and the local media were made aware that the three treaties are part of the law of the city.

On October 26, 2003, police in Fresno, California, shot and killed a man who was unarmed and, according to witnesses, was running away from the police. According to his family, he was running only because he was on parole, not because he had done anything wrong. In the past few years, "Local law enforcement [in Fresno] killed a woman who was hitting cars with a hatchet; they killed a young man who allegedly stole beer from a store; they even shot and killed a man that was handcuffed in the back of a patrol car." Internal Affairs and the Fresno District Attorney found that the law enforcement officers in these situations had acted reasonably and responsibly.[99]

Many residents of Fresno asked the city to set up an independent police oversight committee in order to put an end to the brutality employed by the police. In 2002, the Central California Criminal Justice Committee (CCCJC) met with the Fresno police chief, the mayor, and the city council to present a plan for an Independent Police Auditor. In late 2003, the Fresno City Council rejected a budget item for a police oversight committee.[100]

In late 2003, some of the Fresno activists began including in their demands a request that the City prepare reports to comply with the three human rights treaties, building on the experiences in Berkeley. The Fresno community's attempts to ensure police accountability to citizens have been duplicated in several other US cities, with varying levels of success.

Individuals are beginning to assert their rights in the spirit of the international treaties. This is especially appropriate when a US citizen is denied the right to have a friend from another country visit him after 9/11 because she seems to be an Arab/Muslim/Middle Easterner (Report 11.6).

# 5
# TEXT OF PETITIONS, RESOLUTIONS, AND ORDINANCES

Aﬁer 9/11, many people went to work to try to stop what they thought were violations of human rights and to stop the US military invasions of Afghanistan and Iraq. They tried to force action by a city, county, or state government body calling on the US Congress to repeal a law or calling on the President to act. The most urgent issues were the repeal of the USA PATRIOT Act (A-1) and stopping US military actions (A-2).

These concerned people also urged Congress to write or support a new bill on subjects ranging from the freedom to read (B-1), to an excess profits tax (B-2), to the precautionary principles (B-3), to a sensible budget (B-4). People also tried to get local support for action on a national issue that has local effects, like an approach to asserted corporate constitutional rights (B-5) and an inquiry on impeachment (B-6). Another path is the implementation and enforcement of city resolutions, including the model Human Rights Ordinance adopted in Berkeley, California, in 1990 (C-1) and Berkeley's decision to have city commissions prepare reports for UN committees (C-2). Perhaps the most common local action that regular people can take is for members of an organization to submit a resolution to its governing council. Several unions have passed resolutions on the effects of the US war with Iraq on Iraqi workers (D-1). Some NGOs have filed complaints with the Office of Inspector General (D-2).

## A. CITY/COUNTY/STATE GOVERNMENT RESOLUTIONS AND FEDERAL BILLS FOR NEW US LAWS AND ACTIONS

## 1. AGAINST THE PATRIOT ACT

The Bush Administration's USA PATRIOT ACT has been condemned by more city, county, and state government bodies than any law in recent history, including the states of Alaska, Hawaii, Maine, and Vermont and at least 367 cities in 43 states including Florida, Georgia, Iowa, Kansas, Kentucky, Mississippi, Montana, New Mexico, North Carolina, Ohio, Tennessee, Texas, Utah, Virginia, plus Washington, DC.

**IN THE LEGISLATURE OF THE STATE OF ALASKA**
**SCS CSHJR 22 (JUD) 7/15/03**
**Joint Resolution Passed both Houses and Signed into Law by Governor.**

*A RESOLUTION*

Relating to the USA PATRIOT Act, the Bill of Rights, the Constitution of the State of Alaska, and the civil liberties, peace, and security of the citizens of our country.

*BE IT RESOLVED BY THE LEGISLATURE OF THE STATE OF ALASKA:*

WHEREAS the State of Alaska recognizes the Constitution of the United States as our charter of liberty, and that the Bill of Rights enshrines the fundamental and inalienable rights of Americans, including the freedoms of religion, speech, assembly, and privacy; and

WHEREAS each of Alaska's duly elected public servants has sworn to defend and uphold the United States Constitution and the Constitution of the State of Alaska; and

WHEREAS the State of Alaska denounces and condemns all acts of terrorism, wherever occurring; and

WHEREAS attacks against Americans such as those that occurred on September 11, 2001, have necessitated the crafting of effective laws to protect the public from terrorist attacks; and

WHEREAS any new security measures of federal, state, and local governments should be carefully designed and employed to enhance public safety without infringing on the civil liberties and rights of innocent citizens of the State of Alaska and the nation; and

WHEREAS certain provisions of the "Uniting and Strengthening

America by Providing Appropriate Tools Required to Intercept and Obstruct Terrorism Act of 2001," also known as the USA PATRIOT Act, allow the federal government more liberally to detain and investigate citizens and engage in surveillance activities that may violate or offend the rights and liberties guaranteed by our state and federal constitutions;

BE IT RESOLVED that the Alaska State Legislature supports the government of the United States of America in its campaign against terrorism, and affirms its commitment that the campaign not be waged at the expense of essential civil rights and liberties of citizens of this country contained in the United States Constitution and the Bill of Rights; and be it

FURTHER RESOLVED that it is the policy of the State of Alaska to oppose any portion of the USA PATRIOT Act that would violate the rights and liberties guaranteed equally under the state and federal constitutions; and be it

FURTHER RESOLVED that, in accordance with Alaska state policy, an agency or instrumentality of the State of Alaska, in the absence of reasonable suspicion of criminal activity under Alaska State law, may not

(1) initiate, participate in, or assist or cooperate with an inquiry, investigation, surveillance, or detention;

(2) record, file, or share intelligence information concerning a person or organization, including library lending and research records, book and video store sales and rental records, medical records, financial records, student records, and other personal data, even if authorized under the USA PATRIOT Act;

(3) retain such intelligence information;
the state Attorney General shall review the intelligence information currently held by the state for its legality and appropriateness under the United States and Alaska Constitutions and permanently dispose of it if there is no reasonable suspicion of criminal activity; and be it

**FURTHER RESOLVED** that an agency or instrumentality of the state may not,

(1) use state resources or institutions for the enforcement of federal immigration matters, which are the responsibility of the federal government;

(2) collect or maintain information about the political, religious, or social views, associations, or activities of any individual, group, association, organization, corporation, business, or partnership, unless the information directly relates to an investigation of criminal activities and there are reasonable grounds to suspect the subject of the information is or may be involved in criminal conduct;

(3) engage in racial profiling;
law enforcement agencies may not use race, religion, ethnicity, or

national origin as factors in selecting individuals to subject to investigatory activities except when seeking to apprehend a specific suspect whose race, religion, ethnicity, or national origin is part of the description of the suspect; and be it

**FURTHER RESOLVED** that the Alaska State Legislature implores the United States Congress to correct provisions in the USA PATRIOT Act and other measures that infringe on civil liberties, and opposes any pending and future federal legislation to the extent that it infringes on Americans' civil rights and liberties.

**COPIES** of this resolution shall be sent to the Honorable George W. Bush, President of the United States; the Honorable John Ashcroft, Attorney General of the United States; the Honorable Frank Murkowski, Governor of Alaska; and to the Honorable Ted Stevens and the Honorable Lisa Murkowski, US Senators, and the Honorable Don Young, US Representative, members of the Alaska delegation in Congress.[1]

## 2. AGAINST THE WAR/INVASION IN IRAQ

After President Bush announced that the United States would go to war in Iraq, and after the US Senate agreed to this action, thousands of citizens across the country petitioned their elected officials to send messages opposing these actions.

On March 4, 2003, fifty members of the California State Legislature sent the following letter to the President expressing their opposition to the war and stating their reasons.

### CALIFORNIA LEGISLATORS TO PRESIDENT BUSH

March 4, 2003

The Honorable George W. Bush, President
United States of America
THE WHITE HOUSE
1600 Pennsylvania Avenue, N.W.
Washington, D.C. 20500

Dear Mr. President:

As Members of the California State Legislature, we respectfully write in opposition to a war on Iraq without a formal resolution by the United Nations Security Council and a declaration of war by Congress.

As elected representatives of the largest population and economy in America, we have many concerns over the policies your administration is pursuing. These include:

A lack of credible evidence that meets the standard of "beyond a reasonable doubt" that shows the imminent danger Iraq poses to America's essential interests. Neither Colin Powell nor Hans Blix presented a case sufficient to warrant an attack by American forces.

A failure to persuade other nations to support our intentions. Unlike the aftermath of the Attack on America, you have not been able to enlist the support of other key nations, who presumably have been given even more intelligence data than has the American public. This lack of geopolitical solidarity substantially weakens America's case in the court of world opinion. Further, it enhances the prospects of fighting a war with few allies.

Lack of clarity about the possible instability in the Middle East during the war and subsequent foreign occupation of Iraq. It seems unlikely that the Muslim world will for long passively accept America's incursion—whatever our provocation.

While your administration seems to have financially accommodated key neighboring regimes in return for their neutrality or tactical support, the constituencies these leaders represent are openly hostile to America. Which begs the question: what happens if one or more governments are overthrown and anti-American regimes take control?

Domestically, most economists believe an open-ended war will exacerbate the national recession. They see upward pressure on both interest rates and inflation as the military competes for capital and goods to prosecute the war. (Not to mention the effect on energy prices if Middle East supplies are interrupted or reduced).

California is in the throes of its worst budget deficit in state history, as a result of the most severe, persistent recession in the nation. Your 2003–04 federal budget already reflects your determination to cut state and local assistance for medical and health care services, homeland security and transportation. Can deeper subsequent cuts be far behind when hundreds of billions in war material and nation rebuilding are needed in Iraq? Where will the funds come from, if not the states?

Washington, DC, April 12, 2003: Police officers use sticks to beat back pro-testers against the war in Iraq during a march. Protesters turned out in much smaller numbers than in the months leading up to the conflict, and their focus switched from keeping US troops out of Iraq to bringing them home. (AP Photo/Charles Dharapak)

Finally, the growing world and domestic demonstrations against the war are reminiscent of the ill-fated Vietnam War, when a sitting president was forced to resign and America lost its moral compass as a result of irreparable social and cultural divisions at home. A legacy that sadly still lives.

To conclude, we the undersigned urge that you await a final decision on waging war on Iraq until the United Nations Security Council votes and the Congress acts in accordance with Article I, Section 8 of the United States of America Constitution.

Thank you for your consideration.[2]

# SAN FRANCISCO PROPOSITION N ADOPTED NOVEMBER 2, 2004

The voters in the City and County of San Francisco, California, adopted Proposition N by a vote of 147,533 Yes to 85,207 No: 63.39% to 36.61%.

It is the Policy of the people of the City and Country of San Francisco that:
**The Federal government should take immediate steps to end the US occupation of Iraq and bring our troops safely home now.**

George W. Bush disgracefully lied to the American people to make the case for war in Iraq. His message was one of deceit and fear mongering, linking Saddam Hussein to al Qaeda and weapons of mass destruction. There was never a legitimate case for a preemptive war. Overruling global public opinion and objections from allies, Bush relentlessly led us into a war that has (as of 6-28-04) cost more that 850 American lives and left more than 5,100 wounded.

The US invasion and occupation cost the lives of roughly 10,000 Iraqi civilians in addition to maiming and wounding countless more. It has led to incredible environmental degradation as well as the destruction of homes, schools, sanitation and water treatment plants, and hospitals. Hunger, homelessness and suffering are widespread.

The war and occupation has perpetuated the denial of many labor and human rights. It has sharply increased violence against women and girls. A law issued by Saddam Hussein prohibiting unions where most Iraqis work has continued to be enforced. Systemic and illegal abuse of detainees has been found in the Abu Ghraib prison facility and in other detention centers. During the past two years, there have been consistent allegations of brutality and cruelty by US agents against detainees in violation of international law.

At home, we have witnessed the erosion of civil liberties under the USA PATRIOT ACT, while racism, religious intolerance, and discrimination against immigrants is on the rise.

With Congress appropriating over $150 billion dollars, the war and occupation in Iraq has benefited corporate military contractors while widening economic inequality at home. It has diverted resources away from vital public services and community programs. The war and occupation of Iraq has cost California over $19.5 billion dollars. San Francisco's share of that burden is estimated at over $520 million dollars. With these resources, San Francisco could fund for the next 10 years: health coverage for 1,000 uninsured youth, meals for 5,000 seniors, preschool for 500 low-income children, 100 new school teachers, and supportive housing for the City's estimated 3,000 chronically homeless individuals. Rather than squander more of our precious public resources and sacrifice many more American and Iraqi lives on the occupation, monies should be used to restore life-affirming efforts—public health, welfare, education, jobs, arts and the environment in our country and around the world.

The war and occupation in Iraq has fueled, not lowered, the risk of terrorism here and around the world. We are less safe today than we were when the Bush administration put the nation on this failed course.

We need peace.

The Federal government should take immediate steps to end the US occupation of Iraq and bring our troops safely home now.[3]

## B. LOCAL RESOLUTIONS AND FEDERAL BILLS FOR NEW US LAWS

### 1. FREEDOM TO READ PROTECTION ACT OF 2003

Librarians have become one of the most effective lobbying groups against repression since 9/11. Their militancy spawned a bill to protect people who read books.

### IN THE HOUSE OF REPRESENTATIVES
**March 6, 2003**

108th CONGRESS, 1st Session, H. R. 1157

Mr. SANDERS (for himself, Mr. PAUL, Mr. DEFAZIO, Mr. BLUME-NAUER, Mr. OWENS, Ms. LEE, Mr. FARR, Mr. TOWNS, Mr. GRI-JALVA, Mr. CONYERS, Mr. MCDERMOTT, Ms. JACKSON-LEE of Texas, Mr. HINCHEY, Mr. OLVER, Ms. WOOLSEY, Mr. FRANK of Massachusetts, Mr. JACKSON of Illinois, Mr. MCGOVERN, Ms. BALDWIN, Ms. WATERS, Mr. FORD, Mr. LIPINSKI, Mr. STARK, and Mr. UDALL of Colorado) introduced the following bill; which was referred to the Committee on the Judiciary, and in addition to the Select Committee on Intelligence (Permanent Select), for a period to be subsequently determined by the Speaker, in each case for consideration of such provisions as fall within the jurisdiction of the committee concerned.

### A BILL

To amend the Foreign Intelligence Surveillance Act to exempt bookstores and libraries from orders requiring the production of any tangible things for certain foreign intelligence investigations, and for other purposes.

*Be it enacted by the Senate and House of Representatives of the United States of America in Congress assembled,*

## SECTION 1. SHORT TITLE.

This Act may be cited as the 'Freedom to Read Protection Act of 2003'.

## SEC. 2. EXEMPTION OF BOOKSTORES AND LIBRARIES FROM ORDERS REQUIRING THE PRODUCTION OF ANY TANGIBLE THINGS FOR CERTAIN FOREIGN INTELLIGENCE INVESTIGATIONS.

Section 501 of the Foreign Intelligence Surveillance Act of 1978 (50 U.S.C. 1861) is amended by adding at the end the following new subsection:

(f)(1) No application may be made under this Sectionwith either the purpose or effect of searching for, or seizing from, a bookseller or library documentary materials that contain personally identifiable information concerning a patron of a bookseller or library.

(2) Nothing in this subsection shall be construed as precluding a physical search for documentary materials referred to in paragraph (1) under other provisions of law, including under Section303.

(3) In this subsection:

    (A) The term 'bookseller' means any person or entity engaged in the sale, rental or delivery of books, journals, magazines or other similar forms of communication in print or digitally.

    (B) The term 'library' has the meaning given that term under Section213(2) of the Library Services and Technology Act (20 U.S.C. 9122[2]) whose services include access to the Internet, books, journals, magazines, newspapers, or other similar forms of communication in print or digitally to patrons for their use, review, examination or circulation.

    (C) The term 'patron' means any purchaser, renter, borrower, user or subscriber of goods or services from a library or bookseller.

    (D) The term 'documentary materials' means any document, tape or other communication created by a bookseller or library in connection with print or digital dissemination of a book, journal, magazine, newspaper, or other similar form of communication, including access to the Internet.

    (E) The term 'personally identifiable information' includes information that identifies a person as having used, requested or obtained specific reading materials or services from a bookseller or library.

## SEC. 3. EXPANSION OF REPORTING REQUIREMENTS UNDER FISA.

Section 502 of the Foreign Intelligence Surveillance Act of 1978 (50 U.S.C. 1862) is amended by striking subsections (a) and (b) and inserting the following:

(a) On a semiannual basis, the Attorney General shall fully inform the appropriate congressional committees concerning all requests for the production of tangible things under Section501, including with respect to the preceding 6-month period—

   (1) the total number of applications made for orders approving requests for the production of tangible things under Section501; and
   (2) the total number of such orders either granted, modified, or denied.

(b) In informing the appropriate congressional committees under subsection (a), the Attorney General shall include the following:

   (1) A description with respect to each application for an order requiring the production of any tangible things for the specific purpose for such production.
   (2) An analysis of the effectiveness of each application that was granted or modified in protecting citizens of the United States against terrorism.

(c) In a manner consistent with the protection of the national security of the United States, the Attorney General shall make public the information provided to the appropriate congressional committees under subsection (a).

(d) In this section, the term 'appropriate congressional committees' means—

   (1) the Permanent Select Committee on Intelligence of the House of Representatives and the Select Committee on Intelligence of the Senate; and
   (2) the Committees on the Judiciary of the House of Representatives and the Senate.[4]

## 2. FOR AN EXCESS PROFITS/WINDFALL REVENUE TAX

Daily reports of super profits being paid on Government contracts with companies manufacturing war supplies and providing civilian support for US military actions led to action in at least two California cities in the spring of 2003. The Excess Profits tax proposal built on similar taxes on war contracts adopted by Congress in World War I, World War II, and the Korean War.

The Oakland City Council passed the resolution unanimously on May 20, 2003. The Berkeley City Council had passed a similar resolution on April 8, 2003. On July 13, 2004, Rep. Major Owens (D-NY) introduced H.R. 4825 "To amend the Internal Revenue Code . . . to impose an additional tax on taxable income attributable to contracts with the US for goods and services for the war in Iraq." The excess profits taxed is to be 15 percent.

The Whereas clauses included, "(2) While large corporations continue to net billions of dollars from the War in Iraq, the Bush Administration continues to cut funding for vital domestic programs." Clause (4) lists Halliburton, Bechtel Group, Fluor Corp, Parsons Corp, Louis Berger Groups as benefiting "from the biggest reconstruction projects since the Second World War."[5]

## A RESOLUTION DECLARING THE CITY OF OAKLAND'S SUPPORT FOR FEDERAL LEGISLATION TO LIMIT EXCESS WAR PROFITS

WHEREAS, the people of the City of Oakland believe in the US Constitution and are committed to the rule of law, and support US troops in all lawful actions; and

WHEREAS, excess profit taxes were in place during World Wars I and II and the Korean War, and the reasons are outlined by President Franklin D. Roosevelt in a message to Congress July 1, 1940:

"We are engaged in a great national effort to build up our national defenses to meet any and every potential attack. . . . It is our duty to see that the burden is equitably distributed according to ability to pay so that a few do not gain from the sacrifices of the many. I therefore recommend to the Congress the enactment of a steeply graduated excess profits tax, to be applied to all individuals and all corporate organizations without discrimination," and

WHEREAS, the US Department of Defense is now making contracts for war materiel, and is also making contracts to deal with the "rebuilding" of Iraq after the end of the bombing and military actions; and

WHEREAS, the members of the US Armed Forces are not making excess wages out of this war, but are suffering now, and some will suffer for the rest of their lives, from the actions they are now taking and will take in Iraq; and

WHEREAS, cities have had to bear the burden of increased costs for homeland security without promised help from the federal government, and while the federal government lets contracts for rebuilding Iraq, cities continue to suffer from aging infrastructure due to decreases in federal funding over the years; now therefore, be it

RESOLVED, that the Oakland City Council strongly urges our Congress members in the House and Senate to introduce legislation calling for a high percentage tax on all excess profits on every contract dealing with US military action in Iraq and/or the "rebuilding" of Iraq, including renegotiation of all such contracts made to date to include this tax, which sets aside a portion of this funding to go to cities to address the aforementioned homeland security and infrastructure needs; and be it

FURTHER RESOLVED, that copies of this Resolution be sent to every California Congress Member, to the US Department of Defense, Pres. George W. Bush, and the United Nations Secretary General Kofi Annan.

## 3. FOR THE PRECAUTIONARY PRINCIPLE

Every city, township, county, and state governing body is bombarded with requests for permits to change, enlarge, destroy, or rebuild something: housing, schools, water pipes, roads, sewers, telephone lines. Many decisions require a change or stretching of existing standards for quality control of air, water, sound, and forests. The City and County of San Francisco Board of Supervisors became the first body to vote to change the basis for making these decisions.

### SAN FRANCISCO PRECAUTIONARY PRINCIPLE ORDINANCE
adopted June 17, 2003

### Chapter 1 Precautionary Principle Policy Statement

### Sec. 100. FINDINGS.

The Board of Supervisors finds and declares that:

Every San Franciscan has an equal right to a healthy and safe environment. This requires that our air, water, earth, and food be of a sufficiently high standard that individuals and communities can live healthy, fulfilling, and dignified lives. The duty to enhance, protect and preserve San Francisco's environment rests on the shoulders of government, residents, citizen groups and businesses alike.

Historically, environmentally harmful activities have only been stopped after they have manifested extreme environmental degradation or exposed people to harm. In the case of DDT, lead, and asbestos, for instance, regulatory action took place only after disaster had struck. The delay between first knowledge of harm and appropriate action to deal with it can be measured in human lives cut short.

San Francisco is a leader in making choices based on the least environmentally harmful alternatives, thereby challenging traditional assumptions about risk management. Numerous City ordinances including: the Integrated Pest Management Ordinance, the Resource Efficient Building Ordinance, the Healthy Air Ordinance, the Resource Conservation Ordinance, and the Environmentally Preferable Purchasing Ordinance apply a precautionary approach to specific City purchases and activities. Internationally, this model is called the Precautionary Principle.

As the City consolidates existing environmental laws into a single Environment Code, and builds a framework for new legislation, the City sees the Precautionary Principle approach as its policy framework to develop laws for a healthier and more just San Francisco. By doing so, the City will create and maintain a healthy, viable Bay Area environment for current and future generations, and will become a model of sustainability.

Science and technology are creating new solutions to prevent or mitigate environmental problems. However, science is also creating new compounds and chemicals that are already finding their way into mother's milk and causing other new problems. New legislation may be required to address these situations, and the Precautionary Principle is intended as a tool to help promote environmentally healthy alternatives while weeding out the negative and often unintended consequences of new technologies.

A central element of the precautionary approach is the careful assessment of available alternatives using the best available science. An alternatives assessment examines a broad range of options in order to present the public with different effects of different options considering short-term versus long-term effects or costs, and evaluating and comparing the adverse or potentially adverse effects of each option, noting options with fewer potential hazards. This process allows fundamental questions to be asked: "Is this potentially hazardous activity necessary?" "What less hazardous options are available?" and "How little damage is possible?"

The alternatives assessment is also a public process because, locally or internationally, the public bears the ecological and health consequences of environmental decisions. A government's course of action is necessarily enriched by broadly based public participation when a full range of alternatives is considered based on input from diverse individuals and groups. The public should be able to determine the range of specific reasonable alternatives to be examined. For each alternative the public should consider both immediate and long-term consequences, as well as possible impacts to the local economy. This form of open decision-making is in line with San Francisco's historic Sunshine Act, which allows citizens to have full view of the legislative process. One of the goals of the Precautionary Principle is to include citizens as equal partners in decisions affecting their environment.

San Francisco looks forward to the time when the City's power is generated from renewable sources, when all our waste is recycled, when our vehicles produce only potable water as emissions, when the Bay is free from toxins, and the oceans are free from pollutants. The Precautionary Principle provides a means to help us attain these goals as we evaluate future laws and policies in such areas as transportation, construction, land use, planning, water, energy, health care, recreation, purchasing, and public expenditure.

Transforming our society to realize these goals and achieving a society living respectfully within the bounds of nature will take a behavioral as well as technological revolution. The Precautionary approach to decision-making will help San Francisco speed this process of change by moving beyond finding cures for environmental ills to preventing the ills before they can do harm.

## Sec. 101. THE SAN FRANCISCO PRECAUTIONARY PRINCIPLE.

The following shall constitute the City and County of San Francisco's Precautionary Principle policy. All officers, boards, commissions, and departments of the City and County shall implement the Precautionary Principle in conducting the City and County's affairs:

The Precautionary Principle requires a thorough exploration and a careful analysis of a wide range of alternatives. Based on the best available science, the Precautionary Principle requires the selection of the alternative that presents the least potential threat to human health and the City's natural systems. Public participation and an open and transparent decision making process are critical to finding and selecting alternatives.

Where threats of serious or irreversible damage to people or nature exist, lack of full scientific certainty about cause and effect shall not be viewed as sufficient reason for the City to postpone cost effective measures to prevent the degradation of the environment or protect the health of its citizens. Any gaps in scientific data uncovered by the examination of alternatives will provide a guidepost for future research, but will not prevent protective action being taken by the City. As new scientific data become available, the City will review its decisions and make adjustments when warranted.

Where there are reasonable grounds for concern, the precautionary approach to decision-making is meant to help reduce harm by triggering a process to select the least potential threat. The essential elements of the Precautionary Principle approach to decision-making include:

## Sec. 102. THREE YEAR REVIEW.

No later than three years from the effective date of this ordinance, and after a public hearing, the Commission on the Environment shall submit a report to the Board of Supervisors on the effectiveness of the Precautionary Principle policy.

## Sec. 103 LIST OF ALL ENVIRONMENTAL ORDINANCES AND RESOLUTIONS.

The Director of the Department of the Environment shall produce and maintain a list of all City and County of San Francisco ordinances and resolutions which affect or relate to the environment and shall post this list on the Department of the Environment's website.

## Sec. 104. CITY UNDERTAKING LIMITED TO PROMOTION OF GENERAL WELFARE.

The Board of Supervisors encourages all City employees and officials to take the precautionary principle into consideration and evaluate alternatives when taking actions that could impact health and the environment, especially where those actions could pose threats of serious harm or irreversible damage. This ordinance does not impose specific duties upon any City employee or official to take specific actions. In adopting and undertaking the enforcement of this ordinance, the City and County of San Francisco is assuming an undertaking only to promote the general welfare. It is not assuming, nor is it imposing on its officers and employees, an obligation for breach of which it is liable in money damages to any person who claims that such breach proximately caused injury nor may this ordinance provide any basis for any other judicial relief including, but not limited to a writ of mandamus or an injunction. In adopting this Chapter, the Board of Supervisors does not intend to authorize or require the disclosure to the public of any proprietary information protected under the laws of the State of California.

## 4. SENSIBLE FEDERAL BUDGET RESOLUTION

In Spring 2004, the San Francisco Bay Area Progressive Challenge and the Friends Committee on Legislation, along with supporters, contacted California Assembly members and Senators to have this Resolution introduced at the State Legislature in Sacramento.

## The Resolution

Whereas, the primary purpose of the federal government is to protect and meet the basic needs of its citizens, i.e., the common good; and

Whereas, the President's federal budget proposal calls for greater increases in an already enormous military budget while programs to help urban and rural communities meet their domestic needs would be lowered or kept at current levels; and

Whereas, the budget proposals do not meet the standards for the "common good" of society; adequate health care, affordable housing, more educational assistance, environmental protection; and sufficient food for the hungry; and

Whereas, the security of the nation rests fundamentally on the well-being, equality, and vitality of our citizens, not on military might; and

Whereas, the funds that are provided by the federal government to the states are insufficient to fulfill these responsibilities,

Resolved by the Assembly and Senate of the State of California, jointly, that the Legislature of the State of California hereby respectfully memorializes the Congress and the President of the United States to enact a budget that redirects sufficient amounts of money from the military budget to the states so that the critical needs of rebuilding our communities and inner cities, repairing our schools, educating our children, eliminating hunger, providing affordable housing, improving transportation, protecting our environment, and obtaining a decent level of health care and safety for all of our citizens can be met, thereby increasing fundamentally our security and well-being and

be it further Resolved, that the Chief Clerk of the Assembly transmit copies of this resolution to the President and Vice President of the United States, to the Speaker of the House of representatives, the Secretary of State, and to each Senator and Representative from California in the Congress of the United States.

## 5. AGAINST CORPORATE PERSONHOOD

On June 15, 2004, the Berkeley (California) City Council joined the growing movement questioning the alleged First Amendment rights of corporations when they adopted a resolution proposed by the Berkeley Commission on Peace and Justice.

## Resolution No. 62,539 N.S.

WHEREAS, Chapter 3.68 of the Berkeley Municipal Code, which contains the initiative ordinance creating the Peace and Justice Commission, sets forth several functions of the Peace and Justice Commission, including, but not limited to, "(A) Advise the Berkeley City Council on all matters relating to the City of Berkeley's role in issues of peace and social justice, including, but not limited to support for human rights and self-determination throughout the world; (B) Help create citizen awareness around issues of social justice [and] (C) Help develop proposals for the City Council in furtherance of the goals of peace and justice, and help publicize such actions in the community;" and

WHEREAS, under the United States and California Constitutions, all sovereignty resides with "We the People," such that people hold all inherent political power and government derives its power from the consent of the governed; government is created by the people and for the people for our health, safety, and welfare; our system of government is a representative democracy, through which the people govern; and "We the People" are entitled to inalienable constitutional rights to wield against oppressive governmental regulation; and

WHEREAS, "corporation" is not mentioned in the United States Constitution; our founders did not grant corporations rights; rights were reserved for natural people; historically corporations were created as artificial entities, chartered by state governments to serve the public interest, cause no harm, and be subordinate to the sovereign people; and yet by judicial interpretations, corporations gained personhood status, free speech and other protections guaranteed by the Bill of Rights and the 14th Amendment; and

WHEREAS, with "corporate personhood" and First Amendment rights, corporations dominate the political process and interfere with citizens' control over our government as follows: corporations lobby our legislative and regulatory bodies; with the Supreme Court's assertion that money is a form of free speech, corporations spend vast amounts of money to influence elections; and by virtue of their enormous wealth, corporations wield much more influence over our government and over the media than do "We the People"; and

WHEREAS, this corporate influence is transforming our government from one that is "by and for the people" to one that is by and for corporate interests; corporate influence over our government denies citizens our right to govern through a representative democracy and subjects us to minority rule by the wealthy few; and corporate influence has made it difficult to maintain a living wage, a clean environment, affordable health care, and quality education for all; and

WHEREAS, the citizens of the City of Berkeley consider it to be our sovereign right and civic duty to recognize that corporations remain artificial entities created by the people through our state legislatures; hope to nurture and expand democracy in Berkeley and in our nation; and reject the concept of corporate constitutional rights based on "corporate personhood" or any other factor.

NOW THEREFORE, BE IT RESOLVED that the Council of the City of Berkeley supports amending the United States and California Constitutions to declare that corporations are not granted the protections or rights of persons, and supports amending the United States and California Constitutions to declare that the expenditure of corporate money is not a form of constitutionally protected speech.

BE IT FURTHER RESOLVED, that the City Council directs the City Manager to send a copy of this Resolution to our state and federal government representatives including: Governor Arnold Schwarzenegger, Majority and Minority Leaders of the California Senate Don Perata and James Brulte, California Assemblymember Loni Hancock, United States Senators Barbara Boxer and Diane Feinstein, and United States Representative Barbara Lee.[6]

## *6. FOR AN INQUIRY ON IMPEACHMENT*

On September 10, 2003, the Santa Cruz, California, City Council voted to send a letter to the Senate Judiciary Committee and the Sub-Committee on the Constitution requesting an inquiry into the President's actions and policies after 9/11.

### DRAFT LETTER OF SANTA CRUZ (CALIFORNIA) CITY COUNCIL

Dear Honorable Chairman Sensenbrenner:

The Santa Cruz City Council has asked me to write to convey the widespread concern in our city about President Bush's deeds leading up to and in support of the US war on Iraq. We have received public testimony, petitions, calls, email and letters demanding our support for an impeachment inquiry. As local elected officials and patriots, having sworn to an oath to uphold the constitution, it is our job to relay these concerns to you. By a vote of six to one, local elected officials of the City Council share these concerns. Please determine if one or more of the following represent impeachable offenses by the President:

- Did President Bush violate congressionally ratified international treaties and thus Article VI, the 'supremacy clause', of our own constitution through the invasion and occupation of Iraq?
- Did false or misleading information exaggerate the threat posed by Iraq and was this a part of a conscious effort to mislead the American public?
- Did President Bush exploit the fear generated by the 9/11 terrorist attacks to erode or compromise our constitutionally guaranteed rights and liberties?

We do believe that as patriots it is our job to raise these concerns to your level. Please begin an official inquiry. If your inquiry identifies illegal acts on the part of the leaders of our current administration, we expect that impeachment proceedings would follow immediately.

Sincerely and with the utmost respect,
Emily Reilly, Mayor

[Vice Mayor Jane Kennedy supported adding three points regarding impeachment offenses.]

- Does the Bush administration's plan to develop and deploy yet more nuclear weapons violate the Nuclear Nonproliferation Treaty to which the USA is a signatory?
- Did the United State's use of depleted uranium in both Iraq and Afghanistan violate the United Nations Charter?
- Has the treatment of the prisoners at Guantanamo Bay and elsewhere violated the Geneva Conventions, the Nuremberg Principles, and/or other treaties and conventions to which the US is signatory?[7]

One year later, California lawyers adopted the following resolution introduced by the National Lawyers Guild Chapter at the 2004 convention of the Conference of Delegates of California Bar Associations, by overwhelming vote:

RESOLVED, that the Conference of Delegates of California Bar Associations urges the California Congressional Delegation to commence an independent, bipartisan Congressional investigation into the representations made to Congress and the United Nations used to justify preemptive war on Iraq.

The Problem: . . . The adoption of a preemptive strike doctrine and a "war on terror" without boundaries changes over 200 years of United States foreign policy, and is an issue of extraordinary public concern . . . whether the Separation of Powers Doctrine and established international law have been violated. The lawyers who wrote the Constitution established a public policy contrary to what has occurred, and the public is entitled to hear and review the reasoned discussion by their descendants . . .

(Resolution 11-1-2004, proposed by the National Lawyers Guild San Francisco Northern California Chapter.)

## C. CITY RESOLUTIONS FOR CITY ACTIONS

### 1. HUMAN RIGHTS ORDINANCE

In 1990, the Berkeley Commission on Peace and Justice passed a resolution proposing that the City of Berkeley adopt an ordinance on human rights using the wording of the human rights sections of the UN Charter, Articles 55 and 56. The reasoning was that making this a local city ordinance would cause all city officials to keep it in mind to regulate their actions. The ordinance covers the mayor and council members, local police officers, teachers, all city employees, and people engaged in contracts with the city.

In fact, all of these city officials and contractors were already supposed to live up to the commitments in Articles 55 and 56, since the UN Charter is a treaty and part of the supreme law of the land under the US Constitution, Article VI, Cl. 2. But it turned out that few people in city government had ever carefully read Articles 55 and 56, and even fewer had been reminded that they were committed to carrying out these provisions.

The City Council adopted the resolution on August 16, 1990. It has become the basis for several actions by the City, including the refusal to cooperate with illegal actions by federal agents in the city against noncitizens. The spirit of the Human Rights Ordinance has infused many City Council actions since 9/11, according to Berkeley activists.

## BERKELEY HUMAN RIGHTS ORDINANCE
No. 5985 N.S.

BE IT ORDAINED by the Council of the City of Berkeley as follows:

Section 1. With a view to the creation of conditions of stability and well-being which are necessary for peaceful and friendly relations among the people of this city and region, based on respect for the principle of equal rights of people, the City of Berkeley shall promote:

a. Higher standards of living, full employment, and conditions of economic and social progress and development;
b. Solutions of local economic, social, health and related problems; and regional cultural and educational cooperation, and
c. Universal respect for, and observance of human rights and fundamental freedoms for all without distinction as to race, sex, language or religion.

Section 2. The City of Berkeley pledges to take joint and separate action in cooperation with Alameda County, Association of Bay Area Governments, the State of California and the United States Government for the achievement of the purpose set forth in Section 1, and in cooperation with the United Nations where appropriate.

In effect August 16, 1990.

## 2. FOR REPORTING TO UN COMMITTEES

At its April 20, 1993 meeting, the Berkeley, California, City Council adopted a Resolution that supported the 1992 ratification of the International Covenant on Civil and Political Rights by the United States and encouraged all concerned Berkeley Commissions to establish Task Forces to work with nongovernmental organizations to prepare reports on the enforcement and violations within the city of human rights enunciated in the Covenant. The report was to be sent to the Sate Department for inclusion in the US Report and for study by Berkeley residents.

As a result, the Council received reports from the Commission on the Status of Women and the Berkeley Labor Commission and resolved to forward them to David Stewart of the US Department of State for inclusion in the first US Report to the UN Human Rights Committee, and to Pres. Bill Clinton and Hillary Rodham Clinton.

The Council Set Forth the Basics for Its Resolution in the Whereas Clauses:

WHEREAS, this is the first treaty signed by the U.S. requiring us to report to an international body of experts, the United Nations Human Rights Committee, on the status of all political and civil rights in the U.S. at the federal, state, and local levels, and in all U.S. territories (Puerto Rico, Guam, District of Columbia, etc.); and

WHEREAS, fulfilling this reporting requirement can be a spur to stronger enforcement of existing human rights in the United States, and broadening of the rights in the Constitution (adopted in 1787 and 1791) and in the Reconstruction Amendments (adopted after the Civil War) to include human rights enunciated in the 20th century (rights of children, of women, of indigenous people, of labor unions, immigrant defendants); and

WHEREAS, the City of Berkeley is proud of its efforts to publicize and enforce human rights for all within the City.

## REPORT TO THE UN BY THE CITY OF BERKELEY CALIFORNIA, USA, COMMISSION ON THE STATUS OF WOMEN

September 8, 1993

LAND AND PEOPLE

Berkeley is a city of about 103,000 people. It is somewhat influenced by the proximity of two large metropolitan cities, San Francisco and Oakland, and by the presence of a major university campus—the University of California. The student body at U.C. Berkeley exceeds 30,000; and there are over 10,000 more people connected with the campus as faculty, staff, researchers, and others. Berkeley's social classes run the gamut, from wealthy business or professional people in sumptuous homes in the hills to the desperately poor, many of whom are homeless.

[Re: ICCPR] Articles 6(1), 23(1), 23(4):
Berkeley's women are no strangers to social ills. Women of all ages, all races, and all social classes live under the cloud of threatened violent crime; the perpetrators are thieves, rapists, drug dealers with automatic weapons, physical or sexual abusers of women and children (many of them the husbands or lovers of the women victims), and murderers (again, often husbands and lovers, or would-be lovers). National figures citing battery, gunshots, and other lethal assaults by men as a leading cause of serious injury or death

of women are proportionally true in our City. The poor, and especially homeless women, are most at risk of violence. The National Clearinghouse on Femicide is here in Berkeley, and it is the project of one of our women.

[Re: ICCPR] Articles 3, 23(4), 24(1):
Sexual harassment has probably decreased overall as a result of women's and men's growing awareness and sensitivity brought about through news events, writings and television, although it continues within some social groups and some younger age groups. Sexual abuse of children (usually girls) is widespread throughout the United States, though it is typically practiced in secret, under dire threats from the abuser if the victim should report it. Berkeley is part of Alameda County, and the County's Child Protective Services workers are perpetually overloaded with work and cases to investigate.

Programs exist, predominantly organized and operated by women (both staff and volunteers), to assist homeless women or women victims of violence. These programs offer shelters, free or very low-cost food, drop-in facilities, rape counseling advocates, free legal assistance, and other amenities such as transportation, used clothing, and employment or housing help. These agencies and programs are very good, but they have never been able to address completely the needs of all.

On a middle- and working-class level, women (including those who are other than European-American) have made some strides toward equality in employment over the last 20 years. The same is true of many professions—a number of women doctors, dentists and attorneys practice in Berkeley. A noted exception is the makeup of the faculty and upper-level administrators of the University of California at Berkeley. This bastion of white (European-American) male supremacy has yielded only a few token tenured faculty or high-level administrative appointments to women and minorities.

[Re: ICCPR] Article 25(c):
The root causes of discrimination toward women, violence against women, and other inequities visited upon women and girls are deep in the psyches of American men and women. Violent and dangerous men are glamorized and lionized in the news and entertainment media. Violence is portrayed as an ideal solution to conflict, from children's cartoons to national policy (bombing Iraq when Saddam Hussein displeases American policymakers and presidents). Women are portrayed as sex objects in commercial and entertainment milieux. Parents continue to socialize little boys to be more rough and tough, and to be independent thinkers; and simultaneously they continue to train little girls to be more people-pleasing and dependent. Western Society has spawned this subjugation of women over the past 5,000 years or so, and it will not change or retreat easily, or of its own accord. Per-

sons who care about equity and human rights will have to persevere in trying to recondition those persons who practice, allow, or even advocate male domination over, and abuse or denigration of, women in our American culture. Slowly laws are being struck down that, for example, allowed American men to beat their wives and children, did not allow women to divorce their battering or cruel husbands, and denied women the right to control their own bodies' reproductive organs.

On March 7, 2005, the Berkeley Commission on Peace and Justice considered a resolution asking the Berkeley City Council to send Meiklejohn Institute's report *Challenging US Human Rights Violations Since 9/11* to the US Department of State and the UN High Commissioner for Human Rights.

## D. LABOR UNION AND NONGOVERNMENTAL ORGANIZATION ACTIONS

### 1. UNION RESOLUTIONS OPPOSING US POLICY ON IRAQ AND IRAQI WORKERS

### SERVICE EMPLOYEES INTERNATIONAL UNION (SEIU) NATIONAL CONVENTION RESOLUTION

Adopted June 22, 2004 unanimously by the largest union in the U.S.

Our nation faces growing domestic challenges—unemployment, declining wages and benefits, deunionization of the workforce, reduced public services, crumbling health care and educational systems, cuts in veterans benefits, escalating public debt, and decreased economic, social and personal security. Massive military spending, combined with tax cuts for the rich, is creating massive federal deficits and huge cuts in state public services. This crisis is a product of the Bush Administration's policies (backed by a majority in Congress) of military intervention abroad and attacks on working peoples' rights at home. Only corporations and the wealthy have benefited.

We cannot solve these economic and social problems without addressing U.S. foreign policy and its consequences.

Last January, 2003, with the approval of the International Union Executive Board, International Union President Andrew L. Stern sent a letter to President George Bush expressing our concerns and outlining the following four important principles:

Philadelphia, July 2, 2004: The moving, combat boot memorials to fallen US soldiers in Iraq, organized by the American Friends Service Committee, Chicago, have grown in size from 504 boots in January 2004 to over 1,100 at the end of November 2004. Nearby the array of boots stands as a "wall of remembrance" covered with the names of more than 11,000 Iraqi civilians killed since the US-led invasion. (Terry Foss, AFSC)

1. War involves enormous risks to our families and our communities and must be a last option, not the first.
2. The goal of our foreign policy must be to promote a safer and more just world—promoting peaceful, multilateral solutions for disputes.
3. US foreign policy must give high priority to improving the lives of people around the world.
4. The rights and freedoms our government says it is fighting for abroad must be protected at home.

President Stern's letter ended with these words: We urge you not to invade Iraq in violation of these principles and ask you to work with the Congress and the United Nations to set a course that will provide lasting security for all. That is the best way to honor those who died on September 11, who serve in our armed forces, and who work hard every day to make America work by providing the services our communities depend upon.

As recently confirmed by the 9/11 Commission, in violation of the above principles, and based on deception, lies and false promises to the American people and the World, the Bush Administration launched its unilateral, preemptive war against Iraq. The war in Iraq has resulted in the death of thousands of Iraqis and hundreds of US soldiers. Already more of our soldiers, our sons and daughters, sisters and brothers, have died in this war than any other war since Vietnam. And, this war is costing our nation's taxpayers hundreds of billions of dollars.

Just as President Stern warned in our January, 2003 letter to President Bush, the foreign policy of the Bush administration has weakened rather than strengthened security in the U.S., creating enemies around the world and alienating long-time allies.

In October of 2003 nearly 200 delegates representing over 100 labor organizations, including SEIU Locals representing nearly 400,000 SEIU members, created a permanent coalition called U.S. Labor Against the War (USLAW) to encourage and promote debate within the labor movement on the critical questions of war and peace facing our nation; to work to address the impact that US foreign policy has on workers, their jobs, their rights and liberties, their families, unions and communities; and to promote the extension of labor rights to workers in Iraq now.

## Therefore be it resolved:

That SEIU supports the principles in the Mission Statement adopted at the National Labor Assembly of US Labor Against The War (USLAW), October 25, 2003, namely:

- A Just Foreign Policy based on International law and global justice that promotes genuine security and prosperity at home and abroad;
- An end to the US Occupation of Iraq;
- The Redirecting of the Nation's Resources from inflated military spending to meeting the needs of working families for health care, education, a clean environment, housing and a decent standard of living;
- Supporting Our Troops and their families by bringing our troops home safely, by not recklessly putting them in harms way, by providing adequate veterans' benefits and promoting domestic policies that prioritize the needs of working people who make up the bulk of the military;
- Protecting Workers Rights, Civil Rights, Civil Liberties and the Rights of Immigrants by promoting democracy, not subverting it; and
- Solidarity with workers around the world who are struggling for their own labor and human rights, and with those in the U.S. who want U.S. foreign and domestic policies to reflect our nation's highest ideals.

**Be It Further Resolved:**

That SEIU will work with all religious, community, political, and foreign policy groups (such as USLAW) who support the principles outlined in the January 2004 letter to President Bush and further elaborated in this resolution.[8]

## UNITED TEACHERS LOS ANGELES LOCAL RESOLUTION
Adopted May 16, 2004 by Local 1021 of the American Federation of Teachers AFL-CIO

Whereas, Since George W. Bush declared an end to the war on Iraq in April, 2003, unemployment among Iraqi workers has reached 70%, causing many families to face hunger and dislocation, and

Whereas, Since Bush announced the war's end, the US occupying authority has frozen wages for most Iraqi workers at $60/month, and at the same time eliminating bonuses, profit sharing, and subsidies for food and housing, causing a sharp cut in the income of those Iraqi workers still employed, and

Whereas, $87 billion was appropriated by Congress, for the reconstruction of Iraq, yet nothing is set to be used for raising Iraqi wages or for unemployment benefits, and these extraordinary expenditures will come at the expense of services and jobs here in the US, and

Whereas, The US occupation authority has announced it intends to sell off the factories, refineries, mines and other state enterprises despite the fact that these enterprises belong to the Iraqi people, not to the US, and has issued a new decree, Public Order 39, allowing 100% foreign ownership of Iraqi businesses and the repatriation of profits, in effect making resistance to privatization illegal for Iraqi unions and preventing workers from having any voice in the future of their own jobs, and

Whereas, The privatization of Iraqi businesses would result in massive lay-offs to Iraqi workers, including 28,000 teachers, at a time when unemployment is already at crisis levels, and

Whereas, The US occupation authority has continued to enforce a 1987 law issued by Saddam Hussein prohibiting unions and collective bargaining in the public sector and state enterprises where most Iraqis work, and

Whereas, Since April, 2003, Iraqi workers have begun to reorganize their trade union movement, seeking a better standard of living, and to preserve their jobs and workplaces, despite having no resources; while the US occupying authority withholds welfare funds, buildings and other assets previously held by unions controlled by Saddam Husscin's government, and

Whereas, Workers in the United States have experienced an erosion of our own rights to organize and bargain collectively in defense of our jobs, rights and working conditions and thus understand what the restriction or loss of these rights means to working people, and

Whereas, Since January, 2003, US Labor Against the War, with dozens of affiliated local, state and national unions, along with Central Labor Councils and independent labor organizations, has been in the forefront of educating workers about the labor crisis, mobilizing labor opposition to the war and support for Iraqi trade unionists,

Therefore be it resolved, That AFT call for the institution of full trade union rights in Iraq, for immediate nullification of the 1987 Hussein law banning unions in public enterprises and for the removal of any other restriction on the free exercise of labor rights, and

Be it further resolved, That AFT call on the US occupation authority to immediately implement Conventions 87, 98 and 138 of the International Labor Organization, guaranteeing the right to organize and bargain collectively, and prohibiting child labor, and to immediately halt the process of privatizing Iraqi workplaces and selling off the property of the Iraqi people, and

Be it further resolved, That AFT call for an end to the US occupation of Iraq and return of US troops to their homes and families so that Iraq can be governed by its own people, and

Be it further resolved, That AFT call for a Congressional investigation of the suppression of trade union rights in Iraq and the privatization of Iraqi workplaces and selling off of the property of the Iraqi people, and

Be it further resolved, That AFT become an affiliate member of US Labor Against the War.

Be it finally resolved, AFT will publish information about the plight of Iraqi labor unionists in all its media, and encourage affiliates and members to donate material resources such as computers, telephones, fax machines and office furniture, as well as financial resources to the Fund to Support Iraqi Labor Rights established by US Labor Against the War.

## 2. COMPLAINT TO THE OFFICE OF INSPECTOR GENERAL

An effective complaint about the action of Government officials will include the basic facts, the relevant law, and the issue the OIG should investigate. Public Citizen is an organization with several projects: Buyers Up, Congress Watch, Critical Mass, Global Trade Watch, Health Research Group, and Litigation Group. On December 22, 2003, Public Citizen sent an effective letter to the OIG of the Department of Health and Human Services, and on the same day, Rep. John D. Dingell (D-MI) sent a letter to the OIG on the same subject as Ranking Member of the House Committee on Energy and Commerce. The first point and the conclusion of the Public Citizen letter provide a useful example of an OIG complaint.

### PUBLIC CITIZEN LETTER TO OIG OF HHS

December 22, 2003

Dara Corrigan
Acting Principal Deputy Inspector General
Office of Inspector General
Department of Health and Human Services
200 Independence Avenue, S.W.
Washington, D.C. 20201

Dear Ms. Corrigan:

Public Citizen is writing to express its strong concern about the granting of a waiver from conflict of interest regulations for a senior level employee charged with developing what is one of the nation's most important laws enacted this year: the controversial overhaul of Medicare.

On May 12, 2003, Department of Health and Human Services (HHS) Secretary Tommy Thompson granted a waiver from Executive branch ethics regulations, pursuant to 18 U.S. Code§208(b)(1) and 5 CFR 2640.301, to Thomas Scully, the Administrator of the Centers for Medicare and Medicaid Services. The waiver allowed Mr. Scully, who resigned on Dec. 16, to seek private employment from lobbying firms and investment companies representing the pharmaceutical and other health care industries, while simultaneously allowing him to negotiate a major overhaul of the Medicare program that provided clear and substantial benefits to the potential employers, their clients and Mr. Scully through his potential future employment.

The waiver, which was kept confidential for the most crucial period of Mr. Scully's involvement in the Medicare legislation, ignored the substantial conflicts of interest at stake, runs contrary to some aspects of ethics regulations and was the result of a lackluster process at HHS.

1. The conflict of interest in this situation was so substantial as to render any consideration of exemption unwarranted.

A conflict of interest exists when a public employee involved in an official proceeding, or any person or organization with whom the employee is negotiating potential employment, has a substantial personal financial interest at stake in the outcome of that proceeding such as to "affect the integrity of the employee's service to the Government" [18 USC 208(a) and 5 CFR2640.301(a)].

All parties involved in this conflict of interest—the lobbying firms as potential employers of Mr. Scully, the clients of those lobbying firms, and Mr. Scully himself—stood to gain substantial economic benefit from his involvement in the Medicare legislation.

HHS attempted to downplay the extent of potential economic benefits involved in this situation. According to the waiver, the financial interests of Mr. Scully's potential employers as a class "pose less of a risk that the integrity of an employee's services might be compromised by an interest in any one affected entity." In such matters, "the incentive to please a potential employer . . . [is not] particularly acute."

First, Mr. Scully stood to personally gain a great deal from placing himself on the job market while working on the Medicare bill. This conflict between simultaneously trying to appeal to potential employers and the obligation to serve the public interest reaches to the very heart of conflict of interest issues. At no other point in time are Mr. Scully's services more valuable to prospective employers and, at the same time, so entrusted with the public's interest. This is when Mr. Scully may directly affect the interests of the potential employers in the legislative negotiations, and when potential employers may seek to influence the outcome of those negotiations.

Mr. Scully can undoubtedly benefit from such a commanding position. As a public servant, his government salary was $134,000. The *New York Times* (Dec. 3, 2003) reported that Washington lobbyists are estimating he could earn five times his current salary from these potential employers in the private sector. A partner at one of the law firms Mr. Scully was negotiating employment with said, "Tom's recent experience at the highest levels of the government makes him very attractive to our firm."

Second, the potential employers and, indirectly, their clients have the greatest leverage to influence the legislative process during employment negotiations. Mr. Scully has disclosed the names of three law firms and two investment firms in which he had been in employment discussions [see attachment, "Thomas Scully's Potential Employers and Their Clients"]. These five firms represent at least 41 companies or industry associations that are directly affected by the Medicare legislation and have substantial interests in its outcome.

Among Mr. Scully's potential employer's clients are 12 pharmaceutical companies and their industry association, the Pharmaceutical Research and Manufacturers of America (PhRMA), including five of the top 10 grossing pharmaceutical companies in 2002. These companies are widely acknowledged to be among the biggest beneficiaries of the Medicare bill—receiving a substantial increase in their drug sales, a prohibition against Medicare administrators negotiating lower drug prices for the program, and effectively a prohibition on the reimportation of lower priced drugs from Canada.

In addition to the benefits provided to the pharmaceutical companies, 10 health care providers, four trade associations representing health care providers, and three physician professional organizations are either represented by the three lobby firms or are owned in whole or in part by the two investment firms that held employment discussions with Mr. Scully. Health care providers received numerous huge benefits under the Medicare bill, including the repeal of a scheduled 4.5 percent reduction in physician payments and the substituted 1.5 percent increase in both 2004 and 2005.

Not surprisingly, these potential conflicts of interest bore fruit for Mr. Scully, as he landed choice positions with two of the firms with which he was discussing employment while negotiating, supposedly on behalf of the American people, for an overhaul of Medicare. On December 18, Mr. Scully announced that he will be joining the investment firm Welsh, Carson, Anderson & Stowe and the law firm Alston & Bird.

2. The waiver process was structurally flawed.

This waiver treats conflict of interest regulations more as a nuisance to be readily sidestepped, rather than a cornerstone for public confidence in the governmental process. If this is the rationale and procedure for granting a waiver, then the conflict of interest regulations serve no real purpose—they are effectively nullified as they apply to HHS.

Finally, the public in general, and Congress in particular, were not even informed that a conflict of interest waiver had been granted to Mr. Scully to seek private employment opportunities from those directly affected by the Medicare legislation.

The Associate General Counsel of Ethics at HHS, who recommended this unwarranted waiver, and Secretary Thompson, who approved the waiver without following the appropriate procedural safeguards, acted in possible violation of the conflict of interest regulations. Therefore, Public Citizen requests that the action of granting a waiver for Thomas Scully be reviewed by your office.

In order to prevent future violations of ethical behavior by the Department, Public Citizen also recommends that your office clarify in writing the proper procedures for adherence to the ethics regulations and, if ever appropriate, for granting exemptions to the regulations.

Sincerely,

Joan Claybrook
President
Public Citizen

Frank Clemente
Director
Public Citizen's Congress Watch

cc: The Honorable Tommy Thompson, Secretary, Department of Health and Human Services
Marilyn L. Glynn, Acting Director, Office of Government Ethics

*UPDATE*: On January 6, 2004, the White House issued new guidelines mandating that all ethics waivers like the one granted to Scully be approved by the White House counsel's office. On January 13, Public Citizen, while commending the new guidelines, again called for an investigation into the potential violation of executive branch ethics violations.[9]

# 6
# TEXT OF LAWS VIOLATED AND IGNORED
## (Excerpts)

All of the citizens and noncitizens, detainees and "enemy combatants," travelers and immigrants, professors and students, and demonstrators and activists, who charge that their rights have been violated by the United States Government since 9/11 base their charges on a series of fundamental laws. The most basic laws are presented below. Only the articles or sections that are relevant are reproduced, to save the reader time.

The US Constitution is the bedrock of freedom in the United States and its territories (Section A). The Inspector General Act (Section B) is also referred to in many reports. The second fundamental document is the United Nations Charter. The Charter enunciates basic substantive law in Articles presented here (Section C). (The Charter articles pertaining to how the UN operates are not included.) The treaty-law document that spells out in some detail most of the rights allegedly violated since 9/11 is the International Covenant on Civil and Political Rights (ICCPR). The basic substantive articles are presented here (Section D); only the organizational articles are left out. The Treaty with the Western Shoshone, 1863 (18 Statutes at Large 689), is discussed in Report 18.8. The relevant articles in the Convention on Elimination of Racial Discrimination (CERD) (Section E) and the Convention Against Torture (CAT) (Section F) are also reprinted here, but not the articles on the reporting process and commitments. The Nuremberg Principles (Section G) are basic to all issues arising in times of war, and the Nuclear Non-Proliferation Treaty (Section H) must be considered in all discussions of war and weapons.

There are three additional treaties US Presidents have signed, but the US Senate has not consented to ratify. They enunciate more specific rights and duties described in general terms in the Bill of Rights and the UN Charter human rights articles. They are mentioned in several of the Reports and can be found in any collection of these treaties: the Convention on the Rights of the Child; the Convention on Elimination of Discrimination Against Women; the International Covenant on Economic, Social, and Cultural Rights; the Geneva Convention, and the Geneva Convention Implementation Act. These texts are not included here. For a complete list of the fifty-three UN human rights treaties, including the seventeen the United States has ratified, see *Human Rights: Major International Instruments*, status as of May 31, 2004 (UNESCO).

A series of environmental protection acts are mentioned but not reproduced here. They are accessible in collections of the US Code: the Nuclear Waste Policy Act (42 U.S.C. §10101), the National Environmental Protection Act (42 U.S.C. §4331), the Clean Water Act (33 U.S.C. §1251), and the Clean Air Act (42 U.S.C. §7401). The International Court of Justice Advisory Opinion on the Legality or Illegality of Nuclear Weapons is also mentioned repeatedly but not reproduced here.

# A. US CONSTITUTION

Ratified June 21, 1788

## PREAMBLE

We the people of the United States, in order to form a more perfect union, establish justice, insure domestic tranquility, provide for the common defense, promote the general welfare, and secure the blessings of liberty to ourselves and our posterity, do ordain and establish this Constitution for the United States of America.

## ARTICLE I

### Section 4

The times, places and manner of holding elections for Senators and Representatives, shall be prescribed in each state by the legislature thereof; but the Congress may at any time by law make or alter such regulations, except as to the places of choosing Senators.

The Congress shall assemble at least once in every year, and such meeting shall be on the first Monday in December, unless they shall by law appoint a different day.

## Section 5

Clause 1: Each House shall be the judge of the elections, returns and qualifications of its own members, and a majority of each shall constitute a quorum to do business; but a smaller number may adjourn from day to day, and may be authorized to compel the attendance of absent members, in such manner, and under such penalties as each House may provide.

Each House may determine the rules of its proceedings, punish its members for disorderly behavior, and, with the concurrence of two thirds, expel a member.

## Section 8

Clause 1: The Congress shall have power to lay and collect taxes, duties, imposts and excises, to pay the debts and provide for the common defense and general welfare of the United States; but all duties, imposts and excises shall be uniform throughout the United States;

Clause 2: To borrow money on the credit of the United States;

Clause 3: To regulate commerce with foreign nations, and among the several states, and with the Indian tribes;

Clause 4: To establish a uniform Rule of Naturalization, and uniform laws on the subject of Bankruptcies throughout the United States;

Clause 10: To define and punish piracies and felonies committed on the high seas, and offenses against the law of nations;

Clause 11: To declare war, grant letters of marque and reprisal, and make rules concerning captures on land and water;

Clause 18: To promote the progress of science and useful arts, by securing for limited times to authors and inventors the exclusive right to their respective writings and discoveries;

## Section 9

Clause 2: The privilege of the writ of habeas corpus shall not be suspended, unless when in cases of rebellion or invasion the public safety may require it.

## ARTICLE II

### Section 1

Clause 1: The executive power shall be vested in a President of the United States of America. He shall hold his office during the term of four years, and, together with the Vice President, chosen for the same term, be elected, as follows:

Clause 2: Each state shall appoint, in such manner as the Legislature thereof may direct, a number of electors, equal to the whole number of Senators and Representatives to which the State may be entitled in the Congress: but no Senator or Representative, or person holding an office of trust or profit under the United States, shall be appointed an elector.

Clause 3: The electors shall meet in their respective states, and vote by ballot for two persons, of whom one at least shall not be an inhabitant of the same state with themselves. And they shall make a list of all the persons voted for, and of the number of votes for each; which list they shall sign and certify, and transmit sealed to the seat of the government of the United States, directed to the President of the Senate. The President of the Senate shall, in the presence of the Senate and House of Representatives, open all the certificates, and the votes shall then be counted. The person having the greatest number of votes shall be the President, if such number be a majority of the whole number of electors appointed; and if there be more than one who have such majority, and have an equal number of votes, then the House of Representatives shall immediately choose by ballot one of them for President; and if no person have a majority, then from the five highest on the list the said House shall in like manner choose the President. But in choosing the President, the votes shall be taken by States, the representation from each state having one vote; A quorum for this purpose shall consist of a member or members from two thirds of the states, and a majority of all the states shall be necessary to a choice. In every case, after the choice of the President, the person having the greatest number of votes of the electors shall be the Vice President. But if there should remain two or more who have equal votes, the Senate shall choose from them by ballot the Vice President.

Clause 4: The Congress may determine the time of choosing the electors, and the day on which they shall give their votes; which day shall be the same throughout the United States.

Clause 8: Before he enter on the execution of his office, he shall take the following oath or affirmation:—"I do solemnly swear (or affirm) that I will faithfully execute the office of President of the United States, and will to the best of my ability, preserve, protect and defend the Constitution of the United States."

## Section 2

Clause 1: The President shall be commander in chief of the Army and Navy of the United States, and of the militia of the several states, when called into the actual service of the United States; he may require the opinion, in writing, of the principal officer in each of the executive departments, upon any subject relating to the duties of their respective offices, and he shall have power to grant reprieves and pardons for offenses against the United States, except in cases of impeachment.

Clause 2: He shall have Power, by and with the Advice and Consent of the Senate, to make Treaties, provided two thirds of the Senators present concur; and he shall nominate, and by and with the Advice and Consent of the Senate, shall appoint Ambassadors, other public Ministers and Consuls, judges of the Supreme Court, and all other Officers of the United States, whose Appointments are not herein otherwise provided for, and which shall be established by Law: but the Congress may by Law vest the appointment of such inferior Officers, as they think proper, in the President alone, in the Courts of Law, or in the Heads of Departments.

Clause 3: The President shall have power to fill up all vacancies that may happen during the recess of the Senate, by granting commissions which shall expire at the end of their next session.

## Section 3

He shall from time to time give to the Congress information of the state of the union, and recommend to their consideration such measures as he shall judge necessary and expedient; he may, on extraordinary occasions, convene both Houses, or either of them, and in case of disagreement between them, with respect to the time of adjournment, he may adjourn them to such time as he shall think proper; he shall receive ambassadors and other public ministers; he shall take care that the laws be faithfully executed, and shall commission all the officers of the United States.

Washington, DC, March 19, 2003: US police drag a limp antiwar protester away after arresting him across the street from the White House. (AP Photo/Rich Bowmer)

# ARTICLE III

## Section 2

Clause 1: The judicial Power shall extend to all cases, in law and equity, arising under this Constitution, the laws of the United States, and treaties made, or which shall be made, under their Authority;—to all Cases affecting Ambassadors, other public Ministers and Consuls;—to all Cases of admiralty and maritime Jurisdiction;—to Controversies to which the United States shall be a Party;—to Controversies between two or more States;—between a State and Citizens of another State;—between Citizens of different States;—between Citizens of the same State claiming Lands under grants of different States, and between a State, or the Citizens thereof, and foreign states, Citizens or Subjects.

# ARTICLE IV

### Section 4

The United States shall guarantee to every state in this union a republican form of government, and shall protect each of them against invasion; and on application of the legislature, or of the executive (when the legislature cannot be convened) against domestic violence.

# ARTICLE VI

Clause 2: This Constitution, and the laws of the United States which shall be made in pursuance thereof; and all treaties made, or which shall be made, under the authority of the United States, shall be the supreme law of the land; and the judges in every state shall be bound thereby, anything in the Constitution or laws of any State to the contrary notwithstanding.

Clause 3: The Senators and Representatives before mentioned, and the members of the several state legislatures, and all executive and judicial officers, both of the United States and of the several states, shall be bound by oath or affirmation, to support this Constitution; but no religious test shall ever be required as a qualification to any office or public trust under the United States.

## AMENDMENTS TO THE CONSTITUTION

### Amendment I (1791)

Congress shall make no law respecting an establishment of religion, or prohibiting the free exercise thereof; or abridging the freedom of speech, or of the press; or the right of the people peaceably to assemble, and to petition the government for a redress of grievances.

### Amendment IV (1791)

The right of the people to be secure in their persons, houses, papers, and effects, against unreasonable searches and seizures, shall not be violated, and no warrants shall issue, but upon probable cause, supported by oath or affirmation, and particularly describing the place to be searched, and the persons or things to be seized.

## Amendment V (1791)

No person shall be held to answer for a capital, or otherwise infamous crime, unless on a presentment or indictment of a grand jury, except in cases arising in the land or naval forces, or in the militia, when in actual service in time of war or public danger; nor shall any person be subject for the same offense to be twice put in jeopardy of life or limb; nor shall be compelled in any criminal case to be a witness against himself, nor be deprived of life, liberty, or property, without due process of law; nor shall private property be taken for public use, without just compensation.

## Amendment VI (1791)

In all criminal prosecutions, the accused shall enjoy the right to a speedy and public trial, by an impartial jury of the state and district wherein the crime shall have been committed, which district shall have been previously ascertained by law, and to be informed of the nature and cause of the accusation; to be confronted with the witnesses against him; to have compulsory process for obtaining witnesses in his favor, and to have the assistance of counsel for his defense.

## Amendment VII (1791)

In suits at common law, where the value in controversy shall exceed twenty dollars, the right of trial by jury shall be preserved, and no fact tried by a jury, shall be otherwise re-examined in any court of the United States, than according to the rules of the common law.

## Amendment VIII (1791)

Excessive bail shall not be required, nor excessive fines imposed, nor cruel and unusual punishments inflicted.

## Amendment IX (1791)

The enumeration in the Constitution, of certain rights, shall not be construed to deny or disparage others retained by the people.

## Amendment X (1791)

The powers not delegated to the United States by the Constitution, nor prohibited by it to the states, are reserved to the states respectively, or to the people.

## Amendment XIII (1865)

### Section 1

Neither slavery nor involuntary servitude, except as a punishment for crime whereof the party shall have been duly convicted, shall exist within the United States, or any place subject to their jurisdiction.

### Section 2

Congress shall have power to enforce this article by appropriate legislation.

## Amendment XIV (1868)

### Section 1

All persons born or naturalized in the United States, and subject to the jurisdiction thereof, are citizens of the United States and of the state wherein they reside. No state shall make or enforce any law which shall abridge the privileges or immunities of citizens of the United States; nor shall any state deprive any person of life, liberty, or property, without due process of law; nor deny to any person within its jurisdiction the equal protection of the laws.

### Section 5

The Congress shall have power to enforce, by appropriate legislation, the provisions of this article.

## Amendment XV (1870)

### Section 1

The right of citizens of the United States to vote shall not be denied or abridged by the United States or by any state on account of race, color, or previous condition of servitude.

### Section 2

The Congress shall have power to enforce this article by appropriate legislation.

## Amendment XIX (1920)

The right of citizens of the United States to vote shall not be denied or abridged by the United States or by any state on account of sex.

Congress shall have power to enforce this article by appropriate legislation.

## Amendment XXIV (1964)

Section 1

The right of citizens of the United States to vote in any primary or other election for President or Vice President, for electors for President or Vice President, or for Senator or Representative in Congress, shall not be denied or abridged by the United States or any state by reason of failure to pay any poll tax or other tax.

Section 2

The Congress shall have power to enforce this article by appropriate legislation.

## Amendment XXVI (1971)

Section 1

The right of citizens of the United States, who are 18 years of age or older, to vote, shall not be denied or abridged by the United States or any state on account of age.

Section 2

The Congress shall have the power to enforce this article by appropriate legislation.[1]

# B. INSPECTOR GENERAL ACT OF 1978

§ 2. Purpose and establishment of Offices of Inspector General; departments and agencies involved

In order to create independent and objective units—

(1) to conduct and supervise audits and investigations relating to the programs and operations of the establishments listed in Section11(2);

(2) to provide leadership and coordination and recommend policies for activities designed (A) to promote economy, efficiency, and effectiveness in the administration of, and (B) to prevent and detect fraud and abuse in, such programs and operations; and

(3) to provide a means for keeping the head of the establishment and the Congress fully and currently informed about problems and deficiencies relating to the administration of such programs and operations and the necessity for and progress of corrective action;

there is established—

(A) in each of such establishments an office of Inspector General, subject to subparagraph (B); and

(B) in the establishment of the Department of the Treasury—

    (i) an Office of Inspector General of the Department of the Treasury; and
    (ii) an Office of Treasury Inspector General for Tax Administration.

(Pub. L. 95-452, § 2, Oct. 12, 1978, 92 Stat. 1101; Pub. L. 96-88, title V, § 508(n)(1), Oct. 17, 1979, 93 Stat. 694; Pub. L. 97-113, title VII, § 705(a)(1), Dec. 29, 1981, 95 Stat. 1544; Pub. L. 97-252, title XI, § 1117(a)(1), Sept. 8, 1982, 96 Stat. 750; Pub. L. 99-93, title I, § 150(a)(1), Aug. 16, 1985, 99 Stat. 427; Pub. L. 99-399, title IV, § 412(a)(1), Aug. 27, 1986, 100 Stat. 867; Pub. L. 100-504, title I, § 102(a), (b), Oct. 18, 1988, 102 Stat. 2515; Pub. L. 100-527, § 13(h)(1), Oct. 25, 1988, 102 Stat. 2643; Pub. L. 105-206, title I, § 1103(a), July 22, 1998, 112 Stat. 705.)

§ 3. Appointment of Inspector General; supervision; removal; political activities; appointment of Assistant Inspector General for Auditing and Assistant Inspector General for Investigations

(a) There shall be at the head of each Office an Inspector General who shall be appointed by the President, by and with the advice and consent of the Senate, without regard to political affiliation and solely on the basis of integrity and demonstrated ability in accounting, auditing, financial analysis, law, management analysis, public administration, or investigations. Each Inspector General shall report to and be under the general supervision of the head of the establishment involved or, to the extent such authority is delegated, the officer next in rank below such head, but shall not report to, or be subject to supervision by, any other officer of such establishment. Neither the head of the establishment nor the officer next in rank below such head shall prevent or prohibit the Inspector General from initiating, carrying out, or completing any audit or investigation, or from issuing any subpoena during the course of any audit or investigation.

(b) An Inspector General may be removed from office by the President. The President shall communicate the reasons for any such removal to both Houses of Congress.

(c) For the purposes of Section7324 of title 5, United States Code, no Inspector General shall be considered to be an employee who determines policies to be pursued by the United States in the nationwide administration of Federal laws.

(d) Each Inspector General shall, in accordance with applicable laws and regulations governing the civil service—

(1) appoint an Assistant Inspector General for Auditing who shall have the responsibility for supervising the performance of auditing activities relating to programs and operations of the establishment, and
(2) appoint an Assistant Inspector General for Investigations who shall have the responsibility for supervising the performance of investigative activities relating to such programs and operations.

§ 4. Duties and responsibilities; report of criminal violations to Attorney General

(a) It shall be the duty and responsibility of each Inspector General, with respect to the establishment within which his Office is established—

(1) to provide policy direction for and to conduct, supervise, and coordinate audits and investigations relating to the programs and operations of such establishment;
(2) to review existing and proposed legislation and regulations relating to programs and operations of such establishment and to make recommendations in the semiannual reports required by Section5(a) con-

cerning the impact of such legislation or regulations on the economy and efficiency in the administration of programs and operations administered or financed by such establishment or the prevention and detection of fraud and abuse in such programs and operations;

(3) to recommend policies for, and to conduct, supervise, or coordinate other activities carried out or financed by such establishment for the purpose of promoting economy and efficiency in the administration of, or preventing and detecting fraud and abuse in, its programs and operations;

(4) to recommend policies for, and to conduct, supervise, or coordinate relationships between such establishment and other Federal agencies, State and local governmental agencies, and nongovernmental entities with respect to (A) all matters relating to the promotion of economy and efficiency in the administration of, or the prevention and detection of fraud and abuse in, programs and operations administered or financed by such establishment, or (B) the identification and prosecution of participants in such fraud or abuse; and

(5) to keep the head of such establishment and the Congress fully and currently informed, by means of the reports required by Section 5 and otherwise, concerning fraud and other serious problems, abuses, and deficiencies relating to the administration of programs and operations administered or financed by such establishment, to recommend corrective action concerning such problems, abuses, and deficiencies, and to report on the progress made in implementing such corrective action.[2]

## C. THE UNITED NATIONS CHARTER
Entry into force 24 October, 1945

## Preamble

WE THE PEOPLES OF THE UNITED NATIONS DETERMINED

to save succeeding generations from the scourge of war, which twice in our lifetime has brought untold sorrow to mankind, and

to reaffirm faith in fundamental human rights, in the dignity and worth of the human person, in the equal rights of men and women and of nations large and small, and

to establish conditions under which justice and respect for the obligations arising from treaties and other sources of international law can be maintained, and

to promote social progress and better standards of life in larger freedom,

AND FOR THESE ENDS

to practice tolerance and live together in peace with one another as good neighbours, and

to unite our strength to maintain international peace and security, and

to ensure, by the acceptance of principles and the institution of methods, that armed force shall not be used, save in the common interest, and

to employ international machinery for the promotion of the economic and social advancement of all peoples,

HAVE RESOLVED TO COMBINE OUR EFFORTS TO
ACCOMPLISH THESE AIMS

Accordingly, our respective Governments, through representatives assembled in the city of San Francisco, who have exhibited their full powers found to be in good and due form, have agreed to the present Charter of the United Nations and do hereby establish an international organization to be known as the United Nations.

## Article 1

The Purposes of the United Nations are:

1. To maintain international peace and security, and to that end: to take effective collective measures for the prevention and removal of threats to the peace, and for the suppression of acts of aggression or other breaches of the peace, and to bring about by peaceful means, and in conformity with the principles of justice and international law, adjustment or settlement of international disputes or situations which might lead to a breach of the peace;
2. To develop friendly relations among nations based on respect for the principle of equal rights and self-determination of peoples, and to take other appropriate measures to strengthen universal peace;
3. To achieve international co-operation in solving international problems of an economic, social, cultural, or humanitarian character, and

in promoting and encouraging respect for human rights and for fundamental freedoms for all without distinction as to race, sex, language, or religion; and
4. To be a centre for harmonizing the actions of nations in the attainment of these common ends.

## Article 2

The Organization and its Members, in pursuit of the Purposes stated in Article 1, shall act in accordance with the following Principles.

1. The Organization is based on the principle of the sovereign equality of all its Members.
2. All Members, in order to ensure to all of them the rights and benefits resulting from membership, shall fulfill in good faith the obligations assumed by them in accordance with the present Charter.
3. All Members shall settle their international disputes by peaceful means in such a manner that international peace and security, and justice, are not endangered.
4. All Members shall refrain in their international relations from the threat or use of force against the territorial integrity or political independence of any state, or in any other manner inconsistent with the Purposes of the United Nations.
5. All Members shall give the United Nations every assistance in any action it takes in accordance with the present Charter, and shall refrain from giving assistance to any state against which the United Nations is taking preventive or enforcement action.
7. Nothing contained in the present Charter shall authorize the United Nations to intervene in matters which are essentially within the domestic jurisdiction of any state or shall require the Members to submit such matters to settlement under the present Charter; but this principle shall not prejudice the application of enforcement measures under Chapter VII.

## Article 11

1. The General Assembly may consider the general principles of co-operation in the maintenance of international peace and security, including the principles governing disarmament and the regulation of armaments, and may make recommendations with regard to such principles to the Members or to the Security Council or to both.

3. The General Assembly may call the attention of the Security Council to situations which are likely to endanger international peace and security.

## Article 14

Subject to the provisions of Article 12, the General Assembly may recommend measures for the peaceful adjustment of any situation, regardless of origin, which it deems likely to impair the general welfare or friendly relations among nations, including situations resulting from a violation of the provisions of the present Charter setting forth the Purposes and Principles of the United Nations.

## Article 23

2. The non-permanent members of the Security Council shall be elected for a term of two years. In the first election of the non-permanent members after the increase of the membership of the Security Council from eleven to fifteen, two of the four additional members shall be chosen for a term of one year. A retiring member shall not be eligible for immediate re-election.
3. Each member of the Security Council shall have one representative.

## Article 24

1. In order to ensure prompt and effective action by the United Nations, its Members confer on the Security Council primary responsibility for the maintenance of international peace and security, and agree that in carrying out its duties under this responsibility the Security Council acts on their behalf.
2. In discharging these duties the Security Council shall act in accordance with the Purposes and Principles of the United Nations. The specific powers granted to the Security Council for the discharge of these duties are laid down in Chapters VI, VII, VIII, and XII.
3. The Security Council shall submit annual and, when necessary, special reports to the General Assembly for its consideration.

## Article 25

The Members of the United Nations agree to accept and carry out the decisions of the Security Council in accordance with the present Charter.

## Article 33

1. The parties to any dispute, the continuance of which is likely to endanger the maintenance of international peace and security, shall, first of all, seek a solution by negotiation, enquiry, mediation, conciliation, arbitration, judicial settlement, resort to regional agencies or arrangements, or other peaceful means of their own choice.
2. The Security Council shall, when it deems necessary, call upon the parties to settle their dispute by such means.

## Article 36

3. In making recommendations under this Article the Security Council should also take into consideration that legal disputes should as a general rule be referred by the parties to the International Court of Justice in accordance with the provisions of the Statute of the Court.

## Article 39

The Security Council shall determine the existence of any threat to the peace, breach of the peace, or act of aggression and shall make recommendations, or decide what measures shall be taken in accordance with Articles 41 and 42, to maintain or restore international peace and security.

## Article 51

Nothing in the present Charter shall impair the inherent right of individual or collective self-defence if an armed attack occurs against a Member of the United Nations, until the Security Council has taken measures necessary to maintain international peace and security. Measures taken by Members in the exercise of this right of self-defence shall be immediately reported to the Security Council and shall not in any way affect the authority and responsibility of the Security Council under the present Charter to take at any time such action as it deems necessary in order to maintain or restore international peace and security.

## Article 55

With a view to the creation of conditions of stability and well-being which are necessary for peaceful and friendly relations among nations based on respect for the principle of equal rights and self-determination of peoples, the United Nations shall promote:

a. higher standards of living, full employment, and conditions of economic and social progress and development;
b. solutions of international economic, social, health, and related problems; and international cultural and educational cooperation; and
c. universal respect for, and observance of, human rights and fundamental freedoms for all without distinction as to race, sex, language, or religion.

## Article 56

All Members pledge themselves to take joint and separate action in co-operation with the Organization for the achievement of the purposes set forth in Article 55.

## Article 62

1. The Economic and Social Council may make or initiate studies and reports with respect to international economic, social, cultural, educational, health, and related matters and may make recommendations with respect to any such matters to the General Assembly, to the Members of the United Nations, and to the specialized agencies concerned.
2. It may make recommendations for the purpose of promoting respect for, and observance of, human rights and fundamental freedoms for all.

## Article 68

The Economic and Social Council shall set up commissions in economic and social fields and for the promotion of human rights, and such other commissions as may be required for the performance of its functions.

## Article 71

The Economic and Social Council may make suitable arrangements for consultation with non-governmental organizations which are concerned with matters within its competence. Such arrangements may be made with international organizations and, where appropriate, with national organizations after consultation with the Member of the United Nations concerned.

## Article 73

Members of the United Nations which have or assume responsibilities for the administration of territories whose peoples have not yet attained a full measure of self-government recognize the principle that the interests of the inhabitants of these territories are paramount, and accept as a sacred trust the obligation to promote to the utmost, within the system of international peace and security established by the present Charter, the well-being of the inhabitants of these territories, and, to this end:

   a. to ensure, with due respect for the culture of the peoples concerned, their political, economic, social, and educational advancement, their just treatment, and their protection against abuses;
   b. to develop self-government, to take due account of the political aspirations of the peoples, and to assist them in the progressive development of their free political institutions, according to the particular circumstances of each territory and its peoples and their varying stages of advancement;
   c. to further international peace and security;
   d. to promote constructive measures of development, to encourage research, and to cooperate with one another and, when and where appropriate, with specialized international bodies with a view to the practical achievement of the social, economic, and scientific purposes set forth in this Article; and
   e. to transmit regularly to the Secretary-General for information purposes, subject to such limitation as security and constitutional considerations may require, statistical and other information of a technical nature relating to economic, social, and educational conditions in the territories for which they are respectively responsible other than those territories to which Chapters XII and XIII apply.

## Article 74

Members of the United Nations also agree that their policy in respect of the territories to which this Chapter applies, no less than in respect of their metropolitan areas, must be based on the general principle of good-neighborliness, due account being taken of the interests and well-being of the rest of the world, in social, economic, and commercial matters.

## Article 93

1. All Members of the United Nations are ipso facto parties to the Statute of the International Court of Justice.
2. A state which is not a Member of the United Nations may become a party to the Statute of the International Court of Justice on conditions to be determined in each case by the General Assembly upon the recommendation of the Security Council.

## Article 103

In the event of a conflict between the obligations of the Members of the United Nations under the present Charter and their obligations under any other international agreement, their obligations under the present Charter shall prevail.[3]

## D. INTERNATIONAL COVENANT ON CIVIL AND POLITICAL RIGHTS (ICCPR)

Entry into force 4 January 1969, in accordance with Article 19
999 UNTS 171, entered into force March 23, 1976
United States ratified after Senate advice and consent April 2, 1992: 138 Cong. Rec. S4782.

## Preamble

The States Parties to the present Covenant,

Considering that, in accordance with the principles proclaimed in the Charter of the United Nations, recognition of the inherent dignity and of the equal and inalienable rights of all members of the human family is the foundation of freedom, justice and peace in the world,

Recognizing that these rights derive from the inherent dignity of the human person,

Recognizing that, in accordance with the Universal Declaration of Human Rights, the ideal of free human beings enjoying civil and political freedom and freedom from fear and want can only be achieved if conditions are created whereby everyone may enjoy his civil and political rights, as well as his economic, social and cultural rights,

Considering the obligation of States under the Charter of the United Nations to promote universal respect for, and observance of, human rights and freedoms,

Realizing that the individual, having duties to other individuals and to the community to which he belongs, is under a responsibility to strive for the promotion and observance of the rights recognized in the present Covenant,

Agree upon the following articles:

## PART I

### Article 1

1. All peoples have the right of self-determination. By virtue of that right they freely determine their political status and freely pursue their economic, social and cultural development.
2. All peoples may, for their own ends, freely dispose of their natural wealth and resources without prejudice to any obligations arising out of international economic co-operation, based upon the principle of mutual benefit, and international law. In no case may a people be deprived of its own means of subsistence.
3. The States Parties to the present Covenant, including those having responsibility for the administration of Non-Self-Governing and Trust Territories, shall promote the realization of the right of self-determination, and shall respect that right, in conformity with the provisions of the Charter of the United Nations.

## PART II

### Article 2

1. Each State Party to the present Covenant undertakes to respect and to ensure to all individuals within its territory and subject to its jurisdiction the rights recognized in the present Covenant, without distinction of any kind, such as race, colour, sex, language, religion, political or other opinion, national or social origin, property, birth or other status.
2. Where not already provided for by existing legislative or other measures, each State Party to the present Covenant undertakes to take the necessary steps, in accordance with its constitutional processes and

with the provisions of the present Covenant, to adopt such laws or other measures as may be necessary to give effect to the rights recognized in the present Covenant.

3. Each State Party to the present Covenant undertakes:
   (a) To ensure that any person whose rights or freedoms as herein recognized are violated shall have an effective remedy, notwithstanding that the violation has been committed by persons acting in an official capacity;
   (b) To ensure that any person claiming such a remedy shall have his right thereto determined by competent judicial, administrative or legislative authorities, or by any other competent authority provided for by the legal system of the State, and to develop the possibilities of judicial remedy;
   (c) To ensure that the competent authorities shall enforce such remedies when granted.

## Article 3

The States Parties to the present Covenant undertake to ensure the equal right of men and women to the enjoyment of all civil and political rights set forth in the present Covenant. General comment on its implementation.

## Article 4

1. In time of public emergency which threatens the life of the nation and the existence of which is officially proclaimed, the States Parties to the present Covenant may take measures derogating from their obligations under the present Covenant to the extent strictly required by the exigencies of the situation, provided that such measures are not inconsistent with their other obligations under international law and do not involve discrimination solely on the ground of race, colour, sex, language, religion or social origin.
2. No derogation from articles 6, 7, 8 (paragraphs I and 2), 11, 15, 16 and 18 may be made under this provision.
3. Any State Party to the present Covenant availing itself of the right of derogation shall immediately inform the other States Parties to the present Covenant, through the intermediary of the Secretary-General of the United Nations, of the provisions from which it has derogated and of the reasons by which it was actuated. A further communication shall be made, through the same intermediary, on the date on which it terminates such derogation. General comment on its implementation.

## Article 5

1. Nothing in the present Covenant may be interpreted as implying for any State, group or person any right to engage in any activity or perform any act aimed at the destruction of any of the rights and freedoms recognized herein or at their limitation to a greater extent than is provided for in the present Covenant.
2. There shall be no restriction upon or derogation from any of the fundamental human rights recognized or existing in any State Party to the present Covenant pursuant to law, conventions, regulations or custom on the pretext that the present Covenant does not recognize such rights or that it recognizes them to a lesser extent.

## PART III

## Article 6

1. Every human being has the inherent right to life. This right shall be protected by law. No one shall be arbitrarily deprived of his life.
2. In countries which have not abolished the death penalty, sentence of death may be imposed only for the most serious crimes in accordance with the law in force at the time of the commission of the crime and not contrary to the provisions of the present Covenant and to the Convention on the Prevention and Punishment of the Crime of Genocide. This penalty can only be carried out pursuant to a final judgement rendered by a competent court.
3. When deprivation of life constitutes the crime of genocide, it is understood that nothing in this article shall authorize any State Party to the present Covenant to derogate in any way from any obligation assumed under the provisions of the Convention on the Prevention and Punishment of the Crime of Genocide.
4. Anyone sentenced to death shall have the right to seek pardon or commutation of the sentence. Amnesty, pardon or commutation of the sentence of death may be granted in all cases.
5. Sentence of death shall not be imposed for crimes committed by persons below eighteen years of age and shall not be carried out on pregnant women.
6. Nothing in this article shall be invoked to delay or to prevent the abolition of capital punishment by any State Party to the present Covenant.

## Article 7

No one shall be subjected to torture or to cruel, inhuman or degrading treatment or punishment. In particular, no one shall be subjected without his free consent to medical or scientific experimentation.

## Article 8

1. No one shall be held in slavery; slavery and the slave-trade in all their forms shall be prohibited.
2. No one shall be held in servitude.
3. (a) No one shall be required to perform forced or compulsory labour;
   (b) Paragraph 3 (a) shall not be held to preclude, in countries where imprisonment with hard labour may be imposed as a punishment for a crime, the performance of hard labour in pursuance of a sentence to such punishment by a competent court;
   (c) For the purpose of this paragraph the term "forced or compulsory labour" shall not include:
      (i) Any work or service, not referred to in subparagraph (b), normally required of a person who is under detention in consequence of a lawful order of a court, or of a person during conditional release from such detention;
      (ii) Any service of a military character and, in countries where conscientious objection is recognized, any national service required by law of conscientious objectors;
      (iii) Any service exacted in cases of emergency or calamity threatening the life or well-being of the community;
      (iv) Any work or service which forms part of normal civil obligations.

## Article 9

1. Everyone has the right to liberty and security of person. No one shall be subjected to arbitrary arrest or detention. No one shall be deprived of his liberty except on such grounds and in accordance with such procedure as are established by law.
2. Anyone who is arrested shall be informed, at the time of arrest, of the reasons for his arrest and shall be promptly informed of any charges against him.
3. Anyone arrested or detained on a criminal charge shall be brought promptly before a judge or other officer authorized by law to exercise

judicial power and shall be entitled to trial within a reasonable time or to release. It shall not be the general rule that persons awaiting trial shall be detained in custody, but release may be subject to guarantees to appear for trial, at any other stage of the judicial proceedings, and, should occasion arise, for execution of the judgement.

4. Anyone who is deprived of his liberty by arrest or detention shall be entitled to take proceedings before a court, in order that court may decide without delay on the lawfulness of his detention and order his release if the detention is not lawful.
5. Anyone who has been the victim of unlawful arrest or detention shall have an enforceable right to compensation.

## Article 10

1. All persons deprived of their liberty shall be treated with humanity and with respect for the inherent dignity of the human person.
2. (a) Accused persons shall, save in exceptional circumstances, be segregated from convicted persons and shall be subject to separate treatment appropriate to their status as unconvicted persons;
   (b) Accused juvenile persons shall be separated from adults and brought as speedily as possible for adjudication.
3. The penitentiary system shall comprise treatment of prisoners the essential aim of which shall be their reformation and social rehabilitation. Juvenile offenders shall be segregated from adults and be accorded treatment appropriate to their age and legal status.

## Article 11

No one shall be imprisoned merely on the ground of inability to fulfil a contractual obligation.

## Article 12

1. Everyone lawfully within the territory of a State shall, within that territory, have the right to liberty of movement and freedom to choose his residence.
2. Everyone shall be free to leave any country, including his own.
3. The above-mentioned rights shall not be subject to any restrictions except those which are provided by law, are necessary to protect national security, public order (ordre public), public health or morals or the rights and freedoms of others, and are consistent with the other rights recognized in the present Covenant.

4. No one shall be arbitrarily deprived of the right to enter his own country.

## Article 13

An alien lawfully in the territory of a State Party to the present Covenant may be expelled therefrom only in pursuance of a decision reached in accordance with law and shall, except where compelling reasons of national security otherwise require, be allowed to submit the reasons against his expulsion and to have his case reviewed by, and be represented for the purpose before, the competent authority or a person or persons especially designated by the competent authority.

## Article 14

1. All persons shall be equal before the courts and tribunals. In the determination of any criminal charge against him, or of his rights and obligations in a suit at law, everyone shall be entitled to a fair and public hearing by a competent, independent and impartial tribunal established by law. The press and the public may be excluded from all or part of a trial for reasons of morals, public order (ordre public) or national security in a democratic society, or when the interest of the private lives of the parties so requires, or to the extent strictly necessary in the opinion of the court in special circumstances where publicity would prejudice the interests of justice; but any judgement rendered in a criminal case or in a suit at law shall be made public except where the interest of juvenile persons otherwise requires or the proceedings concern matrimonial disputes or the guardianship of children.
2. Everyone charged with a criminal offence shall have the right to be presumed innocent until proved guilty according to law.
3. In the determination of any criminal charge against him, everyone shall be entitled to the following minimum guarantees, in full equality:
   (a) To be informed promptly and in detail in a language which he understands of the nature and cause of the charge against him;
   (b) To have adequate time and facilities for the preparation of his defence and to communicate with counsel of his own choosing;
   (c) To be tried without undue delay;
   (d) To be tried in his presence, and to defend himself in person or through legal assistance of his own choosing; to be informed, if he does not have legal assistance, of this right; and to have legal assistance assigned to him, in any case where the interests of jus-

tice so require, and without payment by him in any such case if he does not have sufficient means to pay for it;

(e) To examine, or have examined, the witnesses against him and to obtain the attendance and examination of witnesses on his behalf under the same conditions as witnesses against him;

(f) To have the free assistance of an interpreter if he cannot understand or speak the language used in court;

(g) Not to be compelled to testify against himself or to confess guilt.

4. In the case of juvenile persons, the procedure shall be such as will take account of their age and the desirability of promoting their rehabilitation.

5. Everyone convicted of a crime shall have the right to his conviction and sentence being reviewed by a higher tribunal according to law.

6. When a person has by a final decision been convicted of a criminal offence and when subsequently his conviction has been reversed or he has been pardoned on the ground that a new or newly discovered fact shows conclusively that there has been a miscarriage of justice, the person who has suffered punishment as a result of such conviction shall be compensated according to law, unless it is proved that the non-disclosure of the unknown fact in time is wholly or partly attributable to him.

7. No one shall be liable to be tried or punished again for an offence for which he has already been finally convicted or acquitted in accordance with the law and penal procedure of each country.

## Article 15

1. No one shall be held guilty of any criminal offence on account of any act or omission which did not constitute a criminal offence, under national or international law, at the time when it was committed. Nor shall a heavier penalty be imposed than the one that was applicable at the time when the criminal offence was committed. If, subsequent to the commission of the offence, provision is made by law for the imposition of the lighter penalty, the offender shall benefit thereby.

2. Nothing in this article shall prejudice the trial and punishment of any person for any act or omission which, at the time when it was committed, was criminal according to the general principles of law recognized by the community of nations.

## Article 16

Everyone shall have the right to recognition everywhere as a person before the law.

## Article 17

1. No one shall be subjected to arbitrary or unlawful interference with his privacy, family, home or correspondence, nor to unlawful attacks on his honour and reputation.
2. Everyone has the right to the protection of the law against such interference or attacks.

## Article 18

1. Everyone shall have the right to freedom of thought, conscience and religion. This right shall include freedom to have or to adopt a religion or belief of his choice, and freedom, either individually or in community with others and in public or private, to manifest his religion or belief in worship, observance, practice and teaching.
2. No one shall be subject to coercion which would impair his freedom to have or to adopt a religion or belief of his choice.
3. Freedom to manifest one's religion or beliefs may be subject only to such limitations as are prescribed by law and are necessary to protect public safety, order, health, or morals or the fundamental rights and freedoms of others.
4. The States Parties to the present Covenant undertake to have respect for the liberty of parents and, when applicable, legal guardians to ensure the religious and moral education of their children in conformity with their own convictions.

## Article 19

1. Everyone shall have the right to hold opinions without interference.
2. Everyone shall have the right to freedom of expression; this right shall include freedom to seek, receive and impart information and ideas of all kinds, regardless of frontiers, either orally, in writing or in print, in the form of art, or through any other media of his choice.
3. The exercise of the rights provided for in paragraph 2 of this article carries with it special duties and responsibilities. It may therefore be subject to certain restrictions, but these shall only be such as are provided by law and are necessary:

(a) For respect of the rights or reputations of others;
(b) For the protection of national security or of public order (ordre public), or of public health or morals.

## Article 20

1. Any propaganda for war shall be prohibited by law.
2. Any advocacy of national, racial or religious hatred that constitutes incitement to discrimination, hostility or violence shall be prohibited by law.

## Article 21

The right of peaceful assembly shall be recognized. No restrictions may be placed on the exercise of this right other than those imposed in conformity with the law and which are necessary in a democratic society in the interests of national security or public safety, public order (ordre public), the protection of public health or morals or the protection of the rights and freedoms of others.

## Article 22

1. Everyone shall have the right to freedom of association with others, including the right to form and join trade unions for the protection of his interests.
2. No restrictions may be placed on the exercise of this right other than those which are prescribed by law and which are necessary in a democratic society in the interests of national security or public safety, public order (ordre public), the protection of public health or morals or the protection of the rights and freedoms of others. This article shall not prevent the imposition of lawful restrictions on members of the armed forces and of the police in their exercise of this right.
3. Nothing in this article shall authorize States Parties to the International Labour Organisation Convention of 1948 concerning Freedom of Association and Protection of the Right to Organize to take legislative measures which would prejudice, or to apply the law in such a manner as to prejudice, the guarantees provided for in that Convention.

## Article 23

1. The family is the natural and fundamental group unit of society and is entitled to protection by society and the State.
2. The right of men and women of marriageable age to marry and to found a family shall be recognized.
3. No marriage shall be entered into without the free and full consent of the intending spouses.
4. States Parties to the present Covenant shall take appropriate steps to ensure equality of rights and responsibilities of spouses as to marriage, during marriage and at its dissolution. In the case of dissolution, provision shall be made for the necessary protection of any children.

## Article 24

1. Every child shall have, without any discrimination as to race, colour, sex, language, religion, national or social origin, property or birth, the right to such measures of protection as are required by his status as a minor, on the part of his family, society and the State.
2. Every child shall be registered immediately after birth and shall have a name.
3. Every child has the right to acquire a nationality.

## Article 25

Every citizen shall have the right and the opportunity, without any of the distinctions mentioned in article 2 and without unreasonable restrictions:

(a) To take part in the conduct of public affairs, directly or through freely chosen representatives;
(b) To vote and to be elected at genuine periodic elections which shall be by universal and equal suffrage and shall be held by secret ballot, guaranteeing the free expression of the will of the electors;
(c) To have access, on general terms of equality, to public service in his country.

## Article 26

All persons are equal before the law and are entitled without any discrimination to the equal protection of the law. In this respect, the law shall prohibit any discrimination and guarantee to all persons equal and effective protection against discrimination on any ground such as race, colour, sex, language, religion, political or other opinion, national or social origin, property, birth or other status.

## Article 27

In those States in which ethnic, religious or linguistic minorities exist, persons belonging to such minorities shall not be denied the right, in community with the other members of their group, to enjoy their own culture, to profess and practise their own religion, or to use their own language.

## PART IV

## Article 41

1. A State Party to the present Covenant may at any time declare under this article that it recognizes the competence of the Committee to receive and consider communications to the effect that a State Party claims that another State Party is not fulfilling its obligations under the present Covenant. Communications under this article may be received and considered only if submitted by a State Party which has made a declaration recognizing in regard to itself the competence of the Committee. No communication shall be received by the Committee if it concerns a State Party which has not made such a declaration. Communications received under this article shall be dealt with in accordance with the following procedure:

   (a) If a State Party to the present Covenant considers that another State Party is not giving effect to the provisions of the present Covenant, it may, by written communication, bring the matter to the attention of that State Party. Within three months after the receipt of the communication the receiving State shall afford the State which sent the communication an explanation, or any other statement in writing clarifying the matter which should include, to the extent possible and pertinent, reference to domestic procedures and remedies taken, pending, or available in the matter;

   (b) If the matter is not adjusted to the satisfaction of both States Parties concerned within six months after the receipt by the receiving State of the initial communication, either State shall have the right to refer the matter to the Committee, by notice given to the Committee and to the other State;

(c) The Committee shall deal with a matter referred to it only after it has ascertained that all available domestic remedies have been invoked and exhausted in the matter, in conformity with the generally recognized principles of international law. This shall not be the rule where the application of the remedies is unreasonably prolonged;

(d) The Committee shall hold closed meetings when examining communications under this article;

(e) Subject to the provisions of subparagraph (c), the Committee shall make available its good offices to the States Parties concerned with a view to a friendly solution of the matter on the basis of respect for human rights and fundamental freedoms as recognized in the present Covenant;

(f) In any matter referred to it, the Committee may call upon the States Parties concerned, referred to in subparagraph (b), to supply any relevant information;

(g) The States Parties concerned, referred to in subparagraph (b), shall have the right to be represented when the matter is being considered in the Committee and to make submissions orally and/or in writing;

(h) The Committee shall, within twelve months after the date of receipt of notice under subparagraph (b), submit a report:

( i) If a solution within the terms of subparagraph (e) is reached, the Committee shall confine its report to a brief statement of the facts and of the solution reached;

(ii) If a solution within the terms of subparagraph (e) is not reached, the Committee shall confine its report to a brief statement of the facts; the written submissions and record of the oral submissions made by the States Parties concerned shall be attached to the report. In every matter, the report shall be communicated to the States Parties concerned.

2. The provisions of this article shall come into force when ten States Parties to the present Covenant have made declarations under paragraph I of this article. Such declarations shall be deposited by the States Parties with the Secretary-General of the United Nations, who shall transmit copies thereof to the other States Parties. A declaration may be withdrawn at any time by notification to the Secretary-General. Such a withdrawal shall not prejudice the consideration of any matter which is the subject of a communication already transmitted under this article; no further communication by any State Party shall be received after the notification of withdrawal of the declaration has been received by the Secretary-General, unless the State Party concerned has made a new declaration.

## Article 42

1. (a) If a matter referred to the Committee in accordance with article 41 is not resolved to the satisfaction of the States Parties concerned, the Committee may, with the prior consent of the States Parties concerned, appoint an ad hoc Conciliation Commission (hereinafter referred to as the Commission). The good offices of the Commission shall be made available to the States Parties concerned with a view to an amicable solution of the matter on the basis of respect for the present Covenant;

   (b) The Commission shall consist of five persons acceptable to the States Parties concerned. If the States Parties concerned fail to reach agreement within three months on all or part of the composition of the Commission, the members of the Commission concerning whom no agreement has been reached shall be elected by secret ballot by a two-thirds majority vote of the Committee from among its members.

2. The members of the Commission shall serve in their personal capacity. They shall not be nationals of the States Parties concerned, or of a State not Party to the present Covenant, or of a State Party which has not made a declaration under article 41.

3. The Commission shall elect its own Chairman and adopt its own rules of procedure.

4. The meetings of the Commission shall normally be held at the Headquarters of the United Nations or at the United Nations Office at Geneva. However, they may be held at such other convenient places as the Commission may determine in consultation with the Secretary-General of the United Nations and the States Parties concerned.

5. The secretariat provided in accordance with article 36 shall also service the commissions appointed under this article.

6. The information received and collated by the Committee shall be made available to the Commission and the Commission may call upon the States Parties concerned to supply any other relevant information.

7. When the Commission has fully considered the matter, but in any event not later than twelve months after having been seized of the matter, it shall submit to the Chairman of the Committee a report for communication to the States Parties concerned:

   (a) If the Commission is unable to complete its consideration of the matter within twelve months, it shall confine its report to a brief statement of the status of its consideration of the matter;

(b) If an amicable solution to the matter on the basis of respect for human rights as recognized in the present Covenant is reached, the Commission shall confine its report to a brief statement of the facts and of the solution reached;

(c) If a solution within the terms of subparagraph (b) is not reached, the Commission's report shall embody its findings on all questions of fact relevant to the issues between the States Parties concerned, and its views on the possibilities of an amicable solution of the matter. This report shall also contain the written submissions and a record of the oral submissions made by the States Parties concerned;

(d) If the Commission's report is submitted under subparagraph (c), the States Parties concerned shall, within three months of the receipt of the report, notify the Chairman of the Committee whether or not they accept the contents of the report of the Commission.

8. The provisions of this article are without prejudice to the responsibilities of the Committee under article 41.

9. The States Parties concerned shall share equally all the expenses of the members of the Commission in accordance with estimates to be provided by the Secretary-General of the United Nations.

10. The Secretary-General of the United Nations shall be empowered to pay the expenses of the members of the Commission, if necessary, before reimbursement by the States Parties concerned, in accordance with paragraph 9 of this article.

## Article 44

The provisions for the implementation of the present Covenant shall apply without prejudice to the procedures prescribed in the field of human rights by or under the constituent instruments and the conventions of the United Nations and of the specialized agencies and shall not prevent the States Parties to the present Covenant from having recourse to other procedures for settling a dispute in accordance with general or special international agreements in force between them.

## Article 45

The Committee shall submit to the General Assembly of the United Nations, through the Economic and Social Council, an annual report on its activities.

## PART V

### Article 47

Nothing in the present Covenant shall be interpreted as impairing the inherent right of all peoples to enjoy and utilize fully and freely their natural wealth and resources.[4]

## E. CONVENTION ON THE ELIMINATION OF ALL FORMS OF RACIAL DISCRIMINATION (CERD)

Entry into force 4 January 1969, in accordance with Article 19 under CONVENTION ON ELIMINATION OF RACIAL DISCRIMINATION

660 UNTS 195 (1966)

US ratified after Senate advice and consent June 24, 1994: 140 Cong. Rec. S7634 (1994)

The States Parties to this Convention,

Considering that the Charter of the United Nations is based on the principles of the dignity and equality inherent in all human beings, and that all Member States have pledged themselves to take joint and separate action, in co-operation with the Organization, for the achievement of one of the purposes of the United Nations which is to promote and encourage universal respect for and observance of human rights and fundamental freedoms for all, without distinction as to race, sex, language or religion,

Considering that the Universal Declaration of Human Rights proclaims that all human beings are born free and equal in dignity and rights and that everyone is entitled to all the rights and freedoms set out therein, without distinction of any kind, in particular as to race, colour or national origin,

Considering that all human beings are equal before the law and are entitled to equal protection of the law against any discrimination and against any incitement to discrimination,

Considering that the United Nations has condemned colonialism and all practices of segregation and discrimination associated therewith, in whatever form and wherever they exist, and that the Declaration on the Granting of Independence to Colonial Countries and Peoples of 14 December 1960 (General Assembly resolution 1514 [XV]) has affirmed and solemnly proclaimed the necessity of bringing them to a speedy and unconditional end,

Considering that the United Nations Declaration on the Elimination of All Forms of Racial Discrimination of 20 November 1963 (General Assembly resolution 1904 [XVIII]) solemnly affirms the necessity of speedily eliminating racial discrimination throughout the world in all its forms and manifestations and of securing understanding of and respect for the dignity of the human person,

Convinced that any doctrine of superiority based on racial differentiation is scientifically false, morally condemnable, socially unjust and dangerous, and that there is no justification for racial discrimination, in theory or in practice, anywhere,

Reaffirming that discrimination between human beings on the grounds of race, colour or ethnic origin is an obstacle to friendly and peaceful relations among nations and is capable of disturbing peace and security among peoples and the harmony of persons living side by side even within one and the same State,

Convinced that the existence of racial barriers is repugnant to the ideals of any human society,

Alarmed by manifestations of racial discrimination still in evidence in some areas of the world and by governmental policies based on racial superiority or hatred, such as policies of apartheid, segregation or separation,

Resolved to adopt all necessary measures for speedily eliminating racial discrimination in all its forms and manifestations, and to prevent and combat racist doctrines and practices in order to promote understanding between races and to build an international community free from all forms of racial segregation and racial discrimination,

Bearing in mind the Convention concerning Discrimination in respect of Employment and Occupation adopted by the International Labour Organisation in 1958, and the Convention against Discrimination in Education adopted by the United Nations Educational, Scientific and Cultural Organization in 1960,

Desiring to implement the principles embodied in the United Nations Declaration on the Elimination of All Forms of Racial Discrimination and to secure the earliest adoption of practical measures to that end,

Have agreed as follows:

## PART I

### Article 1

1. In this Convention, the term "racial discrimination" shall mean any distinction, exclusion, restriction or preference based on race, colour, descent, or national or ethnic origin which has the purpose or effect of nullifying or impairing the recognition, enjoyment or exercise, on an equal footing, of human rights and fundamental freedoms in the political, economic, social, cultural or any other field of public life.
2. This Convention shall not apply to distinctions, exclusions, restrictions or preferences made by a State Party to this Convention between citizens and non-citizens.
3. Nothing in this Convention may be interpreted as affecting in any way the legal provisions of States Parties concerning nationality, citizenship or naturalization, provided that such provisions do not discriminate against any particular nationality.
4. Special measures taken for the sole purpose of securing adequate advancement of certain racial or ethnic groups or individuals requiring such protection as may be necessary in order to ensure such groups or individuals equal enjoyment or exercise of human rights and fundamental freedoms shall not be deemed racial discrimination, provided, however, that such measures do not, as a consequence, lead to the maintenance of separate rights for different racial groups and that they shall not be continued after the objectives for which they were taken have been achieved.

### Article 2

1. States Parties condemn racial discrimination and undertake to pursue by all appropriate means and without delay a policy of eliminating racial discrimination in all its forms and promoting understanding among all races, and, to this end:
   (a) Each State Party undertakes to engage in no act or practice of racial discrimination against persons, groups of persons or institutions and to ensure that all public authorities and public institutions, national and local, shall act in conformity with this obligation;
   (b) Each State Party undertakes not to sponsor, defend or support racial discrimination by any persons or organizations;

    (c) Each State Party shall take effective measures to review govern-
mental, national and local policies, and to amend, rescind or nul-
lify any laws and regulations which have the effect of creating or
perpetuating racial discrimination wherever it exists;

    (d) Each State Party shall prohibit and bring to an end, by all appro-
priate means, including legislation as required by circumstances,
racial discrimination by any persons, group or organization;

    (e) Each State Party undertakes to encourage, where appropriate,
integrationist multiracial organizations and movements and
other means of eliminating barriers between races, and to discourage anything which tends to strengthen racial division.

2. States Parties shall, when the circumstances so warrant, take, in the
social, economic, cultural and other fields, special and concrete measures to ensure the adequate development and protection of certain
racial groups or individuals belonging to them, for the purpose of
guaranteeing them the full and equal enjoyment of human rights and
fundamental freedoms. These measures shall in no case entail as a
consequence the maintenance of unequal or separate rights for different racial groups after the objectives for which they were taken
have been achieved.

## Article 3

States Parties particularly condemn racial segregation and apartheid and
undertake to prevent, prohibit and eradicate all practices of this nature in territories under their jurisdiction.

## Article 4

States Parties condemn all propaganda and all organizations which are based
on ideas or theories of superiority of one race or group of persons of one
colour or ethnic origin, or which attempt to justify or promote racial hatred
and discrimination in any form, and undertake to adopt immediate and pos-
itive measures designed to eradicate all incitement to, or acts of, such discrimination and, to this end, with due regard to the principles embodied in
the Universal Declaration of Human Rights and the rights expressly set forth
in article 5 of this Convention, inter alia:

    (a) Shall declare an offence punishable by law all dissemination of ideas
based on racial superiority or hatred, incitement to racial discrimination, as well as all acts of violence or incitement to such acts against
any race or group of persons of another colour or ethnic origin, and

also the provision of any assistance to racist activities, including the financing thereof;

(b) Shall declare illegal and prohibit organizations, and also organized and all other propaganda activities, which promote and incite racial discrimination, and shall recognize participation in such organizations or activities as an offence punishable by law;

(c) Shall not permit public authorities or public institutions, national or local, to promote or incite racial discrimination.

## Article 5

In compliance with the fundamental obligations laid down in article 2 of this Convention, States Parties undertake to prohibit and to eliminate racial discrimination in all its forms and to guarantee the right of everyone, without distinction as to race, colour, or national or ethnic origin, to equality before the law, notably in the enjoyment of the following rights:

(a) The right to equal treatment before the tribunals and all other organs administering justice;

(b) The right to security of person and protection by the State against violence or bodily harm, whether inflicted by government officials or by any individual group or institution;

(c) Political rights, in particular the right to participate in elections—to vote and to stand for election—on the basis of universal and equal suffrage, to take part in the Government as well as in the conduct of public affairs at any level and to have equal access to public service;

(d) Other civil rights, in particular:

   (i) The right to freedom of movement and residence within the border of the State;

   (ii) The right to leave any country, including one's own, and to return to one's country;

   (iii) The right to nationality;

   (iv) The right to marriage and choice of spouse;

   (v) The right to own property alone as well as in association with others;

   (vi) The right to inherit;

   (vii) The right to freedom of thought, conscience and religion;

   (viii) The right to freedom of opinion and expression;

   (ix) The right to freedom of peaceful assembly and association;

(e) Economic, social and cultural rights, in particular:

   (i) The rights to work, to free choice of employment, to just and favourable conditions of work, to protection against unemployment, to equal pay for equal work, to just and favourable remuneration;

(ii)   The right to form and join trade unions;

(iii)   The right to housing;

(iv)   The right to public health, medical care, social security and social services;

(v)   The right to education and training;

(vi)   The right to equal participation in cultural activities;

(f) The right of access to any place or service intended for use by the general public, such as transport hotels, restaurants, cafes, theatres and parks.

## Article 6

States Parties shall assure to everyone within their jurisdiction effective protection and remedies, through the competent national tribunals and other State institutions, against any acts of racial discrimination which violate his human rights and fundamental freedoms contrary to this Convention, as well as the right to seek from such tribunals just and adequate reparation or satisfaction for any damage suffered as a result of such discrimination.

## Article 7

States Parties undertake to adopt immediate and effective measures, particularly in the fields of teaching, education, culture and information, with a view to combating prejudices which lead to racial discrimination and to promoting understanding, tolerance and friendship among nations and racial or ethnical groups, as well as to propagating the purposes and principles of the Charter of the United Nations, the Universal Declaration of Human Rights, the United Nations Declaration on the Elimination of All Forms of Racial Discrimination, and this Convention.

## PART II

## Article 8

1. There shall be established a Committee on the Elimination of Racial Discrimination (hereinafter referred to as the Committee) consisting of eighteen experts of high moral standing and acknowledged impartiality elected by States Parties from among their nationals, who shall serve in their personal capacity, consideration being given to equi-

table geographical distribution and to the representation of the different forms of civilization as well as of the principal legal systems.

2. The members of the Committee shall be elected by secret ballot from a list of persons nominated by the States Parties. Each State Party may nominate one person from among its own nationals.

3. The initial election shall be held six months after the date of the entry into force of this Convention. At least three months before the date of each election the Secretary-General of the United Nations shall address a letter to the States Parties inviting them to submit their nominations within two months. The Secretary-General shall prepare a list in alphabetical order of all persons thus nominated, indicating the States Parties which have nominated them, and shall submit it to the States Parties.

4. Elections of the members of the Committee shall be held at a meeting of States Parties convened by the Secretary-General at United Nations Headquarters. At that meeting, for which two thirds of the States Parties shall constitute a quorum, the persons elected to the Committee shall be nominees who obtain the largest number of votes and an absolute majority of the votes of the representatives of States Parties present and voting.

5. (a) The members of the Committee shall be elected for a term of four years. However, the terms of nine of the members elected at the first election shall expire at the end of two years; immediately after the first election the names of these nine members shall be chosen by lot by the Chairman of the Committee;

   (b) For the filling of casual vacancies, the State Party whose expert has ceased to function as a member of the Committee shall appoint another expert from among its nationals, subject to the approval of the Committee.

6. States Parties shall be responsible for the expenses of the members of the Committee while they are in performance of Committee duties. (amendment [see General Assembly resolution 47/111 of 16 December 1992]; status of ratification)

## Article 9

1. States Parties undertake to submit to the Secretary-General of the United Nations, for consideration by the Committee, a report on the legislative, judicial, administrative or other measures which they have adopted and which give effect to the provisions of this Convention:

   (a) within one year after the entry into force of the Convention for the State concerned; and

(b) thereafter every two years and whenever the Committee so requests. The Committee may request further information from the States Parties.

2. The Committee shall report annually, through the Secretary-General, to the General Assembly of the United Nations on its activities and may make suggestions and general recommendations based on the examination of the reports and information received from the States Parties. Such suggestions and general recommendations shall be reported to the General Assembly together with comments, if any, from States Parties.[5]

## F. CONVENTION AGAINST TORTURE AND OTHER CRUEL, INHUMAN, OR DEGRADING TREATMENT OR PUNISHMENT (CAT)

Entry into force 26 June 1987, in accordance with article 27 (1)

Convention Against Torture
1465 UNTS 85
US completed ratification 1994 after Senate advice and consent: 136 Cong. Rec. S17491-2 (Oct. 2, 1990)

Implementation of the Convention Against Torture (8 C.F.R. sec 208.18)

The States Parties to this Convention,

Considering that, in accordance with the principles proclaimed in the Charter of the United Nations, recognition of the equal and inalienable rights of all members of the human family is the foundation of freedom, justice and peace in the world,

Recognizing that those rights derive from the inherent dignity of the human person,

Considering the obligation of States under the Charter, in particular Article 55, to promote universal respect for, and observance of, human rights and fundamental freedoms,

Having regard to article 5 of the Universal Declaration of Human Rights and article 7 of the International Covenant on Civil and Political Rights, both of which provide that no one shall be subjected to torture or to cruel, inhuman or degrading treatment or punishment,

Having regard also to the Declaration on the Protection of All Persons from Being Subjected to Torture and Other Cruel, Inhuman or Degrading Treatment or Punishment, adopted by the General Assembly on 9 December 1975,

Desiring to make more effective the struggle against torture and other cruel, inhuman or degrading treatment or punishment throughout the world,

Have agreed as follows:

# PART I

## Article 1

1. For the purposes of this Convention, the term "torture" means any act by which severe pain or suffering, whether physical or mental, is intentionally inflicted on a person for such purposes as obtaining from him or a third person information or a confession, punishing him for an act he or a third person has committed or is suspected of having committed, or intimidating or coercing him or a third person, or for any reason based on discrimination of any kind, when such pain or suffering is inflicted by or at the instigation of or with the consent or acquiescence of a public official or other person acting in an official capacity. It does not include pain or suffering arising only from, inherent in or incidental to lawful sanctions.
2. This article is without prejudice to any international instrument or national legislation which does or may contain provisions of wider application.

## Article 2

1. Each State Party shall take effective legislative, administrative, judicial or other measures to prevent acts of torture in any territory under its jurisdiction.
2. No exceptional circumstances whatsoever, whether a state of war or a threat of war, internal political instability or any other public emergency, may be invoked as a justification of torture.
3. An order from a superior officer or a public authority may not be invoked as a justification of torture.

## Article 3

1. No State Party shall expel, return ("refouler") or extradite a person to another State where there are substantial grounds for believing that he would be in danger of being subjected to torture.
2. For the purpose of determining whether there are such grounds, the competent authorities shall take into account all relevant considerations including, where applicable, the existence in the State concerned of a consistent pattern of gross, flagrant or mass violations of human rights.

## Article 4

1. Each State Party shall ensure that all acts of torture are offences under its criminal law. The same shall apply to an attempt to commit torture and to an act by any person which constitutes complicity or participation in torture.
2. Each State Party shall make these offences punishable by appropriate penalties which take into account their grave nature.

## Article 5

1. Each State Party shall take such measures as may be necessary to establish its jurisdiction over the offences referred to in article 4 in the following cases:
    (a) When the offences are committed in any territory under its jurisdiction or on board a ship or aircraft registered in that State;
    (b) When the alleged offender is a national of that State;
    (c) When the victim is a national of that State if that State considers it appropriate.
2. Each State Party shall likewise take such measures as may be necessary to establish its jurisdiction over such offences in cases where the alleged offender is present in any territory under its jurisdiction and it does not extradite him pursuant to article 8 to any of the States mentioned in paragraph I of this article.
3. This Convention does not exclude any criminal jurisdiction exercised in accordance with internal law.

## Article 6

1. Upon being satisfied, after an examination of information available to it, that the circumstances so warrant, any State Party in whose terri-

tory a person alleged to have committed any offence referred to in article 4 is present shall take him into custody or take other legal measures to ensure his presence. The custody and other legal measures shall be as provided in the law of that State but may be continued only for such time as is necessary to enable any criminal or extradition proceedings to be instituted.

2. Such State shall immediately make a preliminary inquiry into the facts.

3. Any person in custody pursuant to paragraph I of this article shall be assisted in communicating immediately with the nearest appropriate representative of the State of which he is a national, or, if he is a stateless person, with the representative of the State where he usually resides.

4. When a State, pursuant to this article, has taken a person into custody, it shall immediately notify the States referred to in article 5, paragraph 1, of the fact that such person is in custody and of the circumstances which warrant his detention. The State which makes the preliminary inquiry contemplated in paragraph 2 of this article shall promptly report its findings to the said States and shall indicate whether it intends to exercise jurisdiction.

## Article 7

1. The State Party in the territory under whose jurisdiction a person alleged to have committed any offence referred to in article 4 is found shall in the cases contemplated in article 5, if it does not extradite him, submit the case to its competent authorities for the purpose of prosecution.

2. These authorities shall take their decision in the same manner as in the case of any ordinary offence of a serious nature under the law of that State. In the cases referred to in article 5, paragraph 2, the standards of evidence required for prosecution and conviction shall in no way be less stringent than those which apply in the cases referred to in article 5, paragraph 1.

3. Any person regarding whom proceedings are brought in connection with any of the offences referred to in article 4 shall be guaranteed fair treatment at all stages of the proceedings.

## Article 8

1. The offences referred to in article 4 shall be deemed to be included as extraditable offences in any extradition treaty existing between

States Parties. States Parties undertake to include such offences as extraditable offences in every extradition treaty to be concluded between them.

2. If a State Party which makes extradition conditional on the existence of a treaty receives a request for extradition from another State Party with which it has no extradition treaty, it may consider this Convention as the legal basis for extradition in respect of such offences. Extradition shall be subject to the other conditions provided by the law of the requested State.

3. States Parties which do not make extradition conditional on the existence of a treaty shall recognize such offences as extraditable offences between themselves subject to the conditions provided by the law of the requested State.

4. Such offences shall be treated, for the purpose of extradition between States Parties, as if they had been committed not only in the place in which they occurred but also in the territories of the States required to establish their jurisdiction in accordance with article 5, paragraph 1.

## Article 9

1. States Parties shall afford one another the greatest measure of assistance in connection with criminal proceedings brought in respect of any of the offences referred to in article 4, including the supply of all evidence at their disposal necessary for the proceedings.

2. States Parties shall carry out their obligations under paragraph 1 of this article in conformity with any treaties on mutual judicial assistance that may exist between them.

## Article 10

1. Each State Party shall ensure that education and information regarding the prohibition against torture are fully included in the training of law enforcement personnel, civil or military, medical personnel, public officials and other persons who may be involved in the custody, interrogation or treatment of any individual subjected to any form of arrest, detention or imprisonment.

2. Each State Party shall include this prohibition in the rules or instructions issued in regard to the duties and functions of any such person.

## Article 11

Each State Party shall keep under systematic review interrogation rules, instructions, methods and practices as well as arrangements for the custody and treatment of persons subjected to any form of arrest, detention or imprisonment in any territory under its jurisdiction, with a view to preventing any cases of torture.

## Article 12

Each State Party shall ensure that its competent authorities proceed to a prompt and impartial investigation, wherever there is reasonable ground to believe that an act of torture has been committed in any territory under its jurisdiction.

## Article 13

Each State Party shall ensure that any individual who alleges he has been subjected to torture in any territory under its jurisdiction has the right to complain to, and to have his case promptly and impartially examined by, its competent authorities. Steps shall be taken to ensure that the complainant and witnesses are protected against all ill-treatment or intimidation as a consequence of his complaint or any evidence given.

## Article 14

1. Each State Party shall ensure in its legal system that the victim of an act of torture obtains redress and has an enforceable right to fair and adequate compensation, including the means for as full rehabilitation as possible. In the event of the death of the victim as a result of an act of torture, his dependants shall be entitled to compensation.
2. Nothing in this article shall affect any right of the victim or other persons to compensation which may exist under national law.

## Article 15

Each State Party shall ensure that any statement which is established to have been made as a result of torture shall not be invoked as evidence in any proceedings, except against a person accused of torture as evidence that the statement was made.

**Article 16**

1. Each State Party shall undertake to prevent in any territory under its jurisdiction other acts of cruel, inhuman or degrading treatment or punishment which do not amount to torture as defined in article 1, when such acts are committed by or at the instigation of or with the consent or acquiescence of a public official or other person acting in an official capacity. In particular, the obligations contained in articles 10, 11, 12 and 13 shall apply with the substitution for references to torture of references to other forms of cruel, inhuman or degrading treatment or punishment.
2. The provisions of this Convention are without prejudice to the provisions of any other international instrument or national law which prohibits cruel, inhuman or degrading treatment or punishment or which relates to extradition or expulsion.[6]

## G. THE NUREMBERG PRINCIPLES

*Principles of International Law Recognized in the Charter of the Nürnberg Tribunal and in the Judgment of the Tribunal, 1950*

### Principle I

Any person who commits an act which constitutes a crime under international law is responsible therefor and liable to punishment.

### Principle II

The fact that internal law does not impose a penalty for an act which constitutes a crime under international law does not relieve the person who committed the act from responsibility under international law.

### Principle III

The fact that a person who committed an act which constitutes a crime under international law acted as Head of State or responsible Government official does not relieve him from responsibility under international law.

## Principle IV

The fact that a person acted pursuant to order of his Government or of a superior does not relieve him from responsibility under international law, provided a moral choice was in fact possible to him.

## Principle V

Any person charged with a crime under international law has the right to a fair trial on the facts and law.

## Principle VI

The crimes hereinafter set out are punishable as crimes under international law:

a)  Crimes against peace:
   (i)  Planning, preparation, initiation or waging of a war of aggression or a war in violation of international treaties, agreements or assurances;
   (ii)  Participation in a common plan or conspiracy for the accomplishment of any of the acts mentioned under (i).
b)  War crimes: Violations of the laws or customs of war which include, but are not limited to, murder, ill-treatment or deportation to slave-labour or for any other purpose of civilian population of or in occupied territory; murder or ill-treatment of prisoners of war, of persons on the Seas, killing of hostages, plunder of public or private property, wanton destruction of cities, towns, or villages, or devastation not justified by military necessity.
c)  Crimes against humanity: Murder, extermination, enslavement, deportation and other inhuman acts done against any civilian population, or persecutions on political, racial or religious grounds, when such acts are done or such persecutions are carried on in execution of or in connection with any crime against peace or any war crime.

## Principle VII

Complicity in the commission of a crime against peace, a war crime, or a crime against humanity as set forth in Principle VI is a crime under international law.[7]

# H. NUCLEAR NON-PROLIFERATION TREATY

Signed at Washington, London, and Moscow July 1, 1968
Ratification advised by US Senate March 13, 1969
Ratified by US President November 24, 1969
US ratification deposited at Washington, London, and Moscow
    March 5, 1970
Proclaimed by US President March 5, 1970
Entered into force March 5, 1970

The States concluding this Treaty, hereinafter referred to as the "Parties to the Treaty,"

Considering the devastation that would be visited upon all mankind by a nuclear war and the consequent need to make every effort to avert the danger of such a war and to take measures to safeguard the security of peoples,

Believing that the proliferation of nuclear weapons would seriously enhance the danger of nuclear war,

In conformity with resolutions of the United Nations General Assembly calling for the conclusion of an agreement on the prevention of wider dissemination of nuclear weapons,

Undertaking to cooperate in facilitating the application of International Atomic Energy Agency safeguards on peaceful nuclear activities,

Expressing their support for research, development and other efforts to further the application, within the framework of the International Atomic Energy Agency safeguards system, of the principle of safeguarding effectively the flow of source and special fissionable materials by use of instruments and other techniques at certain strategic points,

Affirming the principle that the benefits of peaceful applications of nuclear technology, including any technological by-products which may be derived by nuclear-weapon States from the development of nuclear explosive devices, should be available for peaceful purposes to all Parties of the Treaty, whether nuclear-weapon or non-nuclear weapon States,

Convinced that, in furtherance of this principle, all Parties to the Treaty are entitled to participate in the fullest possible exchange of scientific information for, and to contribute alone or in cooperation with other States to, the further development of the applications of atomic energy for peaceful purposes,

Declaring their intention to achieve at the earliest possible date the cessation of the nuclear arms race and to undertake effective measures in the direction of nuclear disarmament,

Urging the cooperation of all States in the attainment of this objective,

Recalling the determination expressed by the Parties to the 1963 Treaty banning nuclear weapon tests in the atmosphere, in outer space and under water in its Preamble to seek to achieve the discontinuance of all test explosions of nuclear weapons for all time and to continue negotiations to this end,

Desiring to further the easing of international tension and the strengthening of trust between States in order to facilitate the cessation of the manufacture of nuclear weapons, the liquidation of all their existing stockpiles, and the elimination from national arsenals of nuclear weapons and the means of their delivery pursuant to a Treaty on general and complete disarmament under strict and effective international control,

Recalling that, in accordance with the Charter of the United Nations, States must refrain in their international relations from the threat or use of force against the territorial integrity or political independence of any State, or in any other manner inconsistent with the Purposes of the United Nations, and that the establishment and maintenance of international peace and security are to be promoted with the least diversion for armaments of the worlds human and economic resources,

Have agreed as follows:

## Article I

Each nuclear-weapon State Party to the Treaty undertakes not to transfer to any recipient whatsoever nuclear weapons or other nuclear explosive devices or control over such weapons or explosive devices directly, or indirectly; and not in any way to assist, encourage, or induce any non-nuclear weapon State to manufacture or otherwise acquire nuclear weapons or other nuclear explosive devices, or control over such weapons or explosive devices.

## Article II

Each non-nuclear-weapon State Party to the Treaty undertakes not to receive the transfer from any transferor whatsoever of nuclear weapons or other nuclear explosive devices or of control over such weapons or explosive devices directly, or indirectly; not to manufacture or otherwise acquire nuclear weapons or other nuclear explosive devices; and not to seek or receive any assistance in the manufacture of nuclear weapons or other nuclear explosive devices.

## Article III

1. Each non-nuclear-weapon State Party to the Treaty undertakes to accept safeguards, as set forth in an agreement to be negotiated and concluded with the International Atomic Energy Agency in accordance with the Statute of the International Atomic Energy Agency and the Agencys safeguards system, for the exclusive purpose of verification of the fulfillment of its obligations assumed under this Treaty with a view to preventing diversion of nuclear energy from peaceful uses to nuclear weapons or other nuclear explosive devices. Procedures for the safeguards required by this article shall be followed with respect to source or special fissionable material whether it is being produced, processed or used in any principal nuclear facility or is outside any such facility. The safeguards required by this article shall be applied to all source or special fissionable material in all peaceful nuclear activities within the territory of such State, under its jurisdiction, or carried out under its control anywhere.
2. Each State Party to the Treaty undertakes not to provide: (a) source or special fissionable material, or (b) equipment or material especially designed or prepared for the processing, use or production of special fissionable material, to any non-nuclear-weapon State for peaceful purposes, unless the source or special fissionable material shall be subject to the safeguards required by this article.
3. The safeguards required by this article shall be implemented in a manner designed to comply with article IV of this Treaty, and to avoid hampering the economic or technological development of the Parties or international cooperation in the field of peaceful nuclear activities, including the international exchange of nuclear material and equipment for the processing, use or production of nuclear material for peaceful purposes in accordance with the provisions of this article and the principle of safeguarding set forth in the Preamble of the Treaty.
4. Non-nuclear-weapon States Party to the Treaty shall conclude agree-

ments with the International Atomic Energy Agency to meet the requirements of this article either individually or together with other States in accordance with the Statute of the International Atomic Energy Agency. Negotiation of such agreements shall commence within 180 days from the original entry into force of this Treaty. For States depositing their instruments of ratification or accession after the 180-day period, negotiation of such agreements shall commence not later than the date of such deposit. Such agreements shall enter into force not later than eighteen months after the date of initiation of negotiations.

## Article IV

1. Nothing in this Treaty shall be interpreted as affecting the inalienable right of all the Parties to the Treaty to develop research, production and use of nuclear energy for peaceful purposes without discrimination and in conformity with articles I and II of this Treaty.
2. All the Parties to the Treaty undertake to facilitate, and have the right to participate in, the fullest possible exchange of equipment, materials and scientific and technological information for the peaceful uses of nuclear energy. Parties to the Treaty in a position to do so shall also cooperate in contributing alone or together with other States or international organizations to the further development of the applications of nuclear energy for peaceful purposes, especially in the territories of non-nuclear-weapon States Party to the Treaty, with due consideration for the needs of the developing areas of the world.

## Article V

Each party to the Treaty undertakes to take appropriate measures to ensure that, in accordance with this Treaty, under appropriate international observation and through appropriate international procedures, potential benefits from any peaceful applications of nuclear explosions will be made available to non-nuclear-weapon States Party to the Treaty on a nondiscriminatory basis and that the charge to such Parties for the explosive devices used will be as low as possible and exclude any charge for research and development. Non-nuclear-weapon States Party to the Treaty shall be able to obtain such benefits, pursuant to a special international agreement or agreements, through an appropriate international body with adequate representation of non-nuclear-weapon States. Negotiations on this subject shall commence as soon as possible after the Treaty enters into force. Non-nuclear-weapon States Party to the Treaty so desiring may also obtain such benefits pursuant to bilateral agreements.

## Article VI

Each of the Parties to the Treaty undertakes to pursue negotiations in good faith on effective measures relating to cessation of the nuclear arms race at an early date and to nuclear disarmament, and on a Treaty on general and complete disarmament under strict and effective international control.

## Article VII

Nothing in this Treaty affects the right of any group of States to conclude regional treaties in order to assure the total absence of nuclear weapons in their respective territories.

## Article VIII

1. Any Party to the Treaty may propose amendments to this Treaty. The text of any proposed amendment shall be submitted to the Depositary Governments which shall circulate it to all Parties to the Treaty. Thereupon, if requested to do so by one-third or more of the Parties to the Treaty, the Depositary Governments shall convene a conference, to which they shall invite all the Parties to the Treaty, to consider such an amendment.
2. Any amendment to this Treaty must be approved by a majority of the votes of all the Parties to the Treaty, including the votes of all nuclear-weapon States Party to the Treaty and all other Parties which, on the date the amendment is circulated, are members of the Board of Governors of the International Atomic Energy Agency. The amendment shall enter into force for each Party that deposits its instrument of ratification of the amendment upon the deposit of such instruments of ratification by a majority of all the Parties, including the instruments of ratification of all nuclear-weapon States Party to the Treaty and all other Parties which, on the date the amendment is circulated, are members of the Board of Governors of the International Atomic Energy Agency. Thereafter, it shall enter into force for any other Party upon the deposit of its instrument of ratification of the amendment.
3. Five years after the entry into force of this Treaty, a conference of Parties to the Treaty shall be held in Geneva, Switzerland, in order to review the operation of this Treaty with a view to assuring that the purposes of the Preamble and the provisions of the Treaty are being realized. At intervals of five years thereafter, a majority of the Parties to the Treaty may obtain, by submitting a proposal to this effect to the Depositary Governments, the convening of further conferences with the same objective of reviewing the operation of the Treaty.

## Article IX

1. This Treaty shall be open to all States for signature. Any State which does not sign the Treaty before its entry into force in accordance with paragraph 3 of this article may accede to it at any time.
2. This Treaty shall be subject to ratification by signatory States. Instruments of ratification and instruments of accession shall be deposited with the Governments of the United States of America, the United Kingdom of Great Britain and Northern Ireland and the Union of Soviet Socialist Republics, which are hereby designated the Depositary Governments.
3. This Treaty shall enter into force after its ratification by the States, the Governments of which are designated Depositaries of the Treaty, and forty other States signatory to this Treaty and the deposit of their instruments of ratification. For the purposes of this Treaty, a nuclear-weapon State is one which has manufactured and exploded a nuclear weapon or other nuclear explosive device prior to January 1, 1967.
4. For States whose instruments of ratification or accession are deposited subsequent to the entry into force of this Treaty, it shall enter into force on the date of the deposit of their instruments of ratification or accession.
5. The Depositary Governments shall promptly inform all signatory and acceding States of the date of each signature, the date of deposit of each instrument of ratification or of accession, the date of the entry into force of this Treaty, and the date of receipt of any requests for convening a conference or other notices.
6. This Treaty shall be registered by the Depositary Governments pursuant to article 102 of the Charter of the United Nations.

## Article X

1. Each Party shall in exercising its national sovereignty have the right to withdraw from the Treaty if it decides that extraordinary events, related to the subject matter of this Treaty, have jeopardized the supreme interests of its country. It shall give notice of such withdrawal to all other Parties to the Treaty and to the United Nations Security Council three months in advance. Such notice shall include a statement of the extraordinary events it regards as having jeopardized its supreme interests.
2. Twenty-five years after the entry into force of the Treaty, a conference shall be convened to decide whether the Treaty shall continue in force indefinitely, or shall be extended for an additional fixed period

or periods. This decision shall be taken by a majority of the Parties to the Treaty.

## Article XI

This Treaty, the English, Russian, French, Spanish and Chinese texts of which are equally authentic, shall be deposited in the archives of the Depositary Governments. Duly certified copies of this Treaty shall be transmitted by the Depositary Governments to the Governments of the signatory and acceding States.[8]

# NOTES

## CHAPTER 1

1. Nelson Mandela, *Long Walk to Freedom* (New York: Back Bay Books, 1995); and Amy Goodman and David Goodman, *The Exception to the Rulers* (New York: Hyperion, 2004).

2. U.S. Department of Justice, "Report from the Field: The USA PATRIOT Act at Work," July 13, 2004, http://www.usdoj.gov/ag/speeches/2004/071304_patriot _report_remarks.htm (accessed August 14, 2004).

3. Jack Epstein and Johnny Miller, "The Record in Court of U.S. Charges Brought Against Terrorism Suspects by the Justice Department," *San Francisco Chronicle*, September 17, 2004, p. A3, http://sfgate.com/cgi-bin/article.cgi?file=chronicle/ archive/2004/09/17/MNGK68QJLG1.DTL (accessed December 15, 2004).

4. "Halliburton Contract Probe Opened," *CBSnews.com*, http://www.cbsnews .com/stories/2004/10/28/politics/printable652183.shtml (accessed December 17, 2004).

5. "Annan: Iraq War Hasn't Made the World Safer," *ABC News International*, http://abcnews.go.com/International/wireStory?id=173036 (accessed November 12, 2004).

6. Les Roberts, Riyadh Lafta, Richard Garfield, Jamal Khudhairi, and Gillibert Burnham, "Mortality Before and After the 2003 Invasion of Iraq: Cluster Sample Survey," *Lancet*, http://www.thelancet.com/journal/vol364/iss9445/full/llan.364.9445 .early_online_publication.31137.1 (accessed October 30, 2004).

## CHAPTER 3

1. Nelson Mandela, *Long Walk to Freedom* (New York: Back Bay Books, 1995).

2. Edith M. Lederer, "Belarus Accuses U.S. of Rights Abuses," Associated Press, November 19, 2004, http://news.findlaw.com/ap_stories/i/1103/11-19- 2004/2004 1119044501_04.html (accessed November 22, 2004).

3. UN High Commissioner for Human Rights, Treaty Body Database, Reporting Status, All Reports by Convention, CCPR—International Covenant on Civil and Political Rights, http://www.unhchr.ch/tbs/doc.nsf/RepStatfrset?Open-FrameSet (accessed December 20, 2004).

4. "The 'Bread and Roses' Strike of 1912," Twentieth Annual Bread and Roses Festival, 2004, http://www.breadandroses.net/strike.html (accessed December 20, 2004); Debra Pawlak, "Girl Power: The Story of the Bread and Roses Strike," *Media Drome*, http://www.themediadrome.com/content/articles/history_articles/bread_and_roses.htm (accessed December 20, 2004).

5. See Elizabeth Gurley Flynn, *The Rebel Girl: An Autobiography; My First Life (1906-1926)* (New York: International Publishers, 1973).

6. UN Press Release, "Human Rights Committee Begins Consideration of Canada's Fourth Periodic Report," UN Human Rights Committee, HR/CT/529, March 26, 1999, http://www.unhchr.ch/Huricane/Huricane.nsf/b4aec4dec540ceb68025660 1005b87bd/d80lel7488198eca802567430051cc78?OpenDocument (accessed December 20, 2004).

7. Kareem Shora and Timothy Edgar, "After 9/11, an Assault on Civil Liberties," American-Arab Anti Discrimination Committee, http://www.adc.org/index.php?id=2108 (accessed July 29, 2004).

## CHAPTER 4, A-B

1. Paul Krugman, "Noonday in the Shade," *New York Times*, June 22, 2004, http://www.commondreams.org/views04/0622-04.htm (accessed August 12, 2004).

2. Headlines, *Democracy Now!* September 28, 2004, http://democracynow.org/article.pl?sid=04/09/28/1427234, and October 5, 2004, http://www.democracynow.org/article.pl?sid=04/10/05/1411237 (both accessed December 12, 2004).

3. Victor M. Hwang and Ivy Lee, "Wen Ho Lee Next Time: PATRIOT Act Threatens Asian Americans," *Pacific News Service*, September 12, 2002, http://news.pacificnews.org/news/view_article.html?article_id=4184ec709ae31773ab536eb8f340 6e6c (accessed August 5, 2004).

4. Ibid.

5. Associated Press, "Saying Goodbye to Ousmane Zongo," *cbsnewyork.com*, July 29, 2003, http://cbsnewyork.com/topstories/topstoriesny_story_157220045 .html (accessed June 23, 2004).

6. "As Outrage Mounts in New York Over the Police Killing of Another African Immigrant," *Democracy Now!* May 27, 2003, http://www.democracynow.org/article.pl?sid=03/05/27/1934251 (accessed June 23, 2004).

7. "Alberta Spruill: Victim of NYPD Killer Elite," *Internationalist*, May 2003, http://www.internationalist.org/int16toc.html (accessed July 29, 2004).

8. "Death by Fear: The Case of Alberta Spruill," *Northstar Network*, May 20, 2003, http://www.thenorthstarnetwork.com/news/topstories/181948-1.html (accessed June 23, 2004).

9. Donna Lamb, "Alberta Spruill Murder Taken Seriously by City Council,"

*Caribbean Life*, June 3, 2003, http://indypressny.org/article.php3?ArticleID=895 (accessed June 23, 2004).

10. Jesse L. Jackson Sr., "Death by Police in Cincinnati," *Sacobserver.com*, December 15, 2003, http://www.sacobserver.com/news/commentary/121503/cincinnati _nathaniel_jones.shtml (accessed June 29, 2004).

11. Lisa Cornwell, "Cincinnati Police Cleared in Custody Death," Associated Press, March 23, 2004, http://www.cqservices.com/MyCQ/News/Default.asp?V=7866 (accessed August 6, 2004).

12. Tiana A. Rollinson, "NAACP To Investigate Homicidal Police Beating," *Sacobserver.Com*, December 8, 2003, http://www.sacobserver.com/news/120803/ nathaniel_jones_beating_investigation.shtml (accessed June 29, 2004).

13. "Backlash: When America Turned On Its Own—A Preliminary Report to the 2001 Audit of Violence Against Asian Pacific Americans," *National Asian Pacific American Legal Consortium*, http://www.napalc.org/literature/annual_report/9-11 _report.htm (accessed June 29, 2004).

14. Jim Lobe, "US Police Unprepared To Defend Muslims Post-9/11," *Asheville Global Report*, November 21, 2002, http://www.agrnews.org/issues/201/ nationalnews.html (accessed July 28, 2004).

15. Bob Moser, "Open Season," *Intelligence Report*, Spring 2003, http://www .splcenter.org/intel/intelreport/article.jsp?pid=52 (accessed June 28, 2004).

16. Ibid.

17. *No More Deaths*, http://www.nomoredeaths.org/links.html (accessed July 30, 2004).

18. Jennifer Allen, "Justice on the Line," *Border Action Network*, http://www.borderaction.org/BAN-Justice.pdf (accessed June 28, 2004).

19. Marc W. Herold, "Above the Law and Below Morality: Data on 11 Weeks of U.S. Cluster Bombing of Afghanistan," *Cursor*, February 1, 2002, http://www .cursor.org/stories/abovethelaw.htm (accessed June 23, 2004).

20. Reuters, "Red Cross Warns Afghan Children off Cluster Bombs," June 29, 2002, http://www.rawa.org/cluster2.htm (accessed June 29, 2004).

21. "Civilian Catastrophe as US Bombs Afghan Wedding," *Guardian*, July 1, 2002, http://www.guardian.co.uk/afghanistan/story/0,1284,747529,00.html (accessed June 29, 2004).

22. Luke Harding, "No U.S. Apology Over Wedding Bombing," *Guardian*, July 3, 2002, http://www.guardian.co.uk/international/story/0,3604,748217,00.html (accessed June 29, 2004).

23. Peter Symonds, "Evidence Points to US Cover-up of Afghan Massacre," *World Socialist Web Site*, August 1, 2002, http://www.wsws.org/articles/2002/aug2002/ afgh-a01.shtml (accessed July 29, 2004).

24. "Five in Afghanistan Killed When Blast Destroys Vehicle, UN Says," UN News Centre, October 19, 2004, http://www.un.org/apps/news/storyAr.asp?NewsID =12270&Cr=Afghan&Cr1 (accessed December 3, 2004).

25. Duncan Campbell, "Afghan Prisoners Beaten to Death at US Military Interrogation Base," *Guardian*, March 7, 2003, http://www.guardian.co.uk/ afghanistan/story/0,1284,909294,00.html (accessed June 29, 2004).

26. Andrew McLeod, "US Had Role in Taleban Prisoner Deaths," *Scotsman*,

June 14, 2002, http://www.commondreams.org/headlines02/0614-09.htm (accessed July 29, 2004).

27. Genevieve Roja, "Documenting the Massacre in Mazar," *AlterNet*, July 8, 2002, http://www.alternet.org/story.html?StoryID=13540 (accessed June 23, 2004).

28. Julius Strauss, "Slow Death on the Jail Convoy of Misery," *Daily Telegraph*, March 19, 2002, http://www.telegraph.co.uk/news/main.jhtml?xml=/news/2002/03/19/wafg219.xml (accessed July 29, 2004).

29. "Film Documents Alleged Massacre of 3,000 Taliban Prisoners in Afghanistan," *Democracy Now!* May 22, 2003, http://www.democracynow.org/afghan-film.shtml (accessed June 23, 2004).

30. "Afghan Massacre: The Convoy of Death," *Democracy Now!* May 25, 2003, http://www.democracynow.org/article.pl?std=03/05/23/1637201 (accessed December, 20, 2004).

31. John Heffernan and Barbara Ayotte, "Physicians for Human Rights Renews Calls for Full Forensic Investigation into Alleged Killing of Taliban Prisoners," *Physicians for Human Rights*, June 13, 2002, http://www.phrusa.org/research/afghanistan/report_graves_renewcall.html (accessed July 30, 2004).

32. David Rose, "How We Survived Jail Hell," *Guardian*, March 14, 2004, http://observer.guardian.co.uk/uk_news/story/0,6903,1168937,00.html (accessed June 23, 2004).

33. Medea Benjamin, "The Occupations' Hidden Victims—Innocent Iraqis," *Occupation Watch Center*, August 5, 2003, http://electroniciraq.net/news/1014.shtml (accessed July 30, 2004).

34. "8 Years for Abu Ghraib Soldier," *CNN.com*, October 22, 2004, http://www.cnn.com/2004/WORLD/meast/10/21/iraq.abuse/ (accessed November 16, 2004).

35. Seymour M. Hersh, "Torture at Abu Ghraib," *New Yorker*, May 10, 2004, http://www.newyorker.com/fact/content/?040510fa_fact (accessed July 30, 2004).

36. "Report: Presumption of Guilt: Human Rights Abuses of Post-September 11 Detainees," *Human Rights Watch*, http://www.hrw.org/reports/2002/us911/USA0802-06.htm (accessed August 6, 2004).

37. Mary McGrory, "Bungling on the 9-11 Prisoners," *Washington Post*, February 10, 2002, http://www.commondreams.org/views02/0210-03.htm (accessed July 30, 2004).

38. *Standard*, July 24, 2002, http://www.bcstandard.com/News/2002/0724/Front_Page/003.html (accessed November 19, 2004).

39. Mouhon Paul, "Lettre Ouverte: Jean Toby Oulai Libere," *Abidjan.net*, November 12, 2002, http://www.abidjan.net/lettreouverte/lettre.asp?ID=3555 (accessed November 19, 2004).

40. Winthrop, "Jaoudat Background," *Blue Triangle Network*, http://www.blue-triangle.org/old/jaoudat_detention.htm (accessed August 6, 2004).

41. Jaoudat Abouazza Defense Committee, "The Illegal Detention and Brutalization of Palestinian Activist Jaoudat Abouazza," *Blue Triangle Network*, June 2002, http://www.bluetriangle.org/old/id30.htm (accessed July 30, 2004).

42. "Jaoudat Abouazza Free in Canada, but Struggle for Justice Continues,"

*Progressive Austin*, July 15, 2002, http://www.progressiveaustin.org/jaoudat.htm (accessed June 30, 2004).

43. Matthew Brzezinski, "Hady Hassan Omar's Detention," *New York Times Magazine*, October 27, 2002, http://www.columbia.edu/cu/cssn/cssn-list/2002/10/00157.html (accessed June 30, 2004).

44. "San Diego Material Witness En Route Home," *SanDiegoChannel.com* October 10, 2001, http://www.thesandiegochannel.com/news/1011716/detail.html (accessed August 6, 2004).

45. "Terror Probe Raises Concerns About Civil Rights," *CNN*, October 22, 2001, http://www.cnn.com/2001/US/10/22/inv.civil.rights (accessed June 30, 2004).

46. "San Diego: Prisoners of the Modern American Witch Hunt," *Revolutionary Worker*, no. 1136, (January 27, 2002), http://rwoRorg/a/v23/1130-39/1136/sandiego_arabs.htm (accessed June 30, 2004).

47. Somini Sengupta, "Ill-Fated Path to America, Jail and Death," *New York Times*, November 5, 2001, http://www.crimelynx.com/illfate.html (accessed June 30, 2004).

48. Aamir Latif, "Pakistani Relative Says FBI Tortured Dead Detainee," *Islam Online*, November 1, 2001, http://islamonline.org/english/news/2001-11/02/article4.shtml (accessed July 30, 2004).

49. CCR Legal Team, "*Turkmen v. Ashcroft* Synopsis," *Center for Constitutional Rights*, http://www.ccr-ny.org/v2/legal/september_11th/sept11Article.asp?ObjID=35KQUuFROg&Content=96 (accessed July 28, 2004).

50. Amy Goodman, "Enemy in Their Camp," *Democracy Now!* July 12, 2004, http://www.democracynow.org/article.pl?sid=04/07/12/1345249 (accessed July 12, 2004).

51. Miles Moffeit, "Activists Question Speed of Rape Reforms," *DenverPost.com*, July 12, 2004, http://www.denverpost.com/Stories/0,1413,36~30137~2266964,00.html (accessed July 12, 2004).

52. Amy Goodman, "Enemy in Their Camp."

53. Associated Press, "Lawyer Says Guantanamo Detainees Tortured," *TruthOut*, October 8, 2003, http://truthout.org/docs_03/100903C.shtml (accessed July 1, 2004).

54. AFP, "Former Guantanamo Detainees Write to Bush with Torture Claims," *Channel News Asia*, May 14, 2004, http://www.channelnewsasia.com/stories/afp_world/view/84972/1/.html (accessed August 5, 2004).

55. Associated Press, "Former Guantanamo Detainees Allege Torture," *CNews*, March 13, 2004, http://cnews.canoe.ca/CNEWS/World/2004/03/13/381375-ap.html (accessed August 5, 2004).

56. "Former Guantanamo Detainees Release 115-Page Report, CCR Submits Their Detailed Account of Abuse to Senate Armed Services Committee," *Center for Constitutional Rights*, August 8, 2004, http://www.ccr-ny.org/v2/reports/report.asp?ObjID=4bUT8M23lk&Content=424 (accessed August 6, 2004).

57. "Red Cross: U.S. May Have Committed War Crimes at Guantanamo Bay," *Democracy Now!* August 5th, 2004, http://www.democracynow.org/article.pl?sid=04/08/05/1432259 (accessed August 6, 2004).

58. Irene Khan, "Letter to Donald Rumsfeld," *Amnesty International*, January 7,

2002, http://web.amnesty.org/library/Index/engAMR510052002?OpenDocument& of=COUNTRIES%5CUSA (accessed July 1, 2004).

59. Molly Moore, "Villagers Released by American Troops Say They Were Beaten, Kept in 'Cage,'" *Washington Post Foreign Service*, February 11, 2002, http://www.sunnahonline.com/ilm/contemporary/post_taliban/0001.htm (accessed July 1, 2004).

60. Dana Priest and Barton Gellman, "U.S. Decries Abuse but Defends Interrogations; 'Stress and Duress' Tactics Used on Terrorism Suspects Held in Secret Overseas Facilities," *Washington Post*, December 26, 2002, http://www.washington post.com/ac2/wp-dyn/A37943-2002Dec25 (accessed July 1, 2004).

61. Associated Press, "Iraqi Details Harsh Treatment as Prisoner," *USA Today*, June 30, 2003, http://www.usatoday.com/news/world/iraq/2003-06-30-iraq-amnesty _x.htm (accessed July 1, 2004).

62. "Turkish Soldier: Handcuffs Cut My Wrists, Soldiers Slapped," *Kurdistan Observer*, July 11, 2003, http://home.cogeco.ca/~konuche/11-7-03-turkish-soldier talks-about-his-ordeal.html (accessed July 1, 2004).

63. Louise Christian, "Guantanamo Bay: A Global Experiment In Inhumanity," *Guardian*, January 10, 2004, http://www.guardian.co.uk/comment/story/0,3604, 1119994,00.html (accessed July 30, 2004).

64. Terry Jones, "Spare Our Blushes and Put a Sack On It," *London Observer*, January 6, 2002, http://observer.guardian.co.uk/print/0,3858,4329993-102273,00 .html (accessed July 1, 2004).

65. Neil Mackay, "Did the US Massacre Taliban?" *Sunday Herald*, June 16, 2002, http://www.sundayherald.com/25520 (accessed June 23, 2004).

66. "Probe Opens on U.S. Murder of Afghan Detainees," *Democracy Now!* September 21, 2004, http://www.democracynow.org/article.pl?sid=04/09/21/1347252 (accessed September 21, 2004).

67. David Rose, "US Afghan Allies Committed Massacre: American Experts Find that Northern Alliance Warlords Slaughtered Prisoners of War," *Observer*, March 21, 2004, http://observer.guardian.co.uk/international/story/0,6903,1174554 ,00.html (accessed August 5, 2004).

68. James W. Crawley, "Officials Confirm Dropping Firebombs on Iraqi Troops," *San Diego Union Tribune*, August 5, 2003, http://www.signonsandiego.com /news/military/20030805-9999_1n5bomb.html (accessed July 1, 2004).

69. "U.S. Defends Using Napalm-like Firebombs," *Sydney Morning Herald*, August 8, 2003, http://www.smh.com.au/articles/2003/08/08/1060145827920.html (accessed July 1, 2004).

70. "US Must Ensure Humane Treatment And Access To Justice For Iraqi Detainees," *Amnesty International*, June 30, 2003, http://www.amnestyusa.org/news/ 2003/iraq06302003.html (accessed July 1, 2004).

71. "Iraqi President Frees All Prisoners, Except 'Spies,'" *CNN.com*, October 20, 2002, http://archives.cnn.com/2002/WORLD/meast/10/20/iraq.amnesty (accessed December 21, 2004); "Iraq's Most Feared Prison Open Again for Business Under US Control," *Arab Times Online*, July 13, 2003, http://www.ccmep.org/2003_article/Iraq/ 071303_iraqs_most_feared_prison_open_ag.htm (accessed December 21, 2004).

72. Seymour M. Hersh, "Torture at Abu Ghraib," *New Yorker*, May 10, 2004,

http://www.newyorker.com/fact/content/?040510fa_fact (accessed July 30, 2004); Hersh, "Chain of Command: How the Department of Defense Mishandled the Disaster at Abu Ghraib," *New Yorker*, May 17, 2004, http://www.newyorker.com/fact/content/?040517fa_fact2 (accessed November 16, 2004).

73. Hersh, "Chain of Command."

74. Antonio Ponvert III, "Iraqi Prisoner Abuse: Why Are We Surprised?" *Counterpunch*, http://www.ccmep.org/2004_articles/iraq/061304_counterpunch.htm (accessed December 22, 2004).

75. Gary Younge, "Brutality: The Home Truths," *Guardian*, May 11, 2004, http://www.guardian.co.uk/Iraq/Story/0,2763,1213971.00.html (accessed July 1, 2004).

76. Robert Evans, "UN Says Coalition Troops Violated Rights in Iraq," Reuters, June 4, 2004, http://www.occupationwatch.org/article.php?id=5185 (accessed November 15, 2004).

77. "Family of Iraq Abuse Whistleblower Threatened," Reuters, August 16, 2004, http://www.truthout.org/docs_04/081704U.shtml (accessed November 16, 2004).

78. "CCR Files Lawsuit Against Private Contractors for Torture Conspiracy," *Center for Constitutional Rights*, http://www.ccr-ny.org/v2/reports/report.asp?ObjID=TutDBqRhAY&Content=387 (accessed October 4, 2004); Complaint, *Sami Abbas Al Rawi et al. v. Titan et al.*, filed by local counsel William Aceves, June 9, 2004.

79. Christian Miller, "Army Gives Contract to Company in Jail Scandal," *Los Angeles Times*, August 5, 2004, http://www.latimes.com/news/nationworld/world/la-fg-contract5aug05,1,3952058.story (accessed August 7, 2004).

80. Miller, "Army Gives Contract to Company in Jail Scandal."

81. "Facts about Prisons and Prisoners," *Sentencing Project*, May 2004, http://www.sentencingproject.org/pdfs/1035.pdf (accessed July 2, 2004).

82. Don Thompson, "Prison Horror Stories Continue," *Contra Costa Times*, February 14, 2004, p. A11, http://www.montereyherald.com/mld/cctimes/news/politics/elections/7954213.htm (accessed July 1, 2004).

83. Jane Henderson and Shari Silberstein, "Fundraising Letter," *Equal Justice USA*, Spring 2004, http://www.quixote.org/ej/ (accessed June 24, 2004).

84. "Recently Asked Questions," *School of the Americas Watch*, http://www.soaw.org/new/faq.php (accessed June 25, 2004).

85. "Chile: Armando Fernandez Larios," *Center for Justice and Accountability*, 2003, http://www.cja.org/cases/cabello.shtml (accessed August 7, 2004).

86. Associated Press, "Chilean Court Strips Pinochet of Immunity from Prosecution," *Detroit News*, May 29, 2004, http://www.detnews.com/2004/nation/0405/29/nation-167580.htm (accessed July 2, 2004).

87. "37mm Sting Ball™ Rounds," Combined Tactical Systems Inc., August 5, 2003, http://www.combinedsystems.com/37mmstba.htm (accessed December 21, 2004); "Sting-Ball Rubber Grenade Model 9590," ATD-American Co., http://www.atd.com/catalog/articles/LL020.php (accessed December 21, 2004).

88. Martha Scott to National Lawyers Guild, in Heidi Boghosian, "Assault on Free Speech, Public Assembly, and Dissent," 2004, p. 85.

89. *ACORN v. City of Philadelphia*, Case No. 03-412, [ED PA], September 23, 2003, http://www.aclu.org/FreeSpeech/FreeSpeech.cfm?ID=13698&c=86 (accessed

December 6, 2004).

90. See http://homepage.ntlworld.com/jksonc/docs/acorn-edpa-d21.html (accessed December 26, 2004).

91. Will Potter, "Protest Torture of Animals; Get Arrested as a 'Terrorist': The New War on Terror," *Counterpunch*, May 31, 2004, http://www.counterpunch .com/potter05292004.html (accessed August 7, 2004).

92. "Headlines," *Democracy Now!* October 7, 2004, http://www.democracynow .org/article.pl?sid=04/10/07/1335236 (accessed December 6, 2004).

93. Ian Hoffman, Sean Holstege, and Josh Richman, "State Monitored War Protesters," *Oakland Tribune*, May 18, 2003, http://www.oaklandtribune.com/Stories /0,1413,82%257E1865%257E1400012,00.html (accessed August 5, 2004).

94. Dana Hull, "Police Violence Shocks Activists, Others at Port of Oakland Protest," *San Jose Mercury News*, April 7, 2003, http://www.commondreams .org/headlines03/0407-07.htm (accessed July 20, 2004).

95. Thomas Peele and Carrie Sturrock, "Oakland Police Injure Dozens, Arrest 30 Protesters," Knight Ridder, April 8, 2003, http://www.asuwebdevil.com/issues/ 2003/04/08/sports/411502 (accessed October 23, 2004).

96. Daniel Borgstrom, "The Port of Oakland in the Light of Miami," *SF Indymedia*, December 12, 2003, http://sf.indymedia.org/news/2003/12/1665614.php (accessed July 20, 2004).

97. Hull, "Police Violence Shocks Activists, Others at Port of Oakland Protest."

98. Rachel Lederman, "Bay Area Sues Oakland Over Port Anti-war Demo Shootings," *National Lawyers Guild Notes*, Fall 2003, p. 5.

99. "A Glimpse Behind the Oakland Police Response to Antiwar Protest," *Dubya Report*, April 16, 2003, http://www.thedubyareport.com/opd1.html (accessed August 5, 2004).

100. Jim Zamora, "Crowd Control Policy Changed by Oakland Cops," *San Francisco Chronicle*, December 12, 2003.

101. Associated Press, "Oakland DA Won't Prosecute Port Protestors," *U.S. Labor against the War*, April 22, 2004, http://www.uslaboragainstwar.org/article .php?id=4359 (accessed August 7, 2004).

102. Liv Dillon, "The View From the Middle of the Road," *AlterNet*, May 19, 2003, http://www.alternet.org/story.html?StoryID=15945 (accessed July 20, 2004).

103. Associated Press, "Congressmen Ask Ashcroft To Drop Bursey Prosecution," *TheState.com*, May 27, 2003, http://www.thestate.com/mld/thestate/news /local/5955253.htm (accessed July 20, 2004).

104. Leslie Eaton, "Aftereffects: Questions of Security and Free Speech," *New York Times*, April 27, 2003, http://www.scpronet.com/nytimes20030427.html (accessed July 20, 2004).

105. Associated Press, "Congressmen Ask Ashcroft To Drop Bursey Prosecution."

106. Associated Press, "Bursey Denied Jury Trial," *State.com*, June 9, 2003, http://www.thestate.com/mld/thestate/news/local/6050674.htm (accessed August 7, 2004).

107. Jacob Jordan, "Trial For Bush Protester Delayed Because of Technicality," *Associated Press*, June 24, 2003, http://www.thestate.com/mld/thestate/news/local /6161748.htm (accessed July 8, 2004).

108. Associated Press, "Judge in Bursey Case Says Some Secret Documents May be Disclosed," *Wisconsin 10 TV,* Sept. 19, 2003, http://www.wistv.com /Global/story.asp?S=1448968&nav=0RaPI4tg (accessed July 20, 2004).

109. Laura Longhine, "Bursey Guilty; Gets $500 Fine," *Free Times,* January 7, 2004, http://free-times.com/News&comm/News_Archives/News_2004/news010704 .html (accessed July 20, 2004).

110. James Bovard, "Quarantining Dissent: How the Secret Service Protects Bush from Free Speech," *San Francisco Chronicle,* January 4, 2004, http://www.sfgate.com/cgi-bin/article.cgi?file=/chronicle/archive/2004/01/04 /INGPQ40MB81.DTL (accessed July 20, 2004).

111. Sitara Kapoor and Henry Norr, "Antiwar Demonstrators Win One Over Merchant of Death: Protestors' Solidarity Forces Lockheed Martin to Drop Restitution Claim," *National Lawyers Guild SF Bay Area Chapter NEWS,* October/November 2003, http://www.stoplockheed.org/page1.htm (accessed August 23, 2004).

112. "SF Labor Council Resolution on Amer Jubran/Protest Nov. 6 in SF at 12 noon!" *International Workers of the World,* November 5, 2003, http://lists.iww .org/pipermail/iww-news/2003-November/003830.html (accessed August 5, 2004).

113. "Outcome of Amer Jubran's Final Trial," *Amer Jubran Defense Committee,* November 24, 2003, http://www.notinourname.net/detentions/jubran-final-6nov03 .htm (accessed July 20, 2004).

114. The Independent Review Panel (Jorge E. Reynaardus, Esq., Chair, Civilian Oversight of Miami Police and Corrections and Rehabilitation Departments), *Final Draft Report on the Free Trade Area of the Americas (FTAA) Inquiry,* June 2004, http://miami.staughton.indypgh.org/news/2004/06/107.php (accessed August 1, 2004); Heidi Boghosian, *The Assault on Free Speech, Public Assembly, and Dissent: A National Lawyers Guild Report on Government Violations of First Amendment Rights in the United States* (Great Barrington, MA: North River Press, 2004), pp. 88-89.

115. "Democracy Now!" *Pacifica Radio,* December 22, 2003, http://www.democracy now.org/print.pl?sid=03/12/22/1656255 (accessed November 9, 2004).

116. "USWA Calls for Congressional Investigation into Police-State Assaults in Miami," *United Steelworkers of America,* November 24, 2003, http://www.uswa.org/ uswa/program/content/820.php (accessed August 5, 2004).

117. Associated Press, "Portland, Ore., Police Use Pepper Spray on Protestors at Bush Events," *Infoshop News,* August 23, 2002, http://www.infoshop.org/inews/stories .php?story=02/08/22/7534426 (accessed June 24, 2004).

118. Donald Joughin, "Letter from a Portland Protestor," *World Socialist Web Site,* August 29, 2002, http://www.wsws.org/articles/2002/aug2002/lett-a29 _prn.shtml (accessed June 24, 2004).

119. Phil Busse, "Police Pepper Sprayed My Baby," *Portland Mercury,* September 4, 2002, http://www.portlandmercury.com/2002-08-29/city.html (accessed June 24, 2004).

120. Kerry Taylor, "Soldiers, Families Oppose Bush: Casualties Mount Post Saddam," *War Times,* February-March, 2004, http://www.war-times.org/issues/15art1.html (accessed August 5, 2004).

121. Recardo Gibson, "Vets for Peace on Veteran's Day," *Free Speech Radio News,* November 11, 2003, http://www.fsrn.org/news/20031111_news.html (accessed July 20, 2004).

122. Taylor, "Soldiers, Families Oppose Bush: Casualties Mount Post Saddam."

123. Gibson, "Vets for Peace on Veteran's Day."

124. Sam Husseini, "Bush Accepts Nomination on Final Night of Convention Marked by Historic Protests and Dissent," *Democracy Now!* September 3, 2004, http://www.democracynow.org/article.pl?sid=04/09/031457210 (accessed September 7, 2004).

125. "Manhattan District Attorney Agrees to Dismiss All Charges Against All Cases of People Arrested at Republican National Convention Demonstration," ACLU, October 6, 2004, http://www.aclu.org/news/News Print.cfm?ID=16667&c=206 (accessed November 29, 2004).

126. "NYCLU Grades Policing of Protesters at the RNC," *New York Civil Liberties Union*, September 3, 2004, http://www.nyclu.org/rnc_policing_grades_pr_090304.html (accessed September 7, 2004).

127. ACLU, "Police Trampled Civil Rights during Republican National Convention, NYCLU Charges," October 7, 2004, http://www.aclu.org/news/NewsPrint.cfm?ID=16879&c=86 (accessed November 29, 2004).

128. *McNamara v. New York*, National Lawyers Guild, November 22, 2004, http://www.nlgnyc.org/pdf/rncclassactioncomplaint.pdf (accessed November 29, 2004).

129. *Southern Poverty Law Center Report*, March 2004, http://www.splcenter.org/center/splcreport/article.jsp?aid=71 (accessed August 4, 2004), *SPLC Intelligence Report*, Winter 1999, http://www.splcenter.org/intel/intelreport/archive .jsp?page=2 &yearsBack=0 (accessed August 4, 2004).

130. Nicole Davis, "The Slippery Slope of Racial Profiling," *Color-lines*, December 2001, http://www.alternet.org/story.html?StoryID=12079 (accessed July 1, 2004).

131. Mark Sherman, "Rep. Issa Says Airline Kept Him Off Flight Due To Lebanese Heritage," *Associated Press*, October 26, 2001, http://www.sfgate.com/cgi-bin/article.cgi?file=/news/archive/2001/10/26/national1618EDT0700.DTL (accessed July 1, 2004).

132. Davis, "The Slippery Slope of Racial Profiling."

133. Davar Ardalan, "FBI Probe of Iraqi Americans Nears End," *NPR News*, "All Things Considered," April 5, 2003, http://www.npr.org/templates/story/story.php ?storyId=1220523(accessed December 3, 2004).

134. David Kravets, "ACLU Seeks FBI Data on Muslim Interviews," Associated Press, *MSNBC News*, October 21, 2004, http://www.msnbc.msn.com/id/6303212 (accessed December 3, 2004).

135. "Caught in the Backlash: Stories from Northern California," *ACLU of Northern California*, 2002-2003, http://www.aclunc.org/911/backlash/soza.html (accessed August 7, 2004).

136. "Operation Tarmac: Overkill?" *The Austin Chronicle*, March 14, 2003, http://www.austinchronicle.com/issues/dispatch/2003-03-14/pols_naked6.html (accessed July 1, 2004).

137. Kelli Arena and Terry Frieden, "Operation Tarmac Airport Sweep Widens," *CNN*, April 24, 2002, http://www.cnn.com/2002/TRAVEL/NEWS /04/24/airports.sweep/?related (accessed July 1, 2004).

138. Ben Ehrenreich "Operation Tarnish," *LA Weekly*, October 25-31, 2002,

http://www.laweekly.com/ink/02/49/news-ehrenreich.php (accessed July 1, 2004).

139. "'Operation Tarmac' Hits Texas," *Resource Center of the Americas*, http://www.americas.org/item_8921 (accessed August 7, 2004).

140. The White House, "White House Overview of Fair and Secure Immigration Reform," *U.S. International Information Programs*, January 7, 2004, http://usinfo.state.gov/gi/Archive/2004/Jan/07-872560.html (accessed August 7, 2004).

141. "Fact Sheet: ICE Worksite Enforcement," *U.S. Immigration and Customs Enforcement*, http://www.ice.gov/graphics/news/factsheets/IceWorkEnforcement.htm (accessed August 7, 2004).

142. "Hate Crimes Ballooned After 9/11," *L.A. Daily News*, September 9, 2002, http://www.sbsun.com/Stories/0,1413,200%257E24809%257E848962,00.html (accessed August 7, 2004).

143. Cristina C. Breen, "Immigrants Face Changes Since 9-11", *Charlotte Observer*, September 4, 2002, http://www.charlotte.com/mld/observer/news/3997100.htm?1c (accessed July 2, 2004).

144. Anthony Spangler, "Hate Crimes against Arabs, Muslims Ease," *Star-Telegram*, June 2, 2003, http://www.dfw.com/mld/startelegram/news/local/5995368.htm (accessed July 2, 2004).

145. "Hate Crimes Ballooned After 9/11," *L.A. Daily News*.

146. Spangler, "Hate Crimes against Arabs, Muslims Ease."

147. Heidi Khaled, "Religious Freedom and the War on Islam," *Irvine Progressive*, May 2003, http://irvineprogressive.com/vol1issue2/op5.htm (accessed July 2, 2004).

148. Eric Bradley, "University Professor Was Investigated Under PATRIOT Act," *Oshkosh Northwestern*, March 10, 2003, p.C1.

149. Michael Moss, "False Terrorism Tips to FBI Uproot the Lives of Suspects," *New York Times*, June 19, 2003, http://foi.missouri.edu/terrorintelligence/falseterrorism.html (accessed July 2, 2004).

150. Karl Ross, "Employee Sues Over Demotion," *Miami Herald*, May 9, 2003, http://www.miami.com/mld/miamiherald/5892633.htm (accessed July 2, 2004).

151. "Caught in the Backlash: Stories from Northern California," *ACLU of Northern California*, http://www.aclunc.org/911/backlash/valencia.html (accessed July 2, 2004).

152. David Bacon, "Screened Out," *Nation*, May 12, 2003, http://www.thenation.com/doc.mhtml?i=20030512&c=3&s=bacon (accessed July 2, 2004).

153. "Egyptian Manager Fired Because of National Origin, EEOC Says In Post-9/11 Backlash Discrimination Lawsuit," *U.S. Equal Opportunity Employment Commission*, July 10, 2003, http://www.eeoc.gov/press/7-10-03.html (accessed July 6, 2004).

154. Report: "Muslim/Arab Employment Discrimination Charges Since 9/11," *U.S. Equal Opportunity Employment Commission*, December 2, 2002, http://www.eeoc.gov /origin/z-stats.html (accessed June 11, 2004).

155. "Race/Color Discrimination Statistics," *Equal Employment Opportunity Commission*, http://www.eeoc.gov/types/race.html (accessed August 7, 2004).

156. "United States Border Patrol Mexico-Arizona Border Fencing Project: Facts About the Fence," *Latin American Working Group*, 2003, http://www.lawg .org/docs/what%20is%20the%20fence.pdf (accessed July 26, 2004).

157. Brenda Norrell, "Tohono O'odham and Yaqui: No more walls," *Indian Country Today*, July 20, 2004, http://www.indiancountry.com/?1090337206 (accessed July 26, 2004).

158. Julia Dietz, "Fencing Proposal Threatens Human Life, Environment," *Journal of the Religious Task Force on Central America and Mexico*, May/June 2003, http://www.rtfcam.org/report/volume_23/No_2/article_6.htm (accessed July 26, 2004).

159. *Legal Consequences of the Construction of a Wall in the Occupied Palestinian Territories*, International Court of Justice, July 9, 2004, General List No. 131.

160. Jennifer Allen, "Justice on the Line: The Unequal Impacts of Border Patrol Activities in Arizona Border Communities," *Border Action Network*, http://www.borderaction.org/BAN-Justice.pdf (accessed June 28, 2004).

161. Sherrel Wheeler Stewart, "Blacks Deaths in Iraq War Exceeds Rate in Vietnam," *BlackAmericaWeb.com*, March 17, 2004, http://www.blackamericaweb.com/site.aspx/bawnews/deaths (accessed July 1, 2004).

162. Juliana Maantay, "Addressing Community Concerns: How Environmental Justice Relates to Land Use Planning and Zoning," *National Academy of Public Administration*, July 2003, http://www.napawash.org/Pubs/EJ.pdf (accessed August 7, 2004).

163. Deanne M. Ottaviano et al., "Environmental Justice: New Clean Air Act Regulations & The Anticipated Impact on Minority Communities," a paper delivered at the *Lawyers' Committee for Civil Rights Under Law Conference*, Washington, DC, June 2003, p 7.

164. Luke W. Cole and Shelia R. Foster, *From the Ground Up: Environmental Racism and the Rise of the Environmental Justice Movement*, (New York: New York University Press, 2001), pp. 34–35.

165. Deanne M. Ottaviano, et al., "Environmental Justice: New Clean Air Act Regulations & The Anticipated Impact on Minority Communities."

166. Theodore Cross and Robert Bruce Slater, "How Bans on Race-Sensitive Admissions Severely Cut Black Enrollments at Flagship State Universities," *Journal of Blacks in Higher Education*, Winter 2002/2003, no. 38, http://www.jbhe.com/features/38_race_sensitive.html (accessed July 1, 2004).

167. "CEDAW: Rights that Benefit the Entire Community," *Working Group on Ratification of the UN Convention on the Elimination of All Forms of Discrimination Against Women*, 2004, pp. 49-61.

168. Jim Lobe, *OneWorld US*, October 4, 2004, http://www.oneworld.net (accessed January 31, 2005).

169. "Welfare: NOW Calls for Real Reform," *National Organization for Women*, September 30, 2003, http://www.now.org/issues/economic/welfare/ (accessed July 31, 2004).

170. Jennifer L. Pozner, "Missing Since 9-11: Women's Voices," *Common Dreams*, December 13, 2001, http://www.commondreams.org/views01/1213-04.htm (accessed July 31, 2004).

171. "1,150,000 March on Washington, DC to Voice Opposition to Government Attacks on Women's Reproductive Rights and Health," *March for Women*, April 2004, http://www.marchforwomen.org/content/index.php?pid=119&PHPSESSID=eee953fbf38a0663ef66566e594bd377 (accessed June 30, 2004).

172. Lisa Bennett, "Over One Million March for Women's Lives," *National*

*OrganizationforWomen.org*, Spring 2004, http://www.now.org/nnt/spring-2004/march.html (accessed June 30, 2004).

173. "Iraq: Amnesty International Reveals a Pattern of Torture and Ill Treatment," *Amnesty International*, June 2004, http://web.amnesty.org/pages/irq-torture-eng (accessed August 4, 2004).

174. Associated Press, "Iraqis Tell Grim Stories Of U.S.-Run Camps," *Toronto Star*, October 29, 2003, http://www.occupationwatch.org/article.php?id=1687 (accessed July 30, 2004).

175. ICRC director of operations, Pierre Krähenbühl, "Iraq: ICRC Explains Position over Detention Report and Treatment of Prisoners," *International Committee of the Red Cross/Red Crescent*, May 8, 2004, http://www.icrc.org/Web/Eng/siteeng0.nsf/iwpList74/7EE8626890D74F76C1256E8D005D3861 (accessed August 8, 2004).

176. "Poll: 25% of U.S. Has Negative Stereotypes of Muslims," *Democracy Now!* October 5, 2004, http://www.democracynow.org/article.pl?sid=04/10/05/1411237 (accessed November 17, 2004).

177. David Cole, "Driving While Immigrant," *Nation*, May 12, 2003, http://www.thenation.com/doc.mhtml?i=2003052&s=cole (accessed August 5, 2004).

178. Ibid.

179. *Freeman v. State of Florida, Department of Highway Safety and Motor Vehicles*, Case No. 2002-CA-2828, June 6, 2003.

180. U-Wire, "Minnesota City Council Opposes Homeland Security Orders," *Minnesota Daily*, April 8, 2003, http://www.dailyillini.com/apr03/apr08/news/stories/campus02.shtml (accessed August 5, 2004).

181. Lisa Hoffman, "Fort Jackson a Magnet for Muslim Soldiers," *Scripps Howard News Service*, October 25, 2002, http://www.capitolhillblue.com/cgi-bin/artman/exec/view.cgi?archive=10&num=855 (accessed November 9, 2004).

182. Coralie Carlson "Army Islamic Chaplain To Guantanamo Prisoners Detained," *Associated Press*, September 20, 2003, http://www.centredaily.com/mld/cctimes/news/world/6825347.htm (accessed August 4, 2004).

183. "Muslim US Army Chaplain Arrested on Suspicion of Spying," *AFP*, September 21, 2003, http://quickstart.clari.net/qs_se/webnews/wed/ac/Qus-attacks-guantanamo.Rty9_DSK.html (accessed August 4, 2004).

184. David Cole, "Taking Liberties: The War On Our Rights," *Nation*, December 23, 2003, http://www.thenation.com/doc.mhtml%3Fi=20040112&s=cole (accessed August 4, 2004).

185. Charlie Savage, "Limits Put On New Muslim Chaplain; Role At Guantanamo Won't Include Contact With Camp's Detainees," *Boston Globe*, November 7, 2003, http://www.boston.com/news/world/articles/2003/11/07/limits_put_on_new_muslim_chaplain/.

186. Mike Barger, "All Charges Dropped, but Army Gags Yee," *Seattle Post-Intelligencer*, April 15, 2004, http://seattlepi.nwsource.com/local/169156_yee15.html (accessed August 4, 2004).

187. Gene Johnson, "Muslim Chaplain Who Was Cleared of Charges Resigns," *Seattle Post-Intelligencer*, August 2, 2004, http://seattlepi.nwsource.com/local/aplocal_story.asp?category=6420&slug=WA%20Muslim%20Chaplain (accessed August 4, 2004).

188. "Feds Arrest Va. Man For Libya Ties," *CBSNEWS.com*, September 29, 2003, http://www.cbsnews.com/stories/2003/09/29/attack/main575749.shtml (accessed August 4, 2004).

189. Michael Isikoff and Mark Hosenball, "Who, and What, Does He Know," *Newsweek*, October 1, 2003, http://www.msnbc.com/news/974564.asp?0sl=-12 (accessed August 4, 2004).

190. James Vincini, "FBI Arrests Man Linked to American Muslim Groups," Reuters, September 29, 2003, http://www.asia.reuters.com/newsArticle;html?type=topnews&storyID=3526224 (accessed November 13, 2003).

191. Isikoff and Hosenball, "Who and What Does He Know."

192. "Feds Arrest VA Man For Libya Ties."

193. "ALERT the Case of Abdurahman Alamoudi—Update," *Muslim American Society*, October 2, 2003, http://www.masnet.org/takeaction.asp?id=512 (accessed August 4, 2004).

194. *In re: Terrorist Attacks on September 11, 2001, Federal Insurance Co., et al., v. Al Qaida, et al.*, 2004 WL 1348996 (S.D.N.Y.).

195. "Muslim Teen Files Suit Over Alleged Beating By Orange County Mob: Police Believe Incident Was Hate Crime," *NBC4 TV News*, April 23, 2003, http://www.nbc4.tv/news/2154286/detail.html (accessed August 8, 2004).

196. Ray Henry, "Hate Crime Charges Filed: Second Suspect Arrested in Brutal Beating," *South Coast Today*, June 25, 2003, http://www.southcoasttoday.com/daily/06-03/06-25-03/a01lo005.htm (accessed August 8, 2004).

197. DOJ Civil Rights Division, "Enforcement and Outreach Following the September 11 Terrorist Attacks," *U.S. Department of Justice*, http://www.usdoj.gov/crt/legal info/discrimupdate.htm (accessed August 10, 2004).

198. Don Lattin, "U.S. Muslims Struggle With Faith and Public Image," *San Francisco Chronicle*, March 16, 2003, http://sfgate.com/cgi-bin/article.cgi?file=/chronicle /archive/2003/03/16/MN253692.DTL (accessed July 13, 2004).

199. "Executive Summary: The Status of Muslim Civil Rights in the United States 2004," *Council on American-Islamic Relations*, August 8, 2004, http://www.cairnet .org (accessed August 8, 2004).

200. *US Telecom Ass'n v. FCC*, No. 00-1012b (D.C. Cir. 2004), http://pacer.cadc .uscourts.gov/common/opinions/200403.htm (accessed December 21, 2004).

201. Tom Gutting, "Bush Has Failed to Lead U.S.," *Texas City Sun*, September 22, 2001, http://www.doublestandards.org/gutting1.html (accessed August 5, 2004).

202. Matthew Rothschild, "The New McCarthyism," *Progressive*, http://www.progressive.org/0901/roth0102.html (accessed August 5, 2004).

203. Dan Guthrie, "When the Going Gets Tough, the Tender Turn Tail," *Grant's Pass Daily Courier*, September 15, 2001, http://www.doublestandards .org/lara1.html (accessed August 5, 2004).

204. Robert P. Laurence, "Gag Reflex: We've Met the Enemy, and It Is Us," *Union Tribune*, October 2, 2001, http://www.signonsandiego.com/tvradio/gagreflex .html (accessed August 5, 2004).

205. Vic, "Columnist Stephanie Salter of the Chronicle May Be Getting Fired," *Indymedia*, August 12, 2002, http://sf.indymedia.org/news/2002/08/140546_comment .php (accessed August 5, 2004).

206. Marge Holland, "San Francisco Newspaper Fires Antiwar Reporter," *World Socialist Web Site*, May 2, 2003, http://www.wsws.org/articles/2003/may2003/norr-m02.shtml (accessed August 5, 2004).

207. Sarah Norr, "McCarthyism at the Chronicle?" *Beyond Chron*, July 29, 2004, http://www.beyondchron.org/print_this_story.asp?sdetail=630 (accessed August 13, 2004).

208. Eric Lichtblau, "FBI Admits Secret Seizure of Documents from Associated Press and Opens an Inquiry," *New York Times*, April 24, 2003, p. A20.

209. "Journalist Wins Fight to Remain in United States," *Reporters Committee for Freedom of the Press*, May 20, 2003, http://www.rcfp.org/news/2003/0520mediac.html (accessed August 8, 2004).

210. Monica Lopez, "INS Nabs Journalist in Houston," *KPFT Radio News*, December 13, 2002, http://www.kpft.org/news/121302story1.html (accessed August 5, 2004).

211. "Journalist Wins Fight to Remain in United States."

212. Vikram Dodd, "American Military Bans BBC Crew From Guantanamo Bay for Talking to Inmates," *Guardian*, June 23, 2003, http://www.guardian.co.uk/cuba/story/0,11983,982122,00.html (accessed July 22, 2004).

213. "IFJ Calls For Iraq Probe After Palestinian Journalist Shot Dead By US Troops," *International Federation of Journalists*, August 18, 2003, http://electronicintifada.net/v2/article1828.shtml (accessed August 8, 2004).

214. "New IFJ Demand for Inquiry as Deadly Missile Strike Highlights US Role in Iraq Media Killings," *International Federation of Journalists*, September 13, 2004, http://ifj.org/default.asp?index=2691&Language=EN (accessed November 10, 2004).

215. "Journalists in Danger: Facts on Iraq," *Committee to Protect Journalists*, November 1, 2004, http://www.cpj.org/Briefings/2003/gulf03/iraq_stats.html (accessed November 9, 2004).

216. Peter Phillips, "Corporate Media and Homeland Security Move Towards Total Information Control," *Dissident Voice*, April 26, 2003, http://www.dissidentvoice.org/Articles4/Phillips_Media-TIPS.htm (accessed August 5, 2004).

217. "Freed Iranians Accuse US Of Torture," *Agence France Presse*, November 4, 2003, http://www.theage.com.au/articles/2003/11/04/1067708171880.html (accessed July 22, 2004).

218. National Lawyers Guild, *National Lawyers Guild Notes*, Spring 2004, pp.1, 3, 6.

219. David Cole "13,000 Arabs & Muslims in U.S. Face Deportation & John Ashcroft Attempts to Expand Patriot Act," *Democracy Now!* June 9, 2003, http://www.democracynow.org/print.pl?sid=03/06/09/1652214 (accessed August 5, 2004).

220. "Teenaged Pakistani Brothers Face Deportation," *DAWN*, July 3, 2003, http://www.dawn.com/2003/07/04/nat29.htm (accessed August 5, 2004).

221. Sean Holstege, "Immigration Tears Family Apart," *Oakland Tribune*, July 2, 2003, http://www.amuslimvoice.org/html/body_oakland_tribune_7-2-2003.html (accessed August 5, 2004).

222. "Teenaged Pakistani Brothers Face Deportation."

223. Holstege, "Immigration Tears Family Apart."

224. "Immigrants Targeted for Deportation After Participating in INS Special Registration Program Speak Out," *ACLU of Northern California,* June 30, 2003, http://www.aclunc.org/pressrel/030630-advisory.html (accessed August 5, 2004).

225. Holstege, "Immigration Tears Family Apart."

226. "As Immigrant Registration Deadlines Loom Once Again, ACLU Sees Trap for Arabs and Muslims," *American Civil Liberties Union,* October 30, 2003, http://www.aclu.org/SafeandFree/SafeandFree.cfm?ID=14256&c=206 (accessed August 5, 2004).

227. "US-VISIT System to Be Launched in Early 2004," *Fragomen, Del Rey, Bernsen & Loewy, P.C.,* December 3, 2003, http://pubweb.fdbl.com/news1.nsf /0/bf8a58f73f7e811685256df1007555a4?OpenDocument (accessed August 5, 2004).

228. Mike McPhee, "Police Outline 'Spy File' Revamp: New Curbs Unveiled after Lawsuit Settled," *Denver Post,* April 18, 2003, http://www.ccmep.org/2003_arti- cles /Civil%20Liberties/041803_police_outline_spy_file_revamp.htm (accessed August 5, 2004).

229. Letter from Mark Schlosberg to Fresno Chief of Police Jerry Dyer, Re: Protecting Fresno Residents' Right to Privacy Against Federally Encouraged Intelli- gence Abuses, February 20, 2003, http://www.aclunc.org/police/030220-fresno.pdf (accessed August 5, 2004).

230. Mike Rhodes, "Local Peace Group Infiltrated By Government Agent," *Community Alliance,* November 2003, http://sfbay.indymedia.org/news/2003/10/ 1650550.php (accessed August 8, 2004).

231. Linda Deutsch, "Part of Patriot Act Ruled Unconstitutional," *CNN.Com,* Jan. 26, 2004, http://www.cnn.com/2004/LAW/01/26/patriot.act.ap/ (accessed August 5, 2004).

232. "Frequently Asked Questions about Government Access to Personal Med- ical Information," *American Civil Liberties Union,* May 30, 2003, http://www.aclu.org /privacy/privacy.cfm?ID=12747&c=27 (accessed July 30, 2004).

233. James Ridgeway, "FBI Snoops at Libraries," *Refuse and Resist,* April 8, 2003, http://www.refuseandresist.org/police_state/art.php?aid=690 (accessed August 4, 2004).

234. Dean Murphy, "Librarians Use Shredder to Show Opposition to New FBI Powers," *New York Times,* April 7, 2003, http://www.commondreams.org/headlines03 /0407-03.htm (accessed August 4, 2004).

235. Christine Pelisek, "Check This Out: Libraries Quietly Sound Alarm Against PATRIOT Act," *Los Angeles Weekly,* July 4–10, 2003, http://www.laweekly .com/ink/03/33/features-pelisek.php (accessed August 8, 2004).

236. Associated Press, "Bush Prevails as House Refuses to Curb Patriot Act," *FreeRepublic.com,* July 8, 2004, http://www.freerepublic.com/focus/f-news/1167860 /posts (accessed July 13, 2004).

237. "Technology Alert List Information for Department Advisors and Supervi- sors," *Carnegie Mellon,* June 3, 2003, http://www.studentaffairs.cmu.edu/oie/ forscho/travel2.cfm (accessed July 20, 2004).

238. Jim Dawson, "Post-September 11th Visa Woes Still Plague International Students and Scientists," *Physics Today,* June 2003, http://www.aip.org/pt/vol-56/iss-6 /p25.html (accessed August 5, 2004).

239. Valerie Torres, "New INS Rules to Affect Students," *KPFT Radio News,*

November 22, 2002, http://www.kpft.org/news/112202story2.html (accessed on July 21, 2004).

240. Joseph J. Hindrawan, "International Student Recruitment Since 9-11, Part I: What Is the Fallout from the War on Terrorism?" *World Education and News Reviews*, March/April 2003, http://www.wes.org/ewenr/03March/Feature.htm (accessed July 21, 2004).

241. Robert M. O'Neil, "Academic Freedom and National Security in Times of Crisis," *Academe*, May/June 2003, http://www.aaup.org/publications/Academe/2003/03mj/03mjonei.htm (accessed July 21, 2004).

242. Mark Clayton, "Academia Becomes Target for New Security Laws," *Christian Science Monitor*, September 24 2002, http://www.csmonitor.com/2002/0924/p11s02-lehl.html (accessed July 21, 2004).

243. Dawson, "Post-September 11th Visa Woes Still Plague International Students and Scientists."

244. Ibid.

245. Marjorie S. Smith, "International Student Recruitment Since 9-11," *World Education News and Reviews*, March/April 2003, http://www.wes.org/ewenr/03May/Feature.htm (accessed July 20, 2004).

246. Josh Goodman, "International Students Find a Changed Land of Opportunity," *Cavalier Daily*, September 11, 2002, http://www.cavalierdaily.com/CVArticle.asp?ID=12884&pid=892 (accessed July 21, 2004).

247. Nathan J. Heller and Jessica R. Rubin-Wills, "In Trying Times, Harvard Takes Safe Road," *Harvard Crimson*, June 5, 2003, http://www.thecrimson.com/article.aspx?ref=348387 (accessed on July 21, 2004).

248. "AAU Summarizes 2003 Visa Survey Results For AAU Universities, Makes Recommendations For Improving Process," *Association of American Universities and the Association of International Educators*, November 14, 2003, http://www .aau.edu/resources/aauvisasurveypressrelease.pdf (accessed July 21, 2004).

249. Ben Ehrenreich, "Passport to Hell," *Orange County Weekly*, October 11-17, 2002, http://www.ocweekly.com/ink/03/06/cover-ehrenreich.php (accessed July 21, 2004).

250. Eric Boehlert, "The Prime-Time Smearing of Sami Al-Arian," *Salon.com*, January 19, 2002, http://archive.salon.com/tech/feature/2002/01/19/bubba (accessed July 21, 2004); "Free Sami Al-Arian," *FreeSamiAlArian.com*, http://www.freesamialarian.com/home.htm (accessed July 21, 2004).

251. Amy Goodman interview of Linda Moreno, "The Case of Sami Al-Arian," *Democracy Now!* July 9, 2004, http://www.democracynow.org/article.pl?sid= 04/07/09/144245&mode=thread&tid=25 (accessed August 5, 2004).

252. Meg Dedolph, "Biggert Discusses Immigration," *Naperville Sun*, August 27, 2003, http://www.suburbanchicagonews.com/sunpub/naper/pay-Article-ID:PFS1310308 (accessed July 21, 2004).

253. Pueng Vongs, "Immigrants, Media Cast Wary Eye on US-VISIT," *Berkeley Daily Planet*, January 9, 2004, http://www.berkeleydailyplanet.com/article.cfm ?archiveDate=01-09-04&storyID=18068 (accessed August 5, 2004).

254. "Cat Stevens Saga 'A Spelling Error,'" *Herald Sun* (Australia), September 26, 2004, http://www.heraldsun.news.com.au/printpage/0,5481,10886578,00.html (accessed February 1, 2005).

255. "Caught in the Backlash," American Civil Liberties Union, November 2002, http://www.aclunc.org/911/backlash/adams.html (accessed August 5, 2004).

256. "Protesters Detained in Milwaukee," *Progressive*, April 27, 2002, http://www.progressive.org/webex/wxmc042702.html (accessed August 5, 2004).

257. "Caught in the Backlash," American Civil Liberties Union.

258. Randall Edwards, "CAPPS II Faces Scrutiny Before Funding," *Federal Computer Week*, June 19, 2003, http://www.fcw.com/fcw/articles/2003/0616/web-capps-06-19-03.asp (accessed July 30, 2004).

259. Roy Mark, "Senate Cans CAPPS II Funding," July 14, 2003, *Internetnews*, http://www.internetnews.com/bus-news/article.php/2234511 (accessed July 30, 2004).

260. "CAPPS II Faces Scrutiny Before Funding," *Federal Computer Week*.

261. Roy Mark, "TSA Says CAPPS II Will Fly On," *Internetnews*, August 27, 2003, http://www.internetnews.com/ec-news/print.php/3069271 (accessed July 30, 2004).

262. "Congress Gives CAPPS II a Failing Grade," *Electronic Frontier Foundation*, February 2004, http://www.eff.org/Privacy/cappsii/concern.php (accessed August 8, 2004).

263. Ryan Singel, "Life After Death for CAPPS II?" *Wired News*, July 16, 2004, http://www.wired.com/news/privacy/0,1848,64240,00.html?tw=wn_story_top5 (accessed August 8, 2004).

264. "The Plight of Maher Arar," *911 Review*, March 14, 2003, http://www.911review.org/Wget/freemaherarar.com/ (accessed July 30, 2004).

265. Jeff Sallot, "PM Trying to Repatriate Alleged Al-Qaeda Terrorist," *Globe and Mail*, June 26, 2003, http://www.theglobeandmail.com/servlet/story/RTGAM.20030626.ualqaeda0626/BNPrint/National/ (accessed July 30, 2004).

266. "The Plight of Maher Arar," *911 Review*.

267. Maher Arar, "Now Let Me Tell You Who I Am: Statement Of Maher Arar," *Portland Indymedia*, November 6, 2003, http://portland.indymedia.org/es/2003/11/274764.shtml (accessed July 30, 2004).

268. "Canadian Freed From Syrian Jail Happy To Be Home," *CBC News*, October 7, 2003, http://www.cbc.ca/stories/2003/10/06/arar_back03 (accessed July 30, 2004).

269. "Maher Arar Sues Syria, Jordan," *CBS News*, November 14, 2003, http://www.cbc.ca/stories/2003/11/24/arar_lawsuit031124 (accessed June 7, 2004).

270. "Arar to Sue Ashcroft," *CBC News*, January 22, 2004, http://www.cbc.ca/stories/2003/11/24/arar_lawsuit031124 (accessed July 30, 2004).

271. "Maher Arar: Timeline," *Canadian Broadcasting Company News Online*, July 29, 2004, http://www.cbc.ca/news/background/arar/ (accessed August 7, 2004).

272. Jen Nessel, Communications Dept., Center for Constitutional Rights, e-mail message to MCLI, August 11, 2004.

273. Laura Flanders, "Security threat? Bernadette Devlin McAliskey Barred Entry to the United States," *CounterPunch*, February 22, 2003, http://archives.econ.utah.edu/archives/marxism/2003w07/msg00286.htm (accessed July 23, 2004).

274. Nora Dwyer, "Report from Delegations to the Basque Territory and Spain," *National Lawyers Guild Notes*, Winter 2002.

275. National Lawyers Guild, "Basque Lawyer Refused Entry for Minneapolis Convention," *Twin Cities Independent Media Center,* http://twincities.indymedia .org/newswire/display/14659 (accessed August 8, 2004).

276. Elena Lappin, "A Foreign Reporter Gets a Story of U.S. Paranoia," *Los Angeles Times,* May 11, 2004, http://reclaimdemocracy.org/articles_2004/us_paranoia .html (accessed July 23, 2004).

277. Cindy Domingo, "Peace & Freedom," *WILPF* (Winter 2004): 22.

278. Ibid.

279. "Resist Erosion to Our Limited Right to Travel to Cuba," *Women's International League for Peace and Freedom,* http://www.wilpf.org/campaigns/cuba/CUBA_ actions.htm (accessed February 1, 2005).

280. Pam Zubeck, "Love Can't Get Past the Border," *Colorado Springs Gazette,* October 12, 2003, http://www.unknownnews.net/031013tina.html (accessed June 21, 2004).

281. Trevor Hughes, "An 'Answer' From DHS," *Land of the Free?,* December 16, 2003, http://landofthefree.blogspot.com/archives/2003_12_14_landofthefree_ archive .html (accessed August 14, 2004.); Pam Zubeck, "Wedding Bells or Deportation Cells," *Philly.com,* January 14, 2004, http://www.philly.com/mld/philly/news/nation /7692658.htm?1c (accessed August 14, 2004).

282. "Congress Affirms Bush Electoral Victory," *CNN.com,* January 6, 2001, http://cnnstudentnews.cnn.com/2001/ALLPOLITICS/stories/01/06/electoral.vote/ (accessed July 16, 2004).

283. Peter Philips and Project Censored, *Media Democracy in Action: Censored 2004* (New York: Seven Stories Press, 2003), p. 42.

284. See: http://www.bartcop.com/111102fraud.htm (accessed July 31, 2004).

285. Paul Krugman, "Hack the Vote," *New York Times,* December 2, 2002, http://www.nytimes.com/2003/12/02/opinion/02krug.html (accessed April 20, 2004); Elena Cabral, Oscar Corral, and William Yardly, "Angry Frustrated Voters Fault Officials for Lapses," *Miami Herald,* September 12, 2002, http://www.miami.com/ mld/miami/4054880.htm?1c (accessed July 13, 2004); Alastair Thompson, "American Coup: Mid-Term Election Polls vs Actuals," *Scoop.co.nz,* November 12, 2002, http://www.scoop.co.nz/mason/stories/HL0211/S00078.htm (accessed August 3, 2004); Thom Hartman, "If You Want to Win an Election, Just Control the Voting Machines," *CommonDreams.org,* January 31, 2003, http://www.commondreams.org/ views03/0131-01.htm (accessed July 8, 2004); Lloyd Freeman, "Florida Fouls up State Election: Reno Defeated," Howard University's *The Hilltop,* September 20, 2002, http://www.thehilltoponline.com/global_user_elements/printpage.cfm?storyid =278269 (accessed July 13, 2004); Chris Floyd, "'Disappearing' the Republic at the Push of a Button, Vanishing Act," *Counterpunch,* September 26, 2003, http://www.counterpunch.org/floyd09262003.html (accessed July 10, 2004); R.B. McHam, "A Government Hijacked, The Illegal Coup of '02," *LinkCrusader.com,* July 7, 2003, http://www.linkcrusader.com/vote_machines.htm (accessed July 13, 2004).

286. James Bovard, "Bush's WMD Flimflams," *Freedom Daily,* September 2003, http://www.fff.org/freedom/fd0309d.asp (accessed June 23, 2004).

287. Joseph C. Wilson, "What I Didn't Find in Africa," *New York Times,* July 6, 2003, http://www.commondreams.org/views03/0706-02.htm (accessed July 30,

2004).

288. AFP, "White House Backs Off Iraqi Uranium Claim," *Common Dreams*, July 8, 2003, http://www.commondreams.org/headlines03/0708-09.htm (accessed July 30, 2004).

289. Robert Scheer, "A Diplomat's Undiplomatic Truth: They Lied," *Nation*, July 9, 2003, http://www.thenation.com/doc.mhtml?i=20030721&s=scheer20030708 (accessed July 30, 2004).

290. Lakshmi Chaudhry, "The Importance of Being Joe Wilson," *AlterNet*, November 3, 2003, http://www.alternet.org/story/17091 (accessed July 30, 2004).

291. Bill Nichols and John Diamond, "War Critic at Center of CIA Flap Always Vague on Wife's Job," *USA Today*, October 1, 2003, http://www.usatoday.com/news/washington/2003-09-30-couple_x.htm (accessed July 30, 2004).

292. Associated Press, "White House Staff Investigating CIA Leak," *JSOnline*, October 4, 2003, http://www.jsonline.com/news/nat/ap/oct03/ap-cia-leak100403.asp ?format=print (accessed August 9, 2004).

293. "Valerie Plame 2004 Headlines," *Disinfopedia*, http://www.disinfopedia .org/wiki.phtml?title=Valerie_Plame/External_Links:_2004 (accessed June 21, 2004).

294. Terence Hunt, "Bush Consults Lawyer in CIA Leak Case," *Guardian*, June 3, 2004, http://www.guardian.co.uk/worldlatest/story/0,1280,-4162100,00.html (accessed August 5, 2004).

295. Philip J. Berg, "9-11 Victim's Wife Files RICO Case Against GW," *Scoop New Zealand News*, November 26, 2003, http://www.scoop.co.nz/mason/stories/WO0311/S00261.htm (accessed July 30, 2004).

296. Ellen Mariani, "911 Victim Ellen Mariani Open Letter To The POTUS," *Scoop New Zealand News*, November 27, 2003, http://www.scoop.co.nz/mason/stories/WO0311/S00262.htm (accessed August 5, 2004).

297. Berg, "9-11 Victim's Wife Files RICO Case Against GW."

298. "Bush Asks Daschle to Limit Sept. 11 Probe," *CNN.com*, January 29, 2002, http://www.cnn.com/2002/ALLPOLITICS/01/29/inv.terror.probe/ (accessed July 29, 2004).

299. Brian Montopoli, "Schlep to Judgment," *Washington Monthly*, September 2003, http://www.washingtonmonthly.com/features/2003/0309.montopoli.html (accessed July 27, 2004).

300. Ibid.

301. Laurence Arnold, "Bush Calls White House Data on the 9-11 Attacks 'Sensitive'," Associated Press, October 27, 2003, http://www.apfn.net/messageboard/10-28-03/discussion.cgi.75.html (accessed July 29, 2004).

302. Montopoli, "Schlep to Judgment."

303. Ken Silverstein, "Congress Presses White House For 9/11 Papers," *Los Angeles Times*, October 27, 2003, http://www.commondreams.org/headlines03/1027 -07.htm (accessed July 29, 2003).

304. Patrick Martin, "Terrorism Commission Caves in to White House over 9/11 Documents," *World Socialist Website*, November 24, 2003, http://wsws.org/articles/2003/nov2003/911-n24.shtml (accessed July 27, 2004).

305. Hope Yen, "9/11 Panel Says Iraq Rebuffed Bin Laden," Associated Press, http://apnews.myway.com/article/20040616/D83860A00.html (accessed July 29,

2004, 2004).

306. Editorial, "The Plain Truth," *New York Times*, June 17, 2004, p. A28, http://www.nytimes.com/2004/06/17/opinion/17THU1.html (accessed July 27, 2004).

307. David Johnson and Douglas Jehl, "Report Cites Lapses Across Government and 2 Presidencies," *New York Times*, July 23, 2004, p. A1.

308. Philip Shenon, "9/11 Report Calls for Sweeping Overhaul of Intelligence," *New York Times*, July 23, 2004, p. A10.

309. "A Citizen's Critique: The 9/11 Commission Process," *9/11 Citizens Watch*, http://www.911citizenswatch.org/9-11-Commission-Critique.rtf (accessed July 27, 2004); Ron Hutcheson, "Bush Agreed to Talk to Kean Commission Only with Cheney at His Side," *New Jersey News-Ledger*, http://www.911citizenswatch .org/modules.php?op=modload&name=News&file=article&sid=173 (accessed July 27, 2004).

310. Greg Gordon, "Dayton: FAA, NORAD Hid 9/11 Failures," *Minneapolis Star Tribune*, July 31, 2004, http://www.startribune.com/stories/484/4904237.html (accessed August 3, 2004).

311. "Letter From Sibel Edmonds to the 9/11 Commission," *OpEdNews.com*, August 1, 2004, http://www.opednews.com/edmonds_080304_911_commission _letter.htm (accessed August 4, 2004); and see audio interview with Sibel Edmonds and Daniel Ellsberg at "Sibel Edmonds Story," http://www.kathymcmahon.utvinternet .com/mrn/Sibel-Edmonds.htm (accessed August 9, 2004).

312. Judy Sarasohn, "9/11 Commission Gets Outside PR Help," *Washington Post*, August 5, 2004, http://www.washingtonpost.com/ac2/wp-dyn/A41221-2004Aug 4?language=printer (accessed August 6, 2004); Verena Dobnik, "9/11 Commission's Book Selling Well," Associated Press, July 23, 2004, http://www.guardian .co.uk/worldlatest/story/0,1280,-4344568,00.html (accessed August 6, 2004).

313. Mitch Jeserich, "Bush Responds to 911 Report," *Free Speech Radio News*, August 2, 2004, http://www.fsrn.org/news/20040802_news.html (accessed August 4, 2004); Zachary Coile, "Bush Has Own Plan for New Spy Chief: Job Wouldn't Be in Cabinet as Report Urged," *San Francisco Chronicle*, August 3, 2004, http:// www.sfgate.com/cgi-bin/article.cgi?file=/chronicle/archive/2004/08/03/ MNGDL81RFT1.DTL (accessed August 8, 2004); "Bush Nominated Goss for CIA Head" *Democracy Now!* August 11, 2004, http://www.democracynow .org/article .pl?sid=04/08/11/144246 (accessed August 11, 2004); Benjamin DeMott, "White-wash as Public Service: How the *9/11 Commission Report* Defrauds the Nation," *Harper's*, October 2004, p. 35.

314. Committee On Government Reform—Minority Staff Special Investigations Division, "Iraq on the Record: The Bush Administration's Public Statements on Iraq," *a.k.a* "Waxman Report," *United States House of Representatives*, March 16, 2004, http://www.house.gov/reform/min/pdfs_108_2/pdfs_inves/pdf_admin_iraq_on_the_ record_rep.pdf (accessed August 9, 2004).

315. Tom Carver, "Pentagon Plans Propaganda War," *BBC News*, February 20, 2002, http://www.100777.com/node/view/317 (accessed June 21, 2004).

316. Sonoma State University, "CIA Continues OSI Programs," *Censored Alert* 7, no. 1 (Fall 2003): 4.

317. "The Office of Strategic Influence Is Gone, But Are Its Programs Still In Place?" *Fairness and Accuracy in Reporting*, November 27, 2002, http://www.fair.org/press-releases/osi-followup.html (accessed August 9, 2004).

318. Press Briefing Transcript, "Secretary Rumsfeld Media Availability En Route to Chile," *United States Department of Defense*, November 18, 2002, http://www.defenselink.mil/transcripts/2002/t11212002_t1118sd2.html (accessed August 9, 2004).

319. See http://www.nysd.uscourts.gov/Sept11Litigation.htm.

320. Associated Press, "Voter Purge List Released," *News-Press.com*, July 2, 2004, http://www.southwestfloridaonline.com/news/local_state/040702ruling_lee_bon .html (accessed July 15, 2004).

321. CNN, "Florida Scraps List of Suspected Felons Barred from Voting," *CNN.com*, July 12, 2004, http://www.cnn.com/2004/ALLPOLITICS/07/12/felons (accessed July 15, 2004).

322. Joe Garofoli, "Lawmakers ASK U.N. to Monitor Elections," *San Francisco Chronicle*, July 9, 2004, http://www.sfgate.com/cgi-bin/article.cgi?file=/chronicle/ archive/2004/07/09/BAGBC7I14712.DTL (accessed July 9, 2004).

323. Dan Morgan, "Proposal to Have U.N. Monitor Elections Ends in Partisan Clash," *Washington Post*, July 19, 2004, p. A15, http://www.washingtonpost.com/wp-dyn/ articles/A60143-2004Jul18.html (accessed July 19, 2004).

324. Joseph Farah, "Renewed Push for U.N. to Monitor U.S. Voting," *WorldNet Daily*, July 21, 2004, http://www.worldnetdaily.com/news/article.asp?ARTICLE _ID=39549 (accessed August 9, 2004).

# CHAPTER 4, C-D

1. Askia Muhammad, "Former U.S. Diplomats Want Bush Out," *FinalCall.com*, July 2, 2004, http://www.finalcall.com/artman/publish/article_1489 .shtml (accessed July 12, 2004).

2. "Official Statement," *Diplomats and Military Commanders for Change*, http://www.diplomatsforchange.com/project/statement.shtml (accessed July 12, 2004).

3. Ibid.

4. "The Signatories," *Diplomats and Military Commanders for Change*, http://www.diplomatsforchange.com/signatories/signatories.shtml (accessed July 12, 2004).

5. Oliver Burkeman and Julian Borger, "War Critics Astonished as U.S. Hawk Admits Invasion was Illegal," *Guardian*, http://www.guardian.co.uk/Iraq/Story/ 0,2763,1089159,00.html (accessed May 24, 2004).

6. "Afghanistan: U.S. Bombs Kill Twenty-three Civilians," *Human Rights Watch*, http://www.hrw.org/press/2001/10/afghan1026.htm (accessed July 27, 2004).

7. Mark Herold, "Casualties in Afghanistan and Iraq," *Unknown News*, http://www.unknownnews.net/casualties.html (accessed August 8, 2004).

8. Jonathan Steele, "Forgotten Victims," *Guardian UK*, May 20, 2002,

http://www.guardian.co.uk/analysis/story/0,3604,718635,00.html (accessed July 7, 2004).

9. Reuters, "Red Cross Warns Afghan Children Off Cluster Bombs," *Revolutionary Association of the Women of Afghanistan*, June 29, 2002, http://www.rawa.fancy marketing.net/cluster2.htm (accessed June 21, 2004).

10. "Scores Killed in US Afghan Raid," *BBCNews.com*, July 1, 2002, http://news.bbc.co.uk/1/hi/world/south_asia/2079565.stm (accessed June 21, 2004).

11. Associated Press, "6 Afghan Children Die In U.S. Attack," *MSNBC News*, December 10, 2003, http://msnbc.msn.com/id/3675426/ (accessed June 21, 2004).

12. "U.S. Bombing Kills Afghan Children," *BBCNews.com*, December 7, 2003, http://news.bbc.co.uk/2/hi/south_asia/3297575.stm (accessed August 8, 2004).

13. Associated Press, "Afghan Officials Say U.S. Raid Kills 11, Including 4 Children," *ContraCostaTimes.com*, January 20, 2004, http://www.contracostatimes .com/mld/cctimes/news/world/7751568.htm?1c (accessed June 17, 2004).

14. Saeed Shabazz, "President Aristide Calls for Reparations," *FinalCall.com*, October 8, 2003, http://www.newshaiti.com/index.php?mode=single&n=351 (accessed July 6, 2004).

15. "Resolution of the San Francisco Labor Council Honoring the Bicentennial of Haiti," *San Francisco Labor Council*, December 8, 2003, http://www .iacenter.org/haiti-sflabor03.htm (accessed July 6, 2004).

16. "Aristide: U.S. Forced Me to Leave," *BBC News*, March 2, 2004, http://news.bbc.co.uk/1/hi/world/americas/3524273.stm (accessed July 6, 2004).

17. "Congresswoman Barbara Lee Introduces TRUTH Act," *HaitiAction.com*, March 9, 2004, http://www.haitiaction.com/News/BL/bl3_9_4.html (accessed July 6, 2004).

18. Amy Goodman interviews Max Blumenthal, "Did the Bush Administration Allow a Network of Right-Wing Republicans to Foment a Violent Coup in Haiti?" *Democracy Now!* July 20, 2004, http://www.democracynow.org/article.pl?sid =04/07/20/1327215 (accessed July 20, 2004).

19. Nicolas Watt and Oliver Burkeman, "Bush Asks Congress for Right to Attack," *Guardian UK*, September 20, 2002, http://www.guardian.co.uk/Iraq/Story/ 0,2763,795589,00.html (accessed July 29, 2004).

20. Joint Resolution to Authorize the Use of United States Armed Forces Against Iraq, 2002 PL 107-243, October 16, 2002.

21. "Powell Says U.S.-led War on Iraq 'Consistent with International Law,'" *MSNBC News*, September 17, 2004, http://www.msnbc.msn.com/id/6016893 (accessed December 3, 2004).

22. Les Roberts et al., "Mortality Before and After the 2003 Invasion of Iraq: Cluster Sample Survey," *Lancet*, October 29, 2004, http://pdf.thelancet.com/pdfdownload ?vid=llan.364.9448.primary_research.31264.1&x=x.pdf (accessed December 3, 2004).

23. Fred Abrahams, "Violent Response: The U.S. Army in Al-Fallujah," *Human Rights Watch*, June 2003, http://www.hrw.org/reports/2003/iraqfallujah/Iraqfallujah-09 .htm#P426_64212 (accessed July 29, 2004).

24. Robert H. Reid, "Iraqi Frustration," *San Francisco Examiner*, October 2, 2003, http://www.sfexaminer.com/article/index.cfm/i/100203b_iraq (accessed July 29, 2004).

25. Fred Abrahams, "As U.S. Kills Two Iraqi Demonstrators In Baghdad,

Human Rights Watch Demands Full Investigation Of U.S. Killings In Fallujah," *Democracy Now!* June 18, 2003, http://www.democracynow.org/article.pl?sid=03/ 06/18/1436233 (accessed July 29, 2004).

26. Zehira Houfani, "Human Rights, US Style: The Pupil Is Gone, The Master Has Replaced Him," *Montreal Iraq Solidarity Project,* July 29, 2003, http://electroniciraq .net/news/999.shtml (accessed July 26, 2004).

27. Peter Symonds, "US Occupation Authority Suppresses Study of Iraqi Civilian Casualties," *World Socialist Web Site,* December 15, 2003, http://www.wsws .org/articles/2003/dec2003/iraq-d15.shtml (accessed August 9, 2004).

28. Human Rights Watch, "Off Target: The Conduct of the War and Civilian Casualties in Iraq," *Human Rights Watch,* December 2003, http://www.hrw.org/ reports/2003/usa1203/ (accessed August 9, 2004).

29. Patrick Cockburn and Raymond Whitaker, "Missile Strike by US Kills 22 Civilians in Iraq," *Independent News UK,* June 20, 2004, http://news.independent .co.uk/world/middle_east/story.jsp?story=533378 (accessed August 9, 2004).

30. Mark Benjamin, "US Casualties from Iraq War Top 9,000," *United Press International,* November 14, 2003, http://upi.com/view.cfm?StoryID=20031113-074311-4128r (accessed July 21, 2004).

31. Ibid.

32. Mike Lee, "Casualty Ward: U.S. Medical Center Handles Thousands of Trauma Cases From Iraq War," *ABC News,* August 8, 2004, http://abcnews.go .com/sections/WNT/World/landstuhl_040808.html (accessed August 9, 2004).

33. Suzanne Goldberg, "Pentagon Counts the Psychological Cost of Iraq War as Survey Reveals Suicide Levels," *Guardian Unlimited,* March 29, 2004, http://www .guardian.com.uk/Iraq/Story/0,2763,1180025,00.html (accessed December 3, 2004).

34. Michael Ewens, ed., "Casualties in Iraq: The Human Cost of Occupation," *Antiwar.com,* December 3, 2004, http://www.antiwar.com/casualties (accessed December 3, 2004).

35. Tom Allard, "Check on Execution Claims Promised," *Sydney Morning Herald,* July 20, 2004, http://www.smh.com.au/articles/2004/07/19/1090089101841 .html?oneclick=true (accessed July 19, 2004).

36. Paul McGeough, "Allawi Shot Prisoners in Cold Blood: Witnesses," *Sydney Morning Herald,* July 17, 2004, http://www.smh.com.au/articles/2004/07/16/ 1089694568757.html?oneclick=true (accessed July 19, 2004).

37. "Allawi Ran CIA-backed Bombing Campaigns: Report," *ABC News Online,* June 9, 2004, http://www.abc.net.au/news/newsitems/s1128433.htm (accessed July 19, 2004).

38. McGeough, "Allawi Shot Prisoners in Cold Blood: Witnesses."

39. Allard, "Check on Execution Claims Promised."

40. "Country Reports on Human Rights Practices-Egypt," *Bureau of Democracy, Human Rights, and Labor,* February 25, 2004, http://www.state.gov/g/drl/ rls/hrrpt/2003/27926.htm (accessed June 29, 2004); Clyde R. Mack, Foreign Affairs, Defense, and Trade Division, "Egypt-United States Relations," *Congressional Research Service,* http://fpc.state.gov/documents/organization/23589.pdf (accessed September 14, 2004).

41. "Country Reports on Human Rights Practices—Israel," *Bureau of Democ-*

*racy, Human Rights, and Labor,* February 25, 2004 http://www.state.gov/g/drl/
rls/hrrpt/2003/27929.htm (accessed June 29, 2004); Clyde R. Mack, http://fpc
.state.gov/documents/organization/17876.pdf.

42. *Legal Consequences of the Construction of a Wall in the Occupied Palestinian Territories,* International Court of Justice, July 9, 2004, General List No. 131; Aluf Benn, "ICJ: West Bank Fence Is Illegal, Israel Must Tear It Down," *Ha'aretz,* July 9, 2004, http://www.haaretz.com/hasen/spages/449395.html (accessed July 9, 2004).

43. "Fact Sheet—Colombia: The Pentagon's New Target in Latin America," *International Action Center,* http://www.iacenter.org/colombia_fact.htm (accessed July 28, 2004).

44. Kristine Herwig, "The Environment, Plan Colombia, and U.S. Aid," *Macalester Environmental Review,* September 25, 2002, http://www.macalester .edu/~envirost/MacEnvReview/Colombia.htm (accessed July 28, 2004).

45. Aldo Lale-Demoz, "UNDCP Letter of 2 November to the Sunshine Project," *United Nations Drug Control Program,* November 2, 2000, http://www.sunshine-project .org/agentgreen/laledemoz.html (accessed July 28, 2004).

46. Al Giordano, "Plan Colombia Is Now Called the "Andean Initiative," *Nadir.org,* May 25, 2001, http://www.nadir.org/nadir/initiativ/agp/free/colombia/txt/ 2001/0525andean_initiative.htm (accessed July 28, 2004).

47. Sandra Alvarez and Jason Mark, "Plan Colombia and Mission Creep," *Abu Saleh,* March 14, 2002, http://www.abusaleh.com/index.php?id=154 (accessed July 28, 2004).

48. "U.S. Aid to Colombia Since 1997: Summary Tables," *Center for International Policy's Colombia Program,* February 20, 2004, http://www.ciponline .org/colombia/aidtable.htm (accessed July 28, 2004).

49. "Announcement from Chair Peace Fresno Education Committee," December 3, 2003.

50. Donna Miles, "Army to Expand Stop-Loss Program," *American Forces Information Service,* January 2, 2004, http://www.defenselink.mil/news/Jan2004/ n01022004_200401023.html (accessed November 3, 2004).

51. David Walsh, "US Army's Expanded "Stop-Loss" Program Prevents Thousands from Leaving Military," *World Socialist Web Site,* June 4, 2004, http://www.wsw.org/articles/2004/jun2004/stop-j04_prn.shtml (accessed November 3, 2004).

52. "'Stop Loss' Continues," *Chicago Tribune,* Military.com, September 27, 2004, http://www.military.com/NewsContent/0%2C13319%2CFL_loss_092704 %2C00.html (accessed November 3, 2004).

53. Walsh, "US Army's Expanded 'Stop-Loss.'"

54. Army News Services, "New Army Stop-Loss Program," *About,* November 19, 2003, http://usmilitary.about.com/cs/terrorism/a/arstoploss_p.htm (accessed November 3, 2004).

55. Miles, "Army to Expand Stop-Loss Program."

56. Gabriel Packard, "Hundreds of Soldiers Emerge as Conscientious Objectors," *Common Dreams,* April 15, 2003, http://www.commondreams.org/headlines 03/0415-11.htm (accessed July 13, 2004).

57. Liz Zanoni, "Baxter Speaks on Conscientious Objection in Gulf War,"

*Observer,* February 1, 2001, http://www.nd.edu/~observer/02012001/News/6.html (accessed August 9, 2004).

58. "AWOL GI Refuses Service in 'Gulf War II,'" *IndyMedia,* November 20, 2002, http://www.madison.indymedia.org/newswire/display_pprintable/8411/index .php (accessed July 13, 2004).

59. Pam Belluck, "Absent from Unit in Iraq for Months, Soldier Turns Protester and Surrenders," *New York Times,* March 16, 2004, http://www .refusingtokill.net/CamiloMejiaNYT.htm (accessed July 30, 2004).

60. "Camilo Mejia Seeks Conscientious Objector Status," *Democracy Now!* June 24, 2004, http://www.democracynow.org/article.pl?sid=04/06/24/1422242 (accessed July 12, 2004); Melinda Tuhus, "BTL: Army Conscientious Objector Who Opposed Abuse of Iraqi Civilians and...," *Between the Lines,* June 27, 2004, http://nyc.indymedia .org/newswire/display/95799/index.php (accessed July 12, 2004) and http://www.duck daotsu.org/mejia_testimony.html (accessed November 18, 2004).

61. Pamela J. Podger, "Marine Obeys His Conscience, Reservist Didn't Ship Out With His Unit to Iraq," *Central Committee for Conscientious Objectors,* April 2, 2003, http://www.objector.org/ccco/inthenews/funkco.html (accessed July 30, 2004).

62. Call to Action, "Demand Freedom for Stephen Funk 1st War Resister to be Jailed November 15th 2003—Camp Lejeune Military Base, North Carolina," *Refusing to Kill,* November 10-14, 2003, http://www.refusingtokill.net/USStephenFunk/convergence forstephenfunk.htm (accessed August 9, 2004).

63. NION, "Welcome Home Stephen Funk!" *IndyBay.org,* February 28, 2004, http://www.indybay.org/news/2004/02/1671696.php (accessed August 9, 2004).

64. Podger, "Marine Obeys His Conscience, Reservist Didn't Ship Out With His Unit to Iraq."

65. "Soldier Brings First Challenge to Army Policy Requiring Extended Military Service for Iraq Occupation," *Common Dreams,* August 16, 2004, http://www.commondreams.org/news2004/0816-09.htm (accessed November 3, 2004); *Doc v. Ashcroft,* Law Offices of Michael S. Sorgen, http://www .sorgen.net/id27_stoplosspetition.htm (accessed November 4, 2004).

66. Robert Norris and Hans M. Kristesen, "NRDC: Nuclear Notebook, Global Nuclear Stockpiles, 1945–2002," *Bulletin of Atomic Scientists,* November/December 2002, http://www.thebulletin.org/article_nn.php?art_ofn =nd02norris (accessed December 1, 2004); "Nonviolence on Trial," *Nukewatch,* April 4, 2000, http://www.serve.com/gvaughn/nukewatch/sp00trial.html (accessed December 1, 2004); Steve Fetter, "The Future of Nuclear Arms Control," *American Physical Society Centennial Symposium: History of Physics in National Defense,* World Congress Center, Atlanta, May 24, 1999, http://www.puaf.umd.edu/faculty/ papers/fetter/APS.pdf (accessed December 1, 2004).

67. Nicole Deller, Arjun Makhijani, and John Burroughs, "Multilateral Treaties Are Fundamental Tools for Protecting Global Security," *Lawyers' Committee on Nuclear Policy,* June 2004, http://www.lcnp.org/pubs/rpbflier.htm (accessed July 16, 2004).

68. John Burroughs, "The Shameful U.S. Record in 2003 Disarmament Votes at the United Nations," *Common Dreams,* December 15, 2003, http://www.common dreams .org/views03/1215-04.htm (accessed July 16, 2004); Richard DuBoff, "Mirror, Mirror On The Wall, Who's The Biggest Rogue Of All?" *Z Magazine,* September

2003, http://zmagsite.zmag.org/Sept2003/duboff0903.html (accessed July 14, 2004).

69. John Burroughs, Executive Director, Lawyers' Committee on Nuclear Policy, e-mail communication with the MCLI, July 12, 2004.

70. Donald H. Rumsfeld, Secretary of Defense, "Nuclear Posture Review Report," January 8, 2002, http://www.globalsecurity.org/wmd/library/policy/dod/npr.htm (accessed July 15, 2004).

71. Legality of the Threat or Use of Nuclear Weapons: International Court of Justice Advisory Opinion of July 8, 1996, http://www.icj-cij.org/icjwww/icases/iunan/iunanframe.htm (accessed July 15, 2004).

72. The Center for Defense Information (CDI) in cooperation with the Natural Resources Defense Council (NRDC) and the Stockholm International Peace Research Institute (SIRPI).

73. John Burroughs, "The Nuclear Threat," Presentation at the Barcelona Forum, June 25, 2004, http://www.lcnp.org/disarmament/Barcelona_WMD.pdf (accessed July 15, 2004).

74. Carl Hulse, "Senate Backs New Research on A-Bombs," *New York Times*, June 16, 2004, p. A16

75. William Matthews, "U.S. House Rejects Plea For New Nuclear Arms," *Defense News*, July 12, 2004, http://www.defensenews.com/story.php?F=3055565 &C=america. (accessed July 16, 2004).

76. Ann Fagan Ginger, ed., *Nuclear Weapons Are Illegal: the Historic Opinion of the World Court and How It Will Be Enforced* (New York: Apex Press, 1998), pp. 74-76.

77. Walter C. Uhler, "Policy is a Dangerous Return to Anxieties of the Cold War," *Philadelphia Enquirer*, March 18, 2002, http://www.philly.com/mld/ inquirer/news/editorial/2883600.htm?1c (accessed August 13, 2004).

78. Scott Peterson, "Remains of Toxic Bullets Litter Iraq," *Christian Science Monitor*, May 15, 2003, http://www.csmonitor.com/2003/0515/p01s02-woiq.html (accessed August 8, 2004).

79. Larry Johnson, "Use of Depleted Uranium Weapons Lingers as Health Concern." *Seattle Post Intelligencer*, August 4, 2003, http://seattlepi.nwsource .com/iraq2003/133581_du04.html (accessed July 30, 2004).

80. Sara Flounders, "Another War Crime? Iraqi Cities "Hot" With Depleted Uranium," *International Action Center*, August 18, 2003, http://www.iacenter.org/du-war crime.htm (accessed July 15, 2004).

81. "Legality of the Threat or Use of Nuclear Weapons," *International Court of Justice*, 1996 General List No. 95, (1) ¶¶ 74-87, (2) ¶ 31.

82. Juan Gonzales, "Poisoned?: Shocking Report Reveals Local Troops May Be Victims of America's High-Tech Weapons," *New York Daily News*, April 3, 2004, http://www.nydailynews.com/front/story/180333p-156685c.html (accessed August 9, 2004).

83. Alex Kirby, "Afghans' Uranium Levels Spark Alert," *BBC News Online*, May 23, 2003, http://news.bbc.co.uk/2/hi/science/nature/3050317.stm (accessed July 30, 2004).

84. Mohammed Daud Miraki, "The Silent Genocide from America," *Afghan DU & Recovery Fund*, June 5, 2003, http://www.afghandufund.org/miraki_silent _genocide.pdf (accessed July 30, 2004).

85. Miraki, "The Perpetual Death From America," *World Uranium Weapons Conference*, February 24, 2003, http://www.uranwaffenkonferenz.de/speakers/miraki_perpetual_death.pdf (accessed July 30, 2004).

86. T. Weyman, "Afghan Field Trip #2 Report: Precision Destruction-Indiscriminate Effects," *Uranium Medical Research Center*, November 2002, http://www.mindfully.org/Nucs/2002/Afghan-Destruction-Effects-UMRCNov02.htm (accessed July 30, 2004).

87. "Quotes from Field Team's Trip Report," *Uranium Medical Research Center*, http://www.umrc.net/projectAfghanistan.asp (accessed May 30, 2003).

88. Miraki, "The Silent Genocide from America."

89. Timothy H. Edgar, "Section-by-Section Analysis of Justice Department Draft 'Domestic Security Enhancement Act of 2003' also known as 'PATRIOT Act II,'" *ACLU*, February 14, 2003, http://www.aclu.org/SafeandFree/SafeandFree.cfm?ID=11835&c=206 (accessed June 14, 2004).

90. Charles J. Handy, "Scientists Say Dirty Bomb Would Be A Dud," Associated Press, June 9, 2004, http://www.phillyburbs.com/pb-dyn/news/247-06092004-313952.html (accessed June 11, 2004).

91. Paul Krugman, "Noonday in the Shade: Ashcroft Neglects Real Terrorist Threats Because of His Ideological Biases," *New York Times*, June 22, 2004, http://www.commondreams.org/views04/0622-04.htm (accessed August 6, 2004); Kris Axtman, "The Terror Threat at Home, Often Overlooked," *Christian Science Monitor*, December 29, 2003, http://www.csmonitor.com/2003/1229/p02s01-usju.htm (accessed August 6, 2004).

92. David B. Caruso, "Antiterror Laws Often Used Against Street Criminals," *Mindfully.org*, September 15, 2003, http://www.mindfully.org/Reform/2003/Antiterror-Street-Criminals15sep03.htm (accessed July 30, 2004).

93. Denis Mosgofian, Stan Smith, and Louis Garcia, "OWC CAMPAIGN NEWS—S.F. Labor Council, Open World Conference," *Labor Net*, June 9, 2003, http://www.labornet.org/news/0603/sflcwar.htm (accessed August 10, 2004).

94. David Martin, "Bush Signs Part of PATRIOT Act II into Law—Stealthily," *San Antonio Current*, December 24, 2003, http://www.sacurrent.com/site/news.cfm?newsid=10705756&BRD=2318&PAG=461&dept_id=482778&rfi=6 (accessed July 6, 2004).

95. Susie Day, "Counter-Intelligent: The Surveillance and Indictment of Lynne Stewart," *Monthly Review*, November 2002, http://www.monthlyreview.org/1102day.htm (accessed July 27, 2004); Nat Hentoff, "High Noon for Ashcroft, Stewart, and the Defense Bar," *Village Voice*, April 15, 2002, http://www.villagevoice.com/issues/0216/hentoff.php (accessed August 9, 2004); Elaine Cassel, "The Lynne Stewart Case: When Representing an Accused Terrorist Can Mean the Lawyer Risks Jail, Too," *Counterpunch*, October 12, 2002, http://www.counterpunch.org/cassel1012.html (accessed August 9, 2004).

96. Mark Hamblett, "New Charges Lodged Against Lynne Stewart," *New York Law Journal*, November 20, 2003, http://www.law.com/jsp/article.jsp?id=1069170409840 (accessed July 27, 2004).

97. Homepage Announcement, "Breaking News: Lynne's Trial Blog," *Lynne Stewart Defense Committee*, http://www.lynnestewart.org/ (accessed August 9, 2004).

98. "Justice for Lynne Stewart," *Lynne Stewart Defense Committee*, http://www.lynnestewart.org (accessed February 11, 2005).

99. "The Disappeared," *Independent (UK)*, February 26, 2002, http://news .independent .co.uk/world/americas/story.jsp?story=139913 (accessed July 29, 2004).

100. Louie Meizlish, "Judge Rules Haddad's Trial Must be Open," *Michigan Daily*, April 4, 2002, http://www.michigandaily.com/vnews/display.v/ART/ 2002/04/04/3cabfae765074?in_archive=1 (accessed July 29, 2004). 2002 Fed. App. 0291p [6th Cir. 2002], http://www .ac/umich.org/modules.php?name=News&File= article&sid=246 (accessed October 24, 2004).

101. Associated Press, "Haddad Deported, Family Remains in U.S.," *Refuse & Resist*, July 15, 2003, http://www.refuseandresist.org/detentions/art.php?aid=953 (accessed August 10, 2004).

102. "Rabih Haddad's Wife and Children Deported," *Metro Detroit*, July 28, 2003, http://detroit.about.com/b/a/012965.htm (accessed August 10, 2004).

103. Dan Christenson, "Scrutinizing 'Supersealed' Cases," *Miami Daily Business Review*, December 2, 2003, http://www.law.com/jsp/article.jsp?id=1069801668123 (accessed July 26, 2004).

104. Warren Richey, "Secret 9/11 Case Before High Court," *Christian Science Monitor*, October 30, 2003, http://www.csmonitor.com/2003/1030/p01s02-usju.html (accessed July 29, 2004).

105. Gina Holland, "High Court Asks Details on Detainee," *San Luis Obispo.com*, November 5, 2003, http://www.sanluisobispo.com/mld/inquirer/news/nation/ 7184023.htm (accessed July 29, 2004).

106. Christenson, "Scrutinizing 'Supersealed' Cases."

107. Christenson, "Feds Defend Secret Docketing of Post-9/11 Detainee's Case," *Miami Daily Business Review*, March 5, 2004, http://www.law.com/jsp/ article.jsp?id=1078368923594 (accessed July 26, 2004).

108. Press Release, "Key Provisions of Anti Terrorism Statute Declared Uncon-stitutional," *Center for Constitutional Rights*, December 3, 2003, http://www.ccr-ny .org/v2/newsroom/releases/pReleases.asp?ObjID=NVUclM1aT7&Content=307 (accessed July 29, 2004).

109. David Cole, "The War on Our Rights," *Nation*, December 24, 2003, http://www.thenation.com/doc.mhtml?i=20040112&s=cole (accessed July 29, 2004).

110. David Shepardson, "Terrorism Attorneys May Testify: Detroit Defense Team Is Interviewed by FBI, Told They Could Be Government Witnesses," *Detroit News*, June 21, 2004, http://www.detnews.com/2004/metro/0406/21/b01-189705 .htm (accessed June 25, 2004).

111. Treaty with the Western Shoshoni, October 1, 1863, 18 Stats., 689, ratified June 26, 1866, http://digital.library.okstate.edu/kappler/Vol2/treaties/sho0851.htm (accessed August 9, 2004).

112. "Bush Signs Western Shoshone Legislation: Tribal Leaders View Bill as Massive Land Fraud," *Western Shoshone Defense Project*, July 7, 2004, http://www.wsdp.org/distribution_bill.htm#070904-signs (accessed August 9, 2004).

113. Steven Newcomb, "Failure of the United States Indian Claims Commission to File a Report with Congress in the Western Shoshone Case (Docket 326-K), Pur-

suant to Sections 21 and 22a of the Indian Claims Commission Act," Western Shoshone National Council, January 2003.

114. Carrie Dann, "Statement by Carrie Dann on George W. Bush Signing into 'Law' HR 884," e-mail update from Western Shoshone Defense Project, July 7, 2004, http://www.wsdp.org, (accessed July 18, 2004); "Bush Signs Western Shoshone Legislation: Tribal Leaders View Bill as Massive Land Fraud," *Western Shoshone Defense Project.*

115. Patrick Martin, "Soldier Beaten at Guantanamo in Interrogation Training," *World Socialist Web Site*, May 29, 2004, http://www.wsws.org/articles/2004/may2004/guan-m29_prn.shtml (accessed May 29, 2004).

116. Neil A. Lewis, "Guantanamo Workers Detail Abuse of Detainees," *San Francisco Chronicle*, October 17, 2004, p. A11.

117. "Request for Precautionary Measures," *Center for Constitutional Rights*, February 25, 2002, http://www.ccr-ny.org/v2/legal/september_11th/docs/2-25-02 RequestforPrecautionaryMeasures.pdf (accessed July 28, 2004).

118. "Fact Sheet: Status of Detainees at Guantanamo," *Office of the Press Secretary*, February 7, 2002, http://www.whitehouse.gov/news/releases/2002/02/print/20020207-13.html (accessed May 23, 2004).

119. "Request for Precautionary Measures," *Center for Constitutional Rights.*

120. "Petition to Inter-American Commission on Human Rights on Behalf of the Guantanamo Detainees," *Center for Constitutional Rights*, August 2004, http://www.ccr-ny.org/v2/legal/september_11th/ sept11Article.asp?ObjID=7lt0qa X9CP&Content=134 (accessed August 10, 2004).

121. "U.S. Citizen Detained Without Charge in Saudi Arabia," *Amnesty International*, http://takeaction.amnestyusa.org/action/display/wacmoreinfo.asp?item=10860 (accessed July 29, 2004).

122. "Jailed American's Parents Sue U.S.," Associated Press, July 29, 2004, http://www.washingtontimes.com/functions/print.php?StoryID=20040728-111744 -2431r (accessed July 29, 2004).

123. Mark Corallo, "Statement of Mark Corallo, Director of Public Affairs, Regarding Yaser Hamdi," *Department of Justice*, September 22, 2004, http://www .usdoj.gov/opa/pr/2004/September/04_opa_640.htm (accessed November 10, 2004).

124. *Yaser v. Hamdi*, Case No. 2:02CV439, "Stipulation of Dismissal," http://notablecases.vaed.uscourts.gov/2:02-cv-00439/docs/70269/0.pdf (accessed November 10, 2004).

125. "Yaser Hamdi, Held for Three Years Without Trial, Released to Saudi Arabia," *Human Rights First*, October 12, 2004, http://www.humanrightsfirst .org/media/2004_alerts/1012.htm (accessed November 10, 2004); Elaine Cassel, "Judge Tosses Out Ahmed Abu Ali's Case," *Civil Liberties Watch*, September 12, 2004, http://babelogue.citypages.com:8080/ecassel/2004/09/12 (accessed September 15, 2004).

126. Katty Kay, "No Fast Track at Guantanamo Bay," *BBC News World Edition*, January 11, 2003, http://news.bbc.co.uk/1/low/world/americas/2648547.stm (accessed July 8, 2004).

127. Ted Conover, "In the Land of Guantanamo," *New York Times Magazine*, June 29, 2003, p. 41, http://tedconover.com/gitmo.html, (accessed November 30, 2004).

128. Ibid; Associated Press, Increased Suicide Attempts at Guantanamo," *USA Today*, June 22, 2004, http://www.usatoday.com/news/washington/2004-06-22-guantanamo_x.htm (accessed November 24, 2004).

129. Duncan Campbell, "Six al-Qaeda Suspects to be Tried by American Military Tribunal," *Guardian UK*, July 4, 2003, http://www.guardian.co.uk/international/story/0%2C3604%2C991271%2C00.html (accessed July 8, 2004).

130. Associated Press, "Guantanamo Camp Expands," *Sydney Morning Herald*, August 25, 2003, http://www.smh.com.au/articles/2003/08/25/1061663742056.html (accessed November 30, 2004).

131. Associated Press, "U.S. Releases 26 Guantanamo Detainees," *Washington-post.com*, March 16, 2004, http://www.washingtonpost.com/ac2/wp-dyn/A61753-2004 Mar15?language=printer (accessed November 24, 2004).

132. Christopher Marquis, "Pentagon Will Permit Captives at Cuba Base to Appeal Status," *New York Times*, July 8, 2004, p. A1.

133. Ibid.

134. Charles Aldinger, "U.S. Airman Charged with Espionage in Guantanamo Case," Reuters, http://www.swisspolitics.org/en/news/index.php?section=int&page=news_inhalt &news_id=4272990 (accessed February 2, 2005).

135. Matt Kelley, "Spy Suspect Eyed Before Guantanamo Posting," Associated Press, September 26, 2003, http://www.newsday.com/news/politics/wire/sns-ap-guantanamo-investigation,0,1699953.story?coll=sns-ap-politics-headlines (accessed July 26, 2003).

136. Barbara Grady, "Judge Frees Accused U.S. Guantanamo Spy From Jail," Reuters *News Service*, May 12, 2004, http://www.reuters.com/newsArticle.jhtml?type=domesticNews&storyID=5124694 (accessed June 25, 2004).

137. BBC News, "Top UK Judge Slams Camp Delta," November 26, 2003, http://news.bbc.co.uk/1/hi/uk_politics/3238624.stm (accessed June 25, 2004).

138. David Rose, "Revealed: The Full Story of the Guantanamo Britons," *Observer*, March 14, 2003, http://observer.guardian.co.uk/uk_news/story/0,6903,1168976,00.html (accessed June 25, 2004).

139. Clare Dyer, "Britain Stands Firm against Guantanamo Bay Trials by Tribunal," *Guardian*, June 25, 2004, http://www.guardian.co.uk/uk_news/story/0,3604,1247119,00.html (accessed June 25, 2004).

140. Tania Branigan, "Guantanamo Bay Prisoner's Letter Claims He Was Witness to Murders," *Guardian*, October 2, 2004, http://www.guardian.co.uk/uk_news/story/0,3604,1318125,00 (accessed October 5, 2004).

141. "Operation Liberty Shield Turns Liberty on its Head," *Human Rights First*, March 18, 2003, http://www.humanrightsfirst.org/media/2003_alerts/0318b.htm (accessed July 29, 2004).

142. "CCR Condemns Justice Department's Targeting of Immigrants and Iraqi Nationals," *Center for Constitutional Rights*, March 2003, http://www.ccr-ny.org/v2/newsroom/releases/pReleases.asp?ObjID=4HM4jgt1EY&Content=214 (accessed July 29, 2004).

143. Karen de Sá, "Caught in the Aftermath: Hard Life of a September 11 Detainee," *Mercury News*, August 12, 2002, http://www.mercurynews.com/mld/mercury news/news/3846979.htm (accessed July 29, 2004).

144. Karen de Sá and Mark Gladstone, "September 11 Detainee Released from Jail: Man Still Faces Immigration, Gun Charges," *Mercury News*, August 24, 2002, http://www.mercurynews.com/mld/mercurynews/3929886.htm (accessed July 29, 2004).

145. James Irby, "Palestinian Family Loses Deportation Battle," *ABC13 Eyewitness News*, March 28, 2003, http://abclocal.go.com/ktrk/news/32803_local_family deported.html (accessed July 29, 2004).

146. "Kesbehs Family," *Blue Triangle Network*, June 3, 2003, http://www.bluetriangle .org/old/id53.htm (accessed July 29, 2004).

147. "No Time for Love," *Boulder Weekly*, June 16, 2003, http://www.boulder weekly.com/archive/061203/coverstory.html (accessed July 29, 2004).

148. "Background," *Ciaran Ferry Legal Defense Fund*, http://www.freeciaranferry .com (accessed July 29, 2004).

149. "No Time for Love," *Boulder Weekly*.

150. "Case Status," *Ciaran Ferry Legal Defense Fund*, http://www.freeciaranferry .com (accessed July 29, 2004).

151. Whitehouse.gov., January 20, 2004, http://www.whitehouse.gov/news/ releases/2004/01/20040120-7.html (accessed January 31, 2005).

152. John Caldwell, "People of the Year: The Mayors," *Advocate*, December 21, 2004, pp. 34–40.

153. Human Rights Campaign, "Statewide Marriage Laws," http://www.hrc.org (accessed January 31, 2005).

154. "First National Survey of Children in Immigration Detention Exposes Mistreatment, Lengthy Detentions, Legal Barriers," *Amnesty International*, June 18, 2003, http://www.amnestyusa.org/news/2003/usa06182003.html (accessed July 29, 2004).

155. Lynda Carson, "Bush's Cuts Cause Crisis in Section 8 Housing Program," *Street Spirit*, June 2004, p. 4.

156. Merlin Chowkwanyun, "A Strange and Tragic Legal Journey: The Case of Sherman Austin," *Counterpunch*, October 11-13, 2003, http://www.counterpunch .org/merlin10112003.html (accessed July 13, 2004).

157. Steven Mikulan, "Accidental Anarchist," *LA Weekly*, July 11-17, 2003, http://www.laweekly.com/ink/03/34/news-mikulan.php (accessed July 13, 2004).

158. Walida Imarisha, "Sherman Austin: Black Anarchist Faces PATRIOT Act Repression," *Clamor*, March/April 2004, http://www.freesherman.org/news.html (accessed July 13, 2004).

159. Chowkwanyun, "A Strange and Tragic Legal Journey: The Case of Sherman Austin."

160. "Sherman Austin Freed, Sort of...," *Independent Media Center*, July 29, 2004, http://www.indymedia.org/en/index.shtml (accessed July 29, 2004).

161. Alex Katz, "Oakland Teacher Calls U.S. Security After Teens Make In-Class Comments Threatening President Bush," *Oakland Tribune*, May 4, 2003, http://sf.indymedia.org/news/2003/05/1607366.php (accessed July 29, 2004).

162. Marcelo Rodriguez, "Secret Service Interrogation of 2 Students Sparks Furor," *Los Angeles Times*, May 13, 2003, http://lists.envirolink.org/pipermail/dti-discuss/ 2003q2/000005.html (accessed July 29, 2004).

163. Mary Jo McConahay, "Family Planning: A Neighborhood Named Desire,"

*Sierra Magazine-Sierra Club*, January/February 2004, http://www.sierraclub.org/ sierra/200401/abstinence.asp (accessed July 29, 2004).

164. "ACLU Hails Federal Court's Decision to Halt Taxpayer Financing of Religion in Abstinence-Only Progams," *ACLU of Louisiana*, July 25, 2002, http://www .laaclu.org/News/2002/July%2025%20Abstinence%20Only.htm (accessed July 29, 2004).

165. "ACLU Announces Settlement in Case Against Taxpayer Financing of Religion in Louisiana Abstinence-Only Programs," *ACLU of Louisiana*, November 13, 2002, http://www.laaclu.org/News/2002/Nov%2013%20GPA%20settlement.htm (accessed July 29, 2004).

166. McConahay, "Family Planning: A Neighborhood Named Desire."

167. "W.H. Ponders Condom Warnings," *CNN.com*, http://www.cnn.org/2004/ ALLPOLITICS/03/11/condom.warnings.ap (accessed June 8, 2004).

168. "Hawaii: Legislation Passed to End Sex Tourism and Hold Sex Tour Operators Accountable," *Equality Now, Women's Action 24.2 Update* (mailing), May 2004.

169. Todd Tavares, "The Real Winners," *Dollars and Sense*, no. 248, July/August 2003, http://www.dollarsandsense.org/archives/2003/0703tavares.html (accessed July 29, 2004).

170. Jonathan Weisman and Anitha Reddy, "Spending on Iraq Sets Off Gold Rush: Lawmakers Fear U.S. Is Losing Control of Funds," *Washington Post*, October 9, 2003, http://www.washingtonpost.com/ac2/wp-dyn/A496-2003Oct8?language=printer (accessed July 29, 2004).

171. "Windfalls of War," *Center for Public Integrity*, http://www.publicintegrity .org/wow/ (accessed July 29, 2004).

172. Tavares, "The Real Winners."

173. Larry Margasak, "Report Links Iraq Deals to Bush Donations," *USA Today*, October 30, 2003, http://www.usatoday.com/news/world/iraq/2003-10-30-iraq-bush -donations_x.htm (accessed July 29, 2004).

174. "The Corporate Invasion of Iraq: Profile of U.S. Corporations Awarded Contracts in U.S./British-Occupied Iraq," *U.S. Labor Against the War*, June 6, 2003, http://www.uslaboragainstwar.org/article.php?id=3484 (accessed July 29, 2004).

175. Margasak, "Report Links Iraq Deals to Bush Donations."

176. Letter from Henry Waxman, California State Representative, to the Honorable Joshua Bolten, Director, Office of Management and Budget, September 30, 2003, http://www.henrywaxman.house.gov/ (accessed July 29, 2004).

177. Senator Edward Kennedy, "Congressional Record (Senate)," pp. S12638–S12643, DOCID:cr16oco3-94, October 16, 2003.

178. Kelly Patricia O'Meara, "DynCorp Disgrace," *Insight on the News*, August 19, 2003, http://www.insightmag.com/main.cfm/include/detail/storyid/163052.html (accessed November 18, 2004); Mary Alice Robbins, "RICO Used in Wrongful Termination Suit," *Texas Lawyer*, April 2, 2001, http://www.globalresearch .ca/articles/ROB108A.html (accessed July 29, 2004).

179. Associated Press, "U.N. Whistleblower Wins Claim," *FreeRepublic.com*, August 2, 2002, http://209.157.64.200/focus/f-news/726842/posts (accessed July 29, 2004).

180. Jamie Wilson, "£110,000 Payout for Sacked Whistleblower," *Guardian*, November 27, 2002, http://www.guardian.co.uk/print/0,3858,4555242-103690,00 .html (accessed July 29, 2004).

181. Dana Priest and Mary Pat Flaherty, "Under Fire, Security Firms Form An Alliance," *Washington Post*, April 8, 2004, p. A1.

182. Russell Mokhiber and Robert Weissman, "The Rising Corporate Military Monster," *CommonDreams.org*, April 23, 2004, http://www.commondreams .org/views04/0423-12.htm (accessed June 30, 2004).

183. Barry Lando, "Soldiers and Fortune," *TomPaine.com*, April 16, 2004, http://www.tompaine.com/feature2.cfm/ID/10243/view/print (accessed June 30, 2004).

184. James Dao, "A Man of Violence, of Just '110 Percent' Gung-Ho?" *New York Times*, June 19, 2004, http://www.nytimes.com/2004/06/19/national/19DETA .html?ei=5007&en=4e8a8b6cece04498&ex=1402977600&partner=USERLAND &pagewanted=all&position (accessed June 30, 2004).

185. "Our Demands," *MillionWorkerMarch.org*, http://www.millionworkermarch .org/whywemarch.html#dem (accessed June 30, 2004).

186. "Join the Million Worker March on Washington, D.C.," *MillionWorker March.org*, http://www.millionworkermarch.org (accessed June 30, 2004).

187. David E. Sanger with Steven Greenhouse, "Bush Invokes Taft-Hartley Act to Open West Coast Ports," *New York Times*, October 9, 2002, http://www .labournet.net/docks2/0210/lockbush2.htm (accessed July 16, 2004).

188. Doug Frechin, "Bush Declares War on West Coast Port Workers," *Justice*, no. 31, September/October 2002, http://www.socialistalternative.org/justice31/7 .html (accessed July 19, 2004).

189. "President's Remarks on West Coast Ports," *The White House*, October 8, 2002, http://www.whitehouse.gov/news/releases/2002/10/20021008-4.html (accessed December 22, 2004).

190. Sanger with Greenhouse, "Bush Invokes Taft-Hartley Act to Open West Coast Ports."

191. Steven Greenhouse, "Cleaner At Wal-Mart Tells Of Few Breaks And Low Pay," *New York Times*, October 25, 2003, http://www.mindfully.org/Industry/2003/ Wal-Mart-Cleaner25oct03.htm (accessed January 14, 2004).

192. David Bacon, interviewed on *The Morning Show*, KPFA radio—Berkeley, CA, October 29, 2003.

193. *Economic Report of the President, 2004*, (Washington, DC: Executive Office of the President, 2004).

194. M. Harvey Brenner, "Estimating the Effects of Economic Change on National Health and Social Well-Being," prepared for the Joint Economic Committee, Subcommittee on Economic Goals and Intergovernmental Policy, 98th Cong. 2nd Session, at p. 53 (J. Rpt. 98-198, Serial No. J-98-17), U.S. G.P.O, June 4, 1984, (accessed at Senate Document Room, July 20, 2004).

195. "The Corporate Invasion of Iraq: Profile of U.S. Corporations Awarded Contracts in U.S./British Occupied Iraq," *U.S Labor Against the War*, June 6, 2003, http://www.uslaboragainstwar.org/downloads/CorpInvasionofIraq.complete.pdf (accessed July 19, 2004).

196. Chris Edwards and Veronique de Rugy, "International Tax Competition: A 21st Century Restraint on Government," Cato Institute: *Policy Analysis*, no. 431, April 12, 2002, http://www.cato.org/pubs/pas/pa431.pdf (accessed December 23, 2004).

197. Alan Maas, "Rise of Iraq's New Labor Movement—Delegation of U.S. Unionists," *Socialist Worker*, October 31, 2003, http://uslaboragainstwar .org/article.php?id=2015 (accessed July 19, 2004).

198. "King County Labor Council Resolution Calling for the End of the Occupation of Iraq—Adopted 5/19/04," *US Labor Against the War*, June 8, 2004, http://www.uslaboragainstwar.org/article.php?id=5245 (accessed July 19, 2004).

199. "US Occupation Forces Raid Iraqi Union Headquarters," *Iraqi Federation of Workers' Trade Unions*, December 11, 2003, http://www.iraqitradeunions.org/ archives/2003_12.html (accessed July 19, 2004).

200. Interview with Lynn Baker and Todd Carlson of the Paper, Allied-Industrial, Chemical, and Energy Workers International Union PACE, *Morning Show*, Berkeley's KPFA—Pacifica Radio Network, June 15, 2004.

201. "Continental Carbon Company," *PACE International*, http://www.fight backonline.org/company_background.htm (accessed on June 16, 2004).

202. "PACE, Taiwanese, and International Labor and Environmental Organizations Confront China Synthetic Rubber Company at Stockholders Meeting," *Fight Back Online*, June 26, 2002, http://www.fightbackonline.org/news_release.htm (accessed on June 16, 2004).

203. Press Release, "PACE Union Has Safety Concerns Over Materials Used in Cooper Tire," April 16, 2004, http://www.fightbackonline.org/march_3,_2004.htm (accessed July 7, 2004).

204. Press Release, "Ponca Tribe and PACE Union Hold Protest March Condemning Environmental Pollution and Employee Lockout," *Corporate Social Responsibility Newswire Service*, August 25, 2003, http://www.csrwire.com/article.cgi/2067 .html (accessed July 7, 2004).

205. "Attorney Calls on Bridgestone/Firestone to Stop Using Substandard Carbon Black Produced by Continental Carbon," *National Association of Independent Insurance Adjusters*, March 26, 2004, http://www.naiia.com/fullnewsstory.cfm ?ID=1261 (accessed July 7, 2004); "Firestone Recalls Nearly 500,000 Tires," *ClickOnDetroit.com*, February 26, 2004, http://www.clickondetroit.com/automotive/ 2878487/detail.html (accessed on July 7, 2004).

206. "American Workers, PACE Union Members End Hunger Strike In Taiwan," *Yahoo News Australia/New Zealand*, June 18, 2004, http://au.news.yahoo .com/040618/3/pio0.html (accessed July 7, 2004).

207. Interview with Lynn Baker and Todd Carlson of PACE.

208. "Application of 1988 Civil Liberties Act," *Global Alliance for Preserving the History of World War II in Asia*, http://www.gainfo.org/SFPT/ApplicationOf1988 CivilLibertiesAct.htm (accessed July 30, 2004).

209. Warren Hoge, "Finnish Prisons: No Gates or Armed Guards," *New York Times*, January 2, 2003, http://www.nytimes.com/2003/01/02/international/europe/ 02FINL.html?ex=1042522922&ei=1&en=6c084f42a4a50692 (accessed August 4, 2004).

210. "The Case of Leonard Peltier, Native American Political Prisoner," *FreePeltier .org* October 28, 2003, http://www.freepeltier.org/story.htm (accessed July 12, 2004).

211. "The Case of Leonard Peltier," *American Indian Cultural Support*, http://www.aics.org/LP/ (accessed on October 28, 2003).

212. "The Case of Leonard Peltier," *American Indian Cultural Support*.

213. Jim Suhr, "U.S. Appeals Court Rejects Peltier's Sentence Reduction Bid," *Duluth News Tribune*, December 12, 2002, http://www.duluthsuperior.com/mld/duluthtribune/4726679.htm (accessed July 12, 2004).

214. Associated Press, "Peltier Sentence Reduction Denied," *Lawrence Journal-World*, December 13, 2002, http://www.ljworld.com/section/peltier/story/115426 (accessed July 12, 2004).

215. "Headlines for August 5, 2004: Leonard Peltier Nominated for President," *Democracy Now!* August 5, 2004, http://www.democracynow.org/print.pl?sid=04/08/05/1432239 (accessed August 5, 2004).

216. "Who is Mumia," *FreeMumia.org* http://www.freemumia.org/intro.html (accessed on October 29, 2003).

217. "Fact Sheet on Mumia Abu-Jamal," *International Action Center*, September 13, 1999, http://www.iacenter.org/majfact.htm (accessed July 14, 2004).

218. Monica Moorehead, "Travesty of Justice: Pennsylvania Court Rules Against Mumia," *International Action Center*, October 16, 2003, http://www.iacenter.org/maj-legal 10-03.htm (accessed November 23, 2003).

219. "A Life in the Balance; The Case of Mumia Abu-Jamal," *Amnesty International USA*, http://www.amnestyusa.org/abolish/reports/mumia/ (accessed on October 29, 2003).

220. International Concerned Family and Friends of Mumia Abu-Jamal, "Death Penalty Again Looms over Mumia's Head," *SouthEndpress.org*, July 12, 2004, http://www.southendpress.org/books/freedomPR3.shtml (accessed August 11, 2004).

221. Dave Lindorff, "Support from NAACP, But a Movement in Shambles," *Counterpunch*, July 16, 2004, http://www.counterpunch.org/lindorff07162004.html (accessed July 19, 2004).

222. "Can't Jail the Spirit: Political Prisoners and POW's in the U.S.," *Prison Activist Resource Center*, April 3, 2004, http://www.prisonactivist.org/pps+pows/pplist-alpha .shtml (accessed August 13, 2004).

223. Press Release, "Governor Ryan Declares Moratorium on Executions," *Illinois Government News Network*, January 31, 2000, http://www.state.il .us/gov/press/00/Jan/morat.htm (accessed July 30, 2004).

224. "List of Defendants Executed by Year," *Death Penalty Information Center*, http://www.deathpenaltyinfo.org/article.php?did=414&scid=8 (accessed August 11, 2004).

225. "Facts about the Death Penalty," *Death Penalty Information Center*, July 23, 2004, http://www.deathpenaltyinfo.org/FactSheet.pdf (accessed July 30, 2004); "Population of the United States by Race and Hispanic/Latino Origin, Census 2000 and July 1, 2003," *InfoPlease*, June 14, 2004, http://print.infoplease.com/ipa/A0762156.html (accessed August 6, 2004).

## CHAPTER 4, E-F

1. "Budget for the Executive Office of the President," *Office of Management and Budget*, August 16, 2004, http://www.whitehouse.gov/omb/budget/fy2005/budget.html (accessed August 16, 2004).

2. Richard Du Boff, "Mirror, Mirror on the Wall, Who's the Biggest Rogue of All?" *Z Magazine*, September 2003, http://www.zmag.org/ZMagSite/Sept2003/duboff0903.html (accessed June 18, 2004).

3. Associated Press, "CBO: Gov't Faces Years of More Deficits," *Kansas City Star*, August 26, 2003, http://www.kansascity.com/mld/kansascity/6616991.htm?1c (accessed June 18, 2004).

4. Bernadette D. Proctor and Joseph Dalakar, "Poverty in the United States: 2002," *U.S. Census Bureau*, September 2003, http://www.census.gov/prod/2003pubs/p60-222.pdf (accessed August 13, 2004).

5. "Welfare: NOW Calls for Real Reform," *National Organization for Women*, September 30, 2003, http://www.now.org/issues/economic/welfare/ index.html (accessed July 14, 2004).

6. "Most Americans Unaware of Cancer Cuts in Pending Medicare Bills, National Poll Shows," *U.S. Newswire*, September 25, 2003, http://releases.usnewswire.com/GetRelease.asp?id=137-09252003 (accessed July 29, 2004).

7. Associated Press, "Bush Urges Passage of Medicare Drug Bill," *Wichita Eagle*, September 25, 2003, http://www.kansas.com/mld/kansas/news/6852505.htm (accessed June 18, 2004).

8. Dale Eisman, "Vet's Drugs Bills May Soar," *El Paso Times*, January 2, 2003, http://www.axisoflogic.com/cgi-bin/exec/view.pl?archive=38&num=4366 (accessed July 29, 2004).

9. Jim Abrams, "GOP Joins Dems, Vets Against Benefit Cuts," *Disabled American Veterans*, September 15, 2003, http://www.dav23.com/news/sept03/GOP%20Joins%20Dems,%20Vets%20Against%20Benefit%20Cuts.htm (accessed July 29, 2004).

10. James Boyne, "Bush Honors Veterans By Slashing Veterans Affairs Budget by $1 Billion," *Irregular Times*, June 1, 2004, http://irregulartimes.com/solvingveterans.html (accessed August 13, 2004).

11. Christopher Hellman, "Highlights of the FY '05 Budget Request," *Center for Arms Control and Nonproliferation*, http://64.177.207.201/static/budget/annual/fy05 (accessed December 9, 2004).

12. "Legislative Update," *National Council for the Social Studies*, August 5, 2004, http://www.socialstudies.org/2004/08/06 (accessed December 9, 2004).

13. Executive Office of the President, Office of Management and Budget, "Fiscal Year 2005: Mid-Session Review, Budget of the U.S. Government," July 30, 2004, http://www.whitehouse.gov/omb/budget/fy2005/05msr.pdf (accessed December 3, 2004).

14. Richmond Resident, "Richmond Budget Bodes Ill for Future," *IndyMedia.org*, April 6, 2004, http://www.indybay.org/news/2004/04/1676346.php (accessed July 12, 2004).

15. Kelly St. John, "Richmond Council Delivers Budget Body Blow," *San Francisco Chronicle*, April 2, 2004, http://sfgate.com/cgi-bin/article.cgi?file=/chronicle/archive/2004/04/02/BAGLV5V8181.DTL (accessed July 12, 2004).

16. Resident, "Richmond Budget Bodes Ill for Future."

17. Rebecca Rosen Lum, "Union To Sue Richmond Over Layoffs," *Contra Costa Times*, April 2, 2004, p. A1.

18. "Bush Social Security Investment Accounts Mean Higher Taxes, Higher Retirement Age, Benefit Cuts," *SeniorJournal.com*, January 15, 2003, http://www.senior journal .com/NEWS/SocialSecurity/3-01-15ReformGOA.htm (accessed July 1, 2004).

19. Richard Stevenson, "Report Predicts Deep Benefit Cuts Under Bush Social Security Plan," *Common Dreams*, June 19, 2002, http://www.commondreams.org/ headlines02/0619-04.htm (accessed July 2, 2004).

20. "America's Mental Health Still Ignored in Terrorism Response," *National Mental Health Association*, September 8, 2003, http://panicdisorder.about .com/b/a/024821.htm (accessed July 30, 2004).

21. Christine Lehman, "Parity Advocates Pick Up Crucial Ally As Bush Calls for Legislation This Year," *Psychiatric News*, May 17, 2002, http://pn.psychiatryonline .org/cgi/content/full/37/10/1 (accessed July 30, 2004).

22. "Mental Health Parity Timeline," *National Mental Health Association*, April 29, 2004, http://www.nmha.org/state/parity/parityTimeline.cfm (accessed July 30, 2004).

23. Charles W. Hoge, et al., "Combat Duty in Iraq and Afghanistan, Mental Health Problems, and Barriers to Care," *New England Journal of Medicine*, July 1, 2004, http://content.nejm.org/cgi/content/full/351/1/13 (accessed August 5, 2004).

24. "ICRC Report on the Treatment by the Coalition Forces of POWs and Other Protected Persons," *International Committee of the Red Cross*, February, 2004, http://www.globalsecurity.org/military/library/report/2004/icrc_report_iraq_feb2004 .htm (accessed July 30, 2004).

25. Sasha Abramsky and Jamie Fellner, "Ill-Equipped: U.S. Prisons and Offenders with Mental Illness," *Human Rights Watch Report*, September 2003, http://www.hrw.org/reports/2003/usa1003/ (accessed July 30, 2004).

26. Jeanne Lenzer, "Bush Plans to Screen Whole US Population for Mental Illness," *British Medical Journal*, June 19, 2004; http://bmj.bmjjournals.com/cgi/content/ full/328/7454/1458?maxtoshow=&eaf (accessed August 5, 2004).

27. *Law Project for Psychiatric Rights*, http://psychrights.org/index.htm (accessed August 5, 2004).

28. Mind Freedom Support Coalition International, http://www.mind freedom.org (accessed August 5, 2004).

29. "Low Income Children in the United States," *National Center for Children in Poverty*, 2004, http://www.nccp.org/pub_cpf04.html (accessed July 12, 2004).

30. Jesse Jackson, "In Rush to Rebuild Iraq, Bush Leaves Poor Children Behind," *Chicago Sun-Times*, September 30, 2003, p. 33.

31. "Bush Signs $368B Defense Bill," *USA Today*, October 1, 2003, http://www.usatoday.com/news/washington/2003-10-01-bush-defense_x.htm (accessed July 29, 2004).

32. Committee on Education and the Workforce, "FY2004 Bush Budget Short-changing Education Reform," *US House of Representatives*, February 3, 2003, http:// edworkforce.house.gov/democrats/bush2004budget.pdf (accessed June 10, 2004).

33. "FY 2004 ED Budget summary: Programs Proposed for Elimination," *US Department of Education*, February 3, 2003, http://www.ed.gov/about/overview/ budget/budget04/summary/edlite-section3.html (accessed July 12, 2004).

34. Ibid.

35. Committee on Education and the Workforce, "FY2004 Bush Budget Short-

changing Education Reform."

36. "Quick Facts 2003-2004," *West Contra Costa Unified School District,* http://www.wccusd.k12.ca.us/about/quickfacts.htm (accessed July 12, 2004).

37. Julio Magana-Saludado, "Governor Reverses Position; Agrees to Meet with Fasters," August 11, 2004, http://www.fast4education.org/index.php?s=35&n=32 (accessed July 8, 2004); Ana Facio Contreras, "Officials Seek Aid for School District" *Contra Costa Times,* March 17, 2004, http://www.contracostatimes.com/mld/ cctimes/news/local/states/california/counties/west_county/8206207.htm (accessed August 11, 2004).

38. "FY 2004 ED Budget summary: Programs Proposed for Elimination," *U.S. Dept. of Education,* February 3, 2003, http://www.ed.gov/about/overview/budget/ budget04/summary/edlite-section3.html (accessed July 29, 2004).

39. "Bush Administration: Ship More U.S. Jobs Overseas," *AFL-CIO,* February 11, 2004, http://www.aflcio.org/yourjobeconomy/jobs/ns02112004).cfm?RenderFor Print=1 (accessed July 29, 2004).

40. "Recent Legislative History of Vouchers," *National Education Association,* 2004, http://www.nea.org/lac/vouchers/vouchhistory.html (accessed July 29, 2004).

41. Press Release, "Competition Open to Select Organization to Run First Federally Funded Opportunity Scholarship Program," *US Department of Education,* February 4, 2004, http://www.ed.gov/news/pressreleases/2004/02/02042004) .html (accessed July 29, 2004).

42. "Protecting Quality Public Education—The Issue: D.C. Vouchers," *People For the American Way,* March 10, 2004, http://www.pfaw.org/pfaw/dfiles/file_300.pdf (accessed July 29, 2004).

43. "Fiscal Year 2004 Budget Summary," *U.S. Department of Education,* February 3, 2003, http://www.ed.gov/about/overview/budget/budget04/summary/edlite -section1.html (accessed July 29, 2004).

44. "No Child Left Behind," *U.S. Department of Education,* 2002, http://www.ed .gov/nclb/landing.jhtml# (accessed July 29, 2004).

45. Press Release, "President Bush's 2004 Budget Will Include an Estimated $756 Million to Expand Options for Parents, Paige Says," *U.S. Department of Education,* January 31, 2003, http://www.ed.gov/news/pressreleases/2003/01/01312003 .html (accessed July 29, 2004).

46. Democratic Staff of the Committee on Education and the Workforce, "FY 2004 Shortchanging Education Reform," *U.S. House of Representatives,* February 3, 2003, http://edworkforce.house.gov/democrats/bush2004budget.pdf (accessed July 29, 2004).

47. Committee on Education and the Workforce, "Bush Administration Cuts Public School Funding to Pay for New Private School Voucher Scheme," *U.S. House of Representatives,* February 3, 2003, http://edworkforce.house.gov/democrats/rel2303 .html (accessed July 29, 2004).

48. "Legislative Update Special Report: Bush Commission Weakens Title IX in Sports," *NOW.org,* February 2003, http://www.now.org/issues/legislat/200302.html (accessed July 29, 2004).

49. Catherine Donaldson-Evans, "Bush Gender Policies Criticized as 'Anti-Women,'" *FOX News,* March 4, 2003, http://www.foxnews.com/story/0,2933,80117 ,00.html (accessed July 29, 2004).

50. "Fiscal Year 2004 ED Budget Summary: Programs Proposed for Elimination," *US Department of Education*, February 3, 2003, http://www.ed.gov/about/overview/budget/budget04/summary/edlite-section3.html (accessed July 29, 2004).

51. "Scientists Accuse White House of Distorting Science for Political Gains," *Natural Resources Defense Council*, February 18, 2004, http://www.nrdc.org/bushrecord/airenergy_warming.asp (accessed June 30, 2004).

52. Bruce Barcott, "Changing All the Rules," *New York Times Magazine*, April 4, 2004, http://www.environmentalintegrity.org/pub117.cfm (accessed August 5, 2004).

53. Zarbock, Janicki, Wade, Heimbuch, and Wilson, "Estimates of Total Nitrogen, Total Phosphorus, and Total Suspended Solids Loadings to Tampa Bay, Florida," *Tampa Bay National Estuary Program*, Technical Publication no. 04–94, 1994, pp. 3–7, 3–8.

54. Robert F. Kennedy Jr., "The Junk Science of George W. Bush," *Nation*, March 8, 2004, http://www.thenation.com/doc.mhtml?i=20040308&c=3&s=kennedy (accessed July 21, 2004).

55. "DOE Weakens Standards for Yucca Nuclear Storage," *Natural Resources Defense Council*, December 14, 2001, http://www.nrdc.org/bushrecord/2001_12.asp (accessed July 26, 2004).

56. Staff, "Bush Cleanup Plan Could Leave Behind More Nuclear Waste," *Natural Resources Defense Council*, July 19, 2002, http://www.nrdc.org/bushrecord/2002_07.asp (accessed July 26, 2004).

57. Christine Kraly, "Study: EPA Knowingly Underreports Toxic Air Emissions from Refineries," *Galveston Houston-Association for Smog Prevention*, June 22, 2004, http://www.ghasp.org/publications/trireport/TRInationalnewsrelease.pdf (accessed July 21, 2004).

58. Bruce Barcott, "Changing All the Rules," *New York Times Magazine*, April 4, 2004, http://www.environmentalintegrity.org/pub117.cfm (accessed August 5, 2004).

59. Kraly, "Study: EPA Knowingly Underreports Toxic Air Emissions from Refineries."

60. "EPA and Justice Department File Government's Briefs in Lawsuits Challenging the Agency's December 2002 Rule Revising Regulatory Requirements for New Source Review," *US Environmental Protection Agency*, http://www.epa.gov/nsr/actions.html (accessed August 13, 2004).

61. Kraly, "Study: EPA Knowingly Underreports Toxic Air Emissions from Refineries."

62. "Bush Administration Finally Admits Big Trouble from Global Warming," *Natural Resources Defense Council*, June 3, 2002, http://www.nrdc.org/bushrecord/2002_06.asp (accessed June 30, 2004).

63. United Nations Framework Convention on Climate Change, http://unfccc.int/resource/convkp.html (accessed July 1, 2004).

64. "Bush Administration Finally Admits Big Trouble from Global Warming," *Natural Resources Defense Council*.

65. "EPA Omits Global Warming Section from Pollution Report," *Natural Resources Defense Council*, September 15, 2002, http://www.nrdc.org/bushrecord/2002_09.asp (accessed June 30, 2004).

66. "Bush Administration Fosters Policy of Delay on Global Warming," *Nat-*

*ural Resources Defense Council*, December 4, 2002, http://www.nrdc.org/bush record/2002_12.asp (accessed June 30, 2004).

67. "White House Whitewashes EPA Environment Report," *Natural Resources Defense Council*, June 23, 2003, http://www.nrdc.org/bushrecord/airenergy_warming .asp (accessed June 30, 2004).

68. "White House Plays Down Global Warming Evidence," *Natural Resources Defense Council*, September 21, 2003, http://www.nrdc.org/bushrecord/airenergy _warming.asp (accessed June 30, 2004).

69. "Secret Pentagon Report Details Global Warming Threat," *Natural Resources Defense Council*, February 22, 2004, http://www.nrdc.org/bushrecord/airenergy _warming.asp (accessed June 30, 2004).

70. Paul Brown, "Global Warming Is Killing Us Too, Say Inuit," *Guardian*, December 11, 2003, http://www.guardian.co.uk/international/story/0,3604 ,1104241,00.html (accessed June 28, 2004).

71. "A Guide to the Climate Change Process: The Kyoto Protocol," *United Nations Framework Convention on Climate Change*, http://unfccc.int/text/resource/ process/components/response/respkp.html (accessed August 6, 2004).

72. Brown, "Global Warming Is Killing Us Too, Say Inuit."

73. William Cole, "Hawaii's Stryker Brigade Approved," *Honolulu Advertiser*, July 7, 2004, http://the.honoluluadvertiser.com/article/2004/Jul/07/br/br01p.html (accessed July 9, 2004).

74. Jim Albertini, "Stryker Protest," *Malu 'Aina Center for Non-Violent Education & Action*, July 7, 2004, http://geocities.com/malu_aina/protest (accessed July 9, 2004).

75. "Community Impact Statement on the Stryker Brigade Combat Team," *DMZ Hawaii Aloha Aina*, July 6, 2004, http://www.malu-aina.org (accessed July 9, 2004).

76. Albertini, "Stryker Protest."

77. Letter from Jane Goodall and 358 other scientists to Chris Nolan, Chief of the Division of Conservation and Classification of the U.S. Fish and Wildlife Service, March 4, 2004, http://www.defenders.org/releases/pr2004b/letter.pdf (accessed February 3, 2005).

78. GreenWatch Today, "A Broken Promise; Species Near Extinction," *Bush Green Watch*, February 6, 2004, http://www.bushgreenwatch.org/mt_archives/ 000045.php (accessed August 17, 2004).

79. Fact Web page, "Agricultural Trade," *World Trade Organization*, 2003, http://lnweb18.worldbank.org/ESSD/ardext.nsf/12ByDocName/AgriculturalTrade (accessed July 22, 2004).

80. Farah Khan, "Chop Agricultural Subsidies, Say World Bank and NGOs," *Inter Press Service*, August 27, 2002, http://www.globalpolicy.org/ngos/role/global act/int-inst/2002/0827subsidy.htm (accessed July 21, 2004).

81. E. C. Pasour Jr., "Ending Farm Subsidies Wouldn't Help the Third World? It Just Ain't So!" *Freeman: Ideas on Liberty*, April 2004, http://www.fee.org/ vnews.php?nid=5873 (accessed July 21, 2004).

82. Fact Web page, "Subsidies, Food Imports and Tariffs Key Issues for Developing Countries," *Food and Agriculture Organization of the United Nations*, September 2003, http://www.fao.org/english/newsroom/focus/2003/wto2.htm (accessed July 22, 2004).

83. Ellen Kaiser, "War Watch: U.S. Farm Subsidies Starve the World," *War Times*, October–November 2003, http://www.war-times.org/issues/13art3.html (accessed July 21, 2004).

84. World Bank Press, "Aid Irrelevant Unless Rich Countries Cut Subsidies," *World*, October 11, 2002, http://www.globalpolicy.org/globaliz/econ/2002/1011wb.htm (accessed July 21, 2004).

85. Patrick Baert, "WTO Proposes Elimination of Farm Subsidies," *Agence France Presse*, July 17, 2004, http://www.arabnews.com/?page=6&section=0&article =48506&d=17&m=7&y=2004 (accessed July 21, 2004).

86. "EPA Factory-Farm Rule Favors Polluters," *Natural Resources Defense Council*, December 15, 2002, http://www.nrdc.org/bushrecord/2002_12.asp (accessed June 30, 2004).

87. "Pollution from Giant Livestock Farms Threatens Public Health: Waste Lagoons and Manure Spray-fields—Two Widespread and Environmentally Hazardous Technologies—Are Poorly Regulated," *Natural Resources Defense Council*, July 24, 2001, http://www.nrdc.org/water/pollution/nspills.asp (accessed June 30, 2004).

88. "EPA Factory-Farm Rule Favors Polluters," *Natural Resources Defense Council*.

89. "EPA Secretly Considering Amnesty for Livestock Farm Polluters," *Natural Resources Defense Council*, May 05, 2003, http://www.nrdc.org/bushrecord/water_pollution.asp (accessed June 30, 2004).

90. Nina Totenberg, "Morning Edition: Federal Courts Face Budgetary Crisis," *National Public Radio*, August 12, 2004, http://www.npr.org/features/feature.php?wfId=3847586 (accessed August 12, 2004).

91. Glenn A. Fine, "The September 11 Detainees: A Review of the Treatment of Aliens Held on Immigration Charges in Connection with the Investigation of the September 11 Attacks," *Office of the Inspector General, DOJ*, April 2003, http://www.usdoj.gov/oig/special/0306/index.htm (accessed July 29, 2004).

92. "NYCOSH Update on Safety and Health Archive," *New York Committee for Occupational Safety and Health*, September 24, 2003, http://www.nycosh.org/Update18_Jul-Sept_2003.html (accessed July 29, 2004).

93. "Study Sees Trade Center Health Issues," *MSNBC News*, September 10, 2003, http://curezone.com/forums/m.asp?f=237&i=209 (accessed July 29, 2004).

94. Ibid.

95. "EPA Covered up Deadly Ground Zero Air Problems," *Albion Monitor*, September 11, 2003, http://www.monitor.net/monitor/0309a/default.html (accessed July 29, 2004).

96. Dorothy Smith Patterson, "Reparations: An African American Movement," *Human Rights Now!* Summer 2003, http://www.mcli.org/projects/newsletters / Summer_2003_NL.pdf (accessed August 4, 2004).

97. Cecil Williams, "U.S. Walks Out on Antiracist Conference: World's People Demand Reparations for Slavery and Colonialism, Support Palestine," *International Action Center*, September 5, 2001, http://www.iacenter.org/durban3.htm (accessed August 11, 2004).

98. Associated Press, "Police Accused of Abusing Demonstrators," *Florida Alliance for Retired Americans*, November 26, 2003, http://www.flara.net/ftaa.htm (accessed June 21, 2004).

99. Mike Rhodes, "Stop Police Violence," *Community Alliance*, December 2003, http://www.fresnoalliance.com/home/magazine/2003/magaz%20Dec%202003.PDF (accessed August 6, 2004).

100. Ellie Bluestein, "It's Happening At Last," *Community Alliance*, December 2003, http://www.fresnoalliance.com/home/magazine/2003/magaz%20Dec%202003.PDF (accessed August 6, 2004); e-mail to MCLI from Howard Watkins, August 5, 2004.

## CHAPTER 5

1. Source: http://legis.state.ak.us/basis/get_bill_text.asp?hsid=HJR022D&Session=23 (accessed November 30, 2004).

2. Source: http://www.passionforpeace-slo.org/pdf/CalifLegisNoAttack-3-5-03.pdf (accessed August 12, 2004).

3. Source: http://web.sfgov.org/site/uploadedfiles/election/Docs/VIP_Nov04 .pdf (accessed December 1, 2004).

4. Source: http://www.fas.org/irp/congress/2003_cr/hr1157.html (accessed August 12, 2004).

5. Major Owens's homepage: http://www.house.gov/owens.

6. Source:http://www.ci.berkeley.ca.us/citycouncil/resos/2004/62539.pdf (accessed August 13, 2004).

7. Source: http://santacruz.indymedia.org/feature/display/5557 (accessed August 13, 2004).

8. "SEIU Convention Calls for End to U.S. Occupation of Iraq and Return of U.S. Troops: Nation's Largest Union Adopts Tough Antiwar Stand Without Dissent," *U.S. Labor Against the War*, June 22, 2004, http://uslaboragainstwar.org/article .php?id=5382 (accessed December 21, 2004).

9. Public Citizen, "Conflict of Interest of Former Medicare Chief Thomas Scully," http://www.citizen.org/congress/govt_reform/ethics/scully/ (accessed August 12, 2004).

## CHAPTER 6

1. Source: http://www.law.cornell.edu/constitution/index.html and http://www .midnightbeach.com/jon/US-Constitution.htm (both accessed August 8, 2004).

2. Source: http://www.access.gpo.gov/uscode/title5a/5a_2_.html (accessed August 10, 2004).

3. Source: http://www.un.org/aboutun/charter/ (accessed August 8, 2004).

4. Source: http://www.unhchr.ch/html/menu3/b/a_ccpr.htm (accessed August 8, 2004).

5. Source: http://www.unhchr.ch/html/menu3/b/d_icerd.htm (accessed August 10, 2004).

6. Source: http://www.unhchr.ch/html/menu3/b/h_cat39.htm (accessed August 10, 2004).

7. Source: http://www.un.org/law/ilc/texts/nurnberg.htm (accessed August 10, 2004).

8. Source: http://www.state.gov/www/global/arms/treaties/npt1.html (accessed August 10, 2004).

# TABLE OF CASES

# INDEX TO CHAPTERS 1-3, 5-6

**NOTE:** This index does not include references to cases—see Table of Cases, page 525;
Does not include numerous references to Pres. G. W. Bush—see issue;
Does not include references to UN—see body or issue; and
Does not include references to the US Government—see agency.

# INDEX TO REPORTS IN CHAPTER 4

**NOTES:**

This book is indexed in three ways:

Starting on page 525 the TABLE OF CASES lists lawsuits described in the entire book, with citations to pages.

Starting on page 527 the INDEX TO CHAPTERS 1–3, 5–6, lists names, events, topics, and laws, with citations to pages.

Starting on page 545 the INDEX TO REPORTS IN CHAPTER 4 lists names, events, laws, and places described in the 180 reports, with citations to the numbers of the reports, not to page numbers.

Each report has a Section number, e.g., 1 through 30, and a Report number within the Section, e.g., Reports 1.1, 1.2, etc., through 30.3.

Each Section begins with a brief description of all of the reports in that Section and ends with a list of the laws relevant to those reports. E.g., Section 1 describes Reports 1.1 through 1.13 and then lists the US and UN laws relevant to those reports. The text of all of the laws referred to in the 30 introductory Sections is in Chapter 6.

A reference to "1" is to the introductory Section 1; a reference to "1.1" is to the first report in that Section, etc.

Letters A–F refer to introductory material: in Part A before Section 1 and Reports 1.1–11.6, in Part B before Section 12 and Reports 12.1–12.9, in Part C before Section 13 and Reports 13.1–17.5, in Part D before Section 18 and Reports 18.1–24.4, in Part E before Section 25 and Reports 25.1–28.1, in Part F before Section 29 and Reports 29.1–30.3.

The references to the Bush Administration, United Nations, and United States are suggestive and not complete.